Making Hard Decisions

Making Hard Decisions

AN INTRODUCTION TO DECISION ANALYSIS

Robert T. Clemen

College of Business Administration
University of Oregon

PWS-KENT PUBLISHING COMPANY ♦ Boston

Sponsoring Editor: Michael Payne   **Interior Designer:** Wanda K. Wilking
Assistant Editor: Marcia Cole   **Cover Designer:** Patricia Adams
Editorial Assistant: Patricia Schumacher   **Typesetter:** Grafacon, Inc.
Production Editor: Patricia Adams   **Printer/Binder:** Maple-Vail Book Manufacturing Group
Manufacturing Coordinator: Marcia A. Locke   **Cover Illustrator:** Jean-Francois Podevin/Image Bank

The following cases and examples are fictional. Any resemblance to actual people or business firms is purely coincidental: Larkin Oil (p. 25); The Value of Patience (p. 30); Early Bird, Inc. (p. 31); GPC's New Product Decision (p. 105); Southern Electronics, Part I (p. 106); Southern Electronics, Part II (p. 107); Strenlar, Part I (p. 108); Eagle Airlines (p. 113); DuMond International, Part I (p. 142); Strenlar, Part II (p. 143); Decision Analysis Monthly (p. 200); Overbooking, Part I (p. 277); Municipal Solid Waste (p. 283); Taco Shells (p. 308); Forecasting Sales (p. 309); Overbooking, Part II (p. 311); Fashions (p. 314); Choosing a Manufacturing Process (p. 333); Organic Farming (p. 334); Overbooking, Part III (p. 337); DuMond International, Part II (p. 358); Interplants, Inc. (p. 398); Strenlar, Part III (p. 402); The Life-Insurance Game (p. 425); Nuclear Power Paranoia (p. 426); The Manager's Perspective (p. 427); A Matter of Ethics (p. 471).

ARBORIST screen shots © 1986. Reprinted with permission from Texas Instruments, Inc. DATA: Decision Analysis by TreeAge, screen shots © 1988 by M. Raker. Reprinted with permission of TreeAge Software, Inc. DAVID screen shots © 1988 by R. Shachter and L. Bertrand. Reprinted with permission from Duke University Center for Academic Computing.
Microsoft™ Excel screen shots © 1985–1989 by Microsoft Corporation. Reprinted with permission from Microsoft Corporation.

PWS-KENT Publishing Company is a division of Wadsworth, Inc.

Printed in the United States of America.
2 3 4 5 6 7 8 9 — 95 94 93 92
International Student Edition ISBN 0-534-98444-4

Library of Congress Cataloging-in-Publication Data

Clemen, Robert T. (Robert Taylor), 1952–
    Making hard decisions : an introduction to decision analysis /
  Robert T. Clemen.
        p.   cm.
    Includes bibliographical references and index.
    ISBN 0–534–92336–4
    1. Decision-making.   I. Title.
HD30.23.C577   1990
658.4'03—dc20

                                   90–41176
                                        CIP

Dedication

Whenever I set out to do something, no matter how difficult the task, my mother and father were very careful never to say that I wouldn't be able to do it. If it hadn't been for their undying faith in me over the years, I might never have been able to write this book. *Making Hard Decisions* is dedicated in their loving memory.

Special Thanks

We wish to extend special thanks to Professor David J. Braden of the William E. Simon Graduate School of Business Administration at the University of Rochester. Professor Braden adopted an early manuscript version of *Making Hard Decisions* for his course on quantitative analysis. He continued to use the manuscript as it was revised, contributing extensively to the revisions. His careful reading, insightful feedback, and genuine enthusiasm proved invaluable to the development of *Making Hard Decisions*.

Robert T. Clemen
Michael Payne, Senior Editor

Preface

This book provides a one-semester overview of decision analysis for advanced undergraduate and Master's degree students. The inspiration to write it has come from many sources, but perhaps most important was a desire to give students access to up-to-date information on modern decision-analysis techniques at a level that could be easily understood without a lot of mathematical background. At some points in the book, the student needs to be familiar with the basic statistical concepts that would be covered in an undergraduate applied-statistics course. In particular, some familiarity with probability and probability distributions would be helpful in Chapters 7 through 12. Algebra is used liberally throughout the book. Calculus concepts are used in a few instances as an explanatory tool. Be assured, however, that the material can be thoroughly understood, and the problems can be worked, without any knowledge of calculus.

Interestingly, since I began teaching decision analysis a few years ago, at least four new decision-analysis textbooks have been published. I am still surprised that I felt compelled to spend a lot of time and effort on this project in the face of competition from both new and existing texts. But in some cases, the other books did not include the material I wanted to cover. Some did not get the students involved in real-world decisions. None were written at a level that I considered really appropriate for nontechnical students. And so I have attempted to bring decision-analysis concepts down to an elementary level.

A common theme prevails in the book. As do most decision analysts, I subscribe to the notion that the objective of decision analysis is to help a decision maker think hard about the specific problem at hand, including his or her preferences and beliefs regarding uncertainty. More specifically, the tools of decision analysis allow the decision maker to model the decision situation. Decision-tree and influence-diagram models of the problem can be created. Probabilistic models can be used to represent the decision maker's understanding of the inherent uncertainty, and utility theory provides tools for modeling the decision maker's preferences. Above all else, I want students to understand that the purpose of studying decision-analysis techniques is to be able to represent real-world problems by using models that can be analyzed to gain insight and understanding. It is through such insight and understanding — the hoped-for result of the modeling process — that decisions can be improved.

◆ GUIDELINES FOR STUDENTS

The book covers most of the concepts that I consider important for a basic understanding of decision analysis. Although I have tried to write an elementary introduction to decision analysis, this does not mean that the material is itself elementary. In fact, the more I teach decision analysis, the more I realize that (1) the technical level of the mathematics is low, while (2) the level of the analysis is high. Students must be willing to think clearly and analytically about the problems and issues that arise in decision problems. Good decision analysis requires clear thinking; sloppy thinking results in worthless analysis.

Of course, some topics are more demanding than others. The more difficult sections are labeled as "optional." My faith in students and readers compels me to say that anyone who can handle the "nonoptional" material can, with a bit more effort and thought, also handle the optional material. Thus the label is perhaps best thought of as a warning regarding the upcoming topic. On the other hand, if the optional material is skipped, no harm will be done.

In general, I believe that really serious learning happens when problems are tackled on one's own. I have included a wide variety of exercises, questions, problems, and case studies. The exercises are relatively easy drills of the material. The questions and problems often require thinking beyond the material in the text. Some concepts are presented and dealt with only in the problems. Don't shy away from them! You can learn a lot by working through each one.

It seems as though many textbooks have case studies these days. *Making Hard Decisions* is no exception. There have been numerous successful real-world decision-analysis applications in the past, and a few of these are described in case studies. In addition, many issues are explored in the case studies in the context of current events. For example, the AIDS case at the end of Chapter 7 demonstrates how probability techniques can be used to interpret the results of medical tests. In addition to the real-world cases, the book contains many hypothetical cases and examples, as well as fictional historical accounts, which I have tried to make as realistic as possible.

Some cases and problems are realistic in the sense that not every bit of information desired is given. In these cases, appropriate assumptions are required. On the one hand, this may cause some frustration. On the other hand, incomplete information is typical in the real world. Being able to work with problems that are "messy" in this way is an important skill.

Finally, many of the cases and problems involve controversial issues. For example, the material on AIDS (Chapter 7) or medical ethics (Chapter 15) may evoke strong emotional responses from some readers. In writing a book like this, there are two choices. We can avoid the hard social problems that might offend some readers. Or we can squarely face these problems that need careful thought and discussion. I have taken the second approach because I believe these issues require our attention. Moreover, even though decision analysis alone does not provide the answers to these problems, it does provide a useful framework for thinking about the difficult decisions that we as a society must make.

◆ COMPUTERS AND DECISION ANALYSIS

Computers play a large role in decision analysis. As a result, considerable discussion in some chapters relates to personal-computer programs that are available for the construction and analysis of decision models. The healthiest doses of computer-oriented discussion are in Chapters 4 and 5 on making choices and sensitivity analysis, and again in Chapter 11 on Monte Carlo simulation. Besides special-purpose decision analysis programs, we spend considerable time discussing the use of electronic spreadsheets such as Lotus® 1-2-3™ and Microsoft® Excel™. Spreadsheets provide a very flexible modeling environment for analyzing decision problems, and many students and decision makers may have access to such spreadsheets rather than special-purpose software. One of the most useful skills that an analytically minded decision maker could have these days is expertise in the use of a spreadsheet. Finally, for those readers interested in a PC-based software program that employs influence diagrams to analyze decisions, the *Student Edition of InDia*™, developed by Decision Focus, Inc., is available from the publisher.

Do not take this business about computers wrong, though. Decision-analysis concepts and techniques can indeed be learned, understood, and used quite well without ever touching a computer. In some cases, however, such as simulation or sensitivity analysis, so much more can be done with a computer.

◆ A WORD TO INSTRUCTORS

Many instructors will want to supplement the material in *Making Hard Decisions* with their own material. In fact, there are topics that I cover in my own courses that are not included here. But in the process of writing this book and obtaining comments from colleagues, it has become apparent that decision making courses take on many different forms. Some instructors prefer to emphasize behavioral aspects, while others prefer analytical tools. Other dimensions have to do with situations involving competition, negotiation, and group decision making. *Making Hard Decisions* does not aim to cover everything for everyone. Instead, I have tried to cover the central concepts and tools of modern decision analysis with adequate references (and occasionally cases or problems) so that instructors can introduce their own special material where appropriate. For example, in Chapters 8 and 14 we discuss judgmental aspects of probability assessment and decision making, and an instructor can introduce more behavioral material in these discussions. Likewise, Chapter 15 presents an additive value function for decision making. Some instructors may wish to present goal programming or the analytic hierarchy process here.

♦ ACKNOWLEDGMENTS

It is a pleasure to acknowledge the help I have had with the preparation of this manuscript. First mention goes to my students, who craved the notes from which the book grew. Their desire has provided much motivation. The College of Business at the University of Oregon supplied a wide array of Macintosh hardware and software, both for the writing of the document as well as for developing classroom computer projects. Thanks also goes to the Fuqua School of Business at Duke University for making laser-printing and copying resources available.

Oddly enough, I owe a special debt of gratitude to the authors of competing decision-analysis texts. Their treatments of various topics typically inspired me to try to find a way to bring the insights I gained from their work to my students. Ron Howard, a man I admire greatly, should have been the one to write this book. His practical experience and insights are invaluable, and his enthusiasm about influence diagrams to some extent influenced my decision to incorporate them into the text. I also have been influenced by Detlof von Winterfeldt and Ward Edwards's advanced text *Decision Analysis and Behavioral Research,* as well as by Derek Bunn's *Applied Decision Analysis.*

Many individuals have provided comments on portions of the book at various stages. Thanks to Deborah Amaral, Cathy Barnes, George Benson, Sam Bodily, Dave Braden, Bill Burns, Peter Farquhar, Ken Gaver, Andy Golub, Max Henrion, Ralph Keeney, Robin Keller, Craig Kirkwood, Allan Murphy, Bob Nau, Roger Pfaffenberger, Steve Powell, H. V. Ravinder, Gerald Rose, Sam Roy, Rakesh Sarin, Ross Shachter, Bob Winkler, and Wayne Winston. Special thanks to Deborah Amaral for guidance in writing the municipal solid waste case in Chapter 9, and to Kevin McCardle for allowing me to use numerous problems from his statistics course. I also owe a special word of thanks to my editors, Michael Payne, Marcia Cole, and Patty Adams, for gingerly and patiently guiding me through the process of preparing the manuscript.

Usually at this point the author thanks those who typed the manuscript and created the figures. Being rather ignorant about what is involved in writing a book, I decided to do most of it myself. Even so, I would like to thank my Macintosh computer (Gordo, a fat Mac), mouse (Algernon), and hard disk (Hardy) for many night and weekend sessions. They worked unfailingly and only overheated on very hot summer days when I should have been relaxing anyway.

Finally, thanks to my wife, Sheri, and my children for their forbearance and support. The kids always were excited about "Daddy's book," even though they must have long ago given up hope that I would ever finish. Sheri never gave up hope, though. She provided encouragement and support when needed and even helped proofread the manuscript in various stages. Sometimes she would just look at the pages and shake her head. Was she amazed, or did she wonder if I knew what I was talking about? I'll probably never know.

Robert T. Clemen
Eugene, Oregon
July, 1990

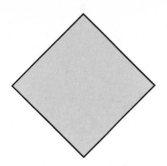

Contents

5   Sensitivity Analysis   113

6   Creativity and Decision Structuring   146

12   Value of Information   339

♦ SECTION THREE: MODELING PREFERENCES   361

13   Risk Attitudes   363

14 Utility Axioms, Paradoxes, and Implications 404

15 Conflicting Objectives I: Some Basic Techniques 430

16 Conflicting Objectives II: Multiattribute Utility Models   474

17 Conclusion and Further Reading   500

Appendixes   503

Answers to Selected Exercises   547

Index   549

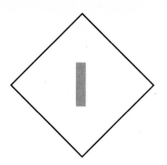

Introduction to Decision Analysis

Have you ever had a difficult decision to make? If so, did you wish for a straightforward way to keep all of the different issues clear? Did you end up making the decision based on your intuition or on a "hunch" that seemed correct? At one time or another, all of us have wished that a hard decision was easy to make. The sad fact is that hard decisions are just that — hard. As individuals we run into such difficult decisions frequently. Business executives and governmental policy makers struggle with hard problems all the time. For example, consider the following problem faced by the Oregon Department of Agriculture (ODA) in 1985.

GYPSY MOTHS AND THE ODA

In the winter of 1985, the ODA grappled with the problem of gypsy moth infestation in Lane County in western Oregon. Forest industry representatives argued strongly for an aggressive eradication campaign using potent chemical insecticides. The ODA instead proposed a plan that involved spraying most of the affected area with BT (*Bacillus thuringiensis*), a bacterial insecticide that is known to be (1) target-specific (that is, it does little damage to organisms other than moths), (2) ecologically safe, and (3) reasonably effective. As well as using BT, the ODA proposed spraying three smaller areas near the city of Eugene with the chemical spray Orthene. Although Orthene was registered as an acceptable insecticide for home garden use, there was some doubt as to its ultimate ecological effects as well as its danger to humans. Forestry officials argued that the chemical insecticide was more potent than BT and was necessary to ensure erad-

1

ication in the most heavily infested areas. Environmentalists argued that the potential danger from the chemical spray was too great to warrant its use. Some individuals argued that spraying would not help because the infestation already was so advanced that no program would be successful. Others argued that an aggressive spray program could solve the problem once and for all, but only if done immediately. Clearly, in making its final decision the ODA would have to deal with many issues.

The ODA has an extremely complex problem on its hands. Before deciding exactly what course of action to take, the agency needs to consider many issues, including the values of different constituent groups and the uncertainties involving the effectiveness and risks of the pesticides under consideration. The ODA must consider these issues carefully and in a balanced way — but how? There is no escaping the problem: This hard decision requires hard thinking.

Decision analysis provides structure and guidance for thinking systematically about hard decisions. With decision analysis , a decision maker can take action with confidence gained through a clear understanding of the problem. Along with a conceptual framework for thinking about hard problems, decision analysis provides analytical tools that can make the required hard thinking easier.

◆ WHY ARE DECISIONS HARD?

What makes decisions hard? Certainly different problems may involve different and often special difficulties. For example, the ODA's problem requires it to think about the interests of various groups as well as to consider only limited information on the possible effects of the sprays. Although every decision may have its own special problems, there are four basic sources of difficulty. A decision-analysis approach can help a decision maker with all four.

First, a decision can be hard simply because of its complexity. In the case of the gypsy moths, the ODA must consider many different individual issues: the uncertainty surrounding the different sprays, the values held by different community groups, the different possible courses of action, the economic impact of any pest-control program, and so on. Simply keeping all of the issues in mind at one time is nearly impossible. Decision analysis provides effective methods for organizing a complex problem into a structure that then can be analyzed. In particular, elements of a decision's structure include the possible courses of action, the possible outcomes that could result, the likelihood of those outcomes, and the costs and benefits to be derived from the different outcomes. Structuring tools that we will consider include decision trees and influence diagrams as well as procedures for analyzing these structures to find solutions and for answering "what if" questions.

Second, a decision can be difficult because of the inherent uncertainty in the situation. In the gypsy moth case, the major uncertainties are the effectiveness of the different sprays in reducing the moth population and their potential for detrimental ecological and health effects. In some decisions the main issue is uncertainty. For example, imagine a firm trying to decide whether to introduce a new product. The size of the market, the market price, eventual competition, and manufacturing and distribution costs all may be uncertain to some extent, and all have some impact on the firm's eventual payoff. Yet the decision must be made without knowing for sure what these uncertain values will be. A decision-analysis approach can help in identifying important sources of uncertainty and representing that uncertainty in a quantitative way.

Third, a decision maker may be interested in working toward multiple objectives, but progress in one direction may impede progress in others. In such a case, a decision maker must trade off benefits in one area against costs in another. In the gypsy moth example, important trade-offs must be made: Are the potential economic benefits to be gained from spraying Orthene worth the potential ecological damage and health risk? In investment decisions a trade-off that we usually must make is between expected return and riskiness. Decision analysis again provides both a framework and specific tools for dealing with multiple objectives.

Fourth and finally, a problem may be difficult if different perspectives lead to different conclusions. Or, even from a single perspective, slight changes in certain inputs may lead to different choices. This source of difficulty is particularly pertinent when more than one person is involved in making the decision. Different individuals may look at the problem from different perspectives, or they may disagree on the uncertainty or value of the various outcomes. The use of the decision-analysis framework and tools can help a decision maker to sort through and resolve these differences.

♦ WHY STUDY DECISION ANALYSIS?

The obvious reason for studying decision analysis is that carefully applying its techniques can lead to better decisions. But what is a good decision? A simple answer might be that it is the one that gives the best outcome. This answer, however, confuses the idea of a lucky outcome with a good decision. Suppose that you are interested in investing an inheritance. After carefully considering all the options available and consulting with investment specialists and financial planners, you decide to invest in stocks. If you purchased a portfolio of stocks in 1982, the investment most likely turned out to be a good one, because stock values increased dramatically during the 1980s. On the other hand, if your stock purchase had been in early 1929, the stock market crash and the following depression would have decreased the value of your portfolio drastically.

Was the investment decision a good one? It certainly could have been if it was made after careful consideration of the available information and thorough deliberation about the goals and possible outcomes. Was the outcome a good one? For the 1929 investor, the answer is no. This example illustrates the difference between a good decision and a lucky outcome: You can make a good decision but still have an unlucky outcome. Of course, you may prefer to have lucky outcomes rather than make good decisions! Although decision analysis cannot improve your luck, it can help you to understand better the problems you face and thus make better decisions. That understanding must include the structure of the problem as well as the uncertainty and trade-offs inherent in the alternatives and outcomes. You may then improve your chances of enjoying a better outcome; more important, you will be less likely to experience unpleasant surprises in the form of unlucky outcomes that were either unforeseen or not fully understood. In other words, you will be making a decision with your eyes open.

The preceding discussion suggests that decision analysis allows people to make effective decisions more consistently. This idea itself warrants discussion. Decision analysis is intended to help people deal with *difficult* decisions. It is a "prescriptive approach designed for normally intelligent people who want to think hard and systematically about some important real problems" (Keeney and Raiffa 1976, p. vii).

This prescriptive view is the most appropriate way to think about decision analysis. It gets across the idea that although we are not perfect decision makers, we can do better through more structure and guidance. We will see that decision analysis is not an idealized theory designed for superrational and omniscient beings. Nor does it describe how people actually make decisions. In fact, ample experimental evidence from psychology shows that people generally do not process information and make decisions in ways that are consistent with the decision-analysis approach. If they did, then there would be no need for decision analysis; why spend a lot of time studying decision analysis if it suggests that you do what you already do?

Although decision analysis provides structure and guidance for systematic thinking in difficult situations, it does not claim to recommend an alternative that must be blindly accepted. Indeed, after the hard thinking that decision analysis fosters, there should be no need for blind acceptance; the decision maker should understand the situation thoroughly. Instead of providing solutions, decision analysis is perhaps best thought of as simply an information source, providing insight about the situation, uncertainty, objectives, and trade-offs, and possibly yielding a recommended course of action. Thus, decision analysis does not usurp the decision maker's job. According to another author,

> [t]he basic presumption of decision analysis is not at all to replace the decision maker's intuition, to relieve him or her of the obligations in facing the problem, or to be, worst of all, a competitor to the decision maker's personal style of analysis, but to complement, augment, and generally work alongside the decision maker in exemplifying the nature of the problem. Ultimately, it is of most value if the decision maker has actually learned something about the problem and his or her own decision-making attitude through the exercise (Bunn 1984, p. 8).

We have been discussing decision analysis as if it were always used to help an individual make a decision. Indeed, this is what it is designed for, but its techniques have many other uses. For example, one might use decision-analysis methods to solve complicated inference problems (that is, answering questions such as "What conclusions can be drawn from the available evidence?"). Structuring a decision problem may be useful for understanding its precise nature, for generating alternative courses of action, and for identifying important objectives and trade-offs. Finally, decision analysis can be used to justify why a previously chosen action was appropriate.

♦ SUBJECTIVE JUDGMENTS AND DECISION MAKING

Personal judgments about uncertainty and values are important inputs for decision analysis. It will become clear through this text that discovering and developing these judgments involves thinking hard and systematically about important aspects of a decision.

Managers and policy makers frequently complain that analytical procedures from management science and operations research ignore subjective judgments. Such procedures often purport to generate "optimal" actions on the basis of purely objective inputs. But the decision-analysis approach allows the inclusion of subjective judgments. In fact, decision analysis *requires* personal judgments; they are important ingredients for making good decisions.

At the same time, it is important to realize that human beings are imperfect information processors. Personal insights about uncertainty and preferences can be both limited and misleading, even while the individual making the judgments may demonstrate an amazing overconfidence. An awareness of human cognitive limitations is critical in developing the necessary judgmental inputs, and a decision maker who ignores these problems can magnify rather than adjust for human frailties. Much current psychological research has a direct bearing on the practice of decision-analysis techniques. In the chapters that follow, many of the results from this research will be discussed and related to decision-analysis techniques. The spirit of the discussion is that understanding the problems people face and carefully applying decision-analysis techniques can lead to better judgments and improved decisions.

♦ THE DECISION-ANALYSIS PROCESS

Figure 1.1 shows a decision-analysis process flow chart. In the first step the decision maker identifies the problem. Although we usually do not have trouble finding decisions to make or problems to solve, we sometimes have trouble identifying them precisely, and thus we sometimes treat the wrong problem. Such a mistake has been called an "error of the third kind." A good decision analysis will always begin with a careful identification of the problem at hand. Perhaps a surface problem is hiding the real issue. For example, in the gypsy moth case, is the decision maker's problem which insecticide to use to control the insects, or is it how to mollify a vocal and ecologically minded minority?

The second step, identifying objectives and alternatives, is an important one in decision making. Identifying objectives involves introspection. What is

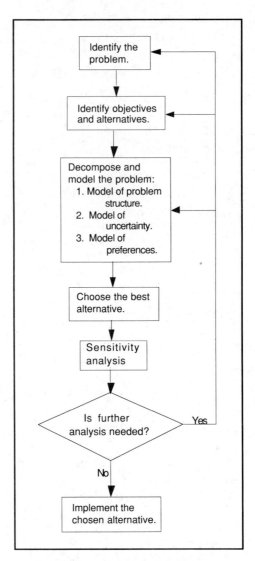

FIGURE 1.1   *A Decision-Analysis Process Flow Chart*

important? What are the objectives? Minimizing cost? Maximizing profit or market share? What about minimizing risks? Does risk mean the chance of a monetary loss, or does it refer to conditions that are potentially damaging to health and the environment? Careful consideration of all aspects of a problem, including pertinent objectives, can lead to the discovery of alternatives that were not obvious at the outset. This is an important benefit of a decision-analysis approach. In addition, research into creativity has led to the development of several techniques that can improve the chance of finding new alternatives.

The next two steps, which might be called "modeling and solution," form the heart of most textbooks on decision analysis, including this one. Much of this book will focus on decomposing problems to understand their structures and measure uncertainty and value; indeed, decomposition is the key to decision analysis. The approach is to "divide and conquer." The first level of decomposition calls for structuring the problem in smaller and more manageable pieces. Subsequent decomposition by the decision maker may entail careful consideration of elements of uncertainty in different parts of the problem or careful thought about different aspects of the objectives.

The idea of *modeling* is critical in decision analysis, as it is in most quantitative or analytical approaches to problems. As indicated in Figure 1.1, we will use models in several ways. We will use influence diagrams or decision trees to create a representation or model of the decision problem. Probability will be used to build models of the uncertainty inherent in the problem. We will assess utility functions in order to model the way in which decision makers value different outcomes and trade off competing objectives. All of these models are mathematical in nature, allowing one to find insights that are not apparent on the surface. Of course, the key advantage from a decision-making perspective is that the mathematical representation of a problem can help the decision maker identify a "preferred" alternative.

Decision analysis is typically an iterative process. Once a model has been built, *sensitivity analysis* is performed. Such analysis answers "what if" questions: "If we make a slight change in one or more aspects of the model, does the optimal decision change?" If so, the decision is said to be sensitive to these small changes, and the decision maker may wish to reconsider more carefully those aspects to which the decision is sensitive. Virtually any part of a decision is fair game for sensitivity analysis. The arrows in Figure 1.1 show that the decision maker may return even to the identification of the problem. It may be necessary to refine the definition of objectives or include objectives that were not previously included in the model. New alternatives may be identified, the model structure may change, and the models of uncertainty and preferences may need to be refined. The term *decision-analysis cycle* best describes the overall process, which may go through several iterations before a satisfactory solution is found.

In this iterative process, the decision maker's perception of the problem changes, beliefs about the likelihood of various uncertain eventualities may develop and change, and preferences for outcomes not previously considered may mature as more time is spent in reflection. Decision analysis not only provides a structured way to think about decisions, but also more fundamentally provides a structure within which a decision maker can develop beliefs and feelings, those subjective judgments that are critical for an adequate solution.

Requisite Decision Models

Phillips (1982, 1984) has introduced the term *requisite decision modeling*. This marvelous term captures the essence of the modeling process in decision analysis. In Phillips's words, "a model can be considered requisite only when no new intuitions emerge about the problem" (1984, p. 37), or when it contains every-thing that is essential for solving the problem. That is, a model is requisite when the decision maker's thoughts about the problem, beliefs regarding uncertainty, and preferences are fully developed. For example, consider a first-time mutual-fund investor who finds high, overall long-term returns appealing. Imagine, though, that in the process of researching the funds the investor begins to un-derstand and become wary of highly volatile stocks and mutual funds. For this investor, a decision model that selected a fund by maximizing the average return in the long run would not be requisite. A requisite model would have to incor-porate a trade-off between long-term returns and volatility.

A careful decision maker may cycle through the process shown in Figure 1.1 several times as the analysis is refined. Sensitivity analysis at appropriate times can help the decision maker choose the next modeling steps to take in develop-ing a requisite model. Successful decision analysts artistically use sensitivity anal-ysis to manage the iterative development of a decision model. An important goal of this book is that you begin to acquire this artistic ability through familiarity and practice with the concepts and tools of decision analysis.

◆ WHERE ARE WE GOING FROM HERE?

This book is divided into three main sections. The first is titled "Modeling Decisions," and it introduces influence diagrams and decision trees as methods for building models of decision problems. The process is sometimes called *struc-turing* because it specifies the elements of the decision and how the elements are interrelated (Chapters 2 and 3). We will find out how to use structuring tools to analyze the available choices in a decision (Chapter 4) and how to conduct sen-sitivity analysis (Chapter 5). In Chapter 6 we discuss creativity and its relation-ship to the decision-structuring process.

The second section is "Modeling Uncertainty." Here we delve into the use of probability for modeling uncertainty in decision problems. First we review basic probability concepts (Chapter 7). Because subjective judgments play a central role in decision analysis, subjective assessments of uncertainty are the topic of Chapter 8. Other ways to use probability include theoretical probability models (Chapter 9), data-based models (Chapter 10), and simulation (Chapter 11). Chapter 12 closes the section with a discussion of information and how to value it in the context of a probability model of uncertainty within a decision problem.

"Modeling Preferences" is the final section. Here we turn to the develop-ment of a mathematical representation of a decision maker's preferences, in-cluding the identification of desirable objectives and trade-offs between conflict-ing objectives. A fundamental issue that we often must confront is how to trade off riskiness and expected value. Typically, if we want to increase our chances at a better outcome, we must accept a simultaneous risk of loss. Chapters 13 and 14 delve into the problem of modeling a decision maker's attitude toward risk. Chapters 15 and 16 complete the section with a treatment of other conflicting objectives. In these chapters you will learn how to construct a mathematical model that reflects subjective feelings about the importance of competing objectives and how they can be traded off one against another.

By the end of the book, you will have learned all of the basic techniques and concepts that are central to the practice of modern decision analysis. This does not mean that your hard decisions will suddenly become easy! But with the decision-analysis framework, and with tools for modeling decisions, uncertainty, and preferences, you will be able to approach your hard decisions systematically. The understanding and insight gained from such an approach will give you confidence in your actions and allow for better decisions in difficult situations. That is what the book is about — an approach that will help you to make hard decisions.

◊ SUMMARY

The purpose of decision analysis is to help a decision maker think systematically about complex problems and to improve the quality of the resulting decisions. In this regard, it is important to distinguish between a good decision and a lucky outcome. A good decision is one that is made on the basis of a thorough understanding of the problem and careful thought regarding the important issues. Outcomes, on the other hand, may be lucky or unlucky, regardless of decision quality.

In general, decision analysis consists of a framework and a tool kit for dealing with difficult decisions. The incorporation of subjective judgments is an important aspect of decision analysis, and to a great extent mature judgments develop as the decision maker reflects on the decision at hand and develops a working model of the problem. The overall strategy is to decompose a complicated problem into smaller chunks that can be more readily analyzed and understood. These smaller pieces then can be brought together to create an overall representation of the decision situation. Finally, the decision-analysis cycle provides the framework within which a decision maker can construct a requisite decision model, one that contains the essential elements of the problem and from which the decision maker can take action.   ◆

◊ QUESTIONS AND PROBLEMS

1.1 Give an example of a good decision that you made in the face of some uncertainty. Was the outcome lucky or unlucky? Can you give an example of a poorly made decision whose outcome was lucky?

1.2 Explain how modeling is used in decision analysis. What is meant by the term "requisite decision model"?

1.3 What role do subjective judgments play in decision analysis?

1.4 At a dinner party, an acquaintance asks whether you have read anything interesting lately, and you mention that you have begun to read a text on decision analysis. Your friend asks what decision analysis is and why anyone would want to read a book about it, let alone write one! How would you answer?

1.5 Your friend in Question 1.4, upon hearing your answer, is delighted! "This is marvelous," she exclaims. "I have this very difficult choice to make at work. I'll tell you the facts, and you can tell me what I should do!" Explain to her why you cannot do the analysis for her.

1.6 Give an example in which a decision was complicated because of difficult preference trade-offs. Give one that was complicated by uncertainty.

1.7 In the gypsy moth example, what are some of the issues that you would consider in making this decision? What are the alternative courses of action? What issues involve uncertainty, and how could you get information to help resolve that uncertainty? What are the values held by opposing groups? How might your decision trade off these values?

1.8 Can you think of some different alternatives that the ODA might consider for controlling the gypsy moths?

1.9 Describe a decision that you have had to make recently that was difficult. What were the major issues? What were your alternatives? Did you have to deal with uncertainty? Were there important trade-offs to make?

1.10 "Socially responsible investing" first became fashionable in the 1980s. Such investing involves consideration of the kinds of businesses that a firm engages in and selection of investments that are as consistent as possible with the investor's sense of ethical and moral business activity. What trade-offs must the socially responsible investor make? How are these trade-offs more complicated than those that we normally consider in making investment decisions?

1.11 Many decisions are simple, preprogrammed, or already solved. For example, retailers do not have to think long to decide how to deal with a new customer. Some operations research models provide "ready-made" decisions, such as finding an optimal inventory level using an order-quantity formula or determining an optimal production mix using linear programming. Contrast these decisions with unstructured or strategic decisions, such as choosing a career or locating a nuclear power plant. What kinds of decisions are appropriate for a decision-analysis approach? Comment on the statement, "Decision making is what you do when you don't know what to do." (For more discussion, see Howard 1980.)

1.12 The argument was made that beliefs and preferences can change as we explore and learn. This even holds for learning about decision analysis! For example, what was your impression of this book before reading the first chapter? Have your beliefs about the value of decision analysis changed? How might this affect your decision about reading more of the book?

▶ CASE STUDIES

Lloyd Bentsen for Vice President?

In the summer of 1988, Michael Dukakis was the Democratic Party's presidential nominee. The son of Greek immigrants, his political career had flourished as governor of Massachusetts, where he had demonstrated excellent administrative and fiscal skills. He chose Lloyd Bentsen, U.S. Senator from Texas, as his running mate. In an analysis of Dukakis's choice, E. J. Dionne of the *New York Times* (July 13, 1988) made the following points:

1. The main job of the vice-presidential nominee is to carry his or her home state. Could Bentsen carry Texas? The Republican presidential nominee was George Bush, whose own adopted state was Texas. Many people thought that Texas would be very difficult for Dukakis to win, even with Bentsen's help. If Dukakis could win Texas's 29 electoral votes, however, the gamble would pay off dramatically, depriving Bush of one of the largest states that he might have taken for granted.

2. Bentsen was a conservative Democrat. Jesse Jackson had run a strong race and had assembled a strong following of liberal voters. Would the Jackson supporters be disappointed in Dukakis's choice? Or would they ultimately come back to the fold and be faithful to the Democratic Party?

3. Bentsen's ties with big business were unusual for a Democratic nominee. Would Democratic voters accept him? The other side of this gamble was that Bentsen was one of the best fund raisers around and might be able to eliminate or even reverse the Republicans' traditional financial advantage. Even if some of the more liberal voters were disenchanted, Bentsen could appeal to a more business-oriented constituency.

4. The safer choice for a running mate would have been Senator John Glenn from Ohio. The polls suggested that with Glenn as his running mate, Dukakis would have no trouble winning Ohio and its 23 electoral votes.

QUESTIONS

1. Why is choosing a running mate a hard decision?
2. What objectives do you think a presidential nominee should consider in making the choice?
3. What elements of risk are involved?
4. The title of Dionne's article was "Bentsen: Bold Choice or Risky Gamble?" In what sense was Dukakis's decision a "bold choice," and in what sense was it a "risky gamble"?

Du Pont and Chlorofluorocarbons

Chlorofluorocarbons (CFC's) are chemicals used as refrigerants in air conditioners and other cooling appliances, propellants in aerosol sprays, and in a variety of other applications. Scientific evidence has been accumulating for some time that CFC's released into the atmosphere can destroy ozone molecules in the ozone layer 15 miles above the earth's surface. This layer shields the earth from dangerous ultraviolet radiation. A large hole in the ozone layer above Antarctica has been found and attributed to CFC's, and a 1988 report by 100 scientists concluded that the ozone shield above the mid-Northern Hemisphere had shrunk by as much as 3% since 1969. Moreover, depletion of the ozone layer appears to be irreversible. Further destruction of the ozone layer could lead to crop failures, damage to marine ecology, and possibly dramatic changes in global weather patterns.

Environmentalists estimate that approximately 30% of the CFC's released into the atmosphere come from aerosols. In 1978, the U.S. government banned their use as aerosol propellants, but many foreign governments still permit them.

Some $2.5 billion of CFC's are sold each year, and Du Pont Chemical Corporation is responsible for 25% of that amount. In early 1988, Du Pont announced that the company would gradually phase out its production of CFC's and that replacements would be developed. Already Du Pont claims to have a CFC substitute for automobile air conditioners, although the new substance is more expensive.

QUESTIONS

Imagine that you are a Du Pont executive charged with making the decision regarding continued production of CFC's.

1. What issues would you take into account?
2. What major sources of uncertainty do you face?
3. What corporate objectives would be important for you to consider? Do you think that Du Pont's corporate objectives and the way the company views the problem might have evolved since the mid-1970s when CFC's were just beginning to become an issue?

(Sources: "A Gaping Hole in the Sky," *Newsweek*, July 11, 1988, pp. 21–23 and A. M. Louis, "Du Pont to Ban Products that Harm Ozone," *San Francisco Chronicle*, March 25, 1988, p. 1.)

◆

◇ REFERENCES

The decision-analysis view is distinctly *prescriptive*. That is, decision analysis is interested in helping people make better decisions; in contrast, a *descriptive* view of decision making focuses on how people actually make decisions. Keeney and Raiffa (1976) explain the prescriptive view as well as anyone. For an excellent summary of the descriptive approach, see Hogarth (1987).

A fundamental element of the prescriptive approach is discerning and accepting the difference between a good decision and a lucky outcome. This issue has been discussed by many authors, both academics and practitioners. An excellent recent reference is Vlek et al. (1984).

Many other books and articles describe the decision-analysis process, and each seems to have its own twist. This chapter has drawn heavily from Ron Howard's thoughts; his 1988 article summarizes his approach. Other books worth consulting include Behn and Vaupel (1982), Bunn (1984), Holloway (1979), Lindley (1985), Raiffa (1968), Samson (1988), and von Winterfeldt and Edwards (1986).

Phillips's (1982, 1984) idea of a requisite decision model is a fundamental concept that we will use throughout the text. For a related view, see Watson and Buede (1987).

BEHN, R. D., and J. D. VAUPEL (1982) *Quick Analysis for Busy Decision Makers.* New York: Basic Books.

BUNN, D. (1984) *Applied Decision Analysis.* New York: McGraw-Hill.

HOGARTH, R. (1987) *Judgement and Choice,* 2nd ed. New York: Wiley.

HOLLOWAY, C. A. (1979) *Decision Making Under Uncertainty: Models and Choices.* Englewood Cliffs, NJ: Prentice-Hall.

HOWARD, R. A. (1988) "Decision Analysis: Practice and Promise." *Management Science,* 34, 679–695.

KEENEY, R., and H. RAIFFA (1976) *Decisions with Multiple Objectives.* New York: Wiley.

LINDLEY, D. V. (1985) *Making Decisions,* 2nd ed. New York: Wiley.

PHILLIPS, L. D. (1982) "Requisite Decision Modelling." *Journal of the Operational Research Society,* 33, 303–312.

PHILLIPS, L. D. (1984) "A Theory of Requisite Decision Models." *Acta Psychologica,* 56, 29–48.

RAIFFA, H. (1968) *Decision Analysis.* Reading, MA: Addison Wesley.

SAMSON, D. (1988) *Managerial Decision Analysis.* Homewood, IL: Irwin.

VLEK, C., W. EDWARDS, I. KISS, G. MAJONE, and M. TODA (1984) "What Constitutes a Good Decision?" *Acta Psychologica,* 56, 5–27.

VON WINTERFELDT, D., and W. EDWARDS (1986) *Decision Analysis and Behavioral Research.* Cambridge: Cambridge University Press.

WATSON, S., and D. BUEDE (1987) *Decision Synthesis.* Cambridge: Cambridge University Press.

◇ EPILOGUE

What did the ODA decide? Its directors decided to use only BT on all 227,000 acres, which were sprayed on three separate occasions in late spring and early summer 1985. At the time, this was the largest gypsy moth–control program ever attempted in Oregon. In 1986, 190,000 acres were sprayed, also with BT. Most of the areas sprayed the second year had not been treated the first year because ODA had found later that the gypsy moth infestation was more widespread than first thought. In the summer of 1986, gypsy moth traps throughout the area indicated that the population was almost completely controlled. In the spring of 1987, the ODA used BT to spray only 7500 acres in 10 isolated pockets of gypsy moth populations on the fringes of the previously sprayed areas. By 1988, the spray program was reduced to a few isolated areas near Eugene, and officials agreed that the gypsy moth population was under control. ◆

Modeling Decisions

This first section is about modeling decisions. Chapter 2 presents a short discussion on the elements of a decision. Through a series of simple examples, the three basic elements are illustrated: decisions to be made, upcoming uncertain events, and the values of different outcomes. The focus is on identifying the basic elements. This skill is necessary for modeling decisions as described in Chapters 3, 4, and 5.

In Chapter 3, we take a close look at the use of influence diagrams and decision trees for representing the basic structure of a decision. Both techniques are graphical modeling tools. An influence diagram is particularly useful for developing the structure of a complex decision problem because it allows many aspects of a problem to be displayed in a compact and intuitive form. A decision-tree representation provides an alternative picture of a decision in which more of the details can be displayed.

Chapters 4 and 5 present the basic tools available to the decision maker for analyzing a decision model. Chapter 4 shows how to solve decision trees and influence diagrams. The basic concept presented is *expected monetary value* (EMV). In analyzing a decision, EMV is calculated for each of the available alternatives. In many decision situations, it is reasonable to choose the alternative with the highest EMV. In Chapter 5 we learn how to use sensitivity-analysis tools in concert with EMV calculations in the iterative decision-structuring and analysis process. After an initial basic model is built, sensitivity analysis can tell which of the input variables really matter in the decision and deserve more attention in the model. Thus, with Chapter 5 we bring the discussion of modeling decisions full circle, showing how structuring and analysis are intertwined in the decision-analysis process.

Finally, Chapter 6 delves into issues of creativity and decision making. One of the critical aspects of constructing a decision model is the determination of viable alternatives. When searching for alternative actions in a decision situation, however, we are subject to a variety of creative blocks that hamper our search for new and different possibilities. Chapter 6 describes these blocks to creativity and also presents several creativity-enhancing techniques.

Elements of Decision Problems

Given a complicated problem, how should one begin? A critical first step is that of identifying the elements of the situation. We will classify the various elements into (1) decisions to make, (2) uncertain events, and (3) the value of specific outcomes. In this chapter, we will discuss briefly these three basic elements and illustrate them in a series of examples.

♦ DECISIONS TO MAKE

Imagine a farmer whose trees are laden with fruit that is not yet ripe. If the weather report forecasts mild weather, the farmer has nothing to worry about, but if the forecast is for freezing weather, it might be appropriate to spend money on protective measures that will save the crop. In such a situation, the farmer has a decision to make, and that decision is whether or not to take protective action. This is a decision that must be made with the available information.

Many situations have as their central issue a decision that must be made immediately. There would always be at least two alternatives, otherwise no decision would need to be made. In the case of the farmer, the alternatives are to take protective action or to leave matters as they are. Of course, there may be a wide variety of alternatives. For example, the farmer may have several strategies for saving the crop, and it may be possible to implement one or more.

Another possibility may be to wait and obtain more information. If the noon weather report suggests the possibility of freezing weather depending on exactly where a weather system travels, then it may be reasonable to wait and listen to the evening report to get better information. Such a strategy, however, may entail a cost. The farmer may have to pay his workers overtime if he decides late in the evening to protect his crop. Some measures may take time to set up; if the farmer waits, there may not be enough time to implement some of these procedures.

Other possible alternatives are taking out insurance or hedging. For example, the farmer might be willing to pay his workers a small amount to be available at night if quick action is needed. Insurance policies also may be available to protect against crop loss (although these typically are not available at the last minute). Any of these alternatives might give the farmer more flexibility, although they would probably cost something up front.

Identifying the immediate decision to be made is a critical first step in understanding a difficult decision situation. Moreover, no model of the decision situation can be built without knowing exactly what decision problem is at hand. In identifying the central decision, it is important also to think about possible alternatives. Some decisions will have specific alternatives (protect the crop or not), while others may involve choosing a specific value out of a range of possible values (deciding on an amount to bid for a company you want to acquire). Other than the obvious alternative courses of action, a decision maker should always consider the possibilities of doing nothing, of waiting to obtain more information, or of somehow hedging bets.

◆ SEQUENTIAL DECISIONS

In many cases, there simply is no single decision to make, but several sequential decisions. The orchard example will demonstrate this. Suppose that several weeks of the growing season remain. Each day the farmer will get a new weather forecast, and each time there is a forecast of adverse weather it will be necessary to decide once again whether to protect the crop.

The example shows clearly that the farmer has many decisions to make, and the decisions are ordered sequentially. If the harvest is tomorrow, then the decision is fairly easy, but if several days or weeks remain, then the farmer really has to think about the upcoming decisions. For example, he may want to adopt a policy whereby the amount spent on protection is less than the value of the crop. One good way to do this would be not to protect during the early part of the growing season; instead, wait until the harvest is closer, and then protect whenever the weather forecast warrants such action. In other words, "If we're going to lose the crop, let's lose it early."

It is important to recognize that in many situations one decision leads eventually to another in a sequence. The orchard example is a special case because the decisions are almost identical from one day to the next: take protective action or not. In many cases, however, the decisions are radically different. For example, a manufacturer considering a new product might first decide whether or not to introduce it. If the decision is to go ahead, the next decision might be whether to produce it or subcontract its production. Once the production decision is made, there may be marketing decisions about distribution, promotion, and pricing.

When a decision situation is complicated by sequential decisions, a decision maker generally will want to consider them when making the immediate decision. Furthermore, the future decision may depend on exactly what happened before. For this reason, we refer to these situations as *dynamic* decision problems. In identifying elements of a decision situation, we want to know not only what specific decisions are to be made, but also the sequence in which they will arise. Figure 2.1 graphically shows a sequence of decisions, represented by squares, mapped along a time line.

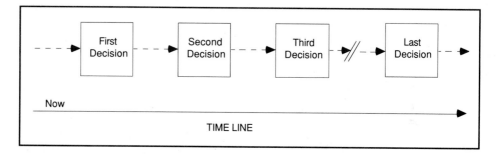

FIGURE 2.1   *Sequential Decisions*
A decision maker must consider decisions to be made now and later.

♦ UNCERTAIN EVENTS

In Chapter 1 we saw that decision problems can be complicated because of uncertainty about what the future holds. Many important decisions must be made without knowing exactly what will happen in the future or exactly what the ultimate outcome will be from a decision made today. A classic example is that of investing in the stock market. An investor may be in a position to buy some stock, but in which company? Some share prices will go up and others down, but it is difficult to tell exactly what will happen. Moreover, the market as a whole may move up or down, depending on economic forces. The best the investor can do is think carefully about the chances associated with each security's price as well as the market as a whole.

In the orchard example, the key uncertain event is the weather. It might or might not damage the crop. With some uncertain events, such as with the orchard, there are only a few possible outcomes. In other cases, such as the stock market, the outcome is a value within some range. That is, next year's price of the security bought today for $50 per share may be anywhere between, say, $0 and $100. (It certainly could never be worth less than zero, but the upper limit is not so well defined: Different individuals might consider different upper limits for the same stock.) The point is that the outcome of the uncertain event that we call "next year's stock price" comes from a range of possible values and may fall anywhere within that range.

Of course, a decision situation often involves more than a single uncertain event. The larger the number of uncertain but relevant events in a given situation, the more complicated the decision situation. Moreover, some uncertain events may depend on others. For example, the price of the specific stock purchased may be more likely to go up if the economy as a whole continues to grow or if the whole stock market increases in value. Thus there may be interdependencies among the uncertain events that a decision maker must consider in a given situation.

How do uncertain events relate to the decisions in Figure 2.1? They must be dovetailed with the time sequence of the decisions to be made; it is important to know at each decision point exactly what information is available and what remains unknown. At the current time ("Now" on the time line), all uncertain events are just that; their outcomes are unknown, although the decision maker can look into the future and specify which uncertainties will be resolved prior to each upcoming decision. For example, in the dynamic orchard decision, on any given day the farmer knows what the weather has been in the past but not what the weather will be in the future.

Sometimes an uncertain event that is resolved before a decision provides information relevant for future decisions. Consider the stock market problem. If the investor is considering an investment in a company that is involved in a lawsuit, one alternative might be to wait until the lawsuit is resolved. Note that the sequence of decisions is (1) wait or buy now, and (2) if waiting, then buy or do not buy after the lawsuit. The decision to buy or not buy may depend crucially on the outcome of the lawsuit that occurs between the two decisions.

What if there are many uncertain events that occur between decisions? There may be a natural order to the uncertain events, or there may not. If there is, then specifying that order during modeling of the decision problem may help the decision maker. But the order of events between decisions is not nearly as crucial as the dovetailing of decisions and events to clarify what events are unknown and what information is available for each decision in the process. It is the time sequence of the decisions that matters, along with the information available at each decision. In Figure 2.2, uncertain events, represented by circles, are dovetailed with a sequence of decisions. An arrow from a group of uncertain events to a decision indicates that the outcomes of those events are known at the time the decision is made. Of course, the decision maker is like the proverbial elephant and never forgets what has happened. For upcoming decisions, he or she should be able to recall (possibly with the aid of notes and documents) everything that happened (decisions and event outcomes) up to that point.

◆ OUTCOMES AND VALUES

After the last decision has been made and the last uncertain event has been resolved, the decision maker's fate is finally determined. It may be a matter of profit or loss as in the case of the farmer. It may be a matter of increase in the investor's portfolio value. In some cases the final outcome may be a "net value"

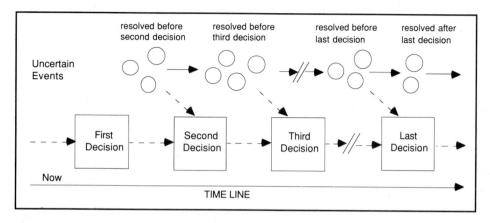

FIGURE 2.2   *Dovetailing Uncertain Events and Sequential Decisions*

figure that accounts for both cash outflows and inflows during the time sequence of the decisions. This might happen in the case of the manufacturer deciding about a new product; certain costs must be incurred (development, raw materials, advertising) before any revenue is obtained.

The examples so far have all had outcomes that could be measured in dollars. In many cases, it will be possible to think in terms of either dollars or some other single measure. More generally, however, the outcome may have more than one dimension. Consider the outcome of a general's decision to storm a hill. The outcome might be good because the army succeeds in taking the hill, but it may be bad at the same time because of lives lost. As we discussed in Chapter 1, the decision may be complicated by conflicting objectives and trade-offs among them.

In our graphical scheme, we must think about the final outcome at the end of the time line after all decisions have been made and all uncertain events resolved. For example, the outcome for the farmer after deciding whether to protect and then experiencing the weather might be a profit of $15,000 or a loss of $3400 or some other dollar amount. For the general it might be "gain the hill, 10 men killed, 20 wounded," or "don't gain the hill, 2 men killed, 5 wounded." Thus, the end of the time line is the point at which the decision maker finds out the results. Looking forward from the current time and decision, the end of the time line is called the *planning horizon.* Figure 2.3 shows how the outcome fits into our graphical scheme.

What is an appropriate planning horizon? For the farmer, the answer is relatively easy; the appropriate planning horizon is the time of harvest. But for the general, this question is not so simple. Is the appropriate horizon the end of the next day when he will know whether his men were able to take the hill? Or is it at the end of the war? Or is it sometime in between — say, the end of next month? For the investor, how far ahead should the planning horizon be? A week? A month? Several years? For individuals planning for retirement, the planning horizon may be years in the future. For speculators trading on the floor of

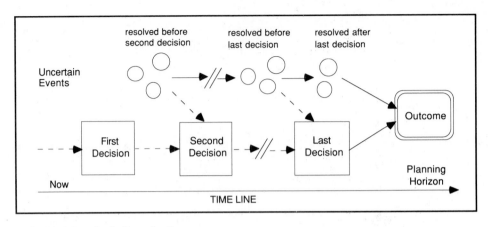

FIGURE 2.3   *Including the Outcome*

a commodity exchange, the planning horizon may be only minutes into the future.

Thus, one of the fundamental issues with which a decision maker must come to grips is how far into the future to look. It always is possible to look farther ahead; there always will be more decisions to make, and earlier decisions may have some effect on the availability of later alternatives. Even death is not an obvious planning horizon because the decision maker may be concerned with effects on future generations; environmental policy decisions provide perfect examples. At some point the decision maker has to stop and say, "My planning horizon is there. It's not worthwhile for me to think beyond that point in time." For the purpose of constructing a requisite model, the idea is to choose a planning horizon such that events and decisions that would follow after are not essential parts of the immediate decision problem.

Once the dimensions of the outcome and the planning horizon have been determined, the next step is to figure out how to value each possible outcome. As mentioned, in many cases it will be possible to work in terms of monetary outcomes. That is, the essential objective of a decision is to make money, so all that matters at the end is profit, cost, or total wealth. Even in cases where several different objectives appear to conflict, it may be possible to *price out* the nonmonetary objectives. For example, a manager might be considering whether to build and run a day care center for the benefit of employees. One dimension of the outcome would be the goodwill between the company and the work force. That goodwill would have certain effects on the operations of the company, including reduced absenteeism, improved ability to recruit, and a better image in the community. Some of these, such as reduced absenteeism and improved recruiting, easily could be translated into dollars. The image may be more difficult to translate, but the manager might assess its value subjectively by determining how much money it would cost in terms of public relations work to improve the firm's image by the same amount.

In some cases, however, it will be difficult to determine exactly how the different objectives should be traded off. For example, how many lives should the general be willing to sacrifice to gain the hill? How much damage to the environment are we willing to accept to increase our supply of domestic oil? How much in the way of health risks are we willing to accept to have blemish-free fruits and vegetables? Many decisions, especially governmental policy decisions, are complicated by trade-offs like these. Even personal decisions, such as taking a job or purchasing a home, require a decision maker to think hard about the trade-offs involved.

◆ THE TIME VALUE OF MONEY: A SPECIAL KIND OF TRADE-OFF

One of the most common outcomes in personal and business decisions is a stream of cash flows. For example, an investor may spend money on a project (an initial cash outflow) to obtain revenue in the future (cash inflows) over a period of years. In such a case, there is a special kind of trade-off: spending dollars today to obtain dollars tomorrow. If a dollar today were worth the same as a dollar next year, there would be no problem, but that is not the case. A dollar today can be invested in a savings account or some kind of interest-bearing security; at the end of a year, one dollar invested now would be worth one dollar plus the interest paid.

Trade-offs between current and future dollars (and between future dollars at different points in time) refer to the fact that the value of a dollar depends on when it is available to the decision maker. Because of this, we often refer to the "time value of money." Fortunately, there is a straightforward way to collapse a stream of cash flows into a single number. This number is called the *present value*, or value in present dollars, of the stream of cash flows.

Suppose you have $100 in your pocket. If you put that money into a savings account that earns 10% per year, paid annually, then you would have $100 × 1.1 = $110 at the end of the year. At the end of two years, the balance in the account would be $110 plus another 10%, or $110 × 1.1 = $121. In fact, you can see that the amount you have is simply the original $100 multiplied by 1.1 twice: $121 = $100 × 1.1 × 1.1 = $100 × 1.1^2. If you keep the money in the account for five years, say, then the interest compounds for five years. The account balance would be $100 × 1.1^5 = $161.05.

We are going to use this idea of interest rates to work backward. Suppose, for example, that someone promises that you can have $110 next year. What is this worth to you right now? If you have available some sort of investment like a savings account that pays 10% per year, then you would have to invest $100 to get $110 next year. Thus, the present value of the $110 that arrives next year is just $110/1.1 = $100. Similarly, the present value of $121 promised at the end of two years is $121/(1.1^2) = 100.

In general, we will talk about the present value of an amount x that will be received at the end of n time periods. Of course, we must know the interest rate that is appropriate. Let r denote the interest rate per time period in decimal form; that is, if the interest rate is 10%, then $r = 0.10$. With this notation, the formula for calculating present value (PV) is:

$$PV(x, n, r) = \frac{x}{(1 + r)^n}.$$

The denominator in this formula is a number greater than one. Thus, dividing x by $(1 + r)^n$ will give a present value that is less than x. For this reason, we often say that we "discount" x back to the present. You can see that if you had the discounted amount now and could invest it at the interest rate r, then after n time periods (days, months, years, and so on) the value of the investment would be the discounted amount times $(1 + r)^n$, which is simply x.

Keeping the interest rate consistent with the time periods is important. For example, a savings account may pay 10% "compounded monthly." Thus, a year is really 12 time periods, and so $n = 12$. The monthly interest rate is 10%/12, or 0.8333%. Thus, the value of $100 deposited in the account and left for a year would be $100 \times (1.00833)^{12} = \$110.47$. Notice that compounding helps because the interest itself earns interest during each time period. Thus, if you have a choice among savings accounts that have the same interest rate, the one that compounds more frequently will have a higher eventual payoff.

We now can talk about the present value of a stream of cash flows. Suppose that a friend is involved in a business deal and offers to let you in on the deal. For $425 paid to him now, he says, you can have $110.00 next year, $121.00 the following year, $133.10 the third year, and $146.41 at the end of the fourth year. This is a great deal, he says, because your payments will total $510.51.

What is the present value of the stream of payments? (You probably can guess already!) Let us suppose you put your money into a savings account at 10%, compounded annually. Then we would calculate the present value of the stream of cash flows as the sum of the present values of the individual cash flows:

$$PV = \frac{110.00}{1.1} + \frac{121.00}{(1.1)^2} + \frac{133.10}{(1.1)^3} + \frac{146.41}{(1.1)^4}$$

$$= \$100 + \$100 + \$100 + \$100 = \$400.$$

Thus, the deal is not so great. You would be paying $425 for a stream of cash flows that has a present value of only $400. The *net present value* (NPV) of the cash flows is the present value of the cash flows ($400) minus the cost of the deal ($425), or −$25; you would be better off keeping your $425 and investing it in the savings account.

The formula for calculating NPV for a stream of cash flows $x_0, \ldots, x_n$ over n periods at interest rate r is:

$$NPV = \frac{x_0}{(1 + r)^0} + \frac{x_1}{(1 + r)^1} + \ldots + \frac{x_n}{(1 + r)^n}$$

$$= \sum_{i=1}^{n} \frac{x_i}{(1 + r)^i}.$$

In general, we can have both outflows (negative numbers) and inflows. In the example, we include the cash outflow of $425 as a negative number in calculating NPV:

$$NPV = \frac{-425.00}{(1.1)^0} + \frac{110.00}{(1.1)^1} + \frac{121.00}{(1.1)^2} + \frac{133.10}{(1.1)^3} + \frac{146.41}{(1.1)^4}$$

$$= -\$425 + \$400$$

$$= -\$25.$$

[Recall that raising any number to the zero power is equal to 1, and so $(1.1)^0 = 1$.] Clearly, we could deal with any stream of cash flows. There could be one big inflow and then several outflows (such as with a loan), or there could be a large outflow (buying a machine), then inflows (revenue), another outflow (maintenance costs), and so on. When NPV is calculated, it reveals the value of the stream of cash flows. A negative NPV for a project indicates that the money would be better invested to earn interest rate r.

We began our discussion by talking about trade-offs. You can see how calculating present values establishes trade-offs between dollars at one point in time and dollars at another. That is, you would be indifferent about receiving $1 now or $1(1 + r)$ at the end of the next time period. More generally, $1 now is worth $1(1 + r)^n$ at the end of n time periods. NPV works by using these trade-off rates to discount all cash flows back to the present.

Knowing the interest rate is the key in using present value analysis. What is the appropriate interest rate? In general, it is the rate that you could get by investing your money in the next best opportunity. Often we use the interest rate from a savings account, a certificate of deposit, or short-term (money market) securities. For a corporation, the appropriate rate to use might be the one that it would have to pay to raise money by issuing bonds. Often the interest rate is called the *hurdle rate*, a term indicating that an acceptable investment must earn more than this rate.

We have talked about the elements of decision problems: decisions to make, uncertain events, and values of outcomes. The discussion of the time value of money showed how an outcome that is a stream of cash flows can be valued through the trade-offs implicit in interest rates. It now is time to put all of this together and try it out in an example. Imagine the problems that an oil company might face in putting together a plan for dealing with a major ocean oil spill.

LARKIN OIL

Bill Mills shuffled his feet. The Oil Spill Contingency Plan Committee was supposed to come up with a concrete proposal for the top management of Larkin Oil, Inc. The committee members had lots of time; the CEO had asked for recommendations within three months. This was their first meeting.

Over the past hour, Peter Wilton and Bob Brown had argued about exactly what level of resources should be committed to planning for a major oil spill in the company's main shipping terminal bay.

"Look," said Peter, "We've been over this so many times. When, and if, an oil spill actually occurs, we will have to move fast to clean up the oil. To do that, we have to have equipment ready to go."

"But having equipment on standby like that means tying up a lot of capital," Bob replied. As a member of the financial staff, Bob was sensitive to committing capital for equipment that would be idle all the time and might actually have to be replaced before it was ever used. "We'd be better off keeping extensive records, maybe just a long list of equipment that would be useful in a major cleanup. We need to know where it is, what it's capable of, what its condition is, and how to transport it."

"Come to think of it, our list will also have to include information on transportation equipment and strategies," Leslie Taylor added.

Bill finally stirred himself. "You know what bothers me? We're talking about these alternatives, and the fact that we need to do thus and so in order to accomplish such and such. We're getting the cart before the horse. We just don't have our hands on the problem yet. I say we go back to basics. First, how could an oil spill happen?"

"Easy," said Peter. "Most likely something would happen at the pipeline terminal. Something goes wrong with a coupling, or someone just doesn't pay attention while loading oil on the ship. The other possibility is that a tanker's hull fails for some reason, probably from running aground because of weather."

"Weather may not be the problem," suggested Leslie. "What about incompetence? What if the pilot gets drunk?"

Tom Kelso always was able to imagine unusual scenarios. "And what about the possibility of sabotage? What if a terrorist decides to wreak environmental havoc?"

"Okay," said Bill. "In terms of the actual cleanup, the more likely terminal spill would require a different kind of response than the less likely event of a hull failure. In planning for a terminal accident, we need to think about having some equipment at the terminal. Given the higher probability of such an accident, we should probably spend money on cleanup equipment that would be right there and available."

"I suppose so," conceded Bob. "At least we would be spending our money on the right kind of thing."

"You know, there's another problem that we're not really thinking about," Leslie offered. "An oil spill at the terminal can be easily contained with relatively little environmental damage. On the other hand, if we ever have a hull failure, we have to act fast. If we don't, and mind you, we may not be able to because of the weather, Larkin Oil will have a terrible time trying to clean up the public relations as well as the beaches. And think about the difference in the PR problem if the spill is due to incompetence on the part of a pilot rather than weather or sabotage."

"Even if we act fast, a huge spill could still be nearly impossible to contain," Bill pointed out. "So what's the upshot? Sounds to me like we need someone who could make a decision immediately about how to respond. We need to recover as much oil as possible, minimize environmental damage, and manage the public relations problem."

"And do this all efficiently," growled Bob Brown. "We still have to do it without having tied up all of the company's assets for years waiting for something to happen."

The committee at Larkin Oil has a huge problem on its hands. The effects of its work now and the policy that is eventually implemented for coping with future accidents will substantially affect the company's resources and possibly the environment. We cannot solve the problem entirely, but we can apply the principles discussed so far in the chapter. Let us look at the basic elements of the decision situation.

First, what is the immediate decision at hand? The immediate decision is what policy to adopt for dealing with oil spills. Exactly what alternatives are available is not clear, but it would appear that a fundamental issue is how much of the company's resources should be committed to standby status waiting for an accident to occur. In general, the more resources committed, the faster the company could respond and the less damage would be done.

Is this a sequential decision problem? Based on Bill's last statement, the immediate decision must anticipate future decisions about responses to specific accident situations. Thus, in figuring out an appropriate policy to adopt now, the committee members may want to think about possible appropriate future decisions and what resources must be available at the time so that the appropriate action could be taken.

The scenario is essentially about uncertain events. Of course, the main uncertain event is whether an oil spill will ever occur. From Bob Brown's point of view, an important issue might be how long the cleanup equipment sits idle, requiring periodic maintenance, until an accident occurs. Also important are events such as the kind of spill, the location, the weather, the cause, and the extent of the damage. At the present time, imagining the first accident, all of these are unknowns, but if and when a decision must be made, some information will be available (location, current weather, cause), while other factors — weather conditions for the cleanup, extent of the eventual damage, and total cleanup cost — probably will not be known.

What is an appropriate planning horizon for Larkin? No indication is given in the case, but the committee members may want to consider this. How far into the future should they look? How long will their policy recommendations be active? They may wish to specify that at some future date (say 10 years from the present) another committee be charged with reviewing and updating the policy in light of scientific and technological advances.

The problem also involves fundamental issues about how the different outcomes are valued. As indicated, the fundamental trade-off is whether to save money by committing fewer resources or to provide better protection against future possible accidents. In other words, just how much is insurance against damage worth to Larkin Oil? In talking about outcomes, the committee can imagine certain possible ones and the overall "cost" (in generic terms) to the company: (1) committing substantial resources and never needing them; (2) committing a lot of resources and using them effectively to contain a major spill; (3) committing few resources and never needing them (the best possible outcome); and (4) committing few resources and not being able to clean up a spill effectively (the worst possible outcome).

Just considering the dollars spent, there is a time-value-of-money problem that Bob Brown eventually will want the committee to address. To some extent, dollars can be spent for protection now instead of later on. Alternative financing schemes can be considered to pay for the equipment required. Different strategies for acquiring and maintaining equipment may have different streams of cash flows. Calculating the present value of these different strategies for providing protection may be an important aspect of the decision.

Finally, the committee members also need to think about exactly how to allocate resources in terms of the other objectives stated by Bill Mills. They need to recover oil, minimize environmental damage, and handle public relations problems. Of course, recovering oil and minimizing environmental damage are linked to some extent. Overall, however, the more resources are committed to one objective, the less available they are to satisfy the others. The committee may want to specify guidelines for resource allocation in its recommendations, but for the most part, this allocation will be made at the time of future decisions that are in turn made in response to specific accidents.

Can we put all of this together? Figure 2.4 shows the sequence of decisions and uncertain events. This is only a rough picture, intended to capture the elements discussed here, a first step toward the development of a requisite decision

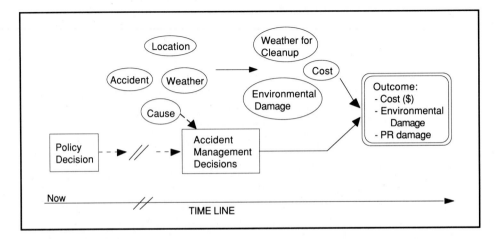

FIGURE 2.4   *A Graphical Representation of Larkin Oil's Problem*

model. Different decision makers most likely would have different representations of the problem, although most probably would agree on the essential elements of the decisions, uncertain events, and values.

◇ SUMMARY

Hard decisions often have many different aspects. The basic elements of decision problems are decisions to be made, uncertain events, and the way in which an outcome is valued. This chapter discussed identification of the immediate decision at hand as well as subsequent decisions. We found that uncertain future events must be dovetailed with the sequence of decisions, showing exactly what is known before each decision is made and what uncertainties still remain. We discussed valuing outcomes in some depth, emphasizing the specification of a planning horizon and the identification of relevant trade-offs. The discussion about the time value of money showed how interest rates imply a special kind of trade-off between cash flows at different points in time. Finally, the Larkin Oil example served to illustrate the identification of the basic elements of a major (and messy) decision problem. ◆

◇ QUESTIONS AND PROBLEMS

2.1 Explain in your own words why it is important in some situations to consider future decisions as well as the immediate decision at hand? Can you give an example from your own experience of an occasion in which you had to make a decision while explicitly anticipating a subsequent decision? How did the immediate decision affect the subsequent one?

2.2 Explain in your own words why it is important to keep track of what information is known and what events are still uncertain for each decision.

2.3 What alternatives other than specific protection strategies might Larkin Oil consider (for example, insurance)?

2.4 Describe a decision problem that you have faced recently or with which you are currently struggling. Identify the basic elements of the decision.

2.5 Imagine the difficulties of an employer who is considering which of several applicants to hire. Identify the basic elements of the employer's decision problem. How does the problem change if the employer has to decide whether to make an immediate offer after each interview?

2.6 Identify the basic elements of a real-estate investor's decision situation. Is the situation dynamic (that is, are there sequential decisions)? What are some of the uncertainties that the investor faces? What kinds of trade-offs should the investor consider? What role does the time value of money play for this investor?

2.7 Calculate the net present value of a business deal that costs $2500 today and will return $1500 at the end of this year and $1700 at the end of the following year. Use an interest rate of 13%.

2.8 A friend asks you to loan him $1000 and offers to pay you back at the rate of $90 per month for 12 months.

a. Using an annual interest rate of 10%, find the net present value of making the loan to him. Repeat using an interest rate of 20%.

b. Find an interest rate that gives a net present value of 0. The interest rate for which NPV = 0 is often called the *internal rate of return.*

2.9 Find the net present value of a project that has cash flows of –$12,000 in Year 1, +$5000 in Years 2 and 3, –$2000 in Year 4, and +$6000 in Years 5 and 6. Use an interest rate of 12%. Find the interest rate that gives a net present value of zero.

2.10 Delores Martinez is considering taking out a loan to purchase a desk. The furniture store manager says he rarely finances purchases, but he will for Delores "as a special favor." He will charge 10% per year, and because the desk costs $600, the interest will come to $60 for a one-year loan. Thus, the total price is $660, and she can pay it off in 12 installments of $55 each.

a. Use the interest rate of 10% per year to calculate Delores's net present value of the loan. (Remember to convert to a monthly interest rate.) Should Delores accept the terms of the loan?

b. Look at this problem from the store manager's perspective. Using the interest rate of 10%, what is the net present value of the loan to the manager?

c. What is the net present value of the loan to the manager if an interest rate of 18% is used? What does this imply for the real rate of interest that Delores is being charged for the loan?

This kind of financing arrangement was widely practiced at one time, and you can see why from your answers to (c). By law lenders now must be sure that the actual annual percentage rate is stated clearly in the loan contract.

2.11 Carl Rasmussen is deciding which sports car to purchase. In his reflection about the decision, he realizes that after a few years he may trade in his car for a new one. Should he count this as an uncertain event or a future decision to make? What are the implications for building a requisite model of the current car-purchase decision if he thinks of trading in the car later as an uncertain event? As a decision?

CASE STUDIES

The Value of Patience

Jack Briggs, a wealthy private investor, had been approached by Union Finance Company the day before. It seemed that Union Finance was interested in loaning money to one of its larger clients, but the client's demands were such that Union could not manage the whole thing. Specifically, the client wanted to obtain a loan for $385,000, offering to repay Union Finance $100,000 per year over seven years.

Union Finance made Briggs the following proposition. Because it was bringing him business, its directors argued, they felt that it was only fair for him to put up a proportionately larger share of the money. If Briggs would put up 60% of the money ($231,000), then Union would put up the remaining 40% ($154,000). The two parties would split the payments evenly, each one getting $50,000 at the end of each year for the next seven years.

QUESTIONS

1. Union Finance usually can earn 18% on its money. Using this interest rate, what is the net present value of the client's offer to Union?
2. Jack Briggs does not have access to the same investments as Union. In fact, if he does nothing else with his money, he will invest it in a certificate of deposit that earns 10% over the next seven years. Using this interest rate, what is Briggs's net present value of the offer made to him by Union? Should he accept the offer?
3. What is the net present value of the deal to Union if Briggs participates as proposed?
4. The title of this case study is "The Value of Patience." Which of these two investors is more patient? Why? How is this difference exploited by them in coming to an agreement?

◆

Early Bird, Inc.

The directors of Early Bird, Inc., were considering whether to begin a sales promotion for their line of specialty coffees earlier than originally planned. "I think we should go ahead with the price cuts," Art Brandon said. "After all, it couldn't hurt! At the very worst, we'll sell some coffee cheap for a little longer than we had planned, and on the other side we could beat New Morning to the punch."

"That's really the question, isn't it," replied Jack Santorini. "If New Morning really is planning its own promotion, and we start our promotion now, we would beat it to the punch. On the other hand, we might provoke a price war. And you know what a price war with that company means. We spend a lot of money fighting with each other. There's no real winner. We both just end up with less profits."

Tom Wheeler, the finance VP for Early Bird, piped up. "Consumers win in a price war. They get to buy things cheaper for a while. We ought to be able to make something out of that."

Ira Press, CEO for Early Bird, looked at the VP thoughtfully. "You've shown good horse sense in situations like these, Tom. How do you see it?"

Tom hesitated. He did not like being put on the spot like this. "You all know what the projections are for the six-week promotion as planned. The marketing group tells us to expect sales of 10 million dollars. The objective is to gain at least two percentage points of market share, but our actual gain could be anywhere from nothing to three points. Profits during the promotion are expected to be down by 10 percent, but after the promotion ends, our increased market share should result in more sales and more profits."

Art broke in. "That's assuming New Morning doesn't come back with its own promotion in reaction to ours. And you know what our report is from Pete. He says that he figures New Morning is up to something."

"Yes, Pete did say that. But you have to remember that Pete works for our advertising agent. His incentive is to sell advertising. And if he thinks that he can talk us into spending more money, he will. Furthermore, you know, he isn't always right. Last time he told us that New Morning was going to start a major campaign, he had the dates right, but it was for a different product line altogether."

Ira would not let Tom off the hook. "But Tom, if New Morning does react to our promotion, would we be better off starting it early?"

Tom thought for a bit. If he were working at New Morning and saw an unexpected promotion begin, how would he react? Would he want to cut prices to match the competition? Would he try to stick with his original plans? Finally he said, "Look, we have to believe that New Morning's managers also have some horse sense. They would not want to get involved in a price war if it could be avoided. At the same time, they aren't going to let us walk away with the market. I think that if we move early, there's about a 30 percent chance that they will react immediately, and we'll be in a price war before we know it."

"We don't have to react to New Morning's reaction, you know," replied Ira.

"You mean," asked Jack Santorini, "we have another meeting like this to decide what to do if it does react?"

"Right."

"So," Tom said, "I guess our immediate options are to start our promotion early or to start it later as planned. If we start it now, a strong reaction from New Morning is possible. If that happens then we can decide whether we want to cut our prices further."

Jack Santorini spoke up. "But if New Morning reacts strongly and we don't, we would probably end up just spending our money for nothing. We would gain no market share at all. We might even lose some market share. If we were to cut prices further, it might hurt profits, but at least we would be able to preserve what market share gains we had made before New Morning's initial reaction."

At this point, several people started to argue among themselves. Sensing that no resolution was immediately forthcoming, Ira Press adjourned the meeting, asking everyone to sleep on the problem and to call him with any suggestions or insights they had.

QUESTIONS

1. What do you think Early Bird's planning horizon should be?
2. Identify the basic elements of Early Bird's decision problem. Construct a diagram like Figure 2.4 to show these elements.

◇ REFERENCES

Identifying the elements of decision situations is implicit in a decision-analysis approach, although most textbooks do not explicitly discuss this initial step in decision modeling. The references listed at the end of Chapter 1 are all appropriate for discussion of decisions, uncertain events, and values of outcomes.

Dynamic decision situations can be very involved, and many articles and books have been written on the topic. A basic textbook that includes dynamic decision analysis is Buchanan (1982). DeGroot (1970) covers many dynamic decision problems at a somewhat more sophisticated level. Murphy et al. (1985) discuss the farmer's dynamic decision problem in detail.

The time value of money is a standard topic in finance courses, and more complete discussions of net present value, internal rate of return (the implied interest rate in a sequence of cash flows), and related topics can be found in most basic financial management textbooks. Two good ones are Brigham (1985) and Schall and Haley (1986).

BRIGHAM, E. F. (1985) *Financial Management: Theory and Practice*, 4th ed. Hinsdale, IL: Dryden.

BUCHANAN, J. T. (1982) *Discrete and Dynamic Decision Analysis.* Chichester: John Wiley.

DEGROOT, M. H. (1970) *Optimal Statistical Decisions.* New York: McGraw-Hill.

MURPHY, A. H., R. W. KATZ, R. L. WINKLER, and W.-R. HSU (1985) "Repetitive Decision Making and the Value of Forecasts in the Cost–Loss Ratio Situation: A Dynamic Model." *Monthly Weather Review*, 113, 801–813.

SCHALL, L. D., and C. W. HALEY (1986) *Introduction to Financial Management*, 4th ed. New York: McGraw-Hill.

◇ EPILOGUE

On March 24, 1989, the Exxon *Valdez* tanker ran aground a reef in Prince William Sound after leaving the Valdez, Alaska, pipeline terminal. More than 11 million gallons of oil spilled into the sound, the largest spill yet in the United States. In the aftermath, it was revealed that Aleyeska, the consortium of oil companies responsible for constructing and managing the pipeline, had instituted an oil spill contingency plan that was inadequate to the task of cleaning up a spill of such magnitude. As a result of the inadequate plan and the adverse weather immediately after the spill, little oil was recovered. Hundreds of miles of environmentally delicate shoreline were contaminated. Major fisheries were damaged, leading to specific economic harm to individuals who relied on fishing for a livelihood. In addition, the spill proved an embarrassment for all of the major oil companies and sparked new interest in environmental issues, especially in upcoming leases for offshore oil drilling. Even though the risk of a major oil spill was quite small, in retrospect one might conclude that the oil companies would have been better off with a much more carefully thought out contingency plan and more resources invested in it. [Source: "Dead Otters and Silent Ducks," *Newsweek*, April 24, 1989, p. 70.]   ◆

Structuring Decisions

Having identified the elements of a decision problem, how should one begin the modeling process? This chapter examines two approaches for structuring problems: influence diagrams and decision trees. These decision-analysis tools have different advantages for modeling difficult decisions. Both approaches are valuable and, in fact, complement one another nicely. The objective of this chapter is to show the roles that each can play in the decision-structuring process.

◆ INFLUENCE DIAGRAMS

An influence diagram provides a simple graphical representation of a decision problem. The elements of a decision problem — decisions to make, uncertain events, and the value of outcomes — show up in the influence diagram as different shapes. These shapes then are linked with arrows in specific ways to show the relationships among the elements.

Squares represent decisions, circles represent chance events, and rectangles with rounded corners represent values. These shapes generally are referred to as *nodes*: decision nodes, chance nodes, and value nodes. Nodes are put together in a *graph*, connected by arrows, or *arcs*. We call a node at the beginning of an arc a *predecessor* and one at the end of an arc a *successor*.

The simplest decision problem is one in which there is a single decision to make, one uncertain event, and an outcome that is affected by both the decision and the uncertain event. As an example, consider a venture capitalist's problem in deciding whether to invest in a small business. The entrepreneur who is seeking the capitalist's investment has impeccable qualifications and generally has done an excellent job of identifying his market, assembling a skilled management and production team, and constructing a suitable business plan. In fact, it is clear that the entrepreneur will be able to obtain financial backing from some source whether the venture capitalist decides to invest or not. The only problem is that the proposed project is extremely risky — more so than most new ventures. Thus, the venture capitalist must decide whether to invest in this highly risky undertaking. If she invests, she may be able to get in on the ground floor of a highly successful business. On the other hand, the operation may fail altogether. Clearly, the capitalist's dilemma is whether the chance of getting in on the ground floor of something big is worth the risk of losing her investment entirely. If she does not invest in this project, she may leave her capital in the stock market or invest in other less risky ventures. Her investment problem appears in influence diagram form in Figure 3.1.

Note that both "Invest?" and "Venture Succeeds or Fails" precede "Value." The implication is that the value of the outcome depends on both the decision and the chance event. In general, the value of the outcome depends on what happens or what is decided in the nodes that precede the value node. Note also that no arc points from the chance node to the decision node. The absence of an arc indicates that when the decision is made, the venture capitalist does not know whether the project will succeed. She may have some feeling for the chance of success, and this information would be included in the influence diagram as probabilities of possible levels of success or failure. Thus, the influence diagram as drawn captures the decision maker's current state of knowledge about the situation.

Also note that no arc points from the decision to the uncertain event. The absence of an arrow here has an important but subtle meaning. The uncertainty node is about the success of the venture. The absence of the arc from "Invest?" to "Venture Succeeds or Fails" means that the venture's chances for success are not affected by the capitalist's decision. In other words, the capitalist does not have to concern herself with her impact on the venture.

It is possible to imagine situations in which the capitalist may be considering different levels of investment as well as managerial involvement. For example,

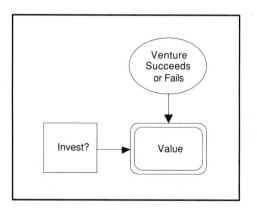

FIGURE 3.1   *Influence Diagram of Venture Capitalist's Decision*

she may be willing to invest $100,000 and leave the entrepreneur alone. But if she invests $500,000, she may wish to be more active in running the company. If she believes her involvement would improve the company's chance of success, then it would be appropriate to include an arrow from the decision node to the chance node; her investment decision — the level of investment and the concomitant level of involvement — would be relevant for determining the company's chance of success. In our simple and stylized example, however, we are assuming that her choice simply is whether to invest and that she has no impact on the company's chance of success.

The rules for using arcs to represent relationships among the nodes are shown in Figure 3.2. In general, two kinds of arcs exist; these are represented by solid and dashed arrows, respectively. The difference between these two arrows is in what kind of node they point to; solid arrows point to chance and value nodes, and dashed arrows point to decisions. A solid arrow pointing into a chance node designates *relevance*, which indicates that the predecessor is relevant for assessing the chances associated with the uncertain event. For example, an arrow from Event A to Event B means that the chances (probabilities) associated with B will be different for different outcomes of A. If an arrow points from a decision node to a chance node, then the specific chosen decision alternative is relevant for assessing the chances associated with the succeeding uncertain event. For instance, the chance that a person will become a millionaire depends to some extent on the choice of a career.

Dashed arrows point to decision nodes. These arrows indicate that the decision is made knowing the outcome of the predecessor node. Thus, a dashed arrow from a chance node to a decision means that the outcome of the chance event is known when the decision is made; this is specific information available

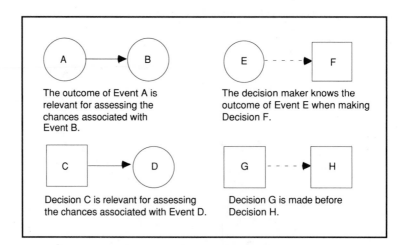

FIGURE 3.2   *Representing Influence with Arrows*
Solid arrows into chance nodes represent relevance, and
dashed arrows into decision nodes represent information.

to the decision maker. An arrow from one decision to another decision simply means that the first decision is made before the second. Thus, the sequential ordering of decisions is shown in an influence diagram by the path through the decision nodes.

Influence diagrams that are properly constructed have no *cycles*; regardless of the starting point, there is no path following the arrows that leads back to the starting point. For example, if there is an arrow from A to B, there is no path that leads back to A from B. Imagine an insect traveling from node to node in the influence diagram, always following the direction of the arrows. In a diagram without cycles, once the insect leaves a particular node, it has no way to get back to that node.

◆ SOME BASIC INFLUENCE DIAGRAMS

In this section, several fundamental influence diagrams are described. Understanding exactly how these diagrams work will provide a basis for understanding and building more complex diagrams.

The Basic Risky Decision

This is the most elementary decision under uncertainty that a decision maker can face. The venture capital example above is a basic risky decision; there is one decision to make and one uncertain event.

Many decisions, in fact, can be reduced to a basic risky decision. For example, imagine that you have $2000 to invest. You could put it into the stock market or keep it in a savings account with a fixed interest rate. If you invest in stocks, the return depends on whether stock prices rise or fall. On the other hand, if you put the money into a savings account, you will earn a certain amount of money in interest regardless of stock price changes.

The influence diagram for this problem is shown in Figure 3.3. This figure also graphically shows the tables that are contained in the decision, chance, and value nodes. The decision node includes the choice of investing in either the stock market or a savings account. The chance node includes whether the stock market goes up or down. The payoff table gives the payoffs for different decisions (stocks versus savings) and different outcomes (market prices rise or fall). In this simplified example, only two possible market outcomes are considered. This payoff table shows clearly that if you invest in stocks, the payoff depends on what the market does. If you put your money into savings, however, the payoff is the same regardless of market activity.

Imperfect Information

Another basic kind of influence diagram reflects the possibility of obtaining imperfect information about some uncertain event that will affect the eventual payoff. This might be a forecast, an estimate or diagnosis from an acknowledged expert, or information from a computer model. In the investment example, you

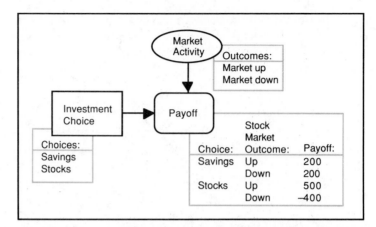

FIGURE 3.3 *Basic Risky Decision with Displayed Choices, Outcomes, and Payoffs*

might subscribe to a service that publishes investment advice, although such services can never predict market conditions perfectly.

Imagine a manufacturing-plant manager who faces a string of defective products and must decide what action to take. He has dispatched his maintenance engineer to do a preliminary inspection on Machine 3, which is suspected to be the source of the problem. The preliminary check will provide some guidance as to whether Machine 3 truly is the culprit, but it requires a day-long series of tests. The manager has two alternatives. First, a replacement for Machine 3 is available and could be brought in at a certain cost. If Machine 3 *is* the problem, then work can proceed and the production schedule will not fall behind. If Machine 3 is not the source of the defects, the problem will remain, and workers will have to change to another product while the problem is tracked down. Second, the workers could be changed immediately to the other product. This action would certainly cause the current product's production schedule to fall behind, but would avoid the risk (and cost) of unnecessarily replacing Machine 3.

Without the engineer's report, this problem would be another basic risky decision; the manager would have to decide whether to take the chance of replacing Machine 3 based on personal knowledge about the chance that it is the source of the defective products. The manager, however, is able to wait for the engineer's preliminary report before taking action. Figure 3.4 shows an influence diagram for the manager's decision problem, with the preliminary report shown as an example of imperfect information. Again, tables show the possible outcomes, choices, and payoffs. The payoff table includes payoffs for combinations of different choices (replace Machine 3 or change products) and whether Machine 3 actually turns out to be the culprit. The engineer's report is not included in the payoff table because it has no direct effect on the payoff.

The dashed arrow from "Engineer's Report" to "Manager's Decision" indicates that the manager will wait to hear from the engineer before deciding.

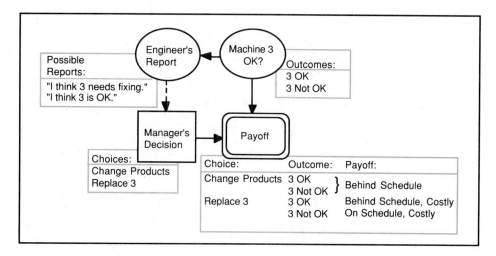

FIGURE 3.4   *Influence Diagram for Manufacturing-Plant Manager's Imperfect Information*

Thus, the engineer's preliminary report is information that is available at the time of the decision. The manager's problem is how to interpret this information. The appropriate action for the manager to take will depend not only on the engineer's report but also on the extent to which the manager believes the engineer is correct. Solving the influence diagram yields a strategy that indicates what the manager should do for each possible preliminary report from the engineer.

Weather forecasting provides another example of imperfect information. Suppose you live in Miami. A hurricane near the Bahama Islands threatens to cause severe damage; as a result, authorities recommend that everyone evacuate. Although evacuation is costly, you will be safe. On the other hand, staying is risky: You could be injured or even killed if the storm comes ashore near Miami. If the hurricane's path changes, however, you would be safe without having incurred the cost of evacuating.

Undoubtedly, you would pay close attention to the weather forecasters who would be predicting the course of the storm. Yet these forecasters are not perfect predictors. They can provide some information about the storm, but they may not perfectly predict its course because not everything is known about hurricanes.

Figure 3.5 shows the influence diagram for the evacuation decision. The arrow from "Hurricane Path" to "Forecast" means that the actual weather situation is relevant for assessing the uncertainty associated with the forecast. If the hurricane actually will hit Miami, then the forecaster (we hope) is more likely to predict a hit than a miss. Conversely, if the hurricane really will miss Miami, the forecaster probably will predict a miss. In either case, however, the forecast may be incorrect because the course of a hurricane is not fully predictable.

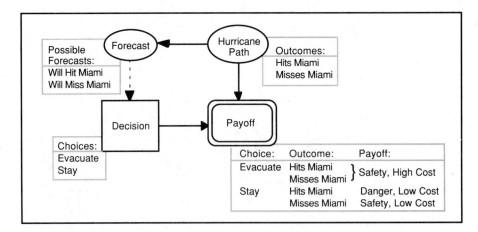

FIGURE 3.5   *Influence Diagram for Evacuation Decision*

Finally, Figure 3.5 represents the decision maker's situation before hearing from the forecaster, and this is where the time structure of the decision problem comes into play. The dashed arrow from the "Forecast" node to the decision node indicates that the decision is made knowing an imperfect weather forecast. The sequence of events, then, is that the decision maker hears the forecast and decides what to do; the hurricane then either hits Miami or misses. Solving the diagram will result in a strategy that recommends a particular decision for each possible statement that the forecaster could make.

The dashed arrow from "Forecast" to "Decision" reflects the fact that the forecast precedes the decision. Note, however, that the solid arrow between "Hurricane Path" and "Forecast" implies neither time sequence nor causality. In fact, the influence diagram is set up in this way because it is relatively easy to model uncertainty in this situation by first thinking about the hurricane path without knowing the forecast and then considering the chances associated with possible forecasts given the actual path. Once these assessments are made, probability manipulations will permit us to reverse the arrow to obtain the chances of specific hurricane paths given a forecast.

Deterministic Nodes

In some cases it is convenient to include an additional node that simply aggregates results from certain predecessor nodes. Suppose, for example, that a firm is deciding whether to introduce a new product. What matters to the firm is the profit level of the enterprise, and so we label the value node "Profit." At a fundamental level, both costs and revenue may be uncertain, and thus a first version of the influence diagram might look like the one shown in Figure 3.6.

On reflection, the firm's chief executive officer (CEO) realizes that substantial uncertainty exists for both variable and fixed costs. With revenue, there is uncertainty about the number of units sold, and a pricing decision must be

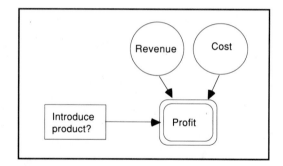

FIGURE 3.6   *Simple Influence Diagram*
for New Product Decision

made. These considerations lead the CEO to consider a somewhat more complicated influence diagram, which is shown in Figure 3.7.

Figure 3.7 is a perfectly adequate influence diagram. Another representation is shown in Figure 3.8. *Deterministic nodes* (double circles) have been included in Figure 3.8 to calculate cost on one hand and revenue on the other.
Deterministic nodes are just that. Given the inputs from the predecessor nodes,
the outcome of the deterministic node can be found immediately. No uncertainty exists after these conditioning variables — decisions and chance events —
are known. Of course, there is no uncertainty only in a conditional sense; the decision maker can look forward in time and know the value of the deterministic
node for any possible combination of the conditioning variables. Before the
conditioning variables are known, however, the deterministic node's eventual
precise value is uncertain.

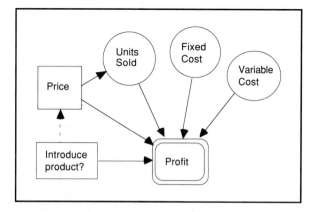

FIGURE 3.7   *New Product Decision*
with Additional Detail

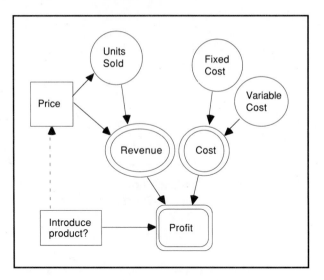

FIGURE 3.8   *New Product Decision with Deterministic Nodes*

In general, deterministic nodes are useful for emphasizing the structure of an influence diagram. Whenever a node has many predecessors, it may be appropriate to include one or more deterministic nodes to define the relationships among the nodes more precisely. In Figure 3.8, the calculation of cost and revenue is represented explicitly, as is the calculation of profit from cost and revenue. The pricing decision and uncertainty about sales are clearly related to revenue, while uncertainty about fixed and variable costs are clearly related to cost.

A value node is a special kind of deterministic node. In constructing the tables contained in a value node, we specify exactly each outcome value for every possible combination of outcomes of the chance and decision nodes that feed into the value node. In other words, once we know the decisions and the results of the chance events, we know the payoff. As in any deterministic node, no uncertainty remains once the conditioning variables are known. As with a regular deterministic node, the value of the outcome is uncertain *a priori* because decisions have not been made and chance events may not have occurred. The uniqueness of the value node is that it can be used as a basis for solving the influence diagram, as we will see in Chapter 4.

Multiple Objectives and Trade-offs

One of the basic elements of a decision problem is the way in which the outcome is valued. The value node allows the decision maker to include this basic element in the influence diagram. In many cases, however, valuing outcomes is a matter of trade-offs among the attributes of the outcomes. In such a case it is possible to show the multiple attributes explicitly with a hierarchical value structure.

Figure 3.9 shows an influence diagram for a multiattribute decision problem. In this problem, the Federal Aviation Administration (FAA) must choose from among several bomb-detection systems for commercial air carriers (Brown and Ulvila, 1983). In making the choice, the agency must try to accomplish several objectives. First, it would like the chosen system to be as effective as possible at detecting various types of explosives. The second objective is to implement the system as quickly as possible. The third is to maximize passenger acceptance, and the fourth is to minimize cost. To make the decision and solve the influence diagram, the FAA would have to score all candidate systems on how well they accomplish each objective, and then use these individual scores to calculate aggregate scores for each system. The "Overall Score" node would contain a formula that aggregates the individual scores, incorporating the appropriate trade-offs among the four objectives. Assessing the trade-off rates and constructing the formula to calculate the overall score is the topic of Chapters 15 and 16.

Sequential Decisions

As indicated in Chapter 2, an immediate decision may lead to later decisions. Returning to Figure 3.8, for example, we see a two-decision sequence: (1) whether to introduce the product, and (2) how to price it. Another example is Figure 1.1 (page 6), the flow-chart representation of a generic decision analysis. At each iteration of the decision-analysis cycle, the analyst decides whether more modeling is needed.

Influence diagrams do not permit the cycles that can be shown in a flow chart (Figure 1.1), primarily because it is critical to account for information that is available or still unknown at each decision. Thus, sequential decisions in an

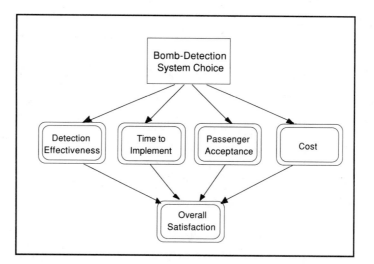

FIGURE 3.9   *Using an Influence Diagram: Multiple Objectives in Selecting a Bomb-Detection System*

influence diagram are strung together via informational arcs that show the specific sequence, in much the same way that we used them in Chapter 2. (In fact, now you can see that the figures in Chapter 2 use essentially the same graphics as influence diagrams!)

For a concrete example, let us take the farmer's decision problem about protecting his trees against adverse weather. Figure 3.10 shows that the influence diagram essentially is a series of imperfect information diagrams strung together. Between decisions (to protect or not) the farmer observes the weather and obtains the forecast for the next day. The arcs from one decision to the next show the time sequence.

The arrows among the weather and forecast nodes from day to day indicate that the observed weather and the forecast both have an effect. That is, yesterday's weather is relevant for assessing the chance of adverse weather today. Not shown explicitly in the influence diagram are arcs from forecast and weather nodes before the previous day. Of course, the decision maker observed the weather and the forecasts for each prior day. These are not included in the influence diagram but are implied by the arcs that connect the decision nodes in a time sequence. The missing arcs sometimes are called *no-forgetting arcs* to indicate that the decision maker would not forget the outcomes of those previous events. Unless the no-forgetting arcs are critical in understanding the problem, it is best not to include them specifically in the diagram because they tend to complicate the representation.

Finally, this decision problem is another example of a multiattribute decision problem, the attributes being the payoffs each day. The total payoff could be the sum of all of the individual payoffs, or it could be a net present value of the individual payoffs over time. The aggregation of individual payoffs is shown in the conventional way as described in the previous section.

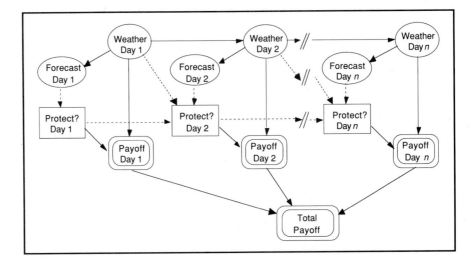

FIGURE 3.10   *Influence Diagram for Farmer's Sequential Decision Problem*

◆ MULTIPLE REPRESENTATIONS

How do you know whether your influence-diagram representation of a decision is the "correct" one? Although this question presupposes that a "correct" diagram exists, for most decision situations, there are, in fact, many ways that an influence diagram could be drawn! Consider the decision modeled in Figures 3.6, 3.7, and 3.8; these figures represent three possible approaches. With respect to uncertainty in a decision problem, several sources of uncertainty may underlie a single chance node. For example, in Figure 3.8, units sold may be uncertain because the CEO is uncertain about the timing and degree of competitive reactions, the nature of consumer tastes, the size of the potential market, the effectiveness of advertising, and so on. In many cases, and certainly for a first-pass representation, the simpler model may be more appropriate. In other cases, more detail may be needed to capture all essential elements of a situation. In the farmer's problem, for example, to understand the issues fully one may need to represent the problem as a sequence of decisions to be considered together rather than making each decision independently. Thus, it is expected that different individuals may create different influence diagrams for the same decision problem, depending on how they view the problem. The real issue is determining whether a diagram is appropriate. Does it really capture and accurately reflect the elements of the decision problem that the decision maker thinks are important?

How can we tell whether our influence diagram is appropriate? The representation that is most appropriate is the one that is *requisite* for the decision maker along the lines of our discussion in Chapter 1. That is, a requisite model contains everything that the decision maker considers important in making the decision. Identifying all of the essential elements may be a matter of working through the problem several times, refining the model on each pass. The only way to get to a requisite decision model is to continue working on the decision until all of the important concerns are fully incorporated. Sensitivity analysis (Chapter 5) will be a great help in determining which elements are important.

◆ BUILDING AN INFLUENCE DIAGRAM

There is no set strategy for building an influence diagram. Because the task is to structure a decision that may be complicated, the best approach may be to put together a simple version of the diagram first and then add details as necessary until the diagram includes all relevant aspects of the problem. In this section, we will demonstrate the construction of an influence diagram for the classic toxic-chemical problem.

TOXIC CHEMICALS AND THE EPA

The Environmental Protection Agency (EPA) often must decide whether to permit the use of an economically beneficial chemical that may be carcinogenic (cancer-causing). Furthermore, the decision often must be made without perfect information about either the long-term benefits or health hazards. Alternative courses of action are to permit the use of the chemical, restrict its use, or ban it altogether. Tests can be run to learn something about the carcinogenic potential of the material, and survey data can indicate the extent of exposure when people use the chemical. These pieces of information are both important in making the decision. For example, if the chemical is only mildly toxic and human exposure is minimal, then restricted use may be reasonable. On the other hand, if the chemical is only mildly toxic, but people are widely exposed, then banning its use may be imperative.

The first step should be to identify the decision. In this case, the decision is what level of use to permit, and this decision clearly will affect the overall value of this decision. Thus, our influence diagram so far would consist of a decision node and a value node.

The next step requires careful consideration of the decision's objectives. These will help to define what is measured by the value node. In most cases we would be able to place a single node and call it something like "Value," "Satisfaction," "Payoff," or "Cost." In this case, the primary objectives are maximizing the economic benefits from the chemicals while minimizing the risk of cancer. It is difficult to measure the value of lives lost to cancer in monetary terms, and so it may be helpful to break down the overall value of the outcomes into two attributes that reflect these objectives: economic value and cancer cost. These two elements of value then feed into an overall value node ("Net Value") that aggregates "Economic Value" and "Cancer Cost" as shown in Figure 3.11.

Now let us think about what affects "Economic Value" and "Cancer Cost" other than the usage decision. Both the uncertain degree of carcinogenicity and the amount of human exposure have effects on the potential cancer cost, thus yielding the diagram shown in Figure 3.12. Because "Carcinogenic Potential" and "Human Exposure" jointly determine the level of risk that is inherent in the chemical, their effects are aggregated in a deterministic node labeled "Cancer Risk." Different values of the predecessor nodes will determine the overall level of "Cancer Risk."

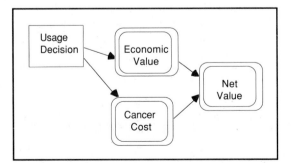

FIGURE 3.11   *Beginning the Toxic-Chemical Influence Diagram*

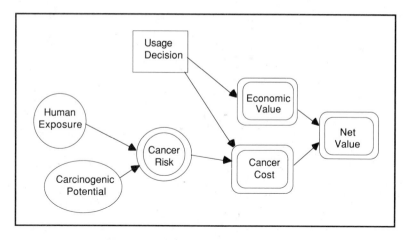

FIGURE 3.12 *Intermediate Influence Diagram for the Toxic-Chemical Decision*

Note that no arrow runs from "Usage Decision" to "Human Exposure," even though such an arrow might appear to make sense. "Human Exposure" refers to the extent of contact when the chemical actually is used and would be measured in terms of a rate (for example, grams of dust inhaled per hour). Here the rate is unknown, and the usage decision does not influence our beliefs concerning the likelihood of various possible rates when the chemical is used.

The influence diagram remains incomplete, however, because we have incorporated neither the test for carcinogenicity nor the survey on exposure. Presumably, results from both the test and the survey would be available to EPA at the time the usage decision is made. Furthermore, it should be clear that the actual degrees of carcinogenic potential and human exposure will influence the test and survey results. The test and survey nodes are included in Figure 3.13 and represent imperfect information; they provide some information regarding carcinogenicity and exposure, respectively. These two nodes are predecessors of the decision node and show that the information is available when the decision is made. This completes the influence diagram.

This example demonstrates the usefulness of influence diagrams for structuring decisions. The toxic-chemicals problem is relatively complex, and yet its influence diagram is compact and, more important, understandable. Of course, the more complicated the problem, the larger the influence diagram. Nevertheless, influence diagrams are useful for creating easily understood overviews of decision problems.

♦ SOME COMMON MISTAKES

First, an easily made mistake in understanding and constructing influence diagrams is to interpret them as flow charts, which depict the sequential nature of a particular process with each node representing an event or activity. For

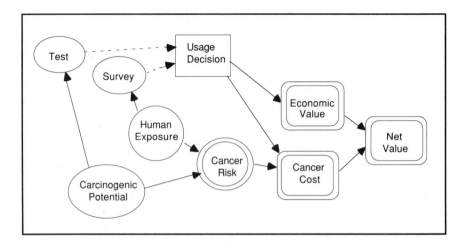

FIGURE 3.13   *Completed Influence Diagram for the Toxic-Chemical Decision*

example, Figure 1.1 (page 6) is a flow chart of a decision-analysis system, and displays the different things a decision analyst does at each stage of the process.

Even though they look a little like flow charts, influence diagrams are quite different. An influence diagram is a picture of the decision situation at a particular time, one that must account for all the decision elements that play a part in the immediate decision. Putting a chance node in an influence diagram means that the decision maker is not sure exactly what will happen, but that he or she has some idea of the likelihood of each of the different possible outcomes. For example, in the toxic-chemical problem, the carcinogenic potential of the chemical is unknown, and in fact will never be known for sure. That uncertainty, however, can be modeled using probabilities for different levels of carcinogenic potential. Likewise, at the time the influence diagram is created, the results of the test are not known. The uncertainty surrounding the test results also can be modeled using probabilities. The informational arrow from "Test" to "Usage Decision," however, means that the decision maker will learn the results of the test before the decision must be made.

The metaphor of a picture of the decision that accounts for all of the decision elements also encompasses the possibility of future decisions that must be considered. For example, a legislator deciding how to vote on a given issue may consider upcoming votes. The outcome of the current issue might affect the legislator's future voting decisions. Thus, at the time of the immediate decision, the decision maker foresees future decisions and models those decisions with the knowledge on hand.

A second common mistake, one related to the perception of an influence diagram as a flow chart, is that of building influence diagrams with many chance nodes having arrows pointing to the primary decision node. The intention usually is to represent the uncertainty in the decision environment. The problem is that the arrows into the decision node indicate that the outcome of these uncertain events will be known when the decision is made, which may not be the case.

The solution requires careful thinking when constructing the influence diagram. An arrow into a decision node means that the decision maker will have a specific bit of information when making the decision; something will be known for sure, with no residual uncertainty. Before drawing an arrow into a decision node, ask whether the decision maker will learn the information before the decision is made. If not, do not draw the arrow! Just by including a chance node with probabilities in the influence diagram in its appropriate place, the decision maker's knowledge regarding the uncertainty of that event is being considered in the decision problem.

A third mistake is the inclusion of cycles (circular paths among the nodes). As already indicated, a properly constructed influence diagram contains no cycles. Cycles are occasionally included in an attempt to denote feedback among the chance and decision nodes. Although this might be appropriate in the case of a flow chart, it is inappropriate in an influence diagram. Think about the diagram as a picture of the decision that accounts for all of the decision elements at a point in time. There is no opportunity for feedback at any point in time, and hence there can be no cycles.

Influence diagrams provide a graphical representation of a decision's structure, a snapshot of the decision environment at one point in time. All of the details (outcomes, choices, payoffs) are present in tables that are contained in the nodes, but usually this information is suppressed in favor of a representation that shows off the decision's structure. In Chapter 4, these hidden tables will be discussed in more detail, along with the calculations for solving influence diagrams.

◆ DECISION TREES

Influence diagrams are excellent for displaying a decision's structure, but they hide many of the details. To reveal more of the decision diagram's surface details, a decision tree, another decision-modeling approach, is used. As with influence diagrams, squares represent decisions to be made, and circles represent chance events. The branches emanating from a square correspond to the choices available to the decision maker, and the branches from a circle represent the possible outcomes of a chance event. The third decision element, the value of the outcomes, is specified at the ends of the branches.

Again consider the venture-capital decision. Figure 3.14 shows the decision tree for this problem. The tree flows from left to right, and so the immediate decision is represented by the square at the left side. The two branches represent the two alternatives, invest or not. If the venture capitalist invests in the project, the next issue is whether the venture succeeds or fails. If the venture succeeds, the capitalist earns a large return, but if it fails, then the amount invested in the project will be lost. If the capitalist decides not to invest in this particular risky project, then she would earn a more typical return on another, less risky project. These outcomes are shown at the ends of the branches at the right.

The interpretation of decision trees requires explanation. First, the options

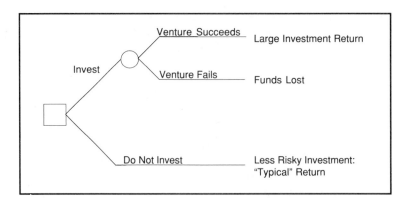

FIGURE 3.14   *Decision-Tree Representation of Venture-Capital Problem*

represented by branches from a decision node must be such that the decision maker can choose only one option. For example, in the venture-capital decision, the decision maker can either invest or not, but not both. In some instances, combination strategies are possible. If the capitalist were considering two separate projects (A and B), for instance, it may be possible to invest in Firm A, Firm B, both, or neither. In this case, all four separate alternatives would be modeled explicitly, yielding four branches from the decision node.

Second, each chance node must have branches that correspond to a set of *mutually exclusive* and *collectively exhaustive* outcomes. "Mutually exclusive" means that only one of the outcomes can happen. In the venture-capital decision, the project can either succeed or fail, but not both. "Collectively exhaustive" means that no other possibilities exist; one of the specified outcomes must occur. Putting these two specifications together means that when the uncertainty is resolved, one and only one of the outcomes occurs.

Third, a decision tree represents all possible paths that the decision maker might follow through time, including all possible decisions and outcomes of chance events. Three such paths exist for the venture capitalist, corresponding to the three branches at the right-hand side of the tree. In a complicated decision situation with many sequential decisions or sources of uncertainty, many such potential paths may exist.

Finally, it is sometimes useful to think of the nodes as occurring in a time sequence. Beginning on the left side of the tree, a decision typically happens first, and then is followed by other decisions or chance events in chronological order. In the venture-capital problem, the capitalist decides first whether or not to invest, and the second step is whether the project succeeds or fails.

As with influence diagrams, the dovetailing of decisions and chance events is critical. Placing a chance event before a decision means that the decision is made conditional on the specific chance outcome having occurred. Conversely, if a chance node is to the right of a decision node, the decision must be made in anticipation of the chance event. The sequence of decisions is shown in a decision tree by order in the tree from left to right. If chance events have a logical time sequence between decisions, they also may be appropriately ordered. If no natural sequence exists then the order in which they appear in the decision tree is not critical, although the order used does suggest the conditioning sequence for modeling uncertainty. For example, it may be easier to think about the chances of a stock price increasing given that the Dow Jones average increases rather than the other way around.

◆ SOME BASIC DECISION TREES

In this section we will look at some basic decision-tree forms. Many correspond to the basic influence diagrams discussed above.

The Basic Risky Decision

Just as the venture-capital decision was the prototypical basic risky decision in our discussion of influence diagrams, so it is here as well. The capitalist's dilemma is whether the potential for large gains in the proposed project is worth the additional risk. If she judges that it is not, then she should not invest in the project.

For another example, consider a politician's decision. A popular political candidate might have the options of: (1) running for reelection to her U.S. House of Representatives seat, in which case reelection is virtually ensured, or (2) running for a Senate seat. If the choice is to pursue the Senate seat, there is a chance of losing (the worst possible outcome), which would result in a job as a lawyer until the next election. On the other hand, winning the Senate race would be the best possible outcome. Figure 3.15 diagrams the decision. The dilemma in the basic risky decision arises because the riskless alternative results in an outcome that, in terms of desirability, falls between the outcomes for the risky alternatives. (If this were not the case, there would be no problem deciding!) The decision maker's problem is to figure out whether the chance of "winning" in the risky alternative is great enough relative to the chance of "losing" to make the risky alternative more valuable than the riskless alternative. The more valuable the riskless alternative, the greater the chance of winning must be for the risky alternative to be preferred.

One variation of the basic risky decision might be called the *double-risk decision dilemma*. Here the problem is deciding between two risky prospects. On the

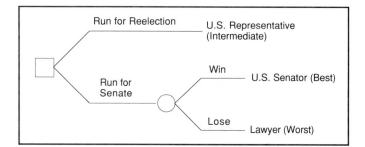

FIGURE 3.15 *The Politician's Basic Risky Decision*

one hand, you are "damned if you do and damned if you don't" because you could lose either way. On the other hand, you could win either way. For example, the political candidate may face the decision represented by the decision tree in Figure 3.16, in which she may enter either of two races and lose either one.

Sometimes the outcome of the chance event will be some value from a range of possible values. For example, an individual deciding whether to accept an out-of-court settlement or go to court faces the decision in Figure 3.17. The crescent shape indicates that the uncertain event (court award) may be any value between the extremes. In this example, the court award may be any positive value up to the amount requested by the plaintiff in the lawsuit. This is still essentially a basic risky decision, but it is sometimes called a *range-of-risk dilemma.*

Imperfect Information

Representing imperfect information with decision trees is a matter of showing that the decision maker will obtain information before making a decision. For example, the evacuation decision problem is shown in Figure 3.18. This decision

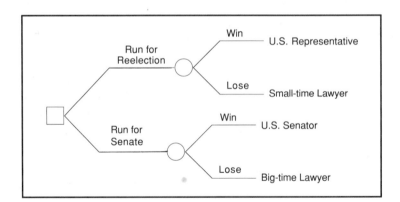

FIGURE 3.16   *Double-Risk Decision Dilemma*

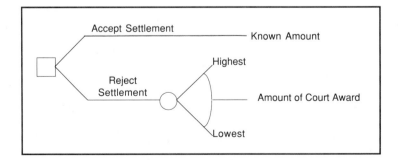

FIGURE 3.17   *Range-of-Risk Decision Dilemma*

tree begins with a chance event, the forecast. The chronological sequence is clear; the forecast arrives, then the evacuation decision is made, and finally the hurricane either hits or misses Miami.

Multiple Objectives and Trade-offs

In its simplest version, uncertainty does not complicate this decision, but the alternatives have high scores on different criteria. The problem is deciding how to trade off the criteria relative to one another. For example, you may have to decide between two jobs. Of course, you would like a higher salary, but you might also prefer to live in in a small city rather than a large one. Suppose you face the decision diagrammed in Figure 3.19. Your decision might be difficult, involving careful thought as to how to trade off salary versus community size.

In the influence-diagram representation (Figure 3.9, the bomb-detection system), the multiple dimensions in which alternatives were evaluated were shown in a hierarchy. In the decision tree, the descriptions at the ends of the branches show how the different outcomes rank on each objective. Collapsing

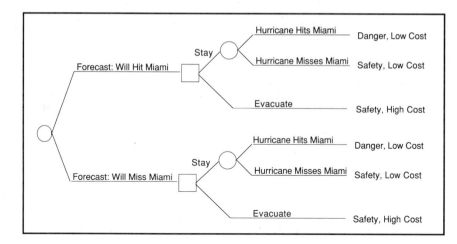

FIGURE 3.18 *Evacuation Decision Represented by Decision Tree*

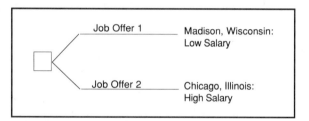

FIGURE 3.19 *Decision Tree for Decision Problem with Multiple Objectives*

the multidimensional description into a single score requires assessment and application of appropriate trade-off weights.

Sequential Decisions

At this point, representing a sequential decision problem with a decision tree may seem to be very difficult indeed because the number of branches increases exponentially as the number of decisions and events increases. In fact, decision trees work poorly for this kind of problem, but it is possible to create a "skeleton" version of a decision tree if (1) the sequential problem repeats itself and (2) the decision tree is symmetric at each stage.

Figure 3.20 shows a skeleton version of the farmer's sequential decision problem. This is the decision-tree version of Figure 3.10. Even though each decision and chance event has only two branches, we use the crescent shape to avoid having the tree explode into a bushy mess. With only the six nodes shown, there would be 2^6 or 64 branches. Moreover, we can string together the crescent shapes sequentially because, regardless of the outcome or decision at any point, the same events and decisions follow in the rest of the tree.

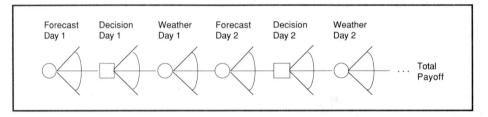

FIGURE 3.20   *Skeleton Version of Farmer's Sequential Decision Problem: Decision-Tree Form*

◆ DECISION TREES AND INFLUENCE DIAGRAMS COMPARED

It is time to step back and compare decision trees with influence diagrams. The discussion and examples have shown that, on the surface at least, decision trees display considerably more information than do influence diagrams. It also should be obvious, however, that decision trees get "messy" much faster than do influence diagrams as decision problems become more complicated. The most complicated decision tree we constructed was the sequential decision problem in Figure 3.20, and it really does not show all of the intricate details contained in the influence-diagram version of the same problem. The level of complexity of the representation is not a small issue. When it comes time to present the results of a decision analysis to upper-level managers, their understanding of the graphical presentation is crucial. Influence diagrams are superior in this regard; they are especially easy for people to understand regardless of mathematical training.

Should you use decision trees or influence diagrams? Both are worthwhile, and they complement each other well. Influence diagrams are particularly valuable for the structuring phase of problem solving and for representing large problems. Decision trees display the details of a problem. The ultimate decision made should not depend on the representation because influence diagrams and decision trees are *isomorphic*; any properly built influence diagram can be converted into a decision tree, and vice versa. One strategy is to start by using an influence diagram to help understand the major elements of the problem and then convert to a decision-tree approach to fill in details.

Influence diagrams and decision trees provide two approaches to modeling a decision problem. Because the two approaches have different advantages, one may be more appropriate than the other, depending on the modeling requirements. For example, if it is important to communicate the overall structure of a model to other people, an influence diagram may be more appropriate. Careful reflection and sensitivity analysis on specific probability and value inputs may work better in the context of a decision tree. Using both approaches together may prove useful; the goal, after all, is to make sure that the model accurately represents the decision situation. Because the two approaches have different strengths, they should be viewed as complementary techniques rather than as competitors in the decision-modeling process.

◆ THE CLARITY TEST

The last topic in structuring is the quite practical problem of ensuring that all elements of the decision problem are clearly defined. Beginning efforts to structure decision problems usually include rather loose specifications of the problem. For example, looking back at the toxic-chemicals example and the influence diagram in Figure 3.11, we see that cancer cost is an element of the net value to society relative to the chemical and its use. How will this cost be measured? In incremental lives lost? Incremental cases of cancer, both treatable and fatal? Consider the "Human Exposure" chance node. What are possible levels of exposure? How will we measure exposure? Are we talking about the number of people exposed to the chemical per day or per hour? Does exposure consist of breathing dust particles, ingesting some critical quantity, or skin contact? Are we concerned about contact over a period of time? Exactly how will we know if an individual has had a high or low level of exposure? The decision maker must give unequivocal answers to these questions before the decision model can be used to resolve EPA's real-world policy problem.

Much of the difficulty in decision making arises when different people have different ideas regarding some aspect of the decision. The solution is to refine the conceptualizations of events and variables associated with the decision enough so that it can be made. How do we know when we have refined enough? The *clarity test* (Howard 1988) provides a simple and understandable answer. Imagine a clairvoyant who has access to all future information: newspapers, instrument readings, technical reports, and so on. Would the clairvoyant be able to determine unequivocally what the outcome would be for any event in the influence diagram? No interpretation or judgment should be required of the clairvoyant. Another approach is to imagine that, in the future, perfect information will be available regarding all aspects of the decision. Would it be possible to tell exactly what happened at every node, again with no interpretation or judgment? The specification of the decision problem passes the clarity test when these questions are answered affirmatively. At this point, the problem should be specified clearly enough that the various people involved in the decision are thinking about the decision elements in exactly the same way. There should be no misunderstandings regarding the definitions of the basic decision elements.

The clarity test is aptly named. It requires absolutely clear definitions of the events and variables. In the case of toxic chemicals, saying that human exposure can be either high or low fails the clarity test; what constitutes a high level of exposure for some people might be low for others. Suppose, however, that human exposure is defined as high if the average skin contact per person on each day of use exceeds 10 milligrams of material per second over 10 minutes. This definition passes the clarity test. It is conceivable that test results could indicate precisely whether the level of exposure exceeded the threshold.

Putting the clarity test to work is straightforward. Once the problem is structured and the decision tree or influence diagram is built, consider each chance node. Does the definition of the event pass the clarity test? If not, refine the definition of the event or the appropriate measurement until the test is satisfied. Defining events and decisions to pass the test means clearly specifying chance outcomes, choices, and payoffs. Thus, all of the action with regard to the clarity test takes place within the tables in an influence diagram or along the individual branches in a decision tree where the critical decision-problem details are specified. Only after every element of the decision passes the clarity test is it appropriate to consider solving the influence diagram or decision tree, which is the topic of Chapter 4.

◇ SUMMARY

This chapter has discussed the general process of structuring decision problems using both influence diagrams and decision trees. This is the first step in modeling the decision problem. It is hard to overemphasize the importance of the structuring step, because it is here that one really understands the problem and all of its different aspects. A decision maker may use both influence diagrams and decision trees as tools in the process of understanding the structure of a problem. Influence diagrams provide a compact representation of a decision problem while suppressing many of the details, and thus are ideal for obtaining an overview, especially for a complex problem. Influence diagrams are especially appropriate for communicating the structure of a decision because they are easily understood by individuals who have no technical background. On the other hand, decision trees display all of the minute details of a problem. Being able to see the details can be an advantage, but in complex decisions the tree may be too large and "bushy" to be of much use in communicating with others. Finally, the clarity test is used to ensure that the problem is defined well enough so that everyone can agree on definitions of the basic decision elements.   ◆

◇ EXERCISES

3.1 Before making an unsecured loan to an individual, a bank orders a report on the applicant's credit history. To justify making the loan, the applicant's credit record must be satisfactory. Describe the bank's decision. What risk does the bank face? What role does the credit report play? Draw an influence diagram of this situation. Your influence diagram should include chance nodes for a credit report and for eventual default; be sure to specify the outcomes in these nodes clearly enough to pass the clarity test.

3.2 When a movie producer decides whether to produce a major motion picture, the main question is how much revenue the movie will generate. Draw a decision tree of this situation. What issues must be considered to ensure that the clarity test is passed?

3.3 You have met an acquaintance for lunch, and he is worried about an upcoming meeting with his boss and certain executives from his firm's headquarters. He has to outline the costs and benefits of some alternative investment strategies. He knows about decision trees and influence diagrams, but cannot decide which presentation to use. In your own words, explain to him the advantages and disadvantages of both.

3.4 Draw the investment decision from Figure 3.3 as a decision tree.

3.5 Draw the politician's decision in Figure 3.15 as an influence diagram. Include the tables showing decision alternatives, chance-event outcomes, and payoffs.

3.6 A dapper young decision maker has just purchased a new suit for $200. Leaving for work, the decision maker considers taking an umbrella, which will protect the suit in the event of rain. Without the umbrella, the suit could be ruined. On the other hand, if it does not rain, carrying the umbrella is an inconvenience.

    a. Draw a decision tree of this situation.

    b. Draw an influence diagram for the situation.

    c. Before deciding, the decision maker considers listening to the weather forecast on the radio. Draw an influence diagram that considers the weather forecast.

3.7 When patients suffered from hemorrhagic fever, M*A*S*H doctors replaced lost sodium by administering a saline solution intravenously. Headquarters (HQ), however, sent an order disallowing the saline solution. With a patient in shock and near death from a disastrously low sodium level, B. J. Hunnicut wanted to administer a low-sodium–concentration saline solution in a last-ditch attempt to save the patient. Colonel Potter looked at B.J. and Hawkeye and summed up the situation. "O.K., let's get this straight. If we go by the new directive from HQ and don't administer saline to replace the sodium, our boy will die for sure. If we try B.J.'s idea, then he may survive, and we'll know how to treat the next two patients who are getting worse. If we try it and he doesn't make it, we're in trouble with HQ and may get court-martialed. I say we have no choice. Let's try it." (*Source*: "Mr. and Mrs. Who." Written by Ronny Graham, directed by Burt Metcalfe, 1980.)

    Structure the doctors' decision. What risk do they face? What trade-offs must they make? Draw a decision tree for their situation.

3.8 Here is an example that provides a way to compare influence diagrams and decision trees.

    a. Suppose you are planning a party. An outdoor barbecue would be best, but only if the sun shines; rain would spoil the barbecue. On the other hand, you could plan an indoor party. This would be a good party, not as nice as an outdoor barbecue in the sunshine, but better than a barbecue in the rain. Of course, it is always possible to forego the party altogether! Construct an influence diagram and a decision tree for this problem.

b. You will, naturally, consult the weather forecast, which will tell you that the weather will be either "sunny" or "rainy." The forecast is not perfect, however. If the forecast is "sunny," then sunshine is more likely than rain, but there still is a small chance of rain. A forecast of "rainy" implies that rain is likely, but the sun may still shine. Now draw an influence diagram for the decision, including the weather forecast. (There should be four nodes in your diagram, including one for the forecast, which will be available at the time you decide what kind of party to have, and one for the actual weather. Which direction should the arrow point between these two nodes? Why?) Now draw a decision tree for this problem. Recall that the events and decisions in a decision tree should be in chronological order.

3.9   The clarity test is an important issue in Problem 3.8. The weather obviously can be somewhere in between full sunshine and rain. Should you include an outcome such as "cloudy"? Would it affect your satisfaction with an outdoor barbecue? How will you define rain? The National Weather Service uses the following definition: Rain has occurred if "measurable precipitation" (more than 0.004 inch) has occurred at the official rain gauge. Would this definition be suitable for your purposes?

3.10   Draw the machine-replacement decision (Figure 3.4) as a decision tree.

◇ QUESTIONS AND PROBLEMS

3.11   In the spring of 1987, Gary Hart, the leading Democratic presidential candidate, told reporters that he was more than willing to have his private life scrutinized carefully. A few weeks later, the *Miami Herald* reported that a woman, Donna Rice, had been seen entering his Washington townhouse on a Friday evening but not leaving until Saturday evening. The result was a political scandal, with Hart contending that Rice had left Friday evening by a back door that the reporter on the scene was not watching. The result was that Hart's credibility as a candidate was severely damaged, thus reducing his chance of winning both the Democratic nomination and the election. The decision he had to make was whether to continue the campaign or to drop out. Compounding the issue was a heavy debt burden that was left over from his unsuccessful 1984 presidential bid.

Using both an influence diagram and a decision tree, structure Hart's decision. What is the main source of uncertainty that he faces? Are there conflicting objectives? If so, what are they? What do you think he should have done? (He decided to drop out of the race, although he eventually reentered, only to drop out again because of poor showings in the primary elections.)

3.12   Occasionally a decision is sensitive to the way it is structured. The following problem shows that leaving out an important part of the problem can affect the way in which we view the situation.

a. Imagine that a close friend has been diagnosed with heart disease. The physician recommends bypass surgery. The surgery should solve the problem. When asked about the risks, the physician replies that a few individuals die during the operation, but most recover and the surgery is completely successful. Thus, your friend can (most likely) anticipate a longer and more healthy life after the surgery. Without surgery, your friend will have a shorter and gradually deteriorating life. Diagram this decision with both an influence diagram and a decision tree.

b. Suppose now that your friend obtains a second opinion. The second physician suggests a third possible outcome: Complications from surgery can develop that will require long and painful treatment. If this happens, the eventual outcome could be full recovery, partial recovery (the patient restricted to a wheelchair until death), or death within a few months. How does this change the decision tree and influence diagram that you created in part a? Draw the decision tree and influence diagram that represent the situation after hearing from both physicians. Given this new structure, does surgery look more or less positive than it did in part a? [For more discussion of this problem, see von Winterfeldt and Edwards (1986) *Decision Analysis and Behavioral Research*, Cambridge, Cambridge University Press, pp. 8–14.]

   c. How does the clarity test relate to this problem? Can you devise a clear definition of the "partial recovery" outcome?

3.13 Create an influence diagram and a decision tree for the difficult decision problem that you described in Problem 1.9 (page 10). Define the events and variables clearly enough to pass the clarity test.

3.14
> To be, or not to be, that is the question:
> Whether 'tis nobler in the mind to suffer
> The slings and arrows of outrageous fortune
> Or to take arms against a sea of troubles,
> And by opposing end them. To die — to sleep —
> No more; and by a sleep to say we end
> The heartache, and the thousand natural shocks
> That flesh is heir to. 'Tis a consummation
> Devoutly to be wished. To die — to sleep.
> To sleep — perchance to dream: ay, there's the rub!
> For in that sleep of death what dreams may come
> When we have shuffled off this mortal coil,
> Must give us pause. There's the respect
> That makes calamity of so long life.
> For who would bear the whips and scorns of time,
> The oppressor's wrong, the proud man's contumely,
> The pangs of despised love, the law's delay,
> The insolence of office, and the spurns
> That patient merit of the unworthy takes,
> When he himself might his quietus make
> With a bare bodkin? Who would these fardels bear,
> To grunt and sweat under a weary life,
> But that the dread of something after death —
> The undiscovered country, from whose bourn
> No traveller returns — puzzles the will,
> And makes us rather bear those ills we have
> Than fly to others that we know not of?

> — *Hamlet*, Act III, Scene 1

Describe Hamlet's decision. What are his choices? What risk does he perceive?

3.15 On July 3, 1988, the USS *Vincennes* was on patrol in the Persian Gulf. On its radar screen a blip appeared that signified an approaching aircraft. After the aircraft repeatedly failed to identify itself, it was tentatively identified as a hostile Iranian F-14 fighter about to attack the *Vincennes*. Captain Will Rogers had little time to make his decision. Should he issue the command to launch a missile and destroy the plane? Or should he wait for positive identification? If he waited too long and the plane was indeed hostile, then it might be impossible to avert the attack and danger to his crew.

Captain Rogers issued the command, and the aircraft was destroyed. It was later revealed to be a civilian Iranian airliner carrying 290 people. There were no survivors.

Draw a decision tree representing Captain Rogers's decision. What trade-offs must he make? What risks does he face?

3.16 In Problem 3.15, the objectives can be framed in terms of either minimizing lives lost or maximizing lives saved. That is, Captain Rogers could think in terms of saving his crew or losing his crew and in terms of saving lives or losing lives of individuals aboard the incoming aircraft. Draw the decision tree for each case. If you were Captain Rogers, would your decision to shoot or not depend on how the problem was framed?

CASE STUDIES

Cold Fusion

On March 23, 1989, Stanley Pons and Martin Fleischmann announced at a press conference at the University of Utah that they had succeeded in creating a small-scale nuclear fusion reaction in a simple apparatus at room temperature. They called the process "cold fusion." Although many details were missing from their description of the experiment, their claim inspired thoughts of a cheap and limitless energy supply, the raw material for which would be ocean water. The entire structure of the world economy potentially would change.

For a variety of reasons, Pons and Fleischmann were reluctant to reveal all of the details of their experiment. If their process really were producing energy from a fusion reaction, and any commercial potential existed, then they could become quite wealthy. The state government of Utah also considered the economic possibilities and even went so far as to approve $5 million to support cold-fusion research. Utah Congressman Wayne Owens introduced a bill in the U.S. House of Representatives requesting $100 million to develop a national cold-fusion research center at the University of Utah campus.

But were the results correct? Experimentalists around the world attempted to replicate Pons and Fleischmann's results. Some reported success while many others did not. A team at Texas A&M University claimed to have detected neutrons, the telltale sign of fusion. Other university teams detected excess heat as had Pons and Fleischmann. Many experiments failed to confirm a fusion reaction, however, and several physicists claimed that the Utah pair simply had made mistakes in their measurements.

QUESTIONS

1. Consider the problem that a member of the U.S. Congress would have in deciding whether to vote for Congressman Owens's bill. What alternatives are

available? What are the key uncertainties? What trade-offs must be considered? Structure the decision problem using an influence diagram and a decision tree.

2. A key part of the experimental apparatus was a core of palladium, a rare metal. Consider a speculator who is thinking of investing in palladium in response to the announcement. Structure the investor's decision. How does it compare to the decision in Question 1?

Sources: "Fusion in a Bottle: Miracle or Mistake," *Business Week*, May 8, 1989, pp. 100–110; "The Race for Fusion," *Newsweek*, May 8, 1989, pp. 49–54.

◆

Prescribed Fire

Using fire in forest management sounds contradictory. Prescribed fire, however, is an important tool for foresters, and a recent article described how decision analysis is used to decide when, where, and what to burn. In one example, several areas in the Tahoe National Forest in California had been logged and were being prepared for replanting. Preparation included prescribed burning, and two possible treatments were available: burning the slash as it lay on the ground or "yarding of unmerchantable material" (YUM) prior to burning. The latter treatment involves using heavy equipment to pile the slash. YUM reduces the difficulty of controlling the burn but costs an additional $100 per acre. In deciding between the two treatments, two uncertainties were considered to be critical. The first was how the fire would behave under each scenario. For example, the fire could be fully successful, problems could arise that could be controlled eventually, or the fire could escape, entailing considerable losses. Second, if problems developed, they could result in high, low, or medium costs.

QUESTION

1. Develop a decision tree and an influence diagram for this situation. Be sure that your definition of costs passes the clarity test. Is the decision tree or influence diagram more appropriate in this situation? Why?

Source: Cohan, D., S. Haas, D. Radloff, and R. Yancik (1984) "Using Fire in Forest Management: Decision Making under Uncertainty," *Interfaces*, 14, 8–19.

◆

The SS Kuniang

In the early 1980s, New England Electric System (NEES) was deciding how much to bid for the salvage rights to a grounded ship, the SS *Kuniang*. If the bid were successful, the ship could be repaired and fitted out to haul coal for the company's power-generation stations. But the value of doing so depended on the outcome of a U.S. Coast Guard judgment about the salvage value of the ship.

The Coast Guard's judgment involved an obscure law regarding domestic shipping in coastal waters. If the judgment indicated a low salvage value, then NEES would be able to use the ship for its shipping needs. If the judgment were high, the ship would be considered ineligible for use in domestic shipping unless a considerable amount of money was spent in fitting her with fancy equipment. The Coast Guard's judgment would not be known until after the winning bid was chosen, and so there was considerable risk associated with actually buying the ship by submission of the winning bid. If the bid failed, the alternatives included purchasing a new ship or a tug and barge combination, both of which were relatively expensive alternatives. One of the major issues was that the higher the bid, the more likely that NEES would win. NEES judged that a bid of $3 million would definitely not win, whereas a bid of $10 million definitely would win. Any bid in between was possible.

QUESTIONS

1. Draw a decision tree and an influence diagram for NEES's decision.
2. Which representation do you think is more appropriate? Why?
3. How would you go about finding the optimal amount to bid?

Source: Bell, D. E. (1984) "Bidding for the S.S. Kuniang," *Interfaces*, 14, 17–23.

◆

◇ REFERENCES

Decision structuring as a topic of discussion and research is relatively new. Traditionally the focus has been on modeling uncertainty and preferences and solution procedures for specific kinds of problems. Recent discussions of structuring include von Winterfeldt and Edwards (1986, Chapter 2), Humphreys and Wisudha (1987), and Keller and Ho (1989).

Influence diagrams are relatively new to the decision-analysis circuit. Developed by Strategic Decisions Group as a consulting aid in the late 1970s, they first appeared in the decision-analysis literature in Howard and Matheson (1984). Bodily (1985) and Shachter and Bertrand's (1988) *Instruction Manual for DAVID* present excellent overviews of influence diagrams. For more technical details, consult Shachter (1986, 1988) and Oliver and Smith (1989).

Decision trees, on the other hand, have been part of the decision-analysis toolkit since the discipline's inception. The textbooks by Holloway (1979) and Raiffa (1968) provide extensive modeling using decision trees. This chapter's discussion of basic decision trees has drawn from Behn and Vaupel's (1982) typology of decisions.

The clarity test is another consulting aid that was invented by Ron Howard and his associates; see Howard (1988).

BEHN, R. D., and J. D. VAUPEL (1982) *Quick Analysis for Busy Decision Makers*. New York: Basic Books.

BODILY, S. E. (1985) *Modern Decision Making*. New York: McGraw-Hill.

BROWN, R. V., and J. ULVILA (1982) "Decision Analysis Comes of Age." *Harvard Business Review* (Sept.–Oct.) 130–141.

HOLLOWAY, C. A. (1979) *Decision Making Under Uncertainty: Models and Choices.* Englewood Cliffs, NJ: Prentice-Hall.

HOWARD, R. A. (1988) "Decision Analysis: Practice and Promise." *Management Science,* 34, 679–695.

HOWARD, R. A., and J. E. MATHESON (1981) "Influence Diagrams." Reprinted in R. Howard and J. Matheson (eds.), *The Principles and Applications of Decision Analysis, Vol. II.* Palo Alto, CA: Strategic Decisions Group (1984), 719–762.

HUMPHREYS, P., and A. WISUDHA (1987) "Methods and Tools for Structuring and Analyzing Decision Problems: A Catalogue and Review," Technical Report No. 87-1. London: Decision Analysis Unit, London School of Economics and Political Science.

KELLER, R., and J. L. HO (1989) "Decision Problem Structuring," in A. P. Sage (ed.), *Concise Encyclopedia of Information Processing in Systems and Organizations.* Oxford: Pergamon Press.

OLIVER, R. M., and J. Q. SMITH (1990) *Influence Diagrams, Belief Nets and Decision Analysis* (Proceedings of an International Conference 1988, Berkeley). New York: John Wiley.

RAIFFA, H. (1968) *Decision Analysis.* Reading, MA: Addison Wesley.

SHACHTER, R. (1986) "Evaluating Influence Diagrams." *Operations Research,* 34, 871–882.

SHACHTER, R. (1988) "Probabilistic Inference and Influence Diagrams." *Operations Research,* 36, 589–604.

SHACHTER, R., and L. BERTRAND (1988) *DAVID: An Interactive Program for Processing Influence Diagrams, Version 1.1.* Durham, NC: Duke University Center for Academic Computing.

VON WINTERFELDT, D., and W. EDWARDS (1986) *Decision Analysis and Behavioral Research.* Cambridge: Cambridge University Press.

◇ EPILOGUE

TOXIC CHEMICALS. The trade-off between economic value and cancer cost can be extremely complicated and can lead to difficult decisions, especially when a widely used substance is found to be carcinogenic. Imposing an immediate ban can have extensive economic consequences. Asbestos is an excellent example of the problem. This material, known since Roman times, was used extensively after World War II. But pioneering research by Dr. Irving Selikoff of the Mt. Sinai School of Medicine showed that breathing asbestos particles can cause lung cancer. This led the EPA to list it as a hazardous air pollutant in 1972. In 1978, the EPA imposed further restrictions and banned spray-on asbestos insulation. In the summer of 1989 the EPA announced a plan that would result in an almost total ban of the substance by the year 1996.

An article in *Science* (Mossman, et al., 1990), however, suggests that EPA's plan may be unnecessary. The authors of this article survey the scientific studies that have been done on asbestos. They conclude that, although substantial evidence exists that asbestos can be dangerous when workers are exposed in mining or manufacturing applications, the typical airborne concentrations of asbestos found in buildings do not harm occupants. [*Sources:* "U.S. Orders Virtual Ban on Asbestos," *Los Angeles Times,* July 7, 1989; "Asbestos Widely Used until Researcher's Warning," *Associated Press*, July 7, 1989; Mossman, B. T., Bignon, J., Corn, M., Seaton, A., & Gee, J. B. L. (1990) "Asbestos: Scientific Developments and Implications for Public Policy," *Science*, 247, 294–301.]

COLD FUSION.   At a conference in Santa Fe, New Mexico, at the end of May 1989, Pons and Fleischmann's results were discussed by scientists from around the world. After many careful attempts by the best experimentalists in the world, no consensus was reached. Some researchers reported observing excess heat, while others had observed neutrons. Many had observed nothing. Many possible explanations still exist for these results, and research will continue to explore these possibilities. [*Source*: Pool, R. (1989) "Cold Fusion: End of Act I." *Science*, 244, 1039–1040.]   ◆

Making Choices

In this chapter, we will learn how to use the details in a structured problem so as to find a preferred alternative. "Using the details" typically means making calculations, and we will see that the kinds of calculations that we make are essentially the same in solving both decision trees and influence diagrams. Following these solution techniques, we will introduce risk profiles and dominance considerations, which are ways to make decisions without doing all those calculations. The chapter concludes with a short discussion of personal-computer programs for decision analysis.

Our main example for this chapter is from the famous Texaco–Pennzoil court case.

TEXACO VERSUS PENNZOIL

In early 1984, Pennzoil and Getty Oil agreed to the terms of a merger. But before any formal documents could be signed, Texaco offered Getty Oil a substantially better price, and Gordon Getty, who controlled most of the Getty stock, reneged on the Pennzoil deal and sold to Texaco. Naturally, Pennzoil felt as if it had been dealt with unfairly and immediately filed a lawsuit against Texaco alleging that Texaco had interfered illegally in the Pennzoil–Getty negotiations. Pennzoil won the case; in late 1985, it was awarded $11.1 billion, the largest judgment ever in the United States. A Texas appeals court reduced the judgment by $2 billion, but interest and penalties drove the total back up to $10.3 billion. James Kinnear, Texaco's chief executive officer, had said that Texaco would file for bankruptcy if Pennzoil obtained court permission to secure the judgment by filing liens against Texaco's assets. Furthermore, Kinnear had promised to fight the case all the way to the U.S. Supreme Court if necessary, arguing in part that Pennzoil had not followed Security and Exchange Commission regulations in its negotiations with Getty. In April 1987, just before Pennzoil began to file the liens, Texaco offered to pay Pennzoil $2 billion to settle the entire case. Hugh Liedtke, chairman of Pennzoil, indicated that his advisors were telling him that a settlement of between $3 billion and $5 billion would be fair.

◆

What do you think Liedtke should do? Should he accept the offer of $2 billion, or should he refuse and make a firm counteroffer? If he refuses the sure $2 billion, then he faces a risky situation. Texaco might agree to pay $5 billion, a reasonable amount in Liedtke's mind. If he counteroffered with $5 billion as a settlement amount, perhaps Texaco would counter with $3 billion or simply pursue further appeals. Figure 4.1 shows a decision tree with a simplified version of Liedtke's problem.

This decision tree is simplified in several ways. The decision alternatives that Liedtke has obviously are more varied than those shown. He could counteroffer a variety of possible dollar values in the initial decision, and in the second decision, he could counteroffer some amount between $3 billion and $5 billion. Likewise, Texaco's counteroffer, if it makes one, need not be exactly $3 billion. The outcome of the final court decision could be anything between zero and the current judgment of $10.3 billion. Finally, our model has not included anything concerning Texaco's option of filing for bankruptcy.

Why all of the simplifications? A straightforward answer (which just happens to have some validity) is that for our purposes in this chapter we need a relatively simple decision tree to work with. But this is just a pedagogical reason. If we were to analyze Liedtke's problem in all of its glory, how much detail should be

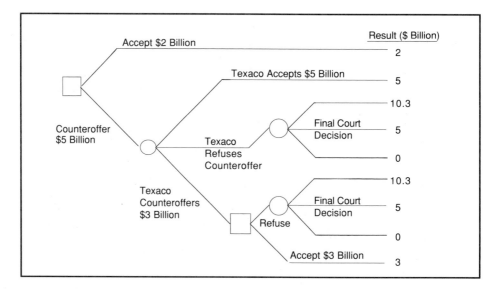

FIGURE 4.1   *Hugh Liedtke's Decision in the Texaco–Pennzoil Affair*

included? As you should now realize, all of the relevant information should be included, and the model should be constructed in a way that makes it easy to analyze. Does our representation accomplish this? Let us consider the following points.

1. *Liedtke's initial counteroffer.* The counteroffer of $5 billion could be replaced by an offer for another amount, and then the decision tree reanalyzed. Different amounts may change the chance of Texaco accepting the counteroffer. At any rate, other possible counteroffers are easily dealt with.
2. *Liedtke's second counteroffer.* Other possible offers could be built into the tree, leading to a Texaco decision to accept, reject, or counter. The reason for leaving these out reflects an impression from news media accounts (especially *Fortune*, May 11, 1987, pp. 50–58) that Kinnear and Liedtke were extremely tough negotiators and that further negotiations were highly unlikely.
3. *Texaco's counteroffer.* The $3-billion counteroffer could be replaced by a fan representing a range of possible counteroffers. It would be necessary to find a "break-even" point, above which Liedtke would accept the offer and below which he would refuse. Another approach would be to replace the $3-billion value with other values, recomputing the tree each time. Thus, we have a variety of ways to deal with this issue.
4. *The final court decision.* We could include more branches, representing additional possible outcomes, or we could replace the three branches with a fan representing a range of possible outcomes. For a first-cut approximation, the possible outcomes we have chosen do a reasonably good job of capturing the uncertainty inherent in the court outcome.
5. *Texaco's bankruptcy option.* One detail left out of the case is that Texaco's net worth is much more than the $10.3 billion judgment. Thus, even if Texaco does file for bankruptcy, Pennzoil probably would still be able to collect. In reality, negotiations can continue even if Texaco has filed for bankruptcy; the purpose of filing is to protect the company from creditors who might seize assets while the company proposes a financial reorganization plan. In fact, this is exactly what Texaco needs to do in order to figure out a way to deal with Pennzoil's claims. In terms of Liedtke's options, however, whether Texaco files for bankruptcy appears to have no impact.

The purpose of this digression has been to explore whether our structure for Liedtke's problem is adequate. The points above suggest that the main issues in the problem have been represented. Although it may be necessary to rework the analysis with slightly different numbers or structure later, the structure in Figure 4.1 should be adequate for a first analysis. The objective is to develop a representation of the problem that captures its essential features so that ensuing analysis will provide the decision maker with insight and understanding.

One small detail remains before we can solve the decision tree. We need to specify the chances associated with Texaco's possible reactions to the $5-billion counteroffer, and we also need to assess the chances of the various court awards. The chances, or probabilities that we assign to the chance branches in the tree, should reflect Liedtke's beliefs about the uncertain events that he faces. For this reason, any numbers that we include to represent these beliefs should be based on what Liedtke has to say about the matter or on information from individuals whose judgments in this matter he would trust. For our purposes, imagine overhearing a conversation between Liedtke and his advisors. Here are some of the issues they might raise:

♦ Given the tough negotiating stance of the two executives, it could be an even chance (50%) that Texaco will refuse to negotiate further. If Texaco does not refuse, then what? What are the chances that Texaco would accept a $5-billion counteroffer? How likely is this outcome compared to the $3-billion counteroffer from Texaco? Liedtke and his advisors might figure that a counteroffer of $3 billion from Texaco is about twice as likely as Texaco accepting the $5 billion. Thus, because there is already a 50% chance of refusal, there must be a 33% chance of a Texaco counteroffer and a 17% chance of Texaco accepting $5 billion.

♦ What are the probabilities associated with the final court decision? In the *Fortune* article cited above, Liedtke is said to admit that Texaco could win its case, leaving Pennzoil with nothing but lawyer bills. Thus, there is a significant possibility that the outcome would be zero. Given the strength of Pennzoil's case so far, there is also a good chance that the court will uphold the judgment as it stands. Finally, the possibility exists that the judgment could be reduced somewhat (to $5 billion in our model). Let us assume that Liedtke and his advisors agree that there is a 20% chance that the court will award the entire $10.3 billion and a slightly larger, or 30%, chance that the award will be zero. Thus, there must be a 50% chance of an award of $5 billion.

Figure 4.2 shows the decision tree with these chances included. The chances have been written in terms of probabilities rather than as percentages.

♦ DECISION TREES AND EXPECTED MONETARY VALUE

One way to choose from among risky alternatives is to pick the alternative with the highest *expected monetary value* (EMV). Finding EMVs when using decision trees is called "folding back the tree" for reasons that will become obvious. We start at the endpoints of the branches on the far right-hand side and move to the left, (1) calculating *expected values* (to be defined momentarily) when we encounter a chance node, or (2) choosing the branch with the highest value or expected value when we encounter a decision node. These instructions sound rather cryptic. It is much easier to understand the procedure through a few examples. We will start with a simple example, the double-risk dilemma shown in Figure 4.3.

Recall that a double-risk dilemma is a matter of choosing between two risky alternatives. Assume that you have a ticket that will let you participate in a game of chance (a lottery) that will pay off $10 with a 45% chance (or a 55% chance

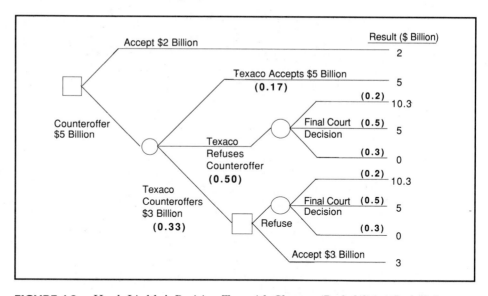

FIGURE 4.2 *Hugh Liedtke's Decision Tree with Chances (Probabilities) Included*

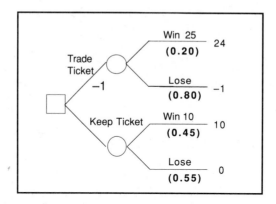

FIGURE 4.3 *Double-Risk Dilemma*

of nothing). Your friend has a ticket to a different lottery that has a 20% chance of paying $25 (that is, an 80% chance of paying nothing). Your friend has offered to let you have his ticket if you will give him your ticket plus one dollar. Should you agree to the trade and play to win $25, or should you keep your ticket and have a better chance of winning $10?

In Figure 4.3 notice that the numbers at the ends of the branches are the net values. The first step in solving a decision tree is to calculate net values for the chain of events and decisions that lead to a particular outcome. Thus, if you trade tickets and win, you will have gained a net $24, having paid one dollar to your friend.

Once the net values at the ends of the branches are calculated, solving the decision tree by using EMV is straightforward. We will start by calculating the expected value of keeping the ticket and playing for $10. The expected value is simply the weighted average of the possible outcomes of the lottery, the weights being the chances with which the outcomes occur. (A more formal definition will be given in Chapter 7.) The calculations are:

$$\text{EMV (Keep Ticket)} = 0.45(10) + 0.55(0)$$
$$= \$4.5.$$

One interpretation of this EMV is that playing this lottery many times would yield on average approximately $4.50 per game. Calculating EMV for trading tickets gives:

$$\text{EMV (Trade Ticket)} = 0.20(24) + 0.80(-1)$$
$$= \$4.$$

Now we can replace the chance nodes in the decision tree with their expected values, as shown in Figure 4.4. Finally, choosing between trading and keeping the ticket amounts to choosing the branch with the highest expected value. The double slash through the "Trade Ticket" branch indicates that this branch would not be chosen.

This simple example is only a warm-up exercise. Now let us see how the solution procedure works when we have a more complicated decision problem. Consider Hugh Liedtke's problem as diagrammed in Figure 4.2. Our strategy, as indicated, will be to work from the right-hand side of the tree. Our first step will be to calculate the expected value of the final court decision. The second step will be to decide whether it is better for Liedtke to accept a $3-billion counteroffer from Texaco or to refuse and take a chance on the final court decision. We will do this by comparing the expected value of the judgment with the sure $3 billion. The third step will be to calculate the expected value of making the $5-billion counteroffer, comparing this expected value with the sure $2 billion that Texaco is offering now.

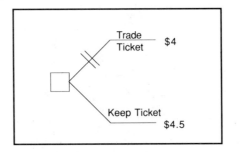

FIGURE 4.4   *Replacing Chance Nodes with EMVs*

The expected value of the court decision is the weighted average of the possible outcomes:

$$\text{EMV(Court Decision)} = [\text{P(Award} = 10.3) \times 10.3] + [\text{P(Award} = 5) \times 5]$$
$$+ [\text{P(Award} = 0) \times 0]$$
$$= [0.2 \times 10.3] + [0.5 \times 5] + [0.3 \times 0]$$
$$= 4.56.$$

We replace both uncertainty nodes representing the court decision with this expected value, as in Figure 4.5. Now, comparing the two options of accepting and refusing Texaco's $3-billion counteroffer, it is obvious that the expected value of $4.56 billion is greater than the certain value of $3 billion, and hence the slash through the "Accept $3 Billion" branch.

To continue folding back the decision tree, we replace the decision node with the preferred alternative. The decision tree as it stands after this replacement is shown in Figure 4.6. The third step is to calculate the expected value of the option "Counteroffer $5 Billion." This expected value is:

$$\text{EMV(Counteroffer \$5 Billion)} = [\text{P(Texaco Accepts)} \times 5]$$
$$+ [\text{P(Texaco Refuses)} \times 4.56]$$
$$+ [\text{P(Texaco Counteroffers)} \times 4.56]$$
$$= [0.17 \times 5] + [0.50 \times 4.56] + [0.33 \times 4.56]$$
$$= 4.63.$$

Replacing the chance node with its expected value results in the decision tree shown in Figure 4.7. Comparing the values of the two branches, it is clear that the expected value of $4.63 billion is preferred to the $2-billion offer from

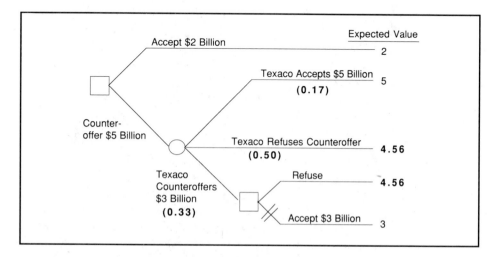

FIGURE 4.5 *Hugh Liedtke's Decision Tree after Expected Value of Court Decision Is Calculated*

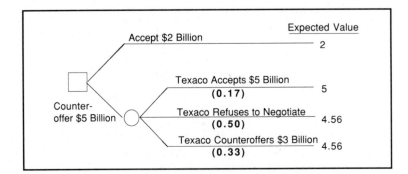

FIGURE 4.6 *Hugh Liedtke's Decision Tree after Decision Node Replaced with Expected Value of Preferred Alternative*

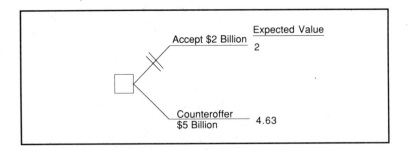

FIGURE 4.7 *Hugh Liedtke's Decision Tree after Original Tree Completely Folded Back*

Texaco. According to this solution, which implies that decisions should be made by comparing expected values, Liedtke should turn down Texaco's offer but counteroffer a settlement of $5 billion. If Texaco turns down the $5 billion and makes another counteroffer of $3 billion, Liedtke should refuse the $3 billion and take his chances in court.

We went through this decision in gory detail to show clearly the steps involved. In fact, in solving a decision tree, we usually do not redraw the tree at each step, but simply indicate on the original tree what the expected values are at each chance node and which alternative is preferred at each decision node. The solved decision tree for Liedtke would look like the tree shown in Figure 4.8, which shows all of the details of the solution. Expected values for the chance nodes are placed above the nodes. The 4.56 above the decision node indicates that if Liedtke gets to this decision point, he should refuse Texaco's offer and take his chances in court for an expected value of $4.56 billion. The decision tree also shows that his best current choice is to make the $5-billion counteroffer with an expected payoff of $4.63 billion.

The decision tree shows clearly what Liedtke should do if Texaco counter-

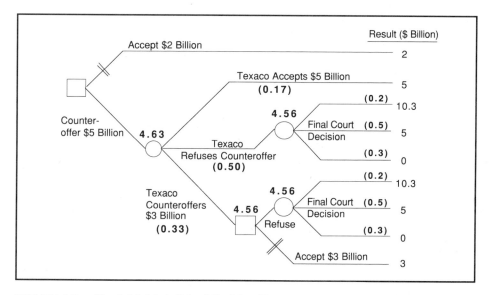

FIGURE 4.8   *Hugh Liedtke's Solved Decision Tree*

offers $3 billion: He should refuse. This is the idea of a contingent strategy. If a particular course of events occurs (Texaco's counteroffer), then there is a specific course of action to take (refuse the counteroffer). Moreover, in deciding whether to accept Texaco's current $2-billion offer, Liedtke must know what he will do in the event that Texaco returns with a counteroffer of $3 billion. This is why the decision tree is solved backward. To make a good decision at the current time, we must know what the appropriate contingent strategies are in the future.

◆ SOLVING INFLUENCE DIAGRAMS

Our discussion so far has shown how to include numerical details in decision trees and how to solve them. We have said nothing about influence diagrams. Although they appear on the surface to be rather simple, much of their complexity is hidden. Our first step is to look closely at how an influence diagram "thinks" about numerical details, and how it translates information into an internal representation. After we understand how the internal representation of the numbers works, we can begin to talk about the influence diagram's solution procedure.

Consider the Texaco–Pennzoil case in influence-diagram form as shown in Figure 4.9. This diagram shows the tables of choices, outcomes (with probabilities), and payoffs that are contained in the nodes. The payoff table in this case is too complicated to include in Figure 4.9. We will work with it later in great detail; it is displayed in Table 4.1 (page 77).

Figure 4.9 needs explanation. The initial decision is whether to accept Texaco's offer of $2 billion. Within this decision node a table shows that the possible

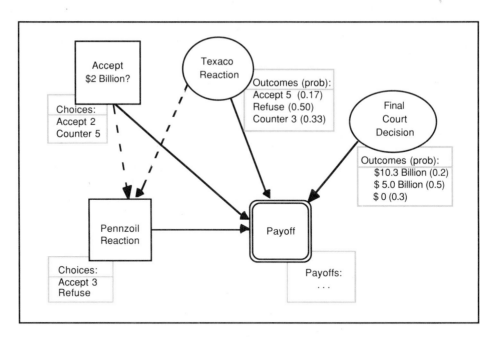

FIGURE 4.9 *Influence Diagram of Liedtke's Decision*

decisions are to accept the offer or make a counteroffer. Likewise, under the "Pennzoil Reaction" node is a table that lists "Accept 3" and "Refuse" as available choices. The chance node "Texaco Reaction" contains a table showing the probabilities of Texaco accepting a counteroffer of $5 billion, making an offer of $3 billion, or refusing to negotiate. Finally, the "Final Court Decision" node has a table with its own outcomes and associated probabilities.

The thoughtful reader should have an immediate reaction to this. After all, whether Texaco reacts depends on whether Liedtke makes his $5-billion counteroffer in the first place! Shouldn't there be an arrow from the decision node "Accept $2 Billion" to the "Texaco Reaction" node? The answer is, yes, there could be such an arrow, but it turns out to be unnecessary and would only complicate matters. The reason is rather subtle, and we will digress with a simple example to explain this phenomenon.

An influence diagram "thinks" about a decision in terms of a symmetric expansion of the decision tree from one node to the next. For example, suppose we have the basic risky decision shown in Figure 4.10, which represents the "umbrella problem." The issue is whether or not to take your umbrella. If you do not take the umbrella, and it rains, your good clothes (and probably your day) are ruined, and your payoff is zero (units of satisfaction). But if you do not take the umbrella and the sun shines, this is the best of all possible outcomes with a payoff of 100. If you decide to take your umbrella, your clothes will not get spoiled, but it is a bit of a nuisance to carry the umbrella around all day. Your payoff is 80, between the other two outcomes.

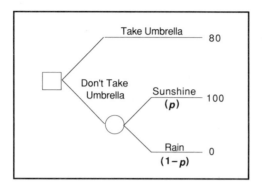

FIGURE 4.10   *Umbrella Problem*

Representing this problem with an influence diagram would yield one like that in Figure 4.11. Now, we have exactly the same situation as we had with Texaco's reaction. It does not matter whether the sun shines if you take the umbrella, just as it does not matter how Texaco would react to a counteroffer if Liedtke accepts the initial offer of $2 billion. If we were to reconstruct exactly how the influence diagram "thinks" about the umbrella problem in terms of a decision tree, the representation would be that shown in Figure 4.12. Note that the uncertainty node on the "Take Umbrella" branch is unnecessary. The payoff is the same regardless of the weather. In a decision-tree model, we can take ad-

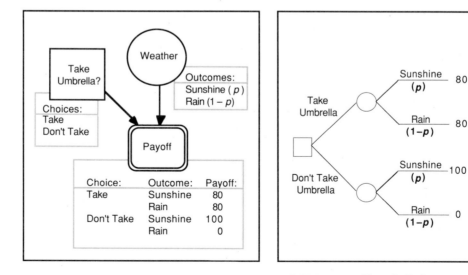

FIGURE 4.11   *Influence Diagram of the Umbrella Problem*

FIGURE 4.12   *How the Influence Diagram "Thinks" about the Umbrella Problem*

vantage of this fact by not even drawing the unnecessary node. Influence diagrams, however, use the symmetric decision tree, even though this may require unnecessary nodes (and hence unnecessary calculations).

Now you should be able to see why there is no arrow in Figure 4.9 between the "Accept $2 Billion" and "Texaco Reaction" nodes. An arrow would indicate that the decision made (accepting or rejecting the $2 billion) would affect the chances associated with Texaco's reaction to a counteroffer. But the uncertainty about Texaco's response to a $5-billion counteroffer does not depend on whether Liedtke accepts the $2 billion. Essentially, the influence diagram is equivalent to a decision tree that is symmetric. Figure 4.13 shows the portion of the tree that deals with Liedtke's initial decision and Texaco's reaction.

For similar reasons, there are no arrows between "Final Court Decision" and the other three nodes. If some combination of decisions comes to pass so that Pennzoil and Texaco agree to a settlement, it does not matter what the court decision would be. The influence diagram implicitly includes the "Final Court Decision" node, with the agreed-upon settlement regardless of the "phantom" court outcome.

How is all of this finally resolved in the influence-diagram representation? Everything is handled in the payoff node, which contains a table that gives Liedtke's payoffs for every possible combination of decisions and outcomes. That table (Table 4.1) shows that the payoff is $2 billion if Liedtke accepts the current offer, regardless of the other outcomes. It also shows that if Liedtke counteroffers $5 billion and Texaco accepts, then the payoff is $5 billion regardless of the court decision or Pennzoil's reaction (neither of which have any impact if Texaco accepts the $5 billion). The table also would show the details of the court outcomes if Texaco refuses to negotiate after Liedtke's counteroffer or if Liedtke refuses a Texaco counteroffer. And so on. The table of payoffs shows exactly what the payoff is to Pennzoil under all possible combinations. The column headings in Table 4.1 represent nodes that are predecessors of the value

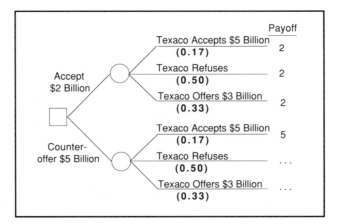

FIGURE 4.13   *How the Influence Diagram "Thinks" about the Texaco–Pennzoil Case*

Accept $2 Billion?	Texaco's Reaction ($ Billion)	Pennzoil's Reaction ($ Billion)	Final Court Decision ($ Billion)	Payoff ($ Billion)
Accept 2	Accept 5	Accept 3	10.3	2.0
			5	2.0
			0	2.0
		Refuse	10.3	2.0
			5	2.0
			0	2.0
	Offer 3	Accept 3	10.3	2.0
			5	2.0
			0	2.0
		Refuse	10.3	2.0
			5	2.0
			0	2.0
	Refuse	Accept 3	10.3	2.0
			5	2.0
			0	2.0
		Refuse	10.3	2.0
			5	2.0
			0	2.0
Offer 5	Accept 5	Accept 3	10.3	5.0
			5	5.0
			0	5.0
		Refuse	10.3	5.0
			5	5.0
			0	5.0
	Offer 3	Accept 3	10.3	3.0
			5	3.0
			0	3.0
		Refuse	10.3	10.3
			5	5.0
			0	0.0
	Refuse	Accept 3	10.3	10.3
			5	5.0
			0	0.0
		Refuse	10.3	10.3
			5	5.0
			0	0.0

TABLE 4.1　*Payoff Table for the Influence Diagram of Liedtke's Decision*

node. In this case, both decision nodes and both chance nodes are included because all are predecessors of the value node.

We now can talk a little about how to solve an influence diagram. Consider the Texaco–Pennzoil diagram in Figure 4.9. In general, our strategy will be to *reduce nodes* one at a time, which means either calculating expected values for a chance node or choosing preferred alternatives for a decision node. The order of reduction is reminiscent of our solution in the case of the decision tree. The first node reduced is the "Final Court Decision," which results in the diagram given in Figure 4.14. In this first step, expected values are calculated using the "Final Court Decision" probabilities, which yields the payoffs shown in Table 4.2.

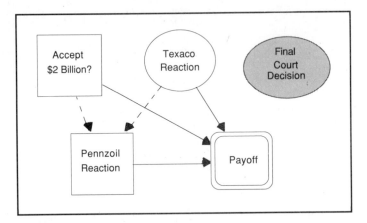

FIGURE 4.14 *First Step in Solving the Influence Diagram*

Accept $2 Billion?	Texaco's Reaction	Pennzoil's Reaction	Expected Payoff ($ Billion)
Accept 2	Accept 5	Accept 3	2
		Refuse	2
	Offer 3	Accept 3	2
		Refuse	2
	Refuse	Accept 3	2
		Refuse	2
Offer 5	Accept 5	Accept 3	5
		Refuse	5
	Offer 3	Accept 3	3
		Refuse	4.56
	Refuse	Accept 3	4.56
		Refuse	4.56

TABLE 4.2 *Payoff Table for Liedtke's Decision after Reducing the "Final Court Decision" Node*

All combinations of decisions and possible outcomes of Texaco's reaction are shown. For example, if Liedtke counteroffers $5 billion and Texaco refuses to negotiate, the expected payoff of $4.56 billion is listed regardless of the decision in the "Pennzoil Reaction" node (because that decision is meaningless if Texaco initially refuses to negotiate). If Liedtke accepts the $2-billion offer, the expected payoff is listed as $2 billion, regardless of other outcomes. (Of course, there is nothing uncertain about this outcome; the value that we know will happen is the expected value.) If Liedtke offers 5, Texaco offers 3, and Liedtke refuses to continue negotiating, the expected value is then given as 4.56. And so on.

The next step is to reduce the "Pennzoil Reaction" node. The resulting influence diagram is shown in Figure 4.15. Now the table in the payoff node (Table 4.3) reflects the fact that Liedtke should choose the alternative with the highest expected value (refuse to negotiate) if Texaco makes the counteroffer of $3 billion. Thus, the table now says that if Liedtke offers $5 billion and Texaco

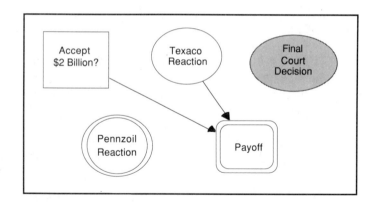

FIGURE 4.15   *Second Step in Solving the Influence Diagram*

Accept $2 Billion?	Texaco's Reaction	Expected Payoff ($ Billion)
Accept 2	Accept 5	2
	Offer 3	2
	Refuse	2
Offer 5	Accept 5	5
	Offer 3	4.56
	Refuse	4.56

TABLE 4.3   *Payoff Table for Influence Diagram of Liedtke's Decision after Reducing "Final Court Decision" and "Pennzoil Reaction" Nodes*

either refuses to negotiate or counters with $3 billion, then the expected value is $4.56 billion. If Texaco accepts the $5-billion counteroffer, the expected value is $5 billion, and if Liedtke accepts the current offer, the expected value is $2 billion. (Again, there is nothing uncertain about these outcomes; the expected value is just the value that we know will occur.)

In addition to the changes in the payoff table at this step, we also have results that we can look at in the table of decisions contained in the "Pennzoil Reaction" node. The node has changed shape and now looks like a deterministic node; this indicates that the table now displays the optimal decisions to make. Specifically, it shows that if Liedtke and Texaco both make counteroffers, the optimal next step is for Liedtke to refuse to negotiate further and to go to court. The table also displays the "optimal" choice for this decision when Liedtke accepts the $2 billion or Texaco either accepts the $5-billion counteroffer or refuses to continue. Of course, in these cases, the Pennzoil reaction decision is vacuous. Even though a reaction is listed in these cases, it is meaningless because the outcome does not depend on that decision.

The third step is to reduce the "Texaco Reaction" node, as shown in Figure 4.16. As with the first step, this involves taking the table of payoffs within the payoff node and recalculating expected values. The payoff table, shown in Table 4.4, now has only two entries. The expected value of Liedtke accepting $2 billion is just $2 billion, and the expected value of countering with $5 billion is $4.63 billion.

The fourth and final step is simply to figure out which decision is optimal in the "Accept $2 Billion?" node and to record the result. This final step is shown in Figure 4.17. The table within the metamorphosed decision node indicates that Liedtke's optimal choice is to counteroffer $5 billion. The payoff table now contains only one value, $4.63 billion, the expected value of the optimal decision.

Reviewing the procedure, you should be able to see that it followed basically the same steps that we followed in folding back the decision tree.

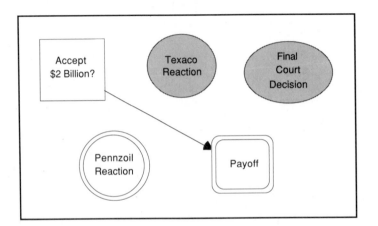

FIGURE 4.16   *Third Step in Solving the Influence Diagram*

Accept $2 Billion?	Expected Payoff ($ Billion)
Accept 2	2
Offer 5	4.63

TABLE 4.4   *Payoff Table after Reducing the "Final Court Decision," "Pennzoil Reaction," and "Texaco Reaction" Nodes*

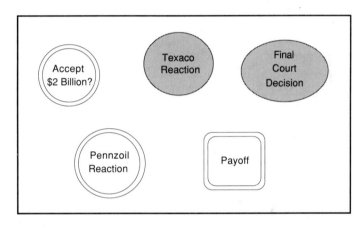

FIGURE 4.17   *Final Step in Solving the Influence Diagram*

◆ SOLVING INFLUENCE DIAGRAMS: AN ALGORITHM (OPTIONAL)

The preceding example should provide some insight into how influence diagrams are solved. Fortunately, you will not typically have to solve influence diagrams by hand; computer programs are available to accomplish this. It is worthwhile, however, to spend a few moments describing the procedure that is used to solve influence diagrams. A set procedure for solving a problem is called an *algorithm*. You already have learned the algorithm for solving a decision tree (the folding-back procedure). Now let us look at an algorithm for solving influence diagrams.

1. First we simply clean up the influence diagram to make sure it is ready for solution. Check to make sure the influence diagram has only one value node (or a series of value nodes that feed into one "super" value node) and that there are no cycles. If your diagram does not pass this test, you must fix it be-

fore it can be solved. In addition, if any nodes other than the value node have arrows into but not out of them, they can be eliminated. Such nodes are called *barren nodes* and have no effect on the decision that would be made. Replace deterministic nodes with chance nodes. For each possible combination of the predecessor node outcomes, the node has only one outcome that happens with probability 1.

2. Second, look for any chance nodes that (a) directly precede the value node and (b) do *not* directly precede any other node. Any such chance node found should be reduced by calculating expected values. The value node then inherits the predecessors of the reduced nodes. (That is, any arrows that went into the node just reduced should be redrawn to go into the value node.)

   This step is just like calculating expected values for chance nodes at the far right-hand side of a decision tree. You can see how this step was implemented in the Texaco–Pennzoil example. In the original diagram, Figure 4.9, the "Final Court Decision" node is the only chance node that directly precedes the value node *and* does not precede any decision node. Thus it is reduced by the expected-value procedure, resulting in the payoff table given in Table 4.2. The value node does not inherit any new direct predecessors as a result of this step because "Final Court Decision" has no direct predecessors.

3. Third, look for a decision node that (a) directly precedes the value node and (b) has as predecessors all other direct predecessors of the value node. *If you do not find any such decision node, go directly to Step 5.* If such a decision node is found, it can be reduced by choosing the optimum value. When decision nodes are reduced, the value node does not inherit any new predecessors. Because of this, new barren nodes may be created. They can be eliminated from the diagram.

   This step is like folding a decision tree back through a decision node at the far right-hand side of the tree. In the Texaco–Pennzoil problem, this step was implemented when we reduced "Pennzoil Reaction." In Figure 4.14, this node satisfies the criteria for reduction because it directly precedes the value node, and the other nodes that directly precede the value node also precede "Pennzoil Reaction." In reducing this node, we choose the option within "Pennzoil Reaction" that gives the highest expected value; as a result we obtain the payoff table shown by Table 4.3. No barren nodes are created in this step.

4. Fourth, return to Step 2 and continue until the influence diagram is completely solved (all nodes reduced). This is like working through a decision tree until all nodes have been processed from right to left.

5. Fifth, you have gotten to this step after reducing all possible chance nodes (if any) and then not finding any decision nodes to reduce. How could this happen? Consider the influence diagram of the hurricane problem in Figure 3.5 (page 40). None of the chance nodes satisfy the criteria for reduction, and the decision node also cannot be reduced. In this case, one of the arrows between chance nodes must be reversed. This is a procedure that requires probability manipulations through the use of Bayes' theorem (Chapter 5). We will not go into the details of the calculations here because most of the simple

influence diagrams that you might be tempted to solve by hand will not require arrow reversals.

Finding an arrow to reverse is a delicate process. First, find the correct chance node. The criteria are that (a) it directly precedes the value node and (b) it does not directly precede any decision node. Call the selected node A. Now look at the arrows out of node A. Find an arrow from A to chance node B (call it A → B) such that there is no other way to get from A to B by following arrows. The arrow A → B can be reversed using Bayes' theorem. Afterward, both nodes inherit each other's direct predecessors *and* keep their own direct predecessors.

After reversing an arrow, return to Step 2 and continue until the influence diagram is solved. (More arrows may need to be reversed before a node can be reduced, but that only means that you may come back to Step 5 one or more times in succession.)

This description of the solution algorithm for influence diagrams is based on the complete (and highly technical) description given in Shachter (1986). The intent here is not to present a "cookbook" for solving an influence diagram, because, as indicated, virtually all but the simplest influence diagrams will be solved by computer program. The description of the algorithm, however, is meant to show the parallels between the influence-diagram solution procedure and the decision-tree solution procedure.

◆ RISK PROFILES

The idea of expected value is appealing, and it is relatively straightforward to compare two alternatives on the basis of their EMVs. For example, Liedtke's expected values are $2 billion and $4.63 billion for his two alternatives. But you might have noticed that these two numbers are not exactly perfect indicators of what might happen. In particular, suppose that Liedtke decides to counteroffer $5 billion: He might end up with $10.3 billion, $5 billion, or nothing, given our simplification of the situation. Moreover, the interpretation of EMV as the average amount that would be obtained by "playing the game" a large number of times is not appropriate here. The "game" in this case amounts to suing Texaco, and this is not a game that Pennzoil will play many times!

That Liedtke could come away with nothing from his dealings with Texaco indicates that choosing to counteroffer is a somewhat risky alternative. In Chapters 11 and 12 we will examine the idea of risk in more detail. For now, however, we can intuitively grasp the relative riskiness of alternatives by studying their *risk profiles*.

A risk profile is a graph that shows the chances associated with possible outcomes. The risk profile for the "Accept $2 Billion" alternative is shown in Figure 4.18. There is a 100% chance that Liedtke will end up with $2 billion. The risk profile for "Counteroffer $5 Billion" is somewhat more complicated and is shown in Figure 4.19. There is a 58.5% chance that the eventual payoff is $5 billion, 16.6% chance of $10 billion, and a 24.9% chance of nothing. These num-

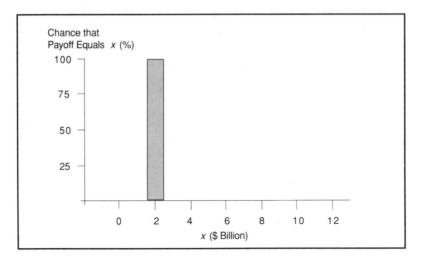

FIGURE 4.18 *Risk Profile for the "Accept $2 Billion" Alternative*

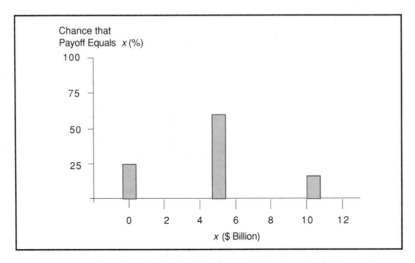

FIGURE 4.19 *Risk Profile for the "Counteroffer $5 Billion" Alternative*

bers are easily calculated. For example, consider the $5-billion outcome. This can happen in three different ways. There is a 17% chance that it happens because Texaco accepts. There is a 25% chance that it happens because Texaco refuses and the judge awards $5 billion (that is, a 50% chance that Texaco refuses times a 50% chance that the award is $5 billion). Finally, the chances are 16.5% that the payoff is $5 billion because Texaco counteroffers $3 billion, Liedtke refuses and goes to court, and the judge awards $5 billion; that is, 16.5% equals 33% times 50%. (Remember that Liedtke's optimal strategy is to refuse the $3-billion counteroffer.)

In constructing a risk profile, we collapse a decision tree by multiplying out the probabilities on sequential chance branches. Of course, decision nodes can be ignored; only the optimal branch from a decision node must be considered. You can think about the process as one in which nodes are gradually removed from the tree in much the same sense as we did with the folding-back procedure, except that here we keep track of the possible outcomes and their probabilities. Figures 4.20, 4.21, and 4.22 show the progression of collapsing the decision tree in order to construct the risk profile for the "Counteroffer $5 Billion" choice.

By looking at the risk profiles, the decision maker can tell a lot about the riskiness of the alternatives. In some cases, he or she can choose from among alternatives on the basis of their risk profiles. Comparing Figures 4.18 and 4.19, it is clear that the worst possible outcome for "Counteroffer $5 Billion" is less than the value for "Accept $2 Billion." On the other hand, the best outcome ($10.3 billion) is much better than $2 billion. Hugh Liedtke has to decide whether the risk of perhaps coming away empty-handed is worth the possibility of getting a settlement higher than $2 billion. This is clearly a case of a basic risky decision, as we can see from the collapsed decision tree in Figure 4.22.

Collapsing a decision tree to find a risk profile has a counterpart in influence diagrams. Thus far we have represented the value node in an influence diagram with a double rounded rectangle. A single rounded rectangle is used in influence diagrams to represent a *value lottery*, as shown in Figure 4.23. If an influence diagram has a value lottery rather than an expected value node, then solving an influence diagram — reducing all the nodes — gives the risk profile in the table within the value-lottery node. That is, once all of the nodes have been reduced, the decision maker can look at the table contained in the value-lottery node to find the risk profile.

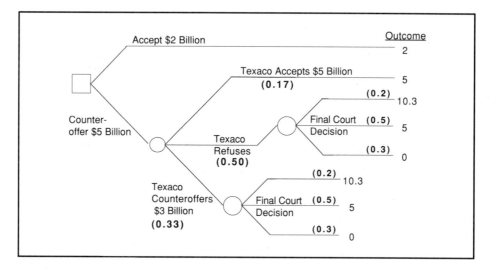

FIGURE 4.20 *First Step in Collapsing the Decision Tree to Make a Risk Profile* The decision node has been removed to leave only the outcomes associated with the "Refuse" branch.

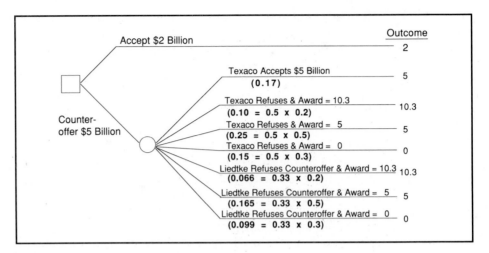

FIGURE 4.21 *Second Step in Collapsing the Decision Tree to Make a Risk Profile* The three chance nodes have been collapsed into one chance node. The probabilities on the branches are the product of the probabilities from the sequential branches in Figure 4.20.

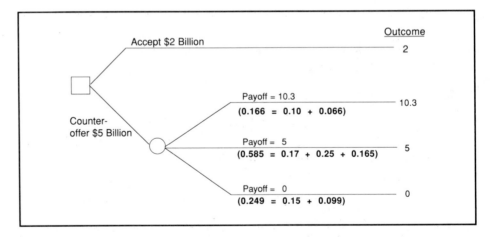

FIGURE 4.22 *Third Step in Collapsing the Decision Tree to Make a Risk Profile* The seven branches from the chance node in Figure 4.21 have been combined into three branches.

As with decision trees, decision nodes that follow the immediate decision essentially are ignored in the process of building the risk profile. The simplest thing to do is to replace the decision nodes with deterministic nodes that specify the optimal alternative. We actually did the same thing with the decision tree in specifying that Liedtke would refuse a counteroffer of $3 billion from Texaco. If

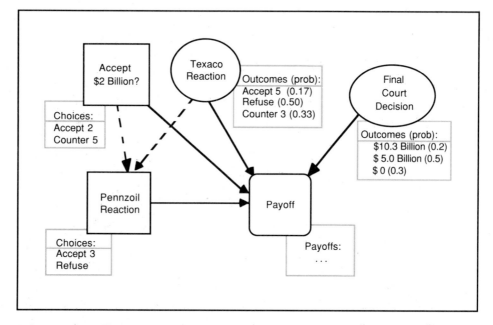

FIGURE 4.23 *Texaco–Pennzoil Influence Diagram with a Value-Lottery Node Instead of an Expected-Value Node*

we had specified that Liedtke would accept, the resulting risk profile would have been different.

Cumulative Risk Profiles

We also can present the risk profile in cumulative form. Figure 4.24 shows the *cumulative risk profile* for "Counteroffer $5 Billion." In this format, the vertical axis is the chance that the payoff is less than or equal to the corresponding value on the horizontal axis. This is only a matter of translating the information contained in the risk profile in Figure 4.19. There is no chance that the payoff is less than zero. At zero, the chance jumps to 24.9%, because there is a substantial chance that the court award will be zero. The graph continues at 24.9% across to $5 billion. (For example, there is a 24.9% chance that the payoff is less than or equal to $3 billion; that is, there is the 24.9% chance that the payoff is zero, and that certainly is less than $3 billion.) At $5 billion, the line jumps to 83.4% (which is 24.9% + 58.5%), because there is an 83.4% chance that the payoff is less than or equal to $5 billion. Finally, at $10.3 billion, the cumulative graph jumps to 100%: The chance is 100% that the payoff is less than or equal to $10.3 billion.

Thus, you can see that creating a cumulative risk profile is simply a matter of adding up, or accumulating, the chances of the individual payoffs. For any specific value along the horizontal axis, we can read off the chance that the pay-

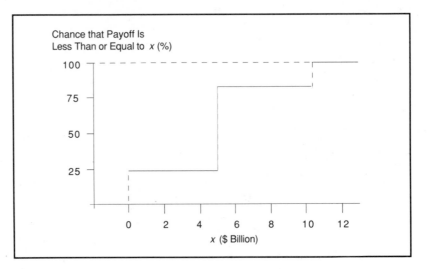

FIGURE 4.24   *Cumulative Risk Profile for the "Counteroffer $5 Billion" Alternative*

off will be less than or equal to that specific value. Cumulative risk profiles will be quite helpful in the next section in our discussion of dominance.

♦ ALTERNATIVES THAT DOMINATE

Expected values are useful, but folding back a tree to find the preferred choice is not always necessary. Suppose we modify Liedtke's problem as shown in Figure 4.2 so that $2.5 billion is the minimum amount that he believes he could get in a court award. Now the decision is diagrammed in Figure 4.25.

Now what should Liedtke do? It is rather obvious. Because he believes that he could do no worse than $2.5 billion if he makes a counteroffer, he should reject Texaco's offer of $2 billion. This kind of dominance is called *deterministic dominance*, which signifies that the dominating alternative pays off at least as much as the one that is dominated.

We can show deterministic dominance in terms of the cumulative risk profiles displayed in Figure 4.26. The cumulative risk profile for "Accept $2 Billion" goes from zero to 100% at $2 billion, because the payoff for this alternative is bound to be $2 billion. The risk profile for "Counteroffer $5 Billion" starts at $2.5 billion, but does not reach 100% until $10.3 billion. Deterministic dominance can be detected in the risk profiles by comparing the value at which one cumulative risk profile reaches 100% with the value at which another risk profile begins. If there is a value x such that the chance of the payoff being less than or equal to x is 100% in Alternative B, and the chance of the payoff being *less than* x is 0% in Alternative A, then A deterministically dominates B. Graphically, continue the vertical line where Alternative A first leaves 0% (the vertical line at $2.5 billion for "Counteroffer $5 Billion"). If that vertical line corresponds to

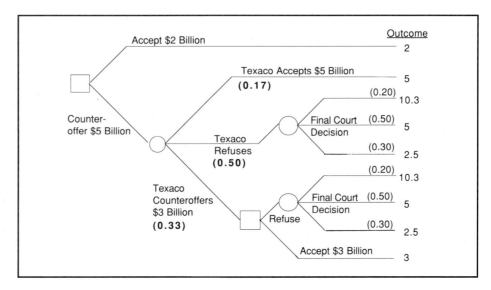

FIGURE 4.25 *Hugh Liedtke's Decision Tree, Assuming $2.5 Billion Is Minimum Court Award*

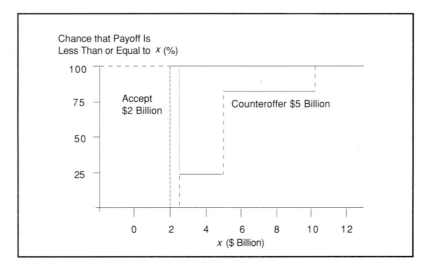

FIGURE 4.26 *Cumulative Risk Profiles for Alternatives in Figure 4.25*

100% for the other cumulative risk profile, then A dominates B. Thus, even if the minimum court award had been $2 billion instead of $2.5 billion, "Counteroffer $5 Billion" still would have dominated "Accept $2 Billion."

The following example shows a similar kind of dominance. Suppose that Liedtke is choosing between two law firms to represent him. He considers both firms to be about equal in their abilities to deal with the case, but one charges

less in the event that the case goes to court. The full decision tree for this problem appears in Figure 4.27. Which choice is preferred? Again, it is rather obvious; the payoffs for choosing Firm A are the same as the corresponding payoffs
for choosing Firm B, except that Pennzoil's payoff is greater with Firm A if the
case results in a damage award in the final court decision. Choosing Firm A is
like choosing Firm B *and* possibly getting a bonus. Firm A is said to display
stochastic dominance over B. Many texts also use the term *probabilistic dominance* to
indicate the same thing. (Strictly speaking, we will discuss first-order stochastic
dominance. Higher-order stochastic dominance comes into play when we consider preferences regarding risk.)

The cumulative risk profiles corresponding to Firms A and B are displayed
in Figure 4.28. The two cumulative risk profiles almost coincide; the only differ-

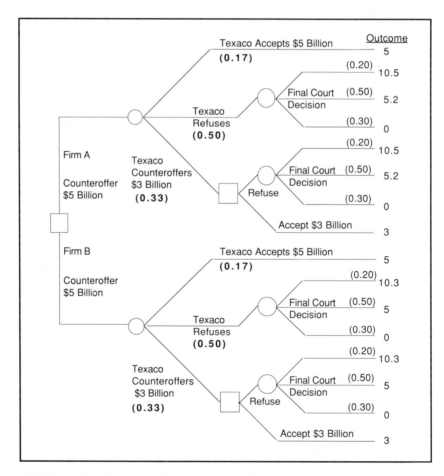

FIGURE 4.27   *A Decision Tree Comparing Two Law Firms*
Firm A charges less than Firm B if Pennzoil is awarded damages
in court.

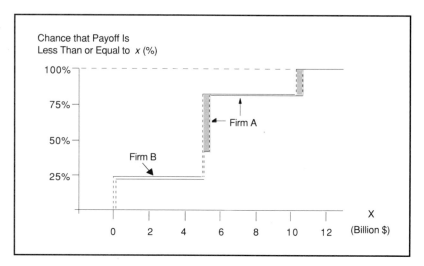

FIGURE 4.28   *Cumulative Risk Profiles for Alternatives in Figure 4.27*
Firm A stochastically dominates Firm B.

ence is that Firm A's profile is slightly to the right of Firm B's at $5 and $10 billion, which represents the possibility of Pennzoil paying less in fees. Stochastic
dominance is represented in the cumulative risk profiles by the fact that the two
profiles do not cross and that there is space between them. That is, if two cumulative risk profiles are such that no part of Profile A lies to the left of B, and at
least some part of it lies to the right of B, then the alternative corresponding to
Profile A stochastically dominates the alternative for Profile B.

The next example demonstrates stochastic dominance in a slightly different
form. Instead of the payoffs, the pattern of the probability numbers makes the
preferred alternative apparent. Suppose that Liedtke's choice is between two law
firms that he considers to be of different abilities. The decision tree is shown in
Figure 4.29. Carefully examine the probabilities in the branches for the final
court decision. Which law firm is preferred? This is a somewhat more subtle situation than the preceding. The essence of the problem is that for Firm C, the
larger outcome values have higher probabilities. The payoffs with Firm C are not
bound to be at least as great or greater than those with Firm D, although the
payoffs with Firm C are more likely to be greater. Think of Firm C as being a better gamble if the situation is decided in court. Situations such as this are characterized by two alternatives that offer the same possible payoffs; the dominating
alternative, however, is more likely to bring a larger payoff.

Figure 4.30 shows the cumulative risk profiles for the two law firms in this
example. As in the last example, the two profiles nearly coincide, although space
is found between the two profiles because of the different probabilities associated with the court award. Because Firm C either coincides with or lies to the
right of Firm D, we can conclude that Firm C stochastically dominates Firm D.

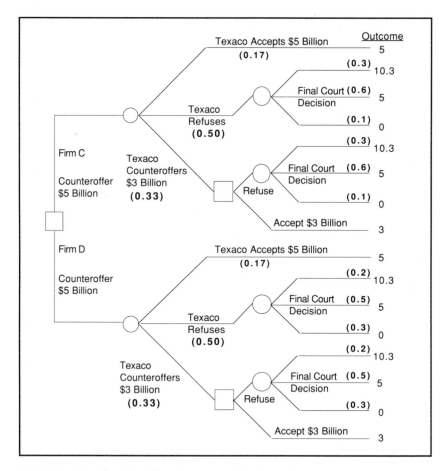

FIGURE 4.29   *Decision Tree Comparing Two Law Firms*
Firm C has a better chance of winning a damage award in court than
does Firm D.

Stochastic dominance can show up in a decision problem in several ways.
One is in terms of the payoffs (as in Figure 4.27), and another is in terms of the
probabilities (as in Figure 4.29). Sometimes stochastic dominance may emerge
as a mixture of the two; both slightly better payoffs and slightly better probabilities may lead to one alternative dominating another.

Why does stochastic dominance work? It turns out that if one alternative
dominates another, then the dominating alternative must have the higher EMV.
This is a property of dominant alternatives that can be proven mathematically.
To get a feeling for why this is true, think about the cumulative risk profiles, and
imagine the EMV for a dominated Alternative B. If Alternative A dominates B,
then its cumulative risk profile must lie at least partly to the right of the profile
for B. Because of this, the EMV for A also must lie to the right of, and hence be
greater than, the EMV for B.

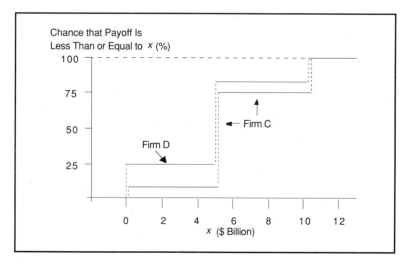

FIGURE 4.30   *Cumulative Risk Profiles for Alternatives in Figure 4.29*
Firm C stochastically dominates Firm D.

Although this discussion of dominance has been fairly brief, one should not conclude that dominance is not important. Indeed, screening alternatives on the basis of dominance begins implicitly in the structuring phase of decision analysis, and, as alternatives are considered, they usually are at least informally compared to other alternatives. Screening alternatives formally on the basis of dominance is an important decision-analysis tool. If an alternative can be eliminated early in the selection process on that basis, considerable costs can be saved in large-scale problems. For example, suppose that the problem is where to build a new electric-power plant. Analysis of proposed alternatives can be exceedingly expensive. If a potential site can be eliminated in an early phase of the analysis on the grounds that another dominates it, then that site need not undergo full analysis.

◆ COMPUTER PROGRAMS FOR DECISION ANALYSIS

In this section we will briefly discuss decision-analysis programs that are currently available for personal computers. All of the programs described here do more than simply calculate EMVs; they also can plot risk profiles and cumulative risk profiles, perform sensitivity analysis, and create a variety of different graphs. Because of the rapidity with which new computer programs are developed and introduced, it is likely that even newer programs are available that are not mentioned here. At the end of the section, we will peek into the future of computerized decision analysis.

Influence-Diagram Programs

Two programs currently exist for interactive creation and processing of influence diagrams: InDia (**In**fluence **Dia**gram) for IBM-compatible computers and DAVID (**D**rawing **A**nd e**V**aluating **I**nfluence **D**iagrams) for the Macintosh. The displays for the two programs are quite similar, and their operation is generally the same. The primary difference between the two is found with the user interface, which actually reflects the differences between the two computers rather than the programs. Interaction with DAVID is through the Macintosh's mouse and keyboard, while interaction for InDia occurs through the keyboard and cursor keys.

The discussion focuses on DAVID, the main screen for which appears in Figure 4.31 with the toxic-chemical influence diagram from Chapter 3. The palette along the left side allows the user to create the various nodes and to place arcs where appropriate. Across the top are the menus, each consisting of a list of commands. The user can select a command using the Macintosh's mouse. For example, under the "Solve" menu is the command "Reduce All Nodes"; the user would choose this to solve a completed influence diagram.

Figure 4.32 shows the information associated with the "Test" node. The upper right-hand corner lists the possible outcomes. The table at the bottom shows a portion of the probability table associated with these outcomes. Figure 4.33 shows the entire table, including all three conditional probability distributions, one for each of the three possible outcomes for "Carcinogenic Potential," the predecessor of "Test." According to the probabilities shown, the test is reason-

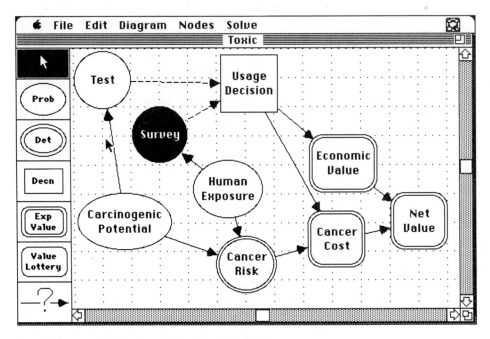

FIGURE 4.31   *Main Screen Display for DAVID*

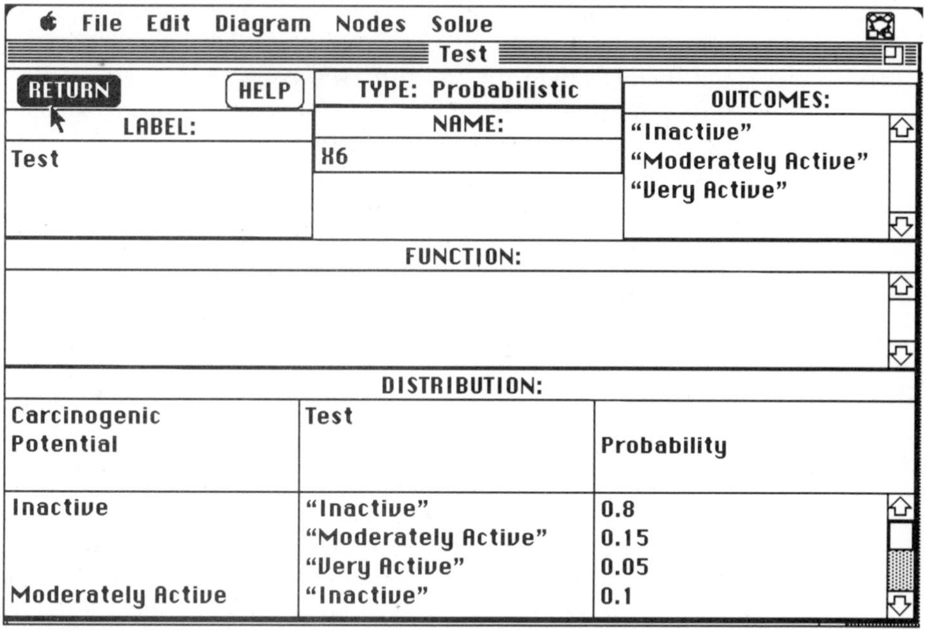

FIGURE 4.32 *Information Contained in the "Test" Chance Node*

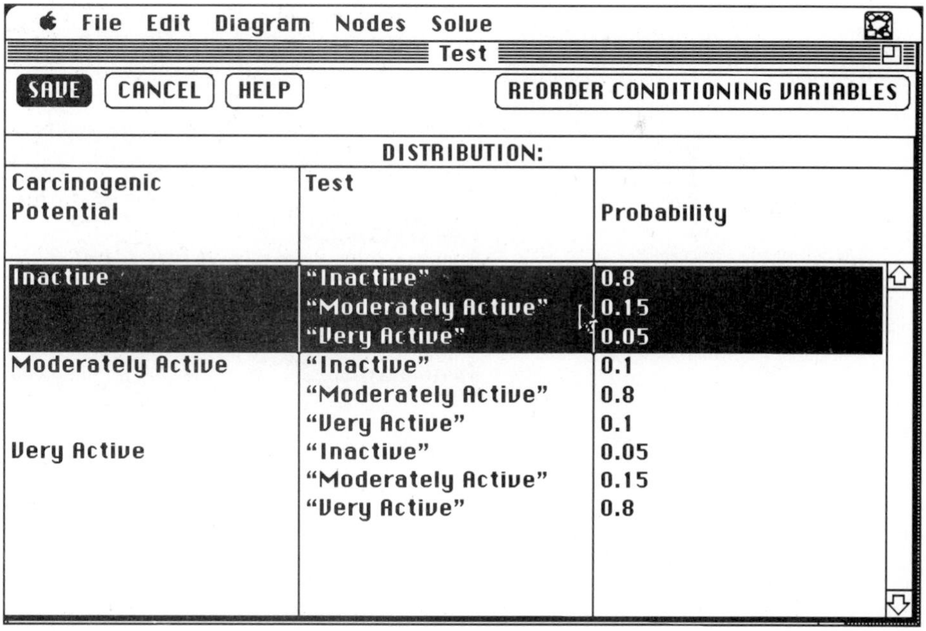

FIGURE 4.33 *Table of Outcomes and Conditional Probabilities Contained in the "Test" Node*

ably good, but not perfect. For instance, if the considered substance is inactive in terms of its carcinogenic potential, then there is an 80% chance that the test will correctly indicate "Inactive." If the substance is very active, however, there is only a 5% chance that the test will incorrectly indicate "Inactive." A perfect test, on the other hand, would be correct 100% of the time, regardless of the substance's actual carcinogenic potential.

Figure 4.34 shows the main screen display for InDia. As you can see, the layout is similar to that for DAVID, with menus listed across the top of the screen. The figure displays the "Node" menu, which contains commands for creating, revising, deleting, and moving nodes as well as for creating arcs through the "Predecessor" and "Successor" commands.

Decision-Tree Programs

Several programs are available for both the IBM-PC and the Macintosh that can create, edit, and process decision trees. Our discussion here will focus on two of the more popular programs, ARBORIST for the IBM personal computer and DATA for the Macintosh. Both provide excellent graphic displays of decision trees and simple ways to enter data so as to modify existing trees. Both programs provide a full arsenal of analysis tools. Again, because of the different computer environments, the user interaction differs significantly between the two.

Figure 4.35 shows the main screen display for ARBORIST. The screen is divided into four windows. The large "Focus Window" on the left displays a close-up view of the currently active portion of the decision tree. Graphs such as risk profiles also appear in this window. The "Macro View Window" in the upper right-hand corner provides an overview of part of the tree, thus making it easier

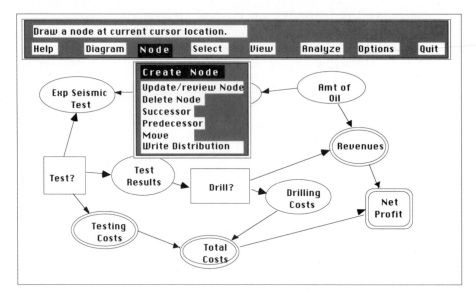

FIGURE 4.34   *Main Screen Display for InDia*

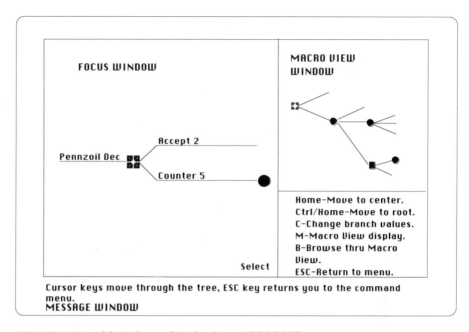

FIGURE 4.35 *Main Screen Display from ARBORIST*

for the user to track exactly which part of a large tree is displayed in the Focus window. The lower right-hand window is the "Menu Window"; this displays available menus and commands. Finally, the "Message Window" runs along the lower edge of the screen. Here is where ARBORIST provides messages to the user, such as what is currently happening, what the user should do next, and error messages.

The main screen display for DATA is shown in Figure 4.36. As with DAVID, the menu titles are listed across the top. The entire Texaco–Pennzoil decision tree fits into the main window, and for larger trees an overview window is available to view the whole tree at one time. Figure 4.37 shows DATA's display of the rolled-back tree. When risk profiles or sensitivity-analysis graphs are created, they appear in their own windows, stacked above the main display window. Changing the view from one window to the next is accomplished with a click of the mouse as in most Macintosh programs.

The specialized programs described here provide convenient environments for modeling decision problems. None is designed for novices, but all can be used effectively by individuals with a bit of training in the use of influence diagrams and decision trees. In general, these programs go hand-in-hand with the training. Having now read Chapters 1 through 4 of *Making Hard Decisions*, you should be reasonably well prepared to try your hand at one of these programs. Working with them will hone your skill in structuring decision problems with influence diagrams and decision trees and will improve your understanding of decision-analysis tools such as risk profiles and dominance.

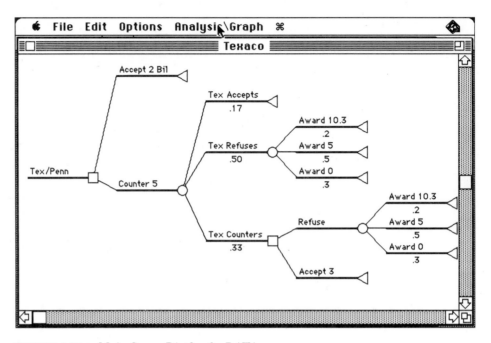

FIGURE 4.36 *Main Screen Display for DATA*

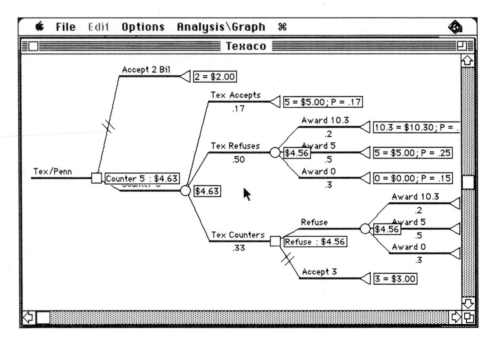

FIGURE 4.37 *DATA's Display of Folded-back Texaco–Pennzoil Tree*

Electronic Spreadsheets

No discussion of decision-analysis software would be complete without considering electronic spreadsheets such as Microsoft® Excel or Lotus® 1-2-3. These programs can be used in a variety of ways in the analysis of decision problems. We will consider two uses here and other uses in later chapters.

First, many decision problems concern accounting information. A spreadsheet environment is ideal for working with accounting data and building financial models for the various possible outcomes in a decision situation. In this way, an analyst may use a spreadsheet to create subsidiary models that provide some of the inputs to a decision tree or influence diagram. In fact, ARBORIST has a built-in interface with Lotus 1-2-3, so it is possible to create financial models in Lotus and then access the appropriate figures on the worksheet directly from ARBORIST.

Second, it is possible to build and process decision trees completely within the spreadsheet. Although building a decision tree within a spreadsheet may appear to be a rather troublesome procedure, the judicious use of spreadsheet *macros*, or collections of commands that can be run with a few keystrokes, can make the process easier. The process will never be as easy and straightforward as using a specialized decision-analysis program, but in some cases the additional flexibility of the spreadsheet will be worthwhile in itself.

Figure 4.38 shows a screen display from Microsoft Excel in which the Texaco–Pennzoil decision tree has been recreated. Macro commands have been used to create chance and decision nodes, each of which includes the necessary calculation, either the EMV for a chance node or the alternative with the greatest EMV for a decision node. The user only has to connect the nodes together by entering simple formulas. For example, the formula in cell B6 is "=D7," indicating that the expected value 4.63 from cell D7 is to be placed into cell B6. The formula in A5 then chooses the greater of the values in B5 and B6. The arrows in Figure 4.38 show the connections among the nodes. Note that there is no need to duplicate the "Court Award" node; the same calculation from cell H5 can be entered in cells I10 and F8.

How useful are electronic spreadsheets really? Much depends on the user's proficiency. A spreadsheet expert can use the program to do many calculations easily, as well as designing decision models and even decision-tree templates and macros to facilitate the process. Moreover, spreadsheet expertise has payoffs in many areas other than decision analysis; these programs can be used to do virtually anything that requires calculations. Of course, gaining such expertise takes time and patience. In the future virtually all managers will have personal computers on their desks with the ability to run sophisticated spreadsheet programs. This suggests that aspiring managers are well advised to become proficient in the use of this flexible tool.

A Peek into the Future

What does the future hold for decision-analysis software? Perhaps we might first expect a program that integrates decision trees, influence diagrams, and a

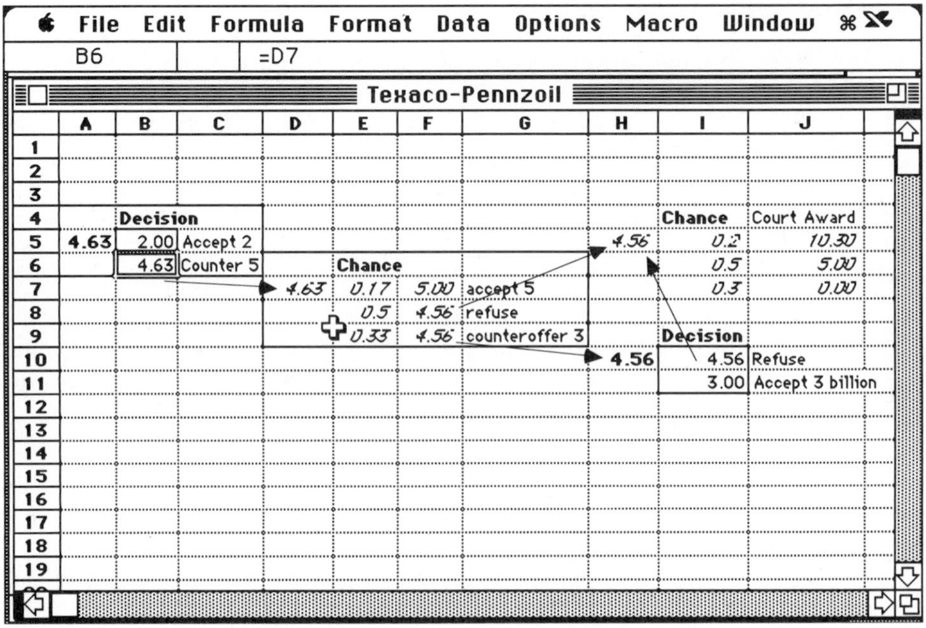

FIGURE 4.38   *Texaco–Pennzoil Decision-Tree Spreadsheet Recreation*
The arrows show the connections among the cells. For example, the expected value 4.63 is calculated in cell D7. A formula is entered into B6, setting it equal to D7.

spreadsheet-like calculator. The decision maker will be able to choose the representation and environment that is most appropriate at the moment and flip back and forth easily among the different parts of the system. This ability will greatly improve modeling flexibility.

Farther into the future we can expect enhancements from the field of artificial intelligence. It may be possible to capture and encode a decision analyst's expertise in model construction, and create an *expert system* program that provides modeling guidance for decision makers. Such a system would be something like having a decision analyst built into your computer, a system that would guide you through the decision-analysis cycle of modeling, sensitivity analysis, refinement, and so on until a requisite model is reached. Such systems probably will be limited to specific domains such as energy-facility location or marketing decisions. Nevertheless, an "intelligent" decision-analysis software system would be a remarkable advance and have the potential of greatly improving decision making at all levels in an organization.

◇ SUMMARY

This chapter has demonstrated a variety of ways to use quantitative tools to make choices in uncertain situations. We first looked at the solution process for decision trees using expected monetary value (EMV). This is the most straightforward way to analyze a decision model; the algorithm for solving a decision tree is relatively easy to apply, and expected values are easy to calculate.

We also explored the process of solving influence diagrams using expected values. To understand the solution process for influence diagrams, we had to look at their internal structures. In a sense, we had to fill in certain gaps left from Chapter 3 about how influence diagrams work. The solution procedure works out easily once we understand how the problem's numerical details are represented internally. The procedure for reducing nodes involves calculating expected values in a way that parallels the solution of a decision tree.

Risk profiles can be developed for comparing alternatives, and we showed how cumulative risk profiles can be used to identify dominated alternatives. The reason for studying dominance criteria for making decisions is that it may be possible to make one without having to calculate expected values. Having seen what can be involved in those calculations, you now should always be on the lookout for dominated alternatives that can be eliminated from consideration.

The chapter ended with an introduction to a few of the available personal-computer programs for performing decision analysis. We also discussed the use of spreadsheets as a flexible modeling tool for decision makers. Such tools can greatly enhance a decision maker's ability to model and analyze a wide variety of decision situations.   ◆

◇ EXERCISES

4.1 Is it possible to solve a decision-tree version of a problem and an equivalent influence-diagram version and come up with different answers? If so, explain. If not, why not?

4.2 Redraw the Texaco–Pennzoil influence diagram using at least one deterministic node.

4.3 The analysis of the Texaco–Pennzoil example shows that the EMV of counteroffering with $5 billion far exceeds $2 billion. Why might Liedtke want to accept the $2 billion anyway? If you were Liedtke, what is the smallest offer from Texaco that you would accept?

4.4 Solve the decision tree in Figure 4.39.

4.5 Draw and solve the influence diagram that corresponds to the decision tree in Figure 4.39.

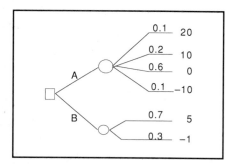

FIGURE 4.39   *Generic Decision Tree for Problem 4.4*

4.6   Solve the decision tree in Figure 4.40. What principle discussed in Chapter 4 is illustrated by this decision tree?

4.7   Solve the decision tree shown in Figure 4.41. Are any calculations required? Explain.

4.8   Solve the decision tree in Figure 4.42.

4.9   Create risk profiles and cumulative risk profiles for Alternatives A and B in Figure 4.42. Does one alternative stochastically dominate the other? Explain.

4.10   Draw and solve the influence diagram that corresponds to the decision tree in Figure 4.42.

4.11   Solve the influence diagram for the umbrella problem in Figure 4.11 (page 75).

4.12   Explain in your own words the ideas of deterministic and stochastic dominance.

4.13   Explain why deterministic dominance is a special case of stochastic dominance.

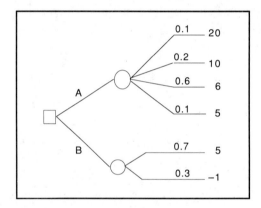

FIGURE 4.40   *Generic Decision Tree for Problem 4.6*

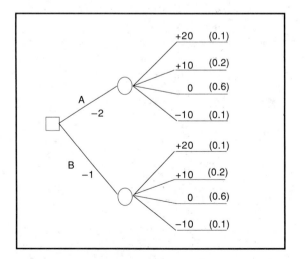

FIGURE 4.41   *Generic Decision Tree for Problem 4.7*

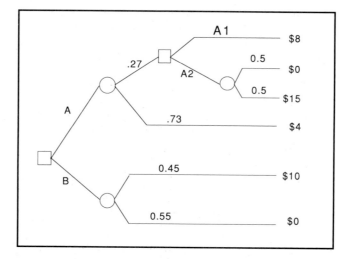

FIGURE 4.42 *Generic Decision Tree for Problem 4.8*

◇ QUESTIONS AND PROBLEMS

4.14 A stock market investor has $500 to spend, and is considering purchasing an option contract on 1000 shares of Apricot Computer. Each share currently sells for $28.50. Apricot is involved in a lawsuit, the outcome of which will be known within a month. If the outcome is in Apricot's favor, analysts expect the company's stock price to increase by $5 per share. If the outcome is unfavorable, then the price is expected to drop by $2.75 per share. The option costs $500, and owning the option would allow the investor to purchase 1000 shares of Apricot stock for $30 per share. Thus, if the investor buys the option and Apricot prevails in the lawsuit, the investor would make an immediate profit. Aside from purchasing the option, the investor could (1) do nothing and earn approximately 8% (annual rate) on his money, or (2) purchase $500 worth of Apricot shares.

   a. Construct cumulative risk profiles for the three alternatives, assuming Apricot has a 25% chance of winning the lawsuit. Can you draw any conclusions?

   b. If the investor believes that Apricot stands a 25% chance of winning the lawsuit, should he purchase the option? What if he believes the chance is only 10%? How large must the probability be for the option to be worthwhile?

4.15 A real-estate investor has the opportunity to purchase an apartment complex. The complex costs $400,000, and is expected to generate a net revenue (after all operating and finance costs) of $6000 per month. Of course, the revenue could vary because the occupancy rate is uncertain. Considering the uncertainty, the revenue could vary from a low of –$1000 to a high of $10,000 per month.

   a. Do you think the investor should buy the apartment complex or invest the $400,000 in a 10-year certificate of deposit earning 9.5% per year? Why?

   b. The city council is currently considering an application to rezone a nearby empty parcel of land. The owner of that land wants to build a small electronics-assembly plant. The proposed plant does not conflict with the city's overall land use plan, but it may have a substantial long-term negative effect on the value of the nearby residential district in which the apartment complex is located. Because the city council currently is divided on the issue and will not make a decision until next month, the real-estate investor is thinking about waiting until the city council makes its decision.

If the investor waits, what could happen? What are the trade-offs that the investor must make in deciding whether to wait or to purchase the complex now?

c. Suppose the investor could pay the seller $1000 in earnest money now, specifying in the purchase agreement that if the council's decision is to approve the rezoning, the investor will forfeit the $1000 and forego the purchase. Draw and solve a decision tree showing the investor's three options. Examine the alternatives for dominance. If you were the investor, which alternative would you choose? Why?

4.16 Analyze the difficult decision situation that you identified in Problem 1.9 (page 10) and structured in Problem 3.13 (page 59). Be sure to examine alternatives for dominance. Does your analysis suggest any new alternatives?

4.17 Johnson Marketing is interested in producing and selling an innovative new food processor. The decision the company faces is the typical "make or buy" decision often faced by manufacturers. On one hand, Johnson could produce the processor itself, subcontracting different subassemblies, such as the motor or the housing. If it does this, the estimates of the costs are as follows.

Alternative: Make Food Processor	
Cost per Unit ($)	**Chance (%)**
35.00	25
42.50	25
45.00	37
49.00	13

The company also could have the entire machine made by a subcontractor. The subcontractor, however, faces similar uncertainties regarding the costs, but has provided Johnson Marketing with the following schedule of costs and chances.

Alternative: Buy Food Processor	
Cost per Unit ($)	**Chance (%)**
37.00	10
43.00	40
46.00	30
50.00	20

If Johnson Marketing wants to minimize its expected cost of production in this case, should it make or buy? Construct cumulative risk profiles to support your recommendation. (*Hint:* Use care when interpreting the graph!)

CASE STUDIES

GPC's New Product Decision

The executives of the General Products Company (GPC) have to decide which of three products to introduce, A, B, or C. Product C is essentially a risk-free proposition, from which the company will obtain a net profit of $1 million. Product B is considerably more risky. Sales may be high, with resulting net profit of $8 million, medium with net profit of $4 million, or low, in which case the company just breaks even. The probabilities for these outcomes are:

P(Sales High for B) = 0.38
P(Sales Medium for B) = 0.12
P(Sales Low for B) = 0.50.

Product A poses some difficulty; a problem with the production system has not yet been solved. The engineering division has indicated its confidence in solving the problem, but there is a slight chance (5%) that devising a workable solution may take a long time. In this event, there will be a delay in introducing the product, and that delay will result in lower sales and profits. Another issue is the price for Product A. The options are to introduce it at either high or low price; the price would not be set until just before the product is introduced. Both of these issues will affect the ultimate net profit.

Finally, once the product is introduced, sales can be either high or low. If the company decides to set a low price, then low sales are just as likely as high sales. If the company sets a high price, the likelihood of low sales depends on whether the product was delayed by the production problem. If there is no delay and the company sets a high price, the probability is 0.4 that sales will be high. But if there is a delay and the price is set high, the probability is only 0.3 that sales will be high. The following table shows the possible net profit figures for Product A:

		High Sales ($ Million)	Low Sales ($ Million)
Time Delay	High Price	5.0	(0.5)
	Low Price	3.5	1.0
No Delay	High Price	8.0	0
	Low Price	4.5	1.5

QUESTIONS

1. Draw an influence diagram for GPC's problem. Specify the possible outcomes and the probability distributions under each chance node. Specify the possible alternatives under each decision node. Write out the complete payoff table under the payoff node. Once you are certain that your representa-

tion of the influence diagram is complete, solve it to find GPC's preferred product. (If possible, do this problem using a computer program for creating and solving influence diagrams.)

2. Draw a complete decision tree for GPC and solve it. What should GPC do? (If possible, do this problem using a computer program for creating and solving decision trees.)

3. Having completed both Questions 1 and 2, comment on the use of both influence diagrams and decision trees.

4. Create cumulative risk profiles for each of the three products. Plot all three profiles on one graph. Can you draw any conclusions?

5. One of the executives of GPC is considerably less optimistic about Product B and assesses the probability of medium sales as 0.3 and the probability of low sales as 0.4. Based on expected value, what decision would this executive make? Do you think he should argue about the probabilities? Why or why not? (*Hint*: Do not forget that probabilities must add to 1!)

◆

Southern Electronics, Part I

Steve Sheffler is president, CEO, and majority stockholder of Southern Electronics, a small firm in the town of Silicon Mountain. Steve faces a major decision: Two firms, Big Red Business Machines and Banana Computer, are bidding for Southern Electronics.

Steve founded Southern 15 years ago, and the company has been extremely successful in developing progressive computer components. Steve is ready to sell the company (as long as the price is right!) so that he can pursue other interests. Last month, Big Red offered Steve $5 million and 100,000 shares of Big Red stock (currently trading at $50 per share and not expected to change substantially in the future). Until yesterday, Big Red's offer sounded good to Steve, and he had planned on accepting it this week. But a lawyer from Banana Computer called last week and indicated that Banana was interested in acquiring Southern Electronics. In discussions this past week, Steve has learned that Banana is developing a new computer, code-named EYF, that, if successful, will revolutionize the industry. Southern Electronics could play an important role in the development of the machine.

In their discussions, several important points have surfaced. First, Banana has said that it believes the probability that the EYF will succeed is 0.6, and if so, the value of Banana's stock will increase from its current value of $30 per share. Although the future price is uncertain, Banana judges that, conditional on the EYF's success, the expected price of the stock will be $50 per share. If the EYF is not successful, the price probably will decrease slightly. Banana judges that if the EYF fails, its share price will be between $20 and $30, with an expected price of $25.

Yesterday Steve discussed this information with his financial analyst, who is an expert regarding the electronics industry and whose counsel Steve trusts completely. The analyst pointed out that Banana has an incentive to be optimistic about the EYF project. "Being realistic, though," said the analyst, "the probability that the EYF succeeds is only 0.4 and if it does succeed, the expected price of the stock would be only $40 per share. On the other hand, I agree with Banana's assessment for the share price if the EYF fails."

Negotiations today have proceeded to the point where Banana has made a final offer to Steve of $5 million and 150,000 shares of Banana stock. The company has stated quite clearly that it cannot pay any more than this in a straight transaction. Furthermore, it does not understand why Steve will not accept the offer because it appears to them to be more valuable than the Big Red offer.

QUESTIONS

1. In terms of expected value, what is the least that Steve should accept from Banana? (This amount is called his *reservation price*.)
2. Steve obviously has two choices: accept the Big Red offer or accept the Banana offer. Draw and solve a complete decision tree representing Steve's decision. (If possible, do this problem using a computer program for creating and solving decision trees.)
3. Draw an influence diagram representing Steve's decision. After specifying all of the necessary details relating to each node, solve the influence diagram. (If possible, do this problem using a computer program to create and solve influence diagrams.)
4. Why is it that Steve cannot accept the Banana offer as it stands?

◆

Southern Electronics, Part II

Steve is well aware of the difference between his probabilities and Banana's, and he realizes that because of this difference, it may be possible to design a contract that benefits both parties. In particular, he is thinking about put options for the stock. A put option gives the owner of the option the right to sell an asset at a specific price. (For example, if you own a put option on 100 shares of General Motors (GM) with an exercise price of $75, you could sell 100 shares of GM for $75 per share before the expiration date of the option. This would be useful if the price of the stock fell below $75.) Steve reasons that if he could get Banana to include a put option on the stock with an exercise price of $30, then he would be protected if the EYF failed.

Steve proposes the following deal: He will sell the company to Banana for $530,000 plus 280,000 shares of Banana stock and a put option that will allow him to sell the 280,000 shares back to Banana for $30 per share any time within the next year (during which time it will become known whether the EYF succeeds or fails).

QUESTIONS

1. Calculate Steve's expected value for this deal. Ignore tax effects and the time value of money.

2. The cost to Banana of its original offer was simply

$$\$5,000,000 + 150,000(\$30) = \$9,500,000.$$

Show that the expected cost to Banana of Steve's proposed deal is less than $9.5 million, and hence in the company's favor. Again, ignore tax effects and the time value of money.

$$\blacklozenge$$

Strenlar, Part I

Fred Wallace scratched his head. By this time tomorrow he had to have an answer for John Sharkey, his former boss at Plastics International (PI). The decision was difficult to make. It involved how he would spend the next 10 years of his life.

Four years ago, when Fred was working at PI, he had come up with an idea for a revolutionary new polymer. A little study — combined with intuition, hunches, and educated guesses — had convinced him that the new material would be extremely strong for its weight. Although it would undoubtedly cost more than conventional materials, Fred discovered that a variety of potential uses existed in the aerospace, automobile manufacturing, robotics, and sporting goods industries.

When he explained his idea to his supervisors at PI, they had patiently told him that they were not interested in pursuing risky new projects. His appeared to be riskier than most because, at the time, many of the details had not been fully worked out. Furthermore, they pointed out that efficient production would require the development of a new manufacturing process. Sure, if that process proved successful, the new polymer could be a big hit. But without that process the company simply could not provide the resources that Fred would need to develop a marketable product.

Fred did not give up. He began to work at home on his idea, consuming most of his evenings and weekends. His intuition and guesses had proven correct, and after some time he had worked out a small-scale manufacturing process. With this process, he was able to turn out small batches of his miracle polymer, which he dubbed Strenlar. At this point he quietly began to assemble capital. He invested $100,000 of his own, managed to borrow another $200,000, and quit his job at PI to devote his time to Strenlar.

That was 15 months ago. In the intervening time he had made substantial progress. The product was refined, and several customers eagerly awaited the first production run. A few problems remained to be solved in the manufacturing process, but Fred was 80% sure that these bugs could be worked out satisfactorily. He was eager to start making profits himself; his capital was running dangerously low. When he became anxious, he tried to soothe his fears by recalling his estimate of the project's potential. His best guess was that sales would be approximately $35 million. After accounting for costs, he would net some $8 million.

Two weeks ago, John Sharkey at PI had surprised him with a telephone call, offering to take Fred to lunch. With some apprehension, Fred accepted the offer. He always had regretted having to leave PI, and was eager to hear how his friends were doing. After some pleasantries, Sharkey came to the point.

"Fred, we're all impressed with your ability to develop Strenlar on your own. I guess we made a mistake in turning down your offer to develop it at PI. But we're interested in helping you out now, and we can certainly make it worth your while. If you will grant PI exclusive rights to Strenlar, we'll hire you back at, say $40,000 a year, and we'll give you a 2.5 percent royalty on Strenlar sales. What do you say?"

Fred did not know whether to laugh or become angry. "John, my immediate reaction is to throw my glass of water in your face! I went out on a limb to develop the product, and now you want to capitalize on my work. There's no way I'm going to sell out to PI at this point!"

The meal proceeded, with Sharkey sweetening his offer gradually, and Fred obstinately refusing. After he got back to his office, Fred felt confused. It would be nice to work at PI again, he thought. At least the future would be secure. But there would never be the potential for the high income that was possible with Strenlar. Of course, he thought grimly, there was still the chance that the Strenlar project could fail altogether.

At the end of the week, Sharkey called him again. PI was willing to go either of two ways. The company could hire him for $50,000 plus a 6% royalty on Strenlar's gross sales. Alternatively, PI could pay him a lump sum of $500,000 now plus options to purchase up to 70,000 shares of PI stock at the current price of $40 any time within the next three years. No matter which offer Fred accepted, PI would pay off Fred's creditors and take over the project immediately. After completing development of the manufacturing process, PI would have exclusive rights to Strenlar. Furthermore, it turned out that PI was deadly serious about this game. If Fred refused both of these offers, PI would file a lawsuit claiming rights to Strenlar on the grounds that Fred had improperly used PI's resources in the development of the product.

Consultation with his attorney just made him feel worse. After reviewing Fred's old contract with PI, the attorney told him that there was a 60% chance that he would win the case. If he won the case, PI would have to pay his court costs. If he lost, his legal fees would amount to approximately $20,000.

Fred's accountant helped him estimate the value of the stock options. First, the exercise date seemed to pose no problem; unless the remaining bugs could not be worked out, Strenlar should be on the market within 18 months. If PI were to acquire the Strenlar project, and the project succeeded, PI's stock would go up to approximately $52 per share. On the other hand, if the project failed, the stock price probably would fall slightly to $39.00.

As Fred thought about all of the problems he faced, he was quite disturbed. On the one hand, he yearned for the comradery he had enjoyed at PI four years ago. He also realized that he might not be cut out to be an entrepreneur. He reacted unpleasantly to the risk he currently faced. His physician had warned him that he may be developing hypertension and had tried to persuade him to relax more. He sighed as he picked up a pencil and pad of paper to see if he could figure out what he should tell John Sharkey.

QUESTION

1. Do a complete analysis of Fred's decision. This may involve drawing and solving either an influence diagram or decision tree, creating risk profiles, checking for stochastic dominance, or whatever else you deem to be appropriate. What do you think he should do? Why? (*Hint*: This case will require you to make certain assumptions in order to do a complete analysis. State clearly any assumptions you make, and be careful that such assumptions are both reasonable and consistent with the information given in the case. Do not forget to consider issues such as the time value of money, riskiness of the alternatives, and so on.)

◆

◇ REFERENCES

The solution of decision trees as presented in this chapter is commonly found in decision-analysis textbooks as well as generally in management-science textbooks. The decision-analysis texts listed at the end of Chapter 1 can provide more guidance in the solution of decision trees if needed. In contrast, the material presented here on the solution of influence diagrams is relatively new. For additional basic instruction in the construction and analysis of decisions using influence diagrams, the user's manual for DAVID (Shachter and Bertrand 1988) is tough to beat. The toxic-chemical example is adapted from a similar example provided with the DAVID system.

The solution algorithm presented here is based on Shachter (1986). The fact that this algorithm deals with a decision problem in a way that corresponds to solving a symmetric decision tree means that the time required for solution rises exponentially with the number of nodes. Thus, the practical upper limit for the size of an influence diagram that can be solved using the algorithm is relatively small. Current researchers are devising solution algorithms that can exploit asymmetric decision characteristics in influence diagrams.

An early and quite readable article on risk profiles is that by Hertz (1964). We have developed them as a way to examine the riskiness of alternatives in a heuristic way and also as a basis for examining alternatives in terms of deterministic and stochastic dominance. Stochastic dominance itself is an important topic in probability. Bunn (1984) gives a good introduction to stochastic dominance, covering higher-order stochastic dominance as well as first-order. Whitmore and Findlay (1978) provide a more thorough review of stochastic dominance.

Sources for the decision-analysis computer programs described in the chapter follow the reference list. In addition, the program Supertree deserves mention. This program was developed by SDG Systems in Menlo Park, California. It is a full-feature decision-analysis system and is appropriate for use by professional decision-analysis consultants. Moreover, McNamee and Celona (1987) provide an excellent introduction to decision analysis and the use of Supertree at a basic level. Supertree's interface is not the most user friendly, however, and thus may prove more difficult for students to use than the programs described above. It is nevertheless a powerful program about which any serious student of decision analysis should be aware.

The use of a spreadsheet as a decision-analysis tool actually is controversial. Everyone agrees that these powerful and flexible programs have a place in the decision-analysis arsenal, although how large a role they should play is the subject of debate. On the one hand, specialized programs would appear to make spreadsheets less important for decision modeling. On the other hand, many important and complicated decision problems have special features that require individualized analysis that can be performed readily in a flexible spreadsheet environment. Furthermore, virtually all managers in the future will have access to electronic spreadsheets and should be encouraged to use these tools to analyze complex decisions. Knowing a few basics of how to build decision models on a spreadsheet will go a long way in this direction.

Jones (1986) describes the use of spreadsheets for decision analysis. Bodily (1985, 1986) discusses their use for modeling decision problems, especially noting their use in building subsidiary models. Bodily (1985) also discusses the IFPS system and its uses in decision modeling in depth. IFPS is a financial-modeling system that uses a command-line interface as opposed to the cell orientation of Lotus 1-2-3 or Microsoft Excel.

Keeping up with developments in the area of intelligent decision systems is difficult. One example that is based on the decision-analysis paradigm is RACHEL, a system to help infertile couples select appropriate medical treatments. RACHEL is discussed in Holtzman and Breese (1986).

BODILY, S. E. (1985) *Modern Decision Making.* New York: McGraw-Hill.

BODILY, S. E. (1986) "Spreadsheet Modeling as a Stepping Stone." *Interfaces,* 16, 34–52.

BUNN, D. (1984) *Applied Decision Analysis.* New York: McGraw-Hill.

DECISION FOCUS, INC. (1988) *InDia, Version 1.0.* Los Altos, CA: Decision Focus, Inc.

HERTZ, D. B. (1964) "Risk Analysis in Capital Investment." *Harvard Business Review.* Reprinted in *Harvard Business Review,* September–October, 1979, 169–181.

HOLTZMAN, S., and J. BREESE (1986) "Exact Reasoning about Uncertainty: On the Design of Expert Systems for Decision Support." In L. N. Kanal and J. F. Lemmer (eds.), *Uncertainty in Artificial Intelligence,* pp. 339–345. Amsterdam: North-Holland.

JONES, J. M. (1986) "Decision Analysis Using Spreadsheets." *European Journal of Operational Research,* 26, 385–400.

McNAMEE, P., and J. CELONA (1987) *Decision Analysis for the Professional with Supertree.* Redwood City, CA: Scientific Press.

MICROSOFT CORPORATION (1989) *EXCEL, Version 2.2.* Redmond, WA: Microsoft Corp.

RAKER, M. (1988) *DATA: Decision Analysis by TreeAge.* Boston, MA: TreeAge Software, Inc.

SHACHTER, R. (1986) "Evaluating Influence Diagrams." *Operations Research,* 34, 871–882.

SHACHTER, R., and L. BERTRAND (1988) *DAVID: An Interactive Program for Processing Influence Diagrams, Version 1.1.* Durham, NC: Duke University Center for Academic Computing.

TEXAS INSTRUMENTS, INC. (1986) *ARBORIST.* Dallas, TX: Texas Instruments, Inc.

WHITMORE, G. A., and M. C. FINDLAY (1978) *Stochastic Dominance.* Lexington, MA: D. C. Heath.

Sources for decision analysis software. Site licenses and educational discounts vary among suppliers.

ARBORIST: Texas Instruments, Inc.
                   P.O. Box 1444
                   Houston, TX 77251
                   1-800-847-2787

DATA: TreeAge Software, Inc.
                   23rd Floor
                   One Post Office Square
                   Boston, MA 02109

DAVID: Center for Academic Computing
                   North Building, Research Drive
                   Duke University
                   Durham, NC 27706-7756

InDia: Decision Focus, Inc.
                   4984 El Camino Real, Suite 200
                   Los Altos, CA 94022

Supertree: SDG Systems, Inc.
                   3000 Sand Hill Road
                   Menlo Park, CA 94025

◇ EPILOGUE

What happened with Texaco and Pennzoil? You may recall that in April 1987 Texaco offered a $2-billion settlement. Hugh Liedtke turned down the offer. Within days of that decision, and only one day before Pennzoil began to file liens on Texaco's assets, Texaco filed for protection from creditors under Chapter 11 of the federal bankruptcy code, fulfilling its earlier promise. In the summer of 1987, Pennzoil submitted a financial reorganization plan on Texaco's behalf. Under its proposal, Pennzoil would receive approximately $4.1 billion, and Texaco's shareholders would be able to vote on the plan. Finally, just before Christmas in 1987, the two companies agreed on a $3-billion settlement as part of Texaco's financial reorganization.   ◆

Sensitivity Analysis

The idea of sensitivity analysis is central to the structuring and solving of decision problems using decision analysis techniques. In this chapter we will discuss sensitivity-analysis issues, think about how sensitivity analysis relates to the overall decision-modeling strategy, and introduce a variety of graphical sensitivity-analysis techniques.

The main example for this chapter is a hypothetical one in which the owner of a small airline considers expanding his fleet.

EAGLE AIRLINES

Dick Carothers, president of Eagle Airlines, had been considering expanding his operation, and now the opportunity was available. An acquaintance had put him in contact with the president of a small airline in the Midwest that was selling an airplane. Many aspects of the situation needed to be thought about, however, and Carothers was having a hard time sorting them out.

Eagle Airlines owned and operated three twin-engine aircraft. With this equipment, Eagle provided both charter flights and scheduled commuter service among several communities in the eastern United States. Scheduled flights constituted approximately 40% of Eagle's flights, averaging only 90 minutes of flying time and a distance of some 300 miles. The remaining 60% of flights were chartered. The mixture of charter flights and short scheduled flights had proved profitable, and Carothers felt that he had found a niche for his company. He was aching to increase the level of service, especially in the area of charter flights, but this was impossible without more aircraft.

A Piper Seneca was for sale at a price of $95,000, and Carothers figured that he could buy it for between $85,000 and $90,000. This twin-engine airplane had been maintained according to FAA regulations. In particular, the engines were almost new, with only 150 hours of operation since a major overhaul. Furthermore, having been used by another small commercial charter service, the Seneca contained all of the navigation and communication equipment that Eagle required. There were seats for five passengers and the pilot, plus room for baggage. Typical airspeed was approximately 175 nautical miles per hour (knots), or 200 statute miles per hour (mph). Operating cost was approximately $245 per hour, including fuel, maintenance, and pilot salary. Annual fixed costs included insurance ($20,000) and finance charges. Carothers figured that he would have to borrow some 40% of the money required, and he knew that the interest rate would be two percentage points above the prime rate (currently 9.5% but subject to change). Based on his experience at Eagle, Carothers knew that he could arrange charters for $300 to $350 per hour or charge a rate of approximately $100 per person per hour on scheduled flights. He could expect on average that the scheduled flights would be half full. He hoped to be able to fly the plane for up to 1000 hours per year, but realized that 800 might be more realistic. In the past his business had been approximately 50% charter flights, but he wanted to increase that percentage if possible.

The owner of the Seneca had told Carothers that he would either sell the airplane outright or sell Carothers an option to purchase it within a year at a specified price. (The current owner would continue to operate the plane during the year.) Although the two had not agreed on a price for the option, the discussions had led Carothers to believe that the option would cost between $2500 and $4000. Of course, he could always invest his cash in the money market and expect to earn about 8%.

As Carothers pondered this information, he realized that many of the numbers that he was using were estimates. Furthermore, some were within his control (for example, the amount financed and prices charged) while others, such as the cost of insurance or the operating cost, were not. How much difference did these numbers make? What about the option? Was it worth considering? Last, but not least, did he really want to expand the fleet? Or was there something else that he should consider?

♦

♦ SENSITIVITY ANALYSIS: A MODELING APPROACH

Sensitivity analysis answers the question, "What matters in this decision?" Returning to the idea of requisite decision models discussed in Chapter 1, you may recall that such a model is one whose form and content are just sufficient to solve a particular problem. That is, the issues that are addressed in a requisite decision model are the ones that matter, and those issues left out are the ones that do not matter. Determining what matters and what does not requires incorporating sensitivity analysis throughout the modeling process.

No "optimal" sensitivity-analysis procedure exists for decision analysis. To a great extent, model building is an art. Because sensitivity analysis is an integral part of the modeling process, its use as part of the process also is an art. Thus, in this chapter we will discuss the philosophy of model building and how sensitivity analysis helps with model development. Several sensitivity-analysis tools are available, and we will see how they work in the context of the Eagle Airlines example.

♦ PROBLEM IDENTIFICATION AND STRUCTURE

The flow chart of the decision-analysis process in Figure 1.1 (page 6) shows that sensitivity analysis can lead the decision maker to reconsider the very nature of the problem. The question that we ask in performing sensitivity analysis at this level is, "Are we solving the right problem?" The answer does not require quantitative analysis, but it does demand careful thought and introspection. Why is this an important sensitivity-analysis concern? The answer is quite simple: Answering a different question, addressing a different problem, or satisfying different objectives can lead to a very different decision.

Solving the wrong problem sometimes is called an "error of the third kind." The terminology contrasts this kind of a mistake with Type I and Type II errors in statistics, where incorrect conclusions are drawn regarding a particular question. An error of the third kind, or Type III error, implies that the wrong question was asked; in terms of decision analysis, the implication is that the wrong problem was identified.

Examples of Type III errors abound; we all can think of times when a symptom was treated instead of a cause. Consider lung disease. Researchers and physicians have developed expensive medical treatments for lung disease. If the objective is to reduce deaths from lung disease, however, these treatments are not as effective as antismoking campaigns. We can, in fact, take the example one step further. Is the objective really to reduce deaths? Or is it to reduce smoking because nonsmokers dislike breathing second-hand smoke? For another example, consider a farmer who decides to use expensive sprays to control pests and disease in an orchard. To a great extent, the presence of pests and disease in orchards result from the practice of monoculture — that is, growing a lot of one crop rather than a little each of many crops. A monoculture does not promote a balanced ecological system in which diseases and pests are kept under control naturally. The solution to the problem is not to use sprays, but to change agricultural practices. Admittedly a long-term project, this requires the development of efficient methods for growing, harvesting, and distributing crops that are grown on a smaller scale.

How can one avoid a Type III error? The best solution is simply to keep asking whether the problem on the surface is the real problem. What exactly is the "unscratched itch" that the decision maker feels? In the case of Eagle Airlines, Carothers appears to be eager to expand operations by acquiring more aircraft. Could he "scratch his itch" by expanding in a different direction? In particular, even though he, like many pilots, may be dedicated to the idea of flying for a living, it might be wise to consider the possibility of helping his customers to communicate more effectively at long distance. To some extent, efficient communication channels such as those provided by computer links and facsimile service, coupled with an air cargo network, can greatly reduce the need for travel. Pursuing ideas such as these might satisfy Carothers's urge to expand while providing a more diversified base of operations. So the real question may be how to satisfy Carothers's desires for expansion rather than simply how to acquire more airplanes.

We also can talk about sensitivity analysis in the context of problem structuring. Problem 3.12 (page 58) gave an example in a medical context in which a decision might be sensitive to the structure. In this situation, the issue is the inclusion of a more complete description of outcomes; coronary bypass surgery can lead to complications that require long and painful treatment. Inclusion of this outcome in a decision tree might make surgery appear considerably less appealing. Von Winterfeldt and Edwards (1986) provide a problem involving the setting of standards for pollution from oil wells in the North Sea. This could have been structured as a standard regulatory problem: Different possible standards and enforcement policies made up the alternatives, and the objective was to minimize pollution while maintaining efficient oil production. The problem, however, was perhaps more appropriately structured as a competitive situation in which the players were the regulatory agency, the industry, and the potential victims of pollution. This is an example of how a decision situation might be represented in a variety of different ways. Sensitivity analysis can aid the resolution of the problem of multiple representations by helping to identify the appropriate perspective on the problem as well as by identifying the specific issues that matter to the decision maker.

Is problem structuring an issue in the Eagle Airlines case? In this case, the alternatives are to purchase the airplane, the option, or neither. A reasonable objective is to maximize expected profits. Carothers could assess the probabilities associated with the various unknown quantities such as operating costs, amount of business, and so on. Thus, it appears that a straightforward decision tree or influence diagram may do the trick.

Figure 5.1 shows an influence diagram for Eagle Airlines, and Table 5.1 provides a description of the variables, including estimates (base values) and reasonable upper and lower bounds. Note that Proportion Financed, Charter Price, and Ticket Price/Hour are shown as decisions, and the other items mentioned in the case are represented as uncertain variables. The case itself includes little information about the influences among the uncertain variables; for now all are shown as independent. As we develop the case, we will give the matter of dependence some consideration. But the real issue in the Eagle Airlines case is, what variables really make a difference in terms of the decision at hand? For example, do different possible interest rates really matter? Does it matter that we can set the ticket price? To answer these questions, we will turn to graphical techniques that can elucidate the relative importance of different variables.

♦ TORNADO DIAGRAMS

One way to find out which variables make the most difference is to create a *tornado diagram*. This diagram shows how much the value of an alternative can vary with changes in a specific quantity. Let us suppose that Carothers is interested in annual profit, and for simplicity let us ignore taxes. The annual profit

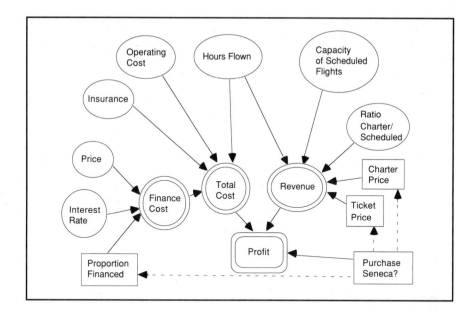

FIGURE 5.1   *Influence Diagram Representing the Eagle Airlines Decision*

Variable	Base Value	Lower Bound	Upper Bound
Hours Flown	800	500	1000
Charter Price/Hour	$325	$300	$350
Ticket Price/Hour	$100	$95	$108
Capacity on Scheduled Flights	50%	40%	60%
Ratio of Charter to Scheduled Flights	50%	45%	70%
Operating Cost/Hour	$245	$230	260
Insurance	$20,000	$18,000	$25,000
Proportion Financed	0.40	0.30	0.50
Interest Rate	11.5%	10.5%	13%
Purchase Price	$87,500	$85,000	$90,000

TABLE 5.1   *Input Variables and Ranges of Possible Values for Eagle Airlines Aircraft-Purchase Decision*

would be the total revenue minus the total cost. Using the base values, we can calculate revenues and costs:

Total Revenue = Revenue from Charters + Revenue from Scheduled Flights

$$= (\text{Charter Ratio} \times \text{Hours Flown} \times \text{Charter Price})$$
$$+ [(1 - \text{Charter Ratio}) \times \text{Hours Flown} \times \text{Ticket Price}$$
$$\times \text{Number of Passenger Seats} \times \text{Capacity on Scheduled Flights}]$$
$$= (0.5 \times 800 \times \$325) + (0.5 \times 800 \times \$100 \times 5 \times 0.5)$$
$$= \$230,000.$$

Total Cost = Variable Cost + Fixed Cost

$$= (\text{Hours Flown} \times \text{Operating Cost}) + \text{Insurance}$$
$$+ (\text{Price} \times \text{Percent Financed} \times \text{Interest Rate})$$
$$= (800 \times \$245) + \$20,000 + (\$87,500 \times 0.4 \times 11.5\%)$$
$$= \$220,025.$$

Thus, his annual profit is estimated to be $230,000 − $220,025 = $9975, using these base values. This represents a return of approximately 19% on his investment of $52,500 (60% of the purchase price).

Imagine that all of the chance nodes in the influence diagram have been changed to deterministic nodes, with each variable having its base value. Now, one at a time, "wiggle" each variable between its high and low values to determine how much change is induced in the expected profit. Figure 5.2 graphically

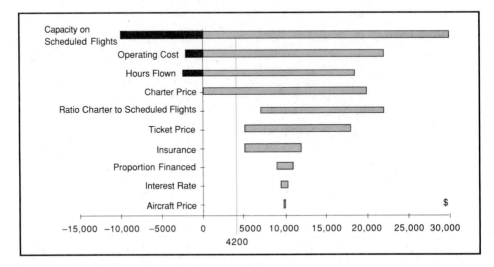

FIGURE 5.2   *Tornado Diagram for the Eagle Airlines Case*
The bars represent the range for the annual profit when the specified quantity is varied from one end of its range to the other, keeping all other variables at their base values.

shows how annual profit varies as the input variables are independently wiggled between the high and low values. For instance, with everything else held at the base value, setting Capacity on Scheduled Flights at 0.4 instead of 0.5 implies a loss of $10,025. That is, plug all the base values into the revenue equation above, except use 0.4 for Capacity on Scheduled Flights:

Total Revenue = Revenue from Charters + Revenue from Scheduled Flights

$$= \text{(Charter Ratio} \times \text{Hours Flown} \times \text{Charter Price)}$$
$$+ [(1 - \text{Charter Ratio}) \times \text{Hours Flown} \times \text{Ticket Price}$$
$$\times \text{Number of Passenger Seats} \times \text{Capacity on Scheduled Flights]}$$
$$= (0.5 \times 800 \times \$325) + (0.5 \times 800 \times \$100 \times 5 \times 0.4)$$
$$= \$210,000.$$

Nothing in the cost equation changes, and so cost still is estimated as $220,025. The estimated loss is just the difference between cost and revenue: $210,000 − $220,025 = −$10,025. This is plotted on the graph as the left end of the bar labeled Capacity on Scheduled Flights. On the other hand, setting Capacity on Scheduled Flights at the high end of its range, 0.6, leads to a profit of $29,975. (Again, plug all of the same values into the revenue equation, but use 0.6 for capacity.) Thus, the right end of the capacity bar is at $29,975.

We follow this same procedure for each input variable. The length of the bar for any given variable represents the extent to which annual profit is sensitive to this variable. The graph is laid out so that the most sensitive variable — the one with the longest bar — is at the top, and the least sensitive is at the bottom. With the bars arranged in this order, it is easy to see why the graph is called a tornado diagram.

The vertical line at $4200 represents what Carothers could make on his investment if he left his $52,500 in the money market account earning 8%. If he does not think he can earn more than $4200, he should not purchase the Seneca.

Interesting insights can be gleaned from Figure 5.2. For example, Carothers's uncertainty regarding Capacity on Scheduled Flights is extremely important. On the other hand, the annual profit is very insensitive to Aircraft Price. What can we do with information like this? The tornado diagram tells us which variables we need to consider more closely and which ones we can leave at their base values. In this case, annual profit is insensitive to Proportion Financed, Interest Rate, and Price, so in further analyzing this decision we simply can leave these variables at their base values. And yet Capacity on Scheduled Flights, Operating Cost, Hours Flown, and Charter Price all have substantial effects on the annual profit; the bars for these four variables cross the critical $4200 line. Charter Ratio, Ticket Price, and Insurance each have a substantial effect on the profit, but the bars for all of these variables lie entirely above the $4200 line. In a first pass, these variables might be left at their base values, and the analyst might perform another sensitivity analysis at a later stage.

◆ DOMINANCE CONSIDERATIONS

In our discussion of making decisions in Chapter 4, we learned that alternatives can be screened on the basis of deterministic and stochastic dominance, and inferior alternatives can be eliminated. Identifying dominant alternatives can be viewed as a version of sensitivity analysis for use early in an analysis. In sensitivity-analysis terms, analyzing alternatives for dominance amounts to asking whether there is any way that one alternative could end up being better than a second. If not, then the first alternative is dominated by the second and can be ignored.

In the case of Eagle Airlines, an immediate question is whether purchasing the option is a dominated alternative. Why would Carothers want to buy the option? There are two possibilities. First, it would allow him to lock in a favorable price on a suitable aircraft while he tried to gather more information. Having constructed a tornado diagram for the problem, we can explore the potential value of purchasing the option by considering the amount of information that we might obtain and the potential impact of this information. A second typical motivation for purchasing an option is to wait and see whether the economic climate for the venture becomes more favorable. In this case, if the commuter/charter air-travel market deteriorates, then Carothers has only lost the cost of the option. (Some individuals also purchase options to lock in a price while they raise the required funds. Carothers, however, appears to have the required capital and credit.)

It is conceivable that Carothers could obtain more accurate estimates of certain input variables. Considering the tornado diagram, he would most like to obtain information about the more critical variables. Some information regarding market variables (Capacity on Scheduled Flights, Hours Flown, and Charter Ratio) might be obtainable through consumer-intentions surveys, but it would be far from perfect as well as costly. The best way to obtain such information would be to purchase or lease an aircraft for a year and try it — but then he might as well buy the Seneca!

What about Operating Cost and Insurance? The main source of uncertainty for Operating Cost is fuel cost, and this is tied to the price of oil, which can fluctuate dramatically. Increases in Insurance are tied to changes in risk as viewed by the insurance companies. Rates have risen dramatically over the years, and stability is not expected. The upshot of this discussion is that good information regarding many of the input variables probably is not available. As a result, if Carothers is interested in acquiring the option in order to have the chance to gather information, he might discover that he is unable to find what he needs.

What about the second motivation, waiting to see whether the climate improves? The question here is whether any uncertainty will be resolved during the term of the option, and whether or not the result would be favorable to Eagle Airlines. In general, considerable uncertainty regarding all of the market variables will remain regardless of how long Carothers waits. Market conditions can fluctuate, oil prices can jump around, and insurance rates can change. On the other hand, if some event is anticipated, such as settlement of a major lawsuit or the creation of new regulations, then the option could protect Carothers until this uncertainty is resolved. (Notice that, even in this case, the option provides Carothers with an opportunity to collect information — all he must do is wait until the uncertain situation is resolved.) But Carothers does not appear to be awaiting the resolution of some major uncertainty. Thus, if his motivation for purchasing the option is to wait to see whether the climate improves, it is not clear whether he would be less uncertain about the economic climate when the option expires.

What are the implications of this discussion? It is fairly clear that, unless an inexpensive information-gathering strategy presents itself, purchasing the option probably is a dominated alternative. For the purposes of the following analysis, we will assume that Carothers has concluded that no such information-gathering strategy exists, and that purchasing the option is unattractive. Thus, we can reduce his alternatives to (1) buying the airplane outright and (2) doing nothing.

◆ TWO-WAY SENSITIVITY ANALYSIS

The tornado-diagram analysis provides considerable insights, although these are limited to what happens when only one variable changes at a time. Suppose we wanted to explore the impact of several variables at one time? This is a difficult problem, but a graphical technique is available for studying the interaction of two variables.

Suppose, for example, that we want to consider the joint impact of changes in the two most critical variables, Operating Cost and Capacity on Scheduled Flights. Imagine a rectangular space (Figure 5.3) that represents all of the possible values that these two variables could take. Now, let us find those values of Operating Cost and Capacity for which the annual profit would be less than $4200.

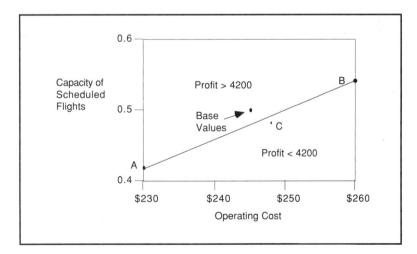

FIGURE 5.3   *Two-Way Sensitivity Graph for Eagle Airlines*
The Line AB represents the points for which profit would be $4200.

If this is to be the case, then we must have total revenues minus total costs less than $4200 or total revenues less than total costs plus $4200:

(Charter Ratio × Hours Flown × Charter Price) + [(1 − Charter Ratio)
× Hours Flown × Ticket Price × Number of Seats
× Capacity on Scheduled Flights]
< (Hours Flown × Operating Cost) + Insurance
+ (Price × Percent Financed × Interest Rate) + 4200.

Inserting the base values for all but the two variables of interest, we obtain

(0.5 × 800 × 325) + [0.5 × 800 × 100 × 5 × Capacity]
< (800 × Operating Cost) + 20,000 + (87,500 × 0.4 × 0.115) + 4200,

which reduces to

130,000 + (200,000 × Capacity) < (800 × Operating Cost) + 28,225.

Now solve this inequality for Capacity in terms of Operating Cost to get

Capacity < 0.004 × Operating Cost − 0.509.

This inequality defines the region in which purchasing the airplane would lead to a profit of less than $4200. When the "<" sign is replaced with an equality, we have the points for which profit equals $4200, or the line of points where the venture just breaks even relative to investing in the money market. To plot this line, notice that we only need two points. The simplest way to come up with these is to plug in the extreme values for Operating Cost and calculate the corresponding values for Capacity. Doing this gives the breakeven points A (Capacity = 0.411 when Operating Cost = 230) and B (Capacity = 0.531 when Operating Cost = 260). These points define Line AB in Figure 5.3. The area below the line (Capacity < 0.004 × Operating Cost − 0.509) represents the region when the profit would be less than $4200. The area above the line represents the region in which the profit would be greater than $4200.

What insight can Carothers gain from Figure 5.3? The point labeled "Base Values" shows that when we plug in the base values for the capacity and operating-cost variables, we get an estimated profit that is greater than $4200, and so the project looks promising. But Carothers might be wondering how likely it is that the two variables might work together to lead to a profit of less than $4200. For example, suppose that Operating Cost was slightly more than the base value, say $248, and that Capacity was just slightly less than the base value, say 48%. Taken individually, these two values do not seem to cause a problem. That is, substituting either one into the profit calculations, while keeping the other at its base value, leads to profit that is still greater than $4200. When we consider these two values jointly (Point C in Figure 5.3), however, they lead to a situation in which it would have been better not to buy the airplane. If Carothers thinks that the two variables might be likely to fall in the "Profit < $4200" region, then he may wish to forego the purchase. But such a situation would indicate that he really needs to model his uncertainty about these variables using probability methods. In the next section we will see how two-way sensitivity analysis can be used in conjunction with probabilities.

♦ SENSITIVITY TO PROBABILITIES

The next step in our analysis will be to model the uncertainty surrounding the critical variables identified by our analysis of the tornado diagram. The four critical variables were (1) Capacity on Scheduled Flights, (2) Operating Cost, (3) Hours, and (4) Charter Price. We only need to think about uncertainty for the first three, because charter price is a decision variable set by Carothers. For the purposes of the example here, let us assume that, in an initial attempt to model the uncertainty, Carothers chooses two values for each variable, one representing an optimistic and one a pessimistic scenario. The influence diagram is shown in Figure 5.4, and the decision tree in Figure 5.5. All of the input variables that are held at their base values (including charter price) are represented as deterministic variables in the influence diagram. Because of the complexity of the decision, details associated with the deterministic variables are suppressed in the decision tree. The decision-tree representation in Figure 5.5 shows the pessimistic and optimistic values for the three variables.

Now that we have simplified the problem somewhat, we can include considerations regarding the interdependence of the remaining chance variables. In

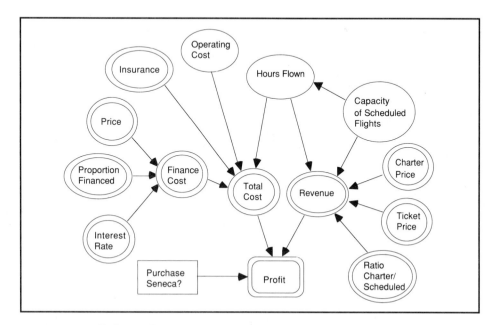

FIGURE 5.4   *Influence Diagram of Eagle Airlines Decision*
Note that only three variables are considered to be uncertain, and that
Hours Flown and Capacity are considered to be probabilistically dependent.

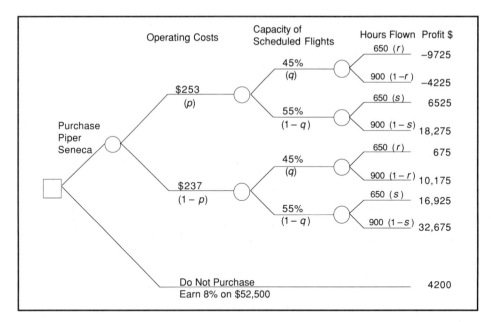

FIGURE 5.5   *Decision Tree for Eagle Airlines with Uncertainty for Three Variables*
Profit is calculated with all other variables held at their base values.

Figures 5.4 and 5.5, the probability distribution for Hours Flown is judged to depend on the Capacity of Scheduled Flights: If Capacity is low, then this may actually result in some flights being cancelled and thus fewer total hours. Thus, a relevance arc leads from Capacity of Scheduled Flights to Hours Flown in the
influence diagram, and in the decision tree the value for $r = P(\text{Low Hours} \mid \text{Low}$
Capacity) may not be the same as the value for $s = P(\text{Low Hours} \mid \text{High Capac-}$
ity). In fact, our argument suggests that r will be greater than s. On the other
hand, Operating Cost is judged to be independent of the other variables.

The next thing to do is to assess some values for probabilities p, q, r, and s.
Let us suppose that Carothers is comfortable with an assessment that $p = 0.5$, or
that Operating Cost is just as likely to be high ($253) as low ($237). Furthermore, suppose that Carothers feels that a reasonable way to represent the dependence between Hours and Capacity is to let s be 80% of r. That is, if Capacity
is high (55%), then the probability that Hours = 650 is only 80% of the probability that Hours = 650 when Capacity is low. With these two specifications, we now
have only two unspecified probabilities left to consider, q and r. Figure 5.6 shows
the modified decision tree with $p = 0.5$ and $s = 0.8r$.

Strategy Regions

We now can create a two-way sensitivity graph for q and r. Such a graph will show
areas for which the expected value of purchasing the Seneca is greater than investing in the money market. Thus, the graph shows regions for which different

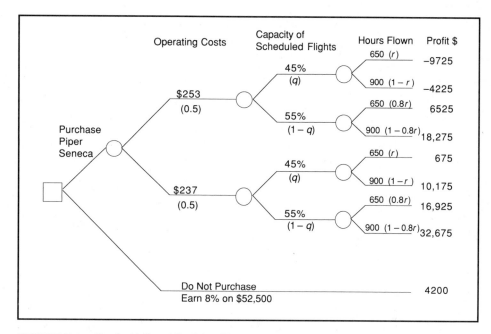

FIGURE 5.6 *Eagle Airlines' Decision Tree with Probabilities Substituted for* p *and* s
This decision tree is now ready for a two-way sensitivity analysis on *q* and *r*.

strategies are optimal, and for that reason this kind of graph is called a *strategy-region graph*.

To create the graph, we first write out the expected value of purchasing the airplane in terms of q and r, including the specifications that $p = 0.5$ and $s = 0.8r$. This equation comes from solving the decision tree:

$$\text{EMV(Purchase)} = 0.5\{q\,[-9725r - 4225(1 - r)] + (1 - q)\,[6525(0.8r)}$$
$$+\ 18{,}275(1 - 0.8r)]\} + 0.5\{q[675r + 10{,}175(1 - r)]$$
$$+\ (1 - q)\,[16{,}925(0.8r) + 32{,}675(1 -\ 0.8r)]\}.$$

After algebraic reduction, this expression becomes:

$$\text{EMV(Purchase)} = q(3500r - 22{,}500) - 11{,}000r + 25{,}475.$$

We would want to purchase the airplane if EMV(Purchase) > 4200. Thus, we can solve the following inequality for q in terms of r:

$$q(3500r - 22{,}500) - 11{,}000r + 25{,}475 > 4200$$
$$25{,}475 - 4200 - 11{,}000r > q(22{,}500 - 3500r)$$

This inequality reduces to:

$$\frac{21{,}275 - 11{,}000r}{22{,}500 - 3500r} > q.$$

Using this inequality, we can create the strategy-region graph for Eagle Airlines (Figure 5.7). The curve separating the two regions represents the values of q and r for which EMV(Purchase) = \$4200. It was plotted by plugging values for r between 0 and 1 into the inequality above. For these values of q and r, Carothers should be indifferent (in terms of EMV) between buying the airplane and not. The area below the line contains points where $q < (21{,}275 - 11{,}000r)/(22{,}500 - 3500r)$; for these (q, r) points, EMV(Purchase) > \$4200. The graph makes sense because q and r are probabilities of the pessimistic scenarios — low Capacity and low number of Hours Flown. If Carothers thinks that the pessimistic scenarios are likely (q and r close to 1), then he would not want to buy the airplane.

The importance of Figure 5.7 is that Carothers may not have especially firm ideas of what the probabilities q and r should be. Suppose, for example, that in the process of coming up with the probabilities he feels that q could be between 0.4 and 0.5 and that r could be between 0.5 and 0.65. These probabilities are represented by the points inside Rectangle A in Figure 5.7. All of these points fall within the "Purchase Seneca" region, and so the conclusion is that the Seneca should be purchased. The decision is not sensitive to the assessment of the probabilities. If, on the other hand, Carothers thinks that reasonable values of p and r fall in Rectangle B, then the optimal choice is not clear. (No wonder the decision is a hard one!) In this situation, he could reflect on the chances associated with Capacity and Hours Flown and try to refine his model of the uncertainty. Decision-analysis tools for modeling uncertainty more carefully are discussed in Chapters 7 through 12.

The value of the strategy-region graph, then, is to provide guidance in determining how much effort is needed to model uncertainty in a decision problem. Looking at it another way, the graph can reveal whether the decision is sensitive to the uncertainty in the problem and to the modeling of that uncertainty.

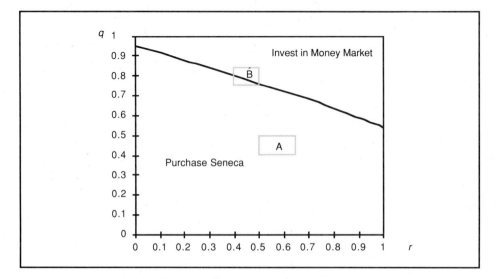

FIGURE 5.7   *Strategy-Region Graph for Eagle Airlines*

◆ SENSITIVITY ANALYSIS BY COMPUTER

Who wants to go through all of that algebra to perform a sensitivity analysis? Fortunately, sensitivity analysis can be done easily by computer. The decision-analysis software packages described in Chapter 4 all have built-in sensitivity-analysis routines. Moreover, creating strategy-region graphs is straightforward by using the "Table" commands in electronic spreadsheets. In this section, we will look briefly at how to use these computer tools for sensitivity analysis.

Deterministic Sensitivity Analysis

Doing the calculations for tornado diagrams by computer is relatively easy. If the choice is to use an electronic spreadsheet, then a spreadsheet is constructed that has one cell for each variable at its base value. A formula for the payoff is entered in another cell. High and low values then are substituted successively for each variable, and the payoff is recorded. This can be done systematically by constructing a table right on the spreadsheet. Figure 5.8 shows one possible layout. In this example, the low value for capacity on scheduled flights (0.4) has been substituted into cell B4; the values in cells B4 through B13 are used to calculate revenue, cost, and profit in cells B15, B16, and B18. The completed calculations indicate which variables are candidates for further modeling of uncertainty. The output from the spreadsheet can be used to create the tornado diagram itself.

	File	Edit	Formula	Format	Data	Options	Macro	Window		
B18			=B15−B16							

Eagle worksheet 2

	A	B	C	D	I	J	K	L
2							Profit:	
3	Variables:	Base	Low	High			min	max
4	Sched Capac	**0.4**	0.4	0.6		Sched Capac	−10025	29975
5	Operating Cost	245	230	260		Operating Cost	−2025	21975
6	Hours	800	500	1000		Hours	−2275	18475
7	Charter price	325	300	350		Charter price	−25	19975
8	Charter ratio	0.5	0.45	0.7		Charter ratio	6975	21975
9	ticket price	100	95	108		ticket price	4975	17975
10	Insurance	20000	18000	25000		Insurance	4975	11975
11	Amt Financed	0.4	0.3	0.5		Amt Financed	8969	10981
12	Interest rate	0.115	0.105	0.13		Interest rate	9450	10325
13	Price	87500	85000	90000		Price	9860	10090
14								
15	Revenue=	210000						
16	Cost=	220025						
17								
18	Annual profit	−10025						
19								
20								

FIGURE 5.8 *Using Microsoft Excel to Perform Deterministic Sensitivity-Analysis Calculations*
Columns K and L show the range of profits when each variable wiggled is between its upper and lower values.

The specialized computer programs also can be used to do the necessary calculations. In particular, this is done easily with the influence-diagram program DAVID. First, an influence diagram is created for the decision problem, with all variables shown as deterministic nodes. Figure 5.9 shows the Eagle Airlines problem in this form. All of the deterministic variables have been set at their base values. Now select a specific variable — say, Capacity on Scheduled Flights — and choose the command "Deterministic Sensitivity"; the computer will calculate the expected payoff for a specified range of values. In this case, we can specify that we want payoff calculated for only two values, the high (0.6) and low (0.4). The resulting output is the graph shown in Figure 5.10. The resulting upper value gives a profit of $30,000, and the lower value gives a profit of −$10,000. Record these values and use them to create Capacity bar in the tornado diagram.

Because the low value for Capacity on Scheduled Flights gives a profit that is less than $4200, this variable is a candidate for uncertainty modeling. Repeating the process with the other variables, of course, will allow you to make the same decision for each variable. At the end of the process, you will know which variables can be left as deterministic ones at their base values and which should be converted to chance variables. At this point, it is a simple matter to change the deterministic nodes to chance nodes, enter the probabilities, and continue with the probabilistic modeling of the decision.

Figures 5.11 and 5.12 show one-way sensitivity-analysis displays from the decision tree programs DATA and ARBORIST for different problems. These programs work in similar ways, asking the user for the variable to be analyzed and

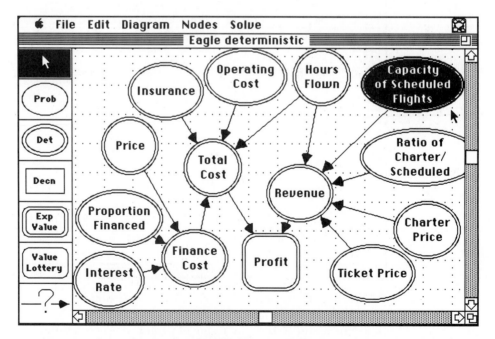

FIGURE 5.9   *Screen Display from DAVID Showing the Deterministic Eagle Airlines Model*

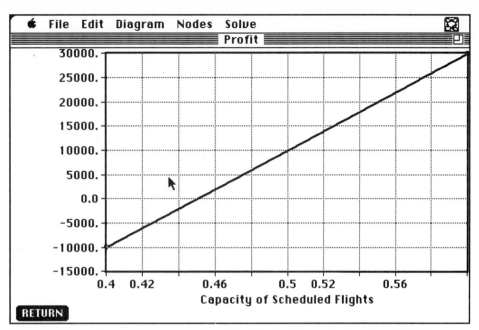

FIGURE 5.10 *Sensitivity-Analysis Graph for Eagle Airlines Produced by DAVID*
The graph shows profit calculated when Capacity on Scheduled Flights
is varied from 0.40 to 0.60.

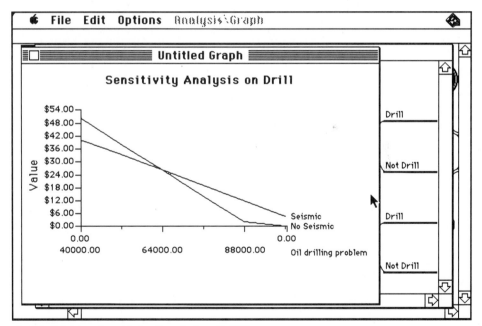

FIGURE 5.11 *Sensitivity Graph from DATA*
The main decision problem is whether to run seismic tests at an oil-well site
prior to drilling. The graph shows the expected value of the two alternatives,
"Seismic" (run the test) and "No Seismic" (do not run the test) when the
cost of drilling is varied from $40,000 to $100,000. Note that the lines cross at
approximately $64,000. Thus, if it is expensive — more than $64,000 — to
drill, then run the test before drilling.

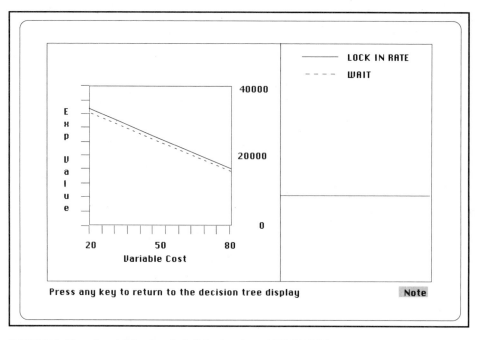

FIGURE 5.12   *Sensitivity-Analysis Display from ARBORIST*
The graph shows that the expected value of the decision decreases
as variable cost increases.

the specified range of values to be tested. The result is a graph showing the expected payoff as a function of the wiggled variable.

Constructing Strategy Regions

In building strategy-region graphs, it is necessary to "wiggle" probabilities rather than values for a specific variable. We showed how it is possible to wiggle two probabilities at once over the entire range from 0 to 1, thus creating a strategy-region graph. Our procedure required considerable algebra, however, and for large-scale problems this may prove infeasible. A less burdensome approach thus would be welcome.

Virtually all decision-analysis packages permit some sort of one-way probabilistic sensitivity analysis; that is, they can wiggle one probability at a time and calculate the expected payoff. For example, consider what is possible with the influence-diagram program DAVID. Figure 5.13 shows the probabilistic version of the Eagle Airlines problem. To perform a one-way sensitivity analysis on, say, operating cost, the operating-cost node is selected first. Choosing the command "Probabilistic Sensitivity" now will create a graph similar to Figure 5.10, but for a specified range of probabilities. Figure 5.14 shows the results after specifying a range of probabilities from 0 to 1 for the outcome that Operating Cost equals $253 per hour. The least expected payoff, when Operating Cost is bound to

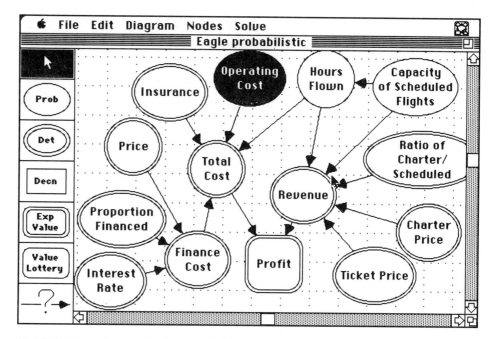

FIGURE 5.13 *Screen Display from DAVID Showing the Influence Diagram for Eagle Airlines*
Operating Cost, Hours Flown, and Capacity of Scheduled Flights are shown as uncertain variables, while all other variables are deterministic.

equal $253, is close to $4000. Thus, on the basis of this analysis we may elect to change Operating Cost back to a deterministic variable.

None of the available specialized programs have built-in routines for creating strategy-region graphs. Creating such graphs, however, is relatively straightforward in a spreadsheet environment. The key is to create a "data table" that does the same calculation using different inputs. This is exactly what we need, a way to calculate expected values for many possible pairs of values for two probabilities.

Figure 5.15 shows a spreadsheet with such a table created for the Eagle Airlines problem. At the top of the spreadsheet in rows 1–15 (not shown), a decision tree model based on Figure 5.6 has been created using the macros discussed in Chapter 4. Cells B5 and B6 contain the expected values for the two alternatives, purchase the Seneca (S) or invest in the money market (M). Cells B18 and B19 contain the values for q and r that are used to calculate the expected values of the tree. Cell A21 then contains a formula that compares the two expected values, returning M or S depending on which expected value is greater. The table is created by selecting the area A21 through L32 and choosing the "Table" command. The row and column inputs are specified as Cells B18 and B19, respectively. The table then evaluates and compares the expected values for each pair of probabilities q and r in the table. The resulting table

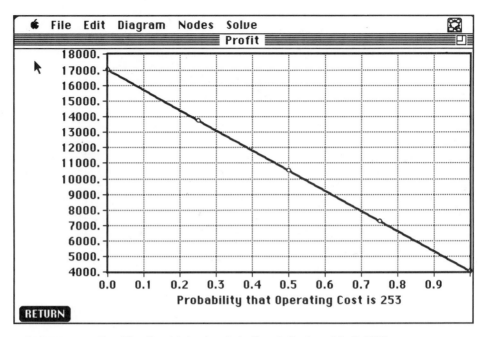

FIGURE 5.14   *One-Way Sensitivity-Analysis Graph Produced by DAVID*
The graph shows the expected profit for values of P(Operating Cost = 253),
ranging from 0 to 1.

File   Edit   Formula   Format   Data   Options   Macro   Window

A21   =IF(B6>B5,"M","S")

Eagle Strategy Region Worksheet

	A	B	C	D	E	F	G	H	I	J	K	L	M
16	EAGLE AIRLINES STRATEGY REGIONS												
17													
18	r=	0.5											
19	q=	0.5											
20							Values for r						
21	S	0	0.1	0.2	0.3	0.4	0.5	0.6	0.7	0.8	0.9	1	
22	1	M	M	M	M	M	M	M	M	M	M	M	
23	0.9	S	M	M	M	M	M	M	M	M	M	M	
24	0.8	S	S	S	S	M	M	M	M	M	M	M	
25	0.7	S	S	S	S	S	S	S	M	M	M	M	
26	0.6	S	S	S	S	S	S	S	S	S	M	M	
27	0.5	S	S	S	S	S	S	S	S	S	S	S	
28	0.4	S	S	S	S	S	S	S	S	S	S	S	
29	0.3	S	S	S	S	S	S	S	S	S	S	S	
30	0.2	S	S	S	S	S	S	S	S	S	S	S	
31	0.1	S	S	S	S	S	S	S	S	S	S	S	
32	0	S	S	S	S	S	S	S	S	S	S	S	
33	Values												
34	for q												

FIGURE 5.15   *Strategy-Region Analysis for Eagle Airlines in Microsoft Excel*

parallels Figure 5.7, indicating that Carothers should invest in the money market only for very pessimistic combinations of q and r.

This overview of sensitivity analysis by computer serves only as an introduction. This book cannot show all of the available ways to conduct such analysis, but you should now have a better appreciation for the available tools and techniques. With practice using these tools, you should be able to avoid a lot of dreary algebra.

◆ STRATEGY REGIONS FOR THREE ALTERNATIVES (OPTIONAL)

As we have analyzed it here, the Eagle Airlines case involves only two alternatives, and so the strategy-region graph has two regions. What happens when there are more than two alternatives? The graph may contain one region for each alternative. Let us consider a stock market–investment problem.

INVESTING IN THE STOCK MARKET

An investor has funds available to invest in one of three choices: a high-risk stock, a low-risk stock, or a savings account that pays a sure $500. If he invests in the stocks, he must pay a brokerage fee of $200.

His payoff for the two stocks depends on what happens to the market. If the market goes up, he will earn $1700 from the high-risk stock and $1200 from the low-risk stock. If the market stays at the same level, his payoffs for the high- and low-risk stocks will be $300 and $400, respectively. Finally, if the stock market goes down, he will lose $800 with the high-risk stock, but still gain $100 with the low-risk stock.

◆

The decision tree is given in Figure 5.16, with unspecified probabilities $t = P(\text{market up})$ and $v = P(\text{market same})$. Of course, $P(\text{market down}) = 1 - t - v$ because the probabilities must sum to 1.

To construct the strategy-region graph, we must compare the alternatives two at a time. First we have to realize that $t + v$ must be less than or equal to 1. Thus, the graph (see Figure 5.17) is a triangle rather than a rectangle because all of the points above a line from ($t = 1$, $v = 0$) to ($t = 0$, $v = 1$) are not feasible. To find the strategy regions, begin by finding the area where the savings account would be preferred to the low-risk stock, or

$$\text{EMV(Savings Account)} > \text{EMV(Low-Risk Stock)}$$
$$500 > t\,(1000) + v\,(200) - (1 - t - v)\,100.$$

Solving for v in terms of t, we get

$$v < 2 - \frac{11t}{3}.$$

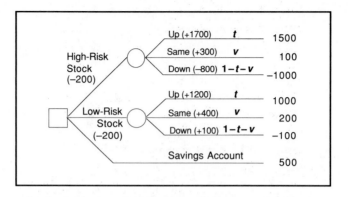

FIGURE 5.16   *Decision Tree for a Stock Market Investor*

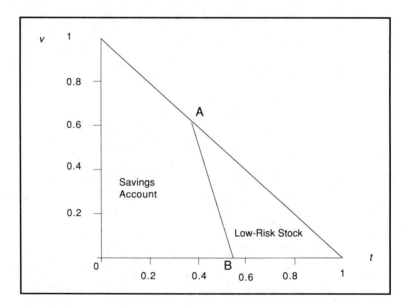

FIGURE 5.17   *Strategy Regions for the Stock Market Problem*
Note that $t + v$ must be less than or equal to 1, and so the only
feasible points are within the large triangular region.

Figure 5.17 shows the regions for the savings account and the low-risk stock divided by line AB.

Now let us find the regions for the high- and low-risk stocks. Begin by setting up the inequality

EMV(Low-Risk Stock) > EMV(High-Risk Stock)

$$t\,(1000) + v\,(200) - (1 - t - v)\,100 > t\,(1500) + v\,(100) - (1 - t - v)\,1000.$$

This reduces to

$$v < \frac{9}{8} - \frac{7t}{4}.$$

Using this inequality, we can add another line to our strategy-region graph (Figure 5.18). Now Line CDE separates the graph into regions in which EMV(Low-Risk Stock) is greater or less than EMV(High-Risk Stock).

From Figure 5.18 we can tell what the optimal strategy is in all but one portion of the graph. For example, in ADEG, we know that the high-risk stock is preferred to the low-risk stock and that the low-risk stock is preferred to the savings account. Thus, the high-risk stock would be preferred overall. Likewise, in HFBDC the savings account would be preferred, and in DBE the low-risk stock would be preferred. But in CDA, all we know is that the low-risk stock is worse than the other two, but we do not know whether to choose the savings account or the high-risk stock.

If the decision maker is sure that the probabilities t and v do not fall into the region CDA, then the sensitivity analysis could stop here. If some question remains (or even if we feel compelled to finish the job), then we can complete the graph by comparing EMV(Savings Account) with EMV(High-Risk Stock):

$$\text{EMV(Savings Account)} > \text{EMV(High-Risk Stock)}$$
$$500 > t\,(1500) + v\,(100) - (1 - t - v)\,1000.$$

This inequality reduces to

$$v < \frac{15}{11} - \frac{25t}{11}.$$

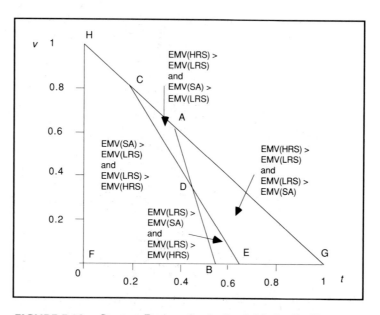

FIGURE 5.18 *Strategy Regions for the Stock Market Problem*
A second inequality has been incorporated. The optimal strategy is clear now for all regions except ACD.

Incorporating this result into the strategy-region graph allows us to see that region CDA actually is split between the high-risk stock and the savings account as indicated by Line ID in Figure 5.19.

With the analysis completed, the investor now can think about probabilities t and v. As in the Eagle Airlines case, it should be possible to tell whether the optimal investment decision is sensitive to these probabilities and whether additional effort should be spent modeling the uncertainty about the stock market.

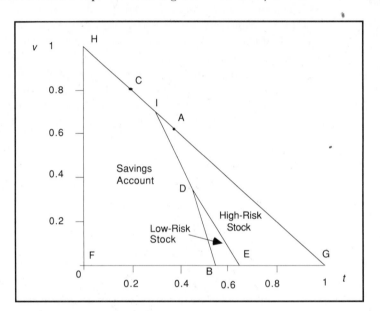

FIGURE 5.19   *Completed Strategy-Region Graph for the Stock Market Problem*
Line ID has split region CDA.

♦ SENSITIVITY ANALYSIS IN ACTION

Is sensitivity analysis ever used in the real world? Indeed it is. This fundamental approach to modeling is the source of important insights and understanding in many real-world problems. The following example comes from the medical field, and shows how sensitivity-analysis graphs can improve decision making in an area where hard decisions are made even harder by the stakes involved.

HEART DISEASE IN INFANTS

Macartney, Douglas, and Spiegelhalter used decision analysis to study alternative treatments of infants who suffered from a disease known as coarctation of the aorta. Difficult to detect, the fundamental uncertainty is whether the disease is present at all. Three alternative treatments exist if an infant is suspected of having the disease. The first is to do nothing, which may be appropriate if the disease is not present. The second is to operate. The third alternative is to catheterize the heart in an attempt to confirm the diagnosis, although it does not always yield a perfect diagnosis. Moreover, catheterizing the heart of a sick infant is itself a dangerous undertaking and may lead to death. The difficulty of the problem is obvious; with all of the uncertainty and the risk of death from operating or catheterization, what is the appropriate treatment? [*Source*: Macartney, F., J. Douglas, and D. Spiegelhalter (1984) "To Catheterise or Not to Catheterise?" *British Heart Journal*, 51, 330–338.]

◆

In their analysis, Macartney et al. created a strategy-region graph (Figure 5.20) showing the sensitivity of the decision to two probabilities. The two probabilities are (1) the disease is present, which is along the horizontal axis; and (2) the mortality rate for cardiac catheterization, which is along the vertical axis. The mortality rate also could be interpreted as the physician's judgment regarding the chance that the infant would die as a result of catheterization.

The graph shows three regions, reflecting the three available alternatives. Note that the location of the three regions makes good sense. If the physician believes that the chances are low that the disease is present and that the risk of catheterizing the infant is high, then the appropriate response is to do nothing. On the other hand, if the risk of catheterization is high relative to the chance that the disease is present, then operating without catheterizing is the pre-

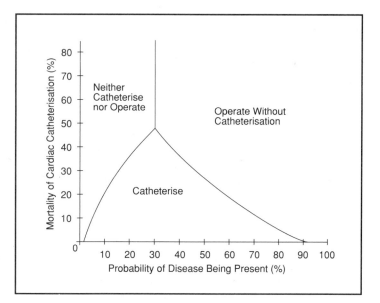

FIGURE 5.20 *Strategy-Region Analysis for the Heart Disease Treatment Decision*

Source: Macartney et al. (1984).

scribed treatment. Catheterization is recommended only for situations with relatively low risk from the procedure.

◆ SENSITIVITY ANALYSIS: A BUILT-IN IRONY

There is a strange irony in sensitivity analysis and decision making. We begin by structuring a decision problem, part of which involves identifying several alternatives. Then some alternatives are eliminated on the grounds of dominance. The remaining ones are difficult to choose from. Being difficult to choose from, they lead us to unveil our array of decision-analysis tools. But also being difficult to choose from, they probably are not too different in expected value; and if so, then it does not matter much which alternative one chooses, does it? For the analyst who wants to be quite sure of making the best possible choice, this realization can be terribly frustrating; almost by definition, hard decisions are sensitive to our assessments. For those who are interested in modeling to improve decision making, the thought is comforting; the better the model, the better the decision, but only a small degree of improvement may be available from rigorous and exquisite modeling of each minute detail. Adequate modeling is all that is necessary. The best way to view sensitivity analysis is as a source of guidance in modeling a decision problem. It provides the guidance for each successive iteration through the decision-analysis cycle. You can see now how the cycle is composed of modeling steps, followed by sensitivity analysis, followed by more modeling, and so on. The ultimate objective of this cycle of modeling and analysis is to arrive eventually at a requisite decision model. By the time the decision maker reaches this point, all important issues will be included in the decision model, and the choice should be clear.

◇ SUMMARY

This chapter has presented an approach and several tools for performing sensitivity analysis. We have considered sensitivity analysis in terms of identifying and structuring problems, dominance among alternatives, and probability assessment. Tornado diagrams and strategy-region graphs were developed, and we discussed ways to perform sensitivity analysis using computers. The purpose of sensitivity analysis in the decision-analysis cycle is to provide guidance for the development of a requisite decision model.   ◆

◇ EXERCISES

5.1   What is the fundamental question that sensitivity analysis answers?

5.2   Some friends of yours have been considering purchasing a new home. They currently live 20 miles from town on a two-acre tract. The family consists of the mother, father, and two small children. They also are considering having more children, and they realize that as the children grow, they may become more involved in activities in town. As it is, most of the family's outings take place in town. Describe the role that sensitivity analysis could play in your friends' decision. What variables could be subjected to sensitivity analysis?

5.3 Over dinner, your father mentions that he is considering retiring from real-estate sales. He has found a small retail business for sale, which he is considering acquiring and running. There are so many issues to think about, however, that he has a difficult time keeping them all straight. After hearing about your decision-analysis course, he asks you whether you have learned anything that might help him in his decision. What kinds of issues are important in deciding whether to buy a retail business? Describe how he might use sensitivity analysis to explore the importance of these issues.

5.4 When purchasing a home, one occasionally hears about the possibility of "renting with an option to buy." This arrangement can take various forms, but a common one is that the renter simply pays rent and may purchase the house at an agreed-upon price. Rental payments typically are not applied toward purchase. The owner is not permitted to sell the house to another buyer unless the renter/option holder waives the right to purchase. The duration of the option may or may not be specified.

Suppose that a buyer is considering whether to purchase a house outright or rent it with an option to buy. Under what circumstances would renting with an option be a dominated alternative? Under what circumstances would it definitely not be dominated?

5.5 What role does sensitivity analysis play in the development of a requisite decision model?

5.6 Explain why the lines separating the three strategy regions in Figure 5.19 all intersect at Point D.

◇ QUESTIONS AND PROBLEMS

5.7 *Cost-to-loss ratio problem.* Consider the decision problem shown in Figure 5.21. This basic decision tree often is called a cost-to-loss ratio problem and is characterized as a decision situation in which the question is whether to take some protective action in the face of possible adverse circumstances. For example, the umbrella problem (Figure 4.10, page 75) is a cost-to-loss ratio problem. Taking the umbrella incurs a fixed cost and protects against possible adverse weather. A farmer may face a cost-to-loss ratio problem if there is a threat of freezing weather that could damage a fruit crop. Steps can be taken to protect the orchard, but they are costly. If no steps are taken, the air temperature may or may not become cold enough to damage the crop.

Sensitivity analysis is easily performed for the cost-to-loss ratio problem. How large can the probability p become before "Take Protective Action" becomes the optimal

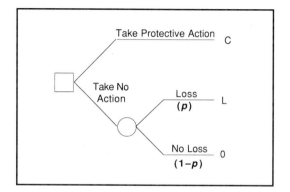

FIGURE 5.21 *Cost-to-Loss Ratio Problem*

(minimum expected cost) alternative? Given your answer, what kind of information does the decision maker need in order to make the decision? (*Hint*: This is an algebra problem. If that makes you uncomfortable, substitute numerical values for C, L, and p.)

5.8 *The cost-to-loss ratio problem continued.* The cost-to-loss ratio problem as shown in Figure 5.21 may be considered a simplified version of the actual situation. The protective action that may be taken may not provide perfect protection. Suppose that, even with protective action, damage D will be sustained with probability q. Thus, the decision tree appears as Figure 5.22. Explain how sensitivity analysis could be used to determine whether it is important to include the upper chance node with probability q and damage D.

5.9 An orange grower in Florida faces a dilemma. The weather forecast is for cold weather, and there is a 50% chance that the temperature tonight will be cold enough to freeze and destroy his entire crop, which is worth some $50,000. He can take two possible actions to try to alleviate his loss if the temperature drops. First, he could set burners in the orchard; this would cost $5000, but he could still expect to incur damage of approximately $15,000 to $20,000. Second, he could set up sprinklers to spray the trees. If the temperature drops, the water would freeze on the fruit and provide some insulation. This method is cheaper ($2000), but less effective. With the sprinklers he could expect to incur as much as $25,000 to $30,000 of the loss with no protective action.

   Compare the grower's expected values for the three alternatives he has, considering the various possible loss scenarios for the burners and the sprinklers. Which alternative would you suggest the grower take?

5.10 A friend of yours can invest in a multiyear project. The cost is $14,000. Annual cash flows are estimated to be $5000 per year for six years, but could vary between $2500 and $7000. Your friend estimates that the cost of capital (interest rate) is 11%, but that it could be as low as 9.5% and as high as 12%. The basis of the decision to invest will be whether the project has a positive net present value. Construct a tornado diagram for this problem. On the basis of the tornado diagram, advise your friend regarding either (1) whether to invest or (2) what to do next in the analysis.

5.11 Reconsider Hugh Liedtke's decision as diagrammed in Figure 4.2 (page 69). Note that three strategies are possible: (1) accept $2 billion, (2) counteroffer $5 billion and then accept $3 billion if Texaco counteroffers, and (3) counteroffer $5 billion and then refuse $3 billion if Texaco counteroffers. Suppose that Liedtke is unsure about the probabilities

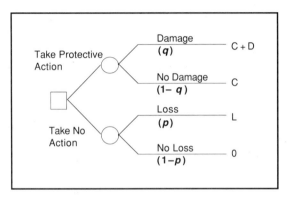

FIGURE 5.22   *More General Version of the Cost-to-Loss Problem*

associated with the final court outcome. Let $p = P(10.3)$ and $q = P(5)$, so that $1 - p - q = P(0)$. Create a strategy-region graph that shows optimal strategies for Liedtke for possible values of p and q. (*Hint*: What is the constraint on $p + q$?) If Liedtke thinks that p must be at least 0.15 and q must be more than 0.35, can he make a decision without further probability assessment?

5.12 Use an electronic spreadsheet to recreate the strategy-region graph for the stock-market problem as shown in Figure 5.19.

CASE STUDIES

The Stars and Stripes

In 1987, the United States won the prestigious America's Cup sailing race, winning the trophy from Australia. The race normally is run every four years, but in 1988 New Zealand invoked an obscure provision in the race charter and challenged the U.S. team to a match. Furthermore, New Zealand proposed to race with the largest boat permitted rather than a standard 12-meter craft. The new yacht, dubbed the *New Zealand*, was 133 feet long, designed and built using space-age material, and equipped with state-of-the-art computer equipment to monitor performance.

Not to be outdone, the U.S. team countered by designing and building a catamaran, the *Stars and Stripes*. A conventional sailboat like the *New Zealand* drags a heavy keel through the water to maintain stability. A catamaran relies on two long, narrow hulls for stability and thus can be considerably lighter and faster. Furthermore, the *Stars and Stripes* was outfitted with a rigid sail designed like an airplane wing. With slots and flaps controlled by wires, the sail could be adjusted precisely for optimum airflow.

New Zealand counterattacked with a lawsuit claiming that the vague deed that established the competition implied that the match was to be between similar boats. But the New York Supreme Court ruled that the race should go on and that protests should be filed afterwards. The race began on September 7, 1988. The *Stars and Stripes* won easily, by 18 minutes in the first race and 21 minutes in the second.

QUESTIONS

1. Designing world-class racing sailboats involves thousands of decisions about shape, size, materials, and countless other details. What are some objectives that might be reasonable in designing a sailboat?
2. What are some specific design decisions that must be made (for example, the shape of the sail)?
3. How can sensitivity analysis be used to decide which design decisions are more important than others?

DuMond International, Part I

"So that's the simplified version of the decision tree based on what appear to be the critical issues," Nancy Milnor concluded. "Calculating expected values, it looks as though we should introduce the new product. Now, I know that we don't all agree on the numbers in the tree, so why don't we play around with them a little bit. I've got the data in the computer here. I can make any changes you want and see what effect they have on the expected value."

Nancy had just completed her presentation to the board of directors of Du-Mond International, which manufactured agricultural fertilizers and pesticides. The decision the board faced was whether to go ahead with a new pesticide product to replace an old one or whether to continue to rely on the current product, which had been around for years and was a good seller. The problem with the current product was that evidence was beginning to surface that showed that the chemical's use could create substantial health risks, and there even was some talk of banning the product. The new product still required more development, and the question was whether all of the development issues could be resolved in time to meet the scheduled introduction date. And once the product was introduced, there was always the question of how well it would be received. The decision tree (Figure 5.23) that Nancy had presented to the board captured these concerns.

The board room was beginning to get warm. Nancy sat back and relaxed as she listened to the comments.

"Well, I'll start," said John Dilts. "I don't have much trouble with the numbers in the top half of the tree. But you have the chance of banning the current product pinned at 30 percent. That's high. Personally, I don't think there's more than a 10 percent chance of an out-and-out ban."

"Yeah, and even if there were, the current product ought to be worth $300,000 at least," added Pete Lillovich. "With a smaller chance of a ban and a higher value, surely we're better off with the old product!"

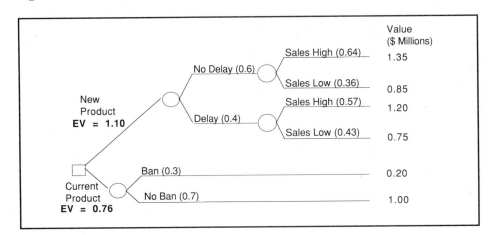

FIGURE 5.23   *DuMond's New Product Decision*

"Well, I don't know about you two," said Marla Jenkins. "I think we have a pretty good handle on what's going on with the current product. But I'd like to play the new product a little more conservatively. I know that the values at the ends of the branches on the top half of the tree are accounting's best guesses based on a complete analysis, but maybe they should all be reduced by $100,000 just to play it safe. And maybe we should just set the probability of high sales equal to 50 percent regardless of the delay."

Steven Kellogg had been involved in the preliminary development of the new product more than anyone else. He piped up, "And the delay is actually more likely than no delay. I'd just reverse those probabilities so that there's a 60 percent chance of a delay. But I wouldn't make any changes on the lower part of the tree. I agree with Marla that we have a good idea about the performance of the current product and the prospects for a ban."

"I don't think it matters," countered Lillovich. "The changes John and I suggest make the current product look better than it does in Nancy's analysis. Marla's and Steven's changes make the new product look worse. Either way, the effect is the same."

Nancy had kept track of the comments and suggested changes. She sat down at the computer and started to enter the changes. After a few moments, she grinned and turned to the board. "In spite of your changes," she said, "I believe I can persuade you that DuMond should go with the new product."

QUESTION

1. Explain why Nancy believes that DuMond should go with the new product.

◆

Strenlar, Part II

QUESTION

1. The Strenlar case study at the end of Chapter 4 (page 108) required substantial modeling. Use sensitivity analysis to refine your model. In particular, you might consider: (1) the interest rate used to calculate net present value, (2) legal fees, (3) the eventual price of PI's stock, (4) Strenlar's gross sales, (5) Fred's profits if Strenlar is successful (remembering that profits are linked to sales), (6) the probability of Strenlar being successful, and (7) the probability of winning the lawsuit. Do you think that Fred's decision is sensitive to any of these variables? Try wiggling one variable at a time away from its base value (the value given in the case), while holding everything else at base value. How much can you wiggle the variable before the decision changes? At the end of your analysis, discuss your results and the implications for Fred's decision model. If he were to refine his model, what refinements should he make?

◆

Facilities Investment and Expansion

Spetzler and Zamora (1984) describe a decision analysis concerning whether a major U.S. corporation should make a $20-million investment in a new plant with the possibility of a $5-million expansion later. The product was a "brightener," and there was some chance that the process also could generate significant quantities of a valuable by-product. Unfortunately, the primary chemical reaction was difficult to control. The exact yields were uncertain, and were subject to the amounts of impurities in the raw material. Other substantial uncertainties surrounded the decision, such as raw material costs, inflation effects, federal regulatory intervention, the development of a full-scale production process based on the pilot project, and so on.

At an early stage of the analysis, the focus was on the numerous uncertain variables that could affect the value of the investment. Table 5.2 shows the effect of 18 different variables on the project's present value.

Variable	Base Case	Tested Range		PV Range ($Million)		Change in PV ($Millions)
		From	To	From	To	
1. By-product Production	36.00 lb/ton	0.00 lb/ton	80.00 lb/ton	−30	35	65
2. Market Price of Brightener in 1980	$0.27/lb	$0.15/lb	$0.35/lb	−12	45	57
3. Raw Material Cost Growth	5.00%/yr	0.00%/yr	8.00%/yr	−7	40	47
4. Raw Material Costs	$7.00/ton	$2.00/ton	$18.00/ton	−9	35	44
5. Impurities in Raw Material	4.00 lb/ton	2.00 lb/ton	6.00 lb/ton	−10	30	40
6. Cost Multiplier on Investment	90.00%	70.00%	125.00%	−12	25	37
7. Brightener Price Growth after 1980	4.00%/yr	2.00%/yr	6.00%/yr	−5	28	33
8. Cost Multiplier on Operations Expenses	110.00%	80.00%	150.00%	3	32	29
9. Cost Multiplier on Maintenance Expenses	100.00%	70.00%	120.00%	2	30	28
10. By-product Price Growth	$0.03/yr	$0.01/yr	$0.06/yr	3	30	27
11. Water Reclamation Costs	$0.03/gal	$0.02/gal	$0.04/gal	4	31	27
12. By-product Price in 1970	$0.50/lb	$0.40/lb	$0.60/lb	3	29	26
13. Plant Efficiency	75.00%	50.00%	110.00%	0	26	26
14. Brightener Production	45.00 lb/ton	40.00 lb/ton	50.00 lb/ton	4	30	26
15. Market Price of Brightener in 1974	$0.25/lb	$0.15/lb	$0.30/lb	4	28	24
16. Government Regulation Costs	$0.02/lb	$0.01/lb	$0.03/lb	3	25	22
17. Market Price of Other By-products	$0.10/lb	$0.07/lb	$0.12/lb	4	24	20
18. Other By-products Produced	84.00 lb/ton	70.00 lb/ton	96.00 lb/ton	4	24	20

TABLE 5.2 *Results of Deterministic Sensitivity Analysis on 18 Different Variables in Facilities Investment Decision*

Source: Spetzler and Zamora (1984).

QUESTION

1. Use the information in the table to create a tornado diagram. Which variables appear to be most critical in this decision? What would be your next step in the analysis?

Source: Spetzler, C. S., and R. M. Zamora (1984) "Decision Analysis of a Facilities Investment and Expansion Decision." In R. A. Howard and J. E. Matheson (eds.), *The Principles and Applications of Decision Analysis*. Menlo Park, CA: Strategic Decisions Group.

◇ REFERENCES

Sensitivity analysis has been one of the more recent additions to the decision analyst's bag of tricks. As more complicated decision problems have been tackled, it has become obvious that sensitivity analysis plays a central role in guiding the analysis and interpreting the results. Recent overviews of sensitivity analysis can be found in Samson (1988), von Winterfeldt and Edwards (1986), and Watson and Buede (1987). In particular, Watson and Buede use real-world examples to show how sensitivity analysis is a central part of the decision-analysis modeling strategy. Phillips (1982) describes an application in which sensitivity analysis played a central part in obtaining consensus among the members of a board of directors.

Howard (1988) presents tornado diagrams and gives them their name. This approach to deterministic sensitivity analysis, along with other sensitivity-analysis tools, is discussed by McNamee and Celona (1987). These authors also show how to perform sensitivity analysis with Supertree and its companion program, Sensitivity.

HOWARD, R. A. (1988) "Decision Analysis: Practice and Promise." *Management Science, 34,* 679–695.

MCNAMEE, P., and J. CELONA (1987) *Decision Analysis for the Professional with Supertree.* Redwood City, CA: Scientific Press.

PHILLIPS, L. D. (1982) "Requisite Decision Modelling." *Journal of the Operational Research Society,* 33, 303–312.

SAMSON, D. (1988) *Managerial Decision Analysis.* Homewood, IL: Irwin.

VON WINTERFELDT, D., and W. EDWARDS (1986) *Decision Analysis and Behavioral Research.* Cambridge: Cambridge University Press.

WATSON, S., and D. BUEDE (1987) *Decision Synthesis.* Cambridge: Cambridge University Press.

◇ EPILOGUE

After the America's Cup race, New Zealand filed its lawsuit against the U.S. team, claiming that the deed of gift that established the race called for a "fair match." The New York Yacht Club, which had held the trophy from 1851 until 1983, even filed an affidavit with the court supporting New Zealand's contention. In April 1989, the court awarded the trophy to New Zealand. But in September 1989, the New York State Supreme Court issued a 4–1 decision that the cup should go back to the United States.   ◆

[*Sources*: "The Cup Turneth Over," *Time,* April 10, 1989, p. 42; *Raleigh News and Observer,* September 20, 1989.]

Creativity and Decision Structuring

All decision analyses involve the evaluation of two or more alternative courses of action. Most practicing decision analysts point out that during analysis new alternatives often may be discovered, apparently resulting from new insights and understanding of a problem. Although the process of understanding and structuring the problem is important in this respect, it is worthwhile to consider seriously the problem of finding alternatives in the first place. The issues have to do with creativity. What makes some people more creative than others? How can we manage and enhance creativity? What keeps us from being able to generate new alternatives? Answers to these questions may be helpful when it comes to thinking up possible solutions to a problem.

A chapter on creativity in a decision-making text makes sense. Everyone is frustrated occasionally by an inability to think creatively and thus can use a hand in being more creative. Perhaps not so clear, however, is the increasing need for creative and innovative solutions. In *Thriving on Chaos*, Tom Peters (1988) depicts the modern business climate as one in which conditions change rapidly. Modern managers must do more than simply cope with radical transformations: They must be on the attack. To be successful, a manager must learn to view new situations as opportunities for beneficial change rather than as problems to overcome somehow without rocking the boat too much. Indeed, Peters argues that the core paradox a manager faces is building an organization that is stable in its ability to innovate rapidly and flexibly. Solving problems creatively must become part of a manager's and a firm's essence.

This chapter presents a short overview of what we know about creativity, with the aim of applying this knowledge in decision-making situations. The literature on creativity is large and growing; interested readers will have no problem locating additional material. As starting points, *Conceptual Blockbusting* by James L. Adams and *Creativity Is Forever* by Gary Davis provide the basis for much of the information in this chapter. Both books are easy to read. Davis provides an overview of creativity, emphasizing psychological theories about differences in creativity and ways of improving creativity that are based on those theories. Adams, on the other hand, is an engineer. His book emphasizes creative solutions to design problems, but the principles he espouses are broadly applicable and as useful in business as anywhere else. Both books provide excellent bibliographies for those interested in further study.

Self-Actualized People

1. Perceive reality more accurately and objectively; tolerate and even like ambiguity; are not threatened by the unknown.
2. Accept themselves, others, and human nature.
3. Are spontaneous, natural, genuine.
4. Are problem-centered (not self-centered), nonegotistical; have a philosophy of life and probably a mission in life.
5. Need some privacy and solitude more than do others; are able to concentrate intensely.
6. Are independent, self-sufficient, and autonomous; have less need for praise or popularity.
7. Have capacity to appreciate again and again simple and commonplace experiences; have zest in living, ability to handle stress, high humor.
8. Have (and are aware of) their rich, alive, fulfilling "peak experiences" — moments of intense enjoyment.
9. Have deep feelings of brotherhood with all mankind; are benevolent, altruistic.
10. Form strong friendship ties with relatively few people; are capable of greater love.
11. Are democratic and unprejudiced in the deepest possible sense.
12. Are strongly ethical and moral in individual (not necessarily conventional) ways; enjoy work in achieving a goal as much as the goal itself; are patient, for the most part.
13. Have a more thoughtful, philosophical sense of humor that is constructive, not destructive.
14. Are creative, original, inventive with a fresh, naive, simple and direct way of looking at life; tend to do things creatively — but do not necessarily possess great talent.
15. Are capable of detachment from their culture; can objectively compare cultures; can take or leave conventions.

Source: Davis: *CREATIVITY IS FOREVER*, 2nd ed. Copyright © 1986 by Kendall/Hunt Publishing Company.

◆ THEORIES OF CREATIVITY

Psychologists disagree about the origins of creative thought, and as a result several different theories have been advanced to explain why some people are more creative than others. Psychoanalytic theorists (Kris 1952, Kubie 1958, Rugg 1963) generally maintain that creative productivity is the result of preconscious mental activity. These theorists have suggested that our brain processes information at a level that is not accessible to our conscious thoughts. Behavioristic theorists (Maltzman 1960, Skinner 1972) argue that our behavior, including creative behavior, is simply a conglomerate of responses to environmental stimuli. Appropriate rewards (stimuli) can lead to more creative behavior. A third approach (Mednick 1962, Staats 1968) suggests that creativity stems from a capacity for making unusual mental associations. In behavioristic terms, creative responses arise from novel combinations of stimuli. Creative people must be good at making new and unusual associations of concepts.

All of these theories have some merit (some more than others), but perhaps the most useful and most optimistic approach to understanding creativity is through Maslow's (1954) concept of self-actualization. Describing self-actualization is easier than defining it. The fifteen traits in the box on page 147 (from Davis 1986) describe self-actualized people. Davis argues that self-actualized people are creative people, and vice versa, and reviews recent psychological evidence to support this proposition.

This view of creativity is very much in the humanistic tradition. It is not so much a matter of explaining how or why someone might be creative, but rather it relates creativity to other qualities of human personality. From the description in the box, it is easy to imagine that a self-actualized person would be quite satisfied with life. Being self-actualized appears to be a good thing for many reasons other than simply being creative, and most of us will try hard to "find ourselves" in the list of traits.

One difficulty with the connection between creativity and self-actualization is that many highly creative individuals (for example, Napoleon, Alexander the Great, and Mozart) were quite talented but not self-actualized at all in the sense of being mentally healthy. Maslow, however, distinguished between special-talent creativity and self-actualized creativity. Individuals who are creative in a self-actualized sense are well adjusted, lead happy lives, and tend to approach their problems in fresh and flexible ways. Individuals with special talents (gifts) in art, music, business, science, or other areas may or may not live well-adjusted, happy lives. Given this distinction, there is both good news and bad news. The bad news is that not everyone can be a da Vinci, Beethoven, or Einstein; few people have the necessary special talents. The good news is that everyone can work toward self-actualization and the enhanced creative potential that it entails. Even more good news, as indicated in Davis's list, is that self-actualization, mental health, and happy lives go together.

Understanding the relationship between self-actualization and creativity is important for understanding blocks to creativity as well as creativity-enhancement techniques. These techniques are meant to enhance the creativity of regular people like us rather than those with special talents. Moreover, understanding individual needs and motivations, especially self-actualization, is critical for the design of groups and organizations that can foster rather than hinder creative thought.

♦ BLOCKS TO CREATIVITY

In *Conceptual Blockbusting*, Adams discusses different kinds of blocks with which an individual may have to cope, among them perceptual, cultural, environmental, and emotional blocks. All have the potential to cause difficulty in finding solutions to business problems.

Perceptual Blocks

Perceptual blocks result in failures to see and understand problems in ways that allow for new solution approaches. The following are common perceptual blocks.

1. DIFFICULTY IN ISOLATING THE PROBLEM. This is a familiar issue. Suppose you are a national sales manager for a line of boots. Sales in the Rocky Mountain states are down. Knowing your regional salesperson, you suspect that the problem is motivational. The "obvious" solution is to threaten or cajole the salesperson into better sales. But is the problem just what you think? Could it be a marketing problem — for example, competition with a regional brand that has been developed specifically for the area? What about a distribution problem? Perhaps it is difficult for the one warehouse in the region to supply the area's special needs. Perhaps customers in the region finally are getting tired of the same old style that has been the company's cash cow for many years. Even if the problem does lie with the salesperson, other possibilities exist, such as personal problems, personality conflicts with local business owners, and so on.

2. DELIMITING THE PROBLEM AREA TOO CLOSELY. Adams uses the classic nine-dot puzzle. Lay out nine dots in a square, three dots per row (Figure 6.1), and then, without lifting your pencil, draw four straight lines that cross all nine dots. Try it before you read on. The epilogue to this chapter gives the standard solution as well as many surprising solutions that Adams has collected from creative readers.

The nine-dot puzzle is a nice example, but what does this perceptual block have to do with decision making? People often look at problems with tacitly imposed constraints, which are sometimes appropriate and sometimes not. Suppose you believe you need more warehouse space for your business, so you have your real-estate agent look for warehouses of a specific size to rent. The size, however, may be an inappropriate constraint. Perhaps so much space is not necessary or may be divided among several smaller warehouses. Perhaps some characteristic of your product would permit a smaller warehouse to be modified in a clever way to provide adequate storage.

3. INABILITY TO SEE THE PROBLEM FROM VARIOUS VIEWPOINTS. This is clearly and closely related to the problem of multiple objectives in decision making and to

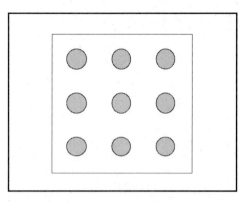

FIGURE 6.1   *Nine-Dot Puzzle*
Connect the dots using four straight
lines without lifting your pencil.

*Source: Conceptual Blockbusting: A Guide To Better
Ideas* by James L. Adams. Copyright 1974, 1976,
1979, 1986 by James L. Adams. Stanford Alumni
Association, Stanford, CA, and James L. Adams.

the problems involved in group decision making. Successful managers must be
able to see a problem from various perspectives and understand the issues that
are important to different parties. Really creative solutions incorporate and satisfy as many competing objectives as possible.

4. STEREOTYPING.   Suppose you are a personnel manager, and an individual
with long hair and no necktie applies for a job as an engineer. Imagine your reaction. What would you think about the person? A typical mental strategy that
most people use is to fit observations (people, things, events, and so on) into a
standard category or stereotype. Much of the time this strategy works well because the categories available are rich enough to represent most observations
adequately. But when new phenomena present themselves, stereotyping and associated preconceived notions can interfere with good judgment.

5. SATURATION.   This is commonly known as "not seeing the forest for the
trees." Many decisions require attention to a large amount of detailed information. For example, consider the issues involved in deciding whether to attempt a
takeover of another firm, or where to site a new manufacturing plant. The sheer
volume of information to be processed can keep the decision maker from seeing
new and promising alternatives.

Emotional Blocks

Here is a great game to play at a party with a lot of friends. Each person is
assigned to be a particular kind of barnyard animal: cow, donkey, chicken, goat,
sheep, or whatever else you designate. The more people, the better. After everyone has been assigned to be an animal, the organizer counts to three. On the
count of three, each person looks directly at his or her nearest neighbor and

makes the sound of his or her animal as loudly as possible. For obvious reasons, this is called the Barnyard Game (Adams 1979), and the participants experience a common emotional block — namely, feeling silly. Other emotional blocks also have to do with uncomfortable emotions that prevent creative activity.

1. FEAR OF TAKING A RISK.   There is nothing inherently wrong with being afraid to take a risk. In fact, risk aversion is a basic concept in decision making under conditions of uncertainty. But being afraid to offer a creative alternative for consideration in a decision problem because it appears "far out" may be counterproductive. What are the consequences of presenting a far-out idea that turns out to be unacceptable? The worst that might happen is that the idea is immediately determined to be infeasible. (Making far-out suggestions can have a more subtle value. Outsiders often have a difficult time understanding exactly what the problem is. Presenting far-out ideas for action is a sure way to get a clear statement of the problem, couched in an explicit and often supercilious explanation of why the idea will not work. Although this technique cannot be used in every situation, when it works the result is better understanding of the decision situation.)

2. JUDGING RATHER THAN GENERATING IDEAS.   Prematurely judging ideas — one's own or someone else's — can prevent new ideas from maturing and gathering enough detail to become usable. Making a habit of judging one's own thoughts inevitably sacrifices some creative potential.

3. INABILITY TO INCUBATE.   If you have ever found yourself with a new solution to a problem you have not considered in some time, you have experienced the phenomenon of incubation. This sometimes is called the "Eureka" effect; Archimedes is said to have exclaimed "Eureka!" (Greek for "I have found it!") when he discovered the principle of specific gravity. The process apparently involves relaxing one's mind and allowing the unconscious to address the problem. Individuals who feel they have to keep working on a problem until they solve it eliminate the creative potential of incubation. In terms of decision making, the message is not to rush into action if there is still time to "sleep on the problem."

The phenomenon of incubation is poorly understood. Perhaps the most satisfactory explanation has been suggested by researchers of artificial intelligence and is based on a "blackboard" model of the human brain. When the brain is in the process of doing other things — when the problem is incubating — parts of the blackboard are erased and new items are put up. Every so often, the new information just happens to be pertinent to the original problem, and the juxtaposition of the new and old information leads to the Eureka effect. An attractive feature of this theory is that it explains why incubation works only a small portion of the time. Too bad it does not work more often!

4. REALITY AND FANTASY.   An individual may have a psychological block that prevents fantasizing. Creative people must be able to control their imagination, and they need complete access to it. Many exercises are available for developing an enhanced imagination and the ability to fantasize. Richard de Mille's *Put Your Mother on the Ceiling* (1976) has many imagination games. Although designed primarily for children, going through one of these games as an exercise in using fantasy can provide a remarkable experience for anyone. An excerpt from one of these games is reproduced in *Breathing* (see below). For the best effect, have a friend read this to you, pausing at the slash marks, while you sit quietly with your eyes closed.

Cultural Blocks

Cultural blocks may be both familiar to you and embarrassing. Many individuals are tightly bound by cultural norms. Valuable alternatives may be impossible to see because they violate some of those norms.

Breathing

Let us imagine that we have a goldfish in front of us. / Have the fish swim around. / Have the fish swim into your mouth. / Take a deep breath and have the fish go down into your lungs, into your chest. / Have the fish swim around in there. / Let out your breath and have the fish swim out into the room again.

Now breathe in a lot of tiny goldfish. / Have them swim around in your chest. / Breathe them all out again.

Let's see what kinds of things you can breathe in and out of your chest. / Breathe in a lot of rose petals. / Breathe them out again. / Breathe in a lot of water. / Have it gurgling in your chest. / Breathe it out again. / Breathe in a lot of dry leaves. / Have them blowing around in your chest. / Breathe them out again. / Breathe in a lot of raindrops. / Have them pattering in your chest. / Breathe them out again. / Breathe in a lot of sand. / Have it blowing around in your chest. / Breathe it out again. / Breathe in a lot of little firecrackers. / Have them all popping in your chest. / Breathe out the smoke and bits of them that are left. / Breathe in a lot of little lions. / Have them roaring in your chest. / Breathe them out again.

Breathe in some fire. / Have it burning and crackling in your chest. Breathe it out again. / Breathe in some logs of wood. / Set fire to them in your chest. / Have them roaring as they burn up. / Breathe out the smoke and ashes. . . .

Be a fish. / Be in the ocean. / Breathe the water of the ocean, in and out. / How do you like that? / Be a bird. / Be high in the air. / Breathe the cold air, in and out. / How do you like that? / Be a camel. / Be on the desert. / Breathe the hot wind of the desert, in and out. / How does that feel? / Be an old-fashioned steam locomotive. / Breathe out steam and smoke all over everything. / How is that? / Be a stone. / Don't breathe. / How do you like that? / Be a boy (girl). / Breathe the air of this room in and out. / How do you like that?

Source: Breathing, a fantasy game from de Mille (1976), *Put Your Mother on the Ceiling*. New York: Viking Penguin.

1. TABOOS.   This type of block has to do with what is "proper behavior" or "acceptable" in a cultural sense; they may exist for no apparently good reason. Suppose one of your co-workers has a new baby and wishes to bring the child to work so that she can continue to nurse the child. Certain taboos are involved here, including nursing in public and having a child in the workplace during "serious" work time. Should the taboos be violated? An important decision problem that demands a creative solution may be to invent ways to accommodate the mother without grossly violating the taboos.

2. HUMOR, PLAYFULNESS, FANTASY, AND REFLECTION.   In the example just given, it is possible that reluctance to allow a child in the workplace is because children represent playfulness, fantasy, and humor — qualities that are not typically appreciated in solving "tough business problems." There is nothing wrong with tough business problems, but being able to play mental games with problems is an important avenue for creative thought. This block obviously is related to the reality and fantasy block discussed under emotional blocks above.

3. PREVALENCE OF REASON AND LOGIC.   There is a clear block against using feelings, intuitions, and emotions in business problem solving. Valuable insights and understanding certainly do come from analytical treatments of any given problem and are important in decision making; any course in decision analysis will teach such skills. But equally valuable cues and ideas can arise by admitting and examining feelings, intuitions, and emotions. For example, managers can benefit from "sensitivity training" that helps them understand and empathize with their employees, which in turn can lead to new and creative solutions to personnel problems and may help solve group decision problems in general. Feelings or intuition in a situation like this may lead a decision maker to consider other attributes (for example, ethical considerations or employee morale) in personnel decisions.

4. ARTISTIC THINKING SKILLS.   In a decision-making course much of the emphasis is on the development of analytical thinking. Unfortunately, little effort is put into more artistic thinking skills, which involve attributes such as beauty, sensitivity, playfulness, feelings, openness, subjectivity, and imagery. These qualities tend to be culturally blocked because of the stress placed on analysis. From this discussion, it would appear that artistic thinking can play an important role in the development of creative solutions to problems. The best possible arrangement is for an individual to be "mentally ambidextrous" — that is, good at switching between thinking styles. Such a skill permits creative development of potential solutions and subsequent careful analysis of the possibilities.

5. TRADITION AND CHANGE.   Decision making automatically means that the decision maker is considering at least one alternative that is different from the status quo. As indicated in the opening of this chapter, the ability to deal with change is becoming increasingly important for managers and decision makers. Those who have a hard time with change and who prefer tradition in general may experience difficulty coming up with creative problem solutions.

Environmental Blocks

Environmental blocks have to do with the extent to which a person's work environment affects creativity.

1. NONSUPPORTIVE ENVIRONMENTS, CRITICISM, AND JUDGING. It is important that interpersonal relationships encourage creativity. New ideas should be accepted gladly and criticized constructively. A supportive environment will make it easier not only to be creative but also to accept and incorporate meaningful criticism. Excessive red tape, lack of trust and cooperation among workers, excessive judgment of new ideas, and general intolerance of change all contribute to a nonsupportive environment.

2. AUTOCRATIC BOSSES. Autocratic bosses are those who solve problems on their own without calling for or using ideas from subordinates. Such a boss may be creative in his or her own right but will tend to inhibit the creativity of subordinates.

3. ORGANIZATIONS. Businesses and other organizations can, by their very nature, impede creative thought. As Adams points out, "the natural tendency of organizations to routinize, decrease uncertainty, increase predictability, and centralize functions and controls is certainly at odds with creativity, and conceptual blocks can abound" (p. 143). On the other hand, more collaborative management systems appear to enhance the creative environment. The reasons for this are manifold and include trust, a spirit of cooperation, more communication up the organizational chart rather than down, and fewer (if any) autocratic bosses. Gains in creativity undoubtedly can be achieved through careful organizational design. But probably the greatest strides can be made by helping individuals become aware of common blocks to the conceptual process.

♦ CREATIVITY-ENHANCING TECHNIQUES

Recognition of the blocks mentioned above goes a long way toward enhancing creativity, but several approaches for consciously and unconsciously breaking through these blocks also can help.

A Questioning Attitude

The single most important way to enhance one's creativity is to adopt a questioning attitude. This is not at all surprising in light of our earlier discussion of the relationship between self-actualization and creativity. A questioning attitude will naturally open up new paths and new directions for exploration. Insatiable curiosity is of paramount importance for the development of creative potential.

Why is it difficult for many of us to adopt a questioning attitude? The answer may lie with our educational system. Observation of very young children at play suggests that they typically have questioning minds. They are naturally curious and creative, and, if encouraged to learn actively (as opposed to watching television or other passive entertainment forms) they seem to retain this natural curiosity. When a child begins school, however, the questioning attitude usually is bent to the standard school curriculum. A typical elementary school teacher has a classroom full of children and a tight schedule of material that is mandated for teaching by the state, school board, and parents. In this situation, the teacher cannot cater to an overly inquisitive child with many apparently impertinent questions. Even curiosity about the subject matter at hand may be discouraged if a child appears to be too far ahead of his or her classmates. In a sense, our educational system may discourage the very questioning attitude that is critical for the development of creativity skills!

Fluent and Flexible Thinking

Fluency and flexibility of thinking are important in enhancing creativity. Fluency is the ability to come up with many new ideas quickly. Flexibility, on the other hand, stimulates variety among these new ideas. An individual who can write down many ideas quickly, regardless of what they may be, would be a fluent thinker. The flexible thinker might have a shorter list of ideas, but the ideas would tend to cover a broader range of possibilities. An individual who is both fluent and flexible can write down many different ideas quickly. One useful analogy compares thinking with digging holes. Fluent thinking is seen as the ability to dig one hole very deep and very quickly by taking a lot of dirt from one place. Flexible thinking, however, is more like the ability to dig many smaller holes in many different places.

A common exercise that is used to demonstrate these ideas is to think of new uses for common red construction bricks. The objective is to come up with marketing ideas that a brickyard owner could pursue to get out of financial difficulties. A list with many uses that are variations on a common theme indicates fluency. For example, many of the uses may be ways to use bricks to build things, or uses that take advantage of a brick's weight (for example, as a paperweight, ballast for hot air balloons, and so on). A list with a lot of variety in different attributes of the bricks indicates flexibility. For example, flexible thinking would use many different attributes of a brick: strength, weight, color, texture, hardness, shape, and so on. Understanding the difference between the two different kinds of thinking is the first step toward developing enhanced thinking skills in either fluency or flexibility or even both.

Idea Checklists

One classic technique for enhancing creativity uses checklists that cover many potential sources of creative solutions to problems. Most of us use lists in a rather natural way. The yellow pages provide a simple and ubiquitous list that can provide many ideas for solutions to specific problems. (Are any plumbers available on Sunday? Any do-it-yourself stores close by?) Mail-order and retail catalogs are examples of lists that we may use to solve a gift-giving problem. Many authors have written general-purpose lists for problem solving. The best known is Osborn's (1963) *73 Idea-Spurring Questions*, reproduced on page 156. Of course, Osborn's list can be extended with other descriptive verbs such as multiply, squeeze, lighten, propel, flatten, and so on.

Osborn's 73 Idea-Spurring Questions

<u>Put to other uses?</u> New ways to use as is? Other uses if modified?

<u>Adapt?</u> What else is like this? What other idea does this suggest? Does the past offer a parallel? What could I copy? Whom could I emulate?

<u>Modify?</u> New twist? Change meaning, color, motion, sound, odor, form, shape? Other changes?

<u>Magnify?</u> What to add? More time? Greater frequency? Stronger? Higher? Longer? Thicker? Extra value? Plus ingredient? Duplicate? Multiply? Exaggerate?

<u>Minify?</u> What to subtract? Smaller? Condensed? Miniature? Lower? Shorter? Lighter? Omit? Streamline? Split up? Understate?

<u>Substitute?</u> Who else instead? What else instead? Other ingredient? Other material? Other process? Other power? Other place? Other approach? Other tone of voice?

<u>Rearrange?</u> Interchange components? Other pattern? Other layout? Other sequence? Transpose cause and effect? Change pace? Change schedule?

<u>Reverse?</u> Transpose positive and negative? How about opposites? Turn it backward? Turn it upside down? Reverse roles? Change shoes? Turn tables? Turn other cheek?

<u>Combine?</u> How about a blend, an alloy, an assortment, an ensemble? Combine units? Combine purposes? Combine appeals? Combine ideas?

Source: Adapted with permission of Macmillan Publishing Company from *Applied Imagination*, 3rd ed., by A. F. Osborn. Copyright © 1963 by Charles Scribner's Sons.

Another creativity-enhancing technique is to write down attributes of a problem, list alternative options under each attribute, and then consider various combinations and permutations of the alternatives. This use of lists was suggested by Koberg and Bagnall (1974), who dubbed the technique *morphological forced connections* to emphasize the combination of morphological attributes in design problems. The technique is not limited to designing new products. In fact, an early variant of this technique was used to think about objectives in a decision situation. Dole et al. (1968) describe an application by the National Aeronautics and Space Administration (NASA) for determining the scientific objectives of space-exploration missions. Action phrases (such as "measure tidal deformations in . . .") were combined with target features (such as "the interior of . . .") and target subjects (Jupiter, for example) to create a possible scientific objective. The candidate objective then was considered to determine whether it was a valid scientific objective. If so, it was included in the list. For example, "Establish the structure of the interior of the sun" was an objective, but "Determine the characteristic circulation patterns in the photosphere of the space environment" was not.

The value of morphological forced connections is not so much to find all possible combinations as much as to provide a framework within which all imaginable combinations can be screened easily to determine the most appropriate candidates. In the NASA example, candidate objectives were generated readily and then screened for validity. Another example, reported by Howard (1988), comes from an advertising claim by a fast food hamburger chain that, with its custom service, one can order 1024 different kinds of hamburgers; that is, a customer could order a burger with or without each of 10 possible ingredients. Not all of the possible combinations are reasonable, however; for example, one combination is a "burger" that consists only of lettuce, or only of ketchup. One is the "nullburger": nothing at all. Most individuals would agree that many of these unusual combinations must be screened out. In fact, a burger may not be a burger without the beef patty and a bun.

A more serious example also comes from Howard (1988), who suggests the *strategy-generation table*. Figure 6.2 shows a typical strategy-generation table for an energy conglomerate that is considering possible expansion. Dividend payout and dividend-to-equity ratio also are important attributes for the conglomerate to consider in strategic planning. For the most part, the table is self-explanatory. An overall strategy is one that has individual elements in each column. As with the hamburger, however, not all combinations make sense. For example, be-

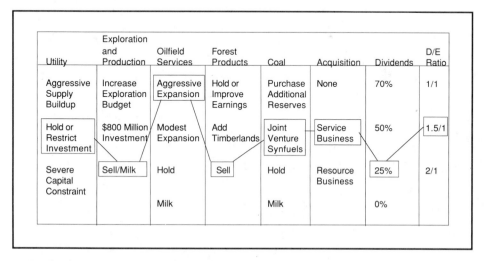

FIGURE 6.2   *Strategy-Generation Table*

Source: Reprinted by permission of Ron Howard, "Decision Analysis: Practice and Promise," *Management Science*, 34, No. 6, June 1988, pp. 679–695. Copyright 1988, The Institute of Management Sciences.

cause of cash constraints it is not likely that the conglomerate could pursue aggressive expansion in each of its five existing businesses, acquire another firm, and also have a high dividend payout. The strategy outlined in Figure 6.2 is one that might be described by executives as a "service business" strategy. Other feasible strategies could be assembled using the strategy-generation table. The point here is that the morphological forced comparisons technique facilitates both generation and screening to come up with a list of reasonable alternatives.

Brainstorming

Brainstorming is another popular way of generating a long list of ideas quickly. To be effective, a brainstorming session should include at least two people, and probably no more than 8 or 10 (it can be difficult to keep up with all of the ideas generated by a group that is very large). The rules for a brainstorming session are simple:

1. No evaluation of any kind is permitted.
2. All participants should think of the wildest ideas possible.
3. The group should be encouraged to come up with as many ideas as possible.
4. Participants should try to build upon or modify the ideas of others.

Brainstorming works well for several reasons. The most important is probably the lack of any judgment, which eliminates an important block for many people. That so many ideas are created rapidly reassures those who have little faith in their own creative potential. The enthusiasm of a few individuals tends to be contagious, and a "one-upmanship" game usually develops as participants try to top previous ideas. Practitioners report that the technique tends to generate a first rash of ideas utilizing common solutions. After this initial phase, participants must come up with new concepts. Naturally, the newer concepts are the most valuable result of the brainstorming exercise.

Metaphorical Thinking

Given our earlier discussion of fantasy and imagination, it should come as no surprise that creativity can be enhanced by the use of metaphors. Much of the work on metaphorical thinking comes from William J. J. Gordon (1961, 1969), who founded Synectics, Inc., a consulting corporation that specializes in creative problem solving. Three kinds of metaphors can be used systematically to enhance creative potential: direct analogy, personal analogy, and fantasy analogy.

Direct analogy involves thinking about how others have solved problems similar to the one under consideration. Often the most productive approach is to examine solutions found in nature. For example, wet leaves, which pack together snugly, suggested metaphorically how potato chips might be packaged. The result was Pringles potato chips, which are stacked and sold in a can. The inventor of Velcro™ was inspired while removing burrs from his dog's fur. Suppose the problem is to design a home security system. What kinds of security systems do plants and animals have? Many animals make a lot of noise when threatened. Perhaps a security system could be designed that could sense intruders and then make noise — by turning on a stereo or TV inside a house — to frighten away intruders.

Personal analogy is closely related to the kinds of games that are played in de Mille's *Put Your Mother on the Ceiling*. The idea is to imagine a variety of personal situations that are pertinent in some way to the problem at hand. Personal analogy can be extremely helpful in computer programming, for example. Imagining the precise steps (and perhaps shortcuts) that would be taken to solve a problem by hand can help in designing a computer program to solve the same kind of problem.

In *fantasy analogy,* the group tries to come up with truly far-fetched, fantastic, and ideal solutions. The classic example arose when a group was trying to design an airtight closure for space suits that would be easily operated. Here is a transcript of part of the session, taken from Gordon (1961):

> *G:* Okay. That's over. Now what we need here is a crazy way to look at this mess. A real insane viewpoint . . . a whole new room with a viewpoint!
>
> *T:* Let's imagine you could will the suit closed . . . and it would do just as you wanted by wishing . . . [fantasy analogy]
>
> *G:* Wishing will make it so . . .
>
> *F:* Ssh, Okay. Wish fulfillment. Childhood dream . . . you wish it closed, and invisible microbes, working for you, cross hands across the opening and *pull* it tight . . .
>
> *B:* A zipper is kind of a mechanical bug [direct analogy]. But not airtight . . . or strong enough . . .
>
> *G:* How do we build a psychological model of "willing-it-to-be-closed"?
>
> *R:* What are you talking about?
>
> *B:* He means that if we could conceive of how "willing-it-to-be-closed" might happen in an actual model — then we . . .
>
> *R:* There are two days left to produce a working model — and you guys are talking about childhood dreams! Let's make a list of all the ways there are of closing things.
>
> *F:* I hate lists. It goes back to my childhood and buying groceries . . .
>
> *R:* F, I can understand your oblique approach when we have time, but now, with this deadline . . . and you still talking about wish fulfillment.
>
> *G:* All the crappy solutions in the world have been rationalized by deadlines.
>
> *T:* Trained insects?
>
> *D:* What?
>
> *B:* You mean, train insects to close and open on orders? 1-2-3 Open! Hup! 1-2-3 Close!
>
> *F:* Have two lines of insects, one on each side of the closure — on the order to close they all clasp hands . . . or fingers . . . or claws . . . whatever they have . . . and then closure closes tight . . .
>
> *G:* I feel like a kind of Coast Guard Insect [personal analogy].
>
> *D:* Don't mind me. Keep talking . . .
>
> *G:* You know the story . . . worst storm of the winter — vessel on the rocks . . . can't use lifeboats . . . some impatient hero grabs the line in his teeth and swims out . . .
>
> *B:* I get you. You've got an insect running up and down the closure, manipulating the little latches . . .

G: And I'm looking for a demon to do the closing for me. When I will it to be closed [fantasy analogy], Presto! It's closed!

B: Find the insect — he'd do the closing for you!

R: If you used a spider . . . he could spin a thread . . . and sew it up [direct analogy].

T: Spider makes thread . . . gives it to a flea . . . Little holes in the closure . . . flea runs in and out of the holes closing as he goes . . .

G: Okay. But those insects reflect a low order of power . . . When the Army tests this thing, they'll grab each lip in a vise one inch wide and they'll pull 150 pounds on it . . . Those idiot insects of yours will have to pull steel wires behind them in order . . . They'd have to stitch with steel. *Steel.*

B: I can see one way of doing that. Take the example of that insect pulling a thread up through the holes . . . You could do it mechanically . . . Same insect . . . put holes in like so . . . and twist a spring like this . . . through the holes all the way up to the damn closure . . . twist, twist, twist, . . . Oh, crap! It would take hours! And twist your damn arm off!

G: Don't give up yet. Maybe there's another way of stitching with steel . . .

B: Listen . . . I have a picture of another type of stitching . . . That spring of yours . . . take two of the . . . let's say you had a long demon that forced its way up . . . like this . . .

R: I see what he's driving at . . .

B: If that skinny demon were a wire, I could poke it up to where, if it got a start, it could pull the whole thing together . . . the springs would be pulled together closing the mouth . . . Just push it up . . . push — and it will pull the rubber lips together . . Imbed the springs in rubber . . . and then you've got it stitched with steel!

[*Source*: Gordon, W. J. J. (1961) *Synectics.* New York: Harper & Row.]

Other Techniques

Several other techniques are available to enhance a group's creative potential. Many rely on methods for improving group interaction in general. For example, Nominal Group Technique (NGT) (Delbecq, Van de Ven, and Gustafson, 1975) begins with no interaction. Individuals in the group each write down as many ideas as they can on pieces of paper. Then each individual in turn presents one of his or her ideas. The group leader records these ideas on a flipchart or chalkboard. Discussion begins after ideas from each participant are written down. At the end, each individual writes down his or her ranking or rating of the ideas. These are then combined mathematically to arrive at a group decision.

The main advantage of NGT is that the group leader manages the interaction of the group in such a way that certain blocks are avoided and the environment is enhanced. For example, discussion is not permitted until after the ideas are presented, thus creating a more supportive environment.

Other techniques actually use a more adversarial approach. Devil's advocacy and dialectical inquiry are techniques in which individuals take sides in a debate. On the surface, this might appear to hamper creative thought, but when such techniques are used only after ideas have been generated and a healthy creative environment has been established, they can work well. It also helps if all participating members understand what the techniques are meant to do. The main advantage of this kind of approach is that it can help a group of individuals consider a problem from multiple perspectives. Being forced into an alternative viewpoint can lead to new creative ideas. Another advantage is that the group is less likely to overlook basic issues that may be hidden from certain vantage points.

The role of the leader in group discussion techniques is paramount. The leader essentially sets the tone of the session and, if good, will promote an atmosphere that is conducive to healthy discussion and that encourages the free flow of ideas. It is easy to see that a group with such a leader probably will have more success in generating creative ideas and solving problems.

◇ SUMMARY

Creativity is important in decision making because it increases the number of available alternatives that determine the boundaries of a decision. Several theories of creativity were presented in this chapter. The idea of self-actualization provides a framework for thinking about creativity and creativity enhancement at both the personal and organizational levels. One way to view the remainder of the chapter is that blocks to creativity are those things that can interfere with the way a person can become self-actualized, while the creativity-enhancing techniques promote an environment in which an individual can become self-actualized. Blocks to creativity include perceptual, emotional, cultural, and environmental barriers. Simple awareness of these blocks can itself improve creative potential. Of the techniques discussed for enhancing creativity, the most important is the adoption of a questioning attitude. Other techniques include becoming proficient in both flexible and fluent thinking, list making, brainstorming, and metaphorical thinking. Group discussion techniques can promote creativity by appropriately managing interaction within a group as well as by enhancing the creative environment. ◆

◇ QUESTIONS AND PROBLEMS

6.1 In talking about cultural blocks, we discussed the matter of a woman bringing an infant into the workplace and the possible reactions of co-workers. Consider the situation in which a classmate wants to bring her child to school in order to continue its nursing. Are the taboos the same? What are the differences between the two situations?

6.2 How can universities get their students to be more creative? What specific exercises can you think of that would help? What kinds of things can an instructor do? Are any changes needed in curricula and requirements? Try some of the creativity-enhancing techniques that we discussed. For example, you might try any of the following:

a. List making, especially morphological forced connections. What are important attributes to list? What are alternatives under those attributes? Can you use Osborn's list? Can you think of extensions to his list?

b. Brainstorming. To do this, find a small group of people with whom to brainstorm. The exact size of the group is not important, but you need at least one other person and probably no more than 8 or 10 people altogether.

c. Metaphorical thinking. Direct analogy is difficult here. How do other disciplines teach students to be creative? How do animals teach offspring to deal with new situations? Personal analogy is somewhat more straightforward. Imagine that you are the boss. What do you want your employee to be able to do? Imagine that you are a professor. Would you want your students to be creative? How would you encourage it? Can you imagine that you are a problem that needs to be solved? How would you like to be solved? Try fantasy analogy. Try to imagine the most fantastic and ideal creativity-training program. Describe it in detail; exercise your imagination! What kinds of resources would be required? How many people? How much time? What kinds of interactions with others? Would there be instructors and students, or just participants, all on the same level? Think of other questions.

You are neither required to use any of these techniques nor limited to them. Your job is to generate creative ideas any way you can.

6.3 How would you design an organization so that it could, in Tom Peters's words, "thrive on chaos"? What characteristics would such an organization have? What kind of people would you try to hire? How would the role of the managers differ from the traditional view of what a manager does?

6.4 In discussing the perceptual block of stereotyping, we used the example of a person with long hair and no necktie applying for a job as an engineer. Did you imagine this person as male or female? Why? Was there a block involved in your perception? Which one?

6.5 In the discussion of the importance of a questioning attitude, the point was made that formal schooling actually can discourage such an attitude. What does this imply for those of us who have attended school for many years? What would you suggest to today's educators as ways to encourage children to be curious?

6.6 Explain in your own words what self-actualization means. Why does it matter? Describe someone you have known who was self-actualized.

6.7 The lists we discussed all focused on the generation of alternatives. The same technique also can be used to determine objectives in a decision situation. Write a list of questions like those on page 156 that you might ask yourself when searching for a job. What do you want to accomplish? For example, do you want to save money? Save time? Improve your life-style? What else is important?

6.8 Describe a situation in which incubation worked for you. Describe one in which it did not. Can you explain why it worked in the first case but not the second?

6.9 One technological problem that we face as a society is the increasing use of plastics in disposable items. Landfills are becoming increasingly expensive and difficult to maintain, and land for new ones can be obtained only at premium prices. Furthermore, the plastics that are dumped in the landfills may release dioxins (toxic chemical substances) into the soil.

Of course, many different kinds of plastic exist. Spend 10 minutes writing down possible ways to recycle one-gallon plastic milk jugs. You can assume that the milk jugs are received rinsed out and reasonably clean, but not sterile. Look at your list. Does it reflect fluent thinking, flexible thinking, or both?

CASE STUDIES

Modular Olympics

Seoul, Korea, was the site of the 1988 Summer Olympic Games. The *Wall Street Journal* (June 29, 1987), however, reported that because of political unrest in Korea, there was concern about holding the games there. Would it have been possible to change sites as late as 1987? It seems unlikely because of the expense and planning associated with staging the games. But wouldn't it be nice to be able to disassemble the games from one site, ship them to a new site, reassemble, and then proceed? Modular Olympics.

QUESTION

1. Use whatever creativity-enhancing techniques you can to help think about ways to modify the Olympics to make changing sites easier than is currently the case.

Burning Grass-Seed Fields

Grass-seed farmers in the Willamette Valley in western Oregon have been burning their fields since the 1940s. After the grass seed is harvested, the left-over straw is burned to remove it and to sterilize the fields. But burning large fields of straw creates a lot of pollution. Another burning method that is less polluting uses a propane torch to burn the stubble in a field after the straw has been removed.

Facing opposition because of the negative effects of burning, the grass seed industry is considering alternative ways to sterilize its fields. The propane method is the most promising, but it requires initial removal of the straw.

QUESTION

1. What can be done with the straw? Spend 10 minutes writing down all the possible uses you can think of for the straw. If possible, form a group and brainstorm. Or try another creativity technique. Does your list demonstrate flexibility or fluency of ideas?

◇ REFERENCES

It is rather unusual for a book on decision theory to include a chapter on creativity. The "management science" tradition would suggest that there is a set way of attacking a specific problem, and that the decision maker only has to apply the appropriate technique. But this is too simple for the complex problems that managers face these days. Hence, this chapter is meant to dispel the notion that analytical thinking is all that is required to solve real problems.

Little literature on creativity exists within management science. Keller and Ho (1989) review and summarize what there is of this literature. Some of Keeney and Raiffa's (1976, Chapter 2) discussion of the structuring of objectives is pertinent to creativity in decision making.

Most of the literature on creativity comes from psychology, as the many references at the beginning of this chapter indicate. Some work, like that of Adams (1979), comes from an engineering/design/inventing perspective. In fact, a recent book by Adams (1986) contains a chapter on decision analysis! He argues that if you are interested in creativity, you probably also have decisions to make; Adams offers a way in which to think systematically about the creative alternatives you come up with.

ADAMS, J. L. (1979) *Conceptual Blockbusting: A Guide to Better Ideas*, 2nd ed. Stanford, CA: Stanford Alumni Association.

ADAMS, J. L. (1986) *The Care and Feeding of Ideas*. Stanford, CA: Stanford Alumni Association.

DAVIS, G. (1986) *Creativity Is Forever*, 2nd ed. Dubuque, IA: Kendall/Hunt.

DELBECQ, A. L., A. H. VAN DE VEN, and D. H. GUSTAFSON (1975) *Group Techniques for Program Planning*. Glenview, IL: Scott, Foresman.

DE MILLE, R. (1976) *Put Your Mother on the Ceiling*. New York: Viking Penguin.

GORDON, W. J. J. (1961) *Synectics*. New York: Harper & Row.

GORDON, W. J. J. (1969) *The Metaphorical Way of Learning and Knowing*. Cambridge, MA: SES Associates.

HOWARD, R. A. (1988) "Decision Analysis: Practice and Promise." *Management Science*, 34, 679–695.

KEENEY, R., and H. RAIFFA (1976) *Decisions with Multiple Objectives*. New York: Wiley.

KELLER, L. R., and J. L. HO (1988) "Decision Problem Structuring: Generating Options." *IEEE Transactions on Systems, Man, and Cybernetics*, 18, 715–728.

KOBERG, D., and J. BAGNALL (1974) *The Universal Traveler*. Los Altos, CA: William Kaufmann, Inc.

KRIS, E. (1952) "On Preconscious Mental Processes." In *Psychoanalytic Explorations in Art*. New York: International Universities Press.

KUBIE, L. S. (1958) *Neurotic Distortion of the Creative Process*. Lawrence, KS: University of Kansas Press.

MALTZMAN, I. (1960) "On the Training of Originality." *Psychological Review*, 67, 229–242.

MASLOW, A. (1954) *Motivation and Personality*. New York: Harper & Row.

MEDNICK, S. A. (1962) "The Associative Basis of the Creative Process." *Psychological Review*, 69, 220–232.

OSBORN, A. F. (1963) *Applied Imagination*, 3rd ed. New York: Scribner's.

PETERS, T. (1988) *Thriving on Chaos*. New York: Knopf.

RUGG, H. (1963) *Imagination: An Inquiry into the Sources and Conditions that Stimulate Creativity*. New York: Harper & Row.

SKINNER, B. F. (1972) *Cumulative Record: A Selection of Papers,* 3rd ed. Englewood Cliffs, NJ: Prentice-Hall.

STAATS, A. W. (1968) *Learning, Language, and Cognition.* New York: Holt, Rinehart & Winston.

◇ EPILOGUE

The basic solution to the nine-dot puzzle is shown in Figure 6.3. Figure 6.4 shows how to connect nine fat dots with three straight lines, removing the block that the line must go through the centers of the dots.

Other solutions include:

♦ Folding the paper in a clever way so that the dots line up in a row. Then one straight line is drawn through all nine dots.

♦ Rolling up the paper and taping it so that a spiral can be drawn through all of the dots.

♦ Cutting the paper into strips and taping them together so that the dots are in one row.

♦ Drawing large dots, wadding the paper up, and then stabbing it with a pencil. Then the paper is unfolded to see whether the pencil went through all the dots. If not, try again. "Everybody wins!"

♦ Folding the paper carefully so that the dots lie one on top of the other. A pencil then is stabbed through the nine layers of paper. A sharp pencil helps.

♦ Drawing very small dots close together in the square pattern and then drawing a fat line through all of them at once. This solution is courtesy of Becky Buechel, who used it when she was 10 years old.   ◆

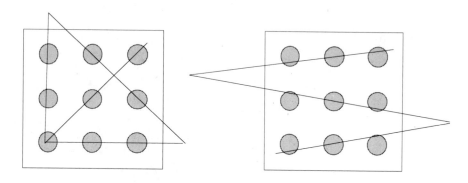

FIGURE 6.3 *Standard Solution to the Nine-Dot Puzzle*

FIGURE 6.4 *An Unblocked Three-Line Solution*

[*Source*: Adams, James L. (1979) *Conceptual Blockbusting: A Guide to Better Ideas,* 2nd ed. Stanford, CA: Stanford Alumni Association.]

Modeling Uncertainty

A s we have seen, uncertainty is a critical element of many decisions that we face. In the next five chapters we will consider a variety of ways to model uncertainty in decision problems by using probability. We begin with a brief introduction to probability in Chapter 7. This introduction has three objectives: to remind you of probability basics, to show some ways that probability modeling can be useful in decision problems, and to give you a chance to polish your ability to manipulate probabilities. The problems and cases at the end of Chapter 7 are recommended especially to help you accomplish the last goal.

Chapter 8 introduces the topic of subjective probability. In the introduction to this text the claim was made that subjective judgments are critical in a decision-analysis approach. Most of us are comfortable making informal statements that reflect our uncertainty. For example, we use terms such as "there's a chance that such-and-such will happen." In a decision-analysis approach, however, there is a need for more precision. We can use probability to model subjective beliefs about uncertainty, and Chapter 8 presents techniques to do this. Thus, our beliefs and feelings about uncertainty can be translated into probability numbers that can be included in a decision tree or influence diagram.

In many cases the uncertainty that we face has characteristics that make it similar to certain prototypical situations. In these cases, it may be possible to represent the uncertainty with a standard mathematical model and then derive probabilities on the basis of the mathematical model. Chapter 9 presents a variety of theoretical probability models that are useful for representing uncertainty in many standard situations.

Chapter 10 discusses the use of historical data as a basis for developing probability distributions. If data about uncertainty in a decision situation are available, a decision maker would surely want to use them. Two approaches are considered. First, we see how to use data alone to create histograms and continuous distributions. Second, we see an approach that uses data to update a decision maker's probability beliefs via Bayes' theorem.

It is also possible to "create data" through computer simulation, or by what is known as Monte Carlo simulation. That is, one can construct a model of a complex decision situation and use a computer to simulate the situation many times. By tracking the outcomes, the decision maker can obtain a fair idea of the probabilities associated with various outcomes. Monte Carlo simulation techniques are discussed in Chapter 11.

When faced with uncertainty most decision makers do their best to reduce it. The basic strategy that we follow is to try to collect information. In this day and age of extensive telecommunications and computer data bases, information is anything but scarce, but determining what information is appropriate and then processing it can be costly. How much is information worth to you? Moreover, in a problem with many sources of uncertainty, calculating the value of information can help to guide the decision analysis, thus indicating where the decision maker can best expend resources to reduce uncertainty. Chapter 12 explores the value of information within the decision-analysis framework.

Probability Basics

One of the central principles of decision analysis is that we can represent uncertainty of any kind through the appropriate use of probability. We already have been using probability in straightforward ways to model uncertainty in decision trees and influence diagrams. This chapter presents some of the basic principles for working with probability and probability models. As we work through the theory, problems, and examples, keep in mind that the objective is to be able to create and analyze a model that represents the uncertainty faced in a decision. The nature of the model created naturally depends on the nature of the uncertainty faced, and the analysis required depends on the exigencies of the decision situation.

We begin with a quick review of certain probability laws and definitions, followed by examples. After reading the chapter and working the problems and cases, you should be (1) reasonably comfortable with probability concepts, (2) comfortable in the use of probability to model simple uncertain situations, (3) able to interpret probability statements in terms of the uncertainty that they represent, and (4) able to manipulate and analyze the models you create.

♦ A LITTLE PROBABILITY THEORY

Probabilities must satisfy the following three requirements.

1. PROBABILITIES MUST LIE BETWEEN 0 AND 1. Every probability (p) must be positive, and between 0 and 1, inclusive ($0 \le p \le 1$). This is a sensible requirement. In informal terms it simply means that nothing can have more than a 100% chance of occurring or less than a 0% chance.

2. PROBABILITIES MUST ADD UP. Suppose two events are mutually exclusive (only one can happen, not both). The probability that one or the other occurs is then the sum of the individual probabilities. Mathematically, we write P(A or B)

= P(A) + P(B) if A and B cannot both happen. For example, consider the stock market. Suppose there is a 30% chance that the market will go up and a 45% chance that it will stay the same (as measured by the Dow Jones average, for example). It cannot do both at once, and so the probability that it will either go up or stay the same must be 75%.

3. TOTAL PROBABILITY MUST EQUAL 1.   Suppose a set of events is mutually exclusive and collectively exhaustive. This means that one (and only one) of the possible outcomes must occur. The probabilities for this set of events must sum to 1. Informally, if we have a set of events such that one of them has to occur, then there is a 100% chance that one of them will indeed come to pass.

We have seen this in decision trees; the branches emanating from a chance node must be such that one and only one of the branches occurs, and the probabilities for all the branches must add to 1. Consider the stock-market example again. If we say that the market can go up, down, or stay the same, then one of these three events must happen. The probabilities for these events must sum to 1 — that is, there is a 100% chance that one of them will occur.

◆ VENN DIAGRAMS

Venn diagrams provide a graphic interpretation of probability. Figure 7.1 shows a simple Venn diagram in which two events, A and B, are displayed. Areas in the diagram represent possible events. The circle labeled A thus represents Event A. The entire rectangle, including Events A and B, represents everything that can occur. Because the areas of A and B do not overlap, A and B cannot both occur at the same time; they are mutually exclusive.

We can use Figure 7.1 to interpret the three requirements of probability mentioned above. The first requirement is that a probability must lie between 0 and 1. Certainly an event cannot be represented by a negative area. Furthermore, an event cannot be represented by an area larger than the entire rectangle. For the second requirement, we see that A and B are mutually exclusive because they do not overlap. Thus, the probability of A or B occurring must be just

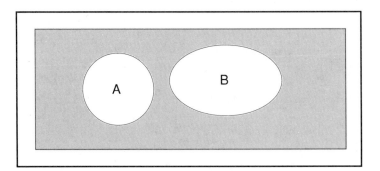

FIGURE 7.1   *A Venn Diagram*
Events A and B are mutually exclusive events.

the sum of the probability of A plus the probability of B. For the third require-ment, label the shaded portion of the rectangle as Event C. This is what must happen if neither A nor B happens. Because A, B, and C together make up the whole rectangle, then one of the three must occur. Moreover, only one of them can occur. The upshot is that their probabilities must sum to 1. Alternatively, there is a 100% chance that A, B, or C will occur.

♦ MORE PROBABILITY FORMULAS

The following definitions and formulas will make it possible to use probabilities in a wide variety of decision situations.

4. CONDITIONAL PROBABILITY.   Suppose that you are interested in whether a par-ticular stock price will increase. You might use a probability P(Up) to represent your uncertainty. If you find out that the Dow Jones average rose, however, you would want to base your probability on this condition. Figure 7.2 represents the situation with a Venn diagram. In the main diagram, the events "Dow Jones Up" and "Stock Price Up" are shown as possible events inside a larger rectangle, indi-cating that other unspecified events also are possible. Because they can both happen at once, the two areas overlap in the diagonally shaded area. It also is possible for one to rise while the other does not, which is represented in the dia-gram by the nonoverlapping portions of the "Dow Jones Up" and "Stock Price Up" areas.

Once we know that the Dow Jones has risen, then the entire rectangle is no longer appropriate. At this point, we can restrict our attention to the "Dow Jones Up" circle. We want to know what the probability is that the stock price will in-

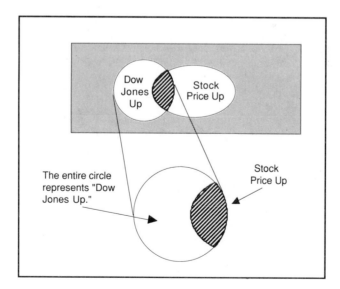

FIGURE 7.2   *A Venn-Diagram Representation of Conditional Probability*

crease given that the Dow Jones average is up, and so we are interested in the probability associated with the area "Stock Price Up" in the restricted space.

Given that we are looking at the restricted space, the conditional probability of "Stock Price Up given Dow Jones Up" would be represented by the proportion of "Dow Jones Up" in the original diagram that is "Stock Price Up" *and* "Dow Jones Up" (the diagonally shaded area). This intuitive approach leads to the conclusion that P(Stock Price Up given Dow Jones Up) = P(Stock Price Up and Dow Jones Up)/P(Dow Jones Up).

Mathematically, we write P(A | B) to represent the conditional probability of A given that B occurs. Read it as "Probability of A given B." The definition is

$$P(A \mid B) = \frac{P(A \text{ and } B)}{P(B)}.$$

Informally, we are looking only at the occasions when B occurs, and P(A | B) is the proportion of those times that A also occurs.

5. INDEPENDENCE. The definition of independence in terms of probability is as follows:

Events A and B are independent if and only if

$$P(A \mid B) = P(A).$$

In words, knowing whether or not B occurred will not help you to find a probability for A. If Events A and B are independent, then we can write

$$P(A) = P(A \mid B) = \frac{P(A \text{ and } B)}{P(B)}.$$

From this we can see that P(A and B) = P(A)P(B). Thus, when two events are independent, we can find the probability that they both occur (their intersection) by multiplying their individual probabilities.

Independence between two events is shown in influence diagrams by the absence of an arrow between chance nodes. This is fully consistent with the definitions given in Chapter 3. If one event is not relevant in determining the chances associated with another event, there is no arrow between the chance nodes. An arrow from chance node B to chance node A would mean that the probabilities associated with A are conditional probabilities that depend on the outcome of B.

As an example of independent events, consider the probability of the Dow Jones index increasing and the probability of the Dow Jones increasing, *given* that it rains tomorrow. It seems reasonable to conclude that

$$P(\text{Dow Jones Up}) = P(\text{Dow Jones Up} \mid \text{Rain}),$$

because knowing about rain does not help to assess the chance of the index going up; the events are independent.

Independent events are not to be confused with mutually exclusive events. Two events are mutually exclusive if only one can happen at a time. Clearly, however, independent events can happen together. For example, it is perfectly possible for the Dow Jones to increase and for rain to occur tomorrow. Rain and No Rain would constitute mutually exclusive events; only one occurs at a time.

Finally, if two events are probabilistically dependent, this does *not* imply that one causes the other to happen. As an example, consider economic indicators. If a leading economic indicator goes up in one quarter, then it is unlikely that a recession will occur in the next quarter; the change in the indicator and the occurrence of a recession are dependent events. But this is not to say that the indicator going up causes the recession not to happen, or vice versa. In some cases there may be a causal chain linking the events, but it may be a very convoluted one. In general, dependence does not imply causality.

Conditional Independence. This is an extension of the idea of independence. Conditional independence is best demonstrated with an influence diagram. In Figure 7.3, Events A and B are conditionally independent given Event C. Note that C can be a chance event or a decision, as in 7.3b. The only connection between A and B goes through C; there is no arrow directly from A to B or vice versa. Mathematically, we would write

> Events A and B are conditionally independent given C if and only if
>
> $$P(A \mid B, C) = P(A \mid C).$$

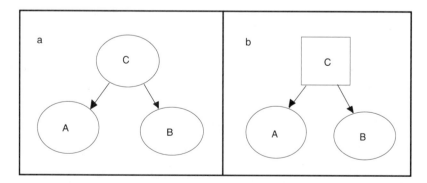

FIGURE 7.3 *Conditional Independence in an Influence Diagram*
In these influence diagrams, A and B are conditionally independent given C. As shown, the conditioning event can be either (a) a chance event or (b) a decision.

In words, suppose we are interested in Event A. If A and B are conditionally independent given C, then learning the outcome of B adds no new information regarding A if the outcome of C already is known. Alternatively, conditional independence means that

$$P(A \text{ and } B \mid C) = P(A \mid C) \, P(B \mid C).$$

Conditional independence is the same as normal (unconditional) independence except that every probability is conditioned on the same event or set of events. When constructing influence diagrams, identification of conditional independence can ease the burden of finding probabilities for the chance events.

As an example of conditional independence, consider a situation in which you wonder whether or not a particular firm will introduce a new product. You are acquainted with the CEO of the firm and may be able to ask about the new product. But one of your suppliers, who has chatted with the CEO's assistant, reports that the company is on the brink of announcing the new product. Your probability that the company will indeed introduce the product thus would change:

$$P(\text{Introduce Product} \mid \text{Supplier's Report}) \neq P(\text{Introduce Product}).$$

Thus, these two events are not independent when considered by themselves. Consider, however, the information from the CEO. Given that information, the supplier's report might not change your probability:

$$P(\text{Introduce Product} \mid \text{Supplier's Report, Information from CEO})$$
$$= P(\text{Introduce Product} \mid \text{Information from CEO}).$$

Thus, given the information from the CEO, the supplier's report and the event of the product introduction are conditionally independent.

6. COMPLEMENTS.   Let $\overline{B}$ ("Not B" or "B-bar") represent the complement of B. This means that if B does not occur, then $\overline{B}$ must occur. Because probabilities must add to 1 (requirement (3) above),

$$P(\overline{B}) = 1 - P(B).$$

The Venn diagram in Figure 7.4 demonstrates complements. If the area labeled B represents Event B, then everything outside of the oval must represent what happens if B does not happen. For another example, the lightly shaded area in Figure 7.2 represents the complement of the event "Dow Jones Up *or* Stock Price Up," the union of the two individual events.

7. TOTAL PROBABILITY OF AN EVENT.   A convenient way to calculate P(A) is with this formula:

$$P(A) = P(A \text{ and } B) + P(A \text{ and } \overline{B})$$
$$= P(A \mid B) \, P(B) + P(A \mid \overline{B}) \, P(\overline{B}).$$

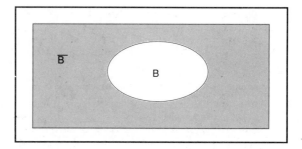

FIGURE 7.4 *Venn Diagram Illustrating the Idea of an Event's Complement*

To understand this formula, examine Figure 7.5. Clearly, Event A is composed of those occasions when A and B occur and when A and $\overline{B}$ occur. Because Events "A and B" and "A and $\overline{B}$" are mutually exclusive, the probability of A must be the sum of the probability of "A and B" plus the probability of "A and $\overline{B}$."

As an example, suppose we want to assess the probability that a stock price will increase. We could use its relationship with the Dow Jones index (Figure 7.2) to help make the assessment:

$$P(\text{Stock Price Up}) = P(\text{Stock Price Up} \mid \text{Dow Jones Up}) \times P(\text{Dow Jones Up})$$
$$+ P(\text{Stock Price Up} \mid \text{Dow Jones Not Up})$$
$$\times P(\text{Dow Jones Not Up}).$$

Although it may appear that we have complicated matters by requiring three assessments instead of one, it may be quite easy to think about (1) the probability of the stock price movement conditional on the change in the Dow Jones index and (2) the probabilities associated with changes in the index.

8. BAYES' THEOREM. Because of the symmetry of the definition of conditional probability, we can write

$$P(B \mid A) \, P(A) = P(A \mid B) \, P(B),$$

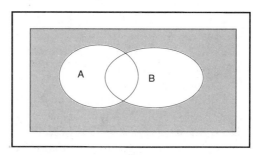

FIGURE 7.5 *Total Probability*
Event A is made up of Events "A and B" and "A and $\overline{B}$."

from which we can derive:

$$P(B \mid A) = \frac{P(A \mid B) \; P(B)}{P(A)} .$$

Now expanding $P(A)$ with the formula for total probability, we obtain

$$P(B \mid A) = \frac{P(A \mid B) P(B)}{P(A \mid B) \; P(B) + P(A \mid \overline{B}) \; P(\overline{B})} .$$

This formula often is referred to as Bayes' theorem. It is extremely useful in decision analysis, especially when using information. We will not bother with an example showing its application here, but we will see numerous applications of Bayes' theorem in the examples at the end of this chapter, as well as in Chapters 9, 10, and 12.

◆ UNCERTAIN QUANTITIES

Many uncertain events are quantitative. For example, we already have mentioned stock prices and the level of the Dow Jones index. Another example would be tomorrow's maximum temperature. Moreover, if an event is not quantitative in the first place, we might define a variable that has a quantitative outcome based on the original event. For example, we might be concerned about precipitation. If we consider the amount of precipitation (in centimeters) that falls tomorrow, this uncertain event is quantitative. Moreover, we could define an unknown quantity X: Let $X = 1$ if precipitation occurs, and $X = 0$ if not.

The set of probabilities associated with all possible outcomes of an uncertain quantity is called its *probability distribution*. For example, consider the probability distribution for the number of raisins in an oatmeal cookie, which we could denote by Y. We might have $P(Y = 0) = 0.02$, $P(Y = 1) = 0.05$, $P(Y = 2) = 0.20$, $P(Y = 3) = 0.40$, and so on. Of course, the probabilities in a probability distribution must add to 1 because the events — numerical outcomes — are mutually exclusive. Uncertain quantities (sometimes called *random variables*) and their probability distributions play a central role in decision analysis.

In general, we will use capital letters to represent uncertain quantities. Thus, we will write $P(X = 3)$ or $P(Y > 0)$, for example, which are read as "the probability that the uncertain quantity X equals 3," and "the probability that the uncertain quantity Y is greater than 0." Occasionally we will need to use a more general form. Lowercase letters will denote outcomes or realizations of an uncertain quantity. An example would be $P(X = x)$, where capital X denotes the uncertain quantity itself, and lowercase x represents the actual outcome.

In general, it is helpful to distinguish between *discrete* and *continuous* uncertain quantities. In the next section we will describe in detail discrete uncertain quantities, their probability distributions, and certain characteristics of those distributions. Then we will turn to continuous uncertain quantities and show how their probability distributions and their characteristics are analogous to the discrete case.

Discrete Probability Distributions

The discrete probability distribution case is characterized by an uncertain quantity that can take only specific values. We already have seen two examples. The first was the precipitation example; we defined a discrete uncertain quantity that could take only the values 0 and 1. The other example was the number of raisins in an oatmeal cookie. Other examples might be the number of operations a computer performs in any given second or the number of games that will be won by the Chicago Cubs next year. Strictly speaking, future stock prices quoted on the New York Stock Exchange are discrete uncertain quantities because they can take only values that are in eighths: $10\frac{5}{8}$, $11\frac{3}{4}$, or $12\frac{1}{2}$, for example.

When we specify a probability distribution for a discrete uncertain quantity, we can express the distribution in several ways. Two approaches are particularly useful. The first is to give the *probability mass function*. This function lists the probabilities for each possible discrete outcome. For example, suppose that you think that no cookie in a batch of oatmeal cookies could have more than five raisins. A possible probability mass function would be:

$P(Y = 0 \text{ raisins}) = 0.02$	$P(Y = 3 \text{ raisins}) = 0.40$
$P(Y = 1 \text{ raisin}) = 0.05$	$P(Y = 4 \text{ raisins}) = 0.22$
$P(Y = 2 \text{ raisins}) = 0.20$	$P(Y = 5 \text{ raisins}) = 0.11.$

This mass function can be displayed in graphical form (Figure 7.6). Such a graph often is called a *histogram*.

The second way to express a probability distribution is as a *cumulative distribution function* (CDF). A cumulative distribution is the probability that an uncer-

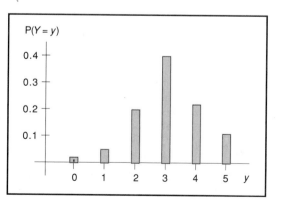

FIGURE 7.6 *A Probability Mass Function Displayed as a Histogram*

tain quantity is less than or equal to a specified value: $P(X \le x)$. For our example, the CDF is given by

$P(Y \le 0 \text{ raisins}) = 0.02$	$P(Y \le 3 \text{ raisins}) = 0.67$
$P(Y \le 1 \text{ raisin}) = 0.07$	$P(Y \le 4 \text{ raisins}) = 0.89$
$P(Y \le 2 \text{ raisins}) = 0.27$	$P(Y \le 5 \text{ raisins}) = 1.00.$

Cumulative probabilities can be graphed; the CDF for the oatmeal cookie is graphed in Figure 7.7.

Note that the graph actually covers all the points along the horizontal axis. That is, we can read from the graph not only $P(Y \le 3)$, but also $P(Y \le 4.67)$, for example. In fact, $P(Y \le 4.67) = P(Y \le 4) = 0.89$, because it is not possible for a cookie to have a fractional number of raisins (assuming whole raisins, of course).

You may recognize this idea of a probability mass function and a CDF. When we constructed risk profiles and cumulative risk profiles in Chapter 4, we were working with these two representations of probability distributions.

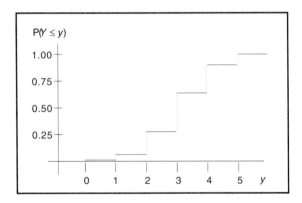

FIGURE 7.7   *Cumulative Distribution Function (CDF) for Number of Raisins in an Oatmeal Cookie*

Expected Value

A discrete uncertain quantity's *expected value* is the probability-weighted average of its possible values. That is, if X can take on any value in the set $\{x_1, x_2, \cdots, x_n\}$, then the expected value of X is simply the sum of x_1 through x_n, each weighted by the probability of its occurrence. Mathematically,

$$\text{Expected value of } X = x_1 P(X = x_1) + x_2 P(X = x_2) + \cdots + x_n P(X = x_n)$$
$$= \sum_{i=1}^{n} x_i P(X = x_i).$$

The expected value of X also is referred to as the average or mean of X, and is denoted by $E(X)$ or occasionally μ_X (Greek mu).

The expected value can be thought of as the "best guess" for the value of an uncertain quantity or random variable. If it were possible to observe many outcomes of the random variable, the average of those outcomes would be very close to the expected value. We already have encountered expected values in calculating EMVs to solve influence diagrams and decision trees. The expected monetary value is the expected value of a random variable that happens to be the monetary outcome in a decision situation.

Suppose that X is used to calculate some other quantity, say Y. Then it is possible to talk about the expected value of Y, or the expected value of this function of X:

> If
>
> $$Y = f(X),$$
>
> Then
>
> $$E(Y) = E[f(X)].$$

A particularly useful function is a linear function of X, one in which X is multiplied by a constant and has a constant added to it. If Y is a linear function of X, then $E(Y)$ is particularly easy to find:

> If
>
> $$Y = a + bX,$$
>
> Then
>
> $$E(Y) = a + bE(X).$$

That is, plug $E(X)$ into the linear formula to get $E(Y)$. Unfortunately, this does not hold for nonlinear functions (log, square root, and so on); in general, it applies only to linear ones.

To go one step further, suppose we have several uncertain quantities, $X_1, \cdots, X_k$, and we add them to get uncertain quantity Y. Then the expected value of Y is the sum of the expected values:

> If
>
> $$Y = X_1 + X_2 + \cdots + X_k,$$
>
> Then
>
> $$E(Y) = E(X_1) + E(X_2) + \cdots + E(X_k).$$

For instance, if we know the expected amount of precipitation for each of the next seven days, the expected amount of precipitation for the entire week is simply the sum of the seven daily expected values.

Variance and Standard Deviation

Another useful measure of a probability distribution is the *variance*. The variance of uncertain quantity X is denoted by $\text{Var}(X)$ or σ_X^2 (Greek sigma), and is calculated mathematically by

$$
\begin{aligned}
\text{Var}(X) &= [x_1 - \text{E}(X)]^2 \text{P}(X = x_1) + [x_2 - \text{E}(X)]^2 \text{P}(X = x_2) \\
&\quad + \cdots + [x_n - \text{E}(X)]^2 \text{P}(X = x_n) \\
&= \sum_{i=1}^{n} [x_i - \text{E}(X)]^2 \text{P}(X = x_i).
\end{aligned}
$$

In words, calculate the difference between the expected value and x_i and square that difference. Do this for each possible x_i. Now find the expected value of these squared differences.

As with expected values, we can find variances of functions for X. In particular, the variance of a linear function of X is easily found:

If
$$
Y = a + bX,
$$
Then
$$
\text{Var}(Y) = b^2 \, \text{Var}(X).
$$

For example, suppose that a firm will sell an uncertain number (X) of units of a product. The expected value of X is 1000 units and the variance is 400. If the price is \$3 per unit, then the revenue (Y) is equal to $3X$. Because this is a linear function of X, $\text{E}(Y) = 3\text{E}(X) = \$3000$, and $\text{Var}(Y) = 3^2 \, \text{Var}(X) = 9(400) = 3600$.

We also can talk about the variance of a sum of independent uncertain quantities. That is, *as long as the uncertain quantities are probabilistically independent* — the probability distribution for one does not depend on the others — then the variance of the sum is the sum of the variances:

If
$$
Y = X_1 + X_2 + \cdots + X_k,
$$
Then
$$
\text{Var}(Y) = \text{Var}(X_1) + \text{Var}(X_2) + \cdots + \text{Var}(X_k).
$$

So, if our firm sells two products, one for $3.00 and another for $5.00, and the variance for these two products is 400 and 750, respectively, then the variance of the firm's revenue is $\mathrm{Var}(Y) = 3^2\,\mathrm{Var}(X_1) + 5^2\,\mathrm{Var}(X_2) = 9(400) + 25(750) = 22{,}350$.

The *standard deviation* of X, denoted by σ_x, is just the square root of the variance. Because the variance is the expected value of the squared differences, the standard deviation can be thought of as a "best guess" as to how far the outcome of X might lie from $E(X)$. A large standard deviation and variance means that the probability distribution is quite spread out; a large difference between the outcome and the expected value is anticipated. For this reason, the variance and standard deviation of a probability distribution are used as measures of variability. A large variance or standard deviation would indicate a situation in which the outcomes are highly variable.

To illustrate the ideas of expected value, variance, and standard deviation, consider the double-risk dilemma depicted in Figure 7.8. Choices A and B both lead to uncertain dollar outcomes. Given Decision A, for example, there are three possible profit outcomes having probability mass function P(Profit = $20 | A) = 0.24, P(Profit = $35 | A) = 0.47, and P(Profit = $50 | A) = 0.29. Likewise, for B we have P(Profit = –$9 | B) = 0.25, P(Profit = $0 | B) = 0.35, and P(Profit = $95 | B) = 0.40. Now we can calculate the expected profits conditional on choosing A or B:

$$E(\text{Profit} \mid A) = 0.24(\$20) + 0.47(\$35) + 0.29(\$50) = \$35.75$$
$$E(\text{Profit} \mid B) = 0.25(-\$9) + 0.35(\$0) + 0.40(\$95) = \$35.75.$$

These two uncertain quantities have exactly the same expected values. (Note that the expected profit does not have to be one of the possible outcomes!)

We also can calculate the variances and standard deviations (σ) for A and B:

$$\mathrm{Var}(\text{Profit} \mid A) = (20 - 35.75)^2(0.24) + (35 - 35.75)^2(0.47)$$
$$+ (50 - 35.75)^2(0.29)$$
$$= 118.69 \text{ "dollars squared."}$$
$$\sigma_A = \sqrt{118.69} = \$10.89.$$

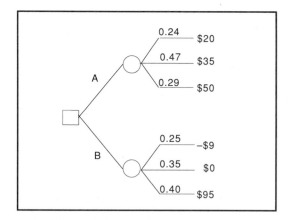

FIGURE 7.8 *A Choice Between Two Uncertain Prospects*

$$\text{Var}(\text{Profit} \mid B) = (-9 - 35.75)^2(0.25) + (0 - 35.75)^2(0.35)$$
$$+ (95 - 35.75)^2(0.40)$$
$$= 2352.19 \text{ "dollars squared."}$$
$$\sigma_B = \sqrt{2352.19} = \$48.50.$$

The variance and standard deviation of B are much larger than those for A. The outcomes in B are more spread out or more variable than the outcomes for A, which are clustered fairly closely around the expected value.

The example also points out the fact that variance, being a weighted sum of squared terms, is expressed in squared units. In this case, the variance is in "dollars squared" because the original outcomes are in dollars. Taking the square root to find the standard deviation brings us back to the original units, or, in this case, dollars. For this reason, the standard deviation is interpreted more easily as a measure of variability.

You might have noticed that, while the variance and standard deviation can be used to gauge the riskiness of an option, the cumulative probabilities also can be useful in this respect. For example, we have $P(\text{Profit} \leq 0 \mid A) = 0$, but $P(\text{Profit} \leq 0 \mid B) = 0.6$, and B thus looks somewhat riskier than A. At the other extreme, of course, B looks better. Project A cannot produce a profit greater than $50: $P(\text{Profit} \leq \$50 \mid A) = 1.00$. For B, however, $P(\text{Profit} \leq \$50 \mid B) = 0.60$.

Continuous Probability Distributions

The discussion above has focused on discrete uncertain quantities. Now we turn briefly to continuous uncertain quantities. In this case, the uncertain quantity can take any value within some range. For example, the temperature tomorrow at O'Hare Airport in Chicago at noon is an uncertain quantity that can be anywhere between, say, –50°F and 120°F. The length of time until some anticipated event (for example, the next major earthquake in California) is a continuous uncertain quantity, as are locations in space (the precise location of the next earthquake), as well as various measurements such as height, weight, and speed (for example, the peak "ground acceleration" in the next major earthquake).

With continuous uncertain quantities, it is not reasonable to speak of the probability that a specific value occurs. In fact, the probability of a particular value occurring is equal to zero: $P(Y = y) = 0$. Intuitively, there are infinitely many possible values, and so the probability of any particular value must be infinitely small. Instead, we typically speak of interval probabilities: $P(a \leq Y \leq b)$. The CDF for a continuous uncertain quantity can be constructed on the basis of such intervals.

The easiest way to understand this process is through a simple example. Let us suppose we are interested in a movie star's age. For a variety of reasons, we may be certain that she is older than 29 and no older than 65. We can translate these into probability statements: $P(\text{Age} \leq 29) = 0$, and $P(\text{Age} \leq 65) = 1$. Now, suppose that you decide that she most likely is between 40 and 50 years old, and that P(40 < Age ≤ 50) = 0.8. Also, suppose you figure that P(Age ≤ 40) = 0.05, and P(Age > 50) = 0.15. Naturally, if you were so inclined, you also could make several other judgments. For example, you might figure that her age is just as likely to be 44 or less as it is to be greater than 44. This would translate into P(Age ≤ 44) = 0.50.

We can take the probabilities from this last example, transform them, and create the following table of cumulative probabilities:

$$P(Age \le 29) = 0.00$$
$$P(Age \le 40) = 0.05$$
$$P(Age \le 44) = 0.50$$
$$P(Age \le 50) = 0.85$$
$$P(Age \le 65) = 1.00.$$

These probabilities then can be displayed in a graph, with years along the horizontal axis and P(Age ≤ Years) along the vertical axis. The graph, shown in Figure 7.9, allows you to select a number of years on the horizontal axis and then read off the probability that the movie star's age is less than or equal to that number of years. As with the discrete case, this graph represents the cumulative distribution function, or CDF.

As before, the CDF allows us to calculate the probability for any interval. For example, P(40 < Age ≤ 44) = P(Age ≤ 44) − P(Age ≤ 40) = 0.45. If we were to make more assessments, the dark line in Figure 7.9 would be smoother, but it should always slope upward. If it were to slope downward, it would imply that some interval had a negative probability!

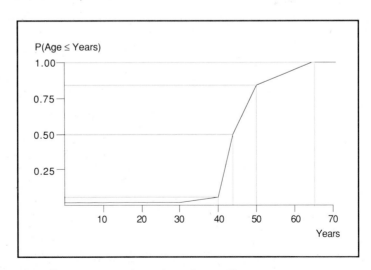

FIGURE 7.9 *Cumulative Distribution Function for Movie Star's Age*

Stochastic Dominance Revisited

Chapter 4 introduced the concept of stochastic dominance as it related to cumulative risk profiles for discrete uncertain quantities. The same principles also hold true in the continuous case.

Figure 7.10 shows CDFs for three investment alternatives, each of which is modeled as a continuous uncertain quantity. Investment B stochastically dominates Investment A because the CDF for B lies entirely to the right of the CDF for A. On the other hand, Investment C neither dominates nor is dominated by the other two alternatives. For instance, Area E represents the portion of B's CDF that lies to the left of the CDF for Investment C. Because C's CDF crosses the other two, no decision can be made between C and B (or between C and A) on the basis of stochastic dominance.

Probability Density Functions

The CDF for a continuous uncertain quantity corresponds closely to the CDF for the discrete case. Is there some representation that corresponds to the probability mass function? The answer is yes, and that representation is called a *probability density function*, which, if we are speaking of uncertain quantity X, would be denoted typically as $f(x)$. The density function $f(x)$ can be built up from the CDF. It is a function in which the area under the curve within a specific interval represents the probability that the uncertain quantity will fall in that interval. For example, the density function $f(\text{Age})$ for the movie star's age might look something like the graph in Figure 7.11. The total area under the curve equals 1 because the uncertain quantity must take on some value. The shaded area in Figure 7.11 corresponds to $P(40 < \text{Age} \leq 50)$ and so this area must be equal to 0.80.

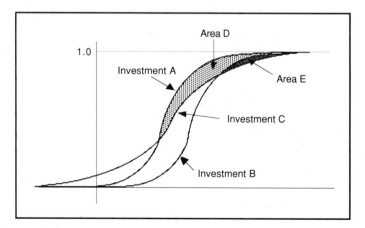

FIGURE 7.10   *CDFs for Three Investment Alternatives*
Investment B stochastically dominates Investment A.

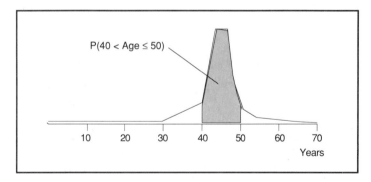

FIGURE 7.11 *Probability Density Function for Movie Star's Age*

Expected Value, Variance, and Standard Deviation: The Continuous Case

As in the discrete case, a continuous probability distribution can have an expected value, variance, and standard deviation. But the definition is not as easy as it was before because now we do not have probabilities for specific values, only probabilities for intervals. Without going into a lot of detail, these characteristics of a continuous probability distribution are defined by using calculus. The definitions for a continuous uncertain quantity X correspond to the discrete case, except that the summation sign is replaced with an integral sign and the density function is used in place of the probabilities:

$$E(X) = \int_{x-}^{x+} x f(x) \ dx$$

$$Var(X) = \sigma_X^2 = \int_{x-}^{x+} [x - E(X)]^2 f(x) \ dx,$$

where $x-$ and $x+$ represent the lower and upper bounds for the uncertain quantity X. As before, the standard deviation σ_X is the square root of the variance.

The interpretation of these formulas also corresponds closely to the summation in the discrete case. It turns out that integration is really the continuous equivalent of the summing operation. Consider the formula for the expected value, for example. Each possible value x between $x-$ and $x+$ is multiplied by (weighted by) the height of the density function $f(x)$. The integration then adds all of these $xf(x)$ products to find $E(X)$. It is as if we had carved up the density function into a very large number of quite narrow but equally wide intervals (Figure 7.12). The relative likelihood of X falling in these different intervals corresponds to the relative height of the density function in each interval. That is, if the density function is (on average) twice as high in one interval as in another, then X is twice as likely to fall into the first interval as the second. As the inter-

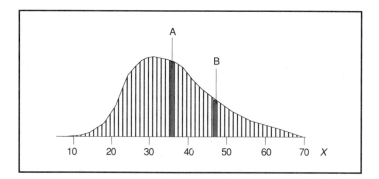

FIGURE 7.12   *A Density Function* f(x) *in Narrow Intervals*
The probability that *X* falls in interval A is about twice as
great as for B because $f(x)$ is about twice as high in A as it
is in B.

vals become infinitesimally narrow, the height of the interval becomes equal to
the value $f(x)$. In the limit, as the width of each interval approaches 0, we take
each *x*, multiply by $f(x)$, add these products (by integration), and — bingo! —
we get E(X).

Rest assured — you will not be required to perform any integration (in this
book anyway). In general, the integration of density functions to obtain expected values and variances is a difficult task and beyond the technical scope of
this textbook. Fortunately, mathematicians have studied many different kinds of
probability distributions and have performed the integration for you, providing
you with formulas for the expected values and variances. We will encounter several of these in Chapter 9.

What about all of those formulas for the expected value and variance of *Y*, a
function of *X*, or for linear combinations of random variables? Fortunately, *all of
those formulas carry over to the continuous case.* If you know the expected value and
variance of several uncertain quantities, you can apply the formulas given above
regardless of whether the uncertain quantities are continuous or discrete. For
example, if $Y = a + bX$, then $E(Y) = a + b\,E(X)$. If $Y = aX_1 + bX_2$, and X_1 and X_2 are
independent, then $\mathrm{Var}(Y) = a^2\mathrm{Var}(X_1) + b^2\mathrm{Var}(X_2)$. It does not matter whether
the *X*'s are discrete or continuous.

The formulas and definitions given above are the essential elements of
probability theory. With these few tools we will be able to go quite a long way in
the construction of uncertainty models for decision situations. The intent has
been to present the tools and concepts so that they are easily grasped. It may be
worthwhile to memorize the formulas, but most important is understanding
them at an intuitive level. To help you cement the concepts in your mind and to
show the formulas in action, we turn now to specific examples.

OIL WILDCATTING

An oil company is considering two sites for an exploratory well. Because of
budget constraints, only one well can be drilled. Site 1 is fairly risky, with sub-

stantial uncertainty about the amount of oil that might be found. On the other hand, Site 2 is fairly certain to produce a low level of oil. The characteristics of the two sites are as follows:

Site 1: Cost to drill $100K

Outcome	Payoff
Dry	–100K
Low producer	150K
High producer	500K

If the rock strata underlying Site 1 are characterized by what geologists call a "dome" structure (see Figure 7.13), the chances of finding oil are somewhat greater than if no dome structure exists. The probability of a dome structure is P(Dome) = 0.6. The conditional probabilities of finding oil at Site 1 are given in Table 7.1.

Site 2 is considerably less complicated. A well there is not expected to be a high producer, so the only outcomes considered are a dry hole and a low producer. The cost, outcomes, payoffs, and probabilities are as follows:

Site 2: Cost to drill $200K

Outcome	Payoff	Probability
Dry	–200K	0.2
Low producer	50K	0.8

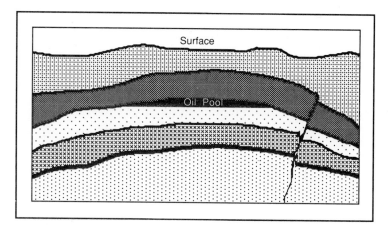

FIGURE 7.13   *Rock Strata Forming a Dome Structure*
Oil tends to pool at the top of the dome in an oil-bearing layer if the layer above is impermeable.

If Dome Structure Exists

Outcome	P(Outcome | Dome)
Dry	0.600
Low	0.250
High	0.150
	1.000

If No Dome Structure Exists

Outcome	P(Outcome | No Dome)
Dry	0.850
Low	0.125
High	0.025
	1.000

TABLE 7.1 *Conditional Probabilities of Outcomes at Site 1*

The decision tree is shown in Figure 7.14. The problem with it as drawn, however, is that we cannot assign probabilities immediately to the outcomes for Site 1. To find these probabilities, we must use the conditional probabilities and the law of total probability to calculate P(Dry), P(Low), and P(High):

$$P(Dry) = P(Dry \mid Dome)\ P(Dome) + P(Dry \mid No\ Dome)\ P(No\ Dome)$$
$$= 0.6(0.6) + 0.85(0.4) = 0.70.$$

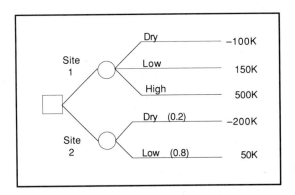

FIGURE 7.14 *Decision Tree for Oil-Wildcatting Problem*

$$P(Low) = P(Low \mid Dome) \, P(Dome) + P(Low \mid No \, Dome) \, P(No \, Dome)$$
$$= 0.25(0.6) + 0.125(0.4) = 0.20.$$

$$P(High) = P(High \mid Dome) \, P(Dome) + P(High \mid No \, Dome) \, P(No \, Dome)$$
$$= 0.15(0.6) + 0.025(0.4) = 0.10.$$

Everything works out as it should. The three probabilities are for mutually exclusive and collectively exhaustive events, and they add to 1, just as they should. Folding back the decision tree, we find that Site 1 has the higher EMV:

$$EMV(Site \ 1) = 0.7 \ (-100K) + 0.2 \ (150K) + 0.1 \ (500K)$$
$$= 10K.$$

$$EMV(Site \ 2) = 0.2 \ (-200K) + 0.8 \ (50K)$$
$$= 0.$$

We also can calculate the variance and standard deviation of the payoffs for each site:

$$\sigma_1^2 = 0.7 \ (-100 - 10)^2 + 0.2 \ (150 - 10)^2 + 0.1 \ (500 - 10)^2$$
$$= 0.7 \ (-110)^2 + 0.2 \ (140)^2 + 0.1 \ (490)^2$$
$$= 36{,}400K^2.$$

$$\sigma_1 = 190.79K.$$

$$\sigma_2^2 = 0.2 \ (-200 - 0)^2 + 0.8 \ (50 - 0)^2$$
$$= 0.2 \ (-200)^2 + 0.8 \ (50)^2$$
$$= 10{,}000K^2.$$

$$\sigma_2 = 100.00K.$$

If we treat these numbers as measures of variability, then it is clear that Site 1, with its higher variance and standard deviation, is more variable than Site 2. In this sense, Site 1 might be considered to be riskier than Site 2.

Note that we could have drawn the decision tree as in Figure 7.15, with "stacked" probabilities. That is, we could have drawn it with a first chance node indicating whether or not a dome is present, followed by chance nodes for the amount of oil. These chance nodes would include the conditional probabilities from Table 7.1.

We also could have created a probability table as in Table 7.2. The probabilities in the cells of the table are the probabilities of both events happening at the same time. Such situations sometimes are called "intersections" or "joint events" to indicate that both events occur together. Calculating probabilities for the table requires the definition of conditional probability in a slightly modified form. For example,

$$P(Low \, and \, Dome) = P(Dome)P(Low \mid Dome)$$
$$= 0.60 \ (0.25)$$
$$= 0.15.$$

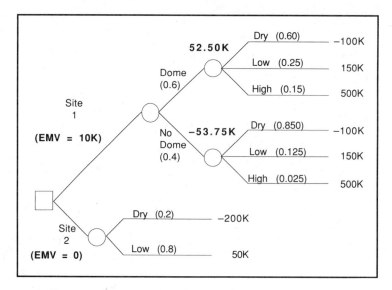

FIGURE 7.15   *An Alternative Decision Tree for the Oil-Wildcatting Problem*

The probability table is easy to construct and easy to understand. Once the probabilities of the joint events are calculated, the probabilities of the individual events then are found by adding across the rows or down the columns. For example, from Table 7.2, we can tell that P(Dry) = 0.36 + 0.34 = 0.70.

Suppose that the company drills at Site 1, and the well is a high producer. In light of this evidence, does it seem more likely that a dome structure exists? Can we figure out P(Dome | High)? This question is part of a larger problem. Figure 7.16 shows a "probability tree" (a decision tree without decisions) that reflects the information that we have been given in the problem. We know P(Dome) and P(No Dome), and we know the conditional probabilities of the amount of oil given the presence or absence of a dome. Thus, our probability tree has the chance node representing the presence or absence of a dome on the left and the chance node representing the amount of oil on the right. Finding P(Dome | High) is a matter of "flipping the tree" so that the chance node for the amount

	Dome	No Dome	
Dry	0.36	0.34	0.70
Low	0.15	0.05	0.20
High	0.09	0.01	0.10
	0.60	0.40	1.00

TABLE 7.2   *Calculating the Probabilities for Site 1*

of oil is on the left and the node for the presence or absence of a dome is on the right, as in Figure 7.17.

Flipping a probability tree is the same as reversing an arrow between two chance nodes in an influence diagram. In Figure 7.18a, the direction of the arrow represents the probabilities as they are given in Table 7.1. Because the arrow points to the "Oil Production" node, the probabilities for the level of oil production are conditioned on whether or not there is a dome. Figure 7.18b shows the arrow reversed. Now the probability of a dome or no dome is conditioned on the amount of oil produced. Changing the direction of the arrow has the same effect as flipping the probability tree.

Simply flipping the tree or turning the arrow around in the influence diagram is not enough. The question marks in Figure 7.17 indicate that we do not yet know what the probabilities are for the flipped tree. The probabilities in the new tree must be consistent with the probabilities in the original version. Consistency means that if we were to calculate P(Dome) and P(No Dome) using the

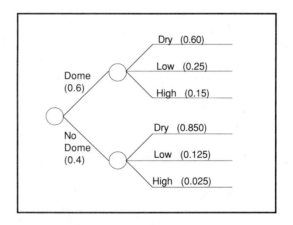

FIGURE 7.16 *Probability Tree for the Uncertainty Faced at Site 1*

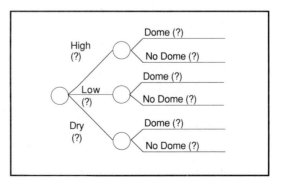

FIGURE 7.17 *Flipping the Probability Tree in Figure 7.16*

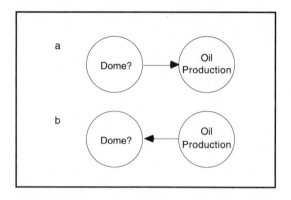

FIGURE 7.18 *Reversing Arrows Between Chance Nodes in an Influence Diagram*

probabilities in the new tree, we would get 0.60 and 0.40, the probabilities we started with in Figure 7.16. How do we ensure consistency?

We can find P(High), P(Low), and P(Dry) by using the law of total probability. We did these calculations above for Figure 7.14, and we found that P(High) = 0.10, P(Low) = 0.20, and P(Dry) = 0.70. How about finding the new conditional probabilities? Bayes' theorem provides the answer. For example:

$$P(\text{Dome} \mid \text{High}) = \frac{P(\text{High} \mid \text{Dome})P(\text{Dome})}{P(\text{High})}$$

$$= \frac{P(\text{High} \mid \text{Dome})P(\text{Dome})}{P(\text{High} \mid \text{Dome})P(\text{Dome}) + P(\text{High} \mid \text{No Dome})P(\text{No Dome})}$$

$$= \frac{0.15\ (0.6)}{0.15\ (0.6) + 0.025\ (0.4)}$$

$$= \frac{0.15\ (0.6)}{0.10}$$

$$= 0.90.$$

Probabilities that have the same conditions must add to 1, and so P(No Dome | High) must be equal to 0.10. Likewise, we can calculate the conditional probabilities of a dome or no dome given a dry hole or a low producer. These probabilities are shown in Figure 7.19.

If you did not enjoy using Bayes' theorem directly to calculate the conditional probabilities required in flipping the tree, you may be pleased to learn that the probability table (Table 7.2) has all the information needed. Recall that the entries in the cells inside the table are the joint probabilities. For example, P(High and Dome) = 0.09. We need P(Dome | High) = P(High and Dome)/P(High), which is just 0.09/0.10 = 0.90. That is, we take the joint probability from inside the table and divide it by the probability of the event on the right side of the vertical bar. This probability is found in the margin of the probability table.

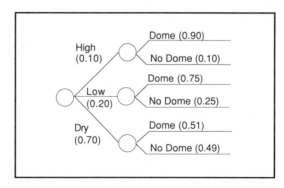

FIGURE 7.19 *The Flipped Probability Tree with New Probabilities*

Whether we use Bayes' theorem directly or the probability table approach to flip the probability tree, the conditional probabilities that we obtain have an interesting interpretation. Recall that we started with P(Dome) = 0.60. After finding that the well was a high producer, we were able to calculate P(Dome | High). This probability sometimes is called a *posterior* probability, indicating that it is the result of revising the original probability after gathering data. In contrast, the probability with which we started, in this case P(Dome) = 0.60, sometimes is called the *prior* probability. One way to think about Bayes' theorem is that it provides a mechanism to update prior probabilities when new information becomes available.

JOHN HINCKLEY'S TRIAL

In 1982 John Hinckley was on trial, accused of having attempted to kill President Reagan. During Hinckley's trial, Dr. Daniel R. Weinberger told the court that when individuals diagnosed as schizophrenics were given computerized axial tomography (CAT) scans, the scans showed brain atrophy in 30% of the cases compared with only 2% of the scans done on normal people. Hinckley's defense attorney wanted to introduce as evidence Hinckley's CAT scan, which showed brain atrophy. The defense argued that the presence of atrophy strengthened the case that Hinckley suffered from mental illness.

◆

We can use Bayes' theorem easily to analyze this situation. We want to know the probability that Hinckley was schizophrenic given that he had brain atrophy. Approximately 1.5% of people in the United States suffer from schizophrenia. This is the "base rate," which we can interpret as the prior probability of schizophrenia before we find out about the condition of an individual's brain. Thus, $P(S) = 0.015$, where S means schizophrenia. We also have $P(A \mid S) = 0.30$ (A means atrophy) and $P(A \mid \overline{S}) = 0.02$. We want $P(S \mid A)$. Bayes' theorem provides the mathematical mechanism for flipping the probability from $P(A \mid S)$ to $P(S \mid A)$:

$$P(S \mid A) = \frac{P(A \mid S)\ P(S)}{P(A \mid S)\ P(S) + P(A \mid \overline{S})P(\overline{S})}$$

$$= \frac{0.30(0.015)}{0.30\ (0.015) + 0.02\ (0.985)}$$

$$= 0.186.$$

Thus, given that his brain showed such atrophy, Hinckley still has less than a 1-in-5 chance of being schizophrenic. Given the situation, this is perhaps a surprisingly low probability. The intuition behind this result is that there are many false positive tests. If we tested 100,000 individuals, some 1500 of them would be schizophrenic and 98,500 would be normal (or at least not schizophrenic). Of the 1500, only 30%, or approximately 450, would show atrophy. Of the 98,500, 2% (some 1970) would show brain atrophy. If a single individual has atrophy, is he one of the 450 with schizophrenia or one of the 1970 without? Note that

$$0.186 = \frac{450}{450 + 1970}.$$

The real question is whether this is good news or bad news for Hinckley. The prosecution might argue that the probability of schizophrenia is too small to make any difference; even in light of the CAT-scan evidence, Hinckley is less than one-fourth as likely to be schizophrenic as not. On the other hand, the defense would counter, 0.186 is much larger than 0.015. Thus, the CAT-scan results indicate that Hinckley was more than 12 times as likely to be schizophrenic than a randomly chosen person on the street.

Now, however, consider what we have done in applying Bayes' theorem. We have used a prior probability of 0.015, which essentially is the probability that a randomly chosen person from the population is schizophrenic. *But Hinckley was not randomly chosen.* In fact, it does not seem reasonable to think of Hinckley, a man accused of attempted assassination, as the typical person on the street.

If 0.015 is not an appropriate prior probability, what is? It may not be obvious what an appropriate prior probability should be, so let us consider a sensitivity-analysis approach and see what different priors would imply. Imagine a juror who, before encountering the CAT-scan evidence, believes that there is only a 10% chance that Hinckley is schizophrenic. For most of us, this would be a fairly strong statement; Hinckley is nine times as likely to be normal as schizophrenic. Now consider the impact of the CAT-scan evidence on this prior probability. We can calculate this juror's posterior probability:

$$P(S \mid A) = \frac{0.30\ (0.10)}{0.30(0.10) + 0.02(0.90)}$$

$$= 0.63.$$

$P(S \mid A) = 0.63$ is a substantial probability. We can do this for a variety of values for the prior probability. Figure 7.20 shows the posterior probability $P(S \mid A)$ graphed as a function of the prior probability that Hinckley was schizophrenic.

As a result of this discussion, it is clear that a juror need not have a very strong prior belief for the CAT-scan evidence to have an overwhelming effect on his or her posterior belief of Hinckley's mental illness. Furthermore, no matter what the juror's prior belief, the CAT-scan result must increase the probability that Hinckley was schizophrenic. [*Source*: Barnett, A., I. Greenberg, and R. Machol (1984) "Hinckley and the Chemical Bath." *Interfaces*, 14, 48–52.]

◇ SUMMARY

The definitions and formulas at the beginning of the chapter are the building blocks of probability theory. Venn diagrams provide a way to visualize these probability "laws." We also discussed uncertain quantities, their probability distributions, and characteristics of those distributions such as expected value, variance, and standard deviation. The use of probability concepts and the manipulation of probabilities were demonstrated in the oil-wildcatting and Hinckley trial examples.   ◆

◇ EXERCISES

7.1   Explain why probability is important in decision analysis.

7.2   Explain in your own words what an uncertain quantity or random variable is. Why is the idea of an uncertain quantity important in decision analysis?

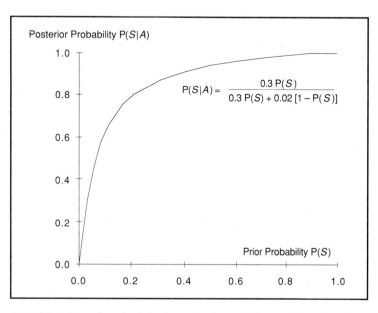

FIGURE 7.20   *Graph of the Posterior Probability that Hinckley Was Schizophrenic Plotted Against the Prior Probability*

7.3   You are given the following probability table:

	A	$\bar{A}$	
B	0.12	0.53	0.65
$\bar{B}$	0.29	0.06	0.35
	0.41	0.59	1.00

Use the probability table to find the following:

$P(A \text{ and } B), P(A \text{ and } \bar{B}), P(A), P(B), P(\bar{B}), P(B \mid A), P(A \mid B), P(\bar{A} \mid \bar{B}).$

7.4   Use the probability table in Exercise 7.3 to find $P(A \text{ or } B)$, or the event where either A occurs or B occurs (or both).

7.5   The Event A or B sometimes is called the union of A and B. The union event occurs if either Event A or Event B (or both) occurs. Suppose that both A and B can happen at the same time (that is, their areas overlap in a Venn diagram). Show that $P(A \text{ or } B) = P(A) + P(B) - P(A \text{ and } B)$. Use a Venn diagram to explain. Why is this result consistent with the second requirement that probabilities add up?

7.6   Often it is difficult to distinguish between the probability of an intersection of events (joint probability) and the probability of a conditional event (conditional probability). Classify the following as joint probability statements or conditional probability statements. [If in doubt, try to write down the probability statement; for example, P(Crash Landing | Out of Fuel) or P(Dow Jones Up and Stock Price Up).]

a. Eight percent of the students in a class were left-handed and red-haired.

b. Of the left-handed students, 20% had red hair.

c. If the Orioles lose their next game, then the Cubs have a 90% chance of winning the pennant.

d. Fifty-nine percent of the people with a positive test result had the disease.

e. For 78% of patients, the surgery is a success and the cancer never reappears.

f. If the surgery is a success, the cancer is unlikely to reappear.

g. Given the drought, food prices are likely to increase.

h. There is an even chance that a farmer who loses his crop will go bankrupt.

i. If the temperature is high and there is no rain, farmers probably will lose their crops.

j. John probably will be arrested because he is trading on insider information.

k. John probably will trade on insider information and get caught.

7.7   Calculate the variance and standard deviation of the payoffs for Products B and C in the GPC case at the end of Chapter 4 (page 105).

7.8 $P(A) = 0.42, P(B \mid A) = 0.66,$ and $P(B \mid \bar{A}) = 0.25.$ Find the following:

$P(\bar{A}), P(\bar{B} \mid A), P(\bar{B} \mid \bar{A}), P(B), P(\bar{B}), P(A \mid B), P(\bar{A} \mid B), P(A \mid \bar{B}), P(\bar{A} \mid \bar{B}).$

7.9 $P(A) = 0.10, P(B \mid A) = 0.39,$ and $P(B \mid \bar{A}) = 0.39.$ Find the following:

$P(\bar{A}), P(\bar{B} \mid A), P(\bar{B} \mid \bar{A}), P(B), P(\bar{B}), P(A \mid B), P(\bar{A} \mid B), P(A \mid \bar{B}), P(\bar{A} \mid \bar{B}).$

How would you describe the relationship between Events A and B?

7.10 $P(A) = 0.68, P(B \mid A) = 0.30,$ and $P(B \mid \bar{A}) = 0.02.$ Find $P(\bar{A}), P(A \text{ and } B),$ and $P(\bar{A} \text{ and } B).$

Use these to construct a probability table. Now use the table to find the following:

$$P(\bar{B} \mid A), P(\bar{B} \mid \bar{A}), P(B), P(\bar{B}), P(A \mid B), P(\bar{A} \mid B), P(A \mid \bar{B}), P(\bar{A} \mid \bar{B}).$$

7.11 Julie Myers, a graduating senior in accounting, is preparing for an interview with a big-eight accounting firm. Before the interview, she sets her chances of eventually getting an offer at 50%. Then, on thinking about her friends who have interviewed and gotten offers from this firm, she realizes that of the people who received offers, 95% had good interviews. On the other hand, of those who did not receive offers, 75% said they had good interviews. If Julie Myers has a good interview, what are her chances of receiving an offer?

7.12 Find the expected value, variance, and standard deviation of X in the following probability distributions:

   a. $P(X = 1) = 0.05$, $P(X = 2) = 0.45$, $P(X = 3) = 0.30$, $P(X = 4) = 0.20$.

   b. $P(X = -20) = 0.13$, $P(X = 0) = 0.58$, $P(X = 100) = 0.29$.

   c. $P(X = 0) = 0.368$, $P(X = 1) = 0.632$.

7.13 If $P(X = 1) = p$ and $P(X = 0) = 1 - p$, show that $E(X) = p$ and $\text{Var}(X) = p(1 - p)$.

7.14 If $P(A \mid B) = p$, must $P(A \mid \bar{B}) = 1 - p$? Explain.

7.15 Suppose that a company produces three different products. The sales for each product is independent of the sales for the others. The information for these products is given below:

Product	Price ($)	Expected Unit Sales	Variance of Unit Sales
A	3.50	2000	1000
B	2.00	10,000	6400
C	1.87	8500	1150

   a. What is the expected revenue and variance of the revenue from Product A alone?

   b. What is the company's overall expected revenue and the variance of its revenue?

7.16 A company owns two different computers, which are in separate buildings and operated entirely separately. Based on past history, Computer 1 is expected to break down 5.0 times a year, with a variance of 6, and costing $200 per breakdown. Computer 2 is expected to break down 3.6 times per year, with a variance of 7, and costing $165 per breakdown. What is the company's expected cost for computer breakdowns and the variance of the breakdown cost? What assumption must you make to find the variance? Is this a reasonable assumption?

7.17 Flip the probability tree shown in Figure 7.21.

7.18 Figure 7.22 shows part of an influence diagram for a chemical that is considered potentially carcinogenic. How would you describe the relationship between the test results and the field results?

7.19 Let CP denote carcinogenic potential, TR test results, and FR field results. Suppose that for Figure 7.22 we have the following probabilities:

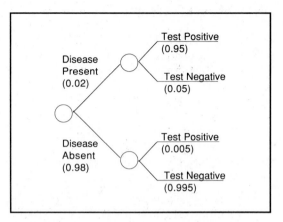

FIGURE 7.21   *A Probability Tree Representing the Diagnostic Performance of a Medical Test*

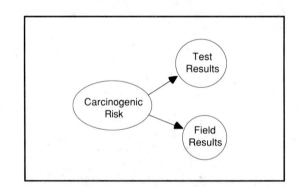

FIGURE 7.22   *An Influence Diagram for a Potentially Carcinogenic Chemical*

P(CP High) = 0.27   P(CP Low) = 0.73

P(TR Positive | CP High) = 0.82   P(TR Positive | CP Low) = 0.21
P(TR Negative | CP High) = 0.18   P(TR Negative | CP Low) = 0.79

P(FR Positive | CP High) = 0.95   P(FR Positive | CP Low) = 0.17
P(FR Negative | CP High) = 0.05   P(FR Negative | CP Low) = 0.83.

Find the following:

P(TR Positive and FR Positive | CP High)
P(TR Positive and FR Negative | CP High)
P(TR Negative and FR Negative | CP Low)
P(TR Negative and FR Positive | CP Low).

◇ QUESTIONS AND PROBLEMS

7.20   Linda is 31 years old, single, outspoken, and very bright. She majored in philosophy. As a student, she was deeply concerned with issues of discrimination and social justice, and also participated in antinuclear demonstrations. Use your judgment to rank the following statements by their probability, using 1 for the most probable statement and 8 for the least probable:

a. Linda is a teacher in an elementary school.

b. Linda works in a bookstore and takes Yoga classes.

c. Linda is active in the feminist movement.

d. Linda is a psychiatric social worker.

e. Linda is a member of the League of Women Voters.

f. Linda is a bank teller.

g. Linda is an insurance salesperson.

h. Linda is a bank teller and is active in the feminist movement.

Source: Tversky, Amos, and Daniel Kahneman (1982) "Judgments of and by Representativeness." In D. Kahneman, P. Slovic, and A. Tversky (eds.), *Judgment Under Uncertainty: Heuristics and Biases*, 84–98. Cambridge: Cambridge University Press.

7.21 The description and statements given in Problem 7.20 often elicit responses that are not consistent with probability requirements. If you are like most people, you ranked statement h (Linda is a bank teller and is active in the feminist movement) as more probable than statement f (Linda is a bank teller).

a. Explain why you ranked statements h and f as you did.

b. Statement h is actually a compound event. That is, for h to be true, Linda must be both a bank teller (Event A) and active in the feminist movement (Event B). Thus, statement h is represented by the Event "A *and* B." Use a Venn diagram to explain why statement h must be less probable than statement f.

c. Suppose that you have presented Problem 7.20 to a friend, who ranks statement h as more probable than statement f. Your friend argues as follows: "Well, it's not very likely that Linda is a bank teller in the first place. But if she is a bank teller, then she is very likely to be active in the feminist movement. So h would appear to be more likely than f." How is your friend interpreting statement h? Explain why this is not an appropriate interpretation.

7.22 Draw an influence diagram for the oil-wildcatting problem. Construct the necessary tables represented by the nodes, including the payoff table, and solve the influence diagram. If possible, use a computer program to do this problem.

7.23 Finding the variance and standard deviation for the payoff from Product A in the GPC case at the end of Chapter 4 (page 105) is somewhat complicated because a pricing decision must be made. How would you calculate the variance and standard deviation for Product A's payoff? (Recall the approach we used in calculating expected values. We were able to "prune" decision branches that were suboptimal.)

7.24 Calculate the variance and standard deviation of the payoffs in the final court decision in the Texaco–Pennzoil case as diagrammed in Figure 4.2 (page 69).

7.25 In the oil-wildcatting problem, suppose that the company could collect information from a drilling core sample and analyze it to determine whether a dome structure exists at Site 1. A positive result would indicate the presence of a dome, and a negative result would indicate the absence of a dome. The test is not perfect, however. The test is highly accurate for detecting a dome; if there is a dome, then the test shows a positive result 99% of the time. On the other hand, if there is no dome, the probability of a negative result is only

0.85. Thus, P(+ | Dome) = 0.99 and P(− | No Dome) = 0.85. Use these probabilities, the information given in the example, and Bayes' theorem to find the posterior probabilities P(Dome | +) and P(Dome | −). If the test gives a positive result, which site should be selected? Calculate expected values to support your conclusion! If the test result is negative, which site should be chosen? Again, calculate expected values.

7.26 In Problem 7.25, calculate the probability that the test is positive and a dome structure exists [P(+ and Dome)]. Now calculate the probability of a positive result, a dome structure, and a dry hole [P(+ and Dome and Dry)]. Finally, calculate P(Dome | + and Dry).

7.27 Referring to the oil-wildcatting decision diagrammed in Figure 7.15 (page 190), suppose that the decision maker has not yet assessed P(Dome) for Site 1. Find the value of P(Dome) for which the two sites have the same EMV. If the decision maker believes that P(Dome) is somewhere between 0.55 and 0.65, what action should be taken?

7.28 Again referring to Figure 7.15, suppose the decision maker has not yet assessed P(Dry) for Site 2 or P(Dome) for Site 1. Let P(Dry) = p and P(Dome) = q. Construct a strategy-region graph for this decision problem.

7.29 Refer to Problems 7.18 and 7.19. Calculate P(FR Positive) and P(FR Positive | TR Positive). [*Hints*: P(FR Positive) is a fairly simple calculation. To find P(FR Positive | TR Positive), first let B = FR Positive, C = TR Positive, A = CP High, and $\bar{A}$ = CP Low. Now expand P(FR Positive | TR Positive) using the law of total probability in this form:

$$P(B \mid C) = P(B \mid A, C) \, P(A \mid C) + P(B \mid \bar{A}, C) \, P(\bar{A} \mid C).$$

Now all of the probabilities on the right-hand side can be calculated using the information in the problem.]

Compare P(FR Positive) and P(FR Positive | TR Positive). Would you say that the test results and field results are independent? Why or why not? Discuss the difference between conditional independence and regular independence.

CASE STUDIES

Decision Analysis Monthly

Peter Finch looked at the numbers for the renewals of subscriptions to *Decision Analysis Monthly* magazine. For both May and June he had figures for the percentage of expiring subscriptions that were gift subscriptions, promotional subscriptions, and from previous subscribers. Furthermore, his data showed what proportion of the expiring subscriptions in each category had been renewed. His information is shown in Table 7.3.

Finch was confused as he considered these numbers. Robert Calloway, who had assembled the data, had told him that the overall proportion of renewals had dropped from May to June. But the figures showed clearly that the proportion renewed had increased in each category. How could the overall proportion possibly have gone down? Peter got a pencil and pad of paper to check Calloway's figures. He had to report to his boss this afternoon and wanted to be able to tell him whether these figures represented good news or bad news.

May Subscription Data	Expiring Subscriptions%	Proportion Renewed
Gift Subscriptions	70	0.75
Promotional Subscriptions	20	0.50
Previous Subscribers	10	0.10
Total	100	

June Subscription Data	Expiring Subscriptions%	Proportion Renewed
Gift Subscriptions	45	0.85
Promotional Subscriptions	10	0.60
Previous Subscribers	45	0.20
Total	100	

TABLE 7.3   *Subscription Data for* Decision Analysis Monthly

AIDS

Acquired Immune Deficiency Syndrome (AIDS) is the most frightening disease of the late twentieth century. The disease attacks and disables the immune system, leaving the body open to other diseases and infection. It is almost always fatal. As of July 31,1990, there were 143,286 confirmed AIDS cases in the United States. Even more frightening is the process by which the disease travels through the population. AIDS appears to be caused by a virus (Human T-lymphotropic virus, Type III, or HTLV-III, although more commonly listed as HIV). The virus is transmitted through semen and blood, and may attack virtually anyone who engages in any of several risky behaviors. The extent of the concern about AIDS among public health officials is reflected in the fact that the U.S. Surgeon General's office mailed brochures on AIDS to 107 million households in May and June 1988, the largest single mailing undertaken by the federal government to that time.

When an individual becomes infected, the body produces a special antibody in an effort to counteract the virus. But it can be as long as 12 weeks before these antibodies appear, and it may be years before any signs or symptoms of AIDS infection appear. During this time the individual may not be aware that he or she is infected and thus spread the disease inadvertently. Studies are not conclusive as to the proportion of infected individuals who actually develop AIDS. Early studies suggested that only some 20% of infected individuals develop full-blown cases of AIDS, and another 30% develop AIDS-related symptoms. But a more recent study of San Francisco gay men who were infected years ago concluded that

99% of those with the virus eventually develop AIDS and die of opportunistic diseases.

Because of the delayed reaction of the virus, there are many more infected individuals than reported AIDS cases. Epidemiologists estimate that as many as 1.7 million Americans may be HIV carriers and potentially infectious of others. Because of this and because of the way the disease is transmitted, the best way to prevent its contraction simply is to avoid risky behavior. Do not share drug needles; use a condom during intercourse unless you are certain that your partner is not infected.

If 1.7 million people in the United States *are* HIV-infected, this amounts to an overall rate of approximately 0.76% in a population of 225 million people. The term *seroprevalence* refers to the incidence of HIV in the population. Seroprevalence rates vary dramatically depending on the particular subpopulation. Table 7.4 shows seroprevalence rates for blood donors and military recruits in each of the 50 states plus the District of Columbia and Puerto Rico. For higher-risk groups the seroprevalence rates are much higher. For example, one study showed that 18% of gay and bisexual men in Oregon were infected, and 21% of those who are both gay and intravenous drug users were infected. As many as 50% of the gay men in San Francisco possibly are infected.

The best tests available for AIDS detect the antibodies rather than the virus. Two such tests are generally available and widely used. The first is the *enzyme-linked immunosorbent assay* (ELISA). An individual is considered to have a positive result on the ELISA test only if both of two separate trials yield positive results. ELISA test kits are manufactured by several pharmaceutical companies, and Petricciani (1985) reports on the performance of the kits from three major manufacturers. In a situation such as this, performance refers to the probabilities associated with correct diagnosis. The probability that an infected individual tests positive, P(ELISA + | Infected), is called the *sensitivity* of the test. The probability that an uninfected individual tests negative, P(ELISA − | Not Infected), is called the *specificity* of the test. A negative result for an infected individual is called a *false negative*, and a positive result for someone who is not infected is called a *false positive*. An ideal test would have 100% sensitivity and 100% specificity, giving correct diagnosis all the time with neither false negatives nor false positives. The three ELISA kits tested by Petricciani had sensitivity and specificity rates as shown in Table 7.5. In actual field use, the sensitivity of the tests may be lower — and the false negative rate higher — because some infected individuals are tested before antibodies appear in the blood.

The *Western Blot* test generally is used to confirm or disconfirm a positive ELISA result. For some time the Western Blot was considered to be a perfect test, but this may not be true. The Western Blot is a labor-intensive test, the results of which require interpretation by a skilled laboratory technician. Little information is available regarding the test's actual performance in field trials. The *Harvard Medical School Health Letter* (September 1987) reports that, for uninfected individuals with a positive ELISA result, the Western Blot could yield as many as 5% false positives. Another study of blood donors in the Atlanta metropolitan area showed that the Western Blot also can give false negative re-

State	Seroprevalence (%)		State	Seroprevalence (%)	
	Military Recruits	Blood Donors		Military Recruits	Blood Donors
Alabama	0.07	0.020	Montana	0.00	0.008
Alaska	0.02	—	Nebraska	0.03	0.002
Arizona	0.06	0.014	Nevada	0.10	0.019
Arkansas	0.08	0.025	New Hampshire	0.01	0.011
California	0.14	0.026	New Jersey	0.30	0.020
Colorado	0.06	0.008	New Mexico	0.04	0.014
Connecticut	0.11	0.004	New York	0.34	0.040
Delaware	0.19	0.039	North Carolina	0.08	0.016
District of Columbia	0.96	0.039	North Dakota	0.00	0.003
Florida	0.18	0.017	Ohio	0.04	0.009
Georgia	0.15	0.032	Oklahoma	0.05	0.016
Hawaii	0.11	—	Oregon	0.05	0.002
Idaho	0.03	0.008	Pennsylvania	0.08	0.020
Illinois	0.10	0.130	Puerto Rico	0.47	—
Indiana	0.07	0.006	Rhode Island	0.04	0.004
Iowa	0.04	0.007	South Carolina	0.09	0.016
Kansas	0.05	0.008	South Dakota	0.01	0.003
Kentucky	0.03	0.013	Tennessee	0.06	0.013
Louisiana	0.10	0.025	Texas	0.12	0.017
Maine	0.00	0.011	Utah	0.04	0.019
Maryland	0.33	0.039	Vermont	0.03	0.011
Massachusetts	0.13	0.004	Virginia	0.07	0.024
Michigan	0.05	0.009	Washington	0.04	0.002
Minnesota	0.04	0.004	West Virginia	0.08	0.009
Mississippi	0.04	0.025	Wisconsin	0.04	0.004
Missouri	0.12	0.011	Wyoming	0.02	0.008

TABLE 7.4   *Seroprevalence Rates for Military Recruits and Blood Donors in the United States*

Source: Oregon AIDS Surveillance Report, 1st Quarter, 1988, State of Oregon Health Division. Data for military recruits were collected from October 1985 to September 1987. Data for blood donors were collected from July 1986 to June 1987. Some states are grouped together to determine aggregate seroprevalence rates.

sults for an individual with a positive ELISA. The false negative rate could be as high as 12.5%. Thus, individuals with a positive ELISA and negative Western Blot cannot be fully confident that they do not have the disease.

QUESTIONS

1. Given that the tests are not perfect, it is worthwhile to calculate the probability of being infected, given the various combinations of results on the tests.

Manufacturer	Sensitivity $P(+ \mid Inf)$	False Negative Rate $P(- \mid Inf)$	Specificity $P(- \mid Not\ Inf)$	False Positive Rate $P(+ \mid Not\ Inf)$
Abbott	0.934	0.066	0.998	0.002
ENI	0.996	0.004	0.992	0.008
Litton	0.989	0.011	0.996	0.004
Average	0.973	0.027	0.995	0.005

TABLE 7.5   *Performance of ELISA Test Kits from Three Major Manufacturers*

Source: Petricciani (1985). These figures are based on repeated tests.

Calculate the probability of being infected given a positive ELISA test result, P(Inf | ELISA+). Use as your prior probability the P(Inf) = 0.0076, the estimated overall rate of infection in the United States. For P(ELISA+ | Inf) and P(ELISA+ | Not Inf), use the average figures from Table 7.5.

2. Create a graph like Figure 7.20 that shows P(Inf | ELISA+) as a function of P(Inf), the prior probability or seroprevalence rate. Indicate on your graph the appropriate prior probability for military recruits in New York, blood donors in Wyoming, and gay men in Oregon.

3. Repeat Questions 1 and 2, but this time finding the probability of being infected given a negative ELISA result, P(Inf | ELISA–).

4. Calculate the probability of being infected given a positive ELISA test result and a positive Western Blot, P(Inf | ELISA+, WB+) and the probability of being infected given a positive ELISA and negative Western Blot, P(Inf | ELISA+, WB–). [*Hint*: All of the information in the case regarding the performance of the Western Blot assumes a positive ELISA. The calculations required here also can be done with Bayes' theorem, using as the prior probability P(Inf | ELISA+), the quantity calculated in Question 1.]

5. Create graphs like those for Questions 2 and 3 that show P(Inf | ELISA+, WB+) and P(Inf | ELISA+, WB–) as functions of the prior probability P(Inf). [*Hint*: Note that this prior probability enters the calculations through P(Inf | ELISA+).]

6. Some public health officials are calling for widespread testing for HIV infection. Certainly there is considerable value to society in identifying HIV carriers, although there are costs inherent in incorrect diagnoses. For example, suppose that you were forced to be tested, and both ELISA and Western Blot tests gave a positive result. Imagine that a later tissue culture revealed no HIV exposure. Thus, for some time you would have been falsely labeled as an AIDS carrier. On the other hand, suppose that the tests had been falsely negative. Then you may have engaged in risky behavior under the assumption

that you had no infection. Discuss the social trade-offs of costs and benefits that are involved in using imperfect screening tests for AIDS.

Sources: This case study was prepared using several publications. The key ones are: "AIDS Tests: When and for Whom?" *Harvard Medical School Health Letter,* September 1987; "A New Attack Against AIDS," *Newsweek,* June 13, 1987, 66–67; Petricciani, J.C. (1985) "Licensed Tests for Antibody to HTLV-III: Sensitivity and Specificity." *Annals of Internal Medicine,* 103, 726–729.

◇ **REFERENCES**

Probability basics appear in a wide variety of books on probability and statistics, presenting the material at various levels of sophistication. Good lower-level introductions can be found in elementary statistics textbooks such as McClave and Benson (1988), Mendenhall et al. (1989), Sincich (1989), and Wonnacott and Wonnacott (1984). Two excellent resources written at higher levels are Olkin, Gleser, and Derman (1980) and Feller (1968).

All decision-analysis textbooks seem to have at least one example about oil wildcatting. True, this is the quintessential decision-analysis problem, and includes many sources of uncertainty, concerns about attitudes toward risk, and opportunities for gathering information. But many problems have these characteristics. Probably the real reason for the oil-wildcatting scenario is that, in 1960, C. J. Grayson published one of the first applied dissertations using decision theory, and its area of application was oil drilling. Decision theorists ever since have used oil drilling as an example!

FELLER, W. (1968) *An Introduction to Probability Theory and Its Applications, Vol. 1,* 3rd ed. New York: Wiley.

GRAYSON, C. J. (1960) *Decisions Under Uncertainty: Drilling Decisions by Oil and Gas Operators.* Cambridge, MA: Division of Research, Harvard Business School.

MCCLAVE, J. T., and P. G. BENSON (1988) *Statistics for Business and Economics,* 4th ed. San Francisco: Dellen.

MENDENHALL, W., J. REINMUTH, and R. BEAVER (1989) *Statistics for Management and Economics,* 6th ed. Boston: PWS-KENT.

OLKIN, I., L. J. GLESER, and C. DERMAN (1980) *Probability Models and Applications.* New York: Macmillan.

SINCICH, T. (1989) *Business Statistics by Example,* 3rd ed. San Francisco: Dellen.

WONNACOTT, T. H., and R. J. WONNACOTT (1984) *Introductory Statistics for Business and Economics.* New York: Wiley.

◇ **EPILOGUE**

JOHN HINCKLEY. Hinckley's defense attorney was not permitted to introduce the CAT scan of Hinckley's brain. In spite of this, the jury's verdict found Hinckley "not guilty by reason of insanity" on all counts, and he was committed to Saint Elizabeth's Hospital in Washington, D.C. The trial caused a substantial commotion among the public, many people viewing the insanity plea and the resulting verdict as a miscarriage of justice. Because of this, some lawmakers initiated efforts to tighten legal loopholes associated with the insanity plea.

AIDS.   New diagnostic tests for AIDS are under continual development as research on this frightening disease continues. When the case study was originally written in 1988, the information was up-to-date. More recent reports, however, indicate that new RNA-based tests are being developed and may be generally available within a year or so. In spite of this, the ELISA and Western Blot tests described in the case study are typical of medical diagnostic tests in general, and the analysis performed shows how to evaluate such tests.   ◆

Subjective Probability

All of us are used to making judgments regarding uncertainty, and we make them frequently. Often our statements involve informal evaluations of the uncertainties that surround an event. Statements such as "The weather is likely to be sunny today," "I doubt that the Democrats will win the next presidential election," or "The risk of cancer from exposure to cigarette smoke is small" all involve a personal, subjective assessment of uncertainty at a fundamental level. As we have seen, subjective assessments of uncertainty are an important element of decision analysis. A basic tenet of modern decision analysis is that subjective judgments of uncertainty can be made in terms of probability. In this chapter we will explore how to make such judgments and what they imply.

Although most people can cope with uncertainty informally, perhaps, it is not clear that it is worthwhile to develop a more rigorous approach to measure the uncertainty that we feel. Just how important is it to deal with uncertainty in a careful and systematic way? The following vignettes demonstrate the importance of uncertainty assessments in a variety of public policy situations.

UNCERTAINTY AND PUBLIC POLICY

FRUIT FROST. Farmers occasionally must decide whether to protect a crop from potentially damaging frost. The decision must be made on the basis of weather forecasts that often are expressed in terms of probability (U.S. National Weather Service is responsible for providing these forecasts). Protecting a crop can be costly, but less so than the potential damage. Because of such potential losses, care in assessing probabilities is important.

EARTHQUAKE PREDICTION. Geologists are beginning to develop ways to assess the probability of major earthquakes for specific locations. In 1988 the U.S. Geological Survey published a report that estimated a 0.60 probability of a major earthquake (7.5–8 on the Richter scale) occurring in Southern California along the southern portion of the San Andreas Fault within the next 30 years. Such an earthquake could cause catastrophic damage in the Los Angeles metropolitan area.

ENVIRONMENTAL IMPACT STATEMENTS.   Federal and state regulations governing environmental impact statements typically require assessments of the risks associated with proposed projects. These risk assessments often are based on the probabilities of various hazards occurring. For example, in projects involving pesticides and herbicides, the chances of cancer and other health risks are assessed.

PUBLIC POLICY AND SCIENTIFIC RESEARCH.   Often scientists learn of the possible presence of conditions that may require action by the government. But action sometimes must be taken without absolute certainty that a condition exists. For example, scientists in 1988 reported that the Earth had begun to warm up because of the "Greenhouse effect," a condition presumably resulting from various kinds of pollution and the destruction of tropical forests. James Hansen of NASA expressed the problem in probabilistic terms, saying that he was 99% certain that the Greenhouse effect was upon us.

◆

Some of the above examples include more complicated and more formal probability assessments as well as subjective judgments. For example, the National Weather Service forecasts are based in part on a large-scale computer model of the global atmospheric system. The computer output is just one bit of information used by a forecaster to develop an official forecast that involves his or her subjective judgment regarding the uncertainty in local weather. Other risk assessments often are based on cancer studies performed on laboratory animals. The results of such studies must be extrapolated subjectively to real-world conditions to derive potential effects on humans. Because of the high stakes involved in these examples and others, it is important for policy makers to exercise care in assessing the uncertainties they face.

At a reduced scale, personal decisions also involve high stakes and uncertainty. Personal investment decisions and career decisions are two kinds of decisions that typically involve substantial uncertainty. Perhaps even harder to deal with are personal medical decisions in which the outcomes of possible treatments are not known in advance. If you suffer from chronic chest pain, would you undergo elective surgery in an attempt to eliminate the pain? Because of the risks associated with open heart surgery, this decision must be made under a condition of uncertainty. You would want to think carefully about your chances on the operating table, considering not only statistics regarding the operation but also what you know about your own health and the skills of your surgeon and the medical staff.

◆ PROBABILITY: A SUBJECTIVE INTERPRETATION

Many introductory textbooks present probability in terms of long-run frequency. For example, if a die is thrown many times, it would land with the five on top approximately one-sixth of the time; thus, the probability of a five on a given throw of the die is one-sixth. In many cases, however, it does not make sense to think about probabilities as long-run frequencies. For example, in assessing the probability that the California condor will be extinct by the year 2010 or the probability of a major nuclear power plant failure in the next 10 years, thinking in terms of long-run frequencies or averages is not reasonable because we cannot rerun the "experiment" many times to find out what proportion of the times the condor becomes extinct or a power plant fails. We often hear references to the chance that a catastrophic nuclear holocaust will destroy life on the planet. Let us not even consider the idea of a long-run frequency in this case!

Even when a long-run frequency interpretation might seem appropriate, there are times when an event has occurred, but we remain unsure of the final outcome. For example, consider the following:

1. You have flipped a coin that has landed on the floor. Neither you nor anyone else has seen it. What is the probability that it is heads?
2. What is the probability that Oregon beat Stanford in their 1970 football game?
3. What is the probability that the coin that was flipped at the beginning of that game came up heads?
4. What is the probability that Millard Fillmore was President in 1850?

For most of us the answers to these questions are not obvious. In every case the actual event has taken place. But unless you know the answer, you are uncertain.

The point of this discussion is that we can view uncertainty in a way slightly different from the traditional long-run frequency approach. In Examples 1 and 3 above, there was a random event (flipping the coin), but the randomness is no longer in the coin. You are uncertain about the outcome because you do not know what the outcome was; the uncertainty is in your mind. In all of the examples, the uncertainty lies in your own brain cells. When we think of uncertainty and probability in this way, we are adopting a subjective interpretation, with a probability representing an individual's *degree of belief* that an event will occur.

Decision analysis requires numbers for probabilities, not phrases such as "common," "unusual," "toss-up," "rare," and so on. In fact, there is considerable evidence from the cognitive psychologists who study such things that the same phrase has different connotations to different people in different contexts. For example, in one study (Beyth-Marom, 1982), the phrase "there is a non-negligible chance . . ." was given specific probability interpretations by individuals that ranged from below 0.36 to above 0.77. Furthermore, it may be the case that we interpret such phrases differently depending on the context. The phrase "a slight chance that it will rain tomorrow" may carry a very different probability interpretation than the phrase "a slight chance that the space shuttle will explode."

One of the main topics of this chapter is how to assess probabilities — the numbers — that are consistent with one's subjective beliefs. Of the many concepts in decision analysis, the idea of subjective probability is one that seems to give students trouble. Some are uncomfortable assessing their degree of belief, because they think there must be a "correct" answer. There are no correct answers when it comes to subjective judgment; different people have different degrees of belief and hence will assess different probabilities.

If you disagree with a friend about the probability that your favorite team will win a game, do you try to persuade your friend that your probability is better? You might discuss different aspects of the situation, such as which team has the home advantage, which players are injured, and so forth. But even after sharing your information, the two of you still might disagree. Then what? You might place a bet. For many people, betting reflects their personal subjective probabilities. Some people bet on anything even if the outcome is based on some "objectively" random event (flipping a coin, playing cards, and so on). One of the most common bets might be investing — betting — in the stock market. For example, you might be willing to purchase a stock now if you think its value is likely to increase.

We will begin with the assessment of probabilities. We will show how you can view different situations in terms of the bets you might place involving small cash amounts or in terms of hypothetical lotteries. Following the discussion of the assessment of discrete probabilities, we will see how to deal with continuous probability distributions (the fan or crescent shape in the range-of-risk dilemma that was introduced in Chapter 3). Special psychological phenomena are associated with probability assessment, and we will explore the cognitive heuristics that we tend to use in probability assessment. The last two sections discuss procedures for decomposing probability assessments and what it means to be "coherent" in assessing probabilities.

◆ ASSESSING DISCRETE PROBABILITIES

There are three basic methods for assessing probabilities. The first is simply to have the decision maker assess the probability directly by asking, "What is your belief regarding the probability that event such-and-such will occur?" The decision maker may or may not be able to give an answer to a direct question like this and may place little confidence in the answer given.

The second method is to ask about the bets that the decision maker would be willing to place. The idea is to find a specific amount to win or lose such that the decision maker is simply indifferent about which side of the bet to take. If he or she is indifferent about which side to bet, then the expected value of the bet must be the same regardless of which is taken. Given these conditions, we can then solve for the probability.

As an example, suppose that the Los Angeles Lakers are playing the Detroit Pistons in the NBA finals this year. We are interested in finding out the decision maker's probability that the Lakers will win the championship. The decision maker is willing to take either of the following two bets:

Bet 1	Win $X if the Lakers win.
	Lose $Y if the Lakers lose.
Bet 2	Lose $X if the Lakers win.
	Win $Y if the Lakers lose.

In these bets, X and Y can be thought of as the amounts that each person puts into the "pot." The winner of the bet takes all of the money therein. Bets 1 and 2 are symmetric in the sense that they are simply opposite sides of the same bet. Figure 8.1 displays the decision tree that the decision maker faces.

   If the decision maker is indifferent between Bets 1 and 2, then in his or her mind their expected values must be equal:

$$X \, P(\text{Lakers Win}) - Y \, [1 - P(\text{Lakers Win})] =$$
$$- \, X \, P(\text{Lakers Win}) + Y \, [1 - P(\text{Lakers Win})],$$

which implies that

$$2\{X \, P(\text{Lakers Win}) - Y \, [1 - P(\text{Lakers Win})]\} = 0.$$

We can divide through by 2 and expand the left-hand side to get

$$X \, P(\text{Lakers Win}) - Y + Y \, P(\text{Lakers Win}) = 0.$$

Collecting terms gives

$$(X + Y) \, P(\text{Lakers Win}) - Y = 0,$$

which reduces to

$$P(\text{Lakers Win}) = \frac{Y}{[X + Y]} \, .$$

For example, a friend of yours might be willing to take either side of the following bet:

Win $2.50 if the Lakers win.

Lose $3.80 if the Lakers lose.

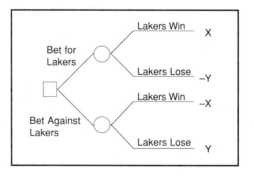

FIGURE 8.1 *Decision Tree Representation for Assessing Subjective Probability via the Betting Method*
The assessor's problem is to find X and Y so that he or she is indifferent about betting for or against the Lakers.

His subjective probability that the Lakers win, as implied by his betting behavior, is simply $3.80/[2.50 + 3.80] = 0.603$.

Finding the bet for which a decision maker would be willing to take either side is fairly straightforward. Begin by offering a bet that is highly favorable to one side or the other, and note which side of the bet she would take. Then offer a bet that favors the opposite side, and ask which side of this new bet she would prefer. Continue offering bets that first favor one side and then the other, gradually adjusting the payoffs on each round. By adjusting the bet appropriately, making it more or less attractive depending on the response to the previous bet, the indifference point can be found.

The third approach is to ask the decision maker to compare two lottery-like games, each of which can result in either Prize A or Prize B. For convenience, set it up so that the decision maker prefers A to B. (Prize A might be a fully paid two-week vacation in Hawaii, and Prize B a coupon for a free beer.) We would ask the decision maker to compare the lottery

Win Prize A (Win) if the Lakers win.

Win Prize B (Lose) if the Lakers lose.

with the lottery

Win Prize A with known probability p.

Win Prize B with probability $1 - p$.

The decision-tree representation is shown in Figure 8.2. The second lottery is called the *reference lottery*, for which the probability mechanism must be well specified. A typical mechanism is drawing a colored ball from an urn in which the proportion of colored balls is known to be p. Another mechanism is to use a "wheel of fortune" with a known area that represents "win"; if the wheel were

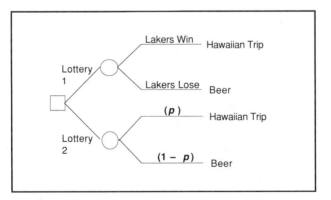

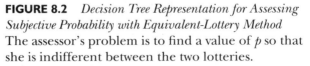

FIGURE 8.2 *Decision Tree Representation for Assessing Subjective Probability with Equivalent-Lottery Method*
The assessor's problem is to find a value of p so that she is indifferent between the two lotteries.

spun and the pointer landed in the win area, then the decision maker would win Prize A.

Once the mechanism is understood by the decision maker, the trick is to adjust the probability of winning in the reference lottery until the decision maker is indifferent between the two lotteries. Indifference in this case means that the decision maker has no preference between the two lotteries, but slightly changing probability p makes one or the other lottery clearly preferable. If the decision maker is indifferent, then her subjective probability that the Lakers win must be the p that makes her indifferent.

How do we find the p that makes the decision maker indifferent? The basic idea is to start with some p_1 and ask which lottery she prefers. If she prefers the reference lottery, then p_1 must be too high; she perceives that the chance of winning in the reference lottery is higher. In this case, choose p_2 less than p_1 and ask her preference again. Continue adjusting the probability in the reference lottery until the indifference point is found. It is important to begin with extremely wide brackets and to converge on the indifference probability slowly. Going slowly allows the decision maker plenty of time to think hard about the assessment, and she probably will be much happier with the final result than she would be if rushed. This is an important point for finding your own probability assessments. Be patient, and home in on your indifference point gradually.

The wheel of fortune is a particularly useful way to assess probabilities. By changing the setting of the wheel to represent the probability of winning in the reference lottery, it is possible to find the decision maker's indifference point quite easily. Furthermore, the use of the wheel avoids the bias that can occur from using only "even" probabilities (0.1, 0.2, 0.3, and so on). With the wheel, a probability can be any value between 0 and 1. Figure 8.3 shows the screen for a simple computer program that permits the decision maker to change the setting of the wheel in order to find the indifference point. Some of the decision-analysis programs we have discussed include such wheels as probability-assessment aids. Figures 8.4 and 8.5 show probability-assessment screens from DAVID and ARBORIST.

The last step in assessing probabilities is to check for consistency. Many problems will require the decision maker to assess several interrelated probabilities. It is important that these probabilities be consistent among themselves; they should obey the probability laws introduced in Chapter 7. For example, if P(A), P($B \mid A$), and P(A and B) were all assessed, then it should be the case that P(A)P($B \mid A$) = P(A and B). If a set of assessed probabilities is found to be inconsistent, then the decision maker should reconsider and modify the assessments as necessary to achieve consistency.

♦ ASSESSING CONTINUOUS PROBABILITIES

The premise of this chapter is that it always is possible to model a decision maker's uncertainty using probabilities. How would this be done in the case of an uncertain but continuous quantity? We already have learned how to assess individual probabilities; we will apply this technique to assess several cumulative

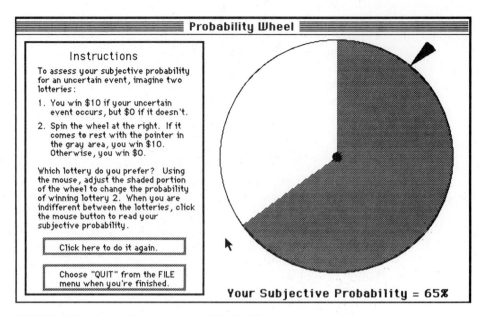

FIGURE 8.3   *Screen Display from a Wheel of Fortune Probability-Assessment Program for the Apple Macintosh Computer*
The "win" (shaded) portion of the wheel changes as the user moves the mouse pointer around the screen. Clicking the mouse button calculates and displays the proportion of the wheel that is shaded.

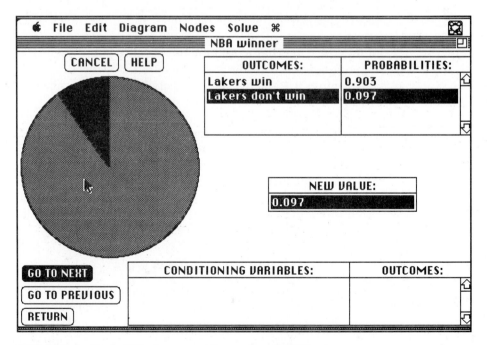

FIGURE 8.4   *Probability-Assessment Screen from DAVID*

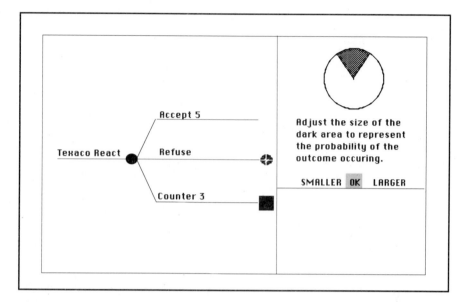

FIGURE 8.5   *Assessing a Probability with ARBORIST*

probabilities and then use these to plot a rough CDF. We will discuss two strategies for assessing a subjective CDF.

Let us reexamine the example of the movie star's age that we introduced in Chapter 7 (page 182). As you recall, the problem was to derive a probability distribution representing a probability assessor's uncertainty regarding a particular movie star's age. In that example, several probabilities were found, and these were transformed into cumulative probabilities.

A typical cumulative assessment would be to assess $P(\text{Age} \leq a)$, where a is a particular value. For example, consider $P(\text{Age} \leq 46)$. The event "Age $\leq$ 46" is an event just like any other, and so a decision maker could assess the probability of this event by using any of the three techniques discussed above. For example, a wheel of fortune might be used as an assessment aid to find the probability p that would make the decision maker indifferent between the two lotteries shown in Figure 8.6.

Using this technique to find a CDF amounts to assessing the cumulative probability for a number of points, plotting them, and drawing a smooth curve through the plotted points. Suppose the following assessments were made:

$$P(\text{Age} \leq 29) = 0.00$$
$$P(\text{Age} \leq 40) = 0.05$$
$$P(\text{Age} \leq 44) = 0.50$$
$$P(\text{Age} \leq 50) = 0.85$$
$$P(\text{Age} \leq 65) = 1.00.$$

Plotting these cumulative probabilities would result in the graph that we originally drew in Figure 7.9, and which is reproduced here as Figure 8.7.

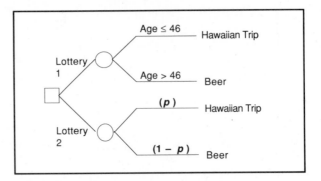

FIGURE 8.6   *Decision-Tree Representation for Assessing P(Age ≤ 46) in Movie Star Example*

The strategy that we have used here is to choose a few values from the horizontal axis (some ages) and then to find the cumulative probabilities that correspond to those ages. This is a perfectly reasonable strategy for assessing a CDF. Another strategy builds up the graph the other way around. That is, we pick a few cumulative probabilities from the vertical axis and find the corresponding ages.

Let us consider this strategy for a moment. Suppose we pick probability 0.35. Now we want the number of years $a_{0.35}$ such that $P(\text{Age} \le a_{0.35}) = 0.35$. The number $a_{0.35}$ is called the 0.35 *fractile* of the distribution. In general, the p fractile of a distribution for X is the value x_p such that $P(X \le x_p) = p$. We can see from Figure 8.7 that the 0.35 fractile of the distribution is approximately 42 years. We

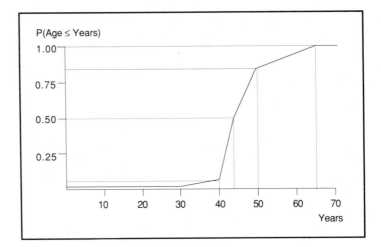

FIGURE 8.7   *Cumulative Distribution Function for Movie Star's Age*

know from the assessments that were made that the 0.05 fractile is 40 years, the 0.50 fractile is 44 years, and the 0.85 fractile is 50 years.

How could you go about assessing a fractile? Figure 8.8 shows a decision tree that represents the process for assessing the 0.35 fractile. In Lottery B, or the reference lottery, the probability of winning is fixed at 0.35. The assessment task is to adjust the number x in Lottery A until indifference between the lotteries is achieved. Indifference would mean that the probability of winning in Lottery A must be 0.35. Hence, there must be a 0.35 chance that X is less than or equal to the assessed x. By definition, then, x must be the 0.35 fractile of the distribution.

It is important to recognize the difference between Figures 8.7 and 8.8. In Figure 8.7 we adjusted p in the reference lottery to find indifference. To assess the 0.35 fractile in Figure 8.8, we fix the probability in the reference lottery at 0.35, and we adjust x in the upper lottery.

The term *fractile* is a general one, but other similar terms are useful for referring to specific fractiles. The idea of a *median* may be familiar. If we can find an amount such that the uncertain quantity is as likely to be above as below that amount, then we have found the median. The median is defined as the 0.50 fractile; the median for the movie star's age is 44 years. We also can speak of *quartiles.* The first quartile is an amount such that P($X \le$ first quartile) = 0.25, or the 0.25 fractile. In our example, the first quartile appears to be around 42 years. Likewise, the third quartile is defined as the 0.75 fractile. The third quartile of our example is approximately 48 years because P(Age $\le$ 48) is approximately 0.75. The second quartile is, of course, the median. Fractiles also can be expressed as *percentiles.* For example, the 90th percentile is defined as the 0.90 fractile of a distribution.

As mentioned above, we can exploit this idea of fractiles so as to assess a continuous distribution. In general, the strategy will be to select specific cumula-

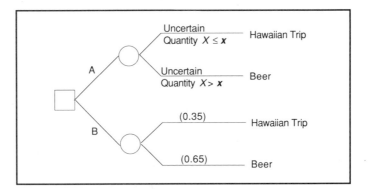

FIGURE 8.8 *Decision Tree for Assessing the 0.35 Fractile of a Continuous Distribution for* X
The decision maker's task is to find x in Lottery A that results in indifference between the two lotteries.

tive probabilities and assess the corresponding fractiles. The first step might be to find the uncertain quantity's extreme values. How small or large could this quantity be? Because it often is difficult, and sometimes even misleading, to think in terms of probabilities of 0 or 1, we take the 0.05 and 0.95 fractiles (or the fifth and 95th percentiles). In our movie star example, the 0.05 fractile is a value $a_{0.05}$ such that there is only a 5% chance that the movie star's age would be less than or equal to $a_{0.05}$. Likewise, the 0.95 fractile is the value $a_{0.95}$ such that there is a 95% chance that the age would be less than or equal to $a_{0.95}$. Informally, we might think of these as the smallest and largest values that the uncertain quantity could reasonably assume. Anything beyond these values would be quite surprising.

After assessing the extreme points, the first and third quartiles might be assessed. For example, Figure 8.9 shows the decision tree that corresponds to the assessment for the first quartile in our example. The task would be for the decision maker to find an age a that makes the two lotteries equivalent. The value of a that leaves the decision maker indifferent is the first quartile of the distribution and can be plotted as a point on the decision maker's subjective CDF. A similar procedure should be followed to assess the third quartile.

Next assess the median. To do this, the decision maker must find a point such that the uncertain quantity is equally likely to fall above or below this point. This assessment can be done in essentially the same way as the assessments for quartiles. Having assessed the extreme points, the median, and the quartiles, we have five points on the cumulative distribution function. These points can be plotted on a graph, and a smooth curve drawn through the points.

As an example, suppose that you have developed a new soft pretzel that you are thinking about marketing through sidewalk kiosks. You are interested in assessing the annual demand for the pretzels as a continuous quantity. You might make the following assessments:

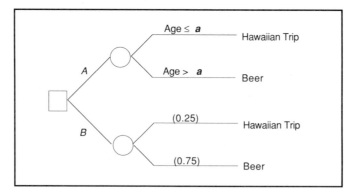

FIGURE 8.9 *Decision Tree for Assessing the First Quartile of the Distribution for the Movie Star's Age*
The assessment task is to adjust the number of years a in Lottery A to achieve indifference.

- 0.05 fractile for demand = 5000.
- 0.95 fractile for demand = 45,000
- There is a 0.25 chance that demand will be below 16,000.
- There is a 0.75 chance that demand will be below 31,000.
- Demand is just as likely to be above 23,000 as below or equal to 23,000.

The last three assessments establish the first quartile to be 16,000, the third quartile to be 31,000, and the median to be 23,000. Plotting the points, we obtain the graph in Figure 8.10. A smooth curve drawn through the five points represents your subjective cumulative probability distribution of demand for the new pretzels.

Once we assess a continuous distribution, how can we use it? Apparently, our motivation for assessing it in the first place was that we faced uncertainty in the form of a range-of-risk dilemma. In our example, we may be deciding whether to go ahead and market the pretzels. We need the probability distribution to fill out our decision tree, calculate expected values, and find an optimum choice. But how will we calculate an expected value for this subjectively assessed distribution? There are several possibilities, some of which we will explore in later chapters. For example, in the next chapter, we will see how to fit a theoretical distribution to an assessed one; we then can use the expected value of the theoretical distribution. Advanced simulation and numerical integration techniques also are possible. At this point, however, we will content ourselves with some simple and useful approximation techniques.

The easiest way to use a continuous distribution in a decision tree or influence diagram is to approximate it with a discrete distribution. The basic idea is to find a few representative points in the distribution and then to assign those points specific probability values. A particularly simple approach, from

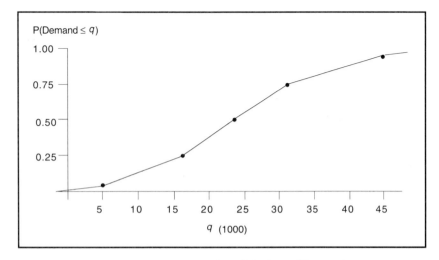

FIGURE 8.10   *A Subjectively Assessed CDF for Pretzel Demand*

Keefer and Bodily (1983), is called the *extended Pearson–Tukey method*. This three-point approximation uses the median and the 0.05 and 0.95 fractiles. Thus, one primary advantage of this method is that we can use assessments that already have been made. In assigning probabilities, the median gets probability 0.63, and the 0.05 and 0.95 fractiles each have probability 0.185. (These probabilities do not appear to admit any obvious interpretation. They arise from a calculus-based analysis of the probability distribution, and in a sense represent approximations to the expected values within certain intervals of the distribution.) For the pretzel-demand example, we can create the three-point discrete approximation as in Figure 8.11. The extended Pearson–Tukey method works best for approximating symmetric distributions. Given its simplicity, however, it also works surprisingly well for asymmetric distributions.

A slightly more complex approximation technique is to find *bracket medians*. Suppose that we consider an interval in which an uncertain quantity could fall: $a \le X \le b$. The bracket median is a value m^* between a and b such that $P(a \le X \le m^*) = P(m^* \le X \le b)$. Figure 8.12 shows how a bracket median relates to the underlying CDF. The bracket median divides the probability of the original interval in half, and is associated with a cumulative probability halfway between the cumulative probabilities for a and b.

To use bracket medians, the typical approach is to break the subjective probability distribution into several equally likely intervals and then to assess the bracket median for each interval. In practice, three, four, or five intervals are typically used; the more intervals used, the better the approximation. With five intervals, the assessor would use the extreme points and the 0.20, 0.40, 0.60, and 0.80 fractiles. These would correspond to cumulative probabilities as follows:

$$P(X \le x_{0.0}) = 0.00$$
$$P(X \le x_{0.2}) = 0.20$$
$$P(X \le x_{0.4}) = 0.40$$

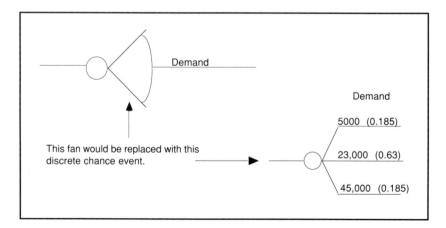

FIGURE 8.11   *Replacing a Continuous Distribution with a Three-Branch Discrete Uncertainty Node in a Decision Tree*

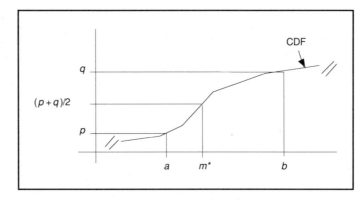

FIGURE 8.12 *Finding the Bracket Median for the Interval Between* a *and* b

The cumulative probabilities p and q correspond to a and b, respectively. Bracket median m^* is associated with a cumulative probability that is halfway between p and q.

$$P(X \leq x_{0.6}) = 0.60$$
$$P(X \leq x_{0.8}) = 0.80$$
$$P(X \leq x_{1.0}) = 1.00.$$

Because these six points define five intervals, we need five bracket medians $(m_1 - m_5)$ with the five cumulative probabilities

$$P(X \leq m_1) = 0.10$$
$$P(X \leq m_2) = 0.30$$
$$P(X \leq m_3) = 0.50$$
$$P(X \leq m_4) = 0.70$$
$$P(X \leq m_5) = 0.90.$$

These bracket medians can be assessed either by using the general assessment technique for assessing fractiles above or by assessing the value m_i so that X is just as likely to be between the lower interval bound and m_i as between m_i and the upper bound.

Figure 8.13 shows the determination of five bracket medians for the pretzel demand distribution. These bracket medians then can be used as "representative points" for their respective brackets. Thus, the discrete approximation to the original distribution would have

$$P(X = m_1 = 8) \ = 0.20$$
$$P(X = m_2 = 18) = 0.20$$
$$P(X = m_3 = 23) = 0.20$$
$$P(X = m_4 = 29) = 0.20$$
$$P(X = m_5 = 39) = 0.20,$$

as shown in Figure 8.14.

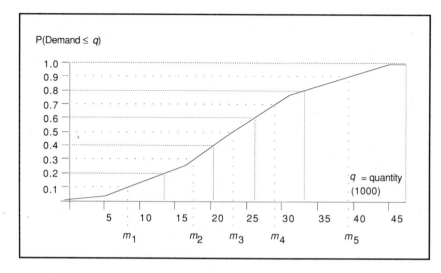

FIGURE 8.13   *Finding Bracket Medians for the Pretzel Demand Distribution*

Both methods that we have described for creating a discrete approximation are straightforward and work reasonably well. The extended Pearson–Tukey method has the advantage of requiring no additional assessments. The advantages of the bracket median approach are its ability to approximate virtually any kind of distribution and the intuitive nature of the bracket median assessments.

Which method should you use? Both work well, but a general strategy exists that dovetails perfectly with the sensitivity-analysis approach we described in

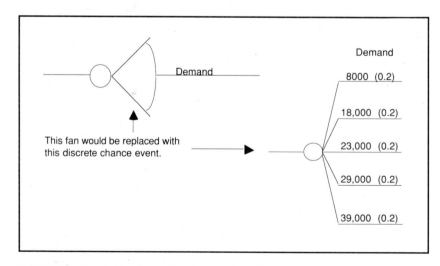

FIGURE 8.14   *Replacing a Continuous Distribution with Bracket Medians in a Decision Tree*

Chapter 5. Suppose that you have constructed a tornado diagram for a decision problem and have identified several variables that are candidates for probabilistic modeling. A simple first step would be to use the extended Pearson–Tukey method with the base value as the median, and the upper and lower values as the 0.95 and 0.05 fractiles, respectively. In many cases, this may be an adequate model of the uncertainty. If not, then it may be worthwhile to use bracket medians to construct a more complete model of the uncertainty.

♦ PITFALLS: HEURISTICS AND BIASES

The methods presented above make probability assessment sound easy. As you probably realize, however, thinking in terms of probabilities is not easy. It takes considerable practice before one is comfortable making probability assessments. Even then, we tend to use rather primitive cognitive techniques to make our probability assessments. Tversky and Kahneman (1974) have labeled these techniques *heuristics*. In general, heuristics can be thought of as rules of thumb for accomplishing tasks. For example, an inventory-control heuristic might be to keep 10% of total yearly demand for any given item on hand. When placing an order for an item that sells some 200 units per year, one then would check the stock and order enough to have 20 units on hand. Heuristics tend to be simple, are easy to perform, and usually do not give optimal answers.

Heuristics for assessing probabilities operate in basically the same way. They are easy and intuitive ways to deal with uncertain situations, but they tend to result in probability assessments that are biased in different ways depending on the heuristic used. In this section we will look at the various heuristics and the biases they can create. Before we begin, however, consider the case of Tom W.

___

TOM W.

"Tom W. is of high intelligence, although lacking in true creativity. He has a need for order and clarity, and for neat and tidy systems in which every detail finds its appropriate place. His writing is rather dull and mechanical, occasionally enlivened by somewhat corny puns and by flashes of imagination of the sci-fi type. He has a strong drive for competence. He seems to have little feel and little sympathy for other people and does not enjoy interacting with others. Self-centered, he nonetheless has a deep moral sense."

The preceding personality sketch of Tom W. was written during his senior year in high school by a psychologist on the basis of projective tests. Tom W. is now a graduate student. Please rank the following nine fields of graduate specialization in order of the likelihood that Tom W. is now a graduate student in each of these fields:

a. Business administration
b. Computer science
c. Engineering

d. Humanities and education

e. Law

f. Library science

g. Medicine

h. Physical and life sciences

i. Social science and social work

Write down your rankings before you read on.

[*Source*: Kahneman, D., and A. Tversky (1973) "On the Psychology of Prediction." *Psychological Review*, 80, 237–251.]

Representativeness

If you are like most people, you wrote down your ranks on the basis of how similar the description of Tom W. is to your preconceived notions of the kinds of people in the nine different fields of study. Specifically, Tom W.'s description makes him appear to be a "nerd," and so most people think that he has a relatively high chance of being in engineering or computer science. But judging the probability of membership in a group on the basis of similarity ignores important information. There are many more graduate students in humanities and education and in social science and social work than in computer science or engineering. Information relating to the incidence or *base rate* of occurrence in the different fields is ignored, however, when we make probability judgments on the basis of similarity.

Making such judgments on similarity is one example of a kind of heuristic that Kahneman and Tversky call *representativeness*. In its most fundamental form, the representativeness heuristic is used to judge the probability that someone or something belongs to a particular category. Using the representativeness heuristic means that the judgment is made by comparing the information known about the person or thing with the stereotypical member of the category. The closer the similarity between the two, the higher the judged probability of membership in the category.

The representativeness heuristic surfaces in many different situations and can lead to a variety of different biases. For example, as in the Tom W. problem, people can be insensitive to base rates or prior probabilities. If one were to consider base rates carefully in the Tom W. problem, humanities and education may well be the most likely category. Insensitivity to sample size is another possible result of the representativeness heuristic. Sometimes termed the "law of small numbers," people (even scientists!) sometimes draw conclusions from highly representative small samples even though small samples are subject to considerably more statistical error than are large samples. Other situations in which representativeness operates include relying on old and unreliable information to make predictions, and making equally precise predictions regardless of the inherent uncertainty in a situation.

Misunderstanding of random processes is another phenomenon attributed to the representativeness heuristic. One of the most important aspects of this situation for managers relates to changes over time and misunderstanding the extent to which a process can be controlled. For example, Kahneman and Tversky relate their experience with a flight instructor in Israel. The instructor had been in the habit of praising students for good landings and scolding them for poor ones. He observed that after receiving praise for a good landing, a pilot's subsequent landing tended to be worse. Conversely, after a pilot received a scolding, his next landing tended to be better. The instructor concluded that scolding was effective feedback and that praise was not. In fact, this phenomenon is more easily explained by what is known as the statistical phenomenon as *regression to the mean*. If performance or measurements are random, then extreme cases will tend to be followed by less extreme ones. Landing a jet is not an easy task, and the pilot must deal with many different problems and conditions on each landing. It is perfectly reasonable to assume that performance for any pilot will vary from one landing to the next. Regression to the mean suggests that a good landing probably will be followed by one that is not as good, and that a poor one will most likely be followed by one that is better.

Availability

Another heuristic that people tend to use to make probability judgments is termed *availability*. According to this heuristic, we judge the probability that an event will occur according to the ease with which we can retrieve similar events from memory. As with the representativeness heuristic, availability comes into play in several ways. External events and influences, for example, can have a substantial effect on the availability of similar incidents. Seeing a traffic accident can increase one's estimate of the chance of being in an accident. Being present at a house fire can have more effect on the retrievability of fire incidents than reading about the fire in the newspaper. Furthermore, differential attention by the news media to different kinds of incidents can result in availability bias. Suppose the local newspaper plays up deaths resulting from homicide but plays down traffic deaths. To some extent, the unbalanced reporting can affect readers' judgments of the relative incidence of homicides and traffic fatalities, thus affecting the community's overall perception.

Bias from availability arises in other ways as well. For example, some situations are simply easier to imagine than others. In other cases, it may be difficult to recall contexts in which a particular event occurs. Another situation involves *illusory correlation*. If a pair of events is perceived as happening together frequently, this perception can lead to an incorrect judgment regarding the strength of the relationship between the two events.

Anchoring and Adjusting

This heuristic refers to the notion that in making estimates we often choose an initial anchor and then adjust that anchor based on our knowledge of the specific event in question. An excellent example is sales forecasting. Many people make such forecasts by considering the sales figures for the most recent period and then adjusting those values based on new circumstances. The problem is that the adjustment usually is insufficient.

The anchor-and-adjust heuristic affects the assessment of probability distributions for continuous uncertain quantities more than it affects discrete assessments. We tend to begin by assessing an anchor, say, the mean or median. Then extreme points or fractiles are assessed by adjusting away from the anchor. Because of the tendency to underadjust, most subjectively assessed probability distributions are too narrow, inadequately reflecting the inherent variability in the uncertain quantity. One of the consequences is that we tend to be overconfident, having underestimated the probability of extreme outcomes, often by a substantial amount (Capen, 1976). The technique described above for assessing a subjective CDF using the median and quartiles is subject to this kind of overconfidence from anchoring and adjusting. This is one reason why we assess the 0.05 and 0.95 fractiles instead of the 0.00 and 1.00 fractiles. Assessing the 0.05 and 0.95 fractiles essentially admits that there is a remote possibility that the uncertain quantity could fall beyond these assessed points. We assess also the 0.05 and 0.95 fractiles, then the quartiles, and finally the median to avoid anchoring on a central value as much as possible.

Motivational Bias

The cognitive biases described above relate to the ways in which we as human beings process information. But we also must be aware of motivational biases. Incentives often exist that lead people to report probabilities or forecasts that do not entirely reflect their true beliefs. For example, a salesperson asked for a sales forecast may be inclined to forecast low so that he will look good (and perhaps receive a bonus) when he sells more than the amount forecast. Occasionally incentives can be quite subtle or even operate at a subconscious level. For example, some evidence suggests that weather forecasters, in assessing the probability of precipitation, persistently err on the high side; they tend to overstate the probability of rain. Perhaps they would rather people were prepared for bad weather (and were pleasantly surprised by sunshine) instead of expecting good weather and being unpleasantly surprised. Even though forecasters generally are good probability assessors and strive for accurate forecasts, their assessments may indeed be slightly affected by such implicit incentives.

This discussion of heuristics and biases in probability judgments sounds quite pessimistic. If people really are subject to such deficiencies in assessing probabilities, is there any hope? There is indeed. First, some evidence suggests that individuals can learn to become good at assessing probabilities. As mentioned, weather forecasters are good probability assessors; in general, they provide accurate probabilities. For example, on those occasions when a forecaster says the probability of rain is 0.20, rain actually occurs very nearly 20% (or slightly less) of the time. Weather forecasters have two advantages; they have a lot of specialized knowledge about the weather, and they receive immediate feedback regarding the outcome. Both of these appear to be important in improving probability-assessment performance.

Second, awareness of the heuristics and biases may help individuals make better probability assessments. If nothing else, knowing about some of the effects, you now may be able to recognize them when they occur. For example, you may be able to recognize regression to the mean, or you may be sensitive to availability effects that result from unbalanced reporting in the news media. Moreover, when you obtain information from other individuals, you should realize that their judgments are subject to these same problems.

Third, the techniques we have discussed for assessing probabilities involve thinking about lotteries and chances in a structured way. These contexts are quite different from the way that most people think about uncertainty. By thinking hard about probabilities using these methods, it may be possible to short-circuit some heuristic reasoning and attendant biases. At the very least, thinking about lotteries provides a new perspective in the assessment process.

Finally, some problems simply cannot be addressed well in the form in which they are presented. In many cases it is worthwhile to decompose a chance event into other events. The result is that more assessments must be made, although they may be easier. In the next section we will see how decomposition may improve the assessment process.

◆ DECOMPOSITION AND PROBABILITY ASSESSMENT

In many cases it is possible to break a probability assessment into smaller and more manageable chunks. This process is known as decomposition. There are at least three different scenarios in which decomposition of a probability assessment may be appropriate. In this section, we will discuss these different scenarios.

In the simplest case, decomposition involves thinking about how the event of interest is related to other events. A simple example might involve assessing the probability that a given stock price increases. Instead of considering only the stock itself, we might think about its relationship to the market as a whole. We could assess the probability that the market goes up (as measured by the Dow Jones average, say), and then assess the conditional probabilities that the stock price increase given that the market increases and given that the market does not increase. Finding the probability that the stock price increases is then a matter of using the law of total probability:

$$P(\text{Stock Price Up}) = P(\text{Stock Price Up} \mid \text{Market Up}) \, P(\text{Market Up})$$
$$+ P(\text{Stock Price Up} \mid \text{Market Not Up}) \, P(\text{Market Not Up}).$$

The reason for performing the assessment in this way is that it may be more comfortable to assess the conditional probabilities and the probability about the market rather than to assess P(Stock Price Up) directly. In terms of an influence diagram or a probability tree, we are adding a chance node that is relevant to the assessment of the probabilities in which we are interested. Figure 8.15 shows the decomposition of the stock-price assessment.

In the second scenario, it is a matter of thinking about what kinds of alternative uncertain events could eventually lead to the event in question. For example, if your car will not start, there are many possible reasons why it will not. The decomposition strategy would be to think about the chances that different possible things could go wrong and the chance that the car will not start given each of these specific underlying problems or some combination of them.

For a more complicated example that we can model, suppose that you are an engineer in a nuclear power plant. Your boss calls you into his office and explains that the Nuclear Regulatory Commission has requested safety information. One item that the commission has requested is an assessment of the probability of an accident resulting in the release of radioactive material into the environment. Your boss knows that you have had a course in decision analysis, and so you are given the job of assessing this probability.

How would you go about this task? Of course, one way is to sit down with a wheel of fortune and think about lotteries. Eventually you would be able to arrive at a probability assessment. Chances are that as you thought about the problem, however, you would realize that many different kinds of situations could lead to an accident. Thus, instead of trying to assess the probability directly, you might construct an influence diagram that includes some of the events that could lead to an accident. Figure 8.16 shows the simple influence diagram that you might draw.

The intuition behind Figure 8.16 is that an accident could result from a failure of the cooling system or of the control system. The cooling system could

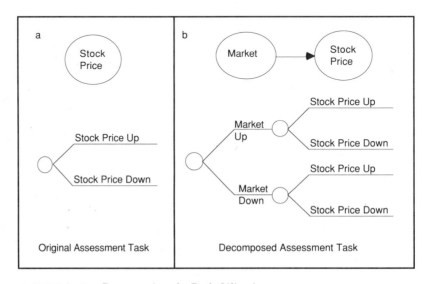

FIGURE 8.15 *Decomposing the Probability Assessment for Stock-Price Movement*

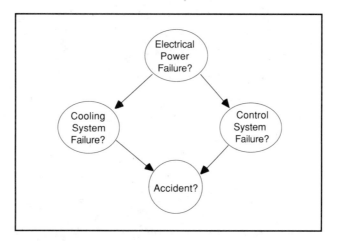

FIGURE 8.16   *Simple Influence Diagram for Assessing the Probability of a Nuclear Power Plant Accident*

either spring a leak itself, thus spilling radioactive material, or its pumps could fail, allowing the reactor core to overheat, and thus resulting in a possible accident. The control system also is critical. If the control system fails, it may become impossible to maintain safe operation of the reactor, and thus possibly result in an accident. Furthermore, the control system and the cooling system do not operate independently: They both depend on the electrical power system within the plant. Thus, failure of the electrical system would make failure of both the cooling and the control systems more likely. (Many other relationships also are possible. An influence diagram to assess the probability of an accident in an actual nuclear power plant would be considerably more complicated than Figure 8.16.)

For each of the four chance nodes in Figure 8.16, we have two possible outcomes. Because failures of both the cooling and control systems are relevant to the assessment of an accident, we have four conditional probabilities to assess. Let A denote the event of an accident, L the event of a cooling system failure, N the event of a control system failure, and E the event of an electrical system failure. The four conditional probabilities we must assess for Event A are $P(A \mid L, N)$, $P(A \mid \overline{L}, N)$, $P(A \mid L, \overline{N})$, and $P(A \mid \overline{L}, \overline{N})$. For the cooling system node, probabilities $P(L \mid E)$ and $P(L \mid \overline{E})$ must be assessed. Likewise, for the control system node $P(N \mid E)$ and $P(N \mid \overline{E})$ must be assessed. Finally, $P(E)$ must be assessed for the electrical system node.

There are nine assessments in all. Again, the reason for decomposing the assessment task into multiple assessments is that you may be more comfortable with the assessments that are required in the decomposed version. For example, you may be able to conclude that $P(A \mid \overline{L}, \overline{N}) = 0$, or that if neither the cooling system nor control system fails, then the probability of an accident is zero.

Assembling the probabilities in this case again is a matter of using the law of total probability, although it must be used more than once. Start out by using the law of total probability to expand $P(A)$:

$$P(A) = P(A \mid L, N)P(L, N) + P(A \mid \overline{L}, N)P(\overline{L}, N)$$
$$+ P(A \mid L, \overline{N})P(L, \overline{N}) + P(A \mid \overline{L}, \overline{N})P(\overline{L}, \overline{N}).$$

Now the problem is to find $P(L, N)$, $P(\overline{L}, N)$, $P(L, \overline{N})$, and $P(\overline{L}, \overline{N})$. Each in turn can be expanded using the law of total probability. For example, consider $P(L, N)$:

$$P(L, N) = P(L, N \mid E)P(E) + P(L, N \mid \overline{E})P(\overline{E}).$$

Now we must find $P(L, N \mid E)$ and $P(L, N \mid \overline{E})$. From the influence diagram, the only connection between the cooling system (L) and the control system (N) is through the electrical system. Thus, cooling and control failures are conditionally independent given the state of the power system. From the definition of conditional independence in Chapter 7, we can write

$$P(L, N \mid E) = P(L \mid E)\, P(N \mid E)$$

and

$$P(L, N \mid \overline{E}) = P(L \mid \overline{E})\, P(N \mid \overline{E})$$

Thus, by expanding out the probabilities, it is possible to build up the probability $P(A)$ from the nine assessments and their complements.

The third scenario is related to the second. In this case, however, it is not a matter of different possible underlying causes, but a matter of thinking through all of the different events that must happen before the event in question occurs. For example, in assessing the probability of an explosion at an oil refinery, an engineer would have to consider the chances that perhaps some critical pipe would fail, that all of the different safety measures also would fail at the same time, and that no one would notice the problem before the explosion occurred. Thus, many different individual events would have to occur before the explosion. In contrast, the nuclear power plant example involved alternative paths that could lead to a failure. Of course, the second and third scenarios can be combined. That is, there may be alternative paths to a failure, each requiring that a certain number of individual events occur. This kind of analysis often is called *fault-tree analysis* because it is possible to build a tree showing the relationship of the prior events to the event in question, which often is the failure of some complicated system.

As you may have noticed in the nuclear power plant example, the probability manipulations can become somewhat complicated. Fortunately, in complicated assessment problems, computer programs can perform the probability manipulations for us. Using such a program allows us to focus on thinking hard about the assessments rather than on the mathematics.

As with many decision-analysis techniques, there may be more than one way to decompose a probability assessment. The whole reason to use decomposition is to make the assessment process easier. The best decomposition to use is the one that is easiest to think about and that gives the clearest view of the uncertainty in the decision problem.

◆ COHERENCE AND THE DUTCH BOOK (OPTIONAL)

Subjective probabilities must obey the same postulates and laws that so-called objective probabilities must obey. That is, probabilities must be between 0 and 1, probabilities for mutually exclusive and collectively exhaustive sets of events must add to 1, and the probability of any event occurring from among a set of mutually exclusive events must be the sum of the probabilities of the individual events. All of the other properties of probabilities follow from these postulates, and subjective probabilities thus also must obey all of the probability "laws" and formulas that we studied in Chapter 7.

If an individual's subjectively assessed probabilities obey the probability postulates, the person is said to be "coherent." What benefit is there in being coherent? The mathematician de Finetti propounded a famous theorem, the Dutch Book Theorem, that says that if a person is not coherent, then it is possible to set up a Dutch book against him or her. A Dutch book is a series of bets that guarantees your opponent will lose and you will win.

For example, suppose that it is nearly the end of the NBA season, and that the Los Angeles Lakers and the Boston Celtics are playing in the finals. A friend of yours says that the probability is 0.4 that the Lakers will win and 0.5 that the Celtics will win. You look at this statement and point out that his probabilities only add to 0.9. Is there some other possible outcome? He sullenly replies that those are his probabilities, and that there is nothing wrong with them.

Let us find what is wrong. If those really are his probabilities, then he should be willing to agree to the following bets:

> **Bet 1**   He wins $40 if the Lakers lose.
> You win $60 if the Lakers win.

> **Bet 2**   You win $50 if the Celtics win.
> He wins $50 if the Celtics lose.

Note that, according to his stated probabilities, his expected value for each bet is 0. In Bet 1 he has a 0.6 chance of winning $40 and a 0.4 chance of losing $60. His expected value is $0.6(40) - 0.4(60) = 0$. In Bet 2, his expected value is $0.5(50) - 0.5(50) = 0$.

What can happen? If the Lakers win (and hence the Celtics lose), then he pays you $60 in Bet 1 and you pay him $50 in Bet 2; he has a net loss of $10. If the Lakers lose and the Celtics win, you pay him $40 in Bet 1 and he pays you $50 in Bet 2. Again he has a net loss of $10. He is bound to pay you $10 no matter what happens!

He wants to know how you figured this out, so we will show him. First, the bets are determined in the following way. Let p represent his stated probability that the Lakers win and q his probability that the Celtics win. To be coherent, $p + q$ should equal 1. To make up the two bets with zero expected value to him, consider his sides of the bets:

Bet 1   He wins the amount $X(p)$ with probability $(1 - p)$
(that is, if the Lakers lose/Celtics win).
You win (he loses) the amount $X(1 - p)$ with probability p.

Bet 2   You win the amount $Y(1 - q)$ with probability q
(that is, if the Celtics win/Lakers lose).
He wins the amount $Y(q)$ with probability $(1 - q)$.

As before, we can think of Y and X as the total stakes that are involved in each bet. For example, in Bet 1 you put $X(p)$ into the pot and he puts in $X(1 - p)$, and whoever wins the bet gets all of the money in the pot. It is easy to verify that his expected value for each bet is zero; for example, in Bet 1 his expected value is:

$$(1 - p)[X(p)] - p[X(1 - p)] = 0.$$

Now, think about the equations that give his net gain or loss. If the Lakers win, his net position is L:

$$-X(1 - p) + Y(q) = L.$$

The two terms on the left-hand side of the equation are his loss from Bet 1 and his gain from Bet 2. Likewise, if the Celtics win, his position is K:

$$X(p) - Y(1 - q) = K.$$

Now, here's the trick. He has supplied p and q. *You have decided to set L and K each equal to –$10 so that he is guaranteed to pay you $10.* Now it is just a matter of solving for X and Y to find the bets necessary to guarantee that he loses $10. There are two equations and two unknowns (X and Y). What could be easier?

"Aha!" he exclaims, "In my linear algebra course, I learned about solving linear equations simultaneously. No matter what L and K are, you should be able to find an X and Y to defeat me. Unless . . . . Oh, I see!" What does he see? Solve the second equation for X to get:

$$X = \frac{[K + Y(1 - q)]}{p}.$$

Now substitute this into the first equation and solve for Y. Rearranging yields

$$Y = \frac{\left[L - K + \dfrac{K}{p}\right]}{1 - \dfrac{(1 - q)}{p}}.$$

This equation always can be solved for Y unless the denominator $[1 - (1 - q)/p]$ on the right-hand side happens to equal 0. That will happen only when $p = 1 - q$, or $p + q = 1$. This was exactly the condition he violated in the first place; his probabilities did not sum to 1. If his probabilities had satisfied this condition, you would not be able to find an X and Y that would solve the two equations, and the Dutch book would have been impossible.

This example points out how incoherence can be exploited. In fact, if a person's probabilities do not conform to the probability laws, it is always possible to do this kind of thing, no matter which probability law is violated. The contribution of de Finetti was to prove that it is only possible not to be exploited if subjective probabilities obey the probability postulates and laws. The practical importance of this is less that you can set up Dutch books against incoherent probability assessors — because no one in his or her right mind would agree to such a series of bets — but to provide insight into why subjective probability should work the same way as "long-run frequency" probability. Because no one in his or her right mind would make decisions in a way that could be exploited, coherence is a reasonable condition to guide our assessments of probabilities for decision-making purposes. When we assess probabilities for use in a decision tree or influence diagram, those probabilities should obey all the normal probability properties.

The idea of coherence has an important implication for assessment when a decision analysis involves assessing several probabilities. Once all probabilities have been assessed, it is important to check for coherence. If the assessments are not coherent, the decision maker should be made aware of this and given the chance to adjust the assessments until they are coherent.

◇ SUMMARY

Many of the decision problems that we face involve uncertain future events. We may have some feeling for such uncertainties, and we can build models of them using subjective probability-assessment techniques. The basic approach to assessing a probability involves either setting up a bet or comparing lotteries. We also have considered assessment methods for continuous uncertain quantities and found that it is straightforward to assess continuous distributions in terms of cumulative distribution functions. A reasonable and practical way to incorporate a continuous distribution into a decision tree is to use a discrete approximation. We discussed bracket medians and the Pearson–Tukey three-point approximation.

Our discussion also touched on the pitfalls of probability assessment. Individuals tend to use cognitive heuristics to judge probabilities. Heuristics such as representativeness, availability, and anchoring and adjustment can lead to bias in probability assessment. Certain ideas for improving probability assessments were discussed, including decomposition of the assessment task.

Finally, we discussed the idea of coherence; that is, that subjective probabilities must obey the same probability laws that "long-run frequency" probabilities do. Being coherent in probability assessment means being sure that one cannot be exploited through a Dutch book.   ◆

◇ EXERCISES

8.1 Explain in your own words the idea of subjective probability.

8.2 An accounting friend of yours has gone to great lengths to construct a statistical model of bankruptcy. Using the model, the probability that a firm will file for bankruptcy within a year is calculated on the basis of financial ratios. On hearing your explanation of subjective probability, your friend says that subjective probability may be all right for decision analysis, but his model gives objective probabilities on the basis of real data. Explain to him how his model is, to a great extent, based on subjective judgments. Comment also on the subjective judgments that a bank officer would have to make in using your friend's model.

8.3   Explain in your own words the difference between assessing the probability for a discrete event and assessing a probability distribution for a continuous unknown quantity.

8.4   For each of the following phrases write down the probability number that you feel is represented by the phrase. After doing so, check your answers to be sure they are consistent [For example, is your answer to e less than your answer to j?]

   a.   "There is a better than even chance that . . ."

   b.   "A possibility exists that . . ."

   c.   ". . . has a high likelihood of occurring."

   d.   "The probability is very high that . . ."

   e.   "It is very unlikely that . . ."

   f.   "There is a slight chance . . ."

   g.   "The chances are better than even . . ."

   h.   "There is no probability, no serious probability, that . . ."

   i.   ". . . is probable."

   j.   ". . . is unlikely."

   k.   "There is a good chance that . . ."

   l.   ". . . is quite unlikely."

   m.   ". . . is improbable."

   n.   ". . . has a high probability."

   o.   "There is a chance that . . ."

   p.   ". . . is very improbable."

   q.   ". . . is likely."

   r.   "Probably . . ."

8.5   Suppose that your father asked you to assess the probability that you would pass your decision-analysis course. How might you decompose this probability assessment? Draw an influence diagram to represent the decomposition.

8.6   Consider the betting method for assessing probabilities. What if the decision maker disliked betting? What if the decision maker's attitude toward risky situations were such that she would rather forego a bet in which she could lose money even if she believed the expected value of the bet to be greater than zero?

◇ QUESTIONS AND PROBLEMS

8.7   Assess your probability that the following events will occur. Use the equivalent-lottery method as discussed in the chapter. If possible, use a wheel of fortune with an adjustable win area, or a computer program that simulates such a wheel. What issues did you account for in making each assessment?

    a. It will rain tomorrow in New York City.

    b. You will have been offered a job before you graduate.

    c. The women's track team at your college will win the NCAA championship this year.

    d. The United States and the Soviet Union will reach an agreement in the coming year to reduce the number of intercontinental ballistic missiles.

    e. The price of crude oil will be more than $30 per barrel on January 1, 2010.

    f. The Dow Jones Industrial Average will go up tomorrow.

    g. Any other uncertain event that interests you.

8.8 Consider the following two events:

    a. You will get an A in your most difficult course.

    b. You will get an A or a B in your easiest course.

    Can you assess the probability of these events occurring? What is different about assessing probabilities regarding your own performance as compared to assessing probabilities for events like those in Problem 8.7?

8.9 Describe a decomposition strategy that would be useful for assessing the probabilities in Problem 8.8.

8.10 Many people deal with uncertainty by assessing odds. For example, in horse racing different horses' odds of winning are assessed. Odds of "a to b for Event E" means that $P(E) = a/(a + b)$. Odds of "c to d against Event E" means that $P(\bar{E}) = c/(c + d)$. For the events in Problem 8.7, assess the odds for that event occurring. Convert your assessed odds to probabilities. Do they agree with the probability assessments that you made in Problem 8.7?

8.11 Should you drop your decision-analysis course? Suppose you faced the following problem:

If you drop the course, the anticipated salary in your best job offer will depend on your current GPA:

$$\text{Anticipated Salary} \mid \text{Drop} = (\$4000 \times \text{Current GPA}) + \$16,000.$$

If you take the course, the anticipated salary in your best job offer will depend on both your current GPA and your overall score (on a scale of 0 to 100) in the course:

$$\begin{aligned}\text{Anticipated Salary} \mid \text{Do Not Drop} = &\ 0.6\ (\$4000 \times \text{Current GPA}) \\ &+ 0.4\ (\$170 \times \text{Course Score}) \\ &+ \$16,000.\end{aligned}$$

The problem is that you do not know how well you will do in the course. You can, however, assess a distribution for your score. Assuming that 90–100 is an A, 80–89 is a B, 70–79 a C, 60–69 a D, and 0–59 an F, assess a continuous probability distribution for your numerical score in the course. Use that distribution to decide whether or not to drop the course. Figure 8.17 shows your decision tree.

8.12 Assess these fractiles for the following uncertain quantities: 0.05 fractile, 0.25 fractile (first quartile), 0.50 (median), 0.75 fractile (third quartile), and 0.95 fractile. Plot your assessments to create graphs of your subjective CDFs.

    a. The closing Dow Jones Industrial Average (DJIA) on the last Friday of the current month.

    b. The closing DJIA on the last Friday of next year.

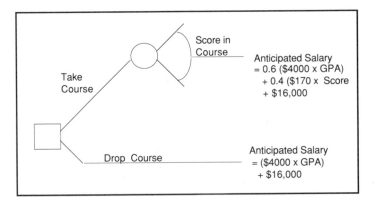

FIGURE 8.17   *Decision Tree for Question 8.11*
Should you drop your decision-analysis course?

   c. The exchange rate, in Japanese yen per dollar, at the end of next Monday.

   d. The official high temperature at O'Hare International Airport tomorrow.

   e. The number of fatalities from airline accidents in the United States next year.

   f. The number of casualties from nuclear power plant accidents in the United States over the next 10 years.

   g. The value of the next jackpot won in the California state lottery.

8.13 Forecasters often provide only point forecasts, which are their best guesses as to an upcoming event. For example, an economic forecaster might predict that U.S. gross national product (GNP) will increase at a 3% annual rate over the next three months. Occasionally a forecaster also will provide an estimate of the degree of confidence in the point forecast to indicate how sure (or unsure) the forecaster is.

     In what sense can your answers to Problem 8.12 be interpreted as forecasts? What advantages do subjective probability distributions have over typical point forecasts? What disadvantages? How could a decision maker use probabilistic forecasts such as those in Problem 8.12?

8.14 Choose a course that you are currently taking in which the final exam is worth 100 points. Treating your score on the exam as if it were a continuous uncertain quantity, assess the subjective probability distribution for your score. After you have finished, check your assessed distribution for consistency by:

   a. choosing any two intervals you have judged to have equal probability content, and

   b. determining whether you would be willing to place small even–odds bets that your score would fall in one of the two intervals. (The bet would be called off if the score fell elsewhere.)

   c. After assessing the continuous distribution, construct a three-point approximation to this distribution with the extended Pearson–Tukey method. Use the approximation to estimate your expected exam score.

   d. Now construct a five-point approximation with bracket medians. Use this approximation to estimate your expected exam score. How does your answer compare with the estimate from part c?

8.15 Compare the discrete-approximation methods by doing the following:

    a. Use the extended Pearson–Tukey method to create three-point discrete approximations for the continuous distributions assessed in Problem 8.12. Use the approximations to estimate the expected values of the uncertain quantities.

    b. Repeat part a, but construct five-point discrete approximations using bracket medians. Compare your estimated expected values from the two methods.

8.16 Assess the probability that the New York Mets will win the World Series (WS) next year. Call this probability p. Now assess the following probabilities: P(Win WS | Win Pennant) and P(Win Pennant). Use these to calculate q = P(Win WS) = P(Win WS | Win Pennant) P(Win Pennant) = P(Win WS and Win Pennant). (To play in the World Series, the team must first win the pennant.)

    a. Does $p = q$? Which of the two assessments are you more confident about? Would you adjust your assessments to make $p = q$? Why or why not?

    b. If you do not like the Mets, do this problem for your favorite major league baseball team.

8.17 Assess the probability that you will be hospitalized for more than one day during the upcoming year. In assessing this probability, decompose the assessment based on whether or not you are in an automobile accident. With this decomposition, you must assess P(Hospitalized | Accident), P(Hospitalized | No Accident), and P(Accident). In what other ways might this assessment be decomposed?

8.18 Choose a firm in which you are particularly interested, perhaps one where you might like to work. Go to the library and read about this firm, about its industry, and about the relationship of this firm and the industry to the economy as a whole. After your reading, assess a subjective CDF for the firm's revenue over the next fiscal year. Discuss the assessment process. In particular, what did you learn in your research that had an impact on the assessment? What kinds of decomposition helped you in your assessment process?

8.19 After observing a long run of red on a roulette wheel, many gamblers believe that black is bound to occur. Such a belief often is called the *gambler's fallacy* because the roulette wheel has no memory. Which probability-assessment heuristic is at work in the gambler's fallacy? Explain.

8.20 Look again at Problems 7.20 and 7.21 (pages 198–199). These problems involve assessments of the relative likelihood of different statements. When an individual ranks "Linda is a bank teller and is active in the feminist movement" as more probable than the statement "Linda is a bank teller," which of the three probability-assessment heuristics may be at work? Explain.

8.21 Suppose that you are a solid B student. Your grades in your courses have always been B's. In your statistics course, you get a D on the midterm. When your parents express concern, what statistical phenomenon might you invoke to persuade them not to worry about the D?

8.22 When we assess our subjective probabilities, we are building a model of the uncertainty we face. If we face a range-of-risk problem, and we begin to assess a continuous distribution subjectively, then clearly it is possible to perform many assessments, which would make the sketched CDF smoother and smoother. How do we know when to stop making assessments and when to keep going? When is the model of our uncertainty adequate for solving the problem, and when is it inadequate?

8.23   Most of us have a hard time assessing probabilities with a lot of precision. For instance, in assessing the probability of rain tomorrow, even carefully considering the lotteries and trying to adjust a wheel of fortune to find the indifference point, many people would eventually say something like this: "If you set p = 0.2, I'd take Lottery A, and if p = 0.3 I'd take Lottery B. My indifference point must be somewhere in between these two numbers, but I am not sure where."

How could you deal with this kind of imprecision in a decision analysis? Illustrate how your approach would work using the umbrella problem (Figure 4.10, page 75). (*Note*: The question is *not* how to get more precise assessments. Rather, given that the decision maker refuses to make precise assessments, and you are stuck with imprecise assessments, can you still apply decision-analysis techniques?)

8.24   It is not necessary to have someone else set up a series of bets against you in order for incoherence to take its toll. It is conceivable that one could inadvertently get oneself into a no-win situation through inattention to certain details and the resulting incoherence, as this problem shows.

Suppose that an executive of a venture-capital investment firm is trying to decide how to allocate his funds among three different projects. The projects are such that one of the three will definitely succeed, but it is not possible for more than one to succeed. Looking at each project as an investment, the anticipated payoff is good, but not wonderful. If a project succeeds, the payoff will be 2.5 times the amount invested, for a net gain of $150,000. Of course, if the project fails, he loses all of the money invested in that project. Because he feels as though he knows nothing about whether a project will succeed or fail, he assigns a probability of 0.5 that each project will succeed, and he decides to invest $100,000 in each project.

a. According to his assessed probabilities, what is the expected profit for each project?

b. What are the possible outcomes of the three investments, and how much will he make in each case?

c. Do you think he invested wisely? Can you explain why he is in such a predicament?

d. If you feel you know nothing about some event, is it reasonable to assess equal probabilities for the outcomes? Give an example where this might be reasonable and another where it might not.

8.25   Could you ever set up a Dutch book against a bookie who places bets for a living? Work through the following problem and think about this question.

Consider a baseball season when the Chicago Cubs and the New York Yankees meet in the World Series. A friend of yours is a Cubs fan, and you are trying to find out how confident he is about the Cubs' chances of winning. He tells you that he would bet on the Cubs at odds of 3:2 *or better*, and on the Yankees at odds of 1:2 *or better*. [Odds of $a:b$ for an event means the probability of the event is $a/(a + b)$.] This means that he would be happy with either of the following bets:

        Bet 1.   He wins $20 if the Cubs win.
                     He loses $30 if the Yankees win.

        Bet 2.   He loses $20 if the Cubs win.
                     He wins $40 if the Yankees win.

a. Explain why he would be happy to accept any modification of these bets as long as the amount he would win increases and the amount he would lose stays the same or is lower. Explain in terms of his expected bet value.

b. Show mathematically that $0.60 \leq P(\text{Cubs Win}) \leq 0.67$. (*Hint*: If he is willing to accept either bet, what does that imply about his expected value for each bet?)

c. Would it be possible to set up a Dutch book against this individual? If your answer is yes, what bets would you place, and how much would you be sure to win? If your answer is no, explain why not. (Be careful! Make sure he is willing to accept the bets you propose.)

d. Most individuals have a hard time assessing subjective probabilities with a very high degree of precision. (See Problem 8.23.) Does this problem shed any light on the issue?

8.26 **Ellsberg Paradox**   A barrel contains a mixture of 90 red, blue, and yellow balls. Thirty of the balls are red, and the remaining 60 are a mixture of blue or yellow, but the proportion of blue and yellow is unknown. A single ball will be taken randomly from the barrel.

a. Suppose you are offered the choice between gambles A and B:

> **A:**   Win $1000 if a red ball is chosen.
>
> **B:**   Win $1000 if a blue ball is chosen.

Would you prefer A or B? Why?

b. Now suppose that you are offered a choice between gambles C and D:

> **C:**   Win $1000 if either a red or a yellow ball is chosen.
>
> **D:**   Win $1000 if either a blue or a yellow ball is chosen.

Would you prefer C or D? Why?

c. Many people prefer A in the first choice and D in the second. Do you think this is inconsistent? Explain.

CASE STUDIES

Assessing Cancer Risk — From Mouse to Man

Cancer is a poorly understood and frightening disease. Its causes are essentially unknown, and the biological process that creates cancerous cells from healthy tissue remains a mystery. Given this state of ignorance, much research has been conducted into how external conditions relate to cancer. For example, we know that smoking leads to substantially higher incidence of lung cancer in humans. Cancer appears spontaneously, however, and its onset seems to be inherently probabilistic, as shown by the fact that some people smoke all their lives without developing lung cancer.

Some commentators claim that the use of new and untested chemicals is leading to a cancer epidemic. As evidence they point to the increase in cancer deaths over the years. Indeed, cancer deaths have increased, but people generally have longer life-spans, and more elderly people now are at risk for the disease. When cancer rates are adjusted for the increased life-span, cancer rates have not increased substantially. In fact, when data are examined this way, some cancer rates (liver, stomach, and uterine cancer) are less common now than they were 50 years ago (American Cancer Society, 1986). Nevertheless, the public fears cancer greatly. The Delaney Amendment to the Food, Drug, and Cosmetics Act of 1954 outlawed residues in processed foods of chemicals that posed any risk of cancer to animals or humans. One of the results of this fear has been an emphasis in public policy on assessing cancer risks from a variety of chemicals.

Scientifically speaking, the best way to determine cancer risk to humans would be to expose one group of people to the chemical while keeping others away from it. But such experiments would not be ethical. Thus, scientists generally rely on experiments performed on animals, usually mice or rats. The laboratory animals in the experimental group are exposed to high doses of the substance being tested. High doses are required because low doses probably would not have a statistically noticeable effect on the relatively small experimental group. After the animals die, cancers are identified by autopsy. This kind of experiment is called a *bioassay*. Typical cancer bioassays involve 600 animals, require two to three years to complete, and cost several hundred thousand dollars.

When bioassays are used to make cancer risk assessments, two important extrapolations are made. First, there is the extrapolation from high doses to low doses. Second, it is necessary to extrapolate from effects on test species to effects on humans. On the basis of data from laboratory experiments and these extrapolations, assessments are made regarding the incidence of cancer when humans are exposed to the substance.

QUESTIONS

1. Clearly, the extrapolations that are made are based on subjective judgments. Because cancer is viewed as being an inherently probabilistic phenomenon, it is reasonable to view these judgments as probability assessments. What kinds of assessments do you think are necessary to make these extrapolations? What issues must be taken into account? What kind of scientific evidence would help in making the necessary assessments?

2. It can be argued that most cancer risk assessments are weak evidence of potential danger or lack thereof. To be specific, a chemical manufacturer and a regulator might argue different sides of the same study. The manufacturer might claim that the study does not conclusively show that the substance is dangerous, while the regulator might claim that the study does not conclusively demonstrate safety. Situations like this often arise, and decisions must be made with imperfect information. What kind of strategy would you adopt for making these decisions? What trade-offs does your strategy involve?

3. In the case of risk assessment, as with many fields of scientific inquiry, some experiments are better than others for many reasons. For example, some experiments may be more carefully designed or use larger samples. In short, some sources of information are more "credible."

    For a simple, hypothetical example, suppose that you ask three "experts" whether a given coin is fair. All three report that the coin is fair; for each one the best estimate of P(Heads) is 0.50. You learn, however, that the first expert flipped the coin 10,000 times and observed heads on 5000 occasions. The second flipped the coin 20 times and observed 10 heads. The third expert did not flip the coin at all, but gave it a thorough physical examination, finding it to be perfectly balanced, as nearly as he could measure.

How should differences in credibility of information be accounted for in assessing probabilities? Would you give the same weight to information from the three examiners of the coin? In the case of putting together information on cancer risk from multiple experiments and expert sources, how might you deal with the information sources' differential credibility?

Source: Freedman, D.A., and H. Zeisel (1988) "From Mouse-to-Man: The Quantitative Assessment of Cancer Risks." *Statistical Science*, 3, 3–56. Includes discussion.

◆

The Space Shuttle Challenger

On January 28, 1986, the space shuttle *Challenger* lifted off from an ice-covered launch pad. Only 72 seconds into the flight, the shuttle exploded, killing all seven astronauts aboard. The United States and the rest of the world saw the accident first-hand as films from NASA were shown repeatedly by the television networks.

Before long the cause of the accident became known. The shuttle's main engines are fueled by liquid hydrogen and oxygen stored in a large tank carried on the shuttle's belly. Two auxiliary rockets that use solid fuel are mounted alongside the main fuel tank and provide additional thrust to accelerate the shuttle away from the launch pad. These boosters use their fuel rapidly and are jettisoned soon after launch.

The solid rocket boosters are manufactured in sections by Morton Thiokol, Inc. (MTI), in Utah. The sections are shipped individually to Kennedy Space Center (KSC) in Florida where they are assembled. The joints between sections of the rocket are sealed by a pair of large rubber O-rings, the purpose of which is to contain the hot gases and pressure inside the rocket. In the case of the *Challenger*, one of the joint seals failed. Hot gases blew past the O-rings and eventually burned through the large belly tank, igniting the highly explosive fuel inside. The resulting explosion destroyed the spacecraft.

Before long it also became known that the launch itself was not without controversy. MTI engineers had been aware of the problems with the O-rings for some time, having observed eroded O-rings in the boosters used on previous flights. A special task force was formed in 1985 to try to solve the problem, but ran into organizational problems. One memo regarding the task force began, "Help! The seal task force is constantly being delayed by every possible means." The problem came to a head when, on the evening before the launch, MTI engineers recommended not launching the shuttle because of the anticipated cold temperatures on the launch pad. After a teleconference involving officials at KSC and the Marshal Space Flight Center (MSFC) in Alabama, management officials at MTI reversed their engineers' recommendation and approved the launch.

QUESTIONS

1. To a great extent, the engineers were concerned about the performance of the O-ring under anticipated cold weather conditions. The coldest previous flight had been 53° F, and, knowing of the existing problems with the seals, the engineers hesitated to recommend a launch under colder conditions. Technically, the problem was that an O-ring stiffens as it gets colder, thus requiring a longer time to seal a joint. The real problem, however, was that the engineers did not know much about the performance of the O-rings at cold temperatures. Robert K. Lund, vice-president of engineering for Morton Thiokol, testified to the presidential commission investigating the accident, "[W]e just don't know how much further we can go below the 51 or 53 degrees or whatever it was. So we were concerned with the unknown. . . . They [officials at MSFC] said they didn't accept that rationale" (*Report of the Presidential Commission on the Space Shuttle* Challenger *Accident*, p. 94).

   The MTI staff felt as if it were in the position of having to prove that the shuttle was unsafe to fly instead of the other way around. Roger Boisjoly, an MTI engineer, testified, "This was a meeting where the determination was to launch, and it was up to us to prove beyond a shadow of a doubt that it was not safe to do so. This is in total reverse to what the position usually is in a preflight conversation or a flight readiness review. It is usually exactly opposite that" (*Report*, p. 93).

   NASA solicited information regarding ice on the launch pad from Rockwell International, the shuttle's manufacturer. Rockwell officials told NASA that the ice was an unknown condition. Robert Glaysher, a vice-president at Rockwell, testified that he had specifically said to NASA, "Rockwell could not 100 percent assure that it is safe to fly" (*Report*, p. 115). In this case, the presidential commission also found that "NASA appeared to be requiring a contractor to prove that it was not safe to launch, rather than proving it was safe" (*Report*, p. 118).

   The issue is how to deal with unknown information. What do you think the policy should be regarding situations in which little or no information is available? Discuss the problems faced by both MTI and NASA. What incentives and pressures might they have faced?

2. Professor Richard Feynman, Nobel Laureate in physics, was a member of the commission. He issued his own statement, published as an appendix to the report, taking NASA to task for a variety of blunders. Some of his complaints revolved around assessments of the probability of failure.

   Failure of the solid rocket boosters.   A study of 2900 flights of solid-fuel rockets revealed 121 failures, or approximately 1 in 25. Because of improved technology and special care in the selection of parts and in inspection, Feynman is willing to credit a failure rate of better than 1 in 100 but not as good as 1 in 1000. But in a risk analysis prepared for the Department of Energy (DOE) that related to DOE radioactive material aboard the shuttle, NASA officials used a figure of 1 in 100,000. Feynman writes:

> If the real probability is not so small [as 1 in 100,000], flights would show troubles, near failures, and possibly actual failures with a reasonable number of trials, and standard statistical methods could give a reasonable estimate. In fact, previous NASA experience had shown, on occasion, just such difficulties, near accidents, and accidents, all giving warning that the probability of flight failure was not so very small. (*Report*, p. F-1)

Failure of the liquid fuel engine.   In another section of his report, Feynman discussed disparate assessments of the probability of failure of the liquid fuel engine. His own calculations suggested a failure rate of approximately 1 in 500. Engineers at Rocketdyne, the engine manufacturer, estimated the probability to be approximately 1 in 10,000. NASA officials estimated 1 in 100,000. An independent consultant for NASA suggested that a failure rate of 1 or 2 per 100 would be a reasonable estimate.

How is it that these probability estimates could vary so widely? How should a decision maker deal with probability estimates that are so different?

3. To arrive at their overall reliability estimates, NASA officials may have decomposed the assessment, estimated the reliability of many different individual components, and then aggregated their assessments. Suppose that, because of an optimistic viewpoint, each probability assessment had been slightly overoptimistic (that is, a low assessed probability of failure). What effect might this have on the overall reliability estimate?

4. In an editorial in *Space World* magazine, editor Tony Reichhardt commented on the accident:

> One person's safety is another's paranoia. How safe is safe? What is acceptable risk? It's no small question, in life or in the space program. It's entirely understandable that astronauts would come down hard on NASA policies that appear to be reckless with their lives. But unless I'm misreading the testimony [before the commission], at the end of the teleconference that night of January 27, most of the participating engineers believed that it was safe to go ahead and launch. A few argued that it was not safe *enough*. There was an element of risk in the decision, and in many others made prior to *Challenger*'s launch, and seven people were killed.
>
> Whether this risk can be eliminated is a question of monumental importance to the space program. Those who have put the blame squarely on NASA launch managers need to think hard about the answer. If no Shuttle takes off until everyone at every level of responsibility is in complete agreement, then it may never be launched again.

No single person can be absolutely sure that the whole system will work. On this vehicle, or on some other spacecraft next year or 30 years from now — even if we ease the financial and scheduling pressures — something will go wrong again. [*Source*: Reichhardt, T., "Acceptable Risk," *Space World*, April 1986, p. 3.]

Comment on Reichhardt's statement. What is an acceptable risk? Does it matter whether we are talking about risks to the general public from cancer or risks to astronauts in the space program? Would your answer change if you were an astronaut? A NASA official? A manufacturer of potentially carcinogenic chemicals? A cancer researcher? How should a policy maker take into account the variety of opinions regarding what constitutes an acceptable risk?

Source: Information for this case was taken from many sources, but by far the most important was the report by the Rogers Commission, *Report of the Presidential Commission on the Space Shuttle Challenger Accident*, Washington, DC: U.S. Government Printing Office, 1986.

◆

◇ REFERENCES

The subjective interpretation of probability is one of the distinguishing characteristics of decision theory and decision analysis. This interpretation was presented first by Savage (1954) and has been debated by probabilists and statisticians ever since. Winkler (1972) provides an excellent introduction to subjective probability and "Bayesian" statistics (so called because of the reliance on Bayes' theorem for inference), as well as extensive references to the literature.

Spetzler and Staël von Holstein (1975) is the standard reference on probability assessment. Winkler (1972) also covers this topic. Wallsten and Budescu (1983) review the field from a psychological perspective.

The debate on appropriate ways to discretize a continuous distribution is far more complex than is portrayed in this chapter. Keefer and Bodily tested many different approximation schemes, including bracket medians. Their extended Pearson–Tukey method worked the best, and bracket medians performed poorly. On the other hand, bracket medians are not only intuitive, but also apparently superior in ways not considered by Keefer and Bodily. Furthermore, ongoing research in this area is uncovering new approximation methods.

The literature on heuristics and biases is extensive. One reference that covers the topic at an introductory level is Tversky and Kahneman (1974). Hogarth (1987) provides a unique overview of this material in the context of decision analysis. Kahneman, Slovic, and Tversky (1982) have collected key research papers in the area. With respect to the issue of overconfidence in particular, Capen (1976) reports an experiment that demonstrates the extent of overconfidence in subjective probability assessments and possible ways to cope with this phenomenon.

Probability decomposition is a topic that has not been heavily researched, although there are many applications. For example, see Bunn (1984) and von Winterfeldt and Edwards (1986) for discussions and examples of fault trees. A recent research paper by Ravinder, Kleinmuntz, and Dyer (1988) discusses when decomposition is worth doing.

As mentioned, the concept of coherence was first introduced by de Finetti (1937). Thinking in terms of coherence as did de Finetti contrasts with the axiomatic approach taken by Savage (1954). The idea of coherence has been developed considerably; examples of ways in which various decision rules or probability assessments are incoherent are given by Bunn (1984), French (1986), and Lindley (1985).

Finally, a topic that arose in Problems 8.23–8.26 deserves mention. This is the matter of vagueness or ambiguity in probability assessments. Problem 8.26 is the classic paradox of Ellsberg (1961), essentially showing that people shy away from risky prospects with vague probabilities. Ongoing research is attempting to understand this phenomenon both descriptively and prescriptively. Einhorn and Hogarth (1985) present a psychological model of the process. Frisch and Baron (1988) define vagueness in terms of the lack of information that could have an impact on a probability assessment. The set-up in Problem 8.25 is a simplified version of Nau's (1990) model in which a decision maker places constraints on the size of the bets that would be acceptable at different odds levels.

BEYTH-MAROM, R. (1982) "How Probable Is Probable? A Numerical Translation of Verbal Probability Expressions." *Journal of Forecasting*, 1, 257–269.

BUNN, D. (1984) *Applied Decision Analysis.* New York: McGraw-Hill.

CAPEN, E. C., (1976) "The Difficulty of Assessing Uncertainty." *Journal of Petroleum Technology*, August 1976, 843–850. Reprinted in R. Howard and J. Matheson (eds.), *The Principles and Applications of Decision Analysis.* Menlo Park, CA: Strategic Decisions Group.

DE FINETTI, B. (1937) "La Prévision: Ses Lois Logiques, Ses Sources Subjectives." *Annales de l'Institut Henri Poincaré*, 7, 1–68. Translated by H. E. Kyburg in H. E. Kyburg, Jr., and H. E. Smokler (eds.) (1964) *Studies in Subjective Probability.* New York: Wiley.

EINHORN, H., and R. M. HOGARTH (1985) "Ambiguity and Uncertainty in Probabilistic Inference." *Psychological Review*, 92, 433–461.

ELLSBERG, D. (1961) "Risk, Ambiguity, and the Savage Axioms." *Quarterly Journal of Economics*, 75, 643–669.

FRENCH, S. (1986) *Decision Theory: An Introduction to the Mathematics of Rationality.* London: Wiley.

FRISCH, D., and J. BARON (1988) "Ambiguity and Rationality." *Journal of Behavioral Decision Making*, 1, 149–157.

HOGARTH, R. M. (1987) *Judgement and Choice*, 2nd ed. New York: Wiley.

KAHNEMAN, D., P. SLOVIC, and A. TVERSKY (eds.) (1982) *Judgment under Uncertainty: Heuristics and Biases.* Cambridge: Cambridge University Press.

KAHNEMAN, D., and A. TVERSKY (1973) "On the Psychology of Prediction." *Psychological Review*, 80, 237–251.

KEEFER, D., and S. E. BODILY (1983) "Three-Point Approximations for Continuous Random Variables." *Management Science*, 29, 595–609.

LINDLEY, D. V. (1985) *Making Decisions*, 2nd ed. New York: Wiley.

NAU, R. (1990) "Indeterminate Probabilities and Utilities on Finite Sets." Working Paper No. 8929, Fuqua School of Business, Duke University.

RAVINDER, H. V., D. KLEINMUNTZ, and J. S. DYER (1988) "The Reliability of Subjective Probabilities Obtained Through Decomposition." *Management Science*, 34, 186–199.

SAVAGE, L. J. (1954) *The Foundations of Statistics.* New York: Wiley.

SPETZLER, C. S., and C.-A. STAËL VON HOLSTEIN (1975) "Probability Encoding in Decision Analysis." *Management Science*, 22, 340–352.

TVERSKY, A., and D. KAHNEMAN (1974) "Judgments Under Uncertainty: Heuristics and Biases." *Science*, 185, 1124–1131.

TVERSKY, A., and D. KAHNEMAN (1982) "Judgments of and by Representativeness." In D. Kahneman, P. Slovic, and A. Tversky (eds.), *Judgment under Uncertainty: Heuristics and Biases*, pp. 84–98. Cambridge: Cambridge University Press.

VATTER, P. A., S. P. BRADLEY, S. C. FREY, JR., and B. B. JACKSON (1978) *Quantitative Methods in Management*. Homewood, IL: Irwin.

VON WINTERFELDT, D., and W. EDWARDS (1986) *Decision Analysis and Behavioral Research*. Cambridge: Cambridge University Press.

WALLSTEN, T. S., and D. V. BUDESCU (1983) "Encoding Subjective Probabilities: A Psychological and Psychometric Review." *Management Science*, 29, 151–173.

WINKLER, R. L. (1972) *Introduction to Bayesian Inference and Decision*. New York: Holt, Rinehart, & Winston.

◇ EPILOGUE

Stanford beat Oregon in their 1970 football contest. The score was 33–10. Jim Plunkett was Stanford's quarterback that season and won the Heisman trophy.

Millard Fillmore was Zachary Taylor's vice president. Taylor died in 1850 while in office. Fillmore succeeded him and was president from 1850 through 1853. ◆

Theoretical Probability Models

The last chapter dealt with the subjective assessment of probabilities as a method of modeling uncertainty in a decision problem. Using subjective probabilities often is all that is necessary, although they occasionally are difficult to come up with, and the nature of the uncertainty in a decision situation can be somewhat complicated. In these cases, we need another approach.

An alternative source for probabilities is to use theoretical probability models and their associated distributions. We can consider the characteristics of the system from which the uncertain event of interest arises, and, if the characteristics correspond to the assumptions that give rise to a standard distribution, we may use the distribution to generate the probabilities. It is important to realize, however, that in this situation a substantial subjective judgment is being made: that the physical system can be represented adequately using the model chosen. In this sense, such probability models would be just as "subjective" as a directly assessed probability distribution.

One approach is to assess a subjective probability distribution and then find a standard distribution that provides a close "fit" to those subjective probabilities. A decision maker might do this simply to make the probability and expected-value calculations easier. Of course, in this case the underlying subjective judgment is that the theoretical distribution adequately fits the assessed judgments.

How important are theoretical probability distributions for decision making? Consider the following applications of theoretical models.

THEORETICAL MODELS APPLIED

EDUCATIONAL TESTING. Most major educational and intelligence tests generate distributions of scores that can be well represented by the normal distribution, or the familiar bell-shaped curve. Many colleges and universities admit only individuals whose scores are above a stated criterion that corresponds to a specific percentile of the normal distribution of scores.

MARKET RESEARCH.   In many market research studies, a fundamental issue is whether a potential customer prefers one product to another. The uncertainty involved in these problems often can be modeled using the binomial or closely related distributions.

QUALITY CONTROL.   How many defects are acceptable in a finished product? In some products, the occurrence of defects, such as bubbles in glass or blemishes in cloth, can be modeled quite nicely with a Poisson process. Once the uncertainty is modeled, alternative qualtity-control strategies can be analyzed for their relative costs and benefits.

PREDICTING ELECTION OUTCOMES.   How do the major television networks manage to extrapolate the results of exit polls to predict the outcome of elections? Again, the binomial distribution forms the basis for making probability statements about who wins an election based on a sample of results.

CAPACITY PLANNING.   Do you sometimes feel that you spend too much time standing in lines waiting for service? Service providers are on the other side; their problem is how to provide adequate service when the arrival of customers is uncertain. In many cases, the number of customers arriving within a period of time can be modeled using the Poisson distribution. Moreover, this distribution can be extended to the placement of orders at a manufacturing facility, the breakdown of equipment, and other similar processes.

ENVIRONMENTAL RISK ANALYSIS.   In modeling the level of pollutants in the environment, scientists often use the lognormal distribution, a variant of the normal distribution. With uncertainty about pollutant levels modeled in this way, it is possible to analyze pollution-control policies so as to understand the relative effects of different policies.

◆

You might imagine that many different theoretical probability models exist and have been used in a wide variety of applications. We will be scratching only the surface here, introducing a few of the more common distributions. For discrete probability situations, we will discuss the binomial and Poisson distributions, both of which are commonly encountered and easily used. Continuous distributions that will be discussed are the exponential, normal, and beta distributions. The references at the end of this chapter will direct you to sources on other distributions.

◆ THE BINOMIAL DISTRIBUTION

Perhaps the easiest place to begin is with the *binomial* distribution. Suppose, for example, that you were in a race for mayor of your hometown, and you wanted to find out how you were doing with the voters. You might take a sample, count the number of individuals who indicated a preference for you, and then, based on this information, judge your chances of winning the election. In this situation, each voter interviewed can be either for you or not. This is the kind of situation in which the binomial distribution can play a large part. Of course, it is not limited to the analysis of voter preferences, but also can be used in analyses of quality control where an item may or may not be defective, in market research, and in many other situations.

The binomial distribution arises from a situation that has the following characteristics:

1. *Dichotomous outcomes.* Uncertain events occur in a sequence, each one having one of two possible outcomes — success/failure, heads/tails, yes/no, true/false, on/off, and so on.
2. *Constant probability.* Each event, or *trial* has the same probability of success. Call that probability p.
3. *Independence.* The outcome of each trial is independent of the outcomes of the other trials. That is, the probability of success does not depend on the preceding outcomes. (As we noted in Problem 8.19 ignoring this sometimes is called the *gambler's fallacy*: just because a roulette wheel has come up red five consecutive times does not mean that black is "due" to occur. Given independence from one game to the next, the probability of black still is 0.5, regardless of the previous outcomes.)

Now suppose we look at a sequence of n trials; for example, four tosses of a loaded coin that has P(Heads) = 0.8. How many successes (heads) could there be? Let R denote the uncertain quantity or random variable that is the number of successes in the sequence of trials. Clearly, there can be no more than n successes: $0 \le R \le n$. In our example, $0 \le R \le 4$, or there will be somewhere between zero and four heads.

What is the probability of four heads? Let H_i denote the event that a head occurs on the ith toss. Then four heads can happen only if the following sequence occurs: H_1, H_2, H_3, H_4. What is $P(H_1, H_2, H_3, H_4)$?

$$
\begin{aligned}
P(R = 4 \mid n = 4, p = 0.8) &= P(H_1, H_2, H_3, H_4) \\
&= P(H_1)\, P(H_2 \mid H_1)\, P(H_3 \mid H_2, H_1)\, P(H_4 \mid H_3, H_2, H_1), \\
&\quad \text{(by using conditional probabilities),} \\
&= P(H_1)\, P(H_2)\, P(H_3)\, P(H_4) \\
&\quad \text{(by the independence property)} \\
&= p^4 \quad \text{(by the constant probability property)} \\
&= 0.8^4 \quad \text{(P(Heads) = 0.8 for the loaded coin)} \\
&= 0.41.
\end{aligned}
$$

What is the probability of three heads? In this case, three heads can occur in any of four ways:

$$H_1, H_2, H_3, T$$
$$H_1, H_2, T, H_4$$
$$H_1, T, H_3, H_4$$
$$T, H_2, H_3, H_4.$$

The probability for any one of these sequences is $p^3(1 - p)^1$. Because these four sequences are mutually exclusive, the probability of three heads is simply the sum of the individual probabilities, or P(three heads in four tosses) = $P(R = 3 \mid n = 4, p = 0.8) = 4\,p^3(1 - p)^1 = 4(0.8^3)\,(0.2)$.

In general, the probability of obtaining r successes in n trials is given by

$$P_B(R = r \mid n,\, p) = \frac{n!}{r!\,(n - r)!}\, p^r\,(1 - p)^{\,n - r}, \tag{9.1}$$

where the subscript B indicates that this is a binomial probability. The term with the factorials is called the *combinatorial term*. It gives the number of ways that a sequence of n trials can have r successes. The second term is just the probability associated with a particular sequence with r successes in n trials. The expected number of successes is simply $E(R) = np$. (If I have n trials, I expect proportion p of them to be successes.) The variance of the number of successes is $\mathrm{Var}(R) = np(1 - p)$.

Binomial probabilities are not difficult to calculate using Formula 9.1, but you do not have to calculate them yourself. Individual probabilities [$P_B(r$ successes)] and cumulative terms [$P_B(r$ or fewer successes)] can be found in the tables in Appendixes A and B at the end of this book. For example, $P_B(R = 2 \mid n = 9, p = 0.12)$ is found in the following way, as illustrated in Figure 9.1. First, we find the value $n = 9$ along the left margin, and then the value for $r = 2$. Now read across that row until you find the column headed by $p = 0.12$. The probability you read is 0.212. Thus, $P_B(R = 2 \mid n = 9, p = 0.12) = 0.212$.

The tables can be used to find binomial probabilities in many different

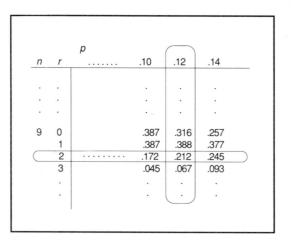

FIGURE 9.1   *Using the Binomial Table to Find*
$P_B(R = 2 \mid n = 9,\ p = 0.12)$

forms. For example, what is $P_B(R > 3 \mid n = 15, p = 0.2)$? To find this probability, all that is necessary is to consider the complement:

$$P_B(R > 3 \mid n = 15, p = 0.2) = 1 - P_B(R \leq 3 \mid n = 15, p = 0.2)$$
$$= 1 - 0.648 \text{ (from Appendix B)}$$
$$= 0.352.$$

You may have noticed that the values for p only go up to 0.50. What if you need to find a binomial probability with a p larger than 0.50? Let's try it. What is $P_B(R \leq 5 \mid n = 8, p = 0.7)$. To do this, we will look at the flip side of the situation. Getting five or fewer successes in eight trials is equivalent to getting three or more failures in eight trials, where $P(\text{failure}) = 1 - P(\text{success})$. Thus, we are arguing that

$$P_B(R \leq 5 \mid n = 8, p = 0.7) = P_B(R' \geq 3 \mid n = 8, p = 0.3),$$

where $R' = n - R$, or the number of failures. Now, to find $P_B(R' \geq 3 \mid n = 8, p = 0.3)$, use the idea of a complement:

$$P_B(R' \geq 3 \mid n = 8, p = 0.3) = 1 - P_B(R' \leq 2 \mid n = 8, p = 0.3)$$
$$= 1 - 0.552$$
$$= 0.448.$$

AN EXAMPLE: MELISSA BAILEY. It is the beginning of winter term at the College of Business at Eastern State. Melissa Bailey says she is eager to study, but she has plans for a ski trip each weekend for 12 weeks. She will go only if there is good weather. The probability of good weather on any weekend during the winter is approximately 0.65. What is the probability that she will be gone for eight or more weekends?

Are all of the requirements satisfied for the binomial distribution? Weekend weather is good or bad, satisfying the dichotomous outcomes property. We will assume that the probabilities are the same from one weekend to the next, and moreover it seems reasonable to assume that the weather on one weekend during the winter is independent of the weather of previous weekends. Given these assumptions, the binomial distribution is an appropriate model for the uncertainty in this problem. Keep in mind that we are building a model of the uncertainty. Although our assumptions may not be exactly true, the binomial distribution should provide a good approximation.

To solve the problem, we must find $P_B(R \geq 8 \mid n = 12, p = 0.65)$. Of course, it is always possible to calculate this probability directly using the formula; however, let us see how to use the tables. The first problem is that the tables only give probabilities for p less than or equal to 0.50. To obtain the probability we want, we look at the problem in terms of bad weather rather than good. Being gone 8 or more weekends (good weather) out of 12 is the same as staying home on 4 or fewer weekends (bad weather). Find $P_B(R' \leq 4 \mid n = 12, p = 0.35)$. Using Appendix B, this is 0.583. Thus, there is more than a 50% chance that Melissa will be home on four or fewer weekends and gone on eight or more weekends.

ANOTHER EXAMPLE: SOFT PRETZELS.   Having just completed your degree in business, you are eager to try your skills as an entrepreneur by marketing a new pretzel that you have developed. You estimate that you should be able to sell them at a competitive price of 50 cents each. The potential market is estimated to be 100,000 pretzels per year. Unfortunately, because of a competing product, you know you will not be able to sell that many. After careful research and thought, you conclude that the following model of the situation captures the relevant aspects of the problem: Your new pretzel might be a hit, in which case it will capture 30% of the market in the first year. On the other hand, it may be a flop, in which case the market share will be only 10%. You judge these outcomes to be equally likely.

Being naturally cautious, you decide that it is worthwhile to bake a few pretzels and test market them. You bake 20, and in a taste test against the competing product, 5 out of 20 people preferred your pretzel. Given this new data, what do you think the chances are that your new pretzel is a hit? The following analysis is one way that you might analyze the situation.

The question we are asking is this: What is P(New Pretzel a hit | 5 of 20 Preferred New Pretzel)? How can we get a handle on this probability? A problem like this that involves finding a probability given some new evidence almost certainly requires an application of Bayes' theorem. Let us use some notation to make our life simpler. Let "Hit" and "Flop" denote the outcomes that the new pretzel is a hit or a flop, respectively. Let R be the number of tasters (out of 20) who preferred the new pretzel. Now we can write down Bayes' theorem using this notation:

$$P(\text{New Pretzel a Hit} \mid 5 \text{ of } 20 \text{ Preferred New Pretzel})$$
$$= P(\text{Hit} \mid R = 5)$$
$$= \frac{P(R = 5 \mid \text{Hit})\ P(\text{Hit})}{P(R = 5 \mid \text{Hit})\ P(\text{Hit}) + P(R = 5 \mid \text{Flop})\ P(\text{Flop})}.$$

Next we must fill in the appropriate probabilities on the right-hand side of the Bayes' theorem equation. The probabilities P(Hit) and P(Flop) are easy. Based on the judgment (stated above) that these two outcomes are considered to be equally likely, we can say that P(Hit) = P(Flop) = 0.50.

What about $P(R = 5 \mid \text{Hit})$ and $P(R = 5 \mid \text{Flop})$? These are a bit trickier. Consider $P(R = 5 \mid \text{Hit})$. This is the binomial probability that 5 out of 20 people prefer your pretzel, given that 30% ($p = 0.3$) of the entire population of pretzel customers would prefer yours. That is, if your pretzel is a hit, you will capture 30% of the market. How does this idea of 30% across the entire population relate to the chance of 5 out of a sample of 20 preferring your pretzel? Provided that we can view the 20 people in our sample as "randomly selected," we can apply the binomial distribution. ("Randomly selected" means that each member of the population had the same chance of being chosen. That is, each taster has the same chance of preferring your pretzel, thus satisfying the independence and constant probabilities for the binomial distribution.) We have $p = 0.30$ (Hit) and $n = 20$ (the sample size), and so $P(R = 5 \mid \text{Hit}) = P_B(R = 5 \mid n = 20, p = 0.30)$. We can use Formula 9.1 or the table to find $P_B(R = 5 \mid n = 20, p = 0.30) = 0.179$.

The same argument can be made regarding $P(R = 5 \mid \text{Flop})$. Now the condition is that the pretzels are a flop. This means that only 10% of the population prefer your pretzel over the other. Thus, we have $p = 0.10$ in this case. This gives us $P(R = 5 \mid \text{Flop}) = P_B(R = 5 \mid n = 20, p = 0.10)$. From the table, this probability is 0.032.

We now have everything we need to do the calculations that are required by Bayes' theorem:

$$P(\text{New Pretzel a Hit} \mid 5 \text{ of } 20 \text{ Preferred New Pretzel})$$

$$= P(\text{Hit} \mid R = 5)$$

$$= \frac{P(R = 5 \mid \text{Hit}) \, P(\text{Hit})}{P(R = 5 \mid \text{Hit}) \, P(\text{Hit}) + P(R = 5 \mid \text{Flop}) \, P(\text{Flop})}$$

$$= \frac{0.179 \, (0.50)}{0.179 \, (0.50) + 0.032 \, (0.50)}$$

$$= 0.848.$$

Thus, this evidence (5 out of 20 people preferring your pretzel) is good news. Your posterior probability that your pretzel will be a hit is almost 85%. Of course, we did the analysis on the basis of prior probabilities being $P(\text{Hit}) = P(\text{Flop}) = 0.50$. If you had assessed different prior probabilities, your answer would be different, although in any case your probability that the pretzel is a hit increases with the evidence.

◆ THE POISSON DISTRIBUTION

While the binomial distribution is particularly good for representing successes in several trials, the *Poisson* distribution is good for representing occurrences of a particular event over time or space. Suppose, for example, that you are interested in the number of customers who arrive at a bank in one hour. Clearly this is an uncertain quantity; there could be none, one, two, three, and so on. The Poisson distribution also may be appropriate for modeling the uncertainty surrounding the number of machine breakdowns in a factory over some period of time. Other Poisson applications include modeling the uncertain number of blemishes in a bolt of fabric, or the number of chocolate chips in a chocolate chip cookie.

The Poisson distribution requires the following:

1. Events can happen at any of a large number of places within the unit of measurement (hour, square yard, and so on), and preferably along a continuum.
2. At any specific point, the probability of an event is small. This simply means that the events do not happen too frequently. For example, we would be interested in a steady flow of customers to a bank, not a run on the bank.
3. Events happen independently of other events. In other words, the probability of an event at any one point is the same regardless of the time (or location) of other events.

4. The average number of events over a unit of measure (time or space) is constant no matter how far or how long the process has gone on.

Let X represent the uncertain number of events in a unit of time or space. Under the conditions given above, the probability that $X = k$ events is given by:

$$P_P(X = k) = \frac{e^{-m} m^k}{k!}, \tag{9.2}$$

where the subscript P indicates this is a Poisson probability, e is the constant 2.718 . . . (the base of the natural logarithms), and m is a parameter that characterizes the distribution. In particular, m turns out to be both the expected number of events and the variance of the number of events. In symbols, $E(X) = m$ and $Var(X) = m$.

It is easy to calculate Poisson probabilities using Formula 9.2 and a good calculator. For example,

$$P_P(X = 2 \mid m = 1.5) = \frac{e^{-1.5}(1.5)^2}{2!}$$

$$= 0.251.$$

Again, however, tables (Appendixes C and D) are available that give both individual Poisson probabilities as well as cumulative probabilities (the probability of x or fewer events) for different values of m. Using these tables is much like using the binomial tables. Find the value for m across the top and the value for k along the left side. Figure 9.2 illustrates the use of the Poisson table in Appendix C to confirm our answer above.

AN EXAMPLE: BLEMISHES IN FABRIC.   As a simple example, suppose that you are interested in estimating the number of blemishes in 200 yards of cloth. Based on earlier experience with the cloth manufacturer, you estimate that a blemish occurs (on average) every 27 yards. At a rate of 1 blemish per 27 yards, this amounts to an approximate 7.4 blemishes in the 200 yards of cloth.

k	m	1.4	1.5	1.6
0		.247	.223	.202
1		.345	.335	.323
2	....	.242	.251	.258
3		.113	.126	.138
.		.	.	.
.		.	.	.

FIGURE 9.2   *Using the Poisson Table to Find*
$P_P(X = 2 \mid m = 1.5)$

Is the Poisson distribution appropriate? Condition 1 is satisfied — we are looking at a continuous 200 yards of fabric. Condition 2 also is satisfied; apparently there are only a few blemishes in the 200 yards. Conditions 3 and 4 both should be satisfied unless blemishes are created by some machine malfunction that results in many of blemishes occurring together. Thus, the Poisson distribution appears to provide an appropriate model of the uncertainty in this problem.

The expected value of 7.4 suggests that we could use a Poisson distribution with $m = 7.4$. Probabilities can be calculated using Formula 9.2. For example, the probability of nine blemishes in the cloth is

$$P_P(X = 9 \mid m = 7.4) = \frac{e^{-7.4}(7.4)^9}{9!}$$

$$= 0.112.$$

We also can confirm this answer by looking in Appendix C, although information from Appendix D may be more useful. For example, the probability of 4 or fewer blemishes is $P_P(X \le 4 \mid m = 7.4) = 0.140$. We also can find the probability of more than 10 blemishes: $P_P(X > 10 \mid m = 7.4) = 1 - P_P(X \le 10 \mid m = 7.4) = 1.000 - 0.871 = 0.129$. Although it is theoretically possible for there to be a very large number of blemishes, we can see that the probability of more than 18 is extremely low. In fact, it is less than 0.0005 (the probabilities in Appendixes C and D are rounded to three decimal places).

SOFT PRETZELS, CONTINUED. Let us continue with the problem of the soft pretzels. You introduced the pretzels, and they are doing quite well. You have been distributing the product through several stores as well as through one street vendor. This vendor has been able to sell an average of 20 pretzels per hour. He had tried a different location earlier, but had to move; sales there were only some 8 pretzels per hour, which was not enough to support his business. Now you are ready to try a second vendor in an altogether different location. The new location could be a "good" one, meaning an average of 20 pretzels per hour, "bad" with an average of only 10 per hour, or "dismal" with an average of 6 per hour. You have carefully assessed the probabilities of good, bad, or dismal using the assessment techniques from Chapter 6. Your judgment is that the new location is likely (probability 0.7) to be a good one. On the other hand, it could be (probability 0.2) a bad location, and it is just possible (probability 0.1) that the sales rate will be dismal.

After having the new stand open for a week, or long enough to establish a presence in the neighborhood, you decide to run a test. In 30 minutes you sell 7 pretzels. Now what are your probabilities regarding the quality of your new location? That is, what are $P(\text{Good} \mid X = 7)$, $P(\text{Bad} \mid X = 7)$, and $P(\text{Dismal} \mid X = 7)$?

As in the binomial case, we are interested in finding posterior probabilities given some new evidence. We will use Bayes' theorem to solve the problem:

$P(\text{Good} \mid X = 7)$

$$= \frac{P(X = 7 \mid \text{Good})P(\text{Good})}{P(X = 7 \mid \text{Good})P(\text{Good}) + P(X = 7 \mid \text{Bad})P(\text{Bad}) + P(X = 7 \mid \text{Dismal})P(\text{Dismal})}.$$

We have our prior probabilities, P(Good) = 0.7, P(Bad) = 0.2, and P(Dismal) = 0.1. What about the probabilities P(X = 7 | Good), P(X = 7 | Bad) and P(X = 7 | Dismal)? First, note that we are talking about a 30-minute period. Thus, the expected number of sales is either 10, 5, or 3 per half hour, depending on whether the location is good, bad, or dismal. If the conditions for the Poisson distribution hold, then P(X = 7 | Good) is the Poisson probability of 7 occurrences when $m = 10$, $P_P(X = 7 | m = 10)$. From Appendix C, this probability is 0.090. Likewise, P(X = 7 | Bad) is the Poisson probability of 7 occurrences when $m = 5$, or 0.104. Finally, P(X = 7 | Dismal) is 0.022.

Now we can plug these values into Bayes' theorem:

P(Good | X = 7)

$$= \frac{P(X = 7 \mid \text{Good})P(\text{Good})}{P(X = 7 \mid \text{Good})P(\text{Good}) + P(X = 7 \mid \text{Bad})P(\text{Bad}) + P(X = 7 \mid \text{Dismal})P(\text{Dismal})}$$

$$= \frac{0.090\ (0.7)}{0.090\ (0.7) + 0.104\ (0.2) + 0.022\ (0.1)}$$

$$= 0.733.$$

Likewise, we can calculate P(Bad | X = 7) = 0.242, and P(Dismal | X = 7) = 0.025. The posterior probabilities P(Good | X = 7) and P(Bad | X = 7) are not much different from the corresponding prior probabilities, so you might conclude that this information did not tell you much. On the basis of the information, however, the probability of the new location being dismal is now quite small.

◆ THE EXPONENTIAL DISTRIBUTION

The Poisson and binomial distributions are examples of discrete probability distributions because the outcome can take on only specific "discrete" values. What about continuous uncertain quantities? For example, tomorrow's high temperature could be any value between, say, 0° and 100° F. The per-barrel price of crude oil at the end of the year 2000 might be anywhere between $10 and $100. As discussed in Chapter 7, it is more natural in these cases to speak of the probability that the uncertain quantity falls within some interval. In the weather example we might look at historical weather patterns and determine that on 50% of days during May in Columbus, Ohio, the daily high temperature has been 70° or lower. On the basis of this, we could assess P(High Temperature in Columbus on May 28th ≤ 60°) = 0.50.

In this section, we will look briefly at the *exponential* distribution for a continuous random variable. In fact, the exponential distribution is closely related to the Poisson. If in the Poisson we were considering the number of arrivals within a specified period of time, then the uncertain time between arrivals (T) has an exponential distribution. The two go hand-in-hand; if the four conditions listed for the Poisson hold, then the time (or space) between events follows an exponential distribution.

For the binomial and Poisson distributions above, we were able to express in

Formulas 9.1 and 9.2 the probability of a specific value for the random variable. The corresponding expression for a continuous random variable is the *density function*. This function shows the relative likelihood for the different values that the uncertain quantity can take. For the exponential, the density function is:

$$f_E(t \mid m) = me^{-mt},$$ (9.3)

where m is the same average rate that we used in the Poisson and t represents the possible values for the uncertain quantity T. An exponential density function with $m = 2$ is illustrated in Figure 9.3. Recall from Chapter 7 that areas under the density function correspond to probabilities. Thus, the area from 0 to a in Figure 9.3 represents $P_E(T \le a \mid m = 2)$, where the subscript E indicates that this is a probability from an exponential distribution.

The exponential distribution turns out to be an easy distribution to work with. Probabilities are calculated by using the following formulas:

$$P_E(T \le a \mid m) = 1 - e^{-am}$$
$$P_E(T > a \mid m) = 1 - P(T \le a \mid m) = e^{-am}$$
$$P_E(b < T \le a \mid m) = P(T \le a \mid m) - P(T \le b \mid m) = e^{-bm} - e^{-am}.$$

For example, we can calculate that

$$P_E(T > 15 \text{ Min} \mid m = 2 \text{ Arrivals per Hr}) = P_E(T > 0.25 \text{ Hr} \mid m = 2 \text{ Arrivals per Hr})$$
$$= e^{-0.25(2)}$$
$$= 0.607.$$

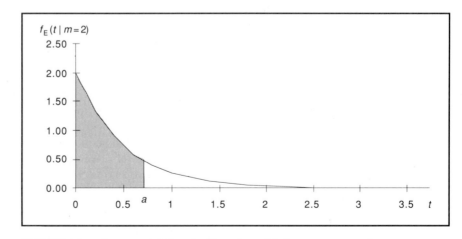

FIGURE 9.3 *Exponential Density Function with Parameter* $m = 2$
The shaded area represents $P_E(T \le a \mid m = 2)$.

Moreover, we can check this particular probability by using the Poisson table! The event "The time until the next arrival is greater than 15 minutes" is equivalent to the event "There are no arrivals in the next 15 minutes." Thus,

$$P_E(T > 15 \text{ Min} \mid m = 2 \text{ Arrivals per Hr})$$
$$= P_P(X = 0 \text{ Arrivals in 15 Min} \mid m = 2 \text{ Arrivals per Hr})$$
$$= P_P(X = 0 \text{ Arrivals in 15 Min} \mid m = 0.5 \text{ Arrivals per 15 Min})$$
$$= 0.607$$

from Appendix C.

The expected value of an exponential random variable is $E(T) = 1/m$, and the variance is $Var(T) = 1/m^2$. Keep in mind that these are in units of time. For example, if $m = 6$ events per hour, then the expected time until the next event is $\frac{1}{6}$ of an hour, or 10 minutes.

SOFT PREZTELS, AGAIN.   The problem at hand is whether a pretzel can be prepared during the time between customers. If it takes 3.5 minutes to cook a pretzel, what is the probability that the next customer will arrive before it is finished, $P(T > 3.5 \text{ Min})$?

This is a difficult calculation because we do not know exactly what the rate m would be for an exponential distribution. But we can expand $P(T > 3.5 \text{ Min})$ by using the total probability formula:

$$P(T > 3.5 \text{ Min}) = P_E(T > 3.5 \text{ Min} \mid m = 20/\text{Hr}) \, P(m = 20)$$
$$+ \, P_E(T > 3.5 \text{ Min} \mid m = 10/\text{Hr}) \, P(m = 10)$$
$$+ \, P_E(T > 3.5 \text{ Min} \mid m = 6/\text{Hr}) \, P(m = 6)$$
$$= P_E(T > 0.0583 \text{ Hr} \mid m = 20/\text{Hr}) \, P(m = 20)$$
$$+ \, P_E(T > 0.0583 \text{ Hr} \mid m = 10/\text{Hr}) \, P(m = 10)$$
$$+ \, P_E(T > 0.0583 \text{ Hr} \mid m = 6/\text{Hr}) \, P(m = 6)$$
$$= e^{-0.0583(20)} \, P(m = 20) + e^{-0.0583(10)} \, P(m = 10)$$
$$+ \, e^{-0.0583(6)} \, P(m = 6)$$
$$= 0.3114 \, P(m = 20) + 0.5580 \, P(m = 10) + 0.7047 \, P(m = 6).$$

Now we can substitute in the posterior probabilities that we calculated above, $P(\text{Good} \mid X = 7) = 0.733$, $P(\text{Bad} \mid X = 7) = 0.242$, and $P(\text{Dismal} \mid X = 7) = 0.025$:

$$P(T > 3.5 \text{ Min}) = 0.3114 \, (0.733) + 0.5580 \, (0.242) + 0.7047 \, (0.025)$$
$$= 0.3809.$$

Thus, the probability is 0.3809 that the time between arrivals is greater than 3.5 minutes. Put another way, the majority of customers will arrive before the next pretzel pops out of the oven.

◆ THE NORMAL DISTRIBUTION

Another particularly useful continuous distribution is the *normal* distribution, which is the familiar bell-shaped curve. The normal distribution is particularly good for modeling situations in which the uncertain quantity is subject to many different sources of uncertainty or error. For example, in measuring something, errors may be introduced by a wide range of environmental conditions, equipment malfunctions, human error, and so on. Many measured biological phenomena (height, weight, length) often follow a bell-shaped curve that can be represented well with a normal distribution.

We will let Y represent an uncertain quantity that follows a normal distribution. If this is the case, the density function for Y is

$$f_N(y \mid \mu, \sigma) = \frac{1}{\sqrt{2\pi}\,\sigma}\, e^{-(y-\mu)^2/2\sigma^2},$$

(9.4)

where μ and σ are parameters of the distribution and y represents the possible values that Y can take. In fact, it turns out that $E(Y) = \mu$ and $\mathrm{Var}(Y) = \sigma^2$. Figure 9.4 illustrates a normal density function. As with the exponential, the area under the density function represents the probability that the random variable falls into the corresponding interval. For example, the shaded area in Figure 9.4 represents $P_N(a \le Y \le b \mid \mu, \sigma)$. Strictly speaking, a normal random variable can take values anywhere between plus and minus infinity. But the probabilities associated with values more than three or four standard deviations from the mean are negligible, so we often use the normal to represent values that have a restricted range (for example, weight or height, which can only be positive) as long as the extreme points are several standard deviations from the mean.

In the case of the normal distribution, there are no simple formulas for finding probabilities as there are for the exponential. A simple rule of thumb exists for the normal, however. The probability is approximately 0.68 that a normal random variable is within one standard deviation of the mean μ, and the probability is approximately 0.95 that it is within two standard deviations of the mean. In symbols:

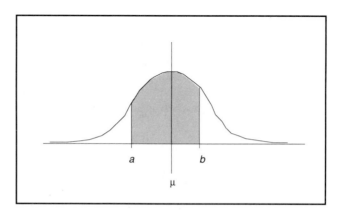

FIGURE 9.4 *Normal Density Function*
The shaded area represents $P_N(a \le Y \le b \mid \mu, \sigma)$.

$$P_N(\mu - \sigma \leq Y \leq \mu + \sigma) \approx 0.68$$
$$P_N(\mu - 2\sigma \leq Y \leq \mu + 2\sigma) \approx 0.95.$$

These are handy approximations for normal random variables and sometimes are called the *Empirical Rule* because these probabilities are found to hold (approximately) in many real-world situations.

A table has been provided in Appendix E so that you can find cumulative normal probabilities. But there is a catch! The table is for a *standard normal* distribution, one that has $\mu = 0$ and $\sigma = 1$. To use this table, we must know how to convert from a normal with any mean and standard deviation to a standard normal. The conversion works by subtracting the mean and dividing by the standard deviation. In symbols,

$$P_N(Y \leq a \mid \mu, \sigma) = P_N\left(Z \leq \frac{a - \mu}{\sigma} \mid \mu = 0, \sigma = 1\right)$$

$$= P_N\left(Z \leq \frac{a - \mu}{\sigma}\right).$$

In most cases, we will leave off the values $\mu = 0$, $\sigma = 1$ when we talk about the standard normal random variable Z.

For example, if Y has a normal distribution with mean 10 and variance 400, then the probability that Y is less than or equal to 35 is

$$P_N(Y \leq 35 \mid \mu = 10, \sigma^2 = 400) = P_N\left(Z \leq \frac{35 - 10}{20}\right)$$

$$= P_N(Z \leq 1.25).$$

Find this probability by looking in Appendix E as illustrated in Figure 9.5. This table has cumulative probabilities listed for values of z from -3.50 up to 3.49. Find $z = 1.25$, and read off $P(Z \leq 1.25) = 0.8944$.

AN INVESTMENT EXAMPLE.   Consider three alternative investments, A, B, and C. Investing in C yields a sure return of $40. Investment A has an uncertain return (X), which is modeled in this case by a normal distribution with mean $50 and standard deviation $10. Investment B's return (represented by Y) also is modeled with a normal distribution having mean of $59 and a standard deviation of $20. On the basis of expected values, B is the obvious choice because $59 is greater than $50 or $40. The decision tree is shown in Figure 9.6.

Although it is obvious that the expected payoff for B is greater than the sure $40 for C, we might be interested in the probability that B's payoff will be less than $40. To find this probability, we must convert the value of 40 in our prob-

....	z	P(Z ≤ z)	....
....	....	....	....
	1.20	.8849	
....	1.21	.8869	....
	1.22	.8888	
	1.23	.8907	
....	1.24	.8925	....
	1.25	.8944	
....	1.26	.8962	....
	1.27	.8980	
	1.28	.8997	
....	1.29	.9015	....
....	....	....	....

FIGURE 9.5   *Using the Normal Distribution Table to Find* $P_N(Z \leq 1.25)$

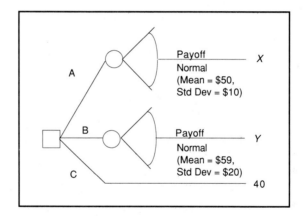

FIGURE 9.6   *Decision Tree for Three Alternative Investments*

lem to a *standardized* value. Subtract the mean and then divide by the standard deviation to get a standardized random variable *Z*:

$$P_N(B \leq 40 \mid \mu = 59, \sigma = 20) = P_N\left(Z \leq \frac{40 - 59}{20}\right)$$

$$= P_N(Z \leq -0.95).$$

From Appendix E we find that

$$P(Z < -0.95) = 0.1711.$$

Doing the same thing for Investment A, we want $P_N(A \leq \$40 \mid \mu = 50, \sigma = 10)$:

$$P_N(A \leq \$40 \mid \mu = 50, \sigma = 10) = P\left(Z \leq \frac{40 - 50}{10}\right)$$
$$= P(Z \leq -1.0)$$
$$= 0.1587.$$

Thus, even though Investment A has a lower expected value than does B, A has a smaller probability of having a return of less than $40. Why? The larger variance for B means that the distribution for B is spread out more than is the distribution for A.

We also might be interested in the probability of a particularly large return, say

$$P_N(B > 78 \mid \mu = 59, \sigma = 20) = P_N\left(Z > \frac{78 - 59}{20}\right)$$
$$= P_N(Z > 0.95).$$

Because Appendix E shows cumulative probabilities $P(Z \leq z)$, we must do extra work in this case. We can find the probability of the complement $P(Z \leq 0.95)$ and subtract this from 1:

$$P_N(Z > 0.95) = 1 - P_N(Z \leq 0.95)$$
$$= 1 - 0.8289$$
$$= 0.1711.$$

The probability $P(Z > 0.95)$ turns out to be the same as $P(Z \leq -0.95)$. This example points out the symmetry of the normal distribution. For any z, $P(Z > z) = P(Z \leq -z)$. To get our probability $P(Z > 0.95)$, we could have found it directly in the table by looking up $P(Z \leq -0.95)$. Figure 9.7 shows this property graphically.

EXAMPLE: QUALITY CONTROL. Suppose that you are the manager for a manufacturing plant that produces disk drives for personal computers. One of your machines produces a part that is used in the final assembly. The width of this part is

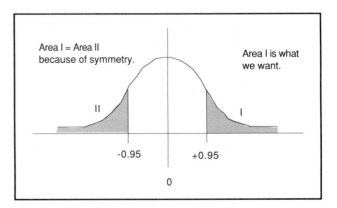

FIGURE 9.7 *The Symmetry of the Normal Distribution*

important to the disk drive's operation; if it falls below 3.995 or above 4.005 millimeters (mm), the disk drive will not work properly and must be repaired at a cost of $10.40.

The machine can be set to produce parts with a width of 4 mm, but it is not perfectly accurate. In fact, the actual width of a part is normally distributed with mean 4 mm, and a variance that depends on the speed of the machine. If the machine is run at a slower speed, the width of the produced parts has a standard deviation of 0.0019 mm. At the higher speed, however, the machine is less precise, producing parts with a standard deviation of 0.0026 mm.

Of course, the higher speed means that more parts can be produced in less time, thus reducing the overall cost of the disk drive. In fact, it turns out that the cost of the disk drive when the machine is set at high speed is $20.45. At low speed, the cost is $20.75.

The question that you as plant manager face is whether it would be better to run the machine at high or low speed. Is the extra expense of lower speed more than offset by the increased precision and hence the lower defect rate? You would like to choose the strategy with the lower expected cost. Your decision tree is shown in Figure 9.8.

To make the decision, we need to know the probability of a defective unit under both of the machine settings. Because the width of the part follows a normal distribution in each case, we can get these probabilities by calculating z values and using Appendix E:

$$P(\text{Defective} \mid \text{Low Speed}) = 1 - P(\text{Not Defective} \mid \text{Low Speed})$$

$$= 1 - P_N(3.995 \leq Y \leq 4.005 \mid \mu = 4, \sigma = 0.0019)$$

$$= 1 - P\left(\frac{3.995 - 4}{0.0019} \leq Z \leq \frac{4.005 - 4}{0.0019}\right)$$

$$= 1 - P(-2.63 \leq Z \leq 2.63)$$

$$= 1 - [P(Z \leq 2.63) - P(Z \leq -2.63)]$$

$$= 1 - [0.9957 - 0.0043]$$

$$= 1 - 0.9914$$

$$= 0.0086.$$

Likewise, we can calculate $P(\text{Defective} \mid \text{High Speed})$:

$$P(\text{Defective} \mid \text{High Speed}) = 1 - P(\text{Not Defective} \mid \text{High Speed})$$

$$= 1 - P_N(3.995 \leq Y \leq 4.005 \mid \mu = 4, \sigma = 0.0026)$$

$$= 1 - P\left(\frac{3.995 - 4}{0.0026} \leq Z \leq \frac{4.005 - 4}{0.0026}\right)$$

$$= 1 - P(-1.92 \leq Z \leq 1.92)$$

$$= 1 - [P(Z \leq 1.92) - P(Z \leq -1.92)]$$

$$= 1 - [0.9726 - 0.0274]$$

$$= 1 - 0.9452$$

$$= 0.0548.$$

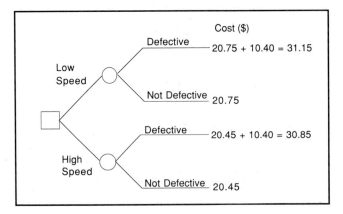

FIGURE 9.8   *Decision Tree for a Quality-Control Problem*

With these probabilities, it now is possible to calculate the expected cost for each alternative:

$$E(\text{Cost} \mid \text{Low Speed}) = 0.9914(\$20.75) + 0.0086(\$31.15)$$
$$= \$20.84.$$
$$E(\text{Cost} \mid \text{High Speed}) = 0.9452(\$20.45) + 0.0548(\$30.85)$$
$$= \$21.02.$$

Thus, in this case the increased cost from the slower speed is more than offset by the increased precision and lower defect rate, and you would definitely choose the slower speed.

◆ THE BETA DISTRIBUTION

Suppose you are interested in the proportion of voters who will vote for the Republican candidate in the next presidential election. If you are uncertain about this proportion, you may want to encode your uncertainty as a continuous probability distribution. Because the proportion can take only values between 0 and 1, neither the exponential nor the normal distribution can adequately reflect the uncertainty you face. The *beta* distribution, however, may be appropriate. Let Q denote an uncertain quantity that can take any value between 0 and 1. Then the beta density function is:

$$f_B(q \mid r, n) = \frac{(n-1)!}{(r-1)! \, (n-r-1)!} \, q^{r-1} \, (1-q)^{n-r-1}. \qquad (9.5)$$

As before, q represents the possible values between 0 and 1 that Q can take.

The numbers r and n are parameters that determine the shape of the density function. If n is large, the distribution is fairly "tight," whereas if n is small, the distribution is more "spread out" (Figure 9.9). If $r = n/2$, the density function is symmetric around 0.5. If this is not the case, however, the distribution is skewed to the right or left depending on whether $r < n/2$ or $r > n/2$, as in Figure 9.10. As usual with density functions, the area under the curve represents probability. Thus, in Figure 9.10 the shaded area represents $P_B(0.2 \leq Q \leq 0.4 \mid n = 6, r = 4)$. A table in Appendix F provides cumulative probabilities for a wide variety of different beta distributions. We will demonstrate this table's use shortly.

Formula 9.5 for the density function looks much like the binomial distribution (Formula 9.1). Keep in mind that the beta distribution is a distribution for Q, a continuous random variable, whereas the binomial distribution is a distribution for R, the number of successes in n trials. Thus, we are considering two entirely different uncertain quantities. The two distributions, however, are closely related.

The expected value of a beta random variable is $E(Q) = r/n$, and the variance is $\mathrm{Var}(Q) = r(n - r)/[n_2(n - 1)]$. Looking at the formula for the expected value, r/n, the relationship between the beta and the binomial becomes apparent. Loosely speaking, r and n still can be interpreted as r successes in n trials. For example, if you had observed 4 successes in 10 trials from a binomial distribution with unknown proportion Q, your best guess for Q would be $\frac{4}{10}$ or 0.40. Moreover, you might concede that Q might not be exactly 0.40, although it is close to 0.40.

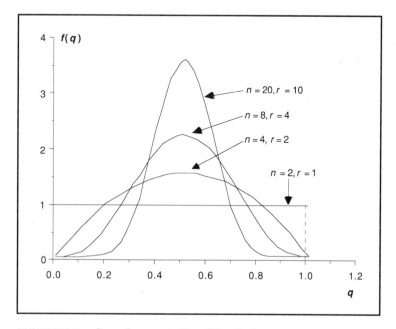

FIGURE 9.9 *Some Symmetric Beta Distributions*

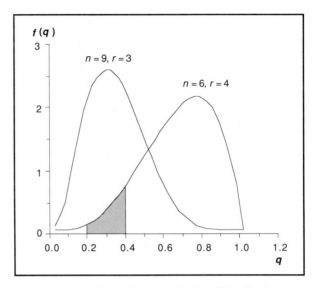

FIGURE 9.10 *Some Asymmetric Beta Distributions*

One way to use a beta distribution to model your subjective beliefs about an uncertain Q is to imagine a sample that would be roughly equivalent to your information. In the case of the proportion of voters who will vote Republican, you may have a feeling that the proportion is "around 0.30," and perhaps you feel as if all of your information (reading newspapers, talking to friends) is roughly equivalent to having polled a random sample of 20 people. These beliefs about Q might be represented by a beta distribution with $r = 6$ and $n = 20$.

Another way to fit a beta distribution is to use the cumulative probability table for the beta distribution (Appendix F). This table works a lot like the others. First, find the appropriate r and n along the left margin; for example, look at a distribution with $r = 6$ and $n = 20$. Read across the row to find the cumulative probabilities for values of q from 0 to 1 (column headings). For example, reading across, you find the number ".11" in the $q = 0.18$ column (Figure 9.11). This means that for a beta distribution with $n = 20$ and $r = 6$, $P_\beta(Q \le 0.18 \mid n = 20, r = 6) = 0.11$, or there is an 11% chance that Q is less than 0.18. Likewise, you can see that $P_\beta(Q \le 0.28 \mid n = 20, r = 6) = 0.45$, and $P_\beta(Q \le 0.30 \mid n = 20, r = 6) = 0.53$. From these two values, we can deduce that the median for this distribution is approximately 0.29. That is, $P_\beta(Q \le 0.29 \mid n = 20, r = 6)$ is approximately 0.50. We also can see that $P_\beta(Q \le 0.48 \mid n = 20, r = 6) = 0.95$. This statement means there is a 95% chance that Q is less than 0.48 in this distribution, and hence only a 5% chance that Q is greater than 0.48.

To use the table to fit a beta distribution to your beliefs, you might assess the median and upper and lower quartiles of your subjective distribution for Q using the techniques discussed in Chapter 6 for assessing a continuous subjective probability distribution. Then look in the table for a combination of r and n that gives a beta distribution with the same (or nearly the same) median and quar-

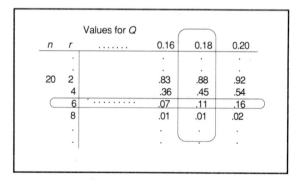

FIGURE 9.11 *Using the Beta Distribution Table to Find $P_\beta(Q \leq 0.18 \mid n = 20, r = 6) = 0.11$*

tiles. For example, suppose you assess the median of your subjective distribution to be 0.40, the lower quartile to be 0.29, and the upper quartile to be 0.55. That is,

$$P(Q \leq 0.29) = 0.25$$
$$P(Q \leq 0.40) = 0.50$$
$$P(Q \leq 0.52) = 0.75.$$

Looking in the table, a beta distribution with $r = 4$ and $n = 10$ has approximately the same median and quartiles:

$$P_\beta(Q \leq 0.29 \mid n = 10, r = 4) = 0.25$$
$$P_\beta(Q \leq 0.40 \mid n = 10, r = 4) = 0.52$$
$$P_\beta(Q \leq 0.52 \mid n = 10, r = 4) = 0.78.$$

Given the closeness between this beta distribution and your subjective assessments, you might find it useful to represent your subjective beliefs with the distribution. Suppose, however, that you had assessed

$$P(Q \leq 0.36) = 0.25$$
$$P(Q \leq 0.40) = 0.50$$
$$P(Q \leq 0.52) = 0.75.$$

No beta distributions have characteristics very close to these. The one with $r = 2$ and $n = 5$ has (roughly) the correct median and upper quartile: $P_\beta(Q \leq 0.40 \mid r = 2, n = 5) = 0.52$ and $P_\beta(Q \leq 0.52 \mid r = 2, n = 5) = 0.72$. On the lower end, however, the approximation is poor: $P_\beta(Q \leq 0.36 \mid r = 2, n = 5) = 0.45$. In this case, we would have three choices. We could be satisfied with a not-so-great approximation, use our subjective assessment directly (perhaps with a discrete approximation), or find another way to approximate our beliefs.

SOFT PRETZELS ONE LAST TIME. Let us return to the issue of how much market share your pretzel will capture. Denote the market share by Q; it is an uncertain quantity that must be between 0 and 1. You might want to model your beliefs about Q with a beta distribution. You know that Q is not likely to be close to 1. Suppose also that you think that the median is approximately 0.20 and the upper quartile is 0.38. To represent these assessments, you might choose a beta distribution with $r = 1$ and $n = 4$. From the table, you can see that this distribution for Q has a median around 0.21 and an upper quartile around 0.37:

$$P_B(Q \le 0.20 \mid r = 1, \; n = 4) = 0.49$$
$$P_B(Q \le 0.38 \mid r = 1, \; n = 4) = 0.76.$$

The expected value of Q is $r/n = \frac{1}{4} = 0.25$.

Should you become a pretzel entrepreneur? Recall that the decision was to price the pretzels at 50 cents each and that the total market is estimated to be 100,000 pretzels. You figure that the total fixed cost of the project amounts to $8000 for marketing, finance costs, and overhead. The variable cost of each pretzel is 10 cents.

You only have one year to prove yourself, and then you will go on to graduate school no matter what happens. It also is apparent that this venture alone will not provide enough income to live on, but embarking on it will not interfere with other plans for gainful employment. Your rich uncle has agreed to help you financially, and you have savings of your own. The only question is whether the net contribution of the project will be positive or negative.

Write the equation for net contribution as the difference between total revenue and total costs:

$$\text{Net Contribution} = Q(100{,}000)\,(0.50) - Q(100{,}000)\,(0.10) - 8000$$
$$= Q(100{,}000)\,(0.40) - 8000.$$

The marginal contribution per pretzel sold is 40 cents, or 0.40. The expected net contribution is:

$$E(\text{Net Contribution}) = 40{,}000\,E(Q) - 8000$$
$$= 40{,}000\,(0.25) - 8000$$
$$= 10{,}000 - 8000$$
$$= 2000.$$

On the basis of expected value, becoming a pretzel entrepreneur is a good idea! But the project also is a pretty risky proposition. What is the probability, for instance, that the pretzels could result in a loss? To answer this, we can find the specific value for Q (call it q^*) that would make the return equal to zero:

$$0 = 40{,}000\, q^* - 8000$$
$$q^* = 8000/40{,}000 = 0.20.$$

If Q turns out to be less than 0.20, you would have been better off with the savings account. We assessed the median of Q to be approximately 0.20. This means that there is just about a 50% chance that the pretzel project will result in a loss. Are you willing to go ahead with the pretzels?

◇ SUMMARY

In this chapter we examined certain ways to use theoretical probability distributions in decision-analysis problems. The distributions we considered were the binomial, Poisson, exponential, normal, and beta. These are only a few of the simpler ones; many other theoretical distributions are available. Each is appropriate in different situations, and a decision analyst must develop expertise in recognizing which distribution provides the best model of the uncertainty in a decision situation.   ◆

◇ EXERCISES

9.1   In the binomial example with Melissa Bailey (page 251), what is the probability that she will be gone six or more weekends?

9.2   Suppose you are interested in an investment with an uncertain return. You think that the return could be modeled as a normal random variable with mean $2000 and standard deviation $1500. What is the probability that the investment will end up with a loss? What is the probability that the return will be greater than $4000?

9.3   If there are, on average, 3.6 chocolate chips per cookie, what is the probability of finding no chocolate chips in a given cookie? Fewer than 5 chocolate chips? More than 10 chips?

9.4   Refer to the discussion of the pretzel problem in the section on the beta distribution (pages 267–268). Find the probability that the net contribution of the pretzel project would be greater than $4500.

9.5   Table look-up and calculation practice

    a. Binomial distribution. Find the following probabilities:

$$P_B(R = 5 \mid n = 10, p = 0.22) \qquad P_B(R = 10 \mid n = 15, p = 0.63)$$
$$P_B(R \leq 1 \mid n = 7, p = 0.04) \qquad P_B(R \leq 3 \mid n = 10, p = 0.35)$$
$$P_B(7 < R \leq 10 \mid n = 12, p = 0.50) \qquad P_B(R > 1 \mid n = 19, p = 0.06)$$
$$P_B(R = 4 \mid n = 6, p = 0.42) \qquad P_B(R < 2 \mid n = 4, p = 0.67).$$

    b. Poisson distribution. Find the following probabilities:

$$P_P(X = 3 \mid m = 2.0) \qquad P_P(X \geq 17 \mid m = 15)$$
$$P_P(X > 4 \mid m = 5.2) \qquad P_P(X < 7 \mid m = 10.0)$$
$$P_P(X \leq 1 \mid m = 3.9) \qquad P_P(3 \leq X < 7 \mid m = 1.5)$$
$$P_P(X = 4 \mid m = 1.75) \qquad P_P(X \leq 2 \mid m = 3.56).$$

    c. Exponential distribution. Find the following probabilities:

$$P_E(T \leq 5 \mid m = 1) \qquad P_E(T \geq 4 \mid m = 0.25)$$
$$P_E(0.25 < T < 1 \mid m = 2) \qquad P_E(T \geq 3.2 \mid m = 2)$$
$$P_E(T = 3.2 \mid m = 2) \qquad P_E(T \geq k \mid m = (1/k)).$$

    d. Normal distribution. Find the following probabilities:

$$P_N(Y \leq 12 \mid \mu = 10, \sigma = 4) \qquad P_N(Y > 50 \mid \mu = 100, \sigma = 30)$$
$$P_N(100 < Y \leq 124 \mid \mu = 133, \sigma = 15) \qquad P_N(Y > 20 \mid \mu = 15, \sigma = 4)$$
$$P_N(Y > 0 \mid \mu = -10, \sigma = 4) \qquad P_N(-44 \leq Y \leq 12 \mid \mu = 10, \sigma = 20)$$
$$P_N(Y = 12 \mid \mu = 10, \sigma = 4) \qquad P_N(Y < 12 \mid \mu = 10, \sigma = 4).$$

   e. Beta distribution. Find the following probabilities:

$$P_B(Q \leq 0.9 \mid n = 10, r = 9)$$ $$P_B(Q \geq 0.5 \mid n = 5, r = 2)$$

$$P_B(Q \leq 0.44 \mid n = 30, r = 20)$$ $$P_B(0.04 < Q \leq 0.38 \mid n = 18, r = 8)$$

$$P_B(0.12 < Q \leq 0.25 \mid n = 14, r = 4)$$ $$P_B(Q = 0.76 \mid n = 18, r = 14).$$

9.6   Find values for z such that:

$$P_N(Z \leq z \mid \mu = 0, \sigma = 1) = 0.05$$ $$P_N(Z > z \mid \mu = 0, \sigma = 1) = 0.25$$

$$P_N(Z \leq z \mid \mu = 0, \sigma = 1) = 0.50$$ $$P_N(Z > z \mid \mu = 0, \sigma = 1) = 0.10.$$

9.7   Find the parameters (μ and σ) for a normal distribution whose first and third quartiles are 125 and 275. That is, $P_N(Y \leq 125 \mid \mu, \sigma) = 0.25$ and $P_N(Y \leq 275 \mid \mu, \sigma) = 0.75$. What are μ and σ?

9.8   An exponential distribution has $P_E(T \geq 5 \mid m) = 0.24$. Find m.

9.9   A Poisson distribution has $P_P(X \geq 12 \mid m) = 0.01$ and $P_P(X \leq 2 \mid m) = 0.095$. Find m.

9.10   A Poisson distribution has $P_P(X = 0 \mid m) = 0.175$. Calculate m.

9.11   Use Appendix E to verify the Empirical Rule (page 260) for normal distributions, which states that the probability is approximately 0.68 that a normal random variable is within one standard deviation of the mean μ, and the probability is approximately 0.95 that the random variable is within two standard deviations of the mean.

◇ QUESTIONS AND PROBLEMS

9.12   The amount of time that a union stays on strike is judged to follow an exponential distribution with a mean of 10 days.

   a. Find the probability that a strike lasts less than one day.

   b. Find the probability that a strike lasts less than six days.

   c. Find the probability that a strike lasts between six and seven days.

   d. Find the conditional probability that a strike lasts less than seven days, given that it already has lasted six days. Compare your answer to part a.

9.13   A photographer works part-time in a shopping center, two hours per day, four days per week. On the average, six customers arrive each hour, and the arrivals appear to occur independently of one another. Twenty minutes after she arrives one day, the photographer wonders what the chances are that exactly one customer will arrive during the next 15 minutes. Find this probability (i) if two customers just arrived within the first 20 minutes, and (ii) if no customers have come into the shop yet on this particular day.

9.14   A consumer is contemplating the purchase of a new compact disc player. A consumer magazine reports data on the major brands. Brand A has lifetime (T_A) which is exponentially distributed with $m = 0.2$; and Brand B has lifetime (T_B), which is exponentially distributed with $m = 0.1$. (The unit of time is one year.)

   a. Find the expected lifetimes for A and B. If a consumer must choose between the two on the basis of maximizing expected lifetime, which one should be chosen?

   b. Find the probability that A's lifetime exceeds its expected value. Do the same for B. What do you conclude?

   c. Suppose one consumer purchases a Brand A compact disc, and another consumer purchases a Brand B compact disc. Find the mean and variance of (i) the average lifetime of the two machines and (ii) the difference between the lifetimes of the two machines. (*Hint*: You must use the rules about means and variances of linear transformations that we discussed in Chapter 7.)

9.15 On the basis of past data, the owner of an automobile dealership finds that, on average, 8.5 cars are sold per day on Saturdays and Sundays during the months of January and February, with the sales rate relatively stable throughout the day. Moreover, purchases appear to be independent of one another. The dealership is open for 10 hours per day on each of these days. There is no reason to believe that the sales for the upcoming year will be any different than in the past.

a. On the first Saturday in February, the dealership will open at 9 A.M. Find the probability that the time until the first sale is more than two hours, $P_E(T \geq 2$ hours $\mid m = 8.5$ cars per 10 hours).

b. Find the probability that the number of sales before 11 A.M. is equal to zero, $P_P(X = 0$ in 2 hours $\mid m = 8.5$ cars per 10 hours). Compare your answer to that from part a. Can you explain why the answers are the same?

c. The owner of the dealership gives her salespeople a bonus, depending on the total number of cars sold. She gives them $20 whenever exactly 13 cars are sold on a given day, $30 whenever 14 cars are sold, $50 whenever 15 cars are sold, and $70 whenever 16 or more cars are sold. On any given Saturday or Sunday in January or February, what is the expected bonus that the dealer will have to pay?

d. Consider the bonus scheme presented in part c. February contains exactly four Saturdays and four Sundays. What is the probability that the owner will have to pay the $20 bonuses exactly twice in those days?

9.16 In the soft pretzels example concerning the taste test — in which we used binomial probabilities — suppose the results had been that 4 out of the 20 people sampled preferred your pretzel. Use Bayes' theorem to find your posterior probability $P(\text{Hit} \mid r = 5, n = 20)$ for the following pairs of prior probabilities:

a. $P(\text{Hit}) = 0.2$, $P(\text{Flop}) = 0.8$

b. $P(\text{Hit}) = 0.4$, $P(\text{Flop}) = 0.6$

c. $P(\text{Hit}) = 0.5$, $P(\text{Flop}) = 0.5$

d. $P(\text{Hit}) = 0.75$, $P(\text{Flop}) = 0.25$

e. $P(\text{Hit}) = 0.90$, $P(\text{Flop}) = 0.10$

f. $P(\text{Hit}) = 1.0$, $P(\text{Flop}) = 0$.

Create a graph of the posterior probability as a function of the prior probability. (We did something similar in Chapter 7 in discussing the Hinckley trial. Refer to Figure 7.20, page 195).

9.17 In a city, 60% of the voters are in favor of building a new park. An interviewer intends to conduct a survey.

a. If the interviewer selects 20 people randomly, what is the probability that more than 15 of them will favor building the park?

b. Instead of choosing 20 people as in part a, suppose that the interviewer wants to conduct the survey until he has found exactly 12 who are in favor of the park. What is the probability that the first 12 people surveyed all favor the park (in which case the interviewer can stop)? What is the probability that the interviewer can stop after interviewing the thirteenth subject? What is the probability that the interviewer can stop after interviewing the eighteenth subject?

9.18   In bottle production, bubbles that appear in the glass are considered defects. Any bottle that has more than two bubbles is classified as "nonconforming" and is sent to recycling. Suppose that a particular production line produces bottles with bubbles at a rate of 1.1 bubbles per bottle. Bubbles occur independently of one another.

   a. What is the probability that a randomly chosen bottle is nonconforming?

   b. Bottles are packed in cases of 12. An inspector chooses one bottle from each case and examines it for defects. If it is nonconforming, she inspects the entire case, replacing nonconforming bottles with good ones. This process is called rectification. If the chosen bottle conforms (has two or fewer bubbles), then she passes the case. In total, 20 cases are produced. What is the probability that at least 18 of them pass?

   c. What is the expected number of nonconforming bottles in the 20 cases after they have been inspected and rectified using the scheme described in part b?

9.19   In our discussion of the Poisson distribution, we used this distribution to represent the process by which customers arrive at the pretzel stand. Is it reasonable to assume that the Poisson distribution is appropriate for finding the probabilities that we need? Why or why not?

9.20   You are the mechanical engineer in charge of maintaining the machines in a factory. The plant manager has asked you to evaluate a proposal to replace the current machines with new ones. The old and new machines perform substantially the same jobs, and so the question is whether the new machines are more reliable than the old. You know from past experience that the old machines break down roughly according to a Poisson distribution, with the expected number of breakdowns at 2.5 per month. When one breaks down, $150 is required to fix it. The new machines, however, have you a bit confused. According to the distributor's brochure, the new machines are supposed to break down at a rate of 1.5 machines per month on average, and should cost $170 to fix. But a friend in another plant that uses the new machines reports that they break down at a rate of approximately 3.0 per month (and do cost $170 to fix). (In either event, the number of breakdowns in any month appears to follow a Poisson distribution.) On the basis of this information, you judge that it is equally likely that the rate is 3.0 or 1.5 per month.

   a. On the basis of minimum expected repair costs, should the new machines be adopted?

   b. Now you learn that a third plant in a nearby town has been using these machines. They have experienced 6 breakdowns in 3.0 months. Use this information to find the posterior probability that the breakdown rate is 1.5 per month.

   c. Given your posterior probability, should your company adopt the new machines in order to minimize expected repair costs?

   d. Consider the information given in part b. If you had read it in the distributor's brochure, what would you think? If you had read it in a trade magazine as the result of an independent test, what would you think? Given your answers, what do you think about using sample information and Bayes' theorem to find posterior probabilities? Should the source of the information be taken into consideration somehow? Could this be done in some way in the application of Bayes' theorem?

9.21   In the soft pretzels example for the beta distribution, suppose you assessed the median of Q to be approximately 0.30 and the upper quartile 0.50. In this case you could use a beta distribution with parameters $r = 1$ and $n = 3$ to represent your beliefs.

   a. Plug the values $r = 1$ and $n = 3$ into the formula for the beta distribution. The expression simplifies considerably. (Recall that 0! = 1 by definition.)

   b. Draw a graph of the distribution of Q.

c. Use what you know about areas of triangles to show that this distribution is a reasonably good representation of your subjective beliefs in the sense that the median and upper quartile are fairly close to your subjectively assessed median and upper quartile.

d. Find the expected profit for the pretzel project with this new distribution.

e. Find the probability that the pretzel project results in a loss under this distribution.

9.22 Sometimes we use probability distributions that are not exact representations of the physical processes that they are meant to represent. (For example, we might use a normal distribution for a distribution of individuals' weights, even though no one can weigh less than zero pounds.) Why do we do this?

9.23 You are an executive at Procter and Gamble, and you are about to introduce a new product. Your boss has asked you to predict the market share (Q, a proportion between 0 and 1) that the new product will capture. You are unsure of Q, and you would like to communicate your uncertainty to the boss. You have made the following assessments:

There is a 1-in-10 chance that Q will be greater than 0.22, and also a 1-in-10 chance that Q will be less than 0.08.

The value for Q is just as likely to be greater than 0.14 as less than 0.14.

a. What should your subjective probabilities $P(0.08 < Q < 0.14)$ and $P(0.14 < Q < 0.22)$ be in order to guarantee coherence?

b. Use Appendix F to find a beta distribution for Q that closely approximates your subjective beliefs.

c. The boss tells you that if you expect that the market share will be less than 0.15, the product should not be introduced. Write him a memo that gives him an expected value and also explains how risky you think it would be to introduce the product. Use your beta approximation.

9.24 Suppose you are considering two investments, and the critical issues are the rates of return (R_1 and R_2). For Investment 1, the expected rate of return (μ_1) is 10%, and the standard deviation (σ_1) is 3%. For the second investment, the expected rate of return (μ_2) is 20%, and the standard deviation (σ_2) is 12%.

a. Does it make sense to decide between these two investments on the basis of expected value alone? Why or why not?

b. Does it make sense to represent the uncertainty surrounding the rates of return with normal distributions? What conditions do we need for the normal distribution to provide a good fit?

c. Suppose you have decided to use normal distributions (either because of or in spite of your answer to part b). Use Appendix E to find the following probabilities:

$$P(R_1 < 0\%)$$
$$P(R_2 < 0\%)$$

$$P(R_1 > 20\%)$$
$$P(R_2 < 10\%)$$

d. How can you find the probability that $R_1 > R_2$? Suppose R_1 and R_2 are correlated (as they would be if, say, both of the investments were stocks). Then the random variable $\Delta R = R_1 - R_2$ is normal with mean $\mu_1 - \mu_2$ and variance $\sigma_1^2 + \sigma_2^2 - 2\rho\sigma_1\sigma_2$, where ρ is the correlation between R_1 and R_2. If $\rho = 0.5$, find $P(R_1 > R_2)$. (*Hint*: Think about it in terms of ΔR, and find $P(\Delta R > 0)$.)

e. How could you use the information from the various probabilities developed in this problem to choose between the two investments?

9.25 Your inheritance, which is in a blind trust, is invested entirely in McDonalds or in U.S. Steel. Because the trustee owns several McDonalds franchises, you believe the probability that the investment is in McDonalds is 0.8. In any one year, the return from an investment in McDonalds is approximately normally distributed with mean 14% and standard deviation 4%, while the investment in U.S. Steel is approximately normally distributed with mean 12% and standard deviation 3%. Assume that the two returns are independent.

a. What is the probability that the investment earns between 6% and 18% (i) if the trust is invested entirely in McDonalds, and (ii) if the trust is invested entirely in U.S. Steel?

b. Without knowing how the trust is invested, what is the probability that the investment earns between 6% and 18%?

c. Suppose you learn that the investment earned more than 12%. Given this new information, find your posterior probability that the investment is in McDonalds.

d. Suppose that the trustee decided to split the investment, and put one-half into each of the two securities. Find the expected value and the variance of this portfolio.

9.26 A continuous random variable X has the following density function:

$$f(x) = 0.5 \text{ for } x \text{ between 3 and 5,}$$

$$0 \text{ otherwise.}$$

a. Draw a graph of this distribution. Verify that the area under the density function equals 1.

b. A density function such as this one is called a *uniform* density, or sometimes a rectangular density. It is extremely easy to work with because probabilities for intervals can be found as areas of rectangles. For example, find $P_U(X \le 4.5 \mid a = 3, b = 5)$. (The parameters a and b are used to denote the lower and upper extremes, respectively.)

c. Find the following uniform probabilities:

$$P_U(X \le 4.3 \mid a = 3, b = 5) \qquad P_U(X > 3.4 \mid a = 0, b = 10)$$
$$P_U(0.25 \le X \le 0.75 \mid a = 0, b = 1) \qquad P_U(X < 0 \mid a = -1, b = 4).$$

d. Plot the CDF for the uniform distribution where $a = 0$, $b = 1$.

e. The expected value of a uniform distribution is $E(X) = (b + a)/2$, and the variance is $\text{Var}(X) = (b - a)^2/12$. Find the expected value and variance of the uniform density with $a = 3$, $b = 5$.

9.27 The length of time until a strike is settled is distributed uniformly from 0 to 10.5 days. (See the previous problem for an introduction to the uniform density.)

a. Find the probability that a strike lasts less than one day.

b. Find the probability that a strike lasts less than six days.

c. Find the probability that a strike lasts between six and seven days.

d. Find the conditional probability that a strike lasts less than seven days, given that it already has lasted six days.

e. Compare your answers with those of Problem 9.12.

9.28 In a survey in a shopping center, the interviewer asks customers how long their shopping trips have lasted so far. The response (T) given by a randomly chosen customer is uniformly distributed from 0 to 1.5 hours.

    a. Find the probability that a customer has been shopping for 36 minutes or less.

    b. The interviewer surveys 18 customers at different times. Find the probability that more than one-half of these customers say that they have been shopping for 36 minutes or less.

9.29 A greeting card shop makes cards that are supposed to fit into 6-inch (in.) envelopes. The paper cutter, however, is not perfect. The length of a cut card is normally distributed with mean 5.9 in. and standard deviation of 0.0365 in. If a card is longer than 5.975 in., it will not fit into a 6-in. envelope.

    a. Find the probability that a card will not fit into a 6-in. envelope.

    b. The cards are sold in boxes of 20. What is the probability that in one box there will be two or more cards that do not fit in 6-in. envelopes?

9.30 You are the maintenance engineer for a plant that manufactures consumer electronic goods. You are just about to leave on your vacation for two weeks, and the boss is concerned about certain machines that have been somewhat unreliable, requiring your expertise to keep them running. The boss has asked you how many of these machines you expect to fail while you are out of town, and you have decided to give him your subjective probability distribution. You have made the following assessments:

    1. There is a 0.5 chance that none of the machines will fail.

    2. There is an approximate 0.15 chance that two or more will fail.

    3. There is virtually no chance that four or more will fail.

    Being impatient with this slow assessment procedure, you decide to try to fit a theoretical distribution.

    a. Many operations researchers would use a Poisson distribution in this case. Why might the Poisson be appropriate? Why might it not be appropriate?

    b. Find a Poisson distribution that provides a good representation of your assessed beliefs. Give a specific value for the parameter m.

    c. Given your answer to b, what is the expected number of machines that will break down during your absence?

9.31 After you have given your boss your information (Problem 9.30), he considers how accurate you have been in the past when you have made such assessments. In fact, he decides you are somewhat optimistic (and he believes in Murphy's Law), so *he assigns a Poisson distribution with m = 1* to the occurrence of machine breakdowns during your two-week vacation. Now the boss has a decision to make. He either can close the part of the plant involving the machines in question, at a cost of $10,000, or he can leave that part up and running. Of course, if there are no machine failures, there is no cost. If there is only one failure, he can work with the remaining equipment until you return, so the cost is effectively zero. If there are two or more failures, however, there will be assembly time lost, and he will have to call in experts to repair the machines immediately. The cost would be $15,000. What should he do?

9.32 Regarding the soft pretzels again, suppose you decide to conduct a taste test of a new recipe at your stand. On average, one person comes to the stand every four minutes, and the arrivals seem to follow a Poisson distribution fairly closely. You decide to check for 30 minutes to see how many customers during that time prefer the new recipe. Suppose the probability is 0.4 that any arriving customer prefers the new recipe over the old one. What is the probability that you will find four or more customers who prefer the new recipe during your 30-minute test period?

9.33   A factory manager must decide whether to stock a particular spare part. The part is absolutely essential to the operation of certain machines in the plant. Stocking the part costs $10 per day in storage and cost of capital. If the part is in stock, a broken machine can be repaired immediately, but if the part is not in stock, it takes one day to get the part from the distributor, during which time the broken machine sits idle. The cost of idling one machine for a day is $65. There are 50 machines in the plant that require this particular part. The probability that any one of them will break and require the part to be replaced on any one day is only 0.004 (regardless of how long since the part was previously replaced). The machines break down independently of one another.

a. If you wanted to use a probability distribution for the number of machines that break down on a given day, would you use the binomial or Poisson distribution? Why?

b. Whichever theoretical distribution you chose in part a, what are appropriate parameters? That is, if you chose the binomial, what are the values for p and n? If you chose the Poisson, what is the value for m?

c. If the plant manager wants to minimize his expected cost, should he keep zero, one, or two parts in stock? Draw a decision tree and solve the manager's problem. (Do not forget that more than one machine can fail in one day!)

9.34   Another useful distribution that is based on the normal is the *lognormal* distribution. Among other applications, this distribution is used by environmental engineers to represent the distribution of pollutant levels, by economists to represent the distribution of returns on investments, and by actuaries to represent the distribution of insurance claims.

Finding probabilities from a lognormal distribution is "as easy as falling off a log"! If X is lognormally distributed with parameters μ and σ, then $Y = \ln(X)$ is normally distributed and has mean μ and variance σ^2. Thus, the simplest way to work with a lognormal random variable X is to work in terms of $Y = \ln(X)$. It is easy to obtain probabilities for Y from the normal table. The expected value and variance of X are given by the following formulas:

$$E(X) = e^{(\mu+0.5\sigma^2)} \qquad Var(X) = (e^{2\mu})(e^{\sigma^2}-1)(e^{\sigma^2})$$

For example, if X is lognormally distributed with parameters $\mu = 0.3$ and $\sigma = 0.2$, then Y is normal with mean 0.3 and standard deviation 0.2. Finding probabilities just means taking logs:

$$P_L(X \geq 1.4 \mid \mu = 0.3, \sigma = 0.2) = P_N(Y \geq \ln(1.4) \mid \mu = 0.3, \sigma = 0.2)$$
$$= P_N(Y \geq 0.336 \mid \mu = 0.3, \sigma = 0.2)$$
$$= P(Z \geq 0.18)$$
$$= 0.4286.$$

The mean and expected value of X are:

$$E(X) = e^{[0.3+(0.5)(0.2)^2]}$$
$$= 1.38.$$
$$Var(X) = (e^{2(0.3)})(e^{(0.2)^2}-1)(e^{(0.2)^2})$$
$$= 0.077.$$

After all that, here is a problem to work. After a hurricane, claims for property damage pour into the insurance offices. Suppose that an insurance actuary models noncommercial property damage claims (X, in dollars) as being lognormally distributed with parameters $\mu = 10$ and $\sigma = 0.3$. Claims on different properties are assumed to be independent.

a. Find the mean and standard deviation of these claims.

b. Find the probability that a claim will be greater than $50,000.

c. The company anticipates 200 claims. If the state insurance commission requires the company to have enough cash on hand to be able to satisfy all claims with probability 0.95, how much money should be in the company's reserve? [*Hint*: The total claims can be represented by the variable $Q = 200X$, and Q will be approximately normally distributed with mean $200\, E(X)$ and variance $200\, \text{Var}(X)$.]

CASE STUDIES

Overbooking

Most airlines practice *overbooking*. That is, they are willing to make more reservations than they have seats on an airplane. Why would they do this? The basic reason is simple; on any given flight a few passengers are likely to be "no-shows." If the airline overbooks slightly, then it still may be able to fill the airplane. Of course, this policy has its risks. If more passengers arrive to claim their reservations than there are seats available, the airline must "bump" some of its passengers. Often this is done by asking for volunteers. If a passenger with a reserved seat is willing to give up his or her seat, the airline typically will give a refund as well as provide a free ticket to the same or another destination. The fundamental trade-off is whether the additional expected revenue gained by flying an airplane that is nearer to capacity on average is worth the additional expected cost of refunds and free tickets.

To study the overbooking policy, let us look at a hypothetical situation. Mockingbird Airlines has a small commuter jet with places for 16 passengers. The airline uses this jet on a route for which it charges $225 for a one-way fare. Every flight has a fixed cost of $900 (for pilot's salary, fuel, airport fees, and so on). Each passenger costs Mockingbird an additional $100. Finally, the no-show rate is 4%. That is, on average approximately 4% of those passengers holding confirmed reservations do not show up. Refunds for unused tickets are made only if the reservation is cancelled at least 24 hours before scheduled departure.

How many reservations should Mockingbird be willing to sell on this airplane? The strategy will be to calculate the expected profit for a given number of reservations. For example, suppose that the Mockingbird manager decides to sell 18 reservations. The revenue is $225 times the number of reservations

$$R = \$225 \ (18)$$
$$= \$4050.$$

The cost consists of two components. The first is the cost of flying the plane and hauling the passengers who arrive (but not more than the airplane's capacity of 16):

$$C_1 = \$900 + \$100 \times \text{Min(Arrivals, 16)}.$$

The second component is the cost of refunds and free tickets that must be issued if 17 or 18 passengers arrive:

$$C_2 = (\$225 + \$100) \times \text{Max}(0, \text{Arrivals} - 16).$$

In this expression for C_2, the \$225 represents the refund for the purchased ticket, and the \$100 represents the cost of the free ticket. The Max( ) expression calculates the number of excess passengers who show up (zero if the number of arrivals is fewer than 16).

QUESTIONS

1. Find the probability that more than 16 passengers will arrive if Mockingbird sells 17 reservations (Res = 17). Do the same for 18 and 19.
2. Find:

   - $E(R \mid \text{Res} = 16)$
   - $E(C_1 \mid \text{Res} = 16)$
   - $E(C_2 \mid \text{Res} = 16)$.

   Finally, calculate

   $$E(\text{Profit} \mid \text{Res} = 16) = E(R \mid \text{Res} = 16) - E(C_1 \mid \text{Res} = 16) - E(C_2 \mid \text{Res} = 16).$$

3. Repeat Question 2 for 17, 18, and 19 reservations. What is your conclusion? Should Mockingbird overbook? By how much?
4. Since the airlines were deregulated in the 1970s, pricing has become more competitive. One of the promotional schemes is the "supersaver" fare that requires early payment and restrictions on refunds. For example, to receive the special fare, a customer may be required to purchase the ticket two weeks in advance, after which no changes or refunds will be made. How do you think this policy has affected the airlines' overbooking policy?

◆

Earthquake Prediction

Because of the potential damage and destruction that earthquakes can cause, geologists and geophysicists have put considerable effort into understanding when and where earthquakes occur. The ultimate aim is the accurate prediction of earthquakes on the basis of movements in the earth's crust, although this goal appears to be some way off. In the meantime, it is possible to examine past data and model earthquakes probabilistically.

Fortunately, considerable data exist on the basis of which to model earthquakes as a probabilistic phenomenon. Gere and Shah (1984) provide the information shown in Table 9.1. Richter magnitude refers to the severity of the earth-quake. For example, if an earthquake is in the 8.0–8.9 category, by definition the ground would shake strongly for 30 to 90 seconds over an area with a diameter of 160 to 320 kilometers. Earthquakes of magnitude less than 4.0 are not dangerous, and, for the most part, are not noticed by laypeople.

An earthquake of magnitude 8.0 or greater could cause substantial damage and a large number of deaths if it were to occur in a highly populated part of the world. In fact, the San Francisco earthquake of April 6, 1906, was calculated later as measuring 8.3 on the Richter scale. The resulting fire burned much of the city, and some 700 people died. California is particularly susceptible to earth-quakes because the state straddles two portions of the earth's crust that are slip-ping past each other, primarily along the San Andreas Fault. For this reason, we will consider the probability of a severe earthquake happening again in Califor-nia in the near future.

QUESTIONS

1. We can model the occurrence of earthquakes using a Poisson distribution. Strictly speaking, the independence requirement for the Poisson is not met for two reasons. First, the geologic processes at work in California suggest that the probability of a large earthquake increases as time elapses following an earlier large quake. Second, large earthquakes often are followed by after-shocks. Our model will ignore these issues and hence can be viewed only as a first-cut approximation at constructing a probabilistic model for earthquakes.

The data from Gere and Shah indicate that, on average, 2493 earth-quakes with magnitude 4.0 or greater will occur in California over a 100-year period. Thus, we might consider using a Poisson distribution with $m = 24.93$ to represent the probability distribution for the number of earthquakes (all

Richter Magnitude	Average Number of Earthquakes per 100 Years in California
8.0–8.9	1
7.0–7.9	12
6.0–6.9	80
5.0–5.9	400
4.0–4.9	2000

TABLE 9.1 *Earthquake Frequency Data for California*

Source: Gere, J. M., and H. C. Shah (1984) *Terra Non Firma: Understanding and Preparing for Earthquakes.* Stanford, CA: Stanford Alumni Association.

magnitudes greater than 4.0) that will hit California during the next year. Use this distribution to find the following probabilities:

$$P_P(X \leq 10 \text{ in Next Year} \mid m = 24.93 \text{ Earthquakes per Year})$$
$$P_P(X \leq 7 \text{ in Six Months} \mid m = 24.93 \text{ Earthquakes per Year})$$
$$P_P(X > 3 \text{ in Next Month} \mid m = 24.93 \text{ Earthquakes per Year}).$$

2. We also can model the probability distribution for the magnitude of an earthquake. For example, the data suggest that the probability of an earthquake in California of magnitude 8.0 or greater is 1/2493, or approximately 0.0004. If we use an exponential distribution to model the distribution of magnitudes, assuming that 4.0 is the least possible, then we might use the following model. Let M denote the magnitude, and let $M' = M - 4$. Then, using the exponential formula, we have $P(M \geq 8) = P(M' \geq 4) = e^{-m(4)} = 0.0004$. Now we can solve for m:

$$e^{-m(4)} = 0.0004$$
$$\ln(e^{-m(4)}) = \ln(0.0004)$$
$$-m(4) = -7.824$$
$$m = 1.96.$$

Thus, the density function for M is given by

$$f(M) = 1.96 \, e^{[-1.96(M-4)]}.$$

Plot this density function.

We now can find the probability that any given earthquake will have a magnitude within a specified range on the Richter scale. For example, use this model to find

$$P_E(M \leq 6.0 \mid m = 1.96)$$
$$P_E(5.0 \leq M \leq 7.5 \mid m = 1.96)$$
$$P_E(M \geq 6.4 \mid m = 1.96).$$

You may find it instructive to use this distribution to calculate the probability that an earthquake's magnitude falls within the five ranges of magnitude shown in Table 9.1. Here is a sensitivity-analysis issue: How might you find other reasonable values for m? What about a range of possible values for m?

3. We now have all of the pieces in the puzzle to find the probability of at least one severe (8.0 magnitude or more) earthquake occurring in California in the near future, say, within the next six months. Our approach will be to find the probability of the complement:

$$P(X_{8+} \geq 1) = 1 - P(X_{8+} = 0),$$

where X_{8+} is used to denote the number of earthquakes having magnitude 8.0 or greater. Now expand $P(X_{8+} = 0)$ using total probability:

$$P(X_{8+} = 0) = P(X_{8+} = 0 \mid X = 0) \ P(X = 0) + P(X_{8+} = 0 \mid X = 1) \ P(X = 1)$$
$$+ \ P(X_{8+} = 0 \mid X = 2) \ P(X = 2)$$
$$+ \cdots + P(X_{8+} = 0 \mid X = k) \ P(X = k) + \cdots$$
$$= \sum_{k=0}^{\infty} P(X_{8+} = 0 \mid X = k) \ P(X = k).$$

The probabilities $P(X = k)$ are just the Poisson probabilities from Question 1:

$$P(X = k) = P_P(X = k \mid m = 12.5),$$

where $m = 12.5$ because we are interested in a 6-month period. The probability of no earthquakes of magnitude 8.0 out of the k that occur is easy to find. If $k = 0$, then $P(X_{8+} = 0 \mid X = 0) = 1$. If $k = 1$, then

$$P(X_{8+} = 0 \mid X = 1) = P_E(M < 8.0 \mid m = 1.96)$$
$$= 1 - e^{-1.96(8-4)}$$
$$= 0.9996.$$

Likewise, if $k = 2$, then

$$P(X_{8+} = 0 \mid X = 2) = (0.9996)^2 = 0.9992,$$

because this is just the probability of two independent earthquakes each having magnitude less than 8.0. Generalizing,

$$P(X_{8+} = 0 \mid X = k) = (0.9996)^k.$$

Now we can substitute these probabilities into the formula:

$$P(X_{8+} \geq 0) = 1 - P(X_{8+} = 0)$$
$$= 1 - \sum_{k=0}^{\infty} P(X_{8+} = 0 \mid X = k) \ P(X = k)$$
$$= 1 - \sum_{k=0}^{\infty} (0.9996)^k \ P_P(X = k \mid m = 12.5).$$

To calculate this, you must calculate with k until the Poisson probability is so small that the remaining probabilities do not matter. It turns out that the probability of at least one earthquake of magnitude 8.0 or more within six months is approximately 0.005.

Now that you have seen how to do this, try calculating the probability of at least one earthquake of magnitude 8.0 or more (i) within the next year and (ii) within the next five years. For these, you may want to use a computer program to calculate the Poisson probabilities. How does the probability of at least one severe earthquake vary as you use the different reasonable values for m from your exponential model in Problem 2? [*Hint*: Calculating the Poisson probabilities may be difficult, even on an electronic spreadsheet, because of the large exponential and factorial terms. An easy way to calculate these probabilities is to use the recursive equation

$$P_P(X = k + 1 \mid m) = \frac{m}{k + 1} \ P_P(X = k \mid m).$$

This equation can be used easily in an electronic spreadsheet or calculator without having to calculate large factorial and exponential terms.]

4. Using the probability model described above, it turns out that the probability of at least one earthquake of magnitude 8.0 or more within the next 20 years in California is approximately 0.2 (or higher, depending on the value used for m in the exponential distribution for the magnitude, M). That is one chance in five. Now imagine that you are a policy maker in California's state government charged with making recommendations regarding earthquake preparedness. How would this analysis affect your recommendations? What kinds of issues do you think should be considered? What about the need for more research regarding precise earthquake prediction at a specific location? What about regulations regarding building design and construction? What other issues are important?

The probabilistic model that we have developed using the information from Gere and Shah is based on a very simplistic model and does not account for geological processes. Geologists do, however, use probability models in some cases as a basis for earthquake predictions. For example, as mentioned at the beginning of Chapter 8, a recent U.S. Geological Survey report concluded that the probability of an earthquake of 7.5–8.0 magnitude along the southern portion of the San Andreas Fault within the next 30 years is approximately 60%. The authors of the report actually constructed separate probability models for the occurrence of large quakes in different segments of major faults using data from the individual segments. Rather than a Poisson model, they used a lognormal distribution to model the uncertainty about the time between large earthquakes. Although their approach permits them to make probability statements regarding specific areas, their results can be aggregated to give probabilities for at least one major earthquake in the San Francisco Bay Area, along the southern San Andreas Fault in Southern California, or along the San Jacinto Fault. Table

Time	USGS Probability	Poisson-Model Probability
Next 5 years	0.27	0.29
Next 10 years	0.49	0.50
Next 20 years	0.71	0.75
Next 30 years	0.90	0.87

TABLE 9.2   *Probabilities for Major Earthquakes in California from Two Different Probability Models*

Source for USGS probabilities: U.S. Geological Survey (1988) "Probabilities of Large Earthquakes Occurring in California on the San Andreas Fault," by the Working Group on California Earthquake Probabilities. USGS Open-File Report No. 88-398, Menlo Park, CA.

9.2 compares their probabilities, which were developed for "large" earthquakes with expected magnitudes of 6.5–8.0, with our Poisson-model probabilities of at least one earthquake having magnitude of 7.0 or greater. It is comforting to know that our model, even with its imperfections, provides probabilities that are not radically different from the geologists' estimates.

◆

Municipal Solid Waste

Linda Butner considered her task. As the risk analysis expert on the city's Incineration Task Force (ITF), she was charged with reporting back to the ITF and to the city regarding the risks posed by constructing an incinerator for disposal of the city's solid waste. It was not a question of whether such an incinerator would be constructed. The city landfill site would be full within three years, and no alternative sites were available at a reasonable cost.

In particular, the state Department of Environmental Quality (DEQ) required information regarding levels of pollutants the incinerator was expected to produce. DEQ was concerned about organic compounds, metals, and acid gases. It was assumed that the plant would incorporate appropriate technology and that good combustion practices would be followed. Residual emissions were expected, however, and the officials were interested in obtaining close estimates of these. Linda's task was to provide an analysis of anticipated emissions of dioxins and furans (organic compounds), particulate matter (PM, representing metals), and sulfur dioxide (SO_2, representing the acid gases). She figured that a thorough analysis of these substances would enable her to answer questions about others.

The current specifications called for a plant capable of burning approximately 250 tons of waste per day. This placed it at the borderline between small- and medium-sized plants according to the Environmental Protection Agency's (EPA) guidelines. In part, this size was chosen because the EPA had proposed slightly different permission levels for these two plant sizes, and the city would be able to choose the plant size that was most advantageous. A smaller (less than 250 tons/day) plant would be expected to have an electrostatic precipitator for reducing particulate matter but would not have a specified SO_2 emission level. A larger plant would have a fabric filter instead of an electrostatic precipitator and would also use dry sorbent injection — the injection of chemicals into the flue — to control the SO_2 level. A summary of EPA's proposed emission levels is shown in Table 9.3.

Standard practice in environmental risk analysis called for assessment and analysis of "worst case" scenarios. But to Linda's way of thinking, this kind of approach did not adequately portray the uncertainty that might exist. Incineration of municipal solid waste (MSW) was particularly delicate in this regard, because the levels of various pollutants could vary dramatically with the content of the waste being burned. Moreover, different burning conditions within the incinera-

| | Plant Capacity (tons of waste per day): | |
Pollutant	Small (Less than 250)	Medium (250 or more)
Dioxins/Furans (ng/Nm^3)	500	125
PM (mg/dscm)	69	69
SO$_2$ (ppmdv)	—	30

TABLE 9.3 *Proposed Pollutant Emission Levels*
Notes: ng/Nm^3 = nanograms per normal cubic meter;
mg/dscm = milligrams per dry standard cubic meter; ppmdv =
parts per million, by dry volume.

tion chamber (more or less oxygen, presence of other gasses, different temperatures, and so on) could radically affect the emissions. To capture the variety of possible emission levels for the pollutants, Linda decided to represent the uncertainty about a pollutant-emission level with a probability distribution.

The lognormal distribution makes sense as a distribution for pollutant-emission levels. (See Problem 9.34 on page 276 for an introduction to the lognormal.) After consulting the available data for the content of pollutants in MSW and the pollutant-emission levels for other incinerators, Linda constructed a table (Table 9.4) to show the parameters for the lognormal distributions for the three pollutants in question. Figure 9.12 illustrates the lognormal distribution for the SO$_2$ emissions.

As Linda looked at this information, she realized that she could make certain basic calculations. For example, it would be relatively straightforward to calculate the probability that the plant's emissions would exceed the proposed levels in Table 9.3. Having these figures in hand, she felt she would be able to make a useful presentation to the task force.

QUESTIONS

1. The plant will be required to meet established emission levels for dioxins/furans and PM on an annual basis. Find the probabilities for exceeding the small-plant levels specified in Table 9.3 for these two pollutants. Repeat the calculations for the medium-plant emission levels.

Pollutant	μ	σ
Dioxins/Furans	3.13	1.20
PM	3.43	0.44
SO$_2$	3.20	0.39

TABLE 9.4 *Lognormal Distribution Parameters μ and σ for Pollutants*

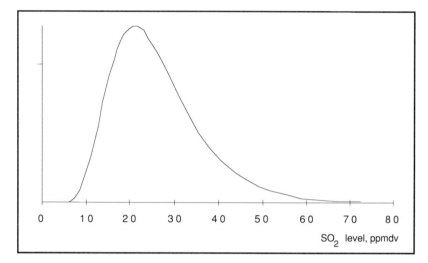

FIGURE 9.12 *Lognormal Density Function for SO₂ Emissions from Incineration Plant*

2. If the plant is subject to SO_2 certification its emissions of this pollutant will be monitored on a continual basis and the average daily emission level must not fall below the specified level in Table 9.3. The numbers in Table 9.4, however, refer to the probability distribution of a single observation. That is, we could use the specified lognormal distribution to find the probability that a single reading of the SO_2 level exceeds the specified level. Finding the probability that an average daily emission exceeds the specified level, though, requires more analysis.

   Let us assume that the average emission level will be calculated by taking n observations and then calculating the *geometric mean*. To do this, we multiply the n observations together and then take the nth root of the product. In symbols, let G denote the geometric mean:

$$G = \left\{ \prod_{i=1}^{n} X_i \right\}^{(1/n)}.$$

It turns out that if each X_i is drawn independently from a distribution that is lognormal with parameters μ and σ, then G has a lognormal distribution with parameters μ and $\sigma/\sqrt{n}$. In our case we will take the 24th root of a product of 24 hourly observations of emission levels.

   Find the probability that the geometric mean of the 24 hourly emission observations exceeds the SO_2 limit specified in Table 9.3. Compare this to the probability that a single observation will exceed the same limit.

3. Discuss the issues that the city should consider in deciding whether to build a small- or medium-sized plant.

Source: Marcus, J., and R. Mills (1988) "Emissions from Mass Burn Resource Recovery Facilities," *Risk Analysis* No. 8, pages 315–327 and "Emission Guidelines: Municipal Waste Combustors" *Federal Register* Vol. 54, No. 243, December 20, 1989, page 52209.

◇ REFERENCES

In this chapter we have scratched only the surface of theoretical probability distributions, although we have discussed most of the truly useful probability models. Theoretical distributions are widely used in operations research and in the construction of formal models of dynamic and uncertain systems. For additional study as well as many illustrative examples, consult the texts by DeGroot (1970), Feller (1968), Olkin, Gleser, and Derman (1980), or Winkler (1972). Johnson and Kotz (1969, 1970a, 1970b, and 1972) have compiled encyclopedic information on a great variety of probability distributions.

DeGroot, M. (1970) *Optimal Statistical Decisions.* New York: McGraw-Hill.

Feller, W. (1968) *An Introduction to Probability Theory and Its Applications, Vol. 1,* 3rd ed. New York: Wiley.

Johnson, N. L., and S. Kotz (1969) *Distributions in Statistics: Discrete Distributions.* New York: Houghton Mifflin.

Johnson, N. L., and S. Kotz (1970a) *Distributions in Statistics: Continuous Univariate Distributions I.* New York: Houghton Mifflin.

Johnson, N. L., and S. Kotz (1970b) *Distributions in Statistics: Continuous Univariate Distributions II.* New York: Houghton Mifflin.

Johnson, N. L., and S. Kotz (1972) *Distributions in Statistics: Continuous Multivariate Distributions.* New York: Wiley.

Olkin, I., L. J. Gleser, and C. Derman (1980) *Probability Models and Applications.* New York: Macmillan.

Winkler, R. L. (1972) *Introduction to Bayesian Inference and Decision.* New York: Holt, Rinehart, & Winston.

◇ EPILOGUE

The case study on earthquake prediction was written in early October 1989, just two weeks before an earthquake of magnitude 7.1 occurred near Santa Cruz, California, on the San Andreas Fault. Strong ground shaking lasted for approximately 15 seconds. The results were 67 deaths, collapsed buildings around the Bay Area, damage to the Bay Bridge between San Francisco and Oakland, and the destruction of a one-mile stretch of freeway in Oakland. This was a small earthquake, however, relative to the 8.3 magnitude quake in 1906. The "big one" is still to come, and may cause even more damage.   ◆

Using Data

We have discussed subjective judgments and theoretical distributions as sources for probabilities when modeling uncertainty in a decision problem. In this chapter we will consider an obvious source for information about probabilities: historical data. It is possible to use data alone to develop probability distributions; we cover the development of discrete and continuous distributions in the first part of the chapter. It also is possible to use data in conjunction with theoretical probability models; that is, the data can provide information to help refine assessments regarding the parameters of a theoretical distribution. In the second part of the chapter, we discuss the use of data in conjunction with some of the theoretical models discussed in Chapter 9.

◆ USING DATA TO CONSTRUCT PROBABILITY DISTRIBUTIONS

Using past data when it is available is a straightforward idea, and most likely you have done something like this in the past, at least informally. Suppose, for example, that you are interested in planning a picnic at the Portland Zoo on an as-yet-undetermined day during February. Obviously, the weather is a concern in this case, and you want to assess the probability of rain. If you were to ask the National Weather Service for advice in this regard, forecasters would report that the probability of rain on any given day in February is approximately 0.47. They base this estimate on analysis of weather during past years; on 47% of the days in February over the past several years rain has fallen in Portland.

We can think about developing both discrete and continuous probability distributions on the basis of empirical data. For the discrete situation, the problem really becomes one of creating a relative frequency histogram from the data. In the case of a continuous situation, we can use the data to draw an empirically based CDF. We will look briefly at each of these.

Histograms

Imagine that you are in charge of a manufacturing plant, and you are trying to develop a maintenance policy for your machines. An integral part of the analysis leading to policy selection most likely would involve an examination of the frequency of machine failures. For example, you might collect the following data over 260 days:

- ◆ No Failures   217 days
- ◆ One Failure   32 days
- ◆ Two Failures   11 days.

These data lead to the following relative frequencies, which could be used as estimates of probabilities of machine failures in your analysis:

No Failures $0.835 = 217/260$
One Failure $0.123 = 32/260$
Two Failures $0.042 = 11/260$.

Thus, we would have a histogram that looks like Figure 10.1, and in a decision tree, we would have a chance node with three branches like that in Figure 10.2.

Our treatment of histograms and estimation of discrete probabilities is brief precisely because the task is simply a matter of common sense. The only serious consideration to keep in mind is that you should have enough data to make a reliable estimate of the probabilities. (One nuclear power plant accident is not enough to develop a probability distribution!) The data requirements depend on the particular problem, but the minimum should be approximately five observations in the least likely category. The other categories, of course, will have more observations.

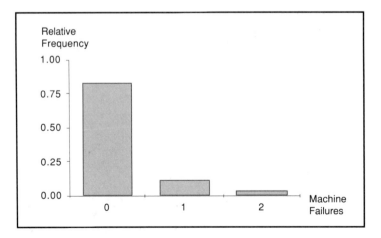

FIGURE 10.1   *Relative Frequency Histogram for Machine Failure Data*

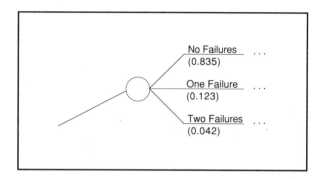

FIGURE 10.2   *The Decision-Tree Representation of Uncertainty Regarding Machine Failures*

Finally, keep in mind that your probability estimates are just that — estimates. The goal is to model uncertainty. Always ask yourself whether the probabilities estimated on the basis of the data truly reflect the uncertainty that you face. If you are not satisfied with the representation based on the data, you may need to model your uncertainty using subjective assessment methods. In particular, this might be the case if you think that the past may not indicate what the future holds.

Empirical CDFs

Continuous probability distributions are common in decision-making situations. We have seen how to assess a continuous probability distribution subjectively through assessment of a CDF. Our use of data to estimate a continuous distribution will follow the same basic strategy. To illustrate the principles, we will use an example and data concerning the costs related to correctional halfway houses.

HALFWAY HOUSES

A halfway house is a facility that provides a residence and some supervision and support for individuals who have been recently released from prison. The purpose of these halfway houses is to ease the transition from prison life to normal civilian life, with the ultimate goal being to improve an ex-convict's chance of successful integration into society. The National Advisory Committee on Criminal Justice Standards and Goals is responsible for providing information pertaining to the costs and resource implications of correctional standards that are related to halfway houses.

◆

The main purpose of the reports made by the advisory committee is to provide cost information to state and local decision makers regarding the many services that halfway houses perform. One important variable is yearly per-bed rental costs. Denote this variable by C. Table 10.1 shows yearly per-bed rental costs (in dollars) — values of C — for a random sample of 35 halfway houses. The data are arranged in ascending order.

To create a smooth CDF from these data, recall the idea of a cumulative probability. Suppose we look at the middle value, 325. Eighteen of the 35 values are less than or equal to 325. It also is true that 18 values are less than or equal to 326, 327, $\cdots$, up to 344.99. So $P(C \leq 325) = P(C \leq 326) = \cdots = P(C \leq 344.99) = 18/35$ or 0.514. So how can we estimate the 0.514 fractile? Take 335 as the best estimate of the 0.514 fractile; 335 is the value that is halfway between 325 and 345. Figure 10.3 shows what we are doing in terms of a CDF graph. The data points define the ends of the flat steps on the graph. Our estimate, the smooth curve, will go through the centers of the flat steps.

To get a CDF, we do the same thing for all data points. The procedure first rank orders the data and then calculates the centers of the flats; this is just a matter of calculating the halfway points between adjacent data points. For example, consider the halfway point between the first and second data points. The halfway point is $(52 + 76)/2 = 64$. Call this x_1. Now calculate $x_2, \cdots, x_{n-1}$, where n is the number of data points. Now associate with each x_i its approximate cumulative probability. The value x_i is in the ith position, and so it has cumulative probability estimated as i/n. In symbols, $P(X \leq x_i)$ is approximately i/n. In our example, $P(C \leq 64)$ is approximately $1/35$ or 0.029. Likewise, $x_{15} = 308$, so $P(C \leq 308)$ is approximately $15/35$, or 0.429. Table 10.2 shows the calculations for all 35 data points. The final step is to plot these points as in Figure 10.4. The tails of the CDF are sketched as smooth extrapolations of the curve.

Although all of the calculations that must be done to obtain a CDF look complicated, these are the kinds of calculations that can be done easily on an electronic spreadsheet. In a spreadsheet environment, the p_i's and cumulative probabilities are calculated easily and then plotted on a graph.

Rental Costs ($)

52	205	303	400	643
76	250	313	402	693
100	257	317	408	732
136	264	325	417	749
137	280	345	422	750
186	282	373	472	791
196	283	384	480	891

TABLE 10.1 *Yearly Bed-Rental Costs for 35 Halfway Houses*

Source: Sincich, T. (1989) *Business Statistics by Example*, 3rd ed. San Francisco, CA: Dellen.

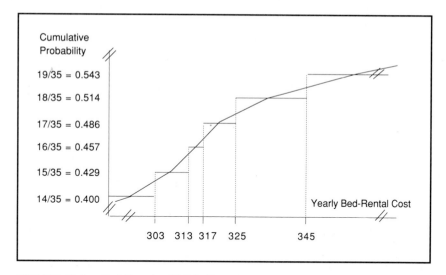

FIGURE 10.3 *Bulding the CDF by Drawing a Smooth Curve Through the Centers of the Flat Steps*

Obs. No.	Cost	x_i	Cumulative Probability	Obs. No.	Cost	x_i	Cumulative Probability
1	52	64.0	0.029	19	345	359.0	0.543
2	76	88.0	0.057	20	373	378.5	0.571
3	100	118.0	0.086	21	384	392.0	0.600
4	136	136.5	0.114	22	400	401.0	0.629
5	137	161.5	0.143	23	402	405.0	0.657
6	186	191.0	0.171	24	408	412.5	0.686
7	196	200.5	0.200	25	417	419.5	0.714
8	205	227.5	0.229	26	422	447.0	0.743
9	250	253.5	0.257	27	472	476.0	0.771
10	257	260.5	0.286	28	480	561.5	0.800
11	264	272.0	0.314	29	643	668.0	0.829
12	280	281.0	0.343	30	693	712.5	0.857
13	282	282.5	0.371	31	732	740.5	0.886
14	283	293.0	0.400	32	749	749.5	0.914
15	303	308.0	0.429	33	750	770.5	0.943
16	313	315.0	0.457	34	791	841.0	0.971
17	317	321.0	0.486	35	891	—	—
18	325	335.0	0.514				

TABLE 10.2 *Estimated Cumulative Probabilities for the Halfway-House Data*

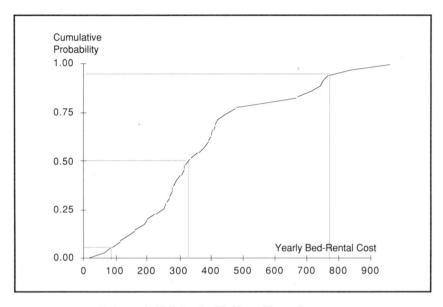

FIGURE 10.4   *Estimated CDF for the Halfway-House Data*

Once we have the CDF, we can use it in the same way as before. For example, we might use it to derive a discrete approximation (Chapter 8) for inclusion in a decision tree. In the case of the halfway-house data, Figure 10.5 shows a three-point discrete approximation that has been constructed using the extended Pearson–Tukey method described in Chapter 8. Recall that the 0.05 and 0.95 fractiles each are given probability 0.185, and the median is given probability 0.63. These fractiles are indicated in Figure 10.4.

There are other alternatives for using data to approximate a continuous distribution. One way that may be familiar to you is to split the data into reasonable groups and create a relative frequency histogram of the grouped data. This procedure is straightforward and similar to the discussion above regarding discrete

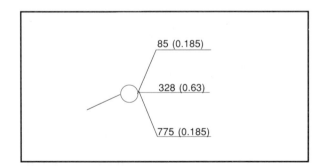

FIGURE 10.5   *Three-Point Approximation for the Halfway-House Data*

probabilities. Again, no category should contain fewer than five observations, and typically the widths of the intervals that define the categories should be the same. If you need more direction on the use of histograms for continuous distributions, consult any introductory statistics textbook. The text by Sincich, from which the halfway-house data were taken, is an excellent source.

◆ USING DATA TO FIT THEORETICAL PROBABILITY MODELS

Another way to deal with data is simply to fit a theoretical distribution to it. Typically, this involves two steps. First, we must decide what kind of distribution is appropriate (binomial, Poisson, normal, and so on). The choice should be based both on an understanding of the situation (for example, whether the uncertain quantity must be between 0 and 1, which suggests a beta distribution, or whether a discrete distribution is appropriate) as well as an inspection of the distribution of the data. For example, it makes little sense to fit a normal distribution, which is symmetric, to data whose distribution is highly skewed.

Having chosen the kind of distribution, the next step is to choose the values of the distribution parameters. In the case of the binomial, for instance, we need values for n and p. For the normal, μ and σ are required. Parameter values can be chosen by calculating some summary statistics (mean, standard deviation, and so on) for a sample, and then simply using those as the parameter values. For example, it is possible to calculate the sample mean ($\bar{x}$) and sample variance (s^2) for the 35 halfway-house observations:

$$n = 35$$

$$\bar{x} = \frac{\sum\limits_{i=1}^{n} x_i}{n} = 380.4$$

$$s^2 = \frac{\sum\limits_{i=1}^{n} (x_i - \bar{x})^2}{n - 1} = 47{,}344.3$$

$$s = \sqrt{47{,}344.3} = 217.6.$$

Thus, we might choose a normal distribution with mean $\mu = 380.4$ and standard deviation $\sigma = 217.6$ to represent the distribution of the yearly bed-rental costs.

Another possibility is to fit a theoretical distribution using fractiles. That is, find a theoretical distribution whose fractiles match as well as possible with the fractiles of the empirical data. This is the data-based counterpart of the procedure discussed in Chapter 9 for fitting a theoretical distribution to a subjectively assessed distribution. In this case we would be fitting a theoretical distribution to a data-based distribution.

For most initial attempts to model uncertainty in a decision analysis, it will be adequate to use the sample mean and variance as estimates of the mean and variance of the theoretical distribution and to establish parameter values in this way. Refinement of the probability model may require more careful judgment about the kind of distribution as well as more care in fitting the parameters. Statisticians have devised many clever parameter-estimation methods. A discussion of these techniques is beyond the scope of this treatment but may be found in advanced textbooks in statistics.

♦ NATURAL CONJUGATE DISTRIBUTIONS (OPTIONAL)

So far we have considered modeling uncertainty using subjective judgments, theoretical models, and data. It is clear that we can mix these techniques to varying degrees. We have seen examples in which we have used a theoretical model to represent a subjective probability distribution (the use of the beta distribution in the soft pretzel problem), others in which data were used to estimate parameters for a theoretical distribution (the halfway-house data), and still others in which data were used to modify subjective probabilities regarding the parameter of a theoretical distribution (the soft pretzel examples using the binomial and Poisson distributions). Our topic now continues in this vein. We will see how to use Bayes' theorem in a systematic way to use data to update beliefs in the context of theoretical models.

Recall the Poisson example in Chapter 9 (page 255) in which we wondered about the quality of a new location for the soft pretzel kiosk. The new location could have been good, bad, or dismal, with P(Good) = 0.7, P(Bad) = 0.2, and P(Dismal) = 0.1. Each characterization is associated with a specific value of m, the expected number of pretzels sold per hour; a good location implies $m = 20$, bad implies $m = 10$, and dismal $m = 6$. The uncertainty about the nature of the location also can be thought of as uncertainty about the parameter m: P($m = 20$) = 0.7, P($m = 10$) = 0.2, and P($m = 6$) = 0.1. Furthermore, we might have had more than three possible values for m; in fact, the location might have been anything between dismal and wonderful, or might have had m values anywhere from 0 to, say, 50 (or even higher).

Uncertainty about a parameter (such as m) often can be modeled with a continuous probability distribution. As before, this would be the prior probability distribution. Then, as in the Poisson example, we may obtain data that also provide information about the parameter of the process. Bayes' theorem provides the mechanism for using the data to update the prior probability distribution in order to arrive at a posterior probability distribution.

In this section, we will explore this process in some detail. It turns out that the mathematical details are such that performing the calculations can be quite difficult unless the prior distribution and the distribution for the data match in a particular way. We will look at two such situations. The first is when the decision maker is uncertain about the parameter p in a binomial distribution and represents that uncertainty with a beta prior distribution. The decision maker then observes data, the outcome of a binomial random variable, and uses these data to update the prior distribution. In the second situation, the decision maker is uncertain about the mean μ of a normal distribution and represents that uncertainty with another normal distribution for μ. Now the decision maker takes a sample, calculates a sample mean, and uses this information to update the prior distribution for μ.

Our plan of attack is as follows. First, we will discuss the overall process. The process is not particularly complicated, but the concepts involved are somewhat demanding. A thorough understanding of the process requires attention to several conceptual issues. Next, we will show how the process works in the two specific situations that were mentioned above, and we will see examples. We will end with a discussion of how the uncertainty about a distribution parameter influences one's prediction or forecast.

Uncertainty About Parameters and Bayesian Updating

The flow chart (*not* an influence diagram) in Figure 10.6 shows the process that we will go through. The symbol θ is used to represent a parameter of a theoretical distribution in which we may be interested. The process goes as follows.

First, the decision maker chooses some theoretical distribution to model his or her beliefs regarding an uncertain quantity X (for example, a normal distribution to model the scores of students on a standardized exam, or a Poisson distribution to model the number of customers who arrive at a soft pretzel kiosk). Let $P(X = x \mid \theta)$ denote this theoretical distribution, which has some parameter θ about which the decision maker is uncertain. Being uncertain about θ, the decision maker assesses a *prior probability distribution,* $f(\theta)$, for the parameter. At this point, $P(X = x \mid \theta)$ and $f(\theta)$ together embody all of the decision maker's beliefs about the possible outcomes of the uncertain quantity X. If necessary, the decision maker can use this model of the uncertainty in solving a decision problem. Our concern here, however, is how to use data. Thus, the next step in the process is the acquisition of data and the incorporation of the new information into the model.

Suppose that the decision maker, having assessed $P(X = x \mid \theta)$ and $f(\theta)$, now observes an x, an outcome from the physical system (for example, a sample of exam scores, or actual arrivals at the soft pretzel kiosk over a period of time). Label the data as x_1. The data contain information that the decision maker can use to refine his or her probabilities. In particular, Bayes' theorem allows for the updating of the prior distribution $f(\theta)$ so that it becomes a posterior distribution $f(\theta \mid x_1)$:

$$f(\theta \mid x_1) = \frac{P(x_1 \mid \theta) \, f(\theta)}{\displaystyle\int_{-\infty}^{+\infty} P(x_1 \mid \theta) \, f(\theta) \, d\theta}. \tag{10.1}$$

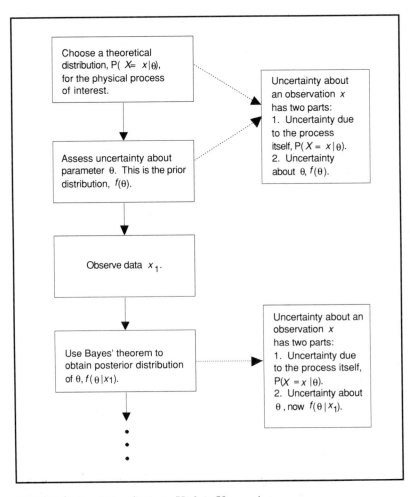

FIGURE 10.6   *Using Data to Update Uncertainty*
about Parameter θ via Bayes' Theorem

Equation (10.1) is simply Bayes' theorem when $f(\theta)$ is a continuous distribution. The output of Bayes' theorem in this case is a posterior distribution of θ after having observed x_1. That is, $f(\theta \mid x_1)$ represents the decision maker's uncertainty about θ after having seen data x_1.

The term $P(x_1 \mid \theta)$ in Equation (10.1) is called the *likelihood function*. We calculated likelihoods for the binomial and Poisson soft pretzel examples in Chapter 9: We did it when we calculated the probability of observing the data for each possible parameter value. In the binomial case, we calculated binomial probabilities for the observed data depending on whether the pretzels were a hit ($p = 0.3$) or a flop ($p = 0.1$). In the Poisson case, we calculated Poisson probabilities for the observed number of arrivals depending on whether the new location was good ($m = 20$ per Hr), bad ($m = 10$ per Hr), or dismal ($m = 6$ per Hr).

The flow chart in Figure 10.6 is shown with three dots at the bottom, indicating that the process can continue. That is, the decision maker now has uncertainty about θ, which is represented by $f(\theta \mid x_1)$. New data (x_2) might be observed, and the decision maker again can incorporate this new information via Bayes' theorem. The result would be $f(\theta \mid x_1, x_2)$. This sequential updating process can continue indefinitely.

In principle, Equation (10.1) can be used regardless of the form of the likelihood function or the prior distribution $f(\theta)$. With specific mathematical expressions for these functions, it always is possible to have a computer crunch the numbers to generate a posterior distribution $f(\theta \mid x_1)$. It may not be possible to write down a mathematical expression for $f(\theta \mid x_1)$, but the computer could grind out the calculations, evaluate $f(\theta \mid x_1)$ for many different values of θ, and finally plot the distribution. But an easier way to do this would be nice.

Fortunately, there is an easier way in certain situations. Recall that we are moving from a prior distribution to a posterior distribution. In certain cases, the prior and posterior distributions have the same form. This form is called the *natural conjugate distribution* for the theoretical distribution that represents the physical process. Moreover, in these cases relatively simple rules guide the use of observed data in adjusting the prior distribution to obtain the posterior. In other words, this elegant result reduces the seemingly complicated Equation (10.1) to a few simple formulas in these cases. Two such cases involve the binomial and normal distributions. We will discuss each one in turn, using examples.

Binomial Distributions: Natural Conjugate Priors for *p*

In this case, the chosen theoretical distribution to represent the physical process is binomial with parameters n and p. That is, the decision maker knows that the process generates many observations that are either successes or failures, and that in a group of n observations, there will be some number X of successes. Thus, $P(X = x \mid \theta)$ in this case is equal to the binomial probability $P_B(X = r \mid n, p)$, which is given in equation (9.1) (page 250).

Of course, $P_B(X = r \mid n, p)$ is easy to calculate for any value of r as long as p is known. In this case, however, we want to incorporate uncertainty about p. The natural conjugate prior distribution for p is a beta distribution. That is, if the decision maker uses the beta distribution to model the prior uncertainty about p, and then updates that beta prior on the basis of an observation from the process, then the posterior distribution of p also will be a beta distribution. Note that the beta distribution is a reasonable model, because p must be between 0 and 1. Here is how the updating process works:

1. The decision maker considers a physical process and concludes that its uncertainty can be represented with a binomial distribution. That is, out of n trials, the probability of r successes is $P_B(X = r \mid n, p)$.
2. The decision maker assesses a beta prior distribution for p, $f_B(p \mid r_0, n_0)$. That is, the decision maker carefully considers the uncertainty about p and concludes that it can be adequately represented with a beta distribution having parameters r_0 and n_0. Based on this prior distribution for p, a good estimate for it would be the mean of this distribution, r_0 / n_0.

3. The decision maker observes n_1 independent trials, and r_1 of these are successes. Based on these data alone, of course, a good estimate for p would be r_1/n_1. The issue is how to combine this information with the prior distribution.

4. Combining the data with the prior distribution via Bayes' theorem gives a posterior distribution for p that is also a beta distribution, $f_B(p \mid r^*, n^*)$, where

$$r^* = r_0 + r_1,$$ (10.2a)

and

$$n^* = n_0 + n_1.$$ (10.2b)

That is, the decision maker only has to add the r's and n's to find the parameters of the posterior distribution for p.

In addition, we can see how this process could continue as new data are observed. The posterior $f_B(p \mid r^*, n^*)$ becomes the prior distribution in the next round. Data r_2 and n_2 are observed. Thus, the parameters for the posterior distribution after observing r_2 and n_2 are $r^{**} = r^* + r_2 = r_0 + r_1 + r_2$ and $n^{**} = n^* + n_2 = n_0 + n_1 + n_2$.

In Chapter 9 we discussed briefly that in subjectively assessing a beta distribution, the decision maker may think of r and n as representing "equivalent information." If the decision maker believes that the available information is equivalent to having observed 5 successes in 10 trials, then appropriate beta parameters would be $r = 5$ and $n = 10$. In performing the updating of a prior distribution via Bayes' theorem here, we can see just how appropriate this analogy is. Essentially, the r's and n's are added together as if they had all resulted from sample observations.

As an example, let us return to the soft pretzel example in Chapter 9, specifically pages 267–268. There we considered whether to proceed with the marketing of your pretzels. Of course, if you are convinced that your new pretzel will be a great seller, you certainly would undertake the project. The problem is that the proportion (Q) of the market that your pretzel might capture is uncertain. In the example, this uncertainty about Q is represented with a beta distribution having parameters $r = 1$ and $n = 4$. Let us take this as a prior distribution, $f_B(Q \mid r_0 = 1, n_0 = 4)$. The expected value of this distribution is $E(Q) = \frac{1}{4} = 0.25$, which would be a good estimate for Q based on the prior distribution.

Now suppose you run a taste test. You bake 20 pretzels, and 7 of 20 tasters prefer your pretzel over the competition's. Thus, $r_1 = 7$ and $n_1 = 20$. Combining these data with the prior distribution, the posterior probability distribution for Q is $f_B(Q \mid r^* = 1 + 7 = 8, n^* = 4 + 20 = 24)$. The posterior expected value of Q is $8/24 = 0.33$. The data have considerably affected your beliefs about Q. Figure 10.7 shows both the prior and posterior distributions. The additional data have greatly reduced the uncertainty about Q.

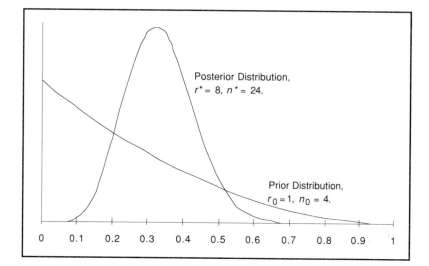

FIGURE 10.7   *Prior and Posterior Distributions for the Market Proportion Captured by the Soft Pretzel*

Normal Distributions: Natural Conjugate Priors for μ

Suppose the decision maker chooses a normal distribution to represent the physical process. That is, the decision maker knows that the outcomes (the x's) that arise from the process are numbers that can take on any value in a continuum, and believes that a normal distribution provides a good representation for the x's distribution. In this case, $P(x \mid \theta)$ is the expression $f_N(x \mid \mu, \sigma)$ from Equation (9.4) (page 259).

We will assume that the standard deviation of the process, σ, is known. The decision maker, however, does not know μ, but is willing to assess a probability distribution for it. The natural conjugate prior distribution for μ also turns out to be a normal distribution. That is, if the decision maker chooses a normal prior distribution to represent the uncertainty about μ, and then updates that prior based on observations from the process, the resulting posterior distribution for μ also will be normal. Let us suppose that the decision maker assesses a normal distribution for μ, $f_N(\mu \mid m_0, \sigma_0)$.

This situation can be a bit confusing because so many different normal distributions are floating around. First, the original distribution is normal, $f_N(x \mid \mu, \sigma)$. But we also have normal distributions for the parameter μ itself. The prior is $f_N(\mu \mid m_0, \sigma_0)$, and the posterior also will be normal, $f_N(\mu \mid m^*, \sigma^*)$. Here are the steps in the updating process:

1. The decision maker considers a physical process and concludes that the uncertainty of the process can be represented with a normal distribution. That is, the distribution of observations from the process is $f_N(x \mid \mu, \sigma)$.
2. The decision maker assesses a normal prior distribution for μ, $f_N(\mu \mid m_0, \sigma_0)$. That is, the decision maker carefully considers the uncertainty about μ and

concludes that it can be modeled with a normal distribution having parameters m_0 and σ_0. Based on this prior distribution for μ, a good estimate for μ would be the mean m_0.

3. The decision maker actually observes n_1 independent observations from the process, and the average of these sample observations is $\bar{x}_1$. Based on these data alone, of course, a good estimate for μ would be $\bar{x}_1$.

4. Combining the data with the prior distribution via Bayes' theorem gives a posterior distribution for μ that also is a normal distribution, $f_N(\mu \mid m^*, \sigma^*)$, where

$$m^* = \frac{m_0 \sigma^2/n_1 + \bar{x}_1 \sigma_0^2}{\sigma^2/n_1 + \sigma_0^2}, \tag{10.3a}$$

and

$$\sigma^* = \sqrt{\frac{\sigma_0^2 \sigma^2/n_1}{\sigma^2/n_1 + \sigma_0^2}}. \tag{10.3b}$$

That is, the decision maker combines the prior information and the data via Equations (10.3a) and (10.3b) to obtain the posterior distribution of μ.

As with the binomial model, one can see how the sequential incorporation of data would be done in this case. Observing the first sample would lead to the posterior as given above. In the next round, m^* and σ^* become the parameters for a new prior distribution that is updated on the basis of a second set of observations, using Equations (10.3a) and (10.3b) with m^* and σ^* in place of m_0 and σ_0. Further sequential updating would follow the same pattern.

In the binomial situation above, it was easy to see how the prior information could be interpreted as "equivalent" sample information. The same is true here, although it is not evident from (10.3a) and (10.3b). Suppose, however, that we write $\sigma_0^2 = \sigma^2/n_0$. Then n_0 is interpreted as our "equivalent sample size." Having made this transformation, Equations (10.3a) and (10.3b) become

$$m^* = \frac{n_0 m_0 + n_1 \bar{x}_1}{n_0 + n_1}, \tag{10.4a}$$

and

$$\sigma^* = \sqrt{\frac{\sigma^2}{n_0 + n_1}}. \tag{10.4b}$$

From these expressions, it is clear how n_0 and n_1 are interacting. The posterior mean m^* is simply a weighted average of m_0 and $\bar{x}_1$, where the weights are based on the "sample sizes" n_0 and n_1. Posterior variance σ^{*2} has the same form as σ_0^2, with the cumulative sample size $n_0 + n_1$ used as the divisor of the process variance σ^2.

As an example of the updating process for the normal distribution, let us again look at the halfway-house data. Suppose that a decision maker believes that yearly bed-rental costs are normally distributed with mean μ and standard deviation $\sigma = \$220$. The expected value μ is unknown, but the decision maker assesses a normal distribution with mean $m_0 = \$345$ and standard deviation $\sigma_0 = \$50$, $f_N(\mu \mid m_0 = \$345, \sigma_0 = \$50)$. For example, this means that the decision maker believes there is roughly a 68% chance that μ is between \$295 and \$395, and roughly a 95% chance that μ is between \$245 and \$445.

Now suppose that the decision maker obtains the 35 observations listed in Table 10.1. The sample mean of these observations is \$380.40. We have $n_1 = 35$ and $\bar{x}_1 = \$380.40$. Applying Equations (10.3a) and (10.3b), we obtain the posterior distribution of μ, a normal distribution with parameters $m^* = \$367.80$ and $\sigma^* = \$29.80$. The prior and posterior distributions are illustrated in Figure 10.8. Notice that, with the added information, the distribution for μ is tighter, reflecting less uncertainty about it.

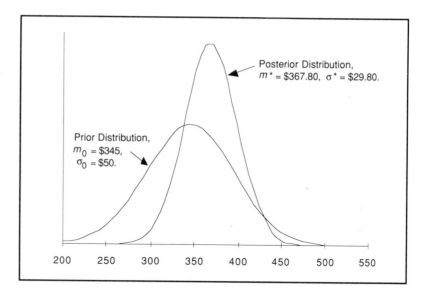

FIGURE 10.8 *Prior and Posterior Distributions for μ in the Halfway-House Example*

Predictive Distributions

We have represented the uncertainty about the physical process under investigation with the distribution $P(X = x \mid \theta)$. That is, if we only knew θ, we would have everything we need for the distribution of the x's. We do not know θ, however, but we do have a probability distribution for it, $f(\theta)$. To give a distribution for the x's, we must combine $P(X = x \mid \theta)$ and $f(\theta)$. As previously mentioned, these two kinds of uncertainty, taken together, provide a complete model of the uncertainty that the decision maker faces regarding the x's. We simply must figure out how to put these pieces together.

To see this, imagine the binomial process. The probability of r successes in n trials is $P_B(X = r \mid n, p)$. But we need to know p in order to calculate probabilities using Equation 9.1. What we can do, however, is take something like an average over all possible values for p. This is exactly the approach we will take.

If we want a distribution for the x's that does not depend on θ, we want $P(X = x)$, not $P(X = x \mid \theta)$. We will call $P(X = x)$ the *predictive distribution* because it describes our uncertainty about X — which x values are most likely, the probability that X will fall into different intervals, and so on. To get $P(X = x)$, we must "integrate out" θ:

$$P(X = x) = \int_{-\infty}^{+\infty} P(X = x \mid \theta)\, f(\theta)\, d\theta.$$

You might recognize this expression as the denominator of Bayes' theorem as it was written in Equation 10.1. Figuring out this integral will not be any easier than it was in Equation 10.1. It will always be possible to use a computer to calculate this integral numerically, but numerical integration techniques are beyond the scope of this text. In cases in which we have a natural conjugate prior distribution for q, it may be possible to find a simple expression for this distribution. We will take a look at the normal and binomial processes.

Predictive Distributions: The Normal Case

If the physical process follows a normal distribution, the integral becomes

$$P(X = x) = \int_{-\infty}^{+\infty} f_N(x \mid \mu, \sigma)\, f(\mu \mid m_0, \sigma_0)\, d\mu$$
$$= f_N(x \mid m_0, \sigma_p = \sqrt{\sigma^2 + \sigma_0^2}\,).$$

We will express this in words. Taking into account the prior uncertainty about μ, the distribution of the next sampled observation from the process is normal with mean m_0 and variance $\sigma_p^2 = \sigma^2 + \sigma_0^2$. The fact that the mean for x is m_0 is reasonable; our best guess for x would be μ, and our best guess for μ is m_0. The fact that the variance is $\sigma^2 + \sigma_0^2$ shows that indeed the overall uncertainty about x is composed of uncertainty about the process that generates the x's (σ^2) and uncertainty about μ (σ_0^2). If we knew exactly what μ was, then the variance of the distribution simply would be σ^2.

What we have just done can be generalized to any normal distribution for μ. If some data already have been collected, and the decision maker has a posterior distribution for μ, $f_N(\mu \mid m^*, \sigma^*)$, then the predictive distribution for x is normal with mean m^* and variance $\sigma_p = \sigma^2 + \sigma^{*2}$.

Continuing our halfway-house example, suppose that, having collected the data and updated the prior distribution for μ, the decision maker would like to express the uncertainty about the next yearly bed rental (x). The distribution desired is the predictive distribution. We know that $\sigma = \$220$, and that the posterior distribution for μ was normal with mean $m^* = \$367.80$ and standard deviation $\sigma^* = \$29.80$. Thus, the predictive distribution will be normal with mean $\$367.80$, and variance $\sigma_p^2 = [(220)^2 + (29.8^2)]$. Performing the calculations, we find that $\sigma_p = \$222$, which is just barely more than the process standard deviation of $\$220$. Thus, as we might have suspected, most of the uncertainty about the bed-rental cost is simply the result of fluctuation in these costs. A little bit of uncertainty results from the uncertainty about μ.

Predictive Distributions: The Binomial Case

If the physical process is one that can be represented with a binomial distribution, then the matter is slightly more complicated. We really want to know how likely we would be to get different numbers of successes in n trials. The integral to find the predictive distribution $P(X = r)$ becomes

$$
\begin{aligned}
P(X = r) &= \int_0^1 P_B(r \mid n, p)\, f_B(p \mid r_0, n_0)\, dp \\[2mm]
&= \frac{(r + r_0 - 1)!\,(n + n_0 - r - r_0 - 1)!\, n!\,(n_0 - 1)!}{r!\,(r_0 - 1)!\,(n - r)!\,(n_0 - r_0 - 1)!\,(n + n_0 - 1)!}.
\end{aligned}
$$

This rather unusual-looking expression is called a *beta-binomial* probability distribution. The number of successes r can take on only discrete values of $0, 1, \cdots, n$. The probability for any of these outcomes can be calculated by plugging values for r, n, r_0, and n_0 into the beta-binomial expression.

As with the normal distribution, this result generalizes as long as the distribution of p is a beta distribution. For example, in the case of our soft pretzels, the posterior distribution for p was a beta distribution with parameters $r^* = 8$ and $n^* = 24$. The predictive distribution of r (the number of tasters out of n who would prefer the new pretzel) would be the same as given above, but with r^* and n^* replacing r_0 and n_0. For example, the probability that 6 out of the next 12 tasters will prefer the new pretzel would be:

$$
\begin{aligned}
P(X = 6) &= \frac{(r + r^* - 1)!\,(n + n^* - r - r^* - 1)!\, n!\,(n^* - 1)!}{r!\,(r^* - 1)!\,(n - r)!\,(n^* - r^* - 1)!\,(n + n^* - 1)!} \\[2mm]
&= \frac{(6 + 8 - 1)!\,(12 + 24 - 6 - 8 - 1)!\, 12!\,(24 - 1)!}{6!\,(8 - 1)!\,(12 - 6)!\,(24 - 8 - 1)!\,(12 + 24 - 1)!} \\[2mm]
&= \frac{13!\, 21!\, 12!\, 23!}{6!\, 7!\, 6!\, 15!\, 35!} \\[2mm]
&= 0.1116.
\end{aligned}
$$

Probabilities for other possible values of r can be calculated in the same way.

The use of data to update information in a systematic way via Bayes' theorem can be very useful in decision analysis. We have spent much time in discussing natural conjugate distributions here, and they can be quite helpful. What is perhaps more critical, however, is that you understand the concept that one can be uncertain about a parameter and encode that uncertainty as a probability distribution. This uncertainty then has an impact on the decision maker's probability of future outcomes. Thus, the underlying ideas of distributions on parameters and predictive distributions for future outcomes are quite basic.

In the next chapter, we will take this process a step further. In simulation we will generate random variables from theoretical probability distributions with specific parameters. This is a standard technique in decision analysis and risk analysis. But we also will be able to specify our parameters as uncertain. By specifying parameters themselves as probabilistic, we will be doing the simulation counterpart of the natural conjugate analysis that we have discussed here. Furthermore, we will not be limited to certain families of distributions. We will be able to specify any kind of probability distribution that seems reasonable; the computer will do the calculations for us.

◇ SUMMARY

In this chapter we have seen some ways in which data can be used in the development of probabilities and probability distributions for decision analysis. We began with the basics of constructing histograms and empirically based CDFs. A short discussion concerned the use of data to estimate parameters for theoretical distributions. The last part of the chapter discussed the use of data to update prior beliefs about parameters of a distribution. This process is based on Bayes' theorem. We saw how natural conjugate distributions worked for both normal and binomial cases. Finally, we discussed predictive distributions, or the distribution for future outcomes of a process when the parameters are uncertain.   ◆

◇ EXERCISES

10.1   Explain in your own words the role that data can play in the development of models of uncertainty in decision analysis.

10.2   Why might a decision maker be reluctant to make subjective probability judgments when historical data are available? In what sense does the use of data still involve subjective judgments?

10.3   Estimate the 0.65 and 0.35 fractiles of the distribution of yearly bed-rental costs, based on the CDF in Figure 10.4 (page 292).

10.4   Choose appropriate intervals and create a relative frequency histogram based on the halfway-house data in Table 10.1 (page 290).

◇ QUESTIONS AND PROBLEMS

10.5   It was suggested that five is the minimum number of data points for the least likely category in constructing histograms. In many cases, however, we must estimate probabilities that are extremely small, or for which relatively few data are available. In the example about machine failures at the beginning of the chapter (page 288–289), suppose that we had one day out of 260 in which three failures occurred. What do you think we should do in such a situation?

10.6 As discussed in the text, it often is possible to use a theoretical distribution as an approximation of the distribution of some sample data. It is always important, however, to check to make sure that your data really do fit the distribution you propose to use.

Consider the halfway-house data again. We calculated the sample mean $\bar{x} = 380.4$ and sample standard deviation $s = 217.6$. Taking these as approximately equal to μ and σ, use the Z table in Appendix E to find normal cumulative probabilities for dollar costs of 200, 300, 400, 500, 600, and 700. How do these theoretical normal probabilities compare with the data-based probabilities from the CDF in Figure 10.4 (page 292)? Do you think that the normal distribution is an appropriate distribution to use in this case? You might sketch the normal distribution CDF and superimpose it on Figure 10.4 to obtain a visual feel for how the normal distribution fits the data.

10.7 A scientist collected the following weights (in grams) of laboratory animals:

9.79	9.23	9.11
9.62	8.73	11.93
10.39	8.68	9.76
9.59	11.49	9.86
11.41	9.60	7.24

a. Use these data to create a data-based CDF for the distribution of weights for lab animals. Estimate the probability that an animal's weight will be less than 9.5 grams.

b. Fit a normal distribution to these data on the basis of the sample mean and sample variance. Use this normal distribution to estimate the probability that an animal's weight will be less than 9.5 grams.

c. Do you think that the normal distribution used in part b is a good choice for a theoretical distribution to fit these data? Why or why not?

10.8 A plant manager is interested in developing a quality-control program for an assembly line that produces light bulbs. To do so, the manager considers the quality of the products that come from the line. The light bulbs are packed in boxes of 12, and the line produces several thousand boxes of bulbs per day. To develop baseline data, some of the workers test all the bulbs in 100 boxes. They obtain the following results:

No. of Defective Bulbs/Box	No. of Boxes
0	68
1	27
2	3
3	2

a. Plot a histogram of these results.

b. What kind of theoretical distribution might fit this situation well? Explain.

c. Estimate parameters for the distribution you chose in part b by calculating the sample mean and variance. Use the theoretical distribution with its estimated parameters to estimate P(0 Defective), P(1 Defective), P(2 Defective), and P(3 Defective). How do these estimates compare to the relative frequency of these events in the data?

10.9 A retail manager in a discount store wants to establish a policy for the number of cashiers to have on hand and also when to open a new cash register. The first step in this process is to determine the rate at which customers arrive at the cash register. One day, the manager observes the following times (in minutes) between arrivals of customers at the cash registers:

0.1	2.6	2.9	0.5
1.2	1.8	4.8	3.3
1.7	0.2	1.5	2.0
4.2	0.6	1.0	2.6
0.9	3.4	1.7	0.4

a. Plot a CDF based on these data.

b. What kind of theoretical distribution do you think would be appropriate for these data? Why?

c. Calculate the sample mean and sample standard deviation of the data, and use these to estimate parameters for the theoretical distribution chosen in part b.

d. Plot a few points from the CDF of your theoretical distribution, and draw a smooth curve through them. How does this theoretical curve compare to the data-based CDF?

10.10 An ecologist studying the breeding habits of birds sent volunteers from the local chapter of the Audubon Society into the field to count nesting sites for a particular species. Each team was to survey five acres of land carefully. Because she was interested in studying the distribution of nesting sites within a particular kind of ecological system, the ecologist was careful to choose survey sites that were as similar as possible. In total, 24 teams surveyed five acres each, and reported the following numbers of nesting sites in each of the five acre parcels:

7	12	6	9
5	2	9	9
7	3	9	9
5	1	7	10
1	8	6	3
4	5	3	13

a. Plot a histogram for these data.

b. What kind of theoretical distribution might you select to represent the distribution of the number of nesting sites? Why?

c. Estimate the parameters of the theoretical distribution by calculating the sample mean and sample variance.

d. Plot the probability distribution based on your theoretical model from parts b and c. How does it compare to your histogram from part a?

10.11 Before performing the experiment, the scientist in Problem 10.7 thought a bit about the animals that he typically used in his lab. He knew (based on information from the animals' supplier) that the standard deviation of their weights was 1.5 grams. But the supplier was unable to specify the average weight precisely. The company did say there was a 68% chance that the average weight was between 9.0 and 9.8 grams, and a 95% chance that the average weight was between 8.6 and 10.2 grams.

a. Use the stated probabilities to find a natural conjugate prior distribution for the average weight of the animals. What is $P(\mu \geq 10 \text{ grams} \mid m_0, \sigma_0)$?

b. Find the posterior distribution for the average weight of the animals after having seen the data in Problem 10.7. What is $P(\mu \geq 10 \text{ grams} \mid m^*, \sigma^*)$?

10.12 Continuing Problem 10.11:

a. Based on the prior probability distribution for μ, find the predictive probability that a single lab animal will weigh more than 11 grams, $P(x \geq 11 \text{ grams} \mid m_0, \sigma_0)$.

b. After having seen the data and updating the beliefs about μ, find the predictive probability that a lab animal weighs more than 11 grams, $P(x \geq 11 \text{ grams} \mid m^*, \sigma^*)$?

10.13 The plant manager in Problem 10.8 actually began her investigation by assessing her subjective probability distribution for Q, the proportion of defective bulbs coming off the assembly line. Her assessed distribution was a beta distribution with parameters $r_0 = 1$, $n_0 = 20$; that is, her distribution was $f_B(q \mid r_0 = 1, n_0 = 20)$.

a. Plot this prior distribution for Q.

b. What would her posterior distribution for Q be after having observed the data in Problem 10.8?

10.14 A political analyst was interested in the proportion C of individuals who would vote for a controversial ballot measure. While he thought that it would be a close call, he was unsure of the precise value for C. He assessed a beta distribution for C with parameters $r_0 = 3$, $n_0 = 6$.

a. Plot this prior distribution for C.

b. The analyst is about to ask four individuals about their preferences. What is the probability that more than two of these individuals will express their support for the ballot measure?

c. Having questioned the four individuals, the analyst found that three would indeed vote for the ballot measure. Find the analyst's posterior distribution for C. Plot this posterior distribution and compare it with the prior distribution plotted in part a.

d. The analyst is now about to survey another 10 people. What is the probability that more than five of these people will support the ballot measure in this new poll?

e. Suppose that 6 of the 10 people surveyed said they would vote for the ballot measure. The analyst now must write up his results. What is his probability that the ballot measure will pass?

10.15 A comptroller was preparing to analyze the distribution of balances in the various accounts receivable for her firm. She knew from studies in previous years that the distribution would be normal with a standard deviation of $1500, but she was unsure of the mean μ. She thought carefully about her uncertainty about this parameter, and assessed a normal distribution for μ with mean $m_0 = \$10,000$ and $\sigma_0 = \$800$.

   Over lunch, she discussed this problem with her friend, who also worked in the accounting division. Her friend commented that she also was unsure of μ, but would have placed it somewhat higher. The friend said that "better" estimates for m_0 and σ_0 would have been $12,000 and $750, respectively.

a. Find $P(\mu > \$11,000)$ for both prior distributions.

b. That afternoon, the comptroller randomly chose nine accounts and calculated $\bar{x} = \$11,003$. Find her posterior distribution for μ. Find the posterior distribution of μ for her friend. Calculate $P(\mu > \$11,000)$ for each case.

c. A week later the analysis had been completed. Of a total of 144 accounts (including the nine reported in part b), the average was $\bar{x} = \$11,254$. Find the posterior distribution for μ for each of the two prior distributions. Calculate $P(\mu > \$11,000)$ for each case.

d. Discuss your answers to parts a, b, and c. What can you conclude?

CASE STUDIES

Taco Shells

Martin Ortiz, purchasing manager for the True Taco fast food chain, was contacted by a salesperson for a food service company. The salesperson pointed out the high breakage rate that was common in the shipment of most taco shells. Martin was aware of this fact, and noted that the chain usually experienced a 10% to 15% breakage rate. The salesperson then explained that his company recently had designed a new shipping container that reduced the breakage rate to less than 5%, and he produced the results of an independent test to support his claim.

When Martin asked about price, the salesperson said that his company charged $25 for a case of 500 taco shells, $1.25 more than True Taco currently was paying. But the salesperson claimed that the lower breakage rate more than compensated for the higher cost, offering a lower cost per usable taco shell than the current supplier. Martin, however, felt that he should try the new product on a limited basis and develop his own evidence. He decided to order a dozen cases and compare the breakage rate in these 12 cases with the next shipment of 18 cases from the current supplier. For each case received, Martin carefully counted the number of usable shells. The results are shown below:

Usable Shells				
New Supplier		**Current Supplier**		
468	467	444	441	450
474	469	449	434	444
474	484	443	427	433
479	470	440	446	441
482	463	439	452	436
478	468	448	442	429

QUESTIONS

1. Martin Ortiz's problem appears to be which supplier to choose to achieve the lowest expected cost per usable taco shell. Draw a decision tree of the problem, assuming he orders one case of taco shells. Should you use continuous fans or discrete chance nodes to represent the number of usable taco shells in one case?

2. Develop CDFs for the number of usable shells in one case for each supplier. Compare these two CDFs. Which appears to have the highest expected number of usable shells? Which one is riskier?

3. Create discrete approximations of the CDFs found in Question 2. Use these approximations in your decision tree to determine which supplier should receive the contract.

4. Based on the sample data given, calculate the average number of usable tacos per case for each supplier. Use these sample means to calculate the cost per usable taco for each supplier. Are your results consistent with your answer to Question 3? Discuss the advantages of finding the CDFs as part of the solution to the decision problem.

5. Should Martin Ortiz account for anything else in deciding which supplier should receive the contract?

Source: This case was adapted from Mendenhall, W., J. Reinmuth, R. Beaver, (1989) *Statistics for Management and Economics*, 6th ed. Boston, MA: PWS-KENT.

◆

Forecasting Sales

Sales documents were scattered all over Tim Hedge's desk. He had been asked to look at all of the available information and to try to forecast the number of microwave ovens that NewWave, Inc., would sell over the upcoming year. He had been with the company for only a month, and had never worked for a microwave company before. In fact, he had never worked for a company that was involved in consumer electronics. He had been hired because the boss had been impressed with his ability to grasp and analyze a wide variety of different kinds of decision problems.

Tim had dug up as much information as he could, and one of the things he had found was that one of NewWave's salespeople, Al Morley, had kept detailed records over the past 14 years of his own annual forecasts of the number of microwaves that the company would sell. Over the years, Morley had been fairly accurate. (His sales performance had been pretty good, too.) Of course, Morley had been only too happy to provide his own forecast of sales for the upcoming year. Tim thought this was fine, and reported back to his boss, Bill Maught.

"Yes," said Bill after he had listened to Tim, "I am aware that Al has been making these forecasts over the years. We have never really kept track of his forecasts, though. Even though he claims to have been fairly accurate over the years, I can remember one or two when he was not very close. For example, I think last year he was off by about 6000 units. Of course, if you ask him about those cases, he can explain them in hindsight. But there is always the possibility of unusual unforeseen circumstances in any given year. Besides, I think he forecasts low. When he does that, his sales quota is set lower, and he's more likely to get a bonus. I'd say there's about a 95 percent chance that on average he underforecasts by 1000 units or more. In fact, I'd bet even money that his average forecast error [sales – forecast] is above 1700 units."

Tim asked the obvious question. "Would you like me to look into this more? Maybe I could get a handle on just how good he is."

"Fine with me," answered Bill. "Besides, if we really could get a handle on how good he is, then his forecast might be a good basis for us to work with each year."

After that discussion, Tim had visited the accounting department to find out the number of units actually sold in each year for which Morley had made a forecast. He now had assembled the data and considered the numbers:

Forecast (Units)	Actual Sales	Error (Sales – Forecast)
39,000	41,553	2553
44,000	46,223	2223
46,000	49,351	3351
54,000	55,393	1393
60,000	61,607	1607
59,000	68,835	9835
99,000	101,647	2647
124,000	123,573	–427
149,000	156,473	7473
145,000	146,333	1333
159,000	155,668	–3332
169,000	167,168	–1832
171,000	171,477	477
179,000	185,529	6529

QUESTIONS

1. Calculate the average and standard deviation of Morley's forecasting errors. What do you think about Bill Maught's opinion of Morley's forecasting?
2. Plot a CDF based on these data. Based on these data alone, what is the probability that Morley's forecast this year will be too low by 1700 units or more?
3. Assume that Morley's forecast errors follow a normal distribution with standard deviation $\sigma = 3000$. Translate Bill Maught's probability assessments into a prior distribution for Morley's average error, μ. On the basis of these data, what would be Maught's posterior distribution? What is his posterior probability that Morley's average error is greater than 1700 units?
4. Morley has forecast sales of 187,000 units for the coming year. Based on Maught's posterior distribution for μ (Morley's average error), what is the probability distribution for sales for this coming year? What is the probability that sales will be greater than 190,000 units? Then sketch a CDF for this distribution.

Overbooking, Part II

Consider again the overbooking issue as discussed in the case study at the end of Chapter 9 (pages 277–278). Suppose that the Mockingbird Airlines operations manager believes that the no-show rate (N) is approximately 0.04, but is not exactly sure of this value. She assesses a probability distribution for N, and finds that a beta distribution with $r_0 = 1$ and $n_0 = 15$ provides a good fit to her subjective beliefs.

QUESTIONS

1. Suppose that Mockingbird sells 17 reservations on the next flight. On the basis of this prior distribution, find the predictive probability that all 17 passengers will show up to claim their reservations. Find the probability that 16 will show up, 15, 14, and so on.
2. Should Mockingbird have overbooked for the next flight? If so, by how much? If not, why not? Support your answer with the necessary calculations.
3. Now suppose 17 reservations are sold, and 17 passengers show up. Find the operations manager's posterior distribution for N.
4. On the basis of this new information and the manager's posterior distribution, should Mockingbird overbook on the next flight? If so, by how much? If not, why not? Support your answer with the necessary calculations. [*Hint*: You may have to be careful in calculating the factorial terms. Many calculators and electronic spreadsheets will not have sufficient precision to do these calculations very well. One trick is to cancel out as many terms in the numerator and denominator as possible. Another is to do the calculation by alternately multiplying and dividing. For example, $5!/6! = (5/6)(4/5)(3/4)(2/3)(1/2)$.]

$\blacklozenge$

$\diamond$ REFERENCES

Using data as the basis for probability modeling is a central issue in statistics. Some techniques that we have discussed, such as creating histograms, are basic tools; any basic statistics textbook will cover these topics. The text by Vatter, et al, (1978) contains an excellent discussion of the construction of a data-based CDF. Fitting a theoretical distribution using sample statistics such as the mean and standard deviation is also a basic and commonly used technique (for example, Olkin, Gleser, and Derman 1980), although it is worth noting that statisticians have many different mathematical techniques for fitting distributions to empirical data.

Bayesian updating and the use of natural conjugate priors is a central element of Bayesian statistics. Winkler (1972) has the most readable fundamental discussion of these issues. For a more complete treatment, including discussion of many more probabilistic processes and analysis using natural conjugate priors, see Raiffa and Schlaifer (1961) or DeGroot (1970).

DeGroot, M. (1970) *Optimal Statistical Decisions*. New York: McGraw-Hill.

Olkin, I., L. J. Gleser, and C. Derman (1980) *Probability Models and Applications*. New York: Macmillan.

RAIFFA, H., and R. SCHLAIFER (1961) *Applied Statistical Decision Theory.* Cambridge, MA: Harvard University Press.

VATTER, P., S. BRADLEY, S. FREY, and B. JACKSON (1978) *Quantitative Methods in Management: Text and Cases.* Homewood, IL: Irwin.

WINKLER, ROBERT L. (1972) *Introduction to Bayesian Inference and Decision.* New York: Holt, Rinehart, & Winston.

Monte Carlo Simulation

The problems we have dealt with so far have allowed us to calculate expected values or to find probability distributions fairly easily. In real-world situations, however, many factors may be subject to some uncertainty. You can imagine what becomes of a decision tree that involves many uncertain events. The only way to prevent it from being a bushy mess is to present a skeleton version as in Figure 11.1, in which A and B represent alternative courses of action, each affected by many different uncertain quantities. We know that consideration of the uncertainties involved is important, but how will we deal with this much uncertainty? It is not at all clear that we will be able to use the techniques we have learned so far. We could, of course, painstakingly develop discrete approximations for all of the continuous distributions and construct the decision tree or influence diagram. In many cases this will work out fine. The decision tree, however, may become extremely complex.

An influence diagram can help somewhat in this kind of a situation. As a more compact representation of a decision problem, an influence diagram can provide a clear picture of the way that multiple sources of uncertainty affect the decision. Figure 11.2 is an influence diagram that corresponds to the skeleton decision tree in Figure 11.1. Careful structuring can lead to a complete influence diagram, especially if the probability distributions can be represented adequately by discrete distributions in the chance nodes. But if there are multiple interrelated uncertain quantities represented by complicated continuous distributions, then even an influence-diagram approach may not be adequate.

In many decision-analysis problems, the ultimate goal is the calculation of an expected value. If a complicated uncertainty model includes several continuous distributions with expected values that are easily found, then analyzing the

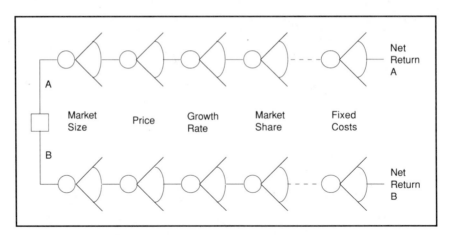

FIGURE 11.1 *Decision Tree Representing a Complex Decision Situation with Many Sources of Uncertainty*

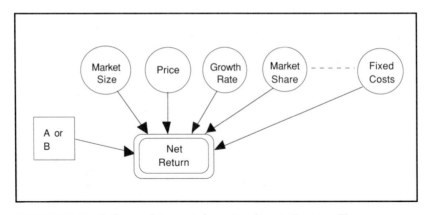

FIGURE 11.2 *Influence Diagram Corresponding to Decision Tree in Figure 11.1*

Interdependencies also may exist among the uncertainty nodes, thus complicating the influence diagram further.

problem may be relatively straightforward. But this is not always true. The following is a realistic example in which it may not be obvious how to calculate an expected value.

FASHIONS

Janet Dawes is in a quandary. She is the purchaser for a factory that produces fashion clothes. Her current task is to choose a supplier who can furnish fabric for a new line of garments. To ensure its supply for the upcoming year, her company must sign a contract with one of several textile suppliers. After a few inquiries, she has narrowed the choice to two specific suppliers. The first will supply as much fabric as she needs during the upcoming year for $2.00 per yard, and will guarantee supply through the year at this price.

The second supplier has a price schedule that depends on how much Janet orders over the next year. The first 20,000 yards will cost $2.10 per yard. The next 10,000 yards will cost $1.90 per yard. After this, the price drops to $1.70 per yard for the next 10,000 yards, and then $1.50 per yard for anything more than 40,000 yards.

After carefully considering the uncertainty about sales for the new garment line, Janet decides to model her uncertainty about the amount of fabric required over the next year as a normal distribution with mean 25,000 yards and standard deviation 5000 yards.

◆

If the new line of garments is successful, Janet Dawes can save considerable money by going with the second supplier. On the other hand, if she signs the contract with Supplier 2, and the new line of garments does not prove successful, the cost of materials will have been higher than it might have been with Supplier 1, thus adding to the cost of an already expensive experiment. What should she do? Her decision tree is shown in Figure 11.3.

In Janet Dawes's problem, it is relatively easy to figure out the expected cost for Supplier 1: It is $2.00 per yard times 25,000 yards, or $50,000. But it is not so

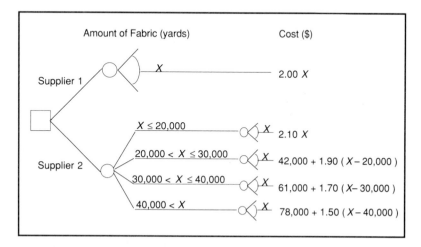

FIGURE 11.3 *Decision Tree for the Fabric Buyer*
The expressions at the ends of the branches for Supplier 2 represent the discounts. For example, if X is between 30,000 and 40,000 yards, the total cost is $42,000 for the first 20,000 yards, plus $19,000 for the next 10,000 yards, plus $1.70 per yard over 30,000.

easy to figure out the expected cost for Supplier 2. To do this, we must know (a) the probability that X is within each interval and (b) the expected value of X for each interval. Part a is no problem; we could figure out the probabilities using the normal distribution as described in Chapter 9. It is not so clear, however, how to find the conditional expected values for X within each interval.

One approach to dealing with complicated uncertainty models such as that discussed above is through computer simulation. Think of the entire decision situation as an uncertain event, and "play the game" represented by the decision tree many times. In Janet Dawes's problem, we could imagine the computer making a random drawing from a normal distribution to find the amount of fabric required. Based on this specific amount, the computer then would calculate the total cost using the expressions given in the decision tree. After performing this procedure many times, it would be possible to draw a histogram or risk profile of the cost figures and thus to calculate the average cost. On the basis of these results, and comparing them with the distribution of costs for Supplier 1 (normal with mean $50,000 and standard deviation $10,000), a choice can be made.

For another example, imagine using a computer simulation to evaluate Alternative A in Figure 11.1. We would let the computer "flip a coin" to find the market size, then flip another to find the price, another to find the growth rate, and so on until all uncertain quantities are chosen, each according to its own probability distribution. Of course, having the computer "flip a coin" means having it choose randomly the market size, price, growth rate, and so on. Once all of the necessary values had been determined in this random fashion, the computer then could calculate the net return. We then would repeat the entire procedure many times and track the results. At the end, it would be possible to graph the distribution of net returns and to examine descriptive statistics such as the mean, standard deviation, and probability of a negative return.

The term *Monte Carlo simulation* often is used to refer to this process because, as in gambling, the eventual results depend on random selections of values. The basic idea is straightforward: if the computer "plays the game" long enough, we will have a very good idea of the distribution of the possible results. Although the concept is easy, its implementation requires attention to many details.

We can use Monte Carlo simulation to cope with situations in which uncertainty abounds; the objective is to represent the uncertainty surrounding the possible payoffs for the different alternatives. How does simulation fit into our perspective of building models to represent decision situations? When we put together all probability distributions for all uncertain quantities, we are building a simulation model that we believe captures the relevant aspects of the uncertainty in the problem. After running the simulation many times, we have an approximation of the probability distribution for the payoffs from the different alternatives. The more simulations we can do, the more accurate that approximation. Finally, the results, both risk profiles and average outcomes, can be used in the decision analysis to make an appropriate decision.

♦ ELECTRONIC SPREADSHEETS AND MONTE CARLO SIMULATION

With the advent of personal computers and electronic spreadsheets, performing relatively simple simulations has become a straightforward task. Spreadsheets such as Lotus 1-2-3 and Microsoft Excel have built-in random-number generators. Typically, a function produces a uniformly distributed random number (x) between 0 and 1. That is, all values between 0 and 1 are possible and equally likely. (See Problems 9.26–9.28, pages 274–275.) Uniform random numbers can be used as building blocks to create other kinds of random numbers.

Let us examine how a simple simulation would be done on an electronic spreadsheet. As an example, we will continue the soft pretzel problem from Chapter 9. You are thinking about manufacturing and marketing soft pretzels using a new recipe, but you face many sources of uncertainty. In the process of analyzing the decision, you might ask whether choosing to go into the soft pretzel business would have a positive expected value. Using Monte Carlo simulation, we can examine the probability distribution of returns that would be associated with your pretzel business.

Let us suppose that the market size is unknown, but your subjective beliefs about the market's size can be represented as a normal random variable with mean 100,000 pretzels and standard deviation 10,000. The proportion of the market that you will capture is unknown and, strictly speaking, is a continuous random variable that could range anywhere between 0 and 100%. You have decided, however, that your beliefs can be modeled adequately with the following discrete distribution:

Proportion (%)	Probability
16	0.15
19	0.35
25	0.35
28	0.15

Your pretzel's selling price is known to be 50 cents. Variable costs are a uniform random variable between 8 and 12 cents per pretzel. Fixed costs also are normally distributed with mean $8000 and standard deviation $500. Putting all of the pieces together to calculate net contribution yields

Net Contribution = (Size × P/100) × (Price – Variable Cost) – Fixed Cost.

Figure 11.4 shows how a spreadsheet might be laid out with the basic information for a Monte Carlo simulation of the soft pretzel problem. To do the simulation, however, you must enter the formulas for generating different kinds of random numbers on the basis of a random number that is uniformly distributed between 0 and 1. To proceed, then, we must discuss how to do this. In

	A	B	C	D	E
1		Market	16	0.15	
2		Proportion	19	0.35	
3		Probabilities	25	0.35	
4			28	0.15	
5					
6	Market	Market	Variable	Fixed	Net
7	Size	Proportion	Cost	Cost	Contribution
8					
9					
10	Put formulas in these cells to generate random				Calculate net
11	numbers according to the specified distributions.				contribution here
12					
13					

FIGURE 11.4   *Entries in an Electronic Spreadsheet for the Soft Pretzels Simulation*

the following we will see how to generate uniform, discrete, exponential, and normal random numbers.

Using Uniform Random Numbers as Building Blocks

Call the random number that the spreadsheet generates x, and recall that x is drawn from a uniform distribution between 0 and 1. One way to use x as a basis for creating random numbers from other distributions is based on the CDF. We require a random number y^* from the distribution $f(y)$. For Step 1, we find the CDF for $f(y)$. Let $F(y)$ denote the CDF; that is, $F(y) = P(Y \leq y)$. An example CDF is plotted in Figure 11.5. In Step 2 we generate a uniform x^* between 0 and 1. Locate that x^* on the vertical axis. For Step 3, read across from x^* to the CDF and down to the horizontal axis. The number on the horizontal axis is the required y^*.

This approach is straightforward and conceptually very intuitive; we first generate a uniform random number and then work backward through the CDF

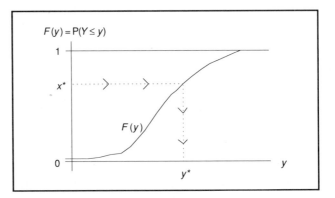

FIGURE 11.5   *Generating a Random Number y* on the Basis of a Uniform Random Number x**

to get y. In principle, we can do this for any distribution. Unfortunately, it is not possible in some cases because of the mathematical form of $F(y)$. In these cases, other methods can be used.

General Uniform Distributions

Suppose that we want to generate a uniform random number between 1 and 2 instead of between 0 and 1. The solution would be simply to calculate

$$y = x + 1.$$

Then y would be uniformly distributed between 1 and 2. If we wanted a random number between 0 and 2, we simply multiply x by 2. This would "stretch out" the uniform distribution so that it would cover the interval from 0 to 2.

In general, suppose you want a uniform random number between a and b ($a < b$). The procedure is to generate x, then move it to the right place and stretch out the distribution to cover the desired interval. The formula is:

$$y = a + x(b - a).$$

Multiplying x by $(b - a)$ stretches out the distribution, and adding a moves the distribution to the right place. If x turns out to be 0, then $y = a$, and if x is 1, then $y = b$.

In our soft pretzel example, variable cost is uniformly distributed between 8 and 12 cents. Thus, the calculation is:

$$\text{Variable Cost} = 0.08 + x(0.12 - 0.08).$$

This procedure for generating general uniform random numbers, which we developed intuitively, is fully compatible with the general simulation approach described above. The CDF for a uniform distribution between a and b is a straight line as shown in Figure 11.6. The line has the equation $F(y) = (y - a)/$

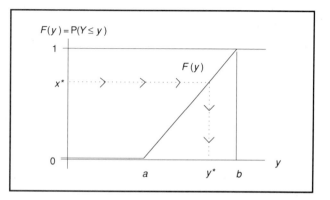

FIGURE 11.6   *Generating a Uniform* y^* *Between* a *and* b

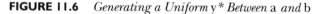

$(b - a)$. (Can you verify this?) To work backward through this CDF, we set the uniform x^* equal to $F(y^*) = (y^* - a)/(b - a)$ and solve for y^*. That is, we need to know what y^* corresponds to our uniform x^* between 0 and 1. Solving for y^*, we obtain $y^* = a + x^*(b - a)$.

Exponential Distributions

Another continuous random variable that can be simulated using our general approach is an exponential random variable T. Suppose that you want to generate a random number that is exponentially distributed with rate m. The CDF for this distribution is $F(t) = 1 - e^{-tm}$. Thus, we generate a uniform x^* and set $x^* = F(t^*) = 1 - e^{-tm}$. Solving for t^* gives

$$t^* = \frac{-\ln(1 - x^*)}{m}.$$

Figure 11.7 shows the CDF and the graphical equivalent of solving for t^*.

The formula derived above can be programmed easily into an electronic spreadsheet. But we can do a little bit better. If x^* is from a uniform distribution between 0 and 1, then so is $1 - x^*$. Thus, we can simplify the procedure by calculating

$$t' = \frac{-\ln(x^*)}{m}.$$

The random number t' also has an exponential distribution with rate m. The reason for the simplification is to avoid unnecessary calculations that would slow down the computer simulation.

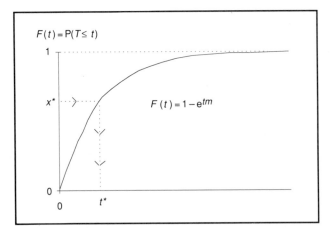

FIGURE 11.7   *Generating an Exponential Random Number*

Discrete Distributions

Discrete distributions also are easy to handle in spreadsheets. Suppose, for example, that we want to simulate flips of a fair coin. We want the probability of a head to be 0.50. First we generate X. Then if $X \leq 0.50$, we will say that we have a head, and if $X > 0.50$, we will have a tail. Because X is uniformly distributed, it has a 50% chance of being between 0 and 0.50, and a 50% chance of being between 0.50 and 1.

The basic strategy obviously is to split the interval from 0 to 1 into intervals corresponding to the outcomes of the discrete event. The outcome of the event then corresponds to the interval into which X falls when it is generated. The probabilities are controlled by the widths of the intervals for X; smaller intervals have smaller probabilities, and larger intervals have larger probabilities.

In our soft pretzel example, we need to generate the market proportion captured (P) using discrete probabilities. The four intervals we need are as follows:

- If $X \leq 0.15$, then P = 16%.
- If $0.15 < X \leq 0.50$, then P = 19%.
- If $0.50 < X \leq 0.85$, then P = 25%.
- If $0.85 < X$, then P = 28%.

How is this accomplished on the spreadsheet itself? The trick is to use "IF" statements, which are part of most major spreadsheets. The details of the IF statements vary slightly among the different programs, but the basic structure involves evaluating an expression. If the expression is true, then the cell has one value, and if false, it has another. To take the heads and tails example, the basic formula to enter in a cell would be:

$$IF(X <= 0.50, \text{"Heads"}, \text{"Tails"})$$

The expression being evaluated is "$X <= 0.50$," or whether X is less than or equal to 0.50. If it is, then "Heads" is the value of the cell. If not, then "Tails" is the value. (In Lotus 1-2-3, the formula would be preceded by an "@" sign. In Microsoft Excel, the formula would be preceded by an "=" sign.)

IF statements can be "nested" to handle more than two outcomes. To handle our market proportion simulation, we would enter the formula

$$IF(X <= 0.15, 16, IF(X <= 0.50, 19, IF(X <= 0.85, 25, 28)))$$

Here we have three nested IF statements. The interpretation is as follows. Generate an X. If X is less than or equal to 0.15, then this cell is 16(%). If not, look at X again. If it is less than or equal to 0.50, then this cell is 19. If not, look at it one more time. If it is less than or equal to 0.85, this cell is 25. If not, this cell is 28.

A random outcome from any discrete distribution can, in principle, be generated in this way. With distributions that involve more than just a few possible outcomes, however, it may be easier to use a table-lookup function rather than nested IF statements. The table would have entries for the possible outcomes and the cumulative probabilities. As an example, we might build a table such as the one in Figure 11.8 in order to generate the market proportion according to our discrete distribution. Note the way the cumulative probabilities are aligned with the possible values of the discrete random variable. The table-lookup functions in both Lotus 1-2-3 and Microsoft Excel are designed to search in the table's first column for the largest value that is still smaller than the target value. In Figure 11.8, the target value is 0.79. The computer runs down Column A until it finds 0.5 in Row 3. This is the largest value that is still smaller than 0.79; the next value in Column A is 0.85, which is larger than the target value. Now the computer looks across Row 3 to find 25%.

You can see how the table-lookup accomplishes the same thing as the string of IF statements. If X is between 0 and 0.15, the probability of which is 0.15, the lookup procedure will find 16%. For X greater than 0.15 and less than 0.5, the lookup returns 19%, and so on. This procedure can be used for any discrete random variable. For example, to generate a binomial random number, we would create a table with outcomes from 0 to n on the right and with cumulative binomial probabilities on the left. (Remember to align the cumulative probabilities correctly for the lookup function. Align the lower boundary for an interval that corresponds to a specific value of the discrete random variable Y with that specific value. In symbols, if $Y = y_i$ when $x_1 \le X \le x_u$, then align x_1 with y_i in your table. At least, this approach is used in most popular spreadsheets. Be sure to consult your user's manual for details.)

Normal Distributions

Generating uniform, exponential, and discrete random numbers is fairly straightforward. How about generating a normally distributed random number? This one is also easy! It turns out that if 12 uniform random numbers are added, the sum is approximately normal with mean 6 and variance 1. Take this sum and subtract 6 to get a random variable that is approximately a standard normal random variable with mean 0 and standard deviation 1:

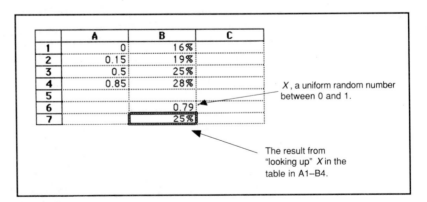

	A	B	C
1	0	16%	
2	0.15	19%	
3	0.5	25%	
4	0.85	28%	
5			
6		0.79	
7		25%	

X, a uniform random number between 0 and 1.

The result from "looking up" X in the table in A1–B4.

FIGURE 11.8   *Using a Table-lookup Approach to Generate a Discrete Random Variable*

$$Z = (\sum_{i=1}^{12} X_i) - 6.$$

Note that this is *not* the same as generating a single uniform random number and then multiplying it by 12. We must generate 12 different uniform random numbers and add them up.

Now suppose that you want a normal random variable Y with mean μ and standard deviation σ. All we must do is adjust Z:

$$Y = \mu + \sigma Z.$$

For example, we need normal random variables for the size of the market and the fixed costs. The size of the market is normal with mean 100,000 and standard deviation 10,000:

$$\text{Size of Market} = 100,000 + [(\sum_{i=1}^{12} X_i) - 6]\, 10,000.$$

Likewise, fixed costs are normal with mean $8000 and standard deviation $500:

$$\text{Fixed Costs} = 8000 + [(\sum_{i=1}^{12} X_i) - 6]\, 500.$$

These formulas, translated into spreadsheet format, would be entered into the cells to generate the normal random variables for market size and fixed costs.

The disadvantage of this approach for generating normally distributed random numbers is that it requires many individual uniform random numbers and thus can take a long time in computational terms. Other methods exist for generating normal random numbers. Most will generate a pair of normals on the basis of a pair of uniforms and use complicated transformations. Thus, these methods save on the number of uniform random numbers, although the complicated transformations can take a long time (unless your computer happens to have a math coprocessor to speed up these calculations). The upshot is that for simple simulations on a run-of-the-mill personal computer, this summing-of-uniforms approach is a reasonable way to proceed.

With these formulas for generating a variety of different kinds of random numbers, we now can see how to perform a simple simulation on a spreadsheet. Let us continue with the soft pretzel example, filling in Row 8 of the spreadsheet that we began back in Figure 11.4 with the appropriate formulas. Doing so amounts to one simulation trial; that is, random numbers are calculated for all of the input variables, and net contribution is calculated on the basis of the inputs. Figure 11.9 shows one possible simulation trial. In this particular trial, the soft pretzel project loses $531.55.

To do many trials, we have two possible strategies. The first and most obvious is to copy this row of formulas down the spreadsheet. The more trials, the

	A	B	C	D	E
1		Market	16%	0.15	
2		Proportion	19%	0.35	
3		Probabilities	25%	0.35	
4			28%	0.15	
5					
6	Market	Market	Variable	Fixed	
7	Size	Proportion	Cost	Cost	Net
8	108820	19%	$0.09	$9,029.72	($531.55)
9					
10					
11					

FIGURE 11.9 *One Simulation Trial in the Soft Pretzel Example* Appropriate formulas for the random variables have been entered into the cells in Row 8; the formula to calculate net contribution is in Cell E8.

better. But spreadsheets are slow when it comes to simulations like this. If you try more than a few hundred trials, it may take a long time to calculate the results. Figure 11.10 shows the spreadsheet after the formulas have been copied and calculated. The random fluctuation of the net contribution is apparent. In one case the project earned $3803.44, but in another it lost $2848.95!

The second possible strategy is to use the spreadsheet's "Table" command. In Chapter 5 we saw how to use a table to perform a two-way sensitivity analysis. Here we will do the same kind of thing, except that we will use the command to trick the spreadsheet into replicating the simulation as many times as required. Figure 11.11 shows the spreadsheet with the table created. To re-create this, first enter the column of integers, starting with a 2 in Cell D9. These numbers play

	A	B	C	D	E
1		Market	16%	0.15	
2		Proportion	19%	0.35	
3		Probabilities	25%	0.35	
4			28%	0.15	
5					
6	Market	Market	Variable	Fixed	
7	Size	Proportion	Cost	Cost	Net
8	100701	19%	$0.08	$7,804.42	$147.61
9	103535	25%	$0.08	$7,059.31	$3,803.44
10	103440	16%	$0.11	$7,824.38	($1,301.54)
11	94144	19%	$0.08	$8,385.84	($902.09)
12	111854	19%	$0.10	$7,574.17	$989.09
13	93215	16%	$0.11	$8,680.97	($2,848.95)
14	92508	25%	$0.09	$7,985.55	$1,425.93
15	94880	25%	$0.08	$8,228.02	$1,725.96
16	87233	19%	$0.11	$7,434.31	($949.66)
17	98370	25%	$0.10	$8,585.46	$1,250.90
18	95443	28%	$0.09	$8,076.78	$2,965.12
19	89977	25%	$0.10	$7,516.57	$1,467.62

FIGURE 11.10 *Soft Pretzel Example After the Simulation Has Been Copied in Several Rows*

	A	B	C	D	E
1		Market	16%	0.15	
2		Proportion	19%	0.35	
3		Probabilities	25%	0.35	
4			28%	0.15	
5					
6	Market	Market	Variable	Fixed	
7	Size	Proportion	Cost	Cost	Net
8	94379	19%	$0.10	$7,624.52	($397.66)
9				2	$3,518.49
10				3	$2,784.69
11				4	$2,907.13
12				5	$2,971.61
13				6	($2,318.56)
14				7	($166.13)
15				8	$1,509.77
16				9	$2,154.19
17				10	$3,843.84
18				11	$1,954.57

FIGURE 11.11 *Performing the Soft Pretzel Simulation by Creating a Table in the Spreadsheet*

no part whatsoever in the calculations; they simply help us track the total number of simulations the spreadsheet will perform. Suppose we want 100 simulations in total; this column of numbers thus will go down to Cell D107, which will contain the integer 100.

The next step is to use the spreadsheet's "Table" command to create the table that covers the range from D8 to E107. The computer will want to know an "input cell" for the net contribution formula in E8. Essentially, it wants to know how to recalculate the net contribution in Column E. We want it to do exactly the same as it did in E8, except with new random numbers; to trick the program into doing the same simulation 100 times, specify *any empty cell* as the column input cell. For example, Cell C12 contains no formula and can be used for the input. When the spreadsheet recalculates, it will display a different result in each row, as in Figure 11.11. Again, the variation in contribution is apparent with a high contribution of $3843.84 in E17, and a loss of $2318.56 in E13. (Note: Not all versions of all spreadsheets allow you to use a Table command to perform a simulation as described here. Your results should have a different outcome for each cell in the table.)

Having performed the calculations, the spreadsheet now contains a column of results from the simulation. These results can be treated like empirical data. In our soft pretzel example the net contribution figures can be summarized and graphed. Appropriate summary measures are the mean, standard deviation, and the percentage of times the result was negative. The risk profile can be graphed as a histogram, or the cumulative risk profile can be graphed as a CDF.

For one run of the soft pretzel simulation with 100 trials, the average net profit was $760.84, with standard deviation $1939.62. There were 40 cases when the net profit was negative, so the probability of a negative net profit appears to be approximately 0.40. This also is apparent from the cumulative risk profile

(Figure 11.12) because the curve crosses the vertical axis at 0.40. The risk profile for the soft pretzel project is presented in histogram form in Figure 11.13. If you try this example, you probably will obtain somewhat different results.

How do we put the results from a Monte Carlo simulation to work? If we were simply interested in comparing the expected values of two projects, we might compare the averages of the simulated results. The point of the simulation, however, has been to obtain an idea of the uncertainty that surrounds the ultimate payoff. Thus, the the risk profile created by using the simulation results

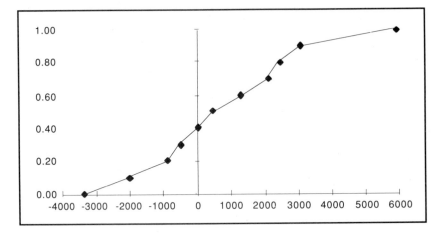

FIGURE 11.12 *Cumulative Risk Profile (CDF) for the Soft Pretzel Project Based on Simulation Results*

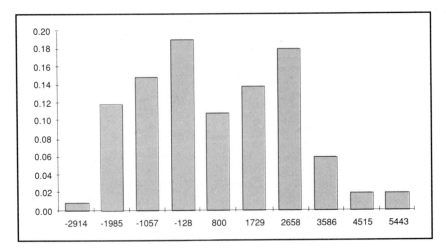

FIGURE 11.13 *Risk Profile for the Soft Pretzel Project Based on Simulation Results*

can be used as discussed in Chapter 4. Visually comparing the histograms of payoffs for two risky projects can reveal the extent to which one project is "riskier" than another, even though they may have similar expected values. You may be able to decide between the two projects simply on the basis of comparing the graphs or by considering P(Profit < 0), say. Finally, a discrete approximation of the distribution could be placed into a decision tree for a rough approximation of the distribution. This strategy might be particularly appropriate if a simulation has been done as an auxiliary analysis to obtain a probability model for part of a complicated decision problem.

♦ SIMULATION AND SENSITIVITY ANALYSIS

Imagine this scenario. You have constructed your simulation model, and as you show it to a colleague, the assumptions that you made are called into question. Suppose your colleague wonders what the effect would be if you had a normal distribution for the market size with mean 120,000 pretzels instead of 100,000. It would be a relatively simple matter to make a change in the spreadsheet and run the simulation again. The results could be compared to the earlier results to determine the effect.

Figure 11.14 demonstrates this idea. The spreadsheet there has cells set aside specifically for the parameters of each of the probability distributions. The simulation formulas in Row 10 then refer to these particular parameter values.

	A	B	C	D	E
1		Market Size	Fixed Cost	Market	
2	Mean	120000	$8,000	Proportion	Probability
3	Std Deviation	10000	$500	16%	0.15
4				19%	0.35
5		Variable Cost		25%	0.35
6	Lower Limit	$0.08		28%	0.15
7	Upper Limit	$0.12			
8					
9	Market	Market	Variable	Fixed	
10	Size	Proportion	Cost	Cost	Net
11	131793	28%	$0.11	$7,896.44	$6,674.43
12				2	$4,223.62
13				3	$933.24
14				4	$553.60
15				5	($39.99)
16				6	$5,055.19
17				7	$1,038.83
18				8	$2,082.06
19				9	($716.18)

FIGURE 11.14 *Soft Pretzel Simulation with Parameter Values Displayed*

By placing the data in accessible cells, sensitivity analysis is now very easy. Notice that the mean for the market size is 120,000 pretzels.

Building the model in this way facilitates sensitivity analysis by simplifying the process of changing one or more model parameters. In fact, it is generally a good idea to put each number (each bit of data) in a cell where it can be modified easily to answer sensitivity-analysis questions. Note in Figure 11.14 that the mean for the market-size distribution has been changed to 120,000 pretzels. Moreover, even in the small sample of the first nine simulation trials the effect of this change is easily seen; the highest net contribution is $6674.43, and the lowest is a loss of $716.18.

Distributions on Parameters (Optional)

Suppose that you cannot settle on a single value for the mean of the distribution for the market size. The uncertainty about this parameter might be modeled with a probability distribution. In fact, this is exactly what was done in Chapter 10 in our discussion of natural conjugate prior distributions for distribution parameters; but here there is no need to restrict ourselves to specific kinds of distributions.

Suppose that you consider carefully your beliefs about the mean of the market-size distribution. You may decide, for example, to model your uncertainty as a uniform random variable between 90,000 and 110,000 pretzels. How would this change the model? The change is straightforward; this uncertain mean simply becomes a new random variable in the simulation. Figure 11.15 demonstrates this. Note that we have displayed the lower and upper limits of the distribution for the market-size mean in Cells C7 and C8. Cell A12 now contains a formula that generates a uniform random number with the specified limits.

	A	B	C	D	E	F
1		Market Size	Fixed Cost	Market		
2	Mean	Unknown	$8,000	Proportion	Probability	
3	Std Deviation	10000	$500	16%	0.15	
4				19%	0.35	
5			Mkt Size	25%	0.35	
6		Var Cost	Mean	28%	0.15	
7	Lower Limit	$0.08	90000			
8	Upper Limit	$0.12	110000			
9						
10	Mean for	Market	Market	Variable	Fixed	
11	Market Size	Size	Proportion	Cost	Cost	Net
12	101288	90740	25%	$0.10	$7,550.64	$1,489.30
13					2	$888.98
14					3	$3,093.26
15					4	($1,697.18)
16			✚		5	$412.27
17					6	$3,025.34
18					7	$1,687.92
19					8	($1,292.02)

FIGURE 11.15 *Incorporating Uncertainty About the Mean of the Distribution for Market Size*
Note that this mean now is treated as a random variable itself with a uniform distribution.

Finally, the formula for market size (B12) uses the random number displayed in A12 as its mean.

Using an electronic spreadsheet as a medium for simulation computations might seem strange. Spreadsheets tend to be slow, taking a long time to do enough calculations for a reasonable simulation; with many personal computers the size of the simulation may be severely constrained. It would not be unreasonable to run 1000 or more simulations of a particular situation. The more sources of uncertainty, the more important it is to run the simulation a very large number of times.

Special-purpose simulation programs do exist, and most statistical packages also provide at least a rudimentary simulation facility. One program in particular that is worth mentioning is @RISK™ by Palisade. This program serves as an "add-on" to Lotus 1-2-3 and Microsoft Excel. Essentially, it provides (1) a wide array of different random-number generators, including all of those that we have mentioned here, as well as many others; and (2) an automatic summary of the simulation results. These two features mean that Monte Carlo simulations on spreadsheets can be done easily. In fact, even the speed of the simulation improves because @RISK is able to perform the calculations using its own programming rather than that of the spreadsheet. To get an idea of how @RISK would work, look again at Figure 11.15. The information would be entered as shown, except that there is no need to create the table to make the spreadsheet perform the simulation many times. Specific random-number generators for the required distributions would be entered into Cells A12–E12. Through a series of commands the number of simulation trials would be set, and the output would be specified. In this case, we would want to see the distribution and summary measures for the net contribution. When @RISK executes the simulation, it stores the simulation results internally and reports back with appropriate graphs and summary statistics. After having gone through the "brute force" spreadsheet simulation of the soft pretzel example, you can imagine how much easier it would be to use a program like @RISK!

◆ SIMULATION, DECISION TREES, AND INFLUENCE DIAGRAMS

Clearly, Monte Carlo simulation provides another modeling tool for decision analysis. Indeed, simulation is an important tool, and probably will become more widely used because of the ease with which small simulations can be performed in a spreadsheet environment. Because of this, it is worthwhile to spend a bit of time thinking about how simulation relates to the other modeling tools in decision analysis.

Simulation is an excellent tool for developing a model of uncertainty. We have used it here to develop risk profiles for decision alternatives; with risk profiles for different alternatives in hand, a decision maker would have some basis in choosing one alternative over the other. As mentioned above, however, simulation also could be used as a subsidiary modeling tool to construct a probability model for a particularly messy part of a problem. For example, if a policy maker is attempting to evaluate alternatives regarding chemical spills, he may ask an analyst to develop a probability model for accidents that lead to spills. Such a model can be developed in the context of a simulation, and once an appropriate probability distribution is constructed, it can be used within a larger analysis.

The ease with which simulation can be performed, along with the flexibility of the simulation environment, makes it an attractive analytical tool. But this ease of use and flexibility does not mean that the decision maker can get away with less effort. In fact, subtle issues in simulation require careful thought. For example, we typically build the simulation in such a way that many of the random numbers are independent draws from their respective distributions. And the analyst may even model uncertainty about parameters through the specification of distributions on those parameters, but still have the parameters independent from one another. But would they be? If the analyst has been optimistic in assessing one parameter, perhaps other estimates have been subject to the same optimism.

A somewhat less subtle issue in simulation modeling is that an analyst may be tempted to include all possible sources of uncertainty in the model. This is relatively easy to do, after all, and somewhat more effort is required to do the sensitivity analysis to determine whether an uncertain quantity really matters in the outcome of the model. Hence, there may be a tendency with simulation not to take certain analysis steps that can lead to real insights as to what matters in a model, what issues should be considered more fully, or what uncertainties may demand more attention, in either more careful assessment or information acquisition.

In short, constructing a Monte Carlo simulation model requires the same careful thought that is required in any decision modeling. Simulation does have its own advantages (flexibility and ease of use) as well as disadvantages (rampant independence assumptions and a tendency to solve problems with brute force), and hence, to some extent, leads to some special problems. But the same is true of simulation that is true of decision modeling in general. The decision maker and the decision analyst still are required to think clearly about the problem at hand and to be sure that the decision model addresses the important issues appropriately. Clear thinking is the key, not fancy quantitative modeling. The objective with any decision-analysis tool is to arrive at a requisite model of the decision, one that appropriately addresses all essential elements of the decision problem. It is through the process of constructing a requisite model, which includes careful thought about the issues, that the decision maker will gain insight and understanding about the problem.

◇ SUMMARY

As we have seen in this chapter, Monte Carlo simulation is another approach to dealing with uncertainty in a decision situation. The basic approach is to construct a model that captures all of the relevant aspects of the uncertainty, and then to translate this model into a form that a computer can use; we focused on the development of such models within the environment of electronic spreadsheets. The computer's job is to simulate the uncertainty by generating the necessary random numbers and then putting them together in an appropriate way. A variety of random-number generators can be constructed on the basis of a uniformly distributed random variable. Our coverage here included general discrete random variables, as well as uniform, normal, and exponential random variables.

Once the model is constructed, the computer runs the simulation many times, keeping track of the results and summarizing them at the end. After all of the calculations, summary statistics can be calculated and graphs created. These results then can be used in decision models in a variety of ways.   ◆

◇ EXERCISES

11.1 Explain in your own words how Monte Carlo simulation may be useful to a decision maker.

11.2 Explain how the simulation process works to produce results that are helpful to a decision maker.

11.3 A simulation model has produced the three cumulative risk profiles displayed in Figure 11.16. What advice would you give a decision maker on the basis of this output?

11.4 A friend of yours has just learned about Monte Carlo simulation methods and has asked you to do a simulation of a complicated decision problem to help her make a choice. She would be happy to have you solve the problem and then recommend what action she should take. Explain why she needs to be involved in the simulation modeling process and what kind of information you need from her.

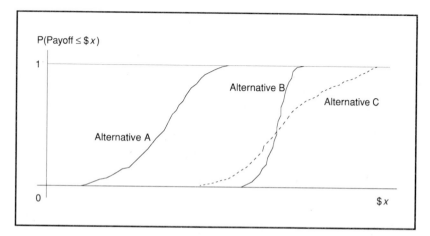

FIGURE 11.16 *Three Cumulative Risk Profiles from a Simulation*

◇ QUESTIONS AND PROBLEMS

11.5   Find the expected cost for Supplier 2 in Janet Dawes's purchasing problem as diagrammed in Figure 11.3 (page 315).

11.6   Simulation is one way to find an expected value for Janet Dawes's problem as diagrammed in Figure 11.3. How could you construct a discrete approximation that would at least provide an approximate expected cost for Supplier 2?

11.7   What other real-world situations involve step functions like the one that Janet Dawes faces?

11.8   Poisson random variables can take on any integer value from zero to infinity. Explain how to simulate a Poisson random variable using the techniques described in the chapter for simulating discrete random numbers.

11.9   An investor has purchased a call option for 100 shares of Alligator stock and intends to hold it until the day the option expires, at which time he will sell it if he can. The option is worth nothing on its expiration date unless the price of Alligator stock is more than $45 per share. For values of the stock greater than $45, the option will be worth 100(Share Price − $45). The reasoning behind this value is that the call option permits the option's owner to purchase 100 shares at $45 per share. Thus, if the share price is greater than $45, then the option owner could buy the shares and immediately resell them at the market price, pocketing the difference. Of course, the investor is uncertain about Alligator's eventual share price on the exercise date, but his uncertainty can be modeled using a normal distribution having mean $45.50 and standard deviation $5.00. Construct a simulation to estimate the expected value of the option on the exercise date.

11.10   Your boss has asked you to work up a simulation model to examine the uncertainty regarding the success or failure of five different investment projects. He provides probabilities for the success of each project individually: $p_1 = 0.50$, $p_2 = 0.35$, $p_3 = 0.65$, $p_4 = 0.58$, $p_5 = 0.45$. Because the projects are run by different people in different segments of the investment market, you both agree that it is reasonable to believe that, given these probabilities, the outcomes of the projects are independent. He points out, however, that he really is not fully confident in these probabilities and that he could be off by as much as 0.05 in either direction on any given probability.

    a.   How can you incorporate his uncertainty about the probabilities into your simulation?

    b.   Now suppose that he says that if he is optimistic about the success of one project, he is likely to be optimistic about the others as well. For your simulation, this means that if one of the probabilities increases, the others also are likely to increase. How might you incorporate this information into your spreadsheet?

11.11   A decision maker is working on a problem that requires her to study the uncertainty surrounding the payoff of an investment. There are three possible levels of payoff — $1000, $5000, and $10,000. As a rough approximation, the decision maker believes that each possible payoff is equally likely. But she is not fully comfortable with the assessment that each probability is exactly $\frac{1}{3}$, and so would like to conduct a sensitivity analysis. In fact, she believes that each probability could range from 0 to $\frac{1}{2}$.

    a.   Show how a Monte Carlo simulation could facilitate a sensitivity analysis of the probabilities of the payoffs.

    b.   Suppose the decision maker is willing to say that each of the three probabilities could be chosen from a uniform distribution between 0 and 1. Could you incorporate this information into your simulation? If so, how? If not, explain why not, or what additional information you would need.

CASE STUDIES

Choosing a Manufacturing Process

AJS, Ltd., is a manufacturing company that performs contract work for a wide variety of firms. It primarily manufactures and assembles metal items, and so most of its equipment is designed for precision machining tasks. The executives of AJS currently are trying to decide between two processes for manufacturing a product. Their main criterion for measuring the value of a manufacturing process is net present value (NPV). The contractor will pay AJS $8 per unit. AJS is using a three-year horizon for its evaluation (the current year and the next two years).

PROCESS 1

Under the first process, AJS's current machinery is used to make the product. The following inputs are used:

DEMAND. Demand for each of the three years is unknown. These three quantities are modeled as discrete random variables denoted D_0, D_1, and D_2 with the following probability distributions:

D_0	$P(D_0)$	D_1	$P(D_1)$	D_2	$P(D_2)$
11K	0.2	8K	0.2	4K	0.1
16K	0.6	19K	0.4	21K	0.5
21K	0.2	27K	0.4	37K	0.4

VARIABLE COST. Variable cost per unit changes each year, depending on the costs for materials and labor. Let V_0, V_1, and V_2 represent the three variable costs. The uncertainty surrounding each variable is represented by a normal distribution with mean $4 and standard deviation $0.40.

MACHINE FAILURE. Each year, AJS's machines fail occasionally, but obviously it is impossible to predict when or how many failures will occur during the year. Each time a machine fails, it costs the firm $8000. Let Z_0, Z_1, and Z_2 represent the number of machine failures in each of the three years, and assume that each is a Poisson random variable with parameter $m = 4$.

FIXED COST. Each year a fixed cost of $12,000 is incurred.

PROCESS 2

The second process involves scrapping the current equipment (it has no salvage value) and purchasing new equipment to make the product at a cost of $60,000. Assume that the firm pays cash for the new machine, and ignore tax effects.

DEMAND.   Because of the new machine, the final product is slightly altered and improved, and consequently the demands are likely to be higher than before, although more uncertain. The new demand distributions are:

D_0	$P(D_0)$	D_1	$P(D_1)$	D_2	$P(D_2)$
14K	0.3	12K	0.36	9K	0.4
19K	0.4	23K	0.36	26K	0.1
24K	0.3	31K	0.28	42K	0.5

VARIABLE COST.   Variable cost still changes each year, but this time V_0, V_1, and V_2 are each judged to be normal with mean $3.50 and standard deviation $1.00.

MACHINE FAILURES.   Equipment failures are less likely with the new equipment, occurring each year according to a Poisson distribution with parameter $m = 3$. They also tend to be less serious, costing only $6000.

FIXED COST.   The fixed cost of $12,000 is unchanged.

QUESTIONS

1. Draw an influence diagram for this decision problem. Do you think it would be feasible to solve this problem with an influence diagram? Explain.
2. Write out the formula for the NPV for both processes described above. Use the variable names as specified, and assume a 10% interest rate.
3. Explain how you might simulate a Poisson random variable.
4. For Process 1, use an electronic spreadsheet to perform 100 simulation trials. Estimate the mean and standard deviation of NPV for this process. Print a histogram of the results, and estimate the probability of a negative NPV occurring.
5. Repeat Question 4 for Process 2.
6. Compare the distribution of NPV for each of the two alternatives. Which process would be better for AJS? Why?

Source: This case was provided by Tom McWilliams.

◆

Organic Farming

Jane Keller surveyed the freshly plowed field on her farm. She and her husband, Tim, had taken over the farm from her parents 10 years ago. Since that time, she and Tim had worked hard to improve the profitability of the farm. Even though the work was hard, the life-style was rewarding. And she found that common sense combined with basics from some business courses had helped her in making difficult decisions.

She faced one such decision now. Over the years, she had noticed more and more of her neighbors adopting a variety of organic farming methods. Many of the techniques were easy to adopt and made good sense. For example, companion planting and promoting a balanced ecology on the farm helped to create an environment in which plants were less susceptible to insect and disease damage. Last year she had grown some produce using only organic methods and had sold it locally. She learned a lot on that small-scale project, and in particular she learned that she did not know much about natural methods for preventing specific diseases and controlling insects.

Still, Jane was intrigued by the possibility of organic farming. Growers who could label their produce as "Organically Grown" commanded premium prices from specialty stores and at the local farmer's market. The Organic Farmers Association (OFA) provided the necessary certification. Meeting OFA's requirements involved (1) documenting the use of the land over a period of years to ensure little or no contamination from nonorganic pesticides, herbicides, and fertilizers; and (2) adhering to the farming methods that OFA deemed "organic."

This year Tim wanted to expand the operation by planting in a new field that had not been farmed in 20 years. Because the new field would be some distance from the other planted areas, it would be an ideal location to grow organic produce. There would be no problem getting the new field certified by the OFA. When she made this suggestion to Tim, he agreed with the idea in principle, but wanted to think seriously about the project. They had several questions to answer. Would they really be able to make money from such a project? What kinds of prices could they anticipate for organic produce? What risks were involved?

Jane agreed to do some research. After visiting with her neighbors and spending a lot of time at the local organic gardening store, she was beginning to develop a plan. Although she could plant a large variety of different vegetables and herbs, most of the area would be devoted to tomatoes, green beans, and potatoes. She and Tim had plenty of experience with these crops, and she felt most comfortable experimenting with them. They would plant enough area so that, if the weather cooperated, they could expect to harvest 250 bushels of each crop. She was very uncertain about the exact yield, however, because of the variety of possible diseases and insects that could cause trouble and because of her own lack of experience with organic methods. For the tomatoes, she judged that there was a 68% chance that the yield would be between 235 and 265 bushels, and she was "almost sure" (95% chance) that the yield would be between 220 and 280 bushels. The green beans and potatoes she judged were somewhat less sensitive; for both of these crops, she estimated a 68% chance that the yield would fall between 242 and 258 bushels, and she was 95% sure that the yield would fall between 234 and 266 bushels.

The uncertain yield was complicated further by the effects of weather. Jane knew that the weather could be either too dry or too rainy for the crops, and that this would reduce her yield somewhat. At the same time, adverse weather would affect all growers in her region, leading to a smaller supply of produce and hence higher prices. The worst possible scenario for the Kellers would be for the weather to be perfect, resulting in a bumper crop around the region, while the Keller's venture into organics resulted in a low yield because of insects, disease, and their own inexperience. Prices would be low and they would have relatively little to sell.

Jane realized that she was facing a difficult judgmental task; ideally she would have to assess her uncertainty for the weather, the yield for each crop under different weather conditions, and the possible prices under the various conditions. To simplify matters, she decided to think about two scenarios. Under the first scenario, the weather would not affect the yield adversely. Under these conditions, she judged that the bushel price of tomatoes could range from $5.00 to $5.80. For potatoes, the range was $4.15 to $4.60; and for green beans, between $5.90 and $6.80. In each case, she figured that all prices in the specified range were equally likely.

Under the second scenario, the weather would have adverse effects on the region's crops. Jane estimated a probability of 0.15 for adverse weather. Because tomatoes were the most sensitive in this regard, the crop size would be reduced by some 20%. With smaller yields in the region, prices would be higher, ranging from $5.50 to $6.00 per bushel. Potatoes were the least sensitive, with only a 7% crop-size reduction, and prices between $4.50 and $4.80. Green beans were not terribly sensitive to the weather in terms of quantity, so Jane estimated a 4% reduction. Under adverse weather conditions, however, the quality of the beans could be highly variable, and so she estimated their price range under this scenario to be between $5.50 and $7.00. Again, she judged that all prices in the specified ranges were equally likely.

Costs also had to be factored in. Organic methods were more labor-intensive than conventional methods, but because Jane and Tim did the work themselves, this did not really affect profits. Even so, Jane estimated that costs for the field would be approximately $800. With the uncertainty about the methods, however, she decided to represent costs with a normal distribution having mean $800 and standard deviation $50.

When she discussed this with Tim, he asked what this meant in terms of a "bottom line." What could they expect their gross sales to be? Could she give him some idea of how uncertain their profit would be? If they went with conventional farming methods, they could expect profits to be approximately $2700, with a standard deviation of some $100. If Jane could develop a probability distribution for profits under organic methods, perhaps the two distributions could be compared.

Tim added another wrinkle. He showed her an advertisement and a related story in the newspaper about a newly developed, genetically engineered bacterial pesticide named VegeTech. The ad claimed (and the story confirmed) that tests with VegeTech in their own geographical area had resulted in an average 10% increase in yield for all kinds of produce. The cost for this increase was approximately 20 cents per bushel. Given anticipated produce prices, this would appear to be cost-effective. The complication was that, while VegeTech had been fully approved by the appropriate federal agencies, OFA had not yet decided whether to approve its use as an organic substance. Proponents argued that it consisted of bacteria that attacked insects, while opponents argued that the bacteria had been synthesized and were not "organic" in the classic sense of the word. OFA had guaranteed that it would run tests and make a decision late this summer about the use of the substance; unfortunately, farmers would have to decide whether or not to use VegeTech before learning of OFA's decision. If the Kellers decided to use VegeTech, and if the OFA failed to certify it as an accepted organic substance, then the Kellers would not be able to label their produce "Organically Grown." The net effect would be a 15% reduction in the prices they could charge. By all indications, there was a 50–50 chance that the OFA would certify VegeTech.

QUESTION

1. Construct a simulation model to address the issues that the Kellers face. Do you think that they should stick with the conventional methods or try organic agriculture? If they go organic, should they try VegeTech this year? Support your conclusions with appropriate simulation outputs (graphs, expected values, and so on).

Overbooking, Part III

Consider again Mockingbird Airlines' problem as described in the overbooking case study in Chapter 9 (pages 277–278).

QUESTIONS

1. Construct a simulation model of the system, and use it to find Mockingbird's optimal policy regarding overbooking. Compare this answer with the one based on the analysis done in Chapter 9.
2. Suppose that you are uncertain about the no-show rate. It could be as low as 0.02 or it could be as high as 0.06, and all values in between are equally likely. Furthermore, the cost of satisfying the bumped passengers may not be constant. That is, the airline may in some cases be able to entice a passenger or two to relinquish their seats in exchange for compensation that would be less than a refund and another free ticket. Alternatively, in some cases the total cost, including loss of goodwill, might be construed as considerably higher. Suppose, for example, that the cost of satisfying an excess customer is normally distributed with mean $300 and standard deviation $40.

   Modify the simulation model constructed in Question 1 to include the uncertainties about the no-show rate and the cost. Do these sources of uncertainty affect the optimal overbooking policy?
3. How else might Mockingbird's analysts address the uncertainty about the no-show rate and the cost?

◇ REFERENCES

Hertz's (1964) article in *Harvard Business Review* extolled the virtues of simulation for the decision-analysis community early on. Hertz and Thomas (1983, 1984) provide discussion and examples of the use of simulation for decision analysis. Other texts that include introductory material on simulation are Holloway (1979) and Samson (1988). Vatter et al. (1978) contains several interesting simulation case studies in decision making. More technical introductions to Monte Carlo simulation at a moderate level are provided by Law and Kelton (1991) and Watson (1989).

With the widespread availability of electronic spreadsheets and personal computers, building simple computerized simulation models has become possible for many students. Hence, in this chapter we have looked at some of the nitty-gritty details involved in the use of spreadsheets for simulation modeling. The availability of programs such as @RISK takes the entire process a step further. With this kind of program, spreadsheet users can easily perform sophisticated Monte Carlo simulation analyses.

HERTZ, D. B. (1964) "Risk Analysis in Capital Investment." *Harvard Business Review.* Reprinted in *Harvard Business Review*, September–October 1979, 169–181.

HERTZ, D. B., and H. THOMAS (1983) *Risk Analysis and Its Applications.* New York: Wiley.

HERTZ, D. B., and H. THOMAS (1984) *Practical Risk Analysis.* New York: Wiley.

HOLLOWAY, C. A. (1979) *Decision Making Under Uncertainty: Models and Choices.* Englewood Cliffs, NJ: Prentice-Hall.

LAW, A. M., and D. KELTON (1991) *Simulation Modeling and Analysis*, 2nd ed. New York: McGraw-Hill.

SAMSON, D. (1988) *Managerial Decision Analysis.* Homewood, IL: Irwin.

VATTER, P., S. BRADLEY, S. FREY, and B. JACKSON (1978) *Quantitative Methods in Management: Text and Cases.* Homewood, IL: Irwin.

WATSON, G. (1989) *Computer Simulation*, 2nd ed. New York: Wiley.

@RISK is available from:
Palisade Corporation
31 Decker Rd.
Newfield, NY 14867
(607) 277-8000

Value of Information

Decision makers who face uncertain prospects often gather information with the intention of reducing uncertainty. Information gathering includes consulting experts, conducting surveys, performing mathematical or statistical analyses, doing research, or simply reading books, journals, and newspapers. The intuitive reason for gathering information is straightforward; to the extent that we can reduce uncertainty about future outcomes, we can make choices that give us a better chance at a good outcome.

In this chapter, we will work a few examples that should help you understand the principles behind information valuation. Naturally, the examples also will demonstrate the techniques used to calculate information value. It turns out that influence diagrams are particularly useful in information-value problems, especially when a computer package is available to solve influence diagrams.

The main example for this chapter is the stock-market example that we introduced in Chapter 5 in our discussion of sensitivity analysis (pages 133–136). For convenience, the details are repeated here.

INVESTING IN THE STOCK MARKET

An investor has some funds available to invest in one of three choices: a high-risk stock, a low-risk stock, or a savings account that pays a sure $500. If he invests in the stocks, he must pay a brokerage fee of $200.

His payoff for the two stocks depends on what happens to the market. If the market goes up, he will earn $1700 from the high-risk stock and $1200 from the low-risk stock. If the market stays at the same level, his payoffs for the high- and low-risk stocks will be $300 and $400, respectively. Finally, if the stock market goes down, he will lose $800 with the high-risk stock, but still gain $100 with the low-risk stock.

♦

The investor's problem can be modeled with either an influence diagram or a decision tree. These two representations are shown in Figure 12.1.

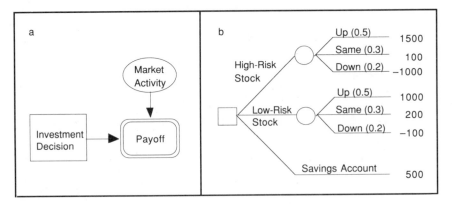

FIGURE 12.1   *(a) Influence-Diagram and (b) Decision-Tree Representations of the Investor's Problem*

◆ VALUE OF INFORMATION: SOME BASIC IDEAS

Before we begin an in-depth study of information from a decision-analysis perspective, let us consider certain fundamental notions. What does it mean for an expert to provide perfect information? How does probability relate to the idea of information? What is an appropriate basis on which to evaluate information in a decision situation? This section addresses these questions and thus sets the stage for a complete development of the value of information in the rest of the chapter.

Probability and Perfect Information

An expert's information is said to be perfect if it is always correct. We can use conditional probabilities to model perfect information. Suppose that when state S will occur, the expert always says so (and never says that some other state will occur). In our stock-market example, imagine an expert who always correctly identifies a situation in which the market will increase:

P(Expert Says "Market Up" | Market Really Does Go Up) = 1.

Because the probabilities must add to 1, we also must have

P(Expert Says "Market Will Stay the Same or Fall"
| Market Really Will Go Up) = 0.

But this is only half the story. The expert also must never say that state S will occur if any other state ($\bar{S}$) will occur. There must be no chance of our expert saying that the market will rise when it really will not:

P(Expert Says "Market Will Go Up"

| Market Really Will Stay the Same or Fall) = 0.

Notice the difference between this probability statement and the preceding. Both are conditional probabilities, but the conditions are different.

If the expert's information is perfect, then upon hearing the expert's report no doubt about the future remains; if the expert says the market will rise, then we know that the market really will rise. Having used conditional probabilities to model the expert's perfect information, we can use Bayes' theorem to "flip" the probabilities as we did in Chapter 7 and show that there is no uncertainty after we have heard the expert. We want to know P(Market Really Will Go Up | Expert Says "Market Will Go Up"). Some notation will make our lives easier:

Market Up = The market really goes up.

Market Down = The market really stays flat or goes down.

Exp Says "Up" = The expert says the market will go up.

Exp Says "Down" = The expert says the market will stay flat or go down.

Now we can apply Bayes' theorem:

P(Market Up | Exp Says "Up")

$$= \frac{(P(\text{Exp Says "Up"}|\text{Market Up})P(\text{Market Up})}{[P(\text{Exp Says "Up"}|\text{Market Up})\, P(\text{Market Up}) + P(\text{Exp Says "Up"}|\text{Market Down})\, P(\text{Market Down})]}$$

$$= \frac{(1\ P(\text{Market Up})}{1\ P(\text{Market Up}) + 0\ P(\text{Market Down})}$$

$$= 1.$$

Observe that the posterior probability P(Market Up | Expert Says "Up") is equal to 1 regardless of the prior probability P(Market Up). This is because of the conditional probabilities that we used to represent the expert's perfect performance. Of course, this situation is not typical of the real world. In real problems we rarely can eliminate uncertainty altogether. If the expert sometimes makes mistakes, these conditional probabilities would not be 1's and 0's and the posterior probability would not be 1 or 0; there still would be some uncertainty about what would actually happen.

This exercise may seem a bit arcane. Its purpose is to introduce the idea of thinking about information in a probabilistic way. We can use conditional probabilities and Bayes' theorem to evaluate all kinds of information in virtually any decision setting.

The Expected Value of Information

How can we place a value on information in a decision problem? For example, how could we decide whether to hire the expert described in the last section? Does it depend on what the expert says? In the investment decision, the optimal choice is to invest in the high-risk stock. Now imagine what could happen. If the expert says that the market will rise, the investor still would choose the high-risk stock. In this case, the information appears to have no value in the sense that the investor would have taken the same action regardless of the expert's information. On the other hand, the expert might say that the market will fall or remain the same, in which case the investor would be better off with the savings account. In this second case, the information has value because it leads to a different action, one with a higher expected value than what would have been experienced without the expert's information.

We can think about information value after the fact, as we have done in the preceding paragraph, but it is much more useful to consider it before the fact — that is, before we actually get the information, or before we hire the expert. What effects do we anticipate the information will have on our decision? We will talk about the *expected value of information.* By considering the expected value, we can decide whether an expert is worth consulting, whether a test is worth performing, or which of several information sources would be the best to consult.

The worst possible case would be that, regardless of the information we hear, we still would make the same choice that we would have made in the first place. In this case, the information has zero expected value! If we would take the same action regardless of what an expert tells us, then why hire the expert in the first place? We are just as well off as we would have been without the expert. Thus, at the worst, the expected value of information is zero. But if there are certain cases — things an expert might say or outcomes of an experiment — on the basis of which we would change our minds and make a different choice, then the expected value of the information must be positive; in those cases, the information leads to a greater expected value. The expected value of information can be zero or positive, but never negative.

At the other extreme, perfect information is the best possible situation. Nothing could be better than resolving all of the uncertainty in a problem. When all uncertainty is resolved, we no longer have to worry about unlucky outcomes; for every choice, we know exactly what the outcome will be. Thus, the expected value of perfect information provides an upper bound for the expected value of information in general. Putting this together with the argument in the previous paragraph, the expected value of any information source must be somewhere between zero and the expected value of perfect information.

Finally, you might have noticed that we continue to consider the expected value of information in terms of the particular choices faced. Indeed, the expected value of information is critically dependent on the particular decision problem at hand. For this reason, different people in different situations may place different values on the same information. For example, General Motors may find that economic forecasts from an expensive forecaster may be a bargain in helping the company refine its production plans. The same economic forecasts may be an extravagant waste of money for a restaurateur in a tourist town.

◆ EXPECTED VALUE OF PERFECT INFORMATION

Now we will see how to calculate the expected value of perfect information (EVPI) in the investment problem. For an expected value–maximizing investor, the optimal choice is the high-risk stock because it has the highest EMV ($580); however, this is partly because the investor is optimistic about what the market will do. How much would he be willing to pay for information about whether the market will move up, down, or sideways?

Suppose he could consult an expert with perfect information — a clairvoyant — who could reveal exactly what the market would do. By including an arrow from "Market Activity" to "Investment Decision," the influence diagram in Figure 12.2 represents the decision situation in which the investor has access to perfect information. Remember, an arrow leading from an uncertainty node to a decision node means that the decision is made knowing the outcome of the uncertainty node. This is exactly what we want to represent in the case of perfect information; the investor knows what the market will do before he invests his money.

With a representation of the decision problem including access to perfect information, how can we find the EVPI? Easy. Solve each influence diagram, Figures 12.1a and 12.2. Find the EMV of each situation. Now subtract the EMV for Figure 12.1a ($580) from the EMV for Figure 12.2 ($1000). The difference ($420) is the EVPI. We can interpret this quantity as the maximum amount that the investor should be willing to pay the clairvoyant for perfect information.

It also is useful to look at the decision-tree representation. To do this, draw a decision tree that includes the opportunity to obtain perfect information (Figure 12.3). As in the influence-diagram representation, the EMV for consulting the clairvoyant is $1000. This is $420 better than the EMV obtained by acting without the information. As before, EVPI is the difference, $420.

Recall that in a decision tree the order of the nodes conforms to a chronological ordering of the events. Is this what happens in the perfect-information branch in Figure 12.3? Yes and no. Yes in the sense that the uncertainty regarding the stock market's activity is resolved before the investment decision is made. This is the important part. But once the decision is made, the market still must go through its performance. It is simply that the investor knows exactly what that performance will be.

This points out a useful aspect of expected-value-of-information analysis with decision trees. If a decision maker faces some uncertainty in a decision, which is represented by those uncertainty nodes that come after his decision in a

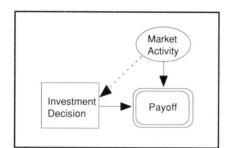

FIGURE 12.2　*Perfect Information in the Investor's Problem*

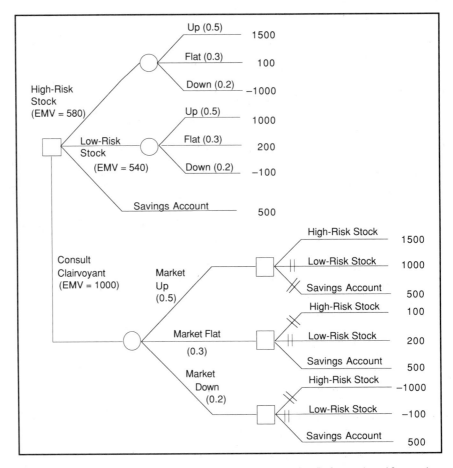

FIGURE 12.3 *Investment Decision Tree with the Perfect-Information Alternative*

decision tree, redrawing the tree to capture the idea of perfect information is easy. Simply reorder the decision and uncertainty nodes! That is, redraw the tree so that the uncertainty nodes for which perfect information is available come before the decision node. This is exactly what we did in the perfect-information branch in Figure 12.3; in this branch, the market-activity and investment-decision nodes are reversed relative to their original positions.

It is worth reiterating that the way we are thinking about the value of information is in a strictly *a priori* sense. The decision-tree representation reinforces this notion because we actually include the decision branch that represents the possibility of consulting the clairvoyant. The investor has not yet consulted the clairvoyant; rather, he is considering whether to consult the clairvoyant in the first place. That action increases the expected value of the decision. Specifically, in this case there is a 50% chance that the clairvoyant will say that the market is not going up, in which case the appropriate decision would be the savings account rather than the high-risk stock.

◆ EXPECTED VALUE OF IMPERFECT INFORMATION

We rarely have access to perfect information. In fact, our information sources usually are subject to considerable error. Thus, we must extend our analysis to deal with imperfect information.

The analysis of imperfect information parallels that of perfect information. We still consider the expected value of the information before obtaining it, and we will call it the "expected value of sample information" (EVSI) to express the notion of collecting some information from a sample.

In the investment example, suppose that the investor hires an economist who specializes in forecasting stock-market trends. Because he can make mistakes, however, he is not a clairvoyant, and his information is imperfect. For example, suppose his track record shows that if the market actually will rise, he says "up" 80% of the time, "flat" 10%, and "down" 10%. We construct a table (Table 12.1) to characterize his performance in probabilistic terms. The probabilities therein are conditional; for example, P(Economist Says "Flat" | Flat) = 0.70. The table shows that he is better when times are good (market up) and worse when times are bad (market down); he is somewhat more likely to make mistakes when times are bad.

How should the investor use the economist's information? Figure 12.4 shows an influence diagram that includes an uncertainty node representing the economist's forecast. The structure of this influence diagram should be familiar from Chapter 3; the economist's information is an example of imperfect information. The arrow from "Market Activity" to "Economic Forecast" means that the probability distribution for the particular forecast is conditioned on what the market will do. This is reflected in the distributions in Table 12.1. In fact, the distributions contained in the "Economic Forecast" node are simply the conditional probabilities from that table.

Solving the influence diagram in Figure 12.4 gives the EMV associated with obtaining the economist's imperfect information before action is taken. The EMV turns out to be $822. As we did in the case of perfect information, we

Economist's Prediction	True Market State		
	Up	Flat	Down
"Up"	0.80	0.15	0.20
"Flat"	0.10	0.70	0.20
"Down"	0.10	0.15	0.60
	1.00	1.00	1.00

TABLE 12.1 *Conditional Probabilities Characterizing Economist's Forecasting Ability*

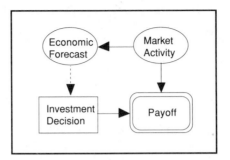

FIGURE 12.4 *Imperfect Information in the Investor's Problem*

calculate EVSI as the difference between the EMVs from Figures 12.4 and 12.1a, or the situation with no information. Thus, EVSI equals $822 – $580 = $242.

The influence-diagram approach is easy to discuss because we actually do not see the detail calculations. On the other hand, the decision-tree approach shows the calculation of EVSI in its full glory. Figure 12.5 shows the decision-tree representation of the situation, with a branch that represents the alternative of consulting the economist. Look at the way in which the nodes are ordered in the "Consult Economist" alternative. The first event is the economist's forecast. Thus, we need probabilities P(Economist Says "Up"), P(Economist Says "Flat"), and P(Economist Says "Down"). Then the investor decides what to do with his money. Finally, the market goes up, down, or sideways. Because the "Market Activity" node follows the "Economists Forecast" node in the decision tree, we must have conditional probabilities for the market such as P(Market Up | Economist Says "Up") or P(Market Flat | Economist Says "Down"). What we have, however, is the opposite. We have probabilities such as P(Market Up) and conditional probabilities such as P(Economist Says "Up" | Market Up).

As we did when we first introduced the notion of the value of an expert's information at the beginning of this chapter, we must use Bayes' theorem to find the posterior probabilities for the actual market outcome. For example, what is P(Market Up | Economist Says "Up")? It stands to reason that after we hear him say "up," we should think it more likely that the market actually will go up than we might have thought before.

We used Bayes' theorem to "flip" probabilities in Chapter 7. There are several ways to think about this situation. First, applying Bayes' theorem is tantamount to reversing the arrow between the nodes "Market Activity" and "Economic Forecast" in Figure 12.4. In fact, reversing this arrow is the first thing that must be done when solving the influence diagram (Figure 12.6). Or we can think in terms of flipping a probability tree as we did in Chapter 7. Figure 12.7a represents the situation we have, and 12.7b represents what we need.

Whether we think of the task as flipping a probability tree or reversing an arrow in an influence diagram, we still must use Bayes' theorem to find the probabilities we need. For example,

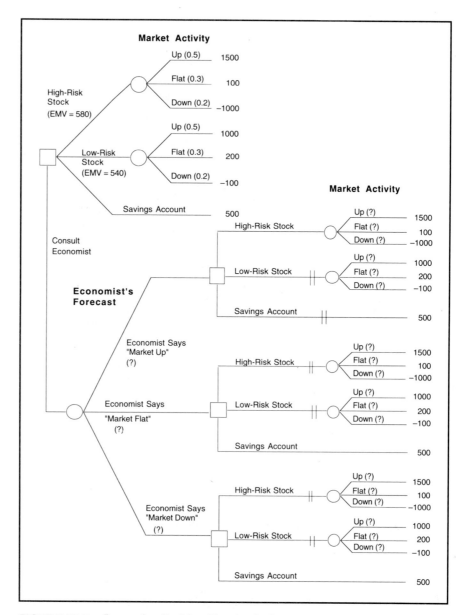

FIGURE 12.5 *Incomplete Decision Tree for the Investment Example,
Including the Alternative for Consulting the Economist*

P(Market Up | Economist Says "Up")

= P(Up | "Up")

$$= \frac{P(\text{"Up"} | Up)\, P(Up)}{P(\text{"Up"} | Up)P(Up) + P(\text{"Up"} | Flat)\, P(Flat) + P(\text{"Up"} | Down)\, P(Down)}.$$

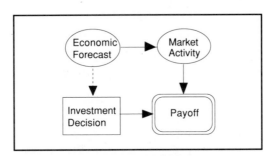

FIGURE 12.6   *First Step in Solving
the Influence Diagram*
We reverse the arrow between "Economic
Forecast" and "Market Activity"

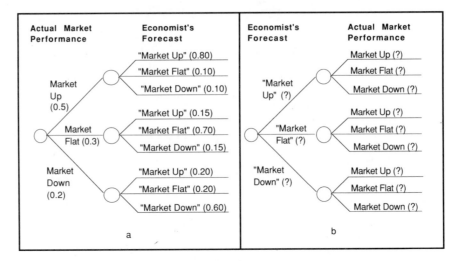

FIGURE 12.7   *Flipping the Probability Tree to Find Posterior Probabilities
Required for Value-of-Information Analysis*
In (a) we see what we have; in (b) we see what we need.

P(Up), P(Flat), and P(Down) are the investor's prior probabilities, while
P(Economist Says "Up" | Up) and so on are the conditional probabilities shown
in Table 12.1. From the principle of total probability, the denominator is
P(Economist Says "Up").

Substituting in values for the conditional probabilities and priors,

$$P(\text{Market Up} \mid \text{Economists Says "Up"}) = \frac{0.8(0.5)}{0.8\,(0.5) + 0.15\,(0.3) + 0.2\,(0.2)}$$

$$= \frac{0.400}{0.485}$$

$$= 0.8247.$$

P(Economist Says "Up") is given by the denominator and is equal to 0.485.

Of course, we need to use Bayes' theorem to calculate nine different posterior probabilities to fill in the gaps in the decision tree in Figure 12.5. Table 12.2 shows the results of these calculations; these probabilities are included on the appropriate branches in the completed decision tree (Figure 12.8).

We also noted that we needed the marginal probabilities P("Up"), P("Flat"), and P("Down"). These probabilities are P("Up") = 0.485, P("Flat") = 0.300, and P("Down") = 0.215; they also are included in Figure 12.8 to represent our uncertainty about what the economist will say. As usual, the marginal probabilities can be found in the process of calculating the posterior probabilities because they simply come from the denominator in Bayes' theorem.

From the completed decision tree in Figure 12.8 we can tell that the EMV for consulting the economist is $822, while the EMV for acting without consulting him is (as before) only $580. The EVSI is the difference between the two EMVs. Thus, EVSI is $242 in this example, just as it was when we solved the problem using influence diagrams. Given this particular decision situation, the investor would never want to pay more than $242 for the economic forecast.

As with perfect information, $242 is the value of the information only in an expected-value sense. If the economist says that the market will go up, then we would invest in the high-risk stock, just as we would if we did not consult him. Thus, if he does tell us that the market will go up, the information turns out to do us no good. But if he tells us that the market will be flat or go down, we would put our money in the savings account and avoid the relatively low expected value associated with the high-risk stock. In those two cases, we would "save" 500 − 187 = 313 and 500 − (−188) = 688, respectively, with the savings in terms of expected value. Thus, EVSI also can be calculated as the "expected incremental savings," which is 0 (0.485) + 313 (0.300) + 688 (0.215) = 242.

Such probability calculations can make value-of-information analysis tedious and time-consuming. This is where computers can play a role. Influence-diagram programs can perform all of the necessary probability calculations and thus make finding EVSI a simple matter. Some decision-tree programs do the same thing, and it always is possible to construct an electronic spreadsheet model that will perform the calculations.

One last note regarding value-of-information calculations. If you have used your calculator to work through the examples in this chapter, you may have

Economist's Prediction	Posterior Probability for:		
	Market Up	**Market Flat**	**Market Down**
"Up"	0.8247	0.0928	0.0825
"Flat"	0.1667	0.7000	0.1333
"Down"	0.2325	0.2093	0.5581

TABLE 12.2 *Posterior Probabilities for Market Trends Depending on Economist's Information*

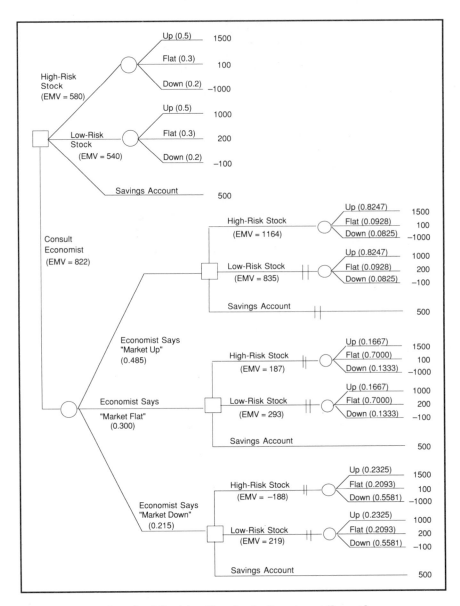

FIGURE 12.8 *Completed Decision Tree for the Investment Example*

found that your answers differed slightly from those in this book. This is because calculations involving Bayes' theorem and value of information tend to be highly sensitive to rounding error. The appropriate strategy is to carry calculations out to many decimal places throughout a given problem, rounding off to dollars or cents only at the end of the problem. Rounding off intermediate results that are used in later calculations sometimes can make a large difference in the final answer.

♦ VALUE OF INFORMATION IN COMPLEX PROBLEMS

The example we have looked at in this section has been a fairly simple one. There was only one uncertain event, the behavior of the market, and we modeled the uncertainty with a simple discrete distribution. As we know, however, most real-world problems involve considerably more complex uncertainty models. In particular, we need to consider two specific situations. First, how can we handle continuous probability distributions? Second, what happens when there are many uncertain events, and information is available about some or all of them?

The answer to the first question is straightforward conceptually, but in practice the calculation of EVPI or EVSI may be difficult when dealing with continuous probability distributions. The principle is the same. Evaluate decision options with and without the information, and find the difference in the EMVs, as we have done in the discrete case. The problem, of course, is calculating the EMVs. Obviously, it always is possible to construct a discrete approximation as discussed in Chapter 8. Another possibility is to construct a Monte Carlo simulation model. Finally, for some theoretical probability models, analytical results are possible. The mathematics for such analysis, however, tend to be somewhat complicated and are beyond the scope of this introductory textbook. References for interested readers are included at the end of the chapter.

The second question asks how we handle value-of-information problems when there are many uncertain events. Again, in principle, the answer is easy, and is most transparent if we think in terms of influence diagrams. Perfect information about any particular event simply implies the presence of an informational arc from the event to the decision node. Naturally, it is possible to include such arcs for a subset of events. The only requirement is that the event not be downstream in the diagram from the decision node, because the inclusion of the information arc would lead to a cycle in the influence diagram. Solving the influence diagram with the informational arcs in place provides the EMV with the information, and this then may be compared to the EMV without the information to obtain the EVPI for the particular information sought.

Consider the same problem when the model is in decision-tree form. In the decision tree in Figure 12.3, the information branch was constructed by reversing the event node and the decision node. The same principle can apply if there are many sources of uncertainty; simply move those chance nodes for which information is to be obtained so that they precede the decision node. Now calculating EMV for the information branch will give the EMV in the case of perfect information for those events that precede the decision node in the decision tree.

For imperfect information, the same general principles apply. For influence diagrams, include an imperfect-information node that provides information to the decision maker. An excellent example is the toxic-chemicals influence diagram in Figure 3.13 (page 48). Two sources of imperfect information are included in that model, the exposure survey and the lab test. In a decision-tree model, it would be a matter of constructing a tree having the appropriate informational chance nodes preceding the decision node. Unfortunately, if there are more than one or two such chance nodes, the decision tree can become extremely unwieldy. Moreover, it may be necessary to calculate and track the marginal and posterior probabilities for the decision tree; these calculations can be done automatically in the influence diagram.

◆ VALUE OF INFORMATION, SENSITIVITY ANALYSIS, AND STRUCTURING

Our motivation for studying value of information has been to examine situations in which information is available and to show how decisions can be made systematically regarding what source of information to select and how much an expert's information might be worth. Strictly speaking, this is precisely what value-of-information analysis can do. But it also can play an elegant and subtle role in the structuring of decisions and in the entire decision-analysis process of developing a requisite decision model. Recall the ideas of sensitivity analysis from Chapter 5. In that chapter we talked about a process of building a decision structure. The first step is to find out, using a tornado diagram, those variables to which the decision was sensitive; these variables require probabilistic modeling. The second step, after constructing a probabilistic model, may be to perform sensitivity analysis on the probabilities.

A third step in the structuring of a probabilistic model would be to calculate the EVPI for each uncertain event. This analysis would indicate where the analyst or decision maker should focus subsequent efforts in the decision-modeling process. That is, if EVPI is very low for an event, then there is little sense in spending a lot of effort in reducing the uncertainty by collecting information. But if EVPI for an event is relatively high, it may indeed be worthwhile to put considerable effort into the collection of information that relates to the event. Such information can have a relatively large payoff by reducing uncertainty and improving the decision maker's EMV. In this way, EVPI analysis can provide guidance to the decision analyst as to what issues should be tackled next in the development of a requisite decision model.

We will end this chapter with a short description of a rather unusual application of value-of-information analysis. Although few applications are as elaborate as this one, this example does provide an idea of how the idea of information value, as developed in decision analysis, can be used to address real-world concerns.

SEEDING HURRICANES

Hurricanes pack tremendous power in their high winds and tides. Recent storms such as Camille (1969) and Hugo (1989) caused damage in excess of a billion dollars, and amply demonstrated the destructive potential of large hurricanes. In the 1960s, the U.S. government experimented with the seeding of hurricanes, or the practice of dropping silver iodide into the storm to reduce peak winds by forcing precipitation. After early limited experiments, Hurricane Debbie was seeded in 1969 with massive amounts of silver iodide on two separate occasions. Each seeding was followed by substantial drops in peak wind speed. Given these results, should hurricanes that threaten highly populated areas be seeded on the basis of current knowledge? Should the government pursue a serious research program on the effects of hurricane seeding?

◆

Howard, Matheson, and North (1972) addressed these specific questions about hurricane seeding. They asked whether it would be appropriate to seed hurricanes, or would a research program be appropriate, or should the federal government simply not pursue this type of weather modification? To answer these questions, they adopted a decision-analysis framework. On the basis of a relatively simple probabilistic model of hurricane winds, along with the relationships among wind speed, damage, and the effect of seeding, they were able to calculate expected dollar losses for two decision alternatives — seeding and not seeding a typical threatening hurricane. On the basis of their model, they concluded that seeding would be the preferred alternative if the federal government wanted to reduce expected damage.

The authors realized that the government might be interested in more than the matter of reducing property damage. What would happen, for example, if the decision was made to seed a hurricane, the wind speed subsequently increased, and increased damage resulted? The government most likely would become the target of many lawsuits for having taken action that appeared to have adverse effects. Thus, the government also faced an issue of responsibility if seeding were undertaken. On the basis of the authors' analysis, however, the government's "responsibility cost" would have to have been relatively high in order for the optimal decision to change.

To address the issue of whether further research on seeding would be appropriate, the authors used a value-of-information approach. They considered the possibility of repeating the seeding experiment that had been performed on Hurricane Debbie, and the potential effects of such an experiment. By modeling the possible outcomes of this experiment and considering the effect on future seeding decisions, the authors were able to calculate the expected value of the research. Including reasonable costs for government responsibility and anticipated damage over a single hurricane season, the expected value of the experiment was determined to be approximately $10.2 million. The authors also extended their analysis to include all future hurricane seasons, discounting future costs by 7% per year. In this case, the expected value of the research was $146 million. To put these numbers in perspective, the cost of the seeding experiment would have been approximately $500,000. [*Source*: Howard, R. A., J. E. Matheson, and D. W. North (1972) "The Decision to Seed Hurricanes." *Science*, 176, 1191–1202.]

◇ SUMMARY

By considering the expected value of information, we can make better decisions about whether to obtain information or which information source to consult. We saw that the expected value of any bit of information must be zero or greater, and it cannot be more than the expected value of perfect information. Both influence diagrams and decision trees can be used as frameworks for calculating expected values. Influence diagrams provide the neatest representation because information available for a decision can be represented through appropriate use of arcs and, if necessary, additional uncertainty nodes representing imperfect information. In contrast, calculating the expected value of imperfect information with decision trees is a more complicated procedure, requiring the calculation of posterior and marginal probabilities. The expected value of information is simply the difference between the EMV calculated both with and without the information.

The final sections in the chapter discussed generally how to solve value-of-information problems in more complex situations. We concluded with a discussion of the role that value-of-information analysis can play in the decision-analysis process of developing a requisite decision model. ◆

◇ EXERCISES

12.1 Explain why in decision analysis we are concerned with the *expected* value of information.

12.2 Calculate the EVPI for the decision shown in Figure 12.9.

12.3 What is the EVPI for the decision shown in Figure 12.10? Must you perform any calculations? Can you draw any conclusions regarding the relationship between value of information and deterministic dominance?

12.4 For the decision tree in Figure 12.11:

   a. Draw the appropriate decision tree and calculate the EVPI for Event E only.

   b. Draw the appropriate decision tree and calculate the EVPI for Event F only.

   c. Draw the appropriate decision tree and calculate the EVPI for both Events E and F: that is, perfect information for both E and F is available before a decision is made.

12.5 Draw the influence diagram that corresponds to the decision tree for Problem 12.4. How would this influence diagram be changed in order to answer parts a, b, and c in Problem 12.4?

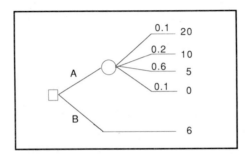

FIGURE 12.9 *Generic Decision Tree for Problem 12.2*

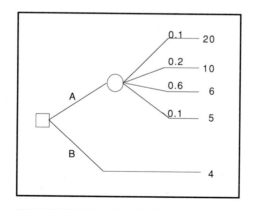

FIGURE 12.10   *Generic Decision Tree for Problem 12.3*

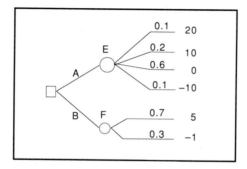

FIGURE 12.11   *Generic Decision Tree for Problem 12.4*

◇ QUESTIONS AND PROBLEMS

12.6   Consider another oil-wildcatting problem. You have mineral rights on a piece of land that you believe may have oil underground. There is only a 10% chance that you will strike oil if you drill, but the payoff is $200,000. It costs $10,000 to drill. The alternative is not to drill at all, in which case your profit is zero.

a. Draw a decision tree to represent your problem. Should you drill?

b. Draw an influence diagram to represent your problem. How could you use the influence diagram to find the EVPI?

c. Calculate the EVPI. Use either the decision tree or the influence diagram.

d. Before you drill you might consult a geologist who can assess the promise of the piece of land. She can tell you whether your prospects are "good" or "poor." But she is not a perfect predictor. If there is oil, the conditional probability is 0.95 that she will say that prospects are good If there is no oil, the conditional probability is 0.85 that she will say poor. Draw a decision tree that includes the "Consult Geologist" alternative. Be careful to calculate the appropriate probabilities to include in the decision tree. Finally, calculate the EVSI for this geologist. If she charges $7000, what should you do?

12.7   In Problem 4.17 (page 104), find:

    a. The EVPI for the cost of making the processor.

    b. The EVPI for the cost of subcontracting the processor.

    c. The EVPI for both uncertain events.

12.8   Look again at Problem 8.11 (page 235), which concerns whether you should drop your decision-analysis course. Estimate the EVPI for your score in the course.

12.9   In Problem 9.31 (page 275), the issue is whether or not to close the plant, and if your boss knew exactly how many machines would fail during your absence, he would be able to decide what to do without the fear of making a mistake.

    a. Find his EVPI concerning the number of machine failures during your absence over the next two weeks.

    b. Suppose that the cost of repairing the broken machines is $30,000. Then what is the EVPI?

    c. Suppose that the cost of repairing the machines is $15,000, but the cost of closing the plant is $20,000. Now calculate the EVPI.

12.10   Consider the Texaco–Pennzoil example from Chapter 4 (pages 65–69).

    a. What is the EVPI to Hugh Liedtke regarding Texaco's reaction to a counteroffer of $5 billion? Can you explain this result intuitively?

    b. The timing of information acquisition may make a difference.

        (i) For example, suppose that Liedtke could obtain information about the final court decision before making his current decision (take the $2 billion or counteroffer $5 billion). What would be the EVPI of this information?

        (ii) Suppose that Liedtke knew he would be able to obtain perfect information only after he has made his current decision, but before he would have to respond to a potential Texaco counteroffer of $3 billion. What would be the EVPI in this case?

    c. In part (b), EVPI for (ii) should be less than EVPI calculated in (i). Can you explain why? (Incidentally, if your results disagree with this, you should check your calculations!)

12.11   In the Texaco–Pennzoil case, what is the EVPI if Liedtke can learn both Texaco's reaction and the final court decision before he makes up his mind about the current $2-billion offer? (*Hint*: Your answer should be more than the sum of the EVPIs for Texaco's reaction and the court decision calculated separately in Problem 12.10.) Can you explain why the interaction of the two bits of information should have this effect?

12.12   In Problem 5.9 (page 140), assume that the grower's loss incurred with the burners would be $17,500, and that the loss incurred with the sprinklers would be $27,500.

    a. Find the EVPI for the weather conditions (freeze or not).

    b. Now assume that the loss incurred with the burners is uniformly distributed between $15,000 and $20,000. Also assume that the loss incurred with the sprinklers is uniformly distributed between $25,000 and $30,000. Now estimate the EVPI regarding these losses, under the assumption that a better weather forecast cannot be obtained.

    c. Do you think the farmer should put more effort into learning his costs more precisely or should he concentrate on obtaining better weather forecasts?

12.13   Reconsider the Eagle Airlines example from Chapter 5, particularly as diagrammed in Figure 5.6 (page 125). Assume that q and r are both 0.5. Calculate the EVPI for each of the three uncertain events individually. What can you conclude from your analysis?

CASE STUDIES

Texaco–Pennzoil Revisited

Often when we face uncertainty, we would like more than simply to know the outcome; it would be nice to control the outcome and bring about the best possible result! A king might consult his wizard as well as his clairvoyant, asking the wizard to cast a spell to cause the desired outcome to occur. How much should such a wizard be paid for these services? The expected value of his wizardry naturally depends on the decision problem at hand, just as the expected value of information does. But the way to calculate the "expected value of wizardry" (to use Ron Howard's term) is very similar to solving the calculations for the expected value of perfect information.

To demonstrate this idea, we again will examine Hugh Liedtke's decision situation as diagrammed in Figure 4.2 (page 69). Now consider the entirely hypothetical possibility that Liedtke could pay someone to influence Texaco's CEO, James Kinnear.

QUESTIONS

1. What would be the most desirable outcome from the "Texaco Reaction" chance node?
2. Construct the decision tree now with three alternatives: "Accept $2 Billion," "Counteroffer $5 Billion," and "Counteroffer $5 billion and Influence Kinnear."
3. Solve your decision tree from Problem 2. What is the maximum amount that Liedtke could afford to pay in order to influence Kinnear?

◆

Medical Tests

One of the principles that arises from a decision-analysis approach to valuing information is that information is worthless if no possible informational outcome will change the decision. For example, suppose that you are considering whether to make a particular investment. You are tempted to hire a consultant recommended by your Uncle Jake (who just went bankrupt last year) to help you analyze the decision. If, however, you think carefully about the things that the consultant might have to say, and conclude that you would (or would not) make the investment regardless of the consultant's recommendation, then you should not hire the consultant. This principle makes perfectly good sense in the light of our approach; do not pay for information that cannot possibly change your mind.

In medicine, however, it is standard practice for physicians to order extensive batteries of tests for patients. Although different kinds of patients may be subjected to different overall sets of tests, it is nevertheless the case that many of these tests provide information that is worthless in a decision-analysis sense; the doctor's prescription would be the same regardless of the outcome of a particular test.

QUESTIONS

1. As a patient, would you be willing to pay for such tests? Why or why not?
2. What incentives do you think the doctor might have for ordering such tests, assuming he realizes that his prescription would not change?
3. How do his incentives compare to yours?

◆

DuMond International, Part II

[Refer back to the DuMond International case study at the end of Chapter 5 (pages 142–143).] Nancy Milnor had returned to her office, still concerned about the decision. Yes, she had persuaded the directors that their disagreements did not affect her analysis; her analysis still showed the new product to be the appropriate choice. The members of the board, however, had not been entirely satisfied. The major complaint was that there was still too much uncertainty. Could she find out more about the likelihood of a ban, or could she get a better assessment from engineering regarding the delay? What about a more accurate sales forecast for the new product?

Nancy gazed at her decision tree (Figure 5.23, page 142). Yes, she could address each of those questions, but where should she start?

QUESTION

1. Calculate the EVPI for the three uncertain events in DuMond's decision as diagrammed in Figure 5.23. Where should Nancy Milnor begin her investigation?

◆

◇ REFERENCES

This chapter has focused primarily on the technical details of calculating the value of information. The most complete, and most highly technical, reference for this kind of analysis is Raiffa and Schlaifer (1961). Winkler (1972) provides an easily readable discussion of value of information. Both texts contain considerably more material than what is included here, including discussion of EVPI and EVSI for continuous distributions. In particular, they delve into questions of the value of sample information for updating natural conjugate prior distributions for model parameters (Chapter 10 in this text) and the selection of appropriate sample sizes, a decision problem intimately related to value of information.

At the end of the chapter, we discussed the way in which the value of information can be related to sensitivity analysis and the decision-analysis process. These ideas are Ron Howard's and have been part of his description of decision analysis since the early 1960s. Many of the articles in Howard and Matheson (1983) explain this process, and illustrative applications show how the process has been applied in a variety of real-world decision problems.

HOWARD, R. A., and J. E. MATHESON (eds.) (1983) *The Principles and Applications of Decision Analysis* (2 volumes). Palo Alto, CA: Strategic Decisions Group.

RAIFFA, H., and R. SCHLAIFER (1961) *Applied Statistical Decision Theory*. Cambridge, MA: Harvard University Press.

WINKLER, R. L. (1972) *Introduction to Bayesian Inference and Decision*. New York: Holt, Rinehart & Winston.

Modeling Preferences

We have come a long way since the first chapters. The first part of the book talked about structuring problems, and the second discussed modeling uncertainty through the use of probability. Now we turn to the problem of modeling preferences.

Why should we worry about modeling preferences? Because virtually every decision involves some kind of trade-off. In decision making under uncertainty, the fundamental trade-off question often is, How much risk is a decision maker willing to assume? After all, expected monetary value is not everything! Often the alternative that has the greatest EMV also involves the greatest risk.

Chapters 13 and 14 look at the role of risk attitudes in decision making. In Chapter 13, basic concepts are presented, and you will learn how to model your own risk attitude. We will develop the concept of a utility function. Modeling your preferences by assessing your utility function is a subjective procedure much like assessing subjective probabilities. Because a utility function incorporates a decision maker's attitude toward risk, the decision maker may decide to choose the alternative that maximizes his or her expected utility rather than expected monetary value.

Chapter 14 discusses some of the foundations that underlie the use of utility functions. The essential reason for choosing alternatives to maximize expected utility is that such behavior is consistent with some fundamental choice and behavior patterns that we call axioms. The paradox is that, even though most of us agree that intuitively the axioms are reasonable, there are cases for all of us when our actual choices are not consistent with the axioms. In many situations these inconsistencies have little effect on a decision maker's choices. But occasionally they can cause trouble, and we will discuss some of these difficulties and their implications.

Dealing with risk attitudes is an important aspect of decision making under uncertainty, but it is only part of the picture. Many problems involve conflicting objectives. Decision makers must balance many different aspects of the problem, and try to accomplish many things at once. Even a simple decision such as deciding where to go for dinner involves trade-offs: How far are you willing to drive? How much should you spend? How badly do you want Chinese food?

Chapters 15 and 16 deal with modeling preferences in situations in which the decision maker has multiple and conflicting objectives. Chapter 15 presents a relatively straightforward approach that is easy and intuitive, and Chapter 16 extends the discussion to the development of multiattribute utility functions. These utility functions allow a decision maker to think about the conflicting objectives that he or she faces and to measure the extent to which each alternative achieves those objectives. In both Chapters 15 and 16, one of the fundamental subjective assessments that the decision maker must make is how to trade off achievement in one dimension against achievement in another.

Risk Attitudes

This chapter marks the beginning of our in-depth study of preferences. Before we begin, let us review where we have been and think about where we are going. The first six chapters provided an introduction to the process of structuring decision problems for decision analysis and an overview of the role that probability and utility theory play in making choices. Chapters 7 through 12 have focused on probability concerns: using probability in a variety of ways to model uncertainty in decision problems, including the modeling of information sources in value-of-information problems.

At this point, we change directions and look at the preference side of decision analysis. How can we model a decision maker's preferences? This chapter looks at the problems associated with risk and return trade-offs. Chapter 14 briefly explores the axiomatic foundations of utility theory and discusses certain paradoxes from cognitive psychology. These paradoxes generally indicate that people do not make choices that are perfectly consistent with the axioms, even though they may agree that the axioms are reasonable! Although such inconsistencies generally do not have serious implications for most decisions, there are certain occasions when they can cause difficulty.

The primary motivating example for this chapter comes from the history of railways in the United States. Imagine what was going through E. H. Harriman's mind as he considered his strategy for acquiring the Northern Pacific Railroad in March 1901.

E. H. HARRIMAN FIGHTS FOR THE NORTHERN PACIFIC RAILROAD

"How could they do it?" E. H. Harriman asked, still angry over the fact that James Hill and J. P. Morgan had bought the Burlington Railroad out from under his nose. "Every U.S. industrialist knows I control the railroads in the West.

I have the Illinois Central, the Union Pacific, the Central and Southern Pacific, not to mention the Oregon Railroad and Navigation Company. Isn't that true?"

"Yes, sir," replied his assistant.

"Well, we will put the pressure on Messrs. Hill and Morgan. They will be surprised indeed to find out that I have acquired a controlling interest in their own railroad, the Northern Pacific. I may even be able to persuade them to let me have the Burlington. By the way, how are the stock purchases going?"

"Sir, we have completed all of the purchases that you authorized so far. You may have noticed that our transactions have driven the price of Northern Pacific stock up to more than $100 per share."

Harriman considered this information. If he bought too fast, he could force the stock price up high enough and fast enough that Hill might begin to suspect that Harriman was up to something. Of course, if Harriman could acquire the shares quickly enough, there would be no problem. On the other hand, if he bought the shares slowly, he would pay lower prices, and Hill might not notice the acquisition until it was too late. His assistant's information, however, suggested that his situation was somewhat risky. If Harriman's plan were discovered, Hill could persuade Morgan to purchase enough additional Northern Pacific shares to enable them to retain control. In that case, Harriman would have paid premium prices for the stock for nothing! On the other hand, if Hill did not make the discovery immediately, the triumph would be that much sweeter.

"How many more shares do we need to have control?" asked Harriman.

"If you could purchase another 40,000 shares, sir, you would own 51 percent of the company."

Another 40,000 shares. Harriman thought about giving Hill and Morgan orders on how to run their own railroad. How enjoyable that would be! Yes, he would gladly increase his investment by that much.

"Of course," his assistant continued, "if we try to purchase these shares immediately, the price will rise very quickly. You will probably end up paying an additional $15 per share above what you would pay if we were to proceed more slowly."

"Well, $600,000 is a lot of money, and I certainly would not want to pay more. But it would be worth the money to be sure that we would be able to watch Hill and Morgan squirm! Send a telegram to my broker in New York right away to place the order. And be quick! It's already Friday. If we are going to do this, we need to do it today. I don't want Hill to have the chance to think about this over the weekend."

◆

◆ RISK

Basing decisions on expected values (EMVs) is convenient, but it can lead to decisions that may not seem intuitively appealing. For example, consider the following two games. Imagine that you have the opportunity to play one game or the other, but only one time. Which one would you prefer to play? Your choice also is drawn in decision-tree form in Figure 13.1.

Game 1	Win $30 with probability 0.5.
	Lose $1 with probability 0.5.

Game 2	Win $2000 with probability 0.5.
	Lose $1900 with probability 0.5.

Game 1 has an expected value of $14.50. Game 2, on the other hand, has an expected value of $50.00. If you were to make your choice on the basis of expected value, then you would choose Game 2. Most of us, however, would consider Game 2 to be riskier than Game 1, and it seems reasonable to suspect that most people actually would prefer Game 1.

Using expected values to make decisions means that the decision maker is considering only the average or expected payoff. If we take a long-run frequency approach, the expected value is the average amount we would be likely to win over many plays of the game. But this ignores the range of possible values. After all, if we play each game 10 times, the worst we could do in Game 1 is to lose $10. On the other hand, the worst we could do in Game 2 is lose $19,000!

Many of the examples and problems that we have considered so far have been analyzed in terms of expected monetary value (EMV). EMV, however, does not capture risk attitudes. For example, consider the Texaco–Pennzoil example in Chapter 4 (pages 65–69). If Hugh Liedtke were afraid of the prospect that Pennzoil could end up with nothing at the end of the court case, he might be willing to take the $2 billion that Texaco offered. To consider the Eagle Airlines case (Chapter 5, pages 113–114), purchasing the airplane is a much riskier alternative than leaving the money in the bank. If Carothers were sensitive to risk, he might prefer to leave the money in the bank. Even someone like E. H. Harriman considered the riskiness of the situations in which he found himself. In our example, Harriman weighed the value of a riskless alternative (immediately purchasing the 40,000 shares that were required to gain control) against the risky

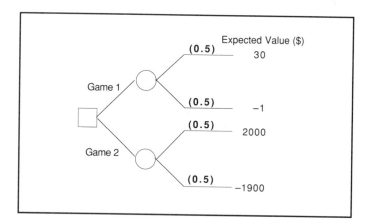

FIGURE 13.1   *Two Lottery Games*
Which game would you choose?

alternative of not purchasing the shares and the possible outcomes that might then follow. Even though all of the dollar amounts were not specified, it is clear that Harriman was not thinking in terms of EMV.

Individuals who are afraid of risk or are sensitive to risk are called *risk-averse.* We can explain risk aversion if we think in terms of a *utility function* (Figure 13.2) that is curved and opening downward (the technical term for a curve with this shape is "concave"). This utility function represents a way to translate dollars into "utility units." That is, if we take some dollar amount (x), we can locate that amount on the horizontal axis. Read up to the curve and then horizontally across to the vertical axis. From that point we can read off the utility value $U(x)$ for the dollars we started with.

A utility function might be specified in terms of a graph, as in Figure 13.2, or given as a table, as in Table 13.1. A third form is a mathematical expression. If graphed, for example, all of the following expressions would have the same general concave shape (opening downward) as the utility function graphed in Figure 13.2:

$$U(x) = \log(x)$$
$$U(x) = 1 - e^{-x/R}$$
$$U(x) = +\sqrt{x} \qquad (\text{or } U(x) = x^{0.5}).$$

Of course, the utility and dollar values in Table 13.1 also could be graphed, as could the functional forms shown above. Likewise, the graph in Figure 13.2 could be converted into a table of values. The point is that the utility function makes the translation from dollars to utility regardless of its displayed form.

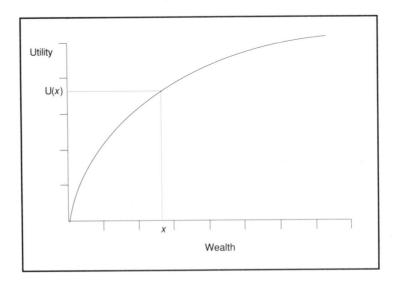

FIGURE 13.2   *A Utility Function that Displays Risk Aversion*

Wealth	Utility Value
2500	1.50
1500	1.24
1000	0.93
600	0.65
400	0.47
0	0.15

TABLE 13.1 *A Utility Function in Tabular Form*

◆ RISK ATTITUDES

We think of a typical utility curve as (1) upward sloping and (2) concave (the curve opens downward). An upward sloping utility curve makes fine sense; it means that more wealth is better than less wealth, everything else being equal. Few people will argue with this. Concavity in a utility curve implies that an individual is risk-averse.

Imagine that you are forced to play the following game:

Win $500 with probability 0.5.

Lose $500 with probability 0.5.

Would you pay to get out of this situation? How much? The game has a zero expected value, so if you would pay something to get out, you are avoiding a risky situation with a zero expected value. Generally, if you would trade a gamble for a sure amount that is less than the expected value of the gamble, you are risk-averse. Purchasing insurance is an example of risk-averse behavior. Insurance companies analyze a lot of data in order to understand the probability distributions associated with claims for different kinds of policies. Of course, this work is costly. To make up these costs and still have an expected profit, an insurance company must charge more for its insurance policy than the policy can be expected to produce in claims. Thus, unless you have some reason to believe that you are more likely than others in your risk group to make a claim, you probably are paying more in insurance premiums than the expected amount you would claim.

Not everyone displays risk-averse behavior all the time, and so utility curves need not be concave. A convex (opening upward) utility curve indicates risk-seeking behavior (Figure 13.3). The risk seeker might be eager to enter into a gamble; for example, he or she might pay to play the game just described. An individual who plays a state lottery exhibits risk-seeking behavior. State lottery tickets typically cost $1.00 and have an expected value of approximately 50 cents.

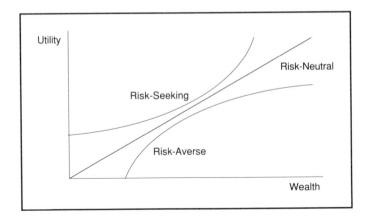

FIGURE 13.3 *Three Different Shapes for Utility Functions*

Finally, an individual can be risk-neutral. Risk neutrality is reflected by a utility curve that is simply a straight line. For this type of person, maximizing EMV is the same as maximizing expected utility. This makes sense; someone who is risk-neutral does not care about risk and can ignore risk aspects of the alternatives that he or she faces. Thus, EMV is a fine criterion for choosing among alternatives, because it also ignores risk.

Although most of us are not risk-neutral, it often is reasonable for a decision maker to assume that his or her utility curve is nearly linear in the range of dollar amounts for a particular decision. This is especially true for large corporations that make decisions involving amounts that are small relative to their total assets. In many cases, it may be worthwhile to use EMV in a first-cut analysis, and then check to see whether the decision would be sensitive to changes in risk attitude. If the decision turns out to be fairly sensitive (that is, if the decision would change for a slightly risk-averse or slightly risk-seeking person), then the decision maker may want to consider modeling his or her risk attitude carefully.

This discussion makes it sound as though individuals can be reduced to their utility functions, and those utility functions can reveal whether the individual is risk-averse or risk-seeking. Keep in mind, however, that the utility function is only a model of an individual's attitude toward risk. Moreover, our development of utility functions in this chapter is intended to help with the modeling of risk attitudes at a fundamental level, and our model may not be able to capture certain complicated psychological aspects. For example, some individuals may be extremely frightened by risk. Others may find that small wagers greatly increase their enjoyment in watching a sporting event, for example. Still others may find that waiting for the uncertainty to be resolved is a source of excitement and exhilaration, although concern about losing money is a source of anxiety. For some people, figuring out exactly what their feelings are toward risky alternatives may be extremely complicated and may depend on the amount at stake, the context of the risk, and the time horizon.

◆ INVESTING IN THE STOCK MARKET, REVISITED

If we have a utility function that translates from dollars to utility, how should we use it? The whole idea of a utility function is that it should help to choose from among alternatives that have uncertain payoffs. Instead of maximizing expected value, the decision maker should maximize expected utility. In a decision tree or influence-diagram payoff table, the net dollar payoffs would be replaced by the corresponding utility values and the analysis performed using those values. The best choice then should be the action with the highest expected utility.

As an example, let us reconsider the stock market–investment example from Chapters 5 and 12. You will recall that an investor has funds that he wishes to invest. He has three choices: a high-risk stock, a low-risk stock, or a savings account that would pay $500. If he invests in the stocks, he must pay a $200 brokerage fee.

With the two stocks his payoff depends on what happens to the market. If the market goes up, he will earn $1700 from the high-risk stock and $1200 from the low-risk stock. If the market stays at the same level, his payoffs for the high- and low-risk stocks will be $300 and $400, respectively. Finally, if the stock market goes down, he will lose $800 with the high-risk stock, but still earn $100 from the low-risk stock. The probabilities that the market will go up, stay the same, or go down are 0.5, 0.3, and 0.2, respectively.

Figure 13.4 shows his decision tree, including the brokerage fee and the payoffs for the two stocks under different market conditions. Note that the values at the ends of the branches are the *net* payoffs, taking into account both the brokerage fee and the investment payoff. Table 13.2 gives his utility function.

We already calculated the expected values of the three investments in Chapter 12. They are:

$$\text{EMV(High-Risk Stock)} = 580$$
$$\text{EMV(Low-Risk Stock)} = 540$$
$$\text{EMV(Savings Account)} = 500.$$

As a result, an expected-value maximizer would choose the high-risk stock.

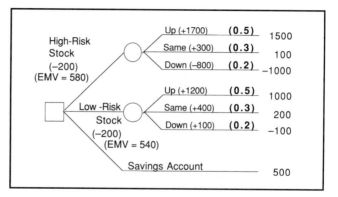

FIGURE 13.4 *Decision Tree for the Stock-Market Investor*

Dollar Value	Utility Value
1500	1.00
1000	0.86
500	0.65
200	0.52
100	0.46
−100	0.33
−1000	0.00

TABLE 13.2   *Utility Function for the Investment Problem*

Figure 13.5 shows the investor's decision tree with the utility values instead of the payoffs. Solving this decision tree, we calculate the expected utility (EU) for the three investments:

$$EU(\text{High-Risk Stock}) = 0.638$$
$$EU(\text{Low-Risk Stock}) = 0.652$$
$$EU(\text{Savings Account}) = 0.650.$$

Now the preferred action is to invest in the low-risk stock because it provides the highest expected utility, although it does not differ much from that for the savings account. You can see how the expected utilities make it possible to rank these investments in order of preference. According to the utility function we are using, this investor dislikes risk enough to find the high-risk stock the least preferred of his three alternatives.

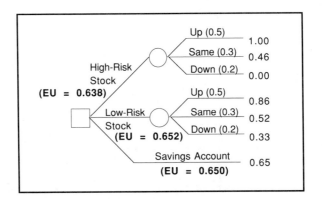

FIGURE 13.5   *Decision Tree for Stock-Market Investor — Utility Values Instead of Dollars*

◆ EXPECTED UTILITY, CERTAINTY EQUIVALENTS, AND RISK PREMIUMS

Two concepts are closely linked to the idea of expected utility. One is that of a *certainty equivalent*, or the amount of money that is equivalent in your mind to a given situation that involves uncertainty. For example, suppose you face the following gamble:

Win $2000 with probability 0.50.

Lose $20 with probability 0.50.

Now imagine that one of your friends is interested in taking your place. "Sure," you reply, "I'll sell it to you." After thought and discussion, you conclude that the least you would sell your position for is $300. If your friend cannot pay that much, then you would rather keep the gamble. (Of course, if your friend were to offer more, you would take it!)

Your certainty equivalent for the gamble is $300. This is a sure thing; no risk is involved. From this, the meaning of certainty equivalent becomes clear. If $300 is the least that you would accept for the gamble, then the gamble must be equivalent in your mind to a sure $300.

In the example at the beginning of the chapter, Harriman decided that he would pay the additional $600,000 simply to avoid the riskiness of the situation. His thinking at the time was that committing the additional money would ensure his control of the Northern Pacific Railroad. He indicated that he did not want to pay more, and so we can think of $600,000 as his certainty equivalent for the gamble of purchasing the shares more slowly and risking detection.

Let us again consider the stock-market investor. We can make certain inferences about his certainty equivalent for the gambles represented by the low-risk and high-risk stocks because we have information about his utility function. For example, his expected utility for the low-risk stock is 0.652, which is just a shade more than $U(\$500) = 0.650$. Thus, his certainty equivalent for the low-risk stock must be only a little more than $500. Likewise, his expected utility for the high-risk stock is 0.638, which is somewhat less than 0.650. Therefore, his certainty equivalent for the high-risk stock must be less that $500 but not as little as $200, which has a utility of 0.520.

You can see also that we can rank the investments by their certainty equivalents. The high-risk stock, having the lowest certainty equivalent, is the least preferred. The low-risk stock, on the other hand, has the highest certainty equivalent, and so is the most preferred. Ranking alternatives by their certainty equivalents is the same as ranking them by their expected utilities. If two alternatives have the same certainty equivalent, then they must have the same expected utility, and the decision maker would be indifferent to a choice between the two.

Closely related to the idea of a certainty equivalent is the notion of *risk premium*. The risk premium is defined as the difference between the EMV and the certainty equivalent:

Risk Premium = EMV − Certainty Equivalent.

Consider the gamble between winning $2000 and losing $20, each with probability 0.50. The EMV of this gamble is $990. On reflection, you assessed your certainty equivalent to be $300, and so your risk premium is

$$\text{Risk Premium} = \$990 - \$300$$
$$= \$690.$$

Because you were willing to trade the gamble for $300, you were willing to "give up" $690 in expected value in order to avoid the risk inherent in the gamble. You can think of the risk premium as the premium you pay (in the sense of a lost opportunity) to avoid the risk.

Figure 13.6 graphically ties together utility functions, certainty equivalents, and risk premiums. Notice that the certainty equivalent and the expected utility of a gamble are points that are "matched up" by the utility function. That is,

$$\text{EU}(\text{Gamble}) = \text{U}(\text{Certainty Equivalent}).$$

In words, the utility of the certainty equivalent is equal to the expected utility of the gamble. Because these two quantities are equal, the decision maker must be indifferent to the choice between them. After all, that is the meaning of certainty equivalent.

Now we can put all of the pieces together in Figure 13.6. Imagine a gamble has expected utility Y. The value Y is in utility units, and so we must first locate Y on the vertical axis. Trace a horizontal line from the expected utility point until the line intersects the utility curve. Now drop down to the horizontal axis to find the certainty equivalent. The difference between the expected value and the certainty equivalent is the risk premium.

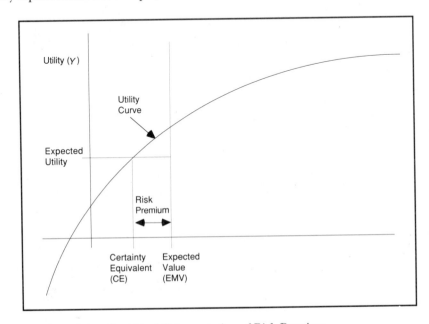

FIGURE 13.6   *Graphical Representation of Risk Premium*

For a risk-averse individual, the horizontal EU line reaches the concave utility curve before it reaches the vertical line that corresponds to the expected value. Thus, for a risk-averse individual the risk premium must be positive. If the utility function were convex, the horizontal EU line would reach the expected value before the utility curve. The certainty equivalent would be greater than the expected value, and so the risk premium would be negative. This would imply that the decision maker would have to be paid to give up an opportunity to gamble.

In any given situation, the certainty equivalent, expected value, and risk premium all depend on two factors: the decision maker's utility function and the probability distribution for the payoffs. The probability distribution for the payoffs determines the expected value. The values that the payoff can take combine with the probabilities to also determine the EMV. The utility function, coupled with the probability distribution, determines the expected utility and hence the certainty equivalent. The degree to which the utility curve is nonlinear determines the distance between the certainty equivalent and the expected payoff.

If the certainty equivalent for a gamble is assessed directly, then finding the risk premium is straightforward — simply calculate the EMV of the gamble and subtract the assessed certainty equivalent. In other cases, the decision maker may have assessed a utility function and now faces a particular gamble that he or she wishes to analyze. If so, there are four steps in finding the gamble's risk premium:

1. Find the EU for the gamble.
2. Find the certainty equivalent, or the sure amount that has the utility value equal to the EU that was found in Step 1.
3. Calculate the EMV for the gamble.
4. Subtract the certainty equivalent from the expected payoff to find the risk premium. This is the difference between the expected value of the risky situation and the sure amount for which the risky situation would be traded.

Here is a simple example. Using the hypothetical utility function given in Figure 13.7, we will find the risk premium for the following gamble:

Win $4000 with probability	0.40.
Win $2000 with probability	0.20.
Win $0 with probability	0.15.
Lose $2000 with probability	0.25.

The first step is to find the expected utility:

$$EU = 0.40 \ U(\$4000) + 0.20 \ U(\$2000) + 0.15 \ U(\$0) + 0.25 \ U(-\$2000)$$
$$= 0.40 \ (0.90) + 0.20 \ (0.82) + 0.15 \ (0.67) + 0.25 \ (0.38)$$
$$= 0.72.$$

The second line is simply a matter of estimating the utilities from Figure 13.7 and substituting them into the equation.

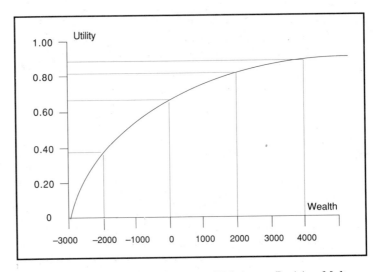

FIGURE 13.7   *Utility Function for a Risk-Averse Decision Maker*

For Step 2, the certainty equivalent is the sure amount that gives the same utility as the expected utility of the gamble. Figure 13.8 shows the process of finding the certainty equivalent for the gamble that has EU = 0.72. We start at the vertical axis with the utility value of 0.72, read across to the utility curve, and then drop down to the horizontal axis. From Figure 13.8, we can see that the certainty equivalent is approximately $400.

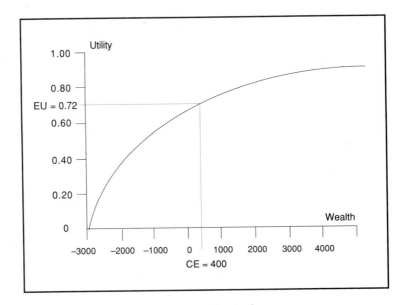

FIGURE 13.8   *Finding a Certainty Equivalent*

Step 3 calculates the expected payoff or EMV:

$$\text{EMV} = 0.40\ (\$4000) + 0.20\ (\$2000) + 0.15\ (\$0) + 0.25\ (-\$2000)$$
$$= \$1500.$$

Finally, in Step 4, we calculate the risk premium by subtracting the certainty equivalent from the expected payoff:

$$\text{Risk Premium} = \$1500 - \$400 = \$1100.$$

◆ KEEPING TERMS STRAIGHT

One problem that students often have is that of confusion about the terms that we use in utility theory. The basic idea, remember, is to use a utility function to translate dollars into utility units. If we compare two risky projects on the basis of expected utility (EU), we are working in utility units. When we calculate certainty equivalents or risk premiums, however, we are working in dollars. Thus, a certainty equivalent is not the same as the expected utility of a gamble. The two measurements provide equivalent information, but only in the sense that the certainty equivalent for a gamble is the sure amount that gives the same utility as the expected utility of the gamble. The translation from certainty equivalent to expected utility and back again is through the utility function, as depicted in Figures 13.6 and 13.8. Again, a certainty equivalent is a dollar amount, whereas expected utility is in utility units. Be careful to use these terms consistently.

◆ UTILITY FUNCTION ASSESSMENT

Different people have different risk attitudes and thus are willing to accept different levels of risk. Some are more prone to taking risks, while others are more conservative and avoid risk. Thus, assessing a utility function is a matter of subjective judgment, just like assessing subjective probabilities. In this section we will look at two utility-assessment approaches that are based on the idea of certainty equivalents. The following section introduces an alternative approach.

It is worth repeating at this point our credo about modeling and decision making. Remember that the objective of the decision-analysis exercise is to help you make a better decision. To do this, we construct a model, or representation, of the decision. When we assess a utility function, we are constructing a mathematical model or representation of preferences. This representation then is included in the overall model of the decision problem and is used to analyze the situation at hand. The objective is to find a way to represent preferences that incorporates risk attitudes. A perfect representation is not necessary. All that is required is a model that represents feelings about risk well enough to understand and analyze the current decision.

Assessment Using Certainty Equivalents

The first assessment method requires the decision maker to assess several certainty equivalents. Suppose you face an uncertain situation in which you may have $10 in the worst case, $100 in the best case, or possibly something in between. You have a variety of options, each of which leads to some uncertain payoff between $10 and $100. To evaluate the alternatives, you must assess your utility for wealth for values from $10 to $100.

We can get the first two points of your utility function by arbitrarily setting $U(100) = 1$ and $U(10) = 0$. This may seem a bit strange, but is easily explained. The idea of the utility function, remember, is to rank order risky situations. We can always take any utility function and rescale it — add a constant and multiply by a positive constant — so that the best outcome has a utility of 1 and the worst has a utility of 0. The rank ordering of risky situations in terms of expected utility will be the same for both the original and rescaled utility functions. What we are doing here is taking advantage of this ability to rescale. We are beginning the assessment process by setting two utility points. The remaining assessments then will be consistent with the scale set by these points. (We could just as well set the endpoints at 100 and 0, or 100 and −50, say. We are using 1 and 0 because this choice of endpoints turns out to be particularly convenient. But we will have to be careful not to confuse these utilities with probabilities!)

Now imagine that you have the opportunity to play the following lottery, which we will call a *reference lottery*:

Win $100 with probability 0.5.

Win $10 with probability 0.5.

What is the minimum amount for which you would be willing to sell your opportunity to play this game? $25? $30? Your job is to find your certainty equivalent (CE) for this reference gamble. A decision tree for your choice is shown in Figure 13.9.

Finding your certainty equivalent is where your subjective judgment comes into play. The CE undoubtedly will vary from person to person. Suppose that for this reference gamble your certainty equivalent is $30. That is, for $31 you would

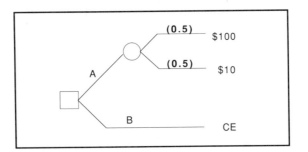

FIGURE 13.9   *A "Reference Gamble" for Assessing a Utility Function*
Your job is to find the certainty equivalent (CE) so that you are indifferent to options A and B.

take the money, but for $29 you would rather play the lottery; $30 must be your true indifference point.

The key to the rest of the analysis is this: *Because you are indifferent between $30 and the risky gamble, the utility of $30 must equal the expected utility of the gamble.* We know the utilities of $10 and $100, so we can figure out the expected utility of the gamble:

$$U(30) = 0.5\ U(100) + 0.5\ U(10)$$
$$= 0.5\ (1) + 0.5\ (0)$$
$$= 0.5.$$

We have found a third point on your utility curve. To find another, take a different reference lottery:

Win $100 with probability 0.5.

Win $30 with probability 0.5.

Now find your certainty equivalent for this new gamble. Again, the certainty equivalent will vary from person to person, but suppose that you settle on $50. We can do exactly what we did before, but with the new gamble. In this case, we can find the utility of $50 because we know $U(100)$ and $U(30)$ from the previous assessment.

$$U(50) = 0.5\ U(100) + 0.5\ U(30)$$
$$= 0.5\ (1) + 0.5\ (0.5)$$
$$= 0.75.$$

This is the fourth point on your utility curve.

Now consider the reference lottery:

Win $30 with probability 0.5.

Win $10 with probability 0.5.

Again you must assess your CE for this gamble. Suppose it turns out to be $18. Now we can do the familiar calculations:

$$U(18) = 0.5\ U(30) + 0.5\ U(10)$$
$$= 0.5\ (0.5) + 0.5\ (0)$$
$$= 0.25.$$

We now have five points on your utility curve, and we can graph and draw a curve through them. The graph is shown in Figure 13.10. A smooth curve drawn through the assessed points should be an adequate representation of your utility function for use in solving your decision problem.

Assessment Using Probabilities

The CE approach requires that you find a dollar amount that makes you indifferent between the gamble and the sure thing in Figure 13.9. Another ap-

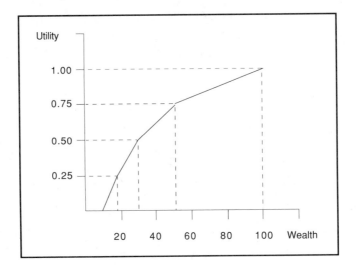

FIGURE 13.10   *Graph of the Utility Function Assessed Using the Certainty-Equivalent Approach*

proach involves setting the sure amount in Alternative B and adjusting the probability in the reference gamble to achieve indifference. We will call this the *probability-equivalent* (PE) assessment technique.

For example, suppose you want to know your utility for $65. This is not one of the certainty equivalents that you assessed, and thus U(65) is unknown. You could make an educated guess. Based on the previous assessments and the graph in Figure 13.10, U(65) must be between 0.75 and 1.00; it probably is around 0.85. But rather than guess, you can assess the value directly. Consider the reference lottery:

Win $100 with probability *p*.

Win $10 with probability (1 − *p*).

This gamble is shown in Figure 13.11.

To find your utility value for $65, adjust *p* until you are indifferent between the sure $65 and the reference gamble. That is, think about various probabilities that make the chance of winning $100 greater or less until you are indifferent between Alternatives C and D in Figure 13.11. Now you can find U(65) because you know that U(100) = 1 and U(10) = 0:

$$U(65) = p\, U(100) + (1 - p)\, U(10)$$
$$= p\,(1) + (1 - p)\,(0)$$
$$= p.$$

The probability that makes you indifferent just happens to be your utility value for $65. For example, if you chose *p* = 0.87 to achieve indifference, then U(65) = 0.87.

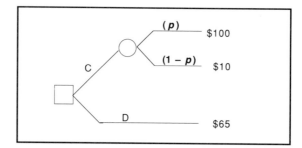

FIGURE 13.11   *A Reference Gamble*
for Assessing the Utility of $65 Using the Probability-
Equivalent Method

◆ RISK TOLERANCE AND THE EXPONENTIAL UTILITY FUNCTION

The assessment process just described works well for assessing a utility function subjectively, and it can be used in any situation, although it can involve a fair number of assessments. An alternative approach is to base the assessment on a particular mathematical function, such as one of those that we introduced early in the chapter. In particular, let us consider the *exponential utility function*:

$$U(x) = 1 - e^{-x/R}.$$

This utility function is based on the constant e = 2.71828 . . . , the base of natural logarithms. This function is concave, and thus can be used to represent risk-averse preferences. As x becomes large, $U(x)$ approaches 1. The utility of zero, $U(0)$, is equal to 0, and the utility for negative x (being in debt) is negative.

In the exponential utility function, R is a parameter that determines how risk-averse the utility function is. In particular, R is called the *risk tolerance*. Larger values of R make the exponential utility function flatter, while smaller values make it more concave or more risk-averse. Thus, if you are less risk-averse — if you can tolerate more risk — you would assess a larger value for R to obtain a flatter utility function. If you are less tolerant of risk, then you would assess a smaller R and have a more curved utility function.

How can R be determined? A variety of ways exist, but it turns out that R has a very intuitive interpretation that makes its assessment relatively easy. Consider the gamble

> Win $\$Y$ with probability 0.5.
>
> Lose $\$Y/2$ with probability 0.5.

Would you be willing to take this gamble if Y were $100? $2000? $35,000? At what point would the risk become intolerable? The decision tree is shown in Figure 13.12.

The largest value of Y for which you would prefer to take the gamble rather than not take it is approximately equal to your risk tolerance. This is the value

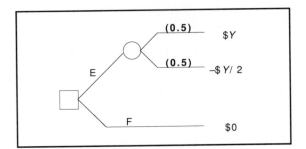

FIGURE 13.12   *Assessing Your Risk Tolerance*
Find the largest value of *Y* for which you
would prefer Alternative E.

that you can use for *R* in your exponential utility function. For example, suppose
that after considering the decision tree in Figure 13.12 you conclude that the
largest *Y* for which you would take the gamble is *Y* = $900. Hence, *R* = $900. Using this assessment in the exponential utility function would result in the utility
function

$$U(x) = 1 - e^{-x/900}.$$

This exponential utility function provides the translation from dollars to utility
units.

Once you have your *R* value and your exponential utility function, it is fairly
easy to find certainty equivalents. For example, suppose that you face the following gamble:

Win $2000 with probability 0.4.

Win $1000 with probability 0.4.

Win $500 with probability 0.2.

The expected utility for this gamble is

$$EU = 0.4 \, U(\$2000) + 0.4 \, U(\$1000) + 0.2 \, U(\$500)$$
$$= 0.4 \, (0.8916) + 0.4 \, (0.6708) + 0.2 \, (0.4262)$$
$$= 0.7102.$$

To find the CE we must work backward through the utility function. We want to
find the value *x* such that $U(x) = 0.7102$. Set up the equation

$$0.7102 = 1 - e^{-x/900}.$$

Subtract 1 from each side to get

$$-0.2898 = -e^{-x/900}.$$

Multiply through to eliminate the minus signs:

$$0.2898 = e^{-x/900}.$$

Now we can take natural logs of both sides to eliminate the exponential term:

$$\ln (0.2898) = \ln(e^{-x/900}) = -x/900.$$

The rule (from algebra) is that $\ln(e^y) = y$. Now we simply solve for x:

$$\ln (0.2898) = -x/900$$
$$x = -900[\ln(0.2898)]$$
$$= \$1114.71.$$

The procedure above requires that you use the exponential utility function to translate the dollar outcomes into utilities, find the expected utility, and finally convert to dollars to find the exact certainty equivalent. That can be a lot of work, especially if there are many outcomes to consider. Fortunately, an approximation is available from McNamee and Celona (1987). Suppose you can figure out the expected value and variance of the payoffs. Then the CE is approximately:

Certainty Equivalent $\approx$ Expected Value -0.5[Variance/Risk Tolerance].

In symbols,

$$CE \approx \mu - \frac{0.5\sigma^2}{R},$$

where μ and σ^2 are the expected value and variance, respectively. For example, in the gamble above, the expected value (EMV or μ) equals \$1300, and the standard deviation (σ) equals \$600. Thus, the approximation gives

$$CE \approx \$1300 - \frac{0.5(\$600)^2}{900}$$
$$\approx \$1100.$$

The approximation is within \$15. That's pretty good! This approximation is especially useful for continuous random variables or problems where the expected value and variance are relatively easy to assess compared to assessing the entire probability distribution. The approximation will be closest to the actual value when the outcome's probability distribution is a symmetric, bell-shaped curve.

What are reasonable R values? For an individual's utility function, the appropriate value for R clearly depends on the individual's risk attitude. As indicated, the less risk-averse a person is, the larger R is. Suppose, however, that an individual or a group (a board of directors, say) has to make a decision on behalf of a corporation. It is important that these decision makers adopt a decision-making attitude that is based on corporate goals and acceptable risk levels for the corporation. This can be quite different from an individual's personal risk attitude; the individual director may be unwilling to risk \$10 million, even though the corporation can afford such a loss. Howard (1988) suggests certain guidelines for determining a corporation's risk tolerance in terms of total sales, net income, or equity. Reasonable values of R appear to be approximately 6.4% of total sales, 1.24 times net income, or 15.7% of equity. These figures are based on observations that Howard has made in the course of consulting with various companies. More research may refine these figures, and it may turn out that different industries have different ratios for determining reasonable R's.

Using the exponential utility function seems like magic, doesn't it? One assessment, and we are finished! Why bother with all of those certainty equivalents that we discussed above? You know, however, that you never get something for nothing, and that definitely is the case here. The exponential utility function has a specific kind of curvature and implies a certain kind of risk attitude. This risk attitude is called *constant risk aversion*. Essentially it means that no matter how much wealth you have — how much money in your pocket or bank account — you would view a particular gamble in the same way. The gamble's risk premium would be the same no matter how much money you have. Is constant risk aversion reasonable? Maybe it is for some people. Many individuals might be less risk-averse if they had more wealth.

In later sections of this chapter we will study the exponential utility function in more detail, especially with regard to constant risk aversion. The message here is that the exponential utility function is most appropriate for people who really believe that they would view gambles the same way regardless of their wealth level. But even if this is not true for you, the exponential utility function can be a useful tool for modeling preferences. The next section shows how sensitivity analysis can be performed in terms of risk tolerance.

◆ RISK TOLERANCE AND SENSITIVITY ANALYSIS: EAGLE AIRLINES, REVISITED

In Chapter 5 we learned how to use sensitivity analysis to help with probability assessment. We also can use sensitivity analysis to deal with preferences. The idea of risk tolerance suggests a tidy way to perform the analysis. Essentially, we will vary the risk tolerance in the exponential utility function to determine at what point the decision changes.

Let us reconsider the Eagle Airlines case that we used for sensitivity analysis in Chapter 5 (pages 113–114). Recall that the question was whether Dick Carothers should purchase an additional aircraft and expand Eagle Airlines' operations. After considerable modeling, we worked the problem down to the consideration of three uncertain variables: the capacity of the scheduled flights (proportion of seats sold), the operating cost, and the total number of hours flown during a year. Figure 13.13 shows the decision tree with specific probabilities on the branches. Using these probabilities, we calculate the EMV for purchasing the airplane as $11,736, which is considerably more than $4200. It also is true, however, that purchasing the airplane is substantially riskier than investing in the money market. If Carothers is risk-averse, just how risk-averse can he be and still be willing to purchase the airplane? Or in terms of his risk tolerance, how low could his risk tolerance be before he would rather invest in the money market?

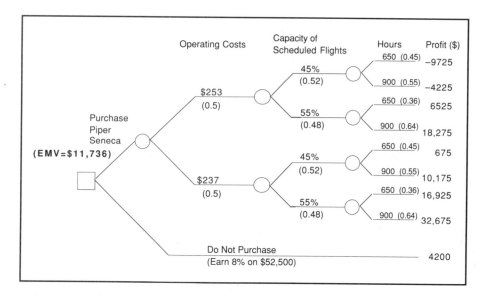

FIGURE 13.13   *Eagle Airlines' Decision Tree*

Answering this question is conceptually simple, but the calculations are tedious. We will use the exponential utility function. Conceptually, all we want to do is find the critical value for R such that the expected utility of purchasing the airplane equals the expected utility of investing in the money market. Then the question is whether Carothers's risk tolerance is above or below the critical value. If it is above the critical value, then he should buy the airplane; if it is less, then he should go with the less risky money market.

What is the easiest way to find the critical value? The simplest is to use a computer and search for the R value that makes the two expected utilities equal. Some decision-analysis programs allow the user to specify a value for R, the risk tolerance. In this case, it is a simple matter to try different values for R until the critical one is found.

An electronic spreadsheet provides a convenient environment for sensitivity analysis with respect to risk tolerance. The expected utility calculations can be programmed easily into the cells of the spreadsheet. Figure 13.14 shows a Microsoft Excel spreadsheet with a table created to perform a sensitivity analysis on the risk tolerance. The decision tree, which is not shown but is in the upper part of the spreadsheet, has been created using macro commands to enter the decision and chance nodes shown in Figure 13.13. Cells B5 and B6 (not shown) contain the final calculations of expected utility for purchasing the Piper Seneca and the utility for earning \$4200 in the money market, each case using the R value specified in Cell B18. In Cell B20, a formula reports which of the two alternatives has the greater expected utility. A table in Cells A20–B33 has been created in which the R values along the right-hand side are used in the expected utility calculations. This table is created by selecting the block of cells, choosing the "Table" command, and specifying B18 as the column-input cell. It may be

Eagle Risk Sensitivity

	A	B	C	D	E
16	EAGLE AIRLINES RISK SENSITIVITY				
17					
18	R=	10250			
19					
20		M			
21	10200	M			
22	10210	M			
23	10220	M			
24	10230	M			
25	10240	M			
26	10250	M			
27	10260	S			
28	10270	S			
29	10280	S			
30	10290	S			
31	10300	S			
32	10310	S			
33	10320	S			
34					

FIGURE 13.14 *Using a Spreadsheet to Find the Critical Value for* R *in the Eagle Airlines Problem*

worthwhile to recalculate the table several times, each time using a narrower range of R values. In the first calculation of the table, using R values over a very wide range helps to find the approximate location of the critical R. Then the table can be calculated several times, each using a finer grid to home in on the precise critical value. As you can see in Figure 13.14, the table checks R values that differ by only \$10.

As Figure 13.14 also shows, the critical R value is approximately \$10,250. Now Carothers must ask whether he would be willing to accept a gamble in which he would have the same chance of winning \$10,250 or losing \$5125. If he concludes that he would not take this gamble, then his risk tolerance must be smaller than \$10,250, and he should not purchase the airplane. But if he would participate gladly in this gamble, then his risk tolerance must be greater than \$10,250, and he should buy the airplane.

♦ DECREASING AND CONSTANT RISK AVERSION (OPTIONAL)

In this section we will consider how individuals might deal with risky investments. Suppose you had \$1000 to invest. How would you feel about investing \$500 in an extremely risky venture in which you might lose the entire \$500? Now suppose you have saved more money and have \$20,000. Now how would you feel about that extremely risky venture? Is it more or less attractive to you? How do you think a person's degree of risk aversion changes with wealth?

Decreasing Risk Aversion

If an individual's preferences show *decreasing risk aversion*, then the risk premium decreases if a constant amount is added to all payoffs in a gamble. Expressed informally, decreasing risk aversion means the more money you have, the less nervous you are about a particular bet.

For example, suppose an individual's utility curve can be described by a logarithmic function:

$$U(x) = \ln(x),$$

where x is the wealth or payoff, and $\ln(x)$ is the natural logarithm of x. Using this logarithmic utility function, consider the gamble:

> Win $10 with probability 0.5.
>
> Win $40 with probability 0.5.

To find the certainty equivalent, we first find the expected utility. The utility values for $10 and $40 are:

$$U(\$10) = \ln(10) = 2.3026.$$
$$U(\$40) = \ln(40) = 3.6889.$$

Calculating expected utility:

$$EU = 0.5\ (2.3026) + 0.5\ (3.6889) = 2.9957.$$

To find the certainty equivalent, you must find the certain value x that has $U(x) = 2.9957$; thus, set the utility function equal to 2.9957:

$$2.9957 = \ln(x).$$

Now solve for x. To remove the logarithm, we take antilogs:

$$e^{2.9957} = e^{\ln(x)} = x.$$

The rule here corresponds to what we did with the exponential function. Here we have $e^{\ln(y)} = y$. Finally, we simply calculate $e^{2.9957}$:

$$x = e^{2.9957} = \$20 = CE.$$

To find the risk premium, we need the expected payoff, which is

$$EMV = 0.5\ (\$10) + .5\ (\$40) = \$25.$$

Thus, the risk premium is $EMV - CE = \$25 - \$20 = \$5$.

Using the same procedure, we can find risk premiums for the lotteries as shown in Table 13.3. Notice that the sequence of lotteries is constructed so that each is like having the previous one plus $10. For example, the $20–$50 lottery is like having the $10–$40 lottery plus a $10 bill. The risk premium decreases with each $10 addition. The decreasing risk premium reflects decreasing risk aversion, which is a property of the logarithmic utility function.

50–50 Gamble Between ($)	Expected Value ($)	Certainty Equivalent ($)	Risk Premium ($)
10, 40	25	20.00	5.00
20, 50	35	31.62	3.38
30, 60	45	42.43	2.57
40, 70	55	52.92	2.08

TABLE 13.3 *Risk Premiums from Logarithmic Utility Function*

An Investment Example

For another example, suppose that an entrepreneur is considering a new business investment. To participate, the entrepreneur must invest $5000. There is a 25% chance that the investment will earn back the $5000, leaving her just as well off as if she had not made the investment. But there is also a 45% chance that she will lose the $5000 altogether, although this is counterbalanced by a 30% chance that the investment will return the original $5000 plus an additional $10,000. Figure 13.15 shows the entrepreneur's decision tree.

We will assume that this entrepreneur's preferences can be modeled with the logarithmic utility function, $U(x) = \ln(x)$, where x is interpreted as total wealth. Suppose that the investor now has $10,000. Should she make the investment or avoid it?

The easiest way to solve this problem is to calculate the expected utility of the investment and compare it with the expected utility of the alternative, which is to do nothing. The expected utility of doing nothing simply is the utility of the current wealth, or $U(10,000)$, which is

$$U(10,000) = \ln(10,000) = 9.2103.$$

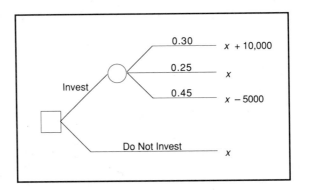

FIGURE 13.15 *Entrepreneur's Investment Decision*
Current wealth is denoted by x.

The expected utility of the investment is easy to calculate:

$$EU = 0.30 \ U(20,000) + 0.25 \ U(10,000) + 0.45 \ U(5000)$$
$$= 0.30 \ (9.9035) + 0.25 \ (9.2103) + 0.45 \ (8.5172)$$
$$= 9.1064.$$

Because the expected utility of the investment is less than the utility of not investing, the investment should not be made.

Now, suppose that several years have passed. The utility function has not changed, but other investments have paid off handsomely, and she currently has $70,000. Should she undertake the project now? Recalculating with a base wealth of $70,000 rather than $10,000, we find that the utility of doing nothing is $U(70,000) = 11.1563$, and the EU for the investment is 11.1630. Now the expected utility of the investment is greater than the utility of doing nothing, and so she should invest.

The point of these examples is to show how decreasing risk aversion determines the way in which a decision maker views risky prospects. As indicated, the wealthier a decreasingly risk-averse decision maker is, the less anxious he or she will be about taking a particular gamble. Generally speaking, decreasing risk aversion makes sense when we think about risk attitudes and the way that many people appear to deal with risky situations. Many would feel better about investing money in the stock market if they were wealthier to begin with. For such reasons, the logarithmic utility function is commonly used by economists and decision theorists as a model of typical risk attitudes.

Constant Risk Aversion

An individual displays constant risk aversion if the risk premium for a gamble does not depend on the initial amount of wealth held by the decision maker. Intuitively, the idea is that a constantly risk-averse person would be just as anxious about taking a bet regardless of the amount of money available.

If an individual is constantly risk-averse, the utility function is exponential. It would have the following form:

$$U(x) = 1 - e^{-x/R}.$$

For example, suppose that the decision maker has assessed a risk tolerance of $35:

$$U(x) = 1 - e^{-x/35}.$$

We can perform the same kind of analysis that we did with the logarithmic utility function above. Consider the gamble:

Win $10 with probability 0.5.

Win $40 with probability 0.5.

As before, the expected payoff is $25. To find the CE, we must find the expected utility, which requires plugging the amounts $10 and $40 into the utility function:

$$U(10) = 1 - e^{-10/35} = 0.2485.$$
$$U(40) = 1 - e^{-40/35} = 0.6811.$$

Thus, EU = 0.5 (0.2485) + 0.5 (0.6811) = 0.4648. To find the certainty equivalent, set the utility function to 0.4648. The value for x that gives the utility of 0.4648 is the gamble's CE:

$$0.4648 = 1 - e^{-x/35}.$$

Now we can solve for x as we did earlier when working with the exponential utility function:

$$0.5352 = e^{-x/35}$$
$$\ln(0.5352) = -0.6251 = -x/35$$
$$x = 0.6251(35) = \$21.88 = CE.$$

Finally, the expected payoff (EMV) is $25, and so the risk premium is

$$\text{Risk Premium} = \text{EMV} - \text{CE} = \$25 - \$21.88 = \$3.12.$$

Using the same procedure, we can find the risk premium for each gamble in Table 13.4. The risk premium stays the same as long as the difference between the payoffs does not change. Adding a constant amount to both sides of the gamble does not change the decision maker's attitude toward the gamble.

Alternatively, you can think about this as a situation where you have a bet in which you may win $15 or lose $15. In the first gamble above, you face this bet with $25 in your pocket. In the constant risk-aversion situation, the way you feel about the bet (as reflected in the risk premium) is the same regardless of how much money is added to your pocket. In the decreasing risk-aversion situation, adding something to your pocket made you less risk-averse toward the bet, thus resulting in a lower risk premium.

Figure 13.16 plots the two utility functions on the same graph. They have been rescaled so that $U(10) = 0$ and $U(100) = 1$ in each case. Note their similarity. It does not take a large change in the utility curve's shape to alter the nature of the individual's risk attitude.

Is constant risk aversion appropriate? Consider the kinds of risks that railroad barons such as E. H. Harriman undertook. Would a person like Harriman

50–50 Gamble Between	Expected Value	Certainty Equivalent	Risk Premium
10, 40	25	21.88	3.12
20, 50	35	31.88	3.12
30, 60	45	41.88	3.12
40, 70	55	51.88	3.12

TABLE 13.4   *Risk Premiums from Exponential Utility Function*

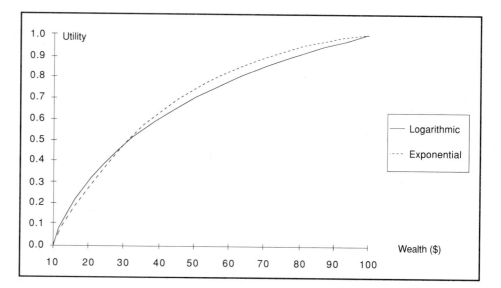

FIGURE 13.16   *Logarithmic and Exponential Utility Functions Plotted over the Range of $10 to $100*

have been willing to risk millions of dollars on the takeover of another railroad had he not already been fairly wealthy? The argument easily can be made that the more wealth one has, the easier it is to take larger risks. Thus, decreasing risk aversion appears to provide a more appropriate model of preferences than does constant risk aversion. This is an important point to keep in mind if you decide to use the exponential utility function and the risk-tolerance parameter; this utility function displays constant risk aversion.

After all is said and done, while the concepts of decreasing or constant risk aversion may be intriguing from the point of view of a decision maker who is interested in modeling his or her risk attitude, precise determination of a decision maker's utility function is not yet possible. Decision theorists still are learning how to elicit and measure utility functions. Many unusual effects arise from human nature; we will study some of these in the next chapter. It would be an overstatement to suggest that it is possible to determine precisely the degree of an individual's risk aversion or whether he or she is decreasingly risk averse. It is a difficult enough problem just to determine whether someone is risk-averse or risk-seeking!

Thus, it may be reasonable to use the exponential utility function as an approximation in modeling preferences and risk attitudes. A quick assessment of risk tolerance, and you are on your way. And if that even seems a bit strained, then it is always possible to use the sensitivity-analysis approach; it may be that a precise assessment of the risk tolerance is not necessary.

◆ SOME CAVEATS

A few things remain to be said about utilities. These are thoughts to keep in mind as you work through utility assessments and use utilities in decision problems.

1. Utilities do not add up. That is, $U(A + B) \neq U(A) + U(B)$. This actually is the whole point of having a nonlinear utility function. Thus, when using utilities in a decision analysis, you must calculate net payoffs or net contributions at the endpoints of the decision tree before transforming to utility values.

2. Utility differences do not express strength of preferences. Suppose that $U(A_1) - U(A_2) > U(A_3) - U(A_4)$. This does not necessarily mean that you would rather go from A_2 to A_1 instead of from A_4 to A_3. Utility only provides a numerical scale for ordering preferences, not a measure of their strengths. Whether this is reasonable is a matter of some debate. For example, von Winterfeldt and Edwards (1986) give the following example: You are first told that you will receive \$100, and then told that you actually will receive \$500, and then finally told that the actual payment will be \$10,000. It would indeed be a pleasant surprise to go from \$100 to \$500, but for most of us, the delight we would experience in going from \$500 to \$10,000 would eclipse the difference between \$100 and \$500. Von Winterfeldt and Edwards argue that we can make judgments of just this sort. Whether one agrees or not, it is necessary to interpret utility carefully in this regard.

3. Utilities are not comparable from person to person. A utility function is a subjective personal statement of an individual's preferences, and so provides no basis for comparing utilities among individuals.

◇ SUMMARY

In this chapter we have explored some basic concepts that underlie risk and return trade-offs, with the aim of being able to understand how to model a decision maker's risk preferences. We discussed the notion of a risk premium (EMV – CE), which can be thought of as a measure of how risk-averse a decision maker is in regard to a particular risky situation. The basic procedure for assessing a utility function requires comparison of lotteries with riskless payoffs. Once a utility function has been determined, the procedure is to replace dollar payoffs in a decision tree or influence diagram with utility values and solve the problem to find the option with the greatest expected utility. We also studied the exponential utility function and the notion of risk tolerance. Because of its nature, the exponential utility function is particularly useful for modeling preferences in decision analysis. The concepts of decreasing and constant risk aversion also were discussed. ◆

◇ EXERCISES

13.1 Why is it important for decision makers to consider their attitudes toward risk?

13.2 We have not given a specific definition of risk. How would you define it? Give examples of lotteries that vary in riskiness in terms of your definition of risk.

13.3 Explain in your own words the idea of a certainty equivalent.

13.4 Explain in your own words the idea of risk tolerance. How does it apply to utility functions other than the exponential utility function?

13.5 Suppose a decision maker has the utility function shown in Table 13.1 (page 367). An investment opportunity has EMV $1236 and expected utility 0.93. Find the certainty equivalent for this investment and the risk premium.

13.6 A decision maker has assessed his risk tolerance as $1210. Assume that his preferences can be modeled with an exponential utility function.

    a. Find U($1000), U($800), U($0), and U(–$1250).

    b. Find the expected utility for an investment that has the following payoff distribution:

$$P(\$1000) = 0.33$$
$$P(\$800) = 0.21$$
$$P(\$0) = 0.33$$
$$P(-\$1250) = 0.13.$$

    c. Find the exact certainty equivalent for the investment and the risk premium.

    d. Find the approximate certainty equivalent using the expected value and variance of the payoffs.

    e. Another investment possibility has expected value $2400 and standard deviation $300. Find the approximate certainty equivalent for this investment.

13.7 Many firms evaluate investment projects individually on the basis of expected value, and at the same time maintain diversified holdings in order to reduce risk. Does this make sense in light of our discussion of risk attitudes in this chapter?

13.8 A friend of yours lives in Reno. He has life insurance, homeowner's insurance, and automobile insurance. He also regularly plays the quarter slot machines in the casinos. What kind of a utility function might explain this kind of behavior? How else might you explain his behavior?

13.9 Two risky gambles were proposed at the beginning of the chapter:

    Game 1   Win $30 with probability 0.5.
                      Lose $1 with probability 0.5.

    Game 2   Win $2000 with probability 0.5.
                      Lose $1900 with probability 0.5.

Many of us would probably pay to play Game 1, but would have to be paid to participate in Game 2. Is this true for you? How much would you pay (or have to be paid) to take part in either game?

◇ QUESTIONS AND PROBLEMS

13.10 **St. Petersburg Paradox.** Consider the following game that you have been invited to play by an acquaintance who always pays his debts. Your acquaintance will flip a fair coin. If it comes up heads, you win $2. If it comes up tails, he flips the coin again. If heads occurs on the second toss, you win $4. If tails, he flips again. If heads occurs on the third toss, you win $8, and if tails, he flips again, and so on. Your payoff is an uncertain amount with the following probabilities:

Payoff	Probability
2	0.50
4	0.25
8	0.125
.	.
.	.
.	.
2^n	0.5^n
.	.
.	.
.	.

(where n is the number of the toss when the first head occurs)

This is a good game to play because you are bound to come out ahead. There is no possible outcome from which you can lose. How much would you pay to play this game? $10? $20? What is the expected value of the game? Would you be indifferent between playing the game and having the expected value for sure?

13.11   Assess your utility function in two different ways.

   a. Use the certainty-equivalent approach to assess your utility function for wealth over a range of $100 to $20,000.

   b. Use the probability-equivalent approach to assess U($1500), U($5600), U($9050), and U($13,700). Are these assessments consistent with the assessments made in part a? Plot these assessments and those from part a on the same graph and compare them.

13.12   Assess your risk tolerance (R). Now rescale your exponential utility function — the one you obtain by substituting your R value into the exponential utility function — so that U($100) = 0 and U($20,000) = 1. (That is, find constants a and b so that $a + b[1 - e^{-100/R}] = 0$ and $a + b[1 - e^{-20,000/R}] = 1$.) Now plot the rescaled utility function on the same graph with the utility assessments from Problem 13.11. How do your assessments compare?

13.13   Let us return to the Texaco–Pennzoil example from Chapter 4 and think about Liedtke's risk attitude. Suppose that Liedtke's utility function is given by the utility function in Table 13.5.

Payoff	Utility
10.3	1.00
5.0	0.75
3.0	0.60
2.0	0.45
0.0	0.00

TABLE 13.5   *Utility Function for Liedtke*

a. Graph this utility function. Based on this graph, how would you classify Liedtke's attitude toward risk?

b. Use the utility function in conjunction with the decision tree sketched in Figure 4.2 (page 69) to solve Liedtke's problem. With these utilities, what strategy should he pursue? Should he still counteroffer $5 billion? What if Texaco counteroffers $3 billion? Is your answer consistent with your response to part a?

c. Based on this utility function, what is the least amount (approximately) that Liedtke should agree to in a settlement? (*Hint*: Find a sure amount that gives him the same expected utility that he gets for going to court.) What does this suggest regarding plausible counteroffers that Liedtke might make?

13.14 Of course, Liedtke is not operating by himself in the Texaco–Pennzoil case; he must report to a board of directors. Table 13.6 gives utility functions for three different directors. Draw graphs of these. How would you classify each director in terms of his or her attitude toward risk? What would be the strategies of each? (That is, what would each one do with respect to Texaco's current offer, and how would each react to a Texaco counteroffer of $3 billion? To answer this question, you must solve the decision tree — calculate expected utilities — for *each* director.)

13.15 How do you think Liedtke (Problem 13.13) and the directors in Problem 13.14 will be able to reconcile their differences?

13.16 Rescale the utility function for Director A in Problem 13.14 so that it ranges between 0 and 1. That is, find constants a and b so that when you multiply the utility function by a and then add b, the utility for $10.30 is 1 and the utility for $0 is 0. Graph the rescaled utility function and compare it to the graph of the original utility function. Use the rescaled utility function to solve the Texaco–Pennzoil decision tree. Is the optimal choice consistent with the one you found in Problem 13.14?

13.17 What if Hugh Liedtke were risk-averse? Based on Figure 4.2 (page 69), find a critical value for Hugh Liedtke's risk tolerance. If his risk tolerance is low enough (very risk-averse), he would accept the $2-billion offer. How small would his risk tolerance have to be for EU(Accept $2 Billion) to be greater than EU(Counteroffer $3 Billion)?

13.18 The idea of dominance criteria and risk aversion come together in an interesting way, leading to a different kind of dominance. If two risky gambles have the same expected payoff, on what basis might a risk-averse individual choose between them without performing a complete utility analysis?

	Utility		
Payoff	**Director A**	**Director B**	**Director C**
10.3	3.0	100	42.05
5.0	2.9	30	23.50
3.0	2.8	15	16.50
2.0	2.6	8	13.00
0.0	1.0	0	6.00

TABLE 13.6   *Utility Functions for Three Pennzoil Directors*

13.19   This problem is related to the ideas of dominance that we discussed in Chapters 4 and 8. Investment D below is said to show "second-order stochastic dominance" over Investment C. In this problem, it is up to you to explain why D dominates C.

You are contemplating two alternative uncertain investments, whose distributions for payoffs are as below.

	Probabilities	
Payoff	Investment C	Investment D
50	1/3	1/4
100	1/3	1/2
150	1/3	1/4

a. If your preference function is given by $U(x) = 1 - e^{-x/100}$, calculate EU for both C and D. Which would you choose?

b. Plot the CDFs for C and D on the same graph. How do they compare? Use the graph to explain intuitively why any risk-averse decision maker would prefer D. (*Hint*: Think about the concave shape of a risk-averse utility function.)

13.20   Utility functions must not necessarily relate to dollar values. Here is a problem in which we know little about five abstract outcomes. What is important, however, is that a person who does know what A–E represent should be able to compare the outcomes using the lottery procedures we have studied.

A decision maker faces a risky gamble in which she may obtain one of five outcomes. Label the outcomes A, B, C, D, and E. A is the most preferred, and E is least preferred. She has made the following three assessments.

◆ She is indifferent between having C for sure or a lottery in which she wins A with probability 0.5 or E with probability 0.5.
◆ She is indifferent between having B for sure or a lottery in which she wins A with probability 0.4 or C with probability 0.6.
◆ She is indifferent between these two lotteries:

No. 1 — a 50% chance at B and a 50% chance at D.
No. 2 — a 50% chance at A and a 50% chance at E.

What are $U(A)$, $U(B)$, $U(C)$, $U(D)$, and $U(E)$?

13.21   You have considered insuring a particular item of property (such as an expensive camera, your computer, or your Stradivarius violin), but after considering the risks and the insurance premium quoted, you have no clear preference for either purchasing the insurance or taking the risk. The insurance company then tells you about a new scheme called "probabilistic insurance." You pay half the above premium, but have coverage only in the sense that in the case of a claim there is a probability of one-half that you will be asked to pay the other half of the premium and will be completely covered, or that you will not be covered and will have your premium returned. The insurance company can be relied on to be fair in flipping the coin to determine whether or not you are covered.

a. Do you consider yourself to be risk-averse?

b. Would you purchase probabilistic insurance?

c. Draw a decision tree for this problem.

d. Show that a risk-averse individual always should prefer the probabilistic insurance.

(*Hint*: This is a difficult problem. To solve it you must be sure to consider that you are indifferent between the regular insurance and no insurance. Write out the equation relating these two alternatives and see what it implies. Another strategy is to select a specific utility function — the log utility function $U(x) = \log(x)$, say — and then find values for the probability of a claim, your wealth, the insurance premium, and the value of your piece of property so that the utility of paying the insurance premium is equal to the expected utility of no insurance. Now use these values to calculate the expected utility of the probabilistic insurance. What is the result?)

13.22 An investor with assets of $10,000 has an opportunity to invest $5000 in a venture that is equally likely to pay either $15,000 or nothing. The investor's utility function can be described by the log utility function $U(x) = \ln(x)$, where x is his total wealth.

a. What should the investor do?

b. Suppose the investor places a bet with a friend before making the investment decision. The bet is for $1000; if a fair coin lands heads up, the investor wins $1000, but if it lands tails up, the investor pays $1000 to his friend. Only after the bet has been resolved will the investor decide whether or not to invest in the venture. What is an appropriate strategy for the investor? If he wins the bet, should he invest? What if he loses the bet?

c. Describe a real-life situation in which an individual might find it appropriate to gamble before deciding on a course of action.

[*Source*: Bell, D. E. (1988) "Value of Pre-Decision Side Bets for Utility Maximizers." *Management Science*, 34, 797–800.]

13.23 A bettor with utility function $U(x) = \ln(x)$, where x is total wealth, has a choice between the following two alternatives:

A: Win $10,000 with probability 0.2.
Win $1000 with probability 0.8.

B: Win $3000 with probability 0.9.
Lose $2000 with probability 0.1.

a. If the bettor currently has $2500, should he choose A or B?

b. Repeat a, assuming the bettor has $5000.

c. Repeat a, assuming the bettor has $10,000.

d. Do you think that this pattern of choices between A and B is reasonable? Why or why not?

[*Source*: Bell, D. E. (1989) "One-Switch Utility Functions and a Measure of Risk." *Management Science*, 34, 1416–1424.]

13.24 Buying and selling prices for risky investments obviously are related to certainty equivalents. This problem, however, shows that the prices depend on exactly what is owned in the first place!

Suppose that Peter Brown's utility for total wealth (*A*) can be represented by the utility function $U(A) = \ln(A)$. He currently has $1000 in cash. A business deal of interest to him yields a reward of $100 with probability 0.5 and $0 with probability 0.5.

a. If he owns this business deal in addition to the $1000, what is the smallest amount for which he would sell the deal?

b. Suppose he does not own the deal. What equation must be solved to find the largest amount he would be willing to pay for the deal?

c. For part b, it turns out that the most he would pay is $48.75, which is not exactly the same as the answer in part a. Can you explain why the amounts are different?

d. (*Extra credit for algebra hotshots.*) Solve your equation in part b to verify the answer ($48.75) given in part c.

[*Source*: This problem was suggested by R. L. Winkler.]

13.25 We discussed decreasing and constant risk aversion. Are there other possibilities? Think about this as you work through this problem.

Suppose that a person's utility function for total wealth is

$$U(A) = 200A - A^2 \qquad \text{for } 0 \le A \le 100,$$

where A represents total wealth in thousands of dollars.

a. Graph this preference function. How would you classify this person with regard to her attitude toward risk?

b. If the person's total assets are currently $10K, should she take a bet in which she will win $10K with probability 0.6 and lose $10K with probability 0.4?

c. If the person's total assets are currently $90K, should she take the bet given in part b?

d. Compare your answers to parts b and c. Does the person's betting behavior seem reasonable to you? How could you intuitively explain such behavior?

[*Source*: Winkler, R. L. (1972) *Introduction to Bayesian Inference and Decision*. New York: Holt, Rinehart, & Winston.]

13.26 Suppose that a decision maker has the following utility function:

$$U(x) = -0.000156 \, x^2 + 0.028125 \, x - 0.265625.$$

Use this utility function to calculate risk premiums for the gambles shown in Tables 13.3 and 13.4; create a similar table but based on this quadratic utility function. How would you classify the risk attitude of a decision maker with this utility function? Does such a risk attitude seem reasonable to you?

13.27 The CEO of a chemicals firm must decide whether to develop a new process that has been suggested by the research division. His decision tree is shown in Figure 13.17. There are two sources of uncertainty. The production cost is viewed as a continuous random variable, uniformly distributed between $1.75 and $2.25, and the size of the market (units sold) for the product is normally distributed with mean 10,300 units and standard deviation 2200 units.

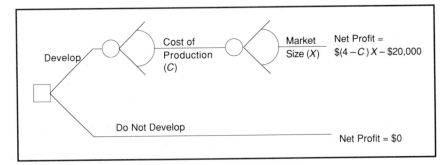

FIGURE 13.17   *Decision Tree for Problem 13.27*

The firm's CEO is slightly risk-averse. His utility function is given by:

$$U(Z) = 1 - e^{-Z/20,000}, \qquad \text{where } Z \text{ is the net profit.}$$

Should the CEO develop the new process? Answer this question by running a computer simulation, using 200 trials. Should the decision maker be concerned about the fact that if he develops the new process, the utility could be less than or greater than the utility for $0? On what basis should he make his decision?

13.28 The year is 2020, and you are in the supercomputer business. Your firm currently produces a machine that is relatively expensive (list price $6 million) and relatively slow (for supercomputers in the twenty-first century). Speed of supercomputers is measured in gigaflops per second (gps), where one "flop" is one calculation. Thus, one 1 gps = 1 billion calculations per second. Your current machine is capable of 150 gps. If you could do it, you would prefer to develop a supercomputer that costs less (to beat the competition) and is faster.

You have a research-and-development (R&D) decision to make based on two alternatives. You can choose one or the other of the following projects, or neither, but budget constraints prevent you from engaging in both projects.

A. The super-supercomputer. This project involves the development of a machine that is extremely fast (800 gps) and relatively inexpensive ($5 million). But this is a fairly risky project. The engineers who have been involved in the early stages estimate that there is only a 50% chance that this project would succeed. If it fails, you will be stuck with your current machine.

B. The better supercomputer. This project would pursue the development of an $8-million machine capable of 500 gps. This project also is somewhat risky. The engineers believe that there is only a 40% chance that this project will achieve its goal. They quickly point out, however, that even if the $8-million, 500-gps machine does not materialize, the technology involved is such that they would at least be able to produce a $5-million machine capable of 350 gps.

The decision tree is shown in Figure 13.18. To decide between the two alternatives, you have made the following assessments:

I. The best possible outcome is the $5-million, 800-gps machine, and the worst outcome is the status quo $6-million, 150-gps machine.

II. If you had the choice, you would be indifferent between Alternatives X and Y shown in Figure 13.19a.

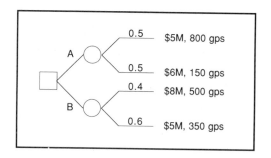

FIGURE 13.18 *Choosing Between Two Risky Supercomputer Development Projects*

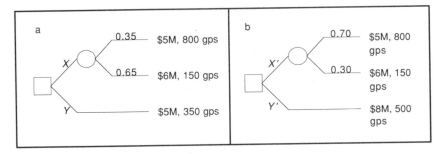

FIGURE 13.19   *Assessments to Assist Your Choice from Among the Supercomputer R&D Projects in Problem 13.28*

III.   If you had the choice, you would be indifferent between Alternatives X' and Y' in Figure 13.19b.

    a.   Using assessments I, II, and III, decide between Projects A and B. Justify your decision.

    b.   Explain why Project A appears to be riskier than Project B. Given that A is riskier than B, would you change your answer to part a? Why or why not?

13.29   Show that the value of Y that yields indifference between the two alternatives in Figure 13.12 (page 380) is approximately within 4% of the risk tolerance R.

CASE STUDIES

Interplants, Inc.

Don Newcomb was perplexed. It had been five years since he had founded Interplants, Inc., a research-and-development firm that developed genetically engineered plants for interplanetary space flight. During that five years, he and his scientists had made dramatic advances in developing special plants that could be used for food and air-purification systems in space stations and transports. In fact, he mused, their scientific success had been far greater than he had ever expected.

Five years ago, after the world superpowers had agreed to share space-travel technology, the outlook had been quite rosy. Everyone had been optimistic. Indeed, he was one of many investors who had jumped at the chance to be involved in the development of such technology. But now, after five tumultuous years, the prospects were less exciting.

First, there had been the disappointing realization that none of the superpowers had made substantial success on an ion engine to power space vehicles. Such an engine was absolutely crucial to the success of interplanetary space flight, because — theoretically, at least — it would make travel 10 times as fast as conventionally powered ships. When the importance of such an engine became obvious, the superpowers had generously funded a huge multinational research project. The project had made substantial progress, but many hurdles remained. Don's risk assessors estimated that there was still a 15% chance that the ion engine would prove an infeasible power source. If this were to happen, of course, Don and the many other investors in space-travel technology would lose out.

Then there was the problem with the settlement policy. The superpowers could not agree on a joint policy for the settlement of interplanetary space, including the deployment of space stations as well as settlements on planets and their satellites. The United American Alliance urged discretion and long-range planning in this matter, suggesting that a multinational commission be established to approve individual settlement projects. Pacificasia and the Allied Soviet Economic Community were demanding that space be divided now. By immediately establishing property rights, they claimed, the superpowers would be able to develop the optimum space economy in which the superpowers could establish their own economic policies within their "colonies" as well as determine trade policies with the other superpowers. Europa favored the idea of a commission, but also was eager to explore other available economic possibilities.

The discussion among the superpowers had been going on since long before the founding of Interplants. Five years ago, progress was being made, and it appeared that an agreement was imminent. But 18 months ago the process stalled. The participants in the negotiations had established positions from which they would not budge. Don had followed the discussions closely and had even provided expert advice to the negotiators regarding the potential for interplanetary agricultural developments. He guessed that there was only a 68% chance that the superpowers would eventually arrive at an agreement. Naturally, until an agreement was reached there would be little demand for space-traveling plants.

Aside from these external matters, Don still faced the difficult issue of developing a full-scale production process for his plants. He and his engineers had some ideas about the costs of the process, but at this point, all they could do was come up with a probability distribution for the costs. In thinking about the distribution, Don had decided to approximate it with a three-point discrete distribution. Thus, he characterized the three branches as "inexpensive," "moderate," and "costly," with probabilities of 0.185, 0.63, and 0.185, respectively. Of course, his eventual profit (or loss) depended on the costs of the final process.

Don also had thought long and hard about the profits that he could anticipate under each of the various scenarios. Essentially, he thought about the uncertainty in two stages. First was the determination of costs, and second was the outcome of the external factors (the ion-engine research and the negotiations regarding settlement policy). If costs turned out to be "inexpensive," then, in the event that the superpowers agreed and the ion engine was successful, he could expect a profit of 125 billion credits. He would lose 15 billion credits if either the engine or the negotiations failed. Likewise, if costs were "moderate," he could anticipate either a 100-billion-credit profit if both of the external factors resulted in a positive outcome, or a loss of 18 billion if either of the external factors were negative. Finally, the corresponding figures in the case of a "costly" production process were profits of 75 billion credits or a loss of 23 billion.

"This is so confusing," complained Don to Paul Fiester, his chief engineer. "I really never expected to be in this position. Five years ago none of these risks were apparent to me, and I guess I just don't tolerate risk well."

After a pause, Paul quietly suggested "Well, maybe you should sell the business."

Don considered that. "Well, that's a possibility. I have no idea how many crazy people out there would want it."

"Some of the other engineers and I might be crazy enough," Paul replied. "Depending on the price, of course. At least we'd be going in with our eyes open. We know what the business is about and what the risks are."

Don gave the matter a lot of thought that night. "What should I sell the company for? I hate to give up the possibility of earning up to 125 billion credits. But I don't like the possibility of losing 23 billion either — no one would!" As he lay awake, he finally decided that he would let the business go — with all its risks — for 20 billion credits. If he could get that much for it, he'd sell. If not, he'd just as soon stick with it, in spite of his frustrations with the risks.

QUESTIONS

1. Draw a decision tree for Don Newcomb's problem.
2. What is the significance of his statement that he would sell the business for 20 billion credits?
3. Suppose that Don's risk attitude can be modeled with an exponential utility function. If his certainty equivalent were 15 billion credits, find his risk tolerance. What would his risk tolerance be if his CE were 20 billion?

◆

Texaco–Pennzoil One More Time

In Problem 12.10 (page 356), we made EVPI calculations for Liedtke's decision in the Texaco–Pennzoil case. Calculating EVPI is somewhat different when the decision maker is risk-averse; that is, we cannot simply fold a tree back using expected values and then compare the expected values with and without information. And we cannot fold back the tree in terms of expected utility and compare the expected utilities. In fact, in general we must find a value C such that, when we subtract that value from each endpoint of the decision tree on the "Acquire Information" branch, the expected utility of this branch is equal to the expected utility of the "no information" branch. Figure 13.20 illustrates the principle by including a branch for acquiring information about Texaco's response.

When using the exponential utility function, however, there is a simple shortcut. Because the exponential utility function displays constant risk aversion, we can work in terms of certainty equivalents. That is, we can calculate CEs for the "Acquire Information" and "No Information" branches and compare

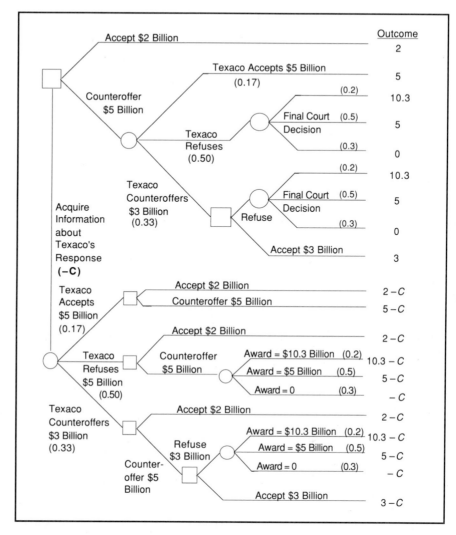

FIGURE 13.20 *Finding EVPI in the Texaco–Pennzoil Decision
when the Decision Maker is Risk-Averse*
Find *C* so that the expected utility of the "Acquire Information" branch
has the same expected utility as the next best alternative

them. The difference between the two is the expected value of the information!
Consider Liedtke's decision as diagrammed in Figure 13.20. Suppose that his decision analyst has modeled Pennzoil's corporate preferences with an exponential utility function and a risk tolerance of $1 billion. An acquaintance of
Liedtke's knows Texaco CEO James Kinnear quite well and has offered to find
out how Kinnear would react to a $5-billion counteroffer. Thus, the third alter-
native available to Liedtke is to acquire information about Texaco.

QUESTION

1. Find the expected value of perfect information regarding the Texaco reaction. Compare your answer to the answer from Problem 12.10a (page 356).

◆

Strenlar, Part III

Consider once again Fred Wallace's decision in the Strenlar case study at the end of Chapter 4 (pages 108–110). What if Fred is risk-averse? Assume that Fred's attitude toward risk in this case can be adequately modeled using an exponential utility function in which the utility is calculated for net present value. Thus,

$$U(NPV) = 1 - e^{-NPV/R}.$$

QUESTION

1. Check the sensitivity of Fred's decision to his risk tolerance, R. What is the critical R value for which his optimal decision changes? What advice can you give to Fred?

◆

◇ REFERENCES

For the most part, the material presented in this chapter has been my own version of familiar material. Good basic treatments of expected utility and risk aversion are available in most decision-analysis textbooks, including Bunn (1984), Holloway (1979), Raiffa (1968), Vatter et al. (1978), von Winterfeldt and Edwards (1986), and Winkler (1972). Keeney and Raiffa (1976) offer a somewhat more advanced treatment that focuses on multiattribute utility models, although it does contain an excellent exposition of the basic material at a somewhat higher mathematical level.

The material on the exponential utility function and risk tolerance is based primarily on Holloway (1979) and McNamee and Celona (1987). Both books contain excellent discussion and problems on this material.

For students who wish more detail on decreasing and constant risk aversion, look in the financial economics literature. In financial models, utility functions for market participants are important for modeling the economic system. An excellent starting point is Copeland and Weston (1979). A classic article that develops the idea of a risk-aversion coefficient (the reciprocal of risk tolerance) is Pratt (1964).

BUNN, D. (1984) *Applied Decision Analysis.* New York: McGraw-Hill.

COPELAND, T. E., and J. F. WESTON (1979) *Financial Theory and Corporate Policy.* Reading, MA: Addison-Wesley.

HOLLOWAY, C. A. (1979) *Decision Making Under Uncertainty: Models and Choices.* Englewood Cliffs, NJ: Prentice-Hall.

HOWARD, R. A. (1988) "Decision Analysis: Practice and Promise." *Management Science*, 34, 679–695.

KEENEY, R., and H. RAIFFA (1976) *Decisions with Multiple Objectives.* New York: Wiley.

MCNAMEE, P., and J. CELONA (1987) *Decision Analysis for the Professional with Supertree.* Redwood City, CA: Scientific Press.

PRATT, J. (1964) "Risk Aversion in the Small and in the Large." *Econometrica*, 32, 122–136.

RAIFFA, H. (1968) *Decision Analysis.* Reading, MA: Addison-Wesley.

VATTER, P. A., S. P. BRADLEY, S. C. FREY, JR., and B. B. JACKSON (1978) *Quantitative Methods in Management.* Homewood, IL: Irwin.

VON WINTERFELDT, D., and W. EDWARDS (1986) *Decision Analysis and Behavioral Research.* Cambridge: Cambridge University Press.

WINKLER, R. L. (1972) *Introduction to Bayesian Inference and Decision.* New York: Holt, Rinehart, & Winston.

◇ EPILOGUE

Harriman's broker, Jacob H. Schiff, was at his synagogue when Harriman's order for 40,000 shares was placed; the shares were never purchased. By the following Monday, Hill had cabled Morgan in France, and they had decided to buy as many Northern Pacific shares as they could. The share price went from $114 on Monday to $1000 on Thursday. In the aftermath, Hill and Morgan agreed that Harriman should be represented on the board of directors. Harriman, however, had little if any influence; James Hill continued to run the Great Northern, Northern Pacific, and Burlington railroads as he saw fit. [*Source*: Holbrook, S. H. (1958) "The Legend of Jim Hill." *American Heritage*, IX (4), 10–13, 98–101]

◆

Utility Axioms, Paradoxes, and Implications

In this chapter we will look at several issues. First, we will consider some of the foundations of utility theory. From the basis of a few behavioral axioms, it is possible to establish logically that people who behave according to the axioms should make choices consistent with the maximization of expected utility. But since the early 1950s, cognitive psychologists have noted that people do not always behave according to expected utility theory, and a large literature now covers these behavioral paradoxes. We review a very small part of that literature here. Because decision analysis depends on foundational axioms, it is worthwhile to consider some implications of these behavioral paradoxes, particularly with regard to the assessment of utility functions.

The following example previews some of the issues we will consider. This one is a participatory example. You should think hard about the choices you are asked to make before reading on.

PREPARING FOR AN INFLUENZA OUTBREAK

The United States is preparing for an outbreak of an unusual Asian strain of influenza. Experts expect 600 people to die from the disease. Two programs are available that could be used to combat the disease, but because of limited resources only one can be implemented.

Program A (Tried and True)   400 people will be saved.
Program B (Experimental)   There is an 80% chance that 600 people will be saved and a 20% chance that no one will be saved.

Which of these two programs do you prefer?

Now consider the following two programs:

Program C   200 people will die.

Program D   There is a 20% chance that 600 people will die and an 80% chance that no one will die.

Would you prefer C or D?

[*Source:* Tversky, A., and D. Kahneman (1981) "The Framing of Decisions and the Psychology of Choice." *Science*, 211, 453–458. Copyright 1981 by the American Association for the Advancement of Science.]

◆

◆ AXIOMS FOR EXPECTED UTILITY

Our first step in this chapter is to look at the behavioral assumptions that form the basis of expected utility. These assumptions, or *axioms*, relate to the consistency with which an individual expresses preferences from among a series of risky prospects. In the following discussion, the axioms are presented at a fairly abstract level. Simple examples are given to clarify their meaning. As we put them to work in the development of the main argument, the importance and intuition behind the axioms should become clearer.

1. *Ordering of outcomes and transitivity.*   A decision maker can order (establish preference or indifference) any two alternatives, and the ordering is transitive. For example, given any alternatives A_1, A_2, and A_3, either A_1 is preferred to A_2 (which is sometimes written as "$A_1 \succ A_2$"), A_2 is preferred to A_1, or the decision maker is indifferent between A_1 and A_2 ($A_1 \sim A_2$). Transitivity means that if A_1 is preferred to A_2, and A_2 is preferred to A_3, then A_1 is preferred to A_3. For example, this axiom says that an individual could express his or her preferences regarding, say, cities in which to reside. If that person preferred Amsterdam to London and London to Paris, then he or she would prefer Amsterdam to Paris.

2. *Reduction of compound uncertain events.*   A decision maker is indifferent between a compound uncertain event (a complicated mixture of gambles or lotteries) and a simple uncertain event as determined by reduction using standard probability manipulations. This comes into play when we reduce compound events into reference gambles. The assumption says that we can perform the reduction without affecting the decision maker's preferences. We made use of this axiom in Chapter 4 in our discussion of risk profiles. The progression from Figure 4.20 through Figure 4.22 (pages 85–86) is a matter of reducing to simpler terms the compound uncertain event that is associated with the counteroffer.

3. *Continuity.*   A decision maker is indifferent between an outcome A (for example, win 100) and some uncertain event involving only two basic outcomes A_1 and A_2, where $A_1 \succ A \succ A_2$. This simply says that we can construct a reference gamble with some probability p, for which the decision maker will be in-

different between the reference gamble and *A*. For example, suppose you find yourself as the plaintiff in a court case. You believe that the court will award you either $5000 or nothing. Now imagine that the defendant offers to pay you $1500 to drop the charges. According to the continuity axiom, there must be some probability *p* of winning $5000 (and the corresponding $1 - p$ probability of winning nothing) for which you would be indifferent between taking or rejecting the settlement offer. Of course, if your subjective probability of winning happens to be lower than *p*, then you would accept the proposal.

4. *Substitutability.*   A decision maker is indifferent between any original uncertain event that includes outcome A and one formed by substituting for A an uncertain event that is judged to be its equivalent. Figure 14.1 shows how this works. This axiom allows the substitution of uncertain reference gambles into a decision for their certainty equivalents and is just the reverse of the reduction axiom already stated. For example, suppose you are interested in playing the lottery, and you are just barely willing to pay 50 cents for a ticket. If I owe you 50 cents, then you should be just as willing to accept a lottery ticket as the 50 cents in cash.

5. *Monotonicity.*   Given two reference gambles with the same possible outcomes, a decision maker prefers the one with the higher probability of winning the preferred outcome. This one is easy to see. Imagine that two different car dealerships each can order the new car that you want. Both dealers offer the same price, delivery, warranty, and financing, but one is more likely to provide good service than the other. To which one would you go? The one that has the better chance of providing good service, of course.

6. *Invariance.*   All that is needed to determine a decision maker's preferences among uncertain events are the payoffs for outcomes and the associated probabilities.

7. *Boundedness.*   No outcomes are considered infinitely bad or infinitely good.

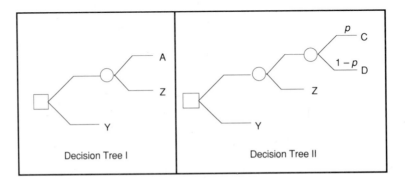

FIGURE 14.1   *Two Decision Trees*
If A is equivalent to a lottery with a *p* chance at C and $(1 - p)$ chance at D, then Decision Tree I is equivalent to Decision Tree II.

Most of us agree that these assumptions are reasonable under almost all circumstances. It is worth noting, however, that many decision theorists find some of the axioms controversial! The reasons for the controversy range from introspection regarding particular decision situations to formal psychological experiments in which human subjects make choices that clearly violate one or more of the axioms. We will discuss some of these experiments in the next section.

For example, the substitutability axiom is a particular point of debate. For some decision makers, the fact of having to deal with two uncertain events in Decision Tree II of Figure 14.1 can be worse than facing the single one in Decision Tree I. Moreover, individuals might make this judgment and at the same time agree that in a single-stage lottery, A is indeed equivalent to the risky prospect with a p chance at C and a $(1 - p)$ chance at D.

As another example, we can pick on the apparently innocuous transitivity axiom. In Figure 14.2, you have two lotteries from which to choose. Each of the six outcomes has probability $\frac{1}{6}$. One way to look at the situation is that the prize in Game B is better than Game A's in five of the six outcomes, and thus it may be reasonable to prefer B, even though the structure of the lotteries is essentially the same. Now consider the games in Figure 14.3. If B was preferred to A in Figure 14.2, then by the same argument C would be preferred to B, D to C, E to D, F to E, and, finally, A would be preferred to F. Thus, these preferences do not obey the transitivity axiom, because transitivity would never permit A to be preferred to something else that is in turn preferred to A.

The controversy about individual axioms notwithstanding, if you accept axioms 1 through 7, then logically you also must accept the following proposition.

Proposition: Given any two uncertain events B_1 and B_2, if assumptions 1 through 7 hold, there are numbers U_1, U_2, . . . , U_n representing preferences (or utilities) associated with the payoffs for outcomes, such that the overall preference between the uncertain events is reflected by the expected values of the U's for each event. In other words, if you accept the axioms, (1) it is possible to find a utility function for you to evaluate the outcomes, and (2) you should be making your decisions in a way that is consistent with maximizing expected utility.

In the following pages we will demonstrate how the axioms permit the transformation of uncertain alternatives into reference gambles (gambles between the best and worst alternatives) with different probabilities. It is on the basis of this kind of transformation that the proposition can be proved.

Suppose you face the simple decision problem shown in Figure 14.4. For convenience, assume the payoffs are in dollars. The continuity axiom says that we can find reference gambles that are equivalent to the outcomes at the ends of the branches. Suppose (hypothetically) that you are indifferent between $15 and the following reference gamble:

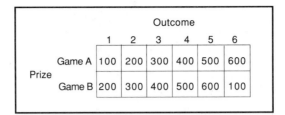

FIGURE 14.2   *A Pair of Lotteries*
Outcomes 1 through 6 each occur with
probability $\frac{1}{6}$. Would you prefer to play
Game A or Game B?

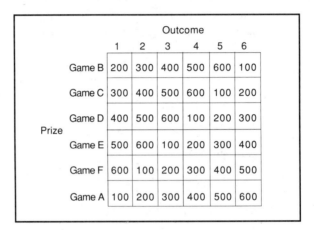

FIGURE 14.3   *More Games to Consider*
Outcomes 1 through 6 each still have probability $\frac{1}{6}$.

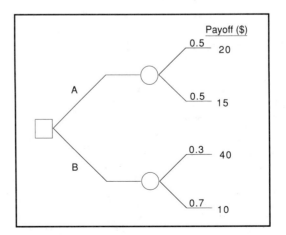

FIGURE 14.4   *A Simple Decision Problem
under Uncertainty*

> Win $40 with probability 0.36.
> Win $10 with probability 0.64.

Likewise, suppose you are indifferent between $20 and the next reference gamble:

> Win $40 with probability 0.60.
> Win $10 with probability 0.40.

The substitutability axiom says that we can replace the original outcomes with their corresponding reference gambles, as in Figure 14.5. (We have replaced the outcomes in Lottery B with "trivial" lotteries. The reason for doing so will become apparent.) The substitutability axiom says that you are indifferent between A and A′ and also between B and B′. Thus, the problem has not changed.

Now use the reduction-of-compound-events axiom to reduce the decision tree (Figure 14.6). In performing this step, the overall probability of winning 40 in A″ is 0.5 (0.60) + 0.5 (0.36), or 0.48; it is similarly calculated for winning 10. For the lower half of the tree, we just retrieve B again. The monotonicity axiom means we prefer A″ to B″, and so by transitivity (which says that $A'' \sim A' \sim A$ and $B'' \sim B' \sim B$) we must prefer A to B in the original decision.

To finish the demonstration, we must show that it is possible to come up with numbers that represent utilities so that a higher expected utility implies a preferred alternative, and vice versa. In this case, we need utilities that result in a higher expected utility for Alternative A. Use the probabilities assessed above in the reference gambles as those utilities. (Now you can see the reason for the extension of B in Figure 14.5; we need the probabilities.) We can redraw the original decision tree, as in Figure 14.7, with the utilities in place of the original monetary payoffs.

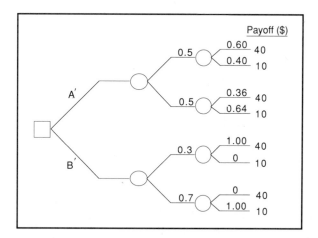

FIGURE 14.5 *Decision Tree After Substituting Reference Gambles for Outcomes*

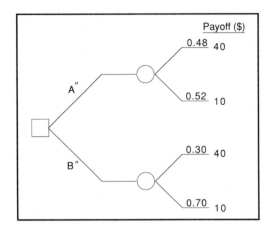

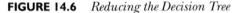

FIGURE 14.6   *Reducing the Decision Tree*

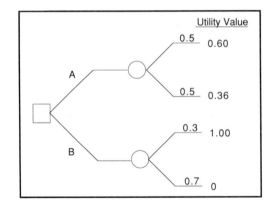

FIGURE 14.7   *Original Decision Tree with Utility Values Replacing Monetary Values*

Calculating expected utilities shows that A has the higher expected utility and hence should be preferred:

$$EU(A) = 0.5 \ (0.60) + 0.5 \ (0.36) = 0.48.$$
$$EU(B) = 0.3 \ (1.00) + 0.7 \ (0) = 0.30.$$

This exercise may seem both arcane and academic. But put simply, if you think it is reasonable to behave according to the axioms at the beginning of the section, then (1) it is possible to find your utility values, and (2) you should make decisions that would be consistent with the maximization of expected utility.

In our initial Chapter 13 discussions of utility assessment, the claim was made that a utility function could be scaled (multiplied by a positive constant and added to a constant) without changing anything. Now you should see clearly that the whole purpose of a utility function is to rank order risky prospects. Take Alternatives A and B. We have concluded that A is preferred to B because EU(A) = 0.48, which is greater than EU(B) = 0.30. Suppose that we take the utility numbers, as shown in Figure 14.7, and scale them. That is, let

$$U'(x) = a + b\,U(x),$$

where $b > 0$, and $U(x)$ is our original utility function (from Figure 14.7). We can calculate the expected utilities of A and B on the basis of the following new utility function:

$$\begin{aligned}
EU'(A) &= 0.5\,[a + b\,U(20)] + 0.5\,[a + b\,U(15)] \\
&= a + b\,[0.5\,U(20) + 0.5\,U(15)] \\
&= a + b\,EU(A) \\
&= a + b\,(0.48).
\end{aligned}$$

$$\begin{aligned}
EU'(B) &= 0.3\,[a + b\,U(40)] + 0.7\,[a + b\,U(10)] \\
&= a + b\,[0.3\,U(40) + 0.7\,U(10)] \\
&= a + b\,EU(B) \\
&= a + b\,(0.30).
\end{aligned}$$

It should be clear that $EU'(A)$ will be greater than $EU'(B)$ as long as $b > 0$. As indicated, the implication is that we can scale our utility functions linearly with the constants a and b without changing the rankings of the risky alternatives in terms of expected utility. Specifically, this means that no matter what the scale of a utility function, we always can rescale it so that the largest value is 1 and the smallest is 0. (For that matter, you can rescale it so that the largest and smallest values are whatever you want!)

If you look carefully at our transformations of the original decision problem above, you will see that we never explicitly invoked either the invariance or boundedness axioms. Why are these axioms important? The invariance axiom says that we need nothing but the payoffs and the probabilities; nothing else matters. (In the context of multiattribute utility as discussed in the next two chapters, we would need outcomes on all relevant dimensions.)

The boundedness axiom assures us that expected utility will never be infinite, and so we always will be able to make meaningful comparisons. To see the problem with unbounded utility, suppose that you have been approached by an evangelist who has told you that unless you accept his religion, you will burn in Hell for eternity. If you attach an infinitely negative utility to an eternity in Hell (and it is difficult to imagine a worse fate), then no matter how small your subjective probability that the evangelist is right, as long as it is even slightly positive you must be compelled to convert. This is simply because any small positive probability multiplied by the infinitely negative utility will result in an infinitely negative expected utility. Similar problems are encountered if an outcome is accorded infinite positive utility; you would do anything at all if doing so gave you even the slightest chance at achieving some wonderful outcome. Thus, if an outcome in your decision problem has unbounded utility, then the expected utility approach does not help much when it comes to making the decision.

♦ PARADOXES

Even though the axioms of expected utility theory appear to be compelling when we discuss them, people do not necessarily make choices in accordance with them. Research into these behavioral paradoxes began almost as early as the original research into utility theory itself, and now a large literature exists for many aspects of human behavior under uncertainty. Much of this literature is reviewed in von Winterfeldt and Edwards (1986) and Hogarth (1987). We will cover a few high points to indicate the nature of the results.

Framing effects are among the most pervasive paradoxes in choice behavior. Tversky and Kahneman (1981) show how an individual's risk attitude can change depending on the way the decision problem is posed — that is, on the "frame" in which a problem is presented. The difficulty is that the same decision problem usually can be expressed in different frames. A good example is the influenza-outbreak problem at the beginning of the chapter. You may have noticed that Program A is the same as C and that B is the same as D. It all depends on whether you think in terms of deaths or lives saved. Many people prefer A on one hand, but D on the other.

To a great extent, the reason for the inconsistent choices appears to be that different points of reference are used to frame the problem in two different ways. That is, in Programs A and B the reference point is that 600 people are expected to die, but some may be saved. Thus, we think about gains in terms of numbers of lives saved. On the other hand, in Programs C and D, the reference point is that no people would be expected to die without the disease. In this case, we tend to think about lives lost. One of the important general principles that Kahneman and Tversky and others have discovered is that people tend to be risk-averse in dealing with gains but risk-seeking in deciding about losses. A typical assessed utility function for changes in wealth is shown in Figure 14.8. These results have been obtained in many different behavioral experiments (for example, see Swalm 1966).

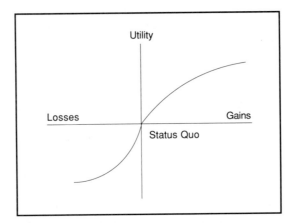

FIGURE 14.8 *Typical Assessed Utility Function for Changes in Wealth*

More fundamental than the risk-averse/risk-seeking dichotomy is that the reference point or status quo can be quite flexible in some situations and inflexible in others. For example, the influenza-outbreak example can be viewed with relative ease from either frame. For many people, the financial status quo changes as soon as they file their income-tax return in anticipation of a refund; they "spend" their refund, usually in the form of credit, long before the check arrives in the mail. In other cases, individuals may maintain a particular reference point far longer than they should. A case in point is that gamblers often try to make up their losses; they throw good money after bad. Here "gamblers" can refer to individuals in casinos as well as to stock-market investors or even managers who maintain a commitment to a project that has obviously gone sour. Typically, such a gambler will argue that backing out of a failed project amounts to a waste of the resources already spent.

Is a specific axiom being violated when a decision maker's choices exhibit a framing effect? The answer to this question is not exactly clear. Although many possibilities exist, the invariance axiom may be the weak link in this case. It may be that payoffs (or utilities) and probabilities are not sufficient to determine a decision maker's preferences. Some understanding of the decision maker's frame of reference also may be required.

For another example, consider the problem:

Allais Paradox

You have two decisions to make.

Decision 1   **A:**   Win $1 million with probability 1.

             B: Win $2 million with probability 0.10.
                    Win $1 million with probability 0.89.
                    Win $0 with probability 0.01.

Before proceeding, choose A or B. Would you give up a sure $1 million for a small chance at $2.5 million and possibly nothing?

Decision 2   **C:**   Win $1 million with probability 0.11.
                    Win $0 with probability 0.89.

             D: Win $2.5 million with probability 0.10.
                    Win $0 million with probability 0.90.

Now choose C or D in Decision 2.

This is the well-known Allais Paradox (Allais, 1953; Allais and Hagen, 1979). The decisions are shown in decision-tree form in Figure 14.9. Experimentally, as many as 82% of subjects prefer A over B and 83% prefer D over C. But we can easily show that choosing A on the one hand and D on the other is contrary to expected utility maximization. Let $U(0) = 0$ and $U(2,500,000) = 1$; they are the best and worst outcomes. Then,

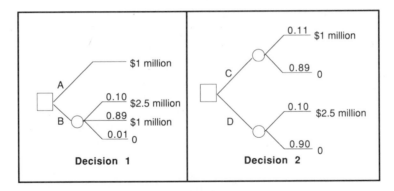

FIGURE 14.9   *Choices in the Allais Paradox*

$$EU(A) = U(\$1 \text{ million})$$
$$EU(B) = 0.10 + 0.89\ U(\$1 \text{ million}).$$

Thus, A is preferred to B if and only if

$$U(\$1 \text{ million}) > 0.10 + 0.89\ U(\$1 \text{ million})$$

or

$$U(\$1 \text{ million}) > 0.91.$$

Now for Decision 2,

$$EU(C) = 0.11\ U(\$1 \text{ million})$$
$$EU(D) = 0.10,$$

so D is preferred to C if and only if $U(1,000,000) < 0.91$.

U($1 million) cannot be both greater than and less than 0.91 at the same time, so choosing A and D is not consistent with expected utility. Consistent choices are A and C or B and D. Kahneman and Tversky have attributed this common inconsistency to the *certainty effect*, whereby individuals tend to place too much weight on a certain outcome relative to uncertain outcomes. In the Allais Paradox, the certainty effect would tend to make individuals overvalue A in Decision 1, possibly leading to an inconsistent choice. When confronted with their inconsistency, some individuals revise their choices. Would you revise yours in light of this discussion?

Another way to look at the Allais Paradox is to structure the decision problem using lottery tickets in a hat. Imagine that 100 tickets are numbered sequentially from 1 to 100 and are placed in a hat. One ticket will be drawn at random, and you will receive a prize depending on the option you choose and the number on the ticket. Prizes for A and B are described in Table 14.1. For A, you would win $1 million regardless of the ticket chosen, but for B you would win nothing if Ticket 1 is chosen, $2.5 million for Tickets 2 through 11, and $1 million for Tickets 12 through 100. Note that you win the same ($1 million) in the

	Tickets		
Option	1	2–11	12–100
A	$1 million	$1 million	$1 million
B	0	$2.5 million	$1 million
C	$1 million	$1 million	0
D	0	$2.5 million	0

TABLE 14.1 *Prizes in the Allais Paradox*
Tickets 1–100 are placed in a hat, and one ticket is drawn randomly. The dollar amounts shown in the table are the prizes for the four options.

two lotteries for tickets 12 through 100. Thus, your choice should depend only on your preferences regarding the outcomes for Tickets 1 through 12.

The same kind of thing can be done for Options C and D, which also are shown in Table 14.1. If you choose C, you win $1 million for Tickets 1–11 and nothing for Tickets 12–100. In D you would win nothing for Ticket 1, $2.5 million for Tickets 2–11, and nothing for Tickets 12-100. Again, you win exactly the same thing (nothing) in both C and D for Tickets 12–100, and so your preferences between C and D should depend only on your preferences regarding Tickets 1–11. As you can see, the prizes associated with Tickets 1–11 are the same for Options A and C on the one hand and B and D on the other. Thus, if you prefer A to B you also should prefer C to D, and vice versa.

It is intuitively reasonable that your preferences should not depend on Tickets 12–100, because the outcome is the same regardless of the decision made. This is an example of the *sure-thing principle*, which says that our preferences over lotteries or risky prospects should depend only on the parts of the lotteries that can lead to different outcomes. The idea of the sure thing is that, in the choice between A and B, winning $1 million is a sure thing if one of the tickets from 12 to 100 is drawn, regardless of your choice. If, as in the Allais choices, there are possible outcomes that have the same value to you regardless of the option you choose, and these outcomes occur with the same probability regardless of the option chosen, then you can ignore this part of the lottery. The sure-thing principle can be derived logically from our axioms. For our purposes, it is best to think of it as a behavioral principle that is consistent with our axioms; if you agree to behave in accordance with the axioms, then you also should obey the sure-thing principle. If your choices in the Allais Paradox were inconsistent, then your preferences violated the sure-thing principle.

◆ IMPLICATIONS

As we learned above, people do not always behave according to the behavioral axioms. This fact has distinct implications for the practice of decision analysis.

First, there are implications regarding how utility assessments should be made. Second, and perhaps more intriguing, are the implications for managers and policy makers whose jobs depend on how people actually do make decisions. It may be important for such managers to consider some of the above-described behavioral phenomena. In this section, we will look at the issues involved in each of these areas.

Implications for Utility Assessment

We rely on assessments of certainty equivalents and other comparisons to find a utility function. Given the discussion above, it is clear that, in the assessment process, we ask decision makers to perform tasks that we know they do not always perform consistently according to the axioms! Thus, it is no surprise that the behavioral paradoxes discussed above may have some impact on the way that utility functions should be assessed. Our discussion here will be brief, not because the literature is particularly large, but because many research questions remain to be answered.

There are several approaches to the assessment of utilities. In Chapter 13 we introduced the certainty-equivalent approach (find a CE for a specified gamble) and the probability-equivalent approach (find a probability that makes a reference lottery equivalent to a specific certain amount). If we think of the general case (Figure 14.10) as being indifferent between CE for sure and the reference lottery:

Win G with probability p
Win L with probability $(1 - p)$,

then it is clear that we must preset three out of the four variables p, CE, G, and L. The selection of the fourth, which makes the decision maker indifferent be-

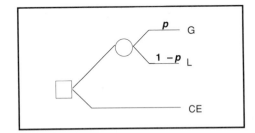

FIGURE 14.10   *A General Framework for Assessing Utilities*
If three of the four variables (G,L, CE, and p) are fixed, assessment of the fourth such that the decision maker is indifferent between the two decision branches permits establishment of utility values.

tween the two prospects, allows the specification of a utility value. Most practitioners use either the CE or PE approaches. Assessing a certainty equivalent involves fixing G, L, and p, and assessing CE; the probability-equivalent method involves fixing CE, G, and L, and assessing p.

The relative merits of the possible assessment techniques have been discussed to some degree. Hershey, Kunreuther, and Shoemaker (1982) report that the use of the CE approach tends to result in more risk-averse responses than does the PE approach when the outcomes are gains. On the other hand, when the outcomes are losses, the CE approach results in more risk-seeking behavior. When using the PE approach, many people appear to exhibit certain forms of probability distortion. Although the evidence is far from conclusive, it indicates that people deal best with 50-50 chances. This empirical result appears to be related to the certainty effect discussed above.

Clearly, these results have an impact on the assessment of utility functions; the nature of the decision maker's responses and hence the deduced risk attitude can depend on the way that questions have been posed in the assessment procedure. McCord and De Neufville (1986) have suggested, in light of the distortion from the certainty effect, that utilities should not be assessed using the CE approach, which requires a decision maker to compare a lottery with a certain quantity. The CE approach, they argue, contains a built-in bias. They suggest that it would be more appropriate to assess utilities by comparing lotteries. For example, suppose that A is the best outcome and C is the worst, and we would like to assess U(B), which is somewhere between A and C. McCord and DeNeufville's technique would have the decision maker assess the probability p that produces indifference between the two lotteries in the decision tree in Figure 14.11. Because p makes the decision maker indifferent, we can set up the equation

$$0.5 \ U(B) + 0.5 \ U(C) = p \ U(A) + (1 - p) \ U(C).$$

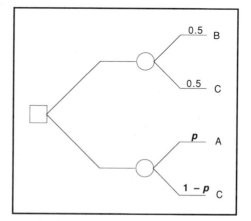

FIGURE 14.11 *The McCord–De Neufville Utility Assessment Procedure*

Substituting U(A) = 1 and U(C) = 0 and rearranging, this becomes

$$U(B) = 2p.$$

Thus, the utility is relatively easy to find once the assessment has been made.

The McCord–De Neufville approach does indeed lead to utility assessments that are less risk-averse than those made with certainty equivalents. Figure 14.12 compares the two methods in terms of hypothetical utility functions that might be assessed. It may be the case, however, that decision makers have a harder time thinking about comparable lotteries than about certainty equivalents.

Managerial and Policy Implications

The idea that people actually make decisions that are sometimes inconsistent with decision-analysis principles is not new. In fact, the premise of a book such as this one is that it is possible to improve one's decision-making skills. But now we have seen that individuals behave in certain specific and predictable ways. What implications does this have for managers and policy makers?

The most fundamental issue has to do with the reference point or status quo. What is the status quo in a particular decision situation? How do people establish a status quo for decision-making purposes? Can the perception of the status quo be manipulated, and, if so, how? Complete answers to these questions are certainly beyond the scope of our discussion here, but we can discuss important examples in which the status quo plays an important role.

First is the problem of "sunk costs." As briefly mentioned earlier, managers frequently remain committed to a project that obviously has gone bad. In decision-analysis terms, the money that already has been spent on the project no longer should influence current and future decisions. Any decisions, particularly whether to continue or abandon a project, must be forward-looking — that is, consider only future cash flows. To account for the sunk costs, they would

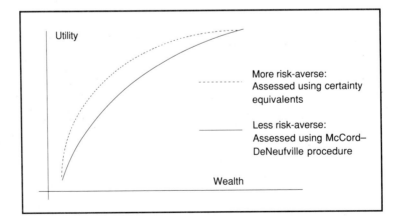

FIGURE 14.12   *Comparing Utility Functions Assessed with Different Approaches*

have to be accounted for on every branch, and hence could not affect the relative ordering of the alternatives.

What do we say to an individual who seems unable to ignore sunk costs? One piece of advice is to make sure that the individual understands exactly what the status quo is. If the individual wants to "throw good money after bad," then he or she may be operating on the basis of a previous status quo; abandoning the project may look like accepting a sure loss of the money already invested. From this perspective, it might seem quite reasonable instead to seek a risky gain by remaining committed to the project. But the real status quo is that the project is unlikely to yield the anticipated benefits. From this new perspective, abandoning the project amounts to the avoidance of a losing venture; funds would be better invested elsewhere.

In other cases, a problem's frame may be specified with equal validity in several ways. Consider the case of seat belts. If people view seat belts as inconvenient and uncomfortable, then they may refuse to wear them; the status quo is the level of comfort when unbuckled. Suppose, however, the status quo were established as how well off people are in general. Who would want to risk the loss of a healthy family, a productive life, and possibly much of one's savings? The use of a seat belt is a form of inexpensive insurance to avoid a possible dramatic loss relative to this new status quo.

A similar argument can be made in the area of environmental protection. People may view environmental programs as anything from inconveniences (being forced to separate recyclable materials from trash) to major economic impediments (adhering to EPA's complex regulations). The implied status quo is the current level of direct costs; the programs represent a sure loss relative to this status quo. If, however, emphasis is given to the current overall condition of the community, nation, or world, then the increased cost induced by the programs can be viewed as a small amount of insurance necessary to avoid a large loss relative to our current overall welfare.

A third situation in which the perception of the status quo can be productively manipulated is in the area of creativity enhancement. In Chapter 6 we discussed removing blocks to creativity. In organizations, one key approach is to make the environment as nonthreatening as possible so that individuals will not be afraid to present new ideas. In the terminology of this section, the goal is to establish a status quo in the organizational environment such that individuals will view the presentation of a new idea as one in which the loss is small if the idea fails but otherwise the potential gain is large.

In the discussion so far we have focused our attention on issues concerning the status quo. We turn now to the certainty effect, or the fact that we tend to overvalue sure outcomes relative to uncertain ones. This psychological phenomenon can have interesting effects on our decision making, especially under conditions of uncertainty.

In our Western culture, we abhor uncertainty. Indeed, it is appropriate to expend resources for information in order to reduce uncertainty. This is true only up to a point, however, as we discussed in Chapter 12. But where may the certainty effect lead? We may try too hard to eliminate uncertainty altogether.

For example, in organizations, there may be a tendency to spend far too much effort and far too many resources on tracking down elusive information in an effort to know the "truth." More insidious is a tendency to ignore uncertainty altogether. We often tend to view forecasts, for example, as perfect indicators of the future, ignoring their inherent uncertainty. The use of carefully assessed probabilistic forecasts is an important way to avoid this problem.

As a society, the certainty effect may be a factor in our preoccupation with certain kinds of health and environmental risks. Many individuals — activists in various causes — would prefer to eliminate risk altogether and thus they call for stringent regulations on projects that appear to pose risks to the population or environment. Certainly these individuals play a valuable role in drawing our attention to important issues, but achieving zero risk in our society is not only impractical, but also impossible. A sound approach to the management of risk in our society requires a consideration of both the benefits and costs of reducing risk to various levels.

In this brief section we have considered certain implications of the behavioral paradoxes for the application of decision analysis (especially utility assessment), as well as for organizational decisions and policy making. But we have only scratched the surface here. As research progresses in this fertile area, many other behavioral paradoxes and their implications will be studied. The examples we have considered illustrate the pervasiveness of the effects as well as their importance.

◆ A FINAL PERSPECTIVE

We have discussed a variety of inconsistencies in human behavior. Do these inconsistencies invalidate expected utility theory? The argument all along has been that people do not seem to make coherent decisions without some guidance. If a decision maker does wish to make coherent decisions, then a careful decision-analysis approach, including a careful assessment of personal preferences, can help the decision maker in looking for better decisions.

It is easy to get the impression that utility and probability numbers reside in a decision maker's mind, and that the assessment procedure simply elicits those numbers. But the process is more than that. Just as the process of structuring a decision problem helps the decision maker understand the problem better and possibly leads to the recognition of new alternatives for action, so may the assessment process provide a medium in which the decision maker actually can develop his or her preferences or beliefs about uncertainty. The assessment process helps to mold the decision maker's subjective preferences and beliefs. How many of us, for example, have given much thought to assessing a utility function for a cup of coffee (Problem 14.14) or considered the probability distribution for a grade in a decision-analysis course (Problem 8.11)? Certainly the assessed numbers do not already exist inside our heads; they come into being through the assessment procedure. This is exactly why assessment often requires hard thinking and why decisions are hard to make. Thus, perhaps the best way to think about the assessment process is in constructive terms. Reflecting on the decision problem faced and considering our preferences and beliefs about uncertainty provides a basis not only for building a model of the problem and necessary beliefs, but also for constructing those beliefs in the first place. This view may explain some of the behavioral paradoxes that we have discussed; individuals who have not thought long and hard in thoroughly developing their preferences and beliefs might be expected to make inconsistent judgments.

This constructive view of the assessment process is a fundamental matter. You may recall that we introduced these ideas way back in Chapter 1 when we suggested that the decision-analysis process actually helps a decision maker develop his or her thoughts about the structure of the problem, beliefs about uncertainty, and preferences. Again, the idea of a requisite model is appropriate. A decision model is requisite in terms of preferences if it captures the essential preference issues that matter to the decision maker for the problem at hand. Thus, this constructive view suggests that decision analysis should provide an environment in which the decision maker can systematically develop his or her understanding of the problem, including preferences and beliefs about uncertainty. But how can we be sure that decision analysis does provide such an environment? More research is required to answer this question completely. The decision-analysis approach, however, does encourage decision makers to think about the issues in a systematic way. Working through the decision-analysis cycle (modeling, analyzing, performing sensitivity analysis, and then modeling again) should help the decision maker to identify and think clearly about the appropriate issues. Thus, the argument is that good initial decision-analysis structuring of a problem will lead to appropriate assessments and careful thought about important issues.

◇ SUMMARY

We have covered a lot of ground in this chapter. We started with the axioms that underlie utility theory and showed how those axioms imply that an individual should make decisions that are consistent with the maximization of expected utility. Then we examined some of the behavioral paradoxes that have been documented. These are situations in which intelligent people make decisions that violate one or more of the axioms, and thus make decisions that are inconsistent with expected utility. These paradoxes do not invalidate the idea that we should still make decisions according to expected utility; recall that the basic goal of decision analysis is to help people improve their decision-making skills. But the paradoxes do have certain implications. We explored some of these implications, including the possibility of assessing equivalent lotteries rather than certainty equivalents and implications for policy makers. We ended with a constructive perspective of assessment, whereby it provides a medium within which the decision maker can explore and develop preferences and beliefs. ◆

◇ EXERCISES

14.1 In your own words explain why the axioms that underlie expected utility are important to decision analysis.

14.2   From a decision-analysis perspective, why is it worthwhile to spend time studying the kinds of paradoxes described in this chapter?

14.3   Most people are learning constantly about themselves and their environment. Our tastes develop and change as our environment changes. As new technologies arise, new risks are discovered. What are the implications of this dynamic environment for decision analysis?

14.4   **a.** Find the value for p that makes you indifferent between

> **Lottery 1**   Win $1000 with probability p.
> Win $0 with probability $(1 - p)$.

and

> **Lottery 2**   Win $400 for sure.

b. Now find the q that makes you indifferent between

> **Lottery 3**   Win $400 with probability 0.50.
> Win $0 with probability 0.50

and

> **Lottery 4**   Win $1000 with probability q.
> Win $0 with probability $(1 - q)$.

c. According to your assessment in part a, $U(\$400) = p$. In part b, $U(\$400) = 2q$. Explain why this is the case.

d. To be consistent, your assessments should be such that $p = 2q$. Were your assessments consistent? Would you change them? Which assessment do you feel most confident about? Why?

◊ QUESTIONS AND PROBLEMS

14.5   Imagine that you collect bottles of wine as a hobby. How would you react to these situations?

a. You have just learned that one of the bottles (Wine A) that you purchased five years ago has appreciated considerably. A friend has offered to buy the bottle from you for $100. His offer is a fair price. Would you sell the bottle of wine?

b. A second bottle of wine (Wine B) is viewed by experts as being equivalent in value to Wine A. You never purchased a bottle of Wine B, but a casual acquaintance did. In conversation at a party, he offers to sell you his bottle of Wine B for $100. Would you buy it?

Many people would neither sell Wine A nor buy Wine B. Explain why this pattern of choices is inconsistent with expected utility. What other considerations might be taken into account?

14.6   Consider the following two scenarios:

a. You have decided to see a show for which tickets cost $20. You bought your ticket in advance, but as you enter the theater, you find that you have lost the ticket. You did not make a note of your seat number, and the ticket is not recoverable or refundable in any way. Would you pay another $20 for a second ticket?

b. You have decided to see a show for which tickets cost $20. As you open your wallet to pay for the ticket, you discover that you have lost a $20 bill. Would you still buy a ticket to see the show?

Many individuals would not purchase a second ticket under the first scenario, but they would under the second. Explain why this is inconsistent with expected utility. How would you explain this kind of behavior?

14.7 Imagine yourself in the following two situations:

a. You are about to go shopping to purchase a stereo system at a local store. Upon reading the newspaper, you find that another stereo store across town has the system you are interested in for $1089.99. You had been planning to spend $1099.95, the best price you had found after considerable shopping. Would you drive across town to purchase the stereo system at the other store?

b. You are about to go shopping to purchase a popcorn popper at a local hardware store for $19.95, the best price you have seen yet. Upon reading the paper, you discover that a department store across town has the same popper for $9.99. Would you drive across town to purchase the popper at the department store?

Many people would drive across town to save money on the popcorn popper, but not on the stereo system. Why is this inconsistent with expected utility? What explanation can you give for this behavior?

14.8 Consider these two scenarios:

a. You have made a reservation to spend the weekend at the coast. To get the reservation, you had to make a nonrefundable $50 deposit. As the weekend approaches, you feel a bit out of sorts. On balance, you decide that you would be happier at home than at the coast. Of course, if you stay home, you forfeit the deposit. Would you stay home or go to the coast? What arguments would you use to support your position?

b. You have decided to spend the weekend at the coast and have made a reservation at your favorite resort. While driving over, you discover a new resort. After looking it over, you realize that you would rather spend your weekend here. Your reservation at the coast can be cancelled easily at no charge. Staying at the new resort, however, would cost $50 more. Would you stay at the new resort or continue to the coast?

Are your decisions consistent in parts a and b? Explain why or why not.

14.9 Even without a formal assessment process, it often is possible to learn something about an individual's utility function just through the preferences revealed by choice behavior. Two persons, A and B, make the following bet: A wins $40 if it rains tomorrow and B wins $10 if it does not rain tomorrow.

a. If they both agree that the probability of rain tomorrow is 0.10, what can you say about their utility functions?

b. If they both agree that the probability of rain tomorrow is 0.30, what can you say about their utility functions?

c. Given no information about their probabilities, is it possible that their utility functions could be identical?

d. If they both agree that the probability of rain tomorrow is 0.20, could both individuals be risk-averse? Is it possible that their utility functions could be identical? Explain.

[*Source*: Winkler, R. L. (1972) *Introduction to Bayesian Inference and Decision*. New York: Holt, Rinehart, & Winston.]

14.10   Assess your utility function for money in the bank over a range from $100 to $20,000 using the McCord–De Neufville procedure described in this chapter. Plot the results of your assessments on the same graph as the assessments made for Problem 13.11 (page 392). Discuss the differences in your assessments from one method to the other. Can you explain any inconsistencies among them?

14.11   Assume that you are interested in purchasing a new model of a personal computer whose reliability has not yet been perfectly established. Measure reliability in terms of the number of days in the shop over the first three years that you own the machine. (Does this definition of reliability pass the clarity test?) Now assess your utility function for computer reliability over the range from 0 days (best) to 50 days (worst). Use whatever assessment technique with which you feel most comfortable, and use computer assessment aids if they are available.

14.12   You are in the market for a new car. An important characteristic is the life-span of the car. (Define life-span as the number of miles driven until the car breaks down, requiring such extensive repairs that it would be cheaper to buy an equivalent depreciated machine.) Assess your utility function for automobile life-span over the range from 40,000 miles to 200,000 miles.

14.13   Being a student, you probably have well-developed feelings about homework. Given the same amount of material learned, the less the better, right? (I thought so!) Define homework as the number of hours spent outside of class on various assignments that enter into your final grade. Now, assuming that the amount of material learned is the same in all instances, assess your utility function for homework over the range from 0 hours per week (best) to 20 hours per week (worst). (*Hint*: You may have to narrow the definition of homework. For example, does it make a difference what kind of course the homework is for? Does it matter whether the homework is term papers, case studies, short written assignments, oral presentations, or something else?)

14.14   We usually think of utility functions as always sloping upward (more is better) or downward (less is better; fewer nuclear power plant disasters, for example). But this is not always the case. In this problem, you must think about your utility function for coffee versus milk.

Imagine that you are about to buy a cup of coffee. Let c ($0 \le c \le 1$) represent the proportion of the contents of the cup accounted for by coffee, and $1 - c$ the proportion accounted for by milk.

  a. Assess your utility function for c for $0 \le c \le 1$. Note that if you like a little milk in your coffee, the high point on your utility function may be at a value of c somewhere between 0 and 1.

  b. Compare (A) the mixture consisting of proportions c of coffee and $1 - c$ of milk in a cup and (B) the lottery yielding a cup of coffee with probability c and a cup of milk with probability $1 - c$. (The decision tree is shown in Figure 14.13.) Are the expected amounts of milk and coffee the same in A and B? (That is, if you calculate $E(c)$, is it the same in A and B?) Is there any value of c for which you are indifferent between A and B? (How about when c is 0 or 1?) Are you indifferent between A and B for the value of c at the high point of your utility function?

  c. How would you describe your risk attitude with respect to c? Are you risk-averse or risk-prone, or would some other term be more appropriate?

14.15   In a court case, a plaintiff claimed that the defendant should pay her $3 million for damages. She did not expect the judge to award her this amount; her expected value actually

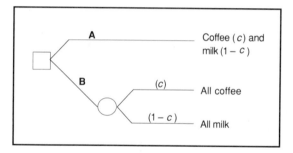

FIGURE 14.13   *Decision Tree for Problem 14.14b*

was $1 million. The defendant also did not believe that the court would award the full $3 million, and shared the plaintiff's expected value of $1 million.

a. Assuming that the plaintiff is thinking about the award in terms of gains, explain why you might expect her to be risk-averse in this situation. If she is risk-averse, what kind of settlement offer might she accept from the defendant?

b. Assuming that the defendant is thinking about the situation in term of losses, explain why you might expect him or her to be risk-seeking. What would this imply about settlement offers to which the defendant might agree? (*Hint*: Draw an example of a risk-seeking utility curve over the possible negative payoffs for the defendant. Now find the certainty equivalent.)

c. Discuss your answers to parts a and b. What are the implications for settlements in real-world court cases? What would happen if the defendant's expected value were less than the plaintiff's?

CASE STUDIES

The Life-Insurance Game

Peggy Ewen sat back in her chair and listened as Tom Pitman tried to explain. "I don't know what's going on," Tom said. "I have no trouble making the phone calls, and I seem to be able to set up in-home visits. I am making at least as many visits as anyone else in the office. For some reason, though, I cannot talk them into buying the product. I seem to be unlucky enough to have run into a lot of people who just are not interested in life insurance."

Peggy thought about this. Tom had been with the company for five months now. He was bright and energetic. He had gone through the training program easily, and had appeared to hit the ground running. His paperwork was always perfect. For some reason, though, his career selling life insurance was virtually stalled. His sales rate was only one-third that of the next best salesperson. Why?

Peggy asked, "How do you feel about going to the in-home visits?"

"Fine," Tom replied. "Well, I'm starting to feel a little apprehensive about it just because I'm becoming less sure of myself. "

"Well, that's something we'll have to work on. But how do the visits go? What do you talk about? Tell me what a typical visit would be like."

"Let's see. Usually I'll come in, sit down, and we'll chat briefly. They'll offer me a cup of coffee. After a short visit, we get right down to business. I go through the presentation material provided by the company. Eventually we get around to talking about the reasons for purchasing life insurance. I really stress the importance of being able to make up for the loss of income. The presentation material stresses the idea of building up savings for sending kids to school or for retirement. You know, the idea of being sure that the extra money will be there down the road. But I really don't think that's why most people buy life insurance. I think they buy it to be sure that their family will be able to make up for a loss. For just a small premium, they can be sure that the loss won't happen, or at least they can minimize the loss."

Peggy seemed interested in Tom's account. "So you really stress the idea that for a little bit of money they can insure against the loss of income."

"Yes," Tom answered. "I'd rather have them look at life insurance as protection against a potential loss, rather than as a savings mechanism that would provide some sure amount in the future. Most of them know that there are better ways to save, anyway."

"And how would you classify your typical client? What kind of income bracket?"

"Mostly young couples just starting out," said Tom. "Maybe they've just had their first child. Not much income yet. Not much savings, either. We usually discuss this early on in the conversation. In general they seem to be quite aware of their financial situation. Occasionally they are even quite sensitive about it."

Peggy looked at Tom and grinned. "Tom, I do believe that there's something you can do right now to improve your sales rate."

QUESTIONS

1. About what issue is Peggy thinking?
2. What are the implications for people interested in selling financial securities such as insurance, annuities, and so on?
3. What are the implications for their customers?

◆

Nuclear Power Paranoia

Ray Kaplan was disgusted. The rally against the power plant had gone poorly. The idea had been to get a lot of people out to show the utility company that the community did not support the idea of nuclear power. It was just too dangerous! Too much chance of an accident. Sure, the officials always pointed out that there had never been a serious nuclear power plant accident in the United

States. They always pointed to the safeguards in the plants, and to the safety features required by federal regulations. "You're safer in our plant than on the freeway," they claimed. Well, the same officials met with the protesters again today and said the same old things. Ray was getting tired of it. He hopped on his motorcycle and rode home. Fast.

He was still ruminating about the rally while he broiled his steak over the charcoal that evening. As he snacked on a bowl of ice cream after dinner, he asked himself, "Can't they see the potential for disaster?"

The next day, Ray decided to mow his lawn and then ride out to the beach. About a mile from his house, he realized that he wasn't wearing his motorcycle helmet. Well, he thought, the beach was only about 20 miles away. Besides, it would be nice to feel the wind in his hair. The ride was nice, even though the traffic was heavier than he had expected. The fumes from one of the trucks really got to him briefly, but fortunately the exit for the beach was right there. As he lay down on his towel to soak up the sunshine, his mind went back to the rally. "Darn," he thought. "I'll probably develop an ulcer just worrying about that silly power plant."

QUESTION

1. What do you think about Ray Kaplan's behavior?

The Manager's Perspective

Ed Freeman just couldn't understand it. Why were the activists so blind? For years the information had been available showing just how safe nuclear power plants were. Study after study had concluded that the risk of fatalities from a nuclear power plant accident was far less than driving a car, flying in a commercial airliner, and many other commonplace activities in which people freely chose to engage. Sure, there had been some close calls, such as Three Mile Island, and there had been the terrible accident at Chernobyl in the Soviet Union. Still, the overall record of the nuclear power industry in the United States was excellent. No one could deny it if they would only compare the industry to others.

His risk assessors had gone through their own paces, documenting the safety features of his plant for the Nuclear Regulatory Commission; it was up to date and, in fact, one of the safest plants in the country. The experts had estimated the probability of an accident at the plant as nearly zero. Furthermore, even if an accident were to occur, the safety systems that had been built in would minimize the public's exposure.

Given all this, he just could not understand the public opposition to the plant. He knew that these were bright people. They were articulate, well read, and were able to marshal their supporters with great skill. But they seemed to ignore all of the data as well as the experts' reports and conclusions.

"I guess it takes all kinds," he sighed as he prepared to go back to work.

QUESTIONS

1. This case and "Nuclear Power Paranoia" go together. People often are willing to engage voluntarily in activities that are far more risky (in the sense of the probability of a serious injury or death) than living near a nuclear power plant. Why do you think this is the case?
2. What makes new technologies seem risky to you?

◆

◇ REFERENCES

The axioms of expected utility, along with the notion of subjective probability, were first discussed by Ramsey (1931), but the world appears to have ignored him. Most economists refer to "von Neumann–Morgenstern utility functions" because in 1947 von Neumann and Morgenstern published their celebrated *Theory of Games and Economic Behavior* in which they also set forth a set of axioms for choice behavior that leads to maximization of expected utility. The axioms subsequently appeared in a wide variety of forms and in many textbooks. Some examples are Luce and Raiffa (1957), Savage (1954), DeGroot (1970), and, more recently, French (1986). French's text is excellent for those interested in the axiomatic mathematics that underlie decision theory.

The various axioms have been debated widely. Our discussion of the transitivity axiom, for example, was suggested by Dr. Peter Fishburn as part of his acceptance speech for the Ramsey Medal, an award for distinguished contributions to decision analysis. If Peter Fishburn, one of the foremost scholars of decision theory, is willing to concede that intransitive preferences might not be unreasonable, perhaps we should pay attention! Fishburn (1989) summarizes many of the recent developments in the axioms and theory.

The text by von Winterfeldt and Edwards (1986) also contains much intriguing discussion of the axioms from the point of view of behavioral researchers and a discussion of the many paradoxes found in behavioral decision theory. Hogarth (1987) also covers this topic. Tversky and Kahneman (1981) provide an excellent and readable treatment of framing effects, and Kahneman and Tversky (1979) present a theory of behavioral decision making that accounts for many anomalies in individual decision behavior.

The constructionist view of decision analysis that is presented in the last section of this chapter does not appear to be widely discussed, although such a view has substantial and fundamental implications for research in decision theory as well as in decision-analysis practice. For more discussion of this topic with regard to utility assessment, see von Winterfeldt and Edwards (1986, p. 356) and Fischer (1979). On the probability side, Shafer and Tversky (1986) view probability and structuring of inference problems in an interesting "constructive" way. Phillips's notion of the development of a requisite model (1982, 1984) and Watson and Buede's (1987) approach to decision analysis contain many of the elements of the constructionist view.

ALLAIS, M. (1953) "Le Comportement de l'Homme Rationnel Devant le Risque: Critique des Postulats et Axiomes de l'École Americaine." *Econometrica*, 21, 503–546.

ALLAIS, M., and J. HAGEN (eds.) (1979) *Expected Utility Hypotheses and the Allais Paradox.* Dordrecht, The Netherlands: Reidel.

FISCHER, G. (1979) "Utility Models for Multiple Objective Decisions: Do They Accurately Represent Human Preferences?" *Decision Sciences*, 10, 451–479.

FISHBURN, P. C. (1989) "Foundations of Decision Analysis: Along the Way." *Management Science*, 35, 387–405.

FRENCH, S. (1986) *Decision Theory: An Introduction to the Mathematics of Rationality.* London: Wiley.

HERSHEY, J. C., H. C. KUNREUTHER, and P. J. H. SHOEMAKER (1982) "Sources of Bias in Assessment Procedures for Utility Functions." *Management Science*, 28, 936–954.

HOGARTH, R. (1987) *Judgment and Choice*, 2nd ed. New York: Wiley.

KAHNEMAN, D., and A. TVERSKY (1979) "Prospect Theory: An Analysis of Decision Under Risk." *Econometrica*, 47, 263–291.

LUCE, R. D., and H. RAIFFA (1957) *Games and Decisions: Introduction and Critical Survey.* New York: Wiley.

MCCORD, M., and R. DE NEUFVILLE (1986) " 'Lottery Equivalents': Reduction of the Certainty Effect Problem in Utility Assessment." *Management Science*, 32, 56–60.

PHILLIPS, L. D. (1982) "Requisite Decision Modelling." *Journal of the Operational Research Society*, 33, 303–312.

PHILLIPS, L. D. (1984) "A Theory of Requisite Decision Models." *Acta Psychologica*, 56, 29–48.

RAMSEY, F. P. (1931) "Truth and Probability." In R. B. Braithwaite (ed.), *The Foundations of Mathematics and Other Logical Essays.* New York: Harcourt Brace.

SAVAGE, L. J. (1954) *The Foundations of Statistics.* New York: Wiley.

SHAFER, G., and A. TVERSKY (1986) "Languages and Designs for Probability Judgment." *Cognitive Science*, 9, 309–339.

TVERSKY, A., and D. KAHNEMAN (1981) "The Framing of Decisions and the Psychology of Choice." *Science*, 211, 453–458.

VON NEUMANN, J., and O. MORGENSTERN (1947) *Theory of Games and Economic Behavior.* Princeton, NJ: Princeton University Press.

VON WINTERFELDT, D., and W. EDWARDS (1986) *Decision Analysis and Behavioral Research.* Cambridge: Cambridge University Press.

WATSON, S. R., and D. M. BUEDE (1987) *Decision Synthesis: The Principles and Practice of Decision Analysis.* Cambridge: Cambridge University Press.

◇ EPILOGUE

We began the chapter with the Asian influenza example. This kind of study has been done repeatedly by many different experimenters, and the results are always the same; many of the subjects make inconsistent choices that depend on the framing of the problem. Of course, many of these experiments have been done using college students and other individuals who are not used to making this kind of decision. It would be nice to think that individuals who make difficult decisions often would not be susceptible to such inconsistencies. Unfortunately, such is not the case. Tversky and Kahneman (1981) report the same kinds of inconsistencies among decisions made by university faculty and physicians.　　　　　　　　　　　　　　　　　　　　　　　◆

Conflicting Objectives I: Some Basic Techniques

The utility functions for money that we have considered have embodied an important fundamental trade-off: monetary return versus riskiness. We have argued all along that the basic reason for using a utility function as a preference model in decision making is to capture our attitudes about risk and return. Accomplishing high returns and minimizing exposure to risk are two conflicting objectives, and we already have learned how to model our preference trade-offs between these objectives using utility functions. Thus, we already have addressed two of the fundamental conflicting objectives that decision makers face.

In Problems 14.11–14.14 in the last chapter (page 424), you were asked to assess utility functions for a variety of things other than money: coffee, computer reliability, life-span of cars, and homework effort. In each case, the utility function that you assessed by comparing lotteries embodied your attitude about risk and return. Furthermore, in all of the cases (except perhaps the coffee), encoding your attitude toward risk was important for decision making. In most decisions involving these things, you would probably be facing an unknown quantity. If you were to purchase a personal computer, you would not know exactly how reliable the computer would turn out to be. Deciding among automobiles to purchase involves weighing your beliefs regarding their probable life-spans. Will they break down in 10,000 miles? Will they last for 200,000 miles? When you decide among courses to take, one of your considerations involves your overall effort spent on assignments outside of class. But you cannot know for sure what degree of effort will be required in any given class. In every case, the risk-to-return trade-off is important, and in general we try hard to manage our decisions in order to improve our chances of achieving the best of something while limiting the risks that we face.

Even though we have indeed been studying two fundamental conflicting objectives, there is one more important step to take. What if more than one aspect of the potential outcome is important? In purchasing cars or computers, we consider not only reliability and life-span, but also price, ease of use, maintenance costs, operating expenses, and so on. In deciding among courses, you might be interested in factors such as the complementarity of courses in terms of material covered, importance in relation to your major and career goals, time schedule, the instructor, and so on. As individuals, we usually can do a fair job of assimilating enough information so that we feel comfortable with a decision. In many cases, we end up saying things like, "Well, I can save some money now and have to buy a new car sooner," "You get what you pay for," and "You can't have everything." These are obvious intuitive statements that reflect the informal trade-offs that we make. Understanding trade-offs in detail, however, may be critical for a company executive who is interested in acquiring hundreds of personal computers or a large fleet of automobiles for the firm.

If you have trouble with conflicting objectives in some of the decisions in your life, consider what it must be like for policy makers who deal with complicated decisions on a daily basis. In Chapter 1 we read about the gypsy moth problem; the ODA wanted to achieve a host of economic, environmental, and health-related objectives, but those objectives conflicted within the framework of the decision that had to be made. The available alternatives simply did not permit high achievement in all directions at once. Compromises and trade-offs are almost always important. Some other examples and possible objectives appear in Figure 15.1 (abstracted from Keeney and Raiffa, 1976).

In this chapter we will present a relatively straightforward way of dealing with conflicting objectives. Essentially, we will create a preference model that is *additive*; that is, we will calculate a utility score for each objective and then add the scores, weighting them appropriately according to the relative importance of the various objectives. The procedure is easy to use and intuitive. Computer programs are available that make the required assessment process fairly simple. But with the simple additive form comes limitations. Some of those limitations will be exposed in the problems at the end of the chapter. In Chapter 16, we will take up multiattribute utility theory and see how to construct more complicated preference models that are less limiting.

Where are we going? This chapter is somewhat involved. Let us consider where we are headed. The first part of the chapter ("What Is Important? Building a Value Tree") addresses the problem of determining what the relevant objectives are. A corresponding issue is how to measure different alternatives' performance in terms of these conflicting objectives. We will specify *attributes*, or operational measures of the extent to which an alternative accomplishes a corresponding objective. In this part of the decision-structuring process, the goal is to construct a *value tree*, a hierarchical representation of the decision maker's objectives and their corresponding attributes.

With the value tree constructed and the attributes specified, we move on to the matter of understanding trade-offs between objectives. In the section titled "Trading Off Conflicting Objectives: The Basics," we will look at an example that

1) A mayor must decide whether to approve a major new electric power generating station. The city needs more power capacity, but the new plant would worsen the city's air quality. The mayor might consider the following issues:

- The health of residents.
- The economic conditions of the residents.
- The psychological state of the residents.
- The economy of the city and the state.
- Businesses.
- Local politics.

2) Imagine the issues involved in the treatment of heroin addicts. A policy maker might like to:

- Reduce the size of the addict pool.
- Reduce costs to the city and its residents.
- Reduce crimes against property and persons.
- Improve the "quality of life" of addicts.
- Improve the "quality of life" of nonaddicts.
- Curb organized crime.
- Live up to the high ideals of civil rights and civil liberties.
- Decrease the alienation of youth.
- Get elected to higher political office.

3) In choosing a site for a new airport near Mexico City, the head of the Ministry of Public Works had to balance such objectives as:

- Minimize the costs to the federal government.
- Raise the capacity of airport facilities.
- Improve the safety of the system.
- Reduce noise levels.
- Reduce access time to users.
- Minimize displacement of people for expansion.
- Improve regional development (roads, for instance).
- Achieve political aims.

4) A doctor prescribing medical treatment must consider a variety of issues:

- Potential health complications for the patient (perhaps death).
- Money cost to the patient.
- Patient's time spent being treated.
- Cost to insurance companies.
- Payments to the doctor.
- Utilization of resources (nurses, hospital space, equipment).
- Information gained in treating this patient (may be helpful in treating others).

FIGURE 15.1   *Four Examples of Decisions Involving Complicated Preference Trade-offs*

Source: Keeney, R., and H. Raiffa *Decisions with Multiple Objectives: Preference and Value Tradeoffs.* Copyright © 1976 by John Wiley & Sons, Inc. Reprinted by permission.

offers a relatively simple choice from among automobiles and involves only two objectives. In this initial discussion, we will develop intuitive ways to trade off two conflicting objectives. In addition, we will see an elementary way to establish scores on each attribute for the alternatives and trade-off weights based on the relative importance of the objectives. We will also discuss indifference curves. The purpose of this discussion is to introduce ideas, help you focus on the primary issues involved, and provide a framework for thinking clearly about trade-offs among objectives.

The simple approach presented can be used in many situations, but it is analogous to making decisions by maximizing EMV. In some cases, this simple approach is inadequate, and there is a need to incorporate risk attitudes. Therefore, in the section titled "Some Alternative Methods for Assessing Scores and Trade-off Weights," we introduce different approaches for determining both attribute scores and trade-off weights. These assessment techniques are preferable in some ways to the simple approach presented earlier in the chapter.

In the last section of the chapter, we will consider an actual example in which the city of Eugene, Oregon, evaluates four candidate sites for a new public library. The example shows the process of defining objectives and attributes, weighting the attributes, ranking the alternatives on the different attributes, and then putting all of the assessments together to obtain an overall ranking of the four sites.

♦ WHAT IS IMPORTANT? BUILDING A VALUE TREE

In Chapter 2, we discussed the process of structuring a decision problem. An important aspect of structuring is to understand exactly what is important. Why does the current decision have to be made, and what are we trying to accomplish? We have argued that in most real-world situations, it is not a matter of maximizing some specific single aspect, but one of trading off conflicting objectives. Thus, at this point, we must return to the problem of structuring and discuss in some detail the process of determining exactly what objectives need to be considered. In short, we must determine the important dimensions of our values. The goal will be to structure those values in a value tree.

What is a value tree? It begins with several fundamental objectives as main branches. Each fundamental objective then is expanded and explained with more specific objectives and values. For example, Figure 15.2 shows a value tree for evaluating alternative-energy technologies (adapted from von Winterfeldt and Edwards, 1986). For example, the "Minimize Risks" branch shows that we would like to minimize risks to environment and human health. Environmental risk can be broken down further into risks to flora and fauna, air and water, history and culture, and aesthetics. Although we generally would like to minimize such risks, choosing an alternative that does so probably will also imply a reduction in benefits gained in the other dimensions.

For another example, consider the possible elements of a value tree for an automobile purchase. Fundamental objectives might include maximizing safety, performance, service availability, and capacity, while cost is minimized. Minimizing cost might be broken down further into purchase price, operating cost, and resale value. Maximizing capacity might lead to considerations of trunk space and seating. And so on.

Identifying the fundamental objectives is a key step in building the value tree. Often this step is taken for granted. At the outset, it is important to think hard about exactly what you want to accomplish. Do you want to improve performance? Minimize cost? Modify something? What things are important to you? Be sure to ask *why* something is important. This question will help you to uncover fundamental objectives. For example, in deciding which computer to purchase, you might say that a good warranty is important and that reputable service technicians must be available. Why are these important? At a more fundamental level you may find that the reliability of the system is important to you, and that a good warranty and quality service will help to ensure a high level of reliability.

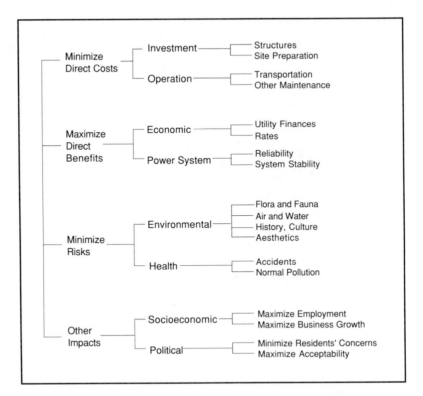

FIGURE 15.2   *Value Tree for Evaluating Alternative-Energy Technologies*

Source: von Winterfeldt, D., and W. Edwards (1986) *Decision Analysis and Behavioral Research*. Cambridge: Cambridge University Press.

A common mistake in constructing value trees is to make them too complicated. Careful thought about objectives can help here. Be sure that the fundamental objectives actually do represent the important dimensions of the decision. If you think hard, you may find that there really are few fundamental objectives. Be sure that the detail objectives indeed help to explain and operationalize the fundamental objectives. The fundamental objectives can be thought of as the *ends* that you want to accomplish, while the detail objectives are the *means* for accomplishing the fundamental objectives.

It may be worthwhile to develop a list of questions like those in Chapter 6 to help identify the objectives. In fact, there is an important relationship between the creativity techniques that we discussed in Chapter 6 and the process of identifying fundamental objectives. Careful development of a complete list of fundamental objectives may lead you to invent new alternatives not previously considered.

Completing the value tree requires identification of *attributes* that correspond to the detail objectives. That is, at the end of each branch, there must be an operational way to measure the extent to which an alternative or outcome accomplishes the detail objective. Finding an operational measurement is an important task and may be difficult. An attribute is operational if you can explain to someone else what information you need and why, that person can provide it to you, and you can pay for it and understand it. As a test, ask yourself these questions: (1) Can you explain to someone else what to measure and why? (2) Is obtaining the measurement a reasonable chore? (3) If you were given the measurement by someone else, would you be able to tell how well the alternative in question achieved the objective? (Or is there something else that you need to know?)

For example, suppose that one of the fundamental objectives in purchasing an automobile is to minimize cost. Two detail objectives might be to minimize the purchase price and to minimize the interest rate of a loan. In each case, there are obvious attributes; the purchase price is the best price that the dealer will give you, and the interest rate can be measured by the annual percentage rate of the loan. It is easy to explain to someone what these attributes are, why they are related to cost, and where to obtain them. Moreover, it would be straightforward for someone else to obtain these numbers and give them to you; no other information is required.

But in other cases, the attribute corresponding to a detail objective may not be so obvious. Take the alternative-energy technology example, and consider the "Normal Pollution" branch. The detail objective is to minimize health risks from normal pollution. But how can these risks be measured? Should we think in terms of expected deaths that can be attributed to the increased pollution? How about workdays lost because of pollution-induced illness? Defining an attribute to measure achievement toward these detail objectives may be a difficult task. Another detail objective is labeled "Accidents" and refers to the detail objective of minimizing accidents that would be dangerous to human health. How could this be measured? Probability of a major accident (suitably defined)? Expected number of lives lost in accidents? Could you explain to another person exactly what measurement to make in this case and why it is important? Could an individual with the appropriate knowledge and skills make the required judgments of probability or expected lives lost? If you ask an expert for his or her subjective assessment, do you need to know anything else (for example, the data considered) in order to make appropriate use of his or her judgment? In many environmental analyses, judgments like these must be made, and careful specification of the attributes is required to ensure that the attributes will be both meaningfully related to the corresponding objective and still obtainable without undue cost or effort.

Construction of a value tree primarily requires careful consideration of what is important to you. There are a few points to keep in mind. Your value tree should meet the following five criteria:

1. A value tree should be complete; it should include all relevant aspects of a decision. If you can think of important issues that are not captured by the value tree, then it may be incomplete.
2. At the same time, the value tree should be as small as possible. A value tree that is too large and too cumbersome is difficult to work with and hard to

understand. Keep in mind that the value tree is meant to be a useful representation or model of objectives that are important to the decision maker. Furthermore, the alternatives should rank differently on the objectives. If all of the alternatives are equivalent in one dimension, then that dimension will not be helpful in making the decision.

3. The attributes at the ends of the branches must be operational. They should provide an easy way to measure the performance of the alternatives or the outcomes on the detail objectives. You should be able to think of both good and bad scenarios for each detail objective.

4. A value tree should not be redundant. That is, the same objectives should be repeated as little as possible through the tree, and the objectives should not be closely related.

5. As far as possible, a value tree should be decomposable. The decision maker should be able to think about one objective easily and without having to consider others. For example, in evaluating construction bids, the cost of the project and the amount of time required may be important attributes. In most cases we can think about these attributes separately; regardless of the cost, it always would be preferable to complete the project sooner, and vice versa. Thus, the value tree would be decomposable into these two attributes, which can be considered independently. On the other hand, if you are deciding from among courses to take, you may want to pick the most interesting topic and at the same time minimize the amount of effort required. These attributes, however, are related in a way that does not permit decomposition, and hence you may have to consider the attributes jointly; whether you want to put in a lot of effort may depend on how interested you are in the material.

◆ TRADING OFF CONFLICTING OBJECTIVES: THE BASICS

The essential problem in multiobjective decision making is deciding how best to trade off increased value on one objective for lower value on another. Making these trade-offs is a subjective matter and requires the decision maker's judgment. In this section, we will look at a simple approach that captures the essence of trade-offs. We will begin with an example that involves only two objectives.

Choosing an Automobile: An Example

Suppose you are buying a car, and you are interested in both price and life-span. You would like a long expected life-span — that is, the length of time until you must replace the car — and a low price. (These assumptions are made for the purpose of this example; some people might enjoy purchasing a new car every three years, and so a long life-span may be meaningless.) Let us further suppose that you have narrowed your choices down to three alternatives — the Portalo (a relatively expensive sedan with a reputation for longevity), the Norushi (renowned for its reliability), and the Standard Motors car (a relatively inexpensive domestic automobile). You have done some library research and have evaluated all three cars on both attributes as shown in Table 15.1. Plotting these three alternatives on a graph with expected life-span on the horizontal axis and price on the vertical axis yields Figure 15.3. The Portalo, Norushi, and Standard show up on the graph as three points arranged on an upward-sloping curve. That the three points are ordered in this way reflects the notion, "You get what you pay for." If you want a longer expected life-span, you have to pay more money.

Occasionally alternatives may be ruled out immediately by means of a dominance argument. For example, consider a hypothetical car that costs $15,000 and has an expected life-span of seven years (Point A in Figure 15.3). Such a car would be a poor choice relative to the Norushi, which gives a longer expected life for less money. Thus, A would be dominated by the Norushi.

On the other hand, none of the cars under consideration is dominated. With this being the case, how can you choose? The question clearly is, "How much are you willing to pay to increase the life-span of your car?" To answer this question, we will start with the Standard, and assume that you will purchase it if

	Portalo	Norushi	Standard Motors
Price ($1000)	17	10	8
Life-Span (Years)	12	9	6

TABLE 15.1 *Automobile Purchase Alternatives*

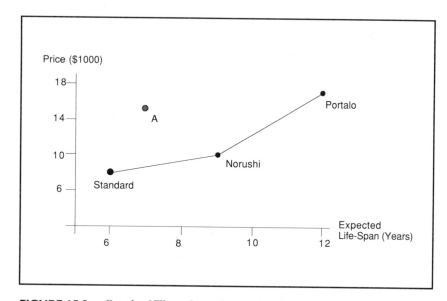

FIGURE 15.3 *Graph of Three Cars, Comparing Price and Expected Life-Span*

the others are not better. Is it worthwhile to switch from the Standard to the Norushi? Note that the slope of the line connecting the Norushi and the Standard is $666.67 per year. The switch would be worthwhile if you were willing to pay at least $666.67 for each additional year of life-span, or $2000 to increase the expected life-span by three years. Would you be willing to pay more than $2000 to increase the expected life of your car by three years? This is a subjective assessment! If you would, then it is worthwhile to switch to the Norushi from the Standard. If not, do not switch.

For the sake of continuing the example, assume that you made the switch, and that you have decided that the Norushi is better for you than the Standard; you would pay at least $2000 for the additional three years of life-span. Now, should you switch to the Portalo? Notice that the slope of the line that connects the Norushi and the Portalo is $2333.33 per year, or $7000 for an additional three years. You were willing to pay at least $666.67 for an extra year. Now, what about an extra $7000 for another three years? Are the extra years of expected life-span worth this much to you? If so, make the switch to the Portalo. If not, stick with the Norushi.

This simple procedure permits you to move systematically through the alternatives. The idea is to start at one corner of the graph (for example, the Standard) and then consider switching with each of the other alternatives, always moving in the same direction. Once a switch is made, there is never a need to reconsider the previous alternative. (After all, the one to which you changed must be better.) If there were many cars to choose from, the procedure would be to plot them all on a graph, eliminate the dominated alternatives, and then systematically move through the non-dominated set, beginning at the lower left-hand side of the graph and considering the alternatives that are to the upper right-hand side.

This procedure works well in the context of two conflicting objectives, and you can see how we are trading off the two. At each step we ask whether the additional benefit from switching (the increase in expected life-span) is worth the cost (the increase in price). The same kind of procedure can be used with three or more attributes. The trade-offs become more complicated, however, and graphical interpretation is difficult.

The automobile example above is intended to give you an intuitive idea of how trade-offs work. This particular example is easy because it seems natural to many of us to think in terms of dollars, and we often can reduce nonmonetary attributes to dollars. But what if we wanted to trade off life-span and reliability? We would like to have a systematic procedure that we can apply in any situation fairly easily. To do this, we must find satisfactory ways to answer two questions. The first question has to do with comparing the attribute levels of the available alternatives. We are comparing three different automobiles. How do they compare on the two attributes? Is the Portalo "twice as good" on life-span as the Norushi? How does the Standard compare (quantitatively) to the Portalo on price? In the energy example, alternative technologies must be ranked on each of their attributes. For example, substantial differences may exist among these technologies on all of the detail attributes. To get anywhere with the construction of a quantitative model of preferences, we must assess numerical scores for each alternative that reflect the comparisons.

The second question asks how the attributes compare in terms of importance. In the automobile example, is life-span twice as important as price, and exactly what does "twice as important" mean? In the alternative-energy example, how do the environmental and health risks compare in terms of importance within the "Minimize Risks" fundamental objective? Again, numerical weights must be assessed for each attribute.

The task at hand, then, is to assess (1) scores for the alternatives on each of the detail attributes and (2) weights for the objectives in the value tree. Then an alternative's overall score can be calculated as a weighted combination of its scores on the individual attributes. We will continue with our automobile example.

Proportional Scores

Comparing the alternatives on the individual attributes is a matter of finding meaningful scores related to the attributes. Of course, we can simply use price and life-span directly. But we also can scale these values, as we did with utility functions, so that the worst has a value of 0 and the best has a value of 1. If we do so, then the scores on price and life-span will be more directly comparable.

The first step is easy. The Standard is best on price and worst on life-span, so assign it a 1 for price and a 0 for life-span. Do the opposite for the Portalo, so that it scores 0 on price and 1 on life-span. Now, how do we derive the scores for the Norushi? Because we have meaningful numerical attributes already, we can simply scale the Norushi's scores. A general formula is handy. Call Norushi's price x. Now calculate

$$S_P(\$10,000) = \frac{(x - \text{Worst Value})}{(\text{Best Value} - \text{Worst Value})}$$

$$= \frac{(10,000 - 17,000)}{(8000 - 17,000)}$$

$$= 0.78.$$

Thus, S_P represents the score for price (indicated by the subscript P). Likewise, Norushi's score on life-span is

$$S_L(9 \text{ Years}) = \frac{(x - \text{Worst Value})}{(\text{Best Value} - \text{Worst Value})}$$

$$= \frac{(9 - 6)}{(12 - 6)}$$

$$= 0.50.$$

The intuition behind these scores is that 9 years is exactly halfway between 6 and 12 years (thus the score of $S_L = 0.50$), while \$10,000 is 78% of the way from \$17,000 to \$8000. The scores for the cars are summarized in Table 15.2. As long as the attributes are numerical, you can see that it will be a straightforward matter to scale those attributes so that the best is 1, the worst is 0, and the intermedi-

	Portalo	Norushi	Standard Motors
Price (S_P)	0.00	0.78	1.00
Life-Span (S_L)	1.00	0.50	0.00

TABLE 15.2   *Scores for Three Cars on Two Attributes*

ate alternatives have scores that reflect the relative distance between the best and worst.

Trade-off Weights: Pricing Out the Attributes

Now we must assess the weights for price and life-span. But before we decide on the weights once and for all, let us look at the implications of various weights. We will use k to denote a trade-off weight, and a subscript will indicate the corresponding attribute. Thus, for the automobile example, we must assess k_P and k_L, which represent the weights for price and life-span, respectively. For convenience, we will have the weights sum to 1.

Suppose you were to decide that price and expected life-span should be weighted equally, or $k_P = k_L = 0.5$. In general, we are going to calculate

$$S(\text{Price, Life-Span}) = k_P S_P(\text{Price}) + k_L S_L(\text{Life-Span}).$$

Thus, the weighted scores would be

$$S(\text{Portalo}) \quad = 0.5\ (0.00) + 0.5\ (1.00) = 0.50$$
$$S(\text{Norushi}) \quad = 0.5\ (0.78) + 0.5\ (0.50) = 0.64$$
$$S(\text{Standard}) = 0.5\ (1.00) + 0.5\ (0.00) = 0.50.$$

The Standard and the Portalo come out with exactly the same weighted score. This is because of the way that price and life-span are traded off against each other. Because the difference between 1 and 0 amounts to $9000 in price versus six years in life-span, the equal weight in this case says that one additional year of life-span is worth $1500. The Norushi comes out on top because you pay less than $1500 per year for the three additional years in expected life-span as compared to the Standard.

Suppose that you have little money to spend on a car. Then you might think that price should be twice as important as life-span. To model this, let $k_P = 0.67$ and $k_L = 0.33$. Now the weighted scores for the cars are: Portalo, 0.33; Norushi, 0.69; and Standard, 0.67. In this case the weights imply that an increase in life-span of one year is only worth an increase in price of $750. (You can verify this by calculating the score for a car that costs $8750 and is expected to last seven years; such a car will have the same weighted score as the Standard.) Again the Norushi comes out as being preferred to the Standard, because its three-year increase in life-span (relative to the Standard) is accompanied by only a $2000 increase in price, whereas the weights indicate that the additional three years would be worth as much as $2250.

You may not be happy with either scheme. Perhaps you have thought carefully about the relative importance of expected life-span and price, and you have decided that you would be willing to pay up to $600 for an extra year of expected life-span. You have thus *priced out* the value of an additional year of expected life-span. How can you translate this price into the appropriate weights? Take the Standard as your base case (although any of the three automobiles could be used for this). Essentially, you are saying that you would be indifferent between paying $8000 for six years of expected life-span and $8600 for seven years of expected life-span. Using the general formula above to calculate scores, we can find that such a hypothetical car (Car B) would score $\frac{1}{6} = 0.167$ on expected life-span (which is one-sixth of the way from the worst to the best case) and 0.933 on price ($8600 is 0.933 of the way from the worst to the best case). Because you would be indifferent between the Standard and the hypothetical Car B, the weights must satisfy:

$$S(\text{Standard}) = S(\text{Car B})$$
$$k_P (1.00) + k_L (0) = k_P (0.933) + k_L (0.167).$$

Simplify this equation to find that

$$k_P (1.00 - 0.933) = k_L (0.167)$$
$$k_P = k_L \frac{0.167}{0.067},$$

or that

$$k_P = 2.50 \, k_L.$$

Including the condition that the weights must sum to 1, we have

$$k_P = 2.50 \, (1 - k_P),$$

or

$$k_P = 0.714 \quad \text{and} \quad k_L = 0.286.$$

Note that these weights are consistent with what we did above. The weight $k_P = 0.667$ implied a price of $750 per additional year of expected life-span. With a still lower price ($600), we obtained a higher weight for k_P.

The final objective, of course, is to compare the cars in terms of their weighted scores:

$$S(\text{Portalo}) \quad = 0.714 \, (0.00) + 0.286 \, (1.00) = 0.286$$
$$S(\text{Norushi}) \quad = 0.714 \, (0.78) + 0.286 \, (0.50) = 0.700$$
$$S(\text{Standard}) = 0.714 \, (1.00) + 0.286 \, (0.00) = 0.714.$$

The Standard comes out only slightly better than the Norushi. This is consistent with the switching approach described earlier. The weights here came from the assessment that one year of life-span was worth only $600, not the $666.67 or more required to switch from the Standard to the Norushi.

Indifference Curves

The assessment that you would trade $600 for an additional year of life-span can be used to construct *indifference curves,* which can be thought of as a set of alternatives (some perhaps being hypothetical) among which the decision maker is indifferent. For example, we already have established that you would be indifferent between the Standard and hypothetical Car B, which costs $8600 and lasts seven years. Thus, in Figure 15.4 we have a line that passes through the points for the Standard and the point for the hypothetical Car B (Point B). All of the points along this line represent cars that would be equivalent to the Standard; all would have the same score, 0.714. Other indifference curves also are shown with their corresponding scores. Note that the indifference curves have higher values as one moves down and to the right because you would rather pay less money and have a longer life-span. You can see that the Norushi and the Portalo are not preferred to the Standard because they lie above the 0.714 indifference curve.

The slope of the indifference curves in Figure 15.4 is related to the trade-off rate that was assessed. Specifically, the slope is $600 per year, the price that was assessed for each year of expected life-span. This also is sometimes called the *marginal rate of substitution,* or the rate at which one attribute can be used to replace another.

Graphing indifference curves is a useful way to obtain insight into one's assessed trade-offs. For example, Figure 15.4 provides a way to understand the trade-offs between life-span and price that complements our discussion in the previous section.

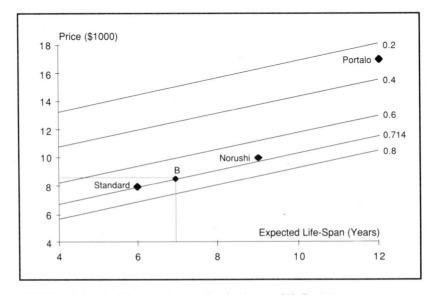

FIGURE 15.4 *Indifference Curves for the Automobile Decision*

A Limitation: Proportional Scores Imply Risk Neutrality

In our example, we developed scores for the Norushi using the notion of proportionality. In fact, we have just taken the original values and scaled them so that they now range from 0 to 1, 0 being the worst and 1 being the best. Figure 15.5 graphs the price relative to a car's score on price. The graph shows a straight line, and we know about straight lines in this context: They imply risk neutrality and all of the unusual behavior associated with risk neutrality. In some cases, this risk-neutral approach may be fine. But even in the case of the automobiles it may be appropriate to consider the utility of money.

Let us think about what risk neutrality implies here with another simple example. Imagine that you face two career choices. You could decide to invest your life savings in an entrepreneurial venture, or you could take a job as a government bureaucrat. After considering the situation carefully, you conclude that your objectives are purely monetary, and you can think in terms of income and savings. (Actually, more than just monetary outcomes should influence your career choice!) The bureaucratic job has a well-defined career path and considerable security. After 10 years, you know with virtual certainty that you will make $30,000 per year and have $60,000 in the bank toward retirement. On the other hand, becoming an entrepreneur is a risky proposition. The income and savings outcomes could range anywhere from zero dollars in the case of failure to some large amount in the event of success. To solve the problem, you decide to assess a continuous distribution and fit a discrete approximation. The decision tree in Figure 15.6 shows your probability assessments and your alternatives. You can

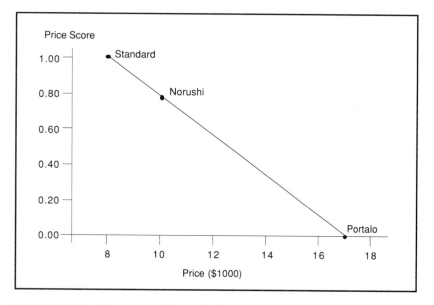

FIGURE 15.5 *Proportional Scores for Prices of Three Cars*

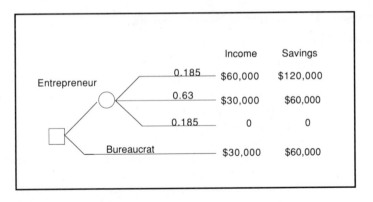

FIGURE 15.6 *A Career Decision*

see that for the entrepreneurial alternative, the expected outcomes are $30,000 in income and $60,000 in savings, the same as the certain values associated with the bureaucratic job.

Now we assign scores to the outcomes. For income, the best is $60,000, the worst is 0, and $30,000 is halfway between. These outcomes receive scores of 1, 0, and $\frac{1}{2}$, respectively. Performing the same analysis for the savings dimension results in similar scores, and the decision tree with these scores appears in Figure 15.7.

We now calculate expected scores for the two alternatives; this requires calculating scores for each of the three possible outcomes. Let k_I and k_S represent the weights that we would assign to income and savings. The scores (S) for the possible outcomes are:

$$S(\$60,000, \$120,000) = k_I (1) + k_S (1) = k_I + k_S$$
$$S(\$30,000, \$60,000) = k_I (\tfrac{1}{2}) + k_S (\tfrac{1}{2}) = \tfrac{1}{2}(k_I + k_S)$$
$$S(0, 0) = k_I (0) + k_S (0) = 0.$$

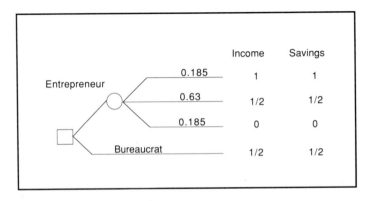

FIGURE 15.7 *A Career Decision with Proportional Scores*

Now we can calculate the expected score (ES) for the entrepreneurial venture. That expected score is obtained by averaging the scores over the three branches:

$$ES(\text{Entrepreneur}) = 0.185\ (k_I + k_S) + 0.63\ [\tfrac{1}{2}\ (k_I + k_S)] + 0.185\ (0)$$
$$= 0.50\ (k_I + k_S)$$
$$= 0.50,$$

because $k_I + k_S = 1$. Of course, the expected score for the bureaucratic option also is 0.50, and so, on the basis of expected scores, the two alternatives are equivalent. (In fact, it is important to note that the two alternatives have the same score regardless of the specific values of k_I and k_S.) It is obvious, however, that being an entrepreneur is riskier. If each job really has the same expected scores in all relevant dimensions, would you be indifferent? (Probably not, but we will not guess about whether you would choose the riskier job or the more secure one!)

The point of this section has been to demonstrate a potential shortcoming of the "proportional scores" method of deriving scores for the individual attributes. As mentioned, it may prove to be a perfectly adequate way to find scores in many cases. But there are other approaches to assess scores and alternative ways to assess trade-offs other than proportional scores and the pricing-out procedure described above, and some of these permit the decision maker to incorporate his or her risk attitude into both scores and trade-off weights. In the next section we will look at some of these alternative methods.

◆ ALTERNATIVE METHODS FOR ASSESSING SCORES AND TRADE-OFF WEIGHTS

Our discussion so far has shown the basics of constructing an additive preference model for two attributes. To make this work, of course, careful thought must be given when trade-off weights and attribute scores are assessed. In this section, we discuss the use of utility functions and ratio assessments for determining scores, and two additional methods for assessing trade-off weights.

Assessing Scores: Utility Functions

A straightforward way to assess attribute scores is simply to assess a utility function for each attribute. For example, we would need to assess a utility function for price (or dollars spent, or wealth) as well as a separate utility function for life-span. Making these assessments would follow the procedures presented in Chapters 13 and 14. If you face a decision that is complicated by both uncertainty and trade-offs, this is the best solution. The utility functions, having been assessed in terms of your preferences over uncertain situations, are models of your preferences in which your attitude toward risk is built in.

We will continue with the example about the two jobs. Suppose we assess a utility function for dollars and find that

$$U_I(\$60,000) = 1$$
$$U_I(\$30,000) = 0.75$$
$$U_I(0) = 0,$$

and

$$U_S(\$120,000) = 1$$
$$U_S(\$60,000) = 0.68$$
$$U_S(0) = 0.$$

Remember that these are two separate utility functions for the two attributes, income and savings, as indicated by the subscripts I and S, respectively.

Now use these utility functions as the scores; that is, let $S_I(x) = U_I(x)$ and $S_S(y) = U_S(y)$. The expected score for becoming an entrepreneur is

$$ES(\text{Entrepreneur}) = 0.185\,[1\ k_I + 1\ k_S] + 0.63\,[0.75\ k_I + 0.68\ k_S]$$
$$+ 0.185\,[0\ k_I + 0\ k_S]$$
$$= 0.658\ k_I + 0.613\ k_S.$$
$$ES(\text{Bureaucrat}) = 0.750\ k_I + 0.680\ k_S.$$

Regardless of the specific values for the weights k_I and k_S, the expected score for being a bureaucrat always will be greater than the expected score for being an entrepreneur because the coefficients for k_I and k_S are larger for the bureaucrat than for the entrepreneur. This makes sense; the expected values (EMVs) for the two alternatives are equal for each attribute, but being an entrepreneur clearly is riskier. When we use a utility function for money that incorporates risk aversion, the riskier alternative ends up with a lower expected utility.

Assessing Scores: Ratios

Another way to assess scores — and one that is particularly appropriate for attributes that are not naturally quantitative — is to assess them on the basis of some ratio comparison. For example, let us return to the automobile example. Suppose that color is an important attribute in your automobile purchase decision. Clearly, this is not something that is readily measurable on a meaningful numerical scale. Using a ratio approach, you might conclude that to you blue is twice as good as red, and that yellow is $2\frac{1}{2}$ times as good as red. We could accomplish the same by assigning some number of points between 0 and 100 to each possible alternative on the basis of performance on the attribute. In this way, for example, you might assign 30 points to red, 60 points to blue, and 75 points to yellow. This could be represented graphically as in Figure 15.8.

Now, however, we must scale these scores so that they range from 0 to 1. We discussed this with utilities. We need to find constants a and b so that:

$$0 = a + b(30)$$
$$1 = a + b(75).$$

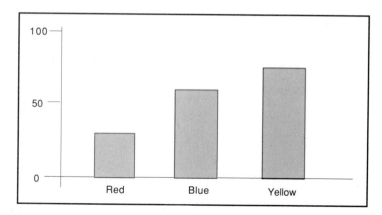

FIGURE 15.8   *Graphically Scoring Alternatives*

Solving these two equations simultaneously gives

$$a = -\tfrac{2}{3}$$

$$b = \tfrac{1}{45}.$$

Applying these scaling constants, we can calculate S_C, the scores for the three colors:

$$S_C(\text{Red}) \quad = -\tfrac{2}{3} + \tfrac{30}{45} = 0$$

$$S_C(\text{Blue}) \quad = -\tfrac{2}{3} + \tfrac{60}{45} = \tfrac{2}{3}$$

$$S_C(\text{Yellow}) = -\tfrac{2}{3} + \tfrac{75}{45} = 1.$$

Figure 15.9 shows the scaled scores, which now represent your relative prefer-ence for the different colors. They may be used to calculate weighted scores for different cars in a decision problem in which color is one attribute to consider. For example, with appropriate trade-off weights for price, color, and life-span, the weighted score for a blue Portalo would be:

$$S(\$17,000, \text{12 Years, Blue}) = k_P(0) + k_L(1) + k_C(0.667).$$

You can see how the ratio approach can be used to compare virtually any set of alternatives whether or not they are quantitatively measured.

Assessing Weights: Swing Weights

The pricing-out approach to assessing trade-offs directly works reasonably well in many situations. Often one can come up with dollar values for nonmonetary attributes, just as we did with life-span. When it is possible to price out attributes in this way, careful thought can clarify the rates at which you would trade off achievement toward one objective against a decrease for another. This is not al-

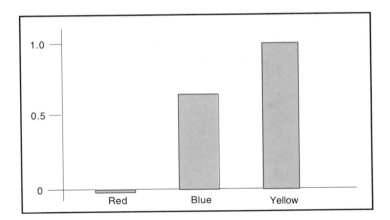

FIGURE 15.9 *Scaled Scores for Colors*

ways possible, however, if only because dollars are not always involved. Here we discuss two additional methods for assessing weights that are both systematic and generally applicable, the first of which is called *swing weighting*.

First, think of the "Worst Conceivable Alternative," one that scores at the lowest level on all of the attributes. Now look at your attributes and think about increasing one of them to its highest level. Identify the attribute that gives you the greatest increase in satisfaction (utility) when you swing it from low to high while leaving the other attributes at their lowest levels. Mentally note the increase in utility that you experience in this case.

Return to your "Worst Conceivable Alternative" and choose another attribute. Swing it through its range, from low to high, while leaving all other attributes at their lowest levels. Compare the improvement in your satisfaction obtained in the two cases. Is the improvement in the second case 50% of the improvement in the first? 75%? Your improvement should never be greater than 1 because the second case involves a less important attribute. Go through this swing-and-compare procedure for each attribute. The percentages that you assess in your comparisons can be used to determine weights for your multiattribute utility function.

Consider the automobile example's three attributes of price, life-span, and color. Let us assume that price is most important, then life-span, and finally color. Imagine a car that is as bad as possible: $17,000, red, with a six-year expected life-span. Now imagine "swinging" the price from $17,000 to the best level, $8000. Keep this hypothetical car in mind. Now return to the worst case. Swing the life-span from 6 years to 12 years. Now compare your increased satisfaction achieved by the life-span change with the increased satisfaction from the price change; this is obviously a subjective assessment. We will assume that this assessment is 75%; that is, your increase in satisfaction from the improvement in life-span is only 75% of the increase in satisfaction that resulted from the price improvement in the first case. Now do the same thing with color. Compare your increase in satisfaction by going from red to yellow with the increased satisfaction from the hypothetical price change. Let us assume that this assessment is 10%.

It turns out that your assessments mean that $k_L = 0.75k_P$ and that $k_C = 0.10k_P$. To find k_L, k_P, and k_C, simply impose the constraint that the three weights add to 1. Thus, we have the three equations:

$$k_L = 0.75k_P$$
$$k_C = 0.10\ k_P$$
$$k_P + k_C + k_L = 1.00.$$

We can substitute from the first two equations into the third:

$$k_P + 0.10\ k_P + 0.75\ k_P = 1.00,$$

or

$$1.85\ k_P = 1.00,$$

which implies that $k_P = 0.541$. Substituting this back into the first two equations gives $k_L = 0.405$ and $k_C = 0.054$. All we have done is find weights that add to 1 and bear the specified relative relationships to each other in terms of ratios. Now use these weights to calculate weighted scores in which scores for every attribute are scaled from 0 to 1 (worst to best). For example, we now can finish calculating the score for a blue Portalo:

$$
\begin{aligned}
S(\$17{,}000,\ 12\ \text{Years, Blue}) &= k_P(0) + k_L(1) + k_C(0.667) \\
&= 0.541(0) + 0.405(1) + 0.054(0.667) \\
&= 0.441.
\end{aligned}
$$

Why do swing weights work? The argument is straightforward. Here are the utilities for the hypothetical cars that you have considered:

$$
\begin{aligned}
U(\text{Worst Conceivable Alternative}) &= U(\$17{,}000,\ 6\ \text{Years, Red}) \\
&= k_P(0) + k_L(0) + k_C(0) \\
&= 0.
\end{aligned}
$$

$$U(\$8000,\ 6\ \text{Years, Red}) = k_P(1) + k_L(0) + k_C(0) = k_P.$$
$$U(\$17{,}000,\ 12\ \text{Years, Red}) = k_P(0) + k_L(1) + k_C(0) = k_L.$$
$$U(\$17{,}000,\ 6\ \text{Years, Yellow}) = k_P(0) + k_L(0) + k_C(1) = k_C.$$

From the first two equations, you can see that the increase in satisfaction from swinging price from worst to best is just k_P. Likewise, the improvement from swinging any attribute from worst to best is simply the value of the corresponding weight. When you compare the relative improvements in utility (the percentages) by swinging the attributes one at a time, you are assessing the ratios k_L/k_P and k_C/k_P. These assessments, along with the constraint that the weights add to 1, allow us to calculate the weights. Figure 15.10 graphically shows how swing weights work.

Swing weights have a built-in advantage in that they are sensitive to the range of values that an attribute takes on. For example, suppose you are comparing two personal computers, and price is an attribute that is included in your value tree. One computer costs $3500 and the other $3600. When you work through the swing-weight assessment procedure, you probably will conclude that the increase in utility from swinging the price is pretty small. This would result,

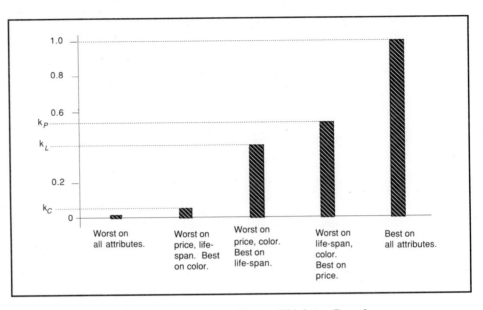

FIGURE 15.10   *Graphic Representation of Swing-Weighting Procedure*

appropriately, in a small weight for price. But if the difference in price is $1000 rather than $100, the increase in utility experienced by swinging from worst to best would be much larger, resulting in a larger weight for price.

If you have a hard time thinking about the "Worst Conceivable Alternative," you might try reversing this procedure. That is, imagine the "Best Conceivable Alternative," best on all attributes, and consider decreases in satisfaction from swinging attributes from high to low. Assess relative decreases in satisfaction, and use those assessments in exactly the same way that we used the relative utility increases.

Assessing Weights: Lotteries

It should come as no surprise that we also can use lottery-comparison techniques to assess weights. In fact, the technique we will use is a version of the probability-equivalent assessment technique introduced in Chapter 13. The general assessment set-up is shown in Figure 15.11.

The assessment of the probability p that makes you indifferent between the lottery and the sure thing turns out to be the weight for the one odd attribute in the sure thing. We will see how this works in the case of the automobiles. Figure 15.12 shows the assessment decision for determining the weight associated with price.

Suppose that the indifference probability in Figure 15.12 turns out to be 0.55. Write down the equation that is implied by the indifference:

$$k_P S_P(\$8000) + k_L S_L(6 \text{ Years}) + k_C S_C(\text{Red})$$
$$= 0.55 \left[k_P S_P(\$8000) + k_L S_L(12 \text{ Years}) + k_C S_C(\text{Yellow}) \right]$$
$$+ 0.45 \left[k_P S_P(\$17,000) + k_L S_L(6 \text{ Years}) + k_C S_C(\text{Red}) \right].$$

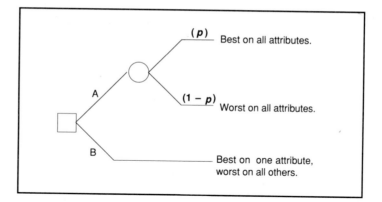

FIGURE 15.11 *Assessing Weights Using a Lottery Technique* The task is to assess the probability *p* that makes you indifferent between the lottery (A) and the sure thing (B).

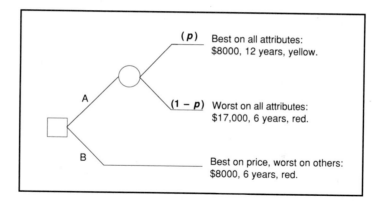

FIGURE 15.12 *Assessing the Weight for Price*

As before, we will have the individual scores range from 0 to 1. This means that

$$S_P(\$8000) = 1.00 \qquad S_P(\$17,000) = 0$$
$$S_L(12 \text{ Years}) = 1.00 \qquad S_L(6 \text{ Years}) = 0$$
$$S_C(\text{Yellow}) = 1.00 \qquad S_C(\text{Red}) = 0.$$

Substitute these values into the equation to obtain

$$k_P = 0.55\,[k_P + k_L + k_C].$$

Because $k_P + k_L + k_C = 1$, we have $k_P = 0.55$, which is simply the indifference probability that was assessed. Thus, we have a direct way to find the trade-off weight for the price attribute. Repeating this procedure one more time for the life-span attribute gives k_L, and then k_C follows because the weights must add to 1. Of course, a simple way to check for consistency is to repeat the procedure a third time for the color attribute. If assessed weights do not add to 1 and are not even close, then the additive model that we are using in this chapter is not appropriate. Chapter 16 discusses more complicated multiattribute utility models that may be able to accommodate such preferences.

In our discussion of utility theory and utility assessment, we found that to include risk attitudes in our utility functions we needed to assess preferences by looking at risky situations or lotteries. The lottery-based assessment of the weights for a multiattribute utility function is the same. If you want to include your risk attitude in your evaluation of multiattribute alternatives, then you should assess the weights for the attributes using the lottery-based approach. (The individual scores also should be based on a lottery-based assessment; that is, those scores should come from assessed utility functions.) Why would you want to incorporate your risk attitude into your utility function? If you face a decision under uncertainty as well as trade-offs, then that risk attitude may be important.

Finally, you may have wondered why we always scale our scores from 0 to 1. The answer is contained in the equations above that underlie the weight-assessment techniques. In each case, we needed the values of 0 and 1 for best and worst cases in order to solve for the weights; the idea that scores are scaled from zero to one is built into these assessment techniques. The result is that weights have very specific meanings. In particular, the swing-weight approach implies that we can interpret the weights in terms of improvements in utility that result from changing one attribute from low to high, and those low and high values are specific to the alternatives being considered. The lottery-assessment method suggests that the weights can be interpreted as an indifference probability in a comparison of lotteries. The specific low and high values among the alternatives are important anchors for interpreting these indifference probabilities.

◆ A RECAP OF SCORING AND WEIGHTING TECHNIQUES

We will stop now to survey the ground we have covered. We began with the development of value trees to specify the objectives for and attributes of a decision problem. Then we turned to the issue of determining the trade-off rate between two competing objectives. This approach let us build an additive weighted score for a particular alternative or outcome:

$$S = k_1\, S_1 + k_2\, S_2.$$

In our initial discussion, we showed how to determine first the weights by a pricing-out procedure and second the scores simply by scaling the attribute values to be between 0 and 1. In our subsequent discussion, we saw how to use utility function assessments or ratio assessments to determine scores, as well as the swing-weighting and lottery techniques for assessing the weights. Thus, we now have three methods for assessing scores and three methods for assessing weights.

Which of these methods should you use? The relative advantages of the three scoring methods are straightforward. The proportional scores (the scaling method) is perhaps the easiest to use, although it implies risk neutrality. If risk is a serious consideration, then assessing a utility function is more appropriate, although more demanding. Using the ratio approach to assess scores is somewhere in the middle, providing a framework to capture important differences in value but not really dealing with risk attitudes.

For the weight-assessment methods, all three proposed methods (pricing out, swing weights, and lottery weights) will work fairly well. If attributes are reduced easily to dollars, then the pricing-out method may be the easiest to use. Swing weights are a bit more demanding, but once a decision maker gets the hang of them the assessments are relatively easy. Finally, the lottery method is both the most demanding, and the only way to incorporate a risk attitude into the trade-off weights in a systematic way. It is important to realize that simply specifying the relative importance of two attributes is not enough; as we saw in the discussion of pricing out, we must understand exactly what the relative importance means in terms of some kind of trade-off rate. All three weight-assessment methods can determine the appropriate trade-off rates.

With these simple examples behind us, we now turn to a more complicated problem. This example will demonstrate the development of an additive weighted score when there are many attributes and the value tree has more than a single layer. The issue is site selection for the new public library.

THE EUGENE PUBLIC LIBRARY

In 1986 a solution was sought for the overcrowded and inadequate conditions at the public library in Eugene, Oregon. The current building, with approximately 38,000 square feet of space, had been built in 1959 with the anticipation that it would serve satisfactorily for some 30 years. In the intervening years, Eugene's population had grown to the point that, on a per-capita basis, the Eugene Public Library was one of the most heavily used public libraries in the western United States. All available space had been used. Even the basement, which had not been designed originally for patron use, had been converted to a periodicals reading room. Low-circulation materials had to be removed from the stacks and placed in storage to make room for patrons and books. Expansion was imperative; consultants estimated that 115,000 square feet of space were needed. The current building could be expanded, but because of the original design it could not be operated as efficiently as a brand new building. Other potential sites were available, but all had their own benefits and drawbacks. After much thought, the possibilities were reduced to four sites in or near downtown Eugene, one of which was the current site. Some were less expensive for one reason or another, others had better opportunities for future expansion, and so on. How could the city choose from among them?

◆

In evaluating the four proposed library sites, the first task was to create a value tree. What aspects of site location were important? The committee in charge of the study created the value tree shown in Figure 15.13 with seven fundamental objectives and detail objectives for each fundamental objective.

Parking, for example, was broken down into patron parking, off-site parking, night staff parking, and bookmobile space. (Without knowledge of Eugene's financial system, certain attributes in the "Related Cost" category may not make sense.) An important objective that is conspicuous by its absence is minimizing the cost of building a library. The committee's strategy was to compare the sites on the seven fundamental criteria first, and then consider the price tags for each. We will see later how this comparison can be made.

Comparing the four candidate sites (alternatives) required these four steps:

1. Score the alternatives on each attribute. This can be done with any of the three scoring methods.

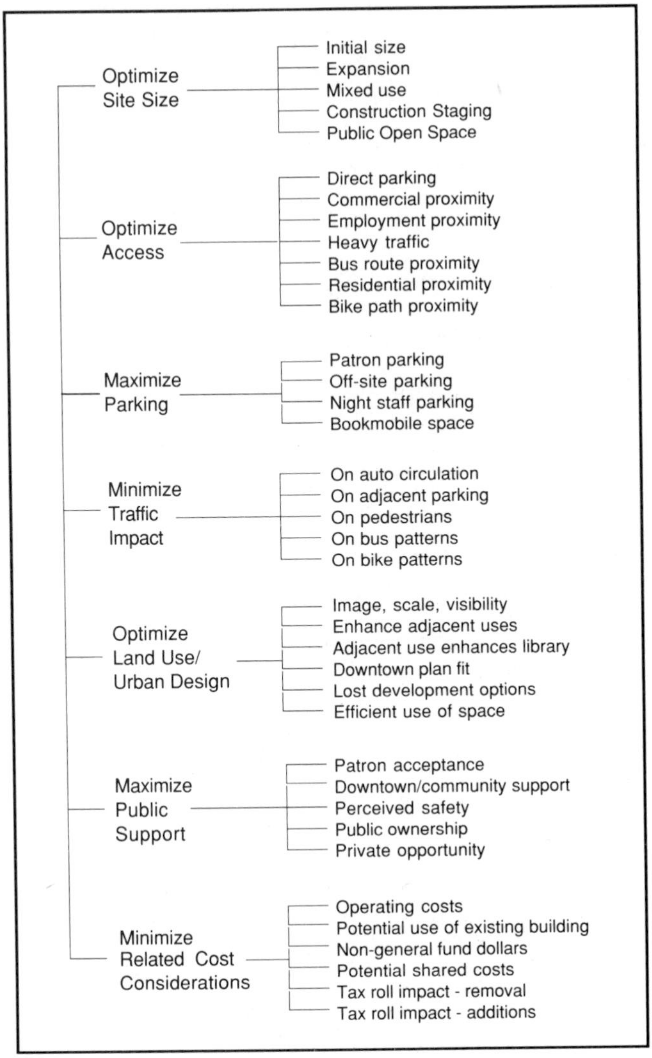

FIGURE 15.13   *Value Tree for the Eugene Public Library Site-Evaluation Study*

2. Weight the attributes in the tree. This can be done with any of the three weight-assessment methods (although pricing out may be difficult because the overall cost is not included in the value tree).
3. Calculate weighted scores.
4. Choose the alternative with the greatest weighted score.

Application of this procedure in the analysis of the four library sites produced the matrix shown in Table 15.3. The relative weights and the individual scores are all shown in this table. (Actually, the committee's analysis did not use scores from 0 to 1. Their scores have been thusly rescaled here, and the weights have been adjusted to be consistent with the rescaled scores. Six detail attributes on which all four sites were scored the same also have been eliminated.)

The weighted score is calculated and shown on a scale from 0 to 100, rather than from 0 to 1; this just makes the table easier to read. Under each fundamental objective is a subtotal for each site. For example, the subtotal for Site 1 under "Parking" is

$$\text{Subtotal (Parking}_1) = [(0.053 \times 0.20 \times 1.00) + (0.053 \times 0.60 \times 0.00)$$
$$+ (0.053 \times 0.20 \times 1.00)] \times 100$$
$$= 2.12.$$

(The factor of 100 at the end simply changes the scale so that it ranges from 0 to 100.) Once all scores have been calculated for each fundamental objective, they are simply added to find the total score for each site. For example,

$$S(\text{Site 1}) = 13.08 + 6.40 + 2.12 + 1.08 + 3.02 + 15.77 + 4.22$$
$$= 45.70.$$

You can see that the overall weight given to a specific detail attribute is the product of the specific weight at the lower level and the overall weight for the fundamental objective. For example, Site 1 has $S(\text{Construction Staging}) = 1.00$. This score then is multiplied by 0.13, the weight for construction staging, and then multiplied by 0.211, the weight for the fundamental attribute of "Site Size." Thus, in this grand scheme, the scores are weighted by a product of the weights at the two levels in the value tree. To express this more formally, let k_i represent the weight of the ith fundamental objective, and k_{ij} and S_{ij} the weight and score, respectively, for the jth attribute under fundamental objective i. If there are m fundamental objectives and m_i detail attributes under fundamental objective i, then the overall score for a site is:

$$S(\text{Site}) = k_1(k_{11} S_{11} + k_{12} S_{12} + k_{13} S_{13} + \cdots + k_{1m_1} S_{1m_1})$$
$$+ k_2(k_{21} S_{21} + k_{22} S_{22} + k_{23} S_{23} + \cdots + k_{2m_2} S_{2m_2})$$
$$+ \cdots + k_m(k_{m1} S_{m1} + k_{m2} S_{m2} + k_{m3} S_{m3} + \cdots + k_{mm_k} S_{mm_k})$$
$$= k_1 k_{11} S_{11} + k_1 k_{12} S_{12} + \cdots + k_m k_{mm_k} S_{mm_k}$$
$$= \sum_{i=1}^{m} k_i \left[\sum_{j=1}^{m_i} k_{ij} S_{ij} \right].$$

Attributes		Scores			
	(%)	Site 1	Site 2	Site 3	Site 4
Site Size (21.1%)					
Initial	38	1.00	0.00	1.00	1.00
Expansion (Horizontal)	13	0.00	0.00	0.00	1.00
Mixed Use	25	0.00	1.00	1.00	1.00
Construction Staging	12	1.00	0.00	0.00	1.00
Public Open Space	12	1.00	0.00	0.00	0.00
Subtotals		*13.08*	*5.28*	*13.29*	*18.57*
Access (20.6%)					
Direct Parking	8	0.00	1.00	0.00	0.00
Commercial Proximity	23	0.00	1.00	0.67	1.00
Employment Proximity	15	0.50	1.00	0.00	1.00
Heavy Traffic	23	0.33	0.33	1.00	0.00
Bus Route Proximity	15	0.00	0.50	0.50	1.00
Residential Proximity	16	1.00	0.00	1.00	0.50
Subtotals		*6.40*	*12.58*	*12.75*	*12.57*
Parking (5.3%)					
Patron Parking	20	1.00	0.00	1.00	1.00
Off-site Parking	60	0.00	1.00	0.33	0.33
Bookmobile Parking	20	1.00	0.00	1.00	1.00
Subtotals		*2.12*	*3.18*	*3.17*	*3.17*
Traffic Impacts (4.5%)					
Auto Circulation	47	0.00	0.75	1.00	0.00
Adjacent Parking	29	0.00	0.00	1.00	0.00
Bus Patterns	24	1.00	1.00	1.00	0.00
Subtotals		*1.08*	*2.67*	*4.50*	*0.00*
Land Use/Design (8.4%)					
Image/Scale/Visibility	13	0.00	1.00	0.00	0.00
Enhance Adjacent Uses	13	0.00	1.00	1.00	1.00
Adj. Uses Enhance Lib.	38	0.00	1.00	1.00	0.00
Downtown Plan Fit	13	1.00	0.00	1.00	1.00
Lost Devel. Options	23	1.00	0.00	0.00	0.00
Subtotals		*3.02*	*5.38*	*5.38*	*2.18*
Public Support (19.0%)					
Patron Acceptance	25	1.00	0.33	0.67	0.00
DT/Community Support	25	1.00	0.67	0.33	0.00
Perceived Safety	25	1.00	0.33	1.00	0.00
Public Ownership	17	0.00	1.00	1.00	0.00
Private Opportunity	8	1.00	0.00	1.00	1.00
Subtotals		*15.77*	*9.55*	*14.25*	*1.52*
Related Costs (21.1%)					
Operating Costs	20	0.00	1.00	1.00	1.00
Use of Existing Building	20	1.00	0.00	0.00	0.00
No General Fund $	30	0.00	1.00	1.00	1.00
Tax Roll Impact, Removal	10	0.00	1.00	1.00	0.00
Tax Roll Impact, Added	20	0.00	1.00	1.00	1.00
Subtotals		*4.22*	*16.88*	*16.88*	*14.77*
Weighted Score		*45.70*	*55.51*	*70.22*	*52.78*

TABLE 15.3 *Matrix of Weights and Scores for Four Library Sites*

[*Source:* Adapted from Robertson/Sherwood/Architects (1987) "Preliminary Draft Report: Eugene Public Library Site Selection Study. Executive Summary." Eugene, OR: Robertson/Sherwood.]

From these expressions, we can see that the scores on the individual attributes are being weighted by the product of the appropriate weights and then added. Thus, we still have an additive score that is a weighted combination of the individual scores, just as we did in the simpler two- and three-attribute examples above. Moreover, it also should be clear that as the value tree grows to have more levels, the formula also grows, multiplying the individual scores by all of the appropriate weights in the value tree.

The result of all of the calculations for the library example? Site 3 ranked the best with 70.02 points, Site 2 was second with 55.51 points, and Sites 4 and 1 (the current location) were ranked third and fourth overall with 52.78 and 45.70 points, respectively.

There is another interesting and intuitive way to interpret this kind of analysis. Imagine that 100 points are available to be awarded for each alternative, depending on how a given alternative ranks on each attribute. In the library case, 21.1 of the 100 points are awarded on the basis of "Site Size," 20.6 on the basis of "Access," 5.3 for "Parking," and so on. Within the "Site Size" category, the weights on the detail factors determine how the 21.1 points for "Site Size" will be allocated; 38% of the 21.1 points (or 8.02 points) will be awarded on the basis of "Initial Size," 13% of the 21.1 points (2.74 points) will be awarded on the basis of "Expansion," and so on. We can see how this subdivision could continue through many layers in a value tree. Finally, when the ends of the branches are reached, we must determine scores for the alternatives. If the scores range from 0 to 1, then the score indicates what proportion of the available points are awarded to the alternative for the particular detail attribute being considered. For example, Site 3 has a score of 0.67 on "Commercial Proximity," so it receives 67% of the points available for this detail attribute. How many points are available? The weight of 23% tells us that 23% of the total points for "Access" are allocated to "Commercial Proximity," and the 20.6% weight for "Access" says that 20.6 points total are available for "Access." Thus, Site 3 earns $0.67 \times 0.23 \times 20.6 = 3.17$ points for "Commercial Proximity." For each detail attribute, calculate the points awarded to Site 3. Now add those points; the total is Site 3's weighted score (70.02) on a scale from 0 to 100.

Recall that cost was an important attribute that was not included in the analysis of the library sites. The committee studying the problem decided to ignore construction costs until the sites were well understood in terms of their other attributes. But now that we have ranked the sites on the basis of the attributes, we must consider money. Table 15.4 shows the costs associated with each site, along with the weighted scores from Table 15.3, and Figure 15.14 shows the same information, graphically plotting cost against weighted score.

Table 15.4 and Figure 15.14 show clearly that Sites 1 and 4 are dominated. That is, if you like Site 4, then you should like Sites 2 or 3 even better, because each has a greater weighted score for less money. Likewise, Site 2 clearly dominates Site 1. Thus, Sites 1 and 4 can be eliminated from the analysis altogether on the basis of dominance. This leaves Sites 2 and 3. Is it worthwhile to pay the additional $5.72 million to gain 14.71 additional points in terms of weighted score? Alternatively, is an increase of one point in the score worth $388,851?

Obviously, we are trying to price out the value of a single point on our 1 to

Site	Cost ($Million)	Weighted Score
1	21.74	45.70
2	18.76	55.51
3	24.48	70.02
4	24.80	52.78

TABLE 15.4 *Costs and Weighted Scores for Four Library Sites*

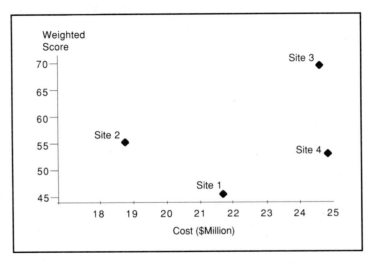

FIGURE 15.14 *Library Site Costs Plotted Against Weighted Scores*

100 scale, just as we previously priced out the value of changes in attributes. But answering this question now is difficult because one point in the weighted score may have many components. One possible approach is to return to the detail attributes, look for specific attributes on which Site 3 is ranked higher than Site 2, and consider how much we would be willing to pay (in dollars) to bring Site 2 up to Site 3's level on this attribute. For example, Site 3 scored much higher than Site 2 for access during heavy traffic periods. The difference is that Site 2 is in a relatively congested area of downtown and on one of the city's main thoroughfares. In contrast, Site 3 is located at the edge of downtown, and access would be through relatively low-volume streets. How much would altering the traffic patterns be worth so that Site 2 would be just as good as Site 3 for this attribute? One million dollars? More?

Let us suppose that we have assessed that the difference between the sites in terms of access during heavy traffic is indeed worth $1 million. It turns out that Site 3's advantage increases its weighted score by 3.17 points. (This is the difference between the sites in points awarded for this attribute.) Thus, the assessment would indicate that 3.17 points of weighted score are worth $1 million, or $315,457 per point of weighted score. This is less than the $388,851 required to switch from Site 2 to Site 3.

A pricing-out approach such as this can be used to assess the dollar value of one point of weighted score. Rather than making only one assessment, however, we should make several on different attributes where the two alternatives differ. For some of these assessments it may be possible to make estimates of true costs in terms of the market price of adjacent land, redesigning traffic patterns, constructing parking lots, and so on, and these cost estimates then might be helpful in assessing the dollar value of specific differences between sites. If the assessments in terms of prices per point of weighted score come out fairly close, then the average of these assessments can be used as a reasonable measure of the value of one point of weighted score. In the case of the library sites, if the final price per point is less than $388,851, then Site 2 is preferred; otherwise Site 3 is preferred. If the price per point turns out to be very close to $388,851, then the two sites are approximately equivalent.

The analysis probably would have been more complete had the committee elected to include minimizing cost as one of its fundamental objectives. In fact, all of the other attributes could have been priced out in terms of dollars, thus making the comparisons and trade-offs more intuitive. But it is not unusual for groups to ignore costs in an initial stage. The motivation often is political; it may be easier to gain constituent support by playing up the benefits of a project such as a new library early before talking about the "bottom line."

◇ SUMMARY

This chapter has introduced the basics of making decisions that involve trade-offs. The basic problem is to create a model of the decision maker's preferences in terms of the various objectives. The first step in building this model is to understand which objectives are most important in making your decision; this requires serious introspection as to fundamental objectives. The goal of this step is to create a value tree that explains these fundamental objectives and decomposes them into detail objectives and a list of operational detail attributes that reflect the performance of the alternatives relative to each detail objective.

The next step is to evaluate the alternatives. To do this, it is necessary to assess scores for each alternative on the various attributes. Deriving these scores is best done through a consistent method of comparison that results in scores that range from 0 to 1. We discussed three methods: calculation of risk-neutral proportional scores, assessment of ratios, and the use of assessed utility functions. All three are viable scoring techniques. Once scores are established, weights for the attributes also must be assessed. Several assessment procedures are possible here, all providing mechanisms for determining the rate at which the attributes can be traded off against one another. Sometimes trade-off rates can be assessed in terms of dollars by pricing out the other attributes. The swing-weighting and lottery-based assessment techniques can be used even if it is difficult to think of the attributes in dollar terms, and these techniques lead to clear interpretations of the assessed weights. The lottery-based method ensures that the decision maker's risk attitude will be incorporated into the weights or trade-offs. With weights and scores both determined, weighted scores are calculated in a straightforward manner. The preferred alternative would be the one with the highest weighted score.

◇ EXERCISES

15.1 Why is it important to think carefully about decision situations that involve multiple conflicting objectives?

15.2 Explain the general decision-analysis approach to dealing with multiple objectives.

15.3 What is a value tree?

15.4 Explain what is meant by the term indifference curve.

15.5 Explain the idea of dominance in the context of multiobjective decision making.

15.6 Imagine that you are working on a committee to develop an employment-conditions policy for your firm. During the discussion of safety, one committee member states that employee safety is twice as important as benefits such as flexible work time, employer-sponsored day care, and so on.

    a. How might you respond to such a statement?

    b. Suppose the statement was that employee safety was twice as important as insurance benefits. How might you translate this statement into a form (perhaps based on dollar values) so that it would be possible to evaluate various policy alternatives in terms of safety and insurance in a way that would be consistent with the statement.

15.7 Explain why proportional scores represent a risk attitude that is risk-neutral.

15.8 An MBA student evaluating weather outcomes for an upcoming party has concluded that a sunny day would be twice as good as a cloudy day, and a cloudy day would be three times as good as a rainy day. Use these assessments to calculate scores that range from 0 to 1 for sunny, rainy, and cloudy days.

15.9 Explain in your own words why swing weights produce meaningful weights for calculating weighted scores for alternatives.

15.10 A decision maker is assessing weights for two attributes using the swing-weight method. When he imagines swinging the attributes individually from worst to best, he concludes that his improvement in satisfaction from Attribute A is 70% of the improvement from swinging Attribute B. Calculate k_A and k_B.

15.11 Explain in your own words why the lottery method works to produce meaningful weights for calculating weighted scores for alternatives.

15.12 A decision maker is assessing weights for three attributes using the lottery-assessment method. In considering the lotteries, she concludes that she is indifferent between:

    A   Win the best possible combination with probability 0.34.
              Win the worst possible combination with probability 0.66.

and

    B   Win a combination that is worst on Attributes 1 and 3, and best on 2.

She also has concluded that she is indifferent between

> **C** Win the best possible combination with probability 0.25.
>   Win the worst possible combination with probability 0.75.

and

> **D** Win a combination that is worst on Attributes 2 and 3, and best on 1.

Find weights k_1, k_2, and k_3.

◇ QUESTIONS AND PROBLEMS

15.13 Suppose that you are searching for an apartment in which to live while you go to school. Apartments near campus generally cost more than equivalent apartments farther away. Five apartments are available. One is right next to campus, and another is one mile away. The remaining apartments are two, three, and four miles away.

   a. Suppose you have a tentative agreement to rent the apartment that is one mile from campus. How much more would you be willing to pay in monthly rent to obtain the one next to campus? (Answer this question on the basis of your own personal experience. Other than rent and distance from campus, the two apartments are equivalent.)

   b. Now suppose you have a tentative agreement to rent the apartment that is four miles away. How much more would you be willing to pay in monthly rent to move to the apartment that is only three miles from campus?

   c. What are the implications of your answers to parts a and b? Would it be appropriate to rank the apartments in terms of distance using the proportional-scoring technique?

   d. Sketch an indifference curve that reflects the way you would trade off rent versus proximity to campus. Is your indifference curve a straight line?

15.14 A friend of yours is in the market for a new computer. Four different machines are under consideration. The four computers are essentially the same, but they vary in price and reliability. The least expensive model is also the least reliable, the most expensive is the most reliable, and the other two are in between.

   a. Describe to your friend how you would approach the decision.

   b. Define reliability in a way that would be appropriate for the decision. Do you need to consider risk?

   c. How might your friend go about establishing a trade-off rate between reliability and price?

15.15 Continuing Problem 15.14, the computers are described as follows:

   A. Price: $998.95   Expected number of days in the shop per year: 4.

   B. Price: $1300.00   Expected number of days in the shop per year: 2.

   C. Price: $1350.00   Expected number of days in the shop per year: 2.5.

   D. Price: $1750.00   Expected number of days in the shop per year: 0.5.

   The computer will be an important part of your friend's livelihood for the next two years. (After two years, the computer will have a negligible salvage value.) In fact, your friend can foresee that there will be specific losses if the computer is in the shop for repairs. The magnitude of the losses are uncertain, but are estimated to be approximately $180 per day that the computer is down.

   a. Can you give your friend any advice without doing any calculations?

b. Use the information given to determine weights k_P and k_R, where R stands for reliability. What assumptions are you making?

c. Calculate weighted scores for the computers. What do you conclude?

d. Sketch three indifference curves that reflect your friend's trade-off rate between reliability and price.

e. What considerations other than losses might be important in determining the trade-off rate between cost and reliability?

15.16 Throughout the chapter we have assessed scores on individual attributes that range from 0 to 1. What is the advantage of doing this?

15.17 You are an up-and-coming developer in downtown Seattle and are interested in constructing a building on a site that you own. You have collected four bids from prospective contractors. The bids include both a cost (millions of dollars) and a time to completion (months):

Contractor	Cost	Time
A	100	20
B	80	25
C	79	28
D	82	26

The problem now is to decide which contractor to choose. B has indicated that for another $20 million he could do the job in 18 months, and you have said that you would be indifferent between that and the original proposal. In talking with C, you have indicated that you would just as soon pay her an extra $4 million if she could get the job done in 26 months. Who gets the job? Explain your reasoning. (It may be convenient to plot the four alternatives on a graph.)

15.18 Consider these simple situations that may involve multiple objectives and create simple value trees.

a. Suppose you want to go out for dinner. What are appropriate objectives to consider? Draw a value tree. How does your tree change if you are going out for lunch instead of dinner?

b. Suppose you are trying to decide where to go for a trip during spring break? What are the appropriate objectives to think about? Draw a value tree.

c. You are about to become a parent (surprise!). You have to choose a name for your child. What are important objectives to consider in choosing a name?

d. Think of any other situation in which choices involve conflicting objectives. Draw a value tree.

15.19 Once you decide that you are in the market for a personal computer, you have many different considerations. You should think about how you will use the computer, and so you need to know whether appropriate software is available and at what price. The nature of the available peripheral equipment (printers, disk drives, and so on) can be important. The "feel" of the computer, which is in some sense determined by the operating system and the user interface, can be critical. Are you an experienced user? Do you want to be able to program the machine, or will you (like most of us) rely on existing or over-the-counter software? If you intend to use the machine for a lot of number crunching, processor speed may be important. Reliability and service are other matters. For many students, an important question is whether the computer will be compatible with other systems in any job they might eventually have. Finally, of course, price and operating costs are important.

Create a value tree to compare your options. Take care in doing this; be sure that you establish the fundamental objectives, the detail objectives, and operational attributes that will allow you to make the necessary comparisons. (Note that the attributes suggested above are *not* exhaustive, and some may not apply to you!) Follow the rules of value-tree construction as described in the chapter.

Use your value tree to choose from among at least three different computers (preferably from different manufacturers). You will have to specify precisely the packages that you compare. It also might be worthwhile to include appropriate software and peripheral equipment. (Exactly what you compare is up to you, but make the packages meaningful.) You will have to assess scores for your alternatives on all of the detail attributes. Be sure that your scores are such that the best alternative gets a 1 and the worst a 0 for each detail attribute. Assess weights using pricing out, swing weighting, or lottery weights. Calculate weighted scores for your alternatives.

Try using the utility functions for money and computer reliability that you assessed in Problems 14.10 and 14.11 (page 424). You may have to rescale the utility functions to obtain scores so that the best alternative in this problem scores 1, and the worst scores 0.

If possible, use a computer-based multiattribute decision program to do this problem.

15.20 When you choose a place to live, what objectives are you trying to accomplish? What makes some apartments better than others? Would you rather live close to campus or farther away and spend less money? What about the quality of the neighborhood? How about amenities such as a swimming pool?

Create a value tree that allows you to compare options. Take care in doing this; be sure to establish the fundamental objectives, detail objectives, and operational attributes that will allow you to make the necessary comparisons.

Once you are satisfied with your value tree, use it to compare available housing alternatives. Try ranking different apartments that are advertised in the classified section of the newspaper, for example. Again, be sure that your scores on detail attributes follow the rules: Best takes a 1 and worst takes 0. (Try using the utility function for money that you assessed in Problem 14.10. You may have to rescale it so that your best alternative gets a 1 and worst gets a 0.) Assess weights using pricing out, swing weighting, or lottery weights. Calculate weighted scores for your alternatives.

If possible, use a computer-based multiattribute decision program to do this problem.

15.21 What is important to you in choosing a job? Certainly salary is important, and for many people location matters a lot. Other considerations might involve promotion potential, the nature of the work, the organization itself, benefits, and so on.

Create a value tree that allows you to compare job offers. Be sure to establish the fundamental objectives, detail objectives, and operational attributes that will allow you to make the necessary comparisons.

Once you are satisfied with your value tree, use it to compare your job offers. You also may want to think about your "ideal" job in order to compare your current offers with your ideal. (You also might consider your imaginary worst possible job in all respects.) Be sure that your scores on detail attributes follow the rules: best (ideal) gets a 1 and worst gets 0. (For the salary attribute, try using the utility function for money that you assessed in Problem 14.10, or some variation of it. You may have to rescale it so that your best alternative is 1 and worst 0.) Assess weights for the attributes using pricing out, swing weighting, or lottery weights, being careful to anchor your judgments in terms of both ideal and worst imaginable jobs. Calculate weighted scores for your various job offers.

If possible, use a computer-based multiattribute decision program to do this problem.

15.22 How can you compare your courses? When you consider those that you have taken, it should be clear that some were better than others, and that the good ones were, perhaps, good for different reasons. What are the important dimensions that affect the quality of a course? Some are obvious, such as the enthusiasm of an instructor, topic, amount and type of work involved, and so on. Other aspects may not be quite so obvious; for example, how you perceive one course may depend on other courses you have had.

In this problem, the objective is to create a "template" that will permit consistent evaluation of your courses. The procedure is essentially the same as it is for any multiattribute decision, except that you will be able to use the template to evaluate future courses. Thus, we do not have a set of alternatives available to use for the determination of scores and weights. (You want to think, however, about current and recent courses in making your assessments.)

First, create a value tree that allows you to compare courses. Be sure to establish the fundamental objectives, detail objectives, and operational attributes that will allow for the necessary comparisons. Constructing a good value tree for comparing courses is considerably more difficult than constructing a tree for comparing computers, apartments, or jobs. You may find that many of the attributes you consider initially will overlap with others, leading to a confusing array of attributes that are interdependent. It may take considerable thought to reduce the degree of redundancy in your value tree and to arrive at a tree that is complete, decomposable, small enough to be manageable, and that involves attributes that are easy to think about.

Once you are satisfied with your value tree, imagine the best and worst courses for each attribute. Write these down clearly enough so that you can use them in the assessment of weights. You also may want to specify intermediate outcomes and appropriate scores. The final outcome of this exercise should be something like a chart for each attribute that specifies the best and worst imaginable outcomes for the attribute, along with a few intermediate outcomes and their respective scores. The idea is to be able to return to these charts with any new course and establish course scores for all attributes with relative ease. [Try using the homework utility function that you developed in Problem 14.13 (page 424). You may have to rescale it so that your best alternative gets a 1 and the worst a 0.)

Once you have identified the best and worst imaginable outcomes for each attribute, you are ready to assess the weights. Try the swing-weighting or lottery approach for assessing the weights. (Pricing out may be difficult to do in this particular example. Can you place a dollar value on your attributes?)

Finally, with the scoring charts and the weights established, you are ready to evaluate courses. Try comparing three or four of your most recent courses. (Try evaluating one that you took more than a year ago. Can you remember enough about the course to establish the individual scores with some degree of confidence?)

If possible, implement your course-evaluation template using a computer-based multiattribute decision program. Alternatively, you might create a spreadsheet template that you could use to evaluate courses.

15.23 Refer to the discussion of the automobiles in the section on "Trading Off Conflicting Objectives: The Basics." We discussed switching first from the Standard to the Norushi, and then from the Norushi to the Portalo. Would it make sense to consider a direct switch from the Standard to the Portalo? Why or why not?

15.24 Critique the library-site selection committee's value tree in Figure 15.13. (page 454). Does this tree satisfy all of the criteria for a good value tree?

15.25 In Chapter 2 we discussed net present value (NPV) as a procedure for evaluating outcomes that yield cash flows at different points in time. If x_i is the cash flow at year i, and r is the discount rate, then the NPV is given by

$$NPV = \Sigma[x_i / (1 + r)^i],$$

where the summation is over all future cash flows including the current x_0.

a. Explain how the NPV criterion is similar to the weighted-scoring technique that was discussed in this chapter. What are the attributes? What are the weights? Describe the way cash at time period i is traded off against cash at time period $i + 1$. (*Hint:* Review Chapter 2!)

b. Suppose that you can invest in one of two different projects. Each costs $20,000. The first project is riskless, and will pay you $10,000 each year for the next three years. The second one is risky. There is a 50% chance that it will pay $15,000 each year for the next three years, and a 50% chance that it will pay only $5000 per year for the next three years. Your discount rate is 9%. Calculate the NPV for both the riskless and risky project. Compare them. What can you conclude about the use of NPV for deciding among risky projects?

c. How might your NPV analysis in part b be modified to take risk into account? Could you use a utility function? How does the idea of a risk-adjusted discount rate fit into the picture? How could the interest rate be adjusted to account for risk? Would this be the same as using a utility function for money?

15.26 Following up Problem 15.25, even though we take riskiness into account, there still is difficulty with NPV as a decision criterion. Suppose that you are facing the two risky projects shown in Figure 15.15.

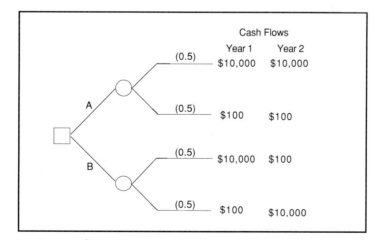

FIGURE 15.15 *Decision Tree for Problem 15.26*
Which of these two risky investments would you prefer?

Project A pays either $10,000 for each of two years or $100 for those two years. Project B pays $10,000 either in the first year or the second year and $100 in the other year. Assume that the cash flows are annual net profits.

a. Which of these two risky investments would you prefer? Why?

b. Calculate the expected NPV for both projects, using the same 9% interest rate from Problem 15.24. Based on expected NPV, in which project would you invest?

c. After careful assessment, you have concluded that you are risk-averse and that your utility function can be adequately represented by $U(X_i) = \ln(X_i)$, where X_i represents cash flow during year i. Calculate the expected net present utility for each project. Net present utility is given by

$$NPU = \sum [U(X_i) / (1 + r)^i].$$

d. NPU in part c should incorporate your attitude toward risk. Are your NPU calculations in part c consistent with your preferences in part a? What is there about these two projects that is not captured by your utility function? Can you think of any other way to model your preferences?

15.27   Instead of calculating a "discounted" utility as we did in Problem 15.26, let us consider calculating $U(NPV)$. That is, calculate NPV first, using an appropriate interest rate, and then calculate a utility value for the NPV. For your utility function, use the exponential utility function $U(NPV) = 1 - e^{-NPV/5000}$. Use this approach to calculate the expected utility of Projects A and B in Figure 15.15. Which would you choose? Are there any problems with using this procedure for evaluating projects?

15.28   A policy maker in the Occupational Safety and Health Administration is under pressure from industry to permit the use of certain chemicals in a newly developed industrial process. Two different versions of the process use two different chemicals, A and B. The risks associated with these chemicals are not known with certainty, but the available information indicates that they may affect two groups of people in the following ways:

♦ *Chemical A*   There is a 50% chance that Group 1 will be adversely affected, while Group 2 is unaffected; and a 50% chance that Group 2 is adversely affected, while Group 1 is unaffected.

♦ *Chemical B*   There is a 50% chance that both groups will be adversely affected, and a 50% chance that neither group will be affected.

Assume that "adversely affected" means the same in every case — an expected increase of one death in the affected group over the next two years. The decision maker's problem looks like the decision tree in Figure 15.16.

a. Calculate the expected number of deaths for each chemical.

b. A decision maker who values outcomes using a weighted score might calculate the score for each outcome as

$$S(\text{Chemical}) = k_1 \, S_1(\text{Group 1 Deaths}) + k_2 \, S_2(\text{Group 2 Deaths}).$$

For both S_1 and S_2, the best and worst possible outcomes are 0 deaths and 1 death, respectively. Thus,

$$S_1(1 \text{ Death}) = 0 \qquad S_1(0 \text{ Deaths}) = 1$$
$$S_2(1 \text{ Death}) = 0 \qquad S_2(0 \text{ Deaths}) = 1.$$

Explain why k_1 and $1 - k_1$ may not be equal.

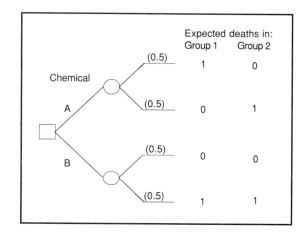

FIGURE 15.16 *Deciding Between Alternative Chemicals in Problem 15.28*

c. Assume that $k_1 = 0.4$. Show that the decision maker who evaluates the two chemicals in terms of their expected weighted scores (as defined above) would be indifferent between them. Does the value of k_1 matter?

d. Why might the decision maker *not* be indifferent between the two programs? (Most people think about the decision maker's risk attitude toward the number of deaths or lives saved. Besides this, think about the following: Suppose you are a member of Group 1, and the decision maker has chosen Chemical A. It turned out that Group 1 was affected. How would you feel? What would you do? What does this imply for the decision maker?)

15.29 Refer to the discussion of the three automobiles in the section "Trading off Conflicting Objectives: The Basics." Suppose we had the following individual utility functions for price and life-span:

Life-Span	Price
$U_L(6 \text{ Years}) = 0.00$	$U_P(17K) = 0.00$
$U_L(9 \text{ Years}) = 0.75$	$U_P(10K) = 0.50$
$U_L(12 \text{ Years}) = 1.00$	$U_P(8K) = 1.00$

The weighted-scoring technique discussed in this chapter would give us the following:

$$S(\text{Price, Life-Span}) = k_L \, U_L(\text{Life-Span}) + (1 - k_L) \, U_P(\text{Price}).$$

a. With $k_L = 0.45$, calculate the utility for the three cars. Which would be chosen?

b. Suppose that you are not completely comfortable with the assessment of $k_L = 0.45$. How *large* could k_L be before the decision changes, and what would be the new choice? How *small* could k_L be before the decision changes, and what would be the new choice? Would you say that the choice among these three cars is very sensitive to the assessment of k_L?

15.30 Refer to Table 15.3 (page 456). Your boss is a member of the library-site selection committee. She is not perfectly satisfied with the assessments shown in the table. Specifically, she wonders to what extent the assessed weights and individual scores on the detail attributes could change without affecting the overall ranking of the four sites. Use an electronic spreadsheet to answer this question, and write a memo that discusses your findings. (*Hint:* There is no specific way to attack a sensitivity analysis like this. One possibility is to establish reasonable ranges for the weights and then create a tornado diagram. Be sure that your weights add to 1 in each category!)

15.31 Refer to Problem 15.12. Suppose that the decision maker has made a third assessment, concluding that she is indifferent between

> **E**   Win the best possible combination with probability 0.18.
> Win the worst possible combination with probability 0.82.

and

> **F**   Win a combination that is worst on Attributes 1 and 2, and best on 3.

What does this assessment imply for the analysis? Is it consistent with your answer for k_3 in Problem 15.12? What should you do now?

CASE STUDIES

The Satanic Verses

In early 1989, the Ayatollah Khomeini of Iran decreed that Salman Rushdie, the British author of *The Satanic Verses*, should be put to death. In many ways, Rushdie's novel satirized Islam and the Prophet Muhammed. Khomeini declared that Rushdie should die and that whoever killed him would go to Heaven.

Many bookstores in both Europe and the United States that carried *The Satanic Verses* found themselves in a bind. Some Muslims threatened violence unless the bookstores stopped selling the book. Some booksellers removed the book from their shelves and sold it only to customers who specifically asked for it. Others refused to sell it altogether on the grounds that it was too risky. Still others defied the threats. One bookseller in Berkeley, California, continued selling the book on the grounds that he would not allow anyone to interfere with the principle of freedom of the press. His store was bombed, and damage was substantial. His reaction? He increased security.

QUESTIONS

1. Imagine that you are the owner of a bookstore faced with the decision of what to do about *The Satanic Verses*. In deciding on a course of action, there are several conflicting objectives. Develop a value tree. Be sure that the detail objectives can be measured in terms of operational attributes.

2. What alternatives do you have?

3. What risks do you face? Do the risks differ depending on the alternative you choose? Sketch a simple influence diagram or decision tree for your problem.

$$\blacklozenge$$

Dilemmas in Medicine

In *Alpha and Omega: Ethics at the Frontiers of Life and Death*, author Ernlé Young specifies four fundamental principles that must be considered in making medical decisions: beneficence, nonmaleficence, justice, and autonomy. The following descriptions of these principles have been abstracted from the book (pp. 21–23):

♦ *Beneficence* implies that the physician's most important duty is to provide services that are beneficial to the patient. In many cases, this can mean taking measures that are intended to preserve the patient's life.

♦ *Nonmaleficence* is the duty not to cause harm to the patient. A medical aphorism of uncertain origin proclaims *primum non nocere* — above all, do no harm. Harm can mean different things in different situations and for different patients, and can include death, disability, separation from loved ones, or deprivation of pleasure or freedom. The difficulty is that many medical procedures entail at least some harm or the potential for harm. This always must be weighed against the potential benefits.

♦ *Justice* in this context refers to the fair use of resources. It is, after all, impossible to do absolutely everything that would be medically justifiable for all patients. Thus, decisions must be made regarding the allocation of scarce resources. The issue is how to make these decisions fairly or equitably. For example, how should we decide what patients have priority for receiving donated organs? Is it appropriate to admit a terminally ill patient to an intensive care unit?

♦ *Autonomy* requires allowing a patient to make his or her own decisions regarding medical treatment as far as is possible. The patient, operating as an independent, self-determining agent, should be able to obtain appropriate information and participate fully in the decisions regarding the course of treatment and, ultimately, the patient's life.

In most medical situations, these principles do not conflict. That is, the physician can provide beneficial care for the patient without causing harm, the treatment can be provided equitably, and the patient can easily make his or her own decisions. In a few cases, however, the principles are in conflict and it is impossible to accomplish all of them at once. For example, consider the case of a terminally ill patient who insists that everything possible be done to extend his or her life. Doing so may violate both nonmaleficence and justice while at the same time providing limited benefit. But not providing the requested services violates autonomy. Thus, the physician would be in a very difficult dilemma.

QUESTIONS

1. Discuss the relationship between the medical ethics here and decision making in the face of conflicting objectives. Sketch a value tree for a physician who must cope with difficult problems such as those described above. Can you suggest any detail objectives to help explain or expand on the four fundamental objectives?

2. Neonatology is the study and treatment of newborn infants. Of particular concern is the treatment of low birth-weight infants who are born prematurely. Often these babies are the victims of poor prenatal care and may be burdened with severe deformities. Millions of dollars are spent annually to save the lives of such infants. Discuss the ways in which the four principles conflict in this situation. Could you give any guidelines to a panel of doctors and hospital administrators groping with such problems?

3. Terminally ill patients face the prospect of death within a relatively short period of time. In the case of cancer victims, their last months can be extremely painful. Increasing numbers of such patients consider taking their own lives, and much controversy has developed concerning euthanasia, or mercy killing. Imagine that a patient is terminally ill and mentions that he or she is considering suicide. If everything reasonable has been done to arrest the disease without success, this may be a reasonable option. Furthermore, the principle of autonomy should be respected here, provided that the patient is mentally stable and sound and understands fully the implications. But how deeply should the physician or loved one be involved? There are varying degrees of involvement. First, the physician might simply provide counseling and emotional support. The next step would be encouraging the patient by removing obstacles. Third, the physician might provide information about how to end one's life effectively and without trauma. The next step would be to assist in the procurement of the means to commit suicide. Helping the patient to end his or her life represents still another step, and actually killing the patient — by lethal injection or removal of a life support system, for example — would represent full involvement.

   Suppose that one of your loved ones were terminally ill and considering suicide. What issues would you want him or her to consider carefully? Draw a value tree for the patient's decision.

   Now suppose that the patient has asked you to assist in his or her suicide. What issues would you want to consider when deciding on your level of involvement? Sketch a value tree for your own decision. Compare this value tree with the patient's.

Source: Young, E. (1989) *Alpha and Omega: Ethics at the Frontiers of Life and Death.* Palo Alto, CA: Stanford Alumni Association.

A Matter of Ethics

Paul Lambert was in a difficult situation. When he had started his current job five years ago, he had understood clearly that he would be working on sensitive defense contracts for the government. In fact, his firm was a subcontractor for some major defense contractors. What he had not realized at the time — indeed, he had only discovered this gradually over the past two years — was that the firm was overcharging. And it was not just a matter of a few dollars. In some cases, the government was overcharged by as much as a factor of 10.

Three weeks ago, he had inadvertently come across an internal accounting memo that documented one particularly flagrant violation. He had quietly made a copy and locked it in his desk. At the time, he had been amazed, then righteously indignant. He had resolved to take the evidence immediately to the appropriate authorities. But the more he thought about it, the more confused he became. Finally, he called his brother-in-law, Jim Grillich. Jim worked for another defense-related firm and agreed to have lunch with Paul. After exchanging stories about their families and comments on recent sporting events, Paul laid his cards on the table.

"Looks as though you could really make some waves," Jim commented, after listening to Paul's story.

"I guess I could. But I just don't know. If I blow the whistle. I'd feel like I'd have to resign. And then it would be tough to find another job. Nancy and I don't have a lot of savings, you know." The thought of dipping into their savings made Paul shake his head. "I just don't know."

The two men were silent for a long time. Then Paul continued, "To make matters worse, I really believe that the work that the company is doing, especially in the research labs, is important. It may have a substantial impact on our society over the next 20 years. The CEO is behind the research 100 percent, and I gather from the few comments I've overheard that he's essentially funding the research by overcharging on the subcontracts. So if I call foul, the research program goes down the drain."

"I know what you mean." Jim went on to recount a similar dilemma that he faced a few years before.

"So what did you do?"

"The papers are still in my desk. I always wanted to talk to someone about it. I even thought about calling you up, but I never did. After a while, it seemed like it was pretty easy just to leave the papers in there, locked up, safe and sound."

QUESTIONS

1. What trade-offs is Paul trying to make? Sketch out a value tree based on his discussion. What appear to be his fundamental objectives?
2. Suppose that Paul's take-home pay is currently $2400 per month. In talking to an employment company, he is told that it will probably take two months to find a similar job if he leaves his current one, and he had better expect three months if he wants a better job. In looking at his savings account of $10,500, he decides that he cannot justify leaving his job, even

though this means keeping quiet about the overcharging incident. Can you say anything about an implicit trade-off rate between the fundamental objectives that you identified above?

3. Have you ever been in a situation in which it was difficult for you to decide whether to take an ethically appropriate action? Describe the situation. What made the decision difficult? What trade-offs did you have to make? What did you finally do?

◆

FDA and the Testing of Experimental Drugs

The Food and Drug Administration (FDA) of the federal government is one of the largest consumer-protection agencies in the world. One of FDA's charges is to ensure that drugs sold to consumers do not pose health threats. As a result, the testing procedure that leads to a new drug's approval is rigorous and demanding. So much so, in fact, that some policy makers are calling for less stringent standards. Below are some of the dilemmas that FDA faces:

◆ If an experimental drug shows promise in the treatment of a dangerous disease such as AIDS, should the testing procedure be abbreviated in order to get the drug to market more quickly?

◆ FDA already is a large and costly bureaucracy. By easing testing standards, substantial dollars could be saved. But would it be more likely that a dangerous drug would be approved? What are the costs of such a mistake?

A fundamental trade-off is involved here. What are we gaining in the way of assurance of safe drugs, and what are we giving up by keeping the drugs away from the general public for an additional year or two?

QUESTIONS

1. What are the consequences (both good and bad) of keeping a drug from consumers for some required period of rigorous testing?

2. What are the consequences (both good and bad) of allowing drugs to reach consumers with less stringent testing?

3. Imagine that you are FDA's commissioner. A pharmaceutical company requests special permission to rush a new AIDS drug to market. On the basis of a first round of tests, the company estimates that the new drug will save the lives of 200 AIDS victims in the first year. Your favorite pharmacologist expresses reservations, however, claiming that without running the complete series of tests, he fears that the drug may have as-yet-undetermined but serious side effects. What decision would you make? Why?

4. Suppose that the drug in Problem 3 was for arthritis. It could be used by any individual who suffers from arthritis, and, according to the preliminary tests, would be able to cure up to 80% of rheumatoid arthritis cases. But your pharmacologist expresses the same reservations as for the AIDS drug. Now what decision would you make? Why?

◆

◇ REFERENCES

The additive weighted score has been described by many authors. The most comprehensive discussion, and the only one that covers swing weights, is that by von Winterfeldt and Edwards (1986). Keeney and Raiffa (1976) and Keeney (1980) also have devoted a lot of material to this preference model.

The basic idea of creating an additive weighted score is fairly common and has been applied in a variety of settings. Moreover, this basic approach also has earned several different names. For example, a cost–benefit analysis typically prices out nonmonetary costs and benefits and then aggregates them. For an interesting critique of a cost–benefit analysis, see Bunn (1984, Chapter 5).

Other decision-aiding techniques also use the additive weighted score implicitly or explicitly, including the Analytic Hierarchy Process (Saaty, 1980) and goal programming with nonpreemptive weights (see Winston, 1986). Conjoint analysis, a statistical technique used in market research to determine preference patterns of consumers on the basis of survey data, often is used to create additive weighted scores. In all of these, some kind of subjective judgment forms the basis for the weights, and yet the interpretation of the weights is not always clear. Clearly, for all of these alternative models, extreme care must be exercised in making the judgments on which the additive value function is based. There is no substitute for thinking hard about trade-off issues. This text's view is that the decision-analysis approach discussed in this chapter provides the best systematic framework for making those judgments.

BUNN, D. (1984) *Applied Decision Analysis.* New York: McGraw-Hill.

KEENEY, R. (1980) *Siting Energy Facilities.* New York: Academic Press.

KEENEY, R., and H. RAIFFA (1976) *Decisions with Multiple Objectives.* New York: Wiley.

SAATY, T. (1980) *The Analytic Hierarchy Process.* New York: McGraw-Hill.

VON WINTERFELDT, D., and W. EDWARDS (1986) *Decision Analysis and Behavioral Research.* Cambridge: Cambridge University Press.

WINSTON, W. (1987) *Operations Research: Applications and Algorithms.* Boston, MA: PWS-KENT .

◇ EPILOGUE

What happened with the Eugene Public Library? After much public discussion, an alternative emerged that had not been anticipated. An out-of-state developer expressed a desire to build a multistory office building in downtown Eugene (at Site 2, in fact) and proposed that the library could occupy the lower two floors of the building. By entering into a partnership with the developer, the city could save a lot in construction costs. Many citizens voiced concerns about the prospect of the city's alliance with a private developer, others were concerned about the complicated financing arrangement, and still others disapproved of the proposed location for a variety of reasons. On the other hand, the supporters pointed out that this might be the only way that Eugene would ever get a new library. In March 1989, the proposal to accept the developer's offer was submitted to the voters. The result? They turned down the offer.   ◆

Conflicting Objectives II: Multiattribute Utility Models

The weighted-scoring procedure described in Chapter 15 is an easy-to-use technique. It is incomplete, however, because it ignores certain fundamental characteristics of choices among multiattribute alternatives. We discussed one problem with proportional scores — they assume risk neutrality. Problem 15.25 (page 465) demonstrated this in the important context of the common NPV choice criterion. More subtle are situations in which attributes interact. For example, two attributes may be substitutes for one another to some extent. Imagine a CEO who oversees several divisions. The simultaneous success of every division may not be terribly important; as long as some divisions perform well, cash flows and profits will be adequate. On the other hand, attributes can be complementary. An example might be the success of various phases of a research-and-development project. The success of each individual project is valuable in its own right. But the success of all phases might make possible an altogether new technology or process, thus leading to substantial synergistic gains in many ways. In this case, high achievement on all attributes (success in the various R&D phases) is worth more than the sum of the value obtained from the individual successes.

Such interactions cannot be captured by our weighted-scoring procedure for modeling preferences. That model is essentially an additive combination of preferences for individual attributes. To capture the kinds of interactions that we are talking about here, as well as risk attitudes within as well as across attributes, we must think more generally. Let us think in terms of a *utility surface*, such as the one depicted in Figure 16.1 for two attributes. Although it is possible to think about many attributes at once, we will develop multiattribute utility theory concepts using only two attributes. The ideas are readily extended to more attributes, and at the end of the chapter we will say a bit about multiattribute utility functions for three or more attributes.

Much of this chapter is fairly abstract and technical. To do a good job with the material, the mathematics are necessary. After theoretical development, which is sprinkled with illustrative examples, we will process a complete example that involves the assessment of a two-attribute utility function for managing a blood bank.

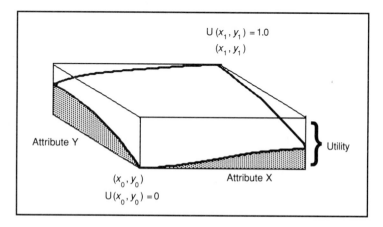

FIGURE 16.1 *A Utility Surface for Two Attributes*

◆ MULTIATTRIBUTE UTILITY FUNCTIONS: DIRECT ASSESSMENT

To assess a utility function like the one in Figure 16.1, we can use the same basic approach that we already have used. For example, consider the reference-gamble method. The appropriate reference gamble has the worst pair (x_0, y_0) and the best pair (x_1, y_1) as the two possible outcomes:

Win (x_1, y_1) with probability p.
Win (x_0, y_0) with probability $1 - p$.

Now for any pair (x, y), where $x_0 \leq x \leq x_1$ and $y_0 \leq y \leq y_1$, find the probability p to use in the reference gamble that will make you indifferent between (x, y) and the reference gamble. As before, you can use p as your utility $U(x, y)$ because $U(x_1, y_1) = 1$, and $U(x_0, y_0) = 0$. Figure 16.2 shows the decision tree that represents the assessment situation. This is simply the standard probability-equivalent utility assessment technique that we have seen before.

You can see that we will wind up with many utility numbers after making this assessment for a reasonable number of (x, y) pairs. There may be several pairs

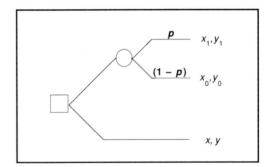

FIGURE 16.2   *Directly Assessing
a Multiattribute Utility*
The probability that makes you
indifferent between the lottery and the
sure thing is your utility value for (x, y).

with the same utility, and you should be indifferent among such pairs. Thus, (x, y) pairs with the same utilities must fall on an indifference curve. One approach to understanding your multiattribute preferences is simply to plot the assessed points on a graph, as in Figure 16.3, and sketch the indifference curves.

To find a good representation of preferences through direct assessment, however, there is a drawback: You must assess utilities for a substantial number of points. And even though it is straightforward to see how this approach might be extended to three or more attributes, the more being considered, the more

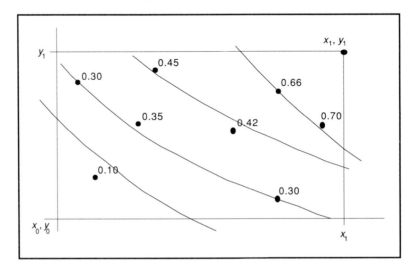

FIGURE 16.3   *Sketching Indifferent Curves*
The point values are the assessed utility values for the
corresponding x, y pair

points you must assess, and the more complicated graphical representations become. An easier way would be nice.

Another approach that would ease the assessment burden would be to think about a multiattribute utility function that is made up of the individual utility functions. Mathematically, we might represent the most general case as:

$$U(x, y) = f\{U_X(x), U_Y(y)\}.$$

The $f\{\cdot, \cdot\}$ notation means that $U(x, y)$ is a function of the individual utility functions $U_X(x)$ and $U_Y(y)$. Of course, we need a specific functional form. The one we will consider is

$$U(x, y) = c_1 + c_2\,U_X(x) + c_3\,U_Y(y) + c_4\,U_X(x)\,U_Y(y).$$

The importance of any such formulation is that it greatly eases the assessment burden; we only require the individual utility functions and enough information to put them together. Being able to break down the multiattribute utility function this way sometimes is called *separability*; the overall utility function can be "separated" into chunks that represent different attributes.

Is such an arrangement possible? Yes, but it requires some interesting conditions for the combined utility function. These conditions concern how the preferences interact among the attributes, a point suggested in the beginning of this chapter. We will digress briefly to discuss these conditions.

♦ INDEPENDENCE CONDITIONS

Preferential Independence

One thing we need in order to have the kind of separability mentioned above is *mutual preferential independence*. An attribute Y is said to be preferentially independent of X if preferences for specific outcomes of Y do not depend on the level of attribute X. As an example, let Y be the time to completion of a project and X its cost. If we prefer a project time of 5 days to one of 10 days, assuming that the cost is 100 in each case, and if we also prefer a project time of 5 days to one of 10 days if the cost is 200 in both cases, then Y is preferentially independent of X; it does not matter what the cost is — we still prefer the shorter completion time.

We need mutual preferential independence, so we also need the cost to be preferentially independent of the completion time. If we prefer lower cost no matter what the completion time, then X is preferentially independent of Y. Then we can say that the two attributes are mutually preferentially independent.

Preferential independence seems to be a pretty reasonable condition to assume, especially in cases like the one involving costs and time to completion. But it is easy to imagine situations in which preferential independence might not hold. For example, in Chapter 15 it was suggested that your preference for amount of homework effort might depend on course topic. Bunn (1984) relates a nice hypothetical example in which preferential independence might not hold. Consider a decision with outcomes that affect both the place where you live and the automobile that you drive. Let X be an outcome variable that could denote either Los Angeles or an African farm, and Y an outcome variable denoting either a Cadillac or a Land Rover. The value of X (whether you live in Los Angeles or on an African farm) may well affect your preference for a Cadillac or a Land Rover. Therefore, Y would not be preferentially independent of X. Consider the reverse: You may prefer Los Angeles to an African farm (or vice versa) regardless of the car you own. Thus, one attribute would be preferentially independent of the other, but the two are not mutually preferentially independent.

It probably is fair to say that mutual preferential independence holds for many people and many situations, or that at least it is a reasonable approximation. Mutual preferential independence is like the decomposability property for a value tree. If a decision maker has done a good job of building a decomposable value tree, mutual preferential independence probably is a reasonable assumption. But it should never be taken for granted.

As indicated, mutual preferential independence among outcomes is necessary to obtain separability of the multiattribute utility function. Unfortunately, it is not quite strong enough. Note that in the above discussion concerning preferential independence we never mentioned the possibility that the outcomes might be uncertain. Preferential independence has to do with outcomes that are certain. As we know, however, many important decisions involve uncertainty.

Utility Independence

Utility independence is slightly stronger than preferential independence. An attribute Y is considered utility independent of attribute X if preferences for *uncertain choices* involving different levels of Y are independent of the value of X. Imagine assessing a certainty equivalent for a lottery involving only outcomes in Y. If our certainty equivalent amount for the Y lottery is the same no matter what the level of X, then Y is utility independent of X. If X also is utility independent of Y, then the two attributes are mutually utility independent.

Utility independence clearly is analogous to preferential independence, except that the assessments are made under conditions of uncertainty. For the project evaluation example above, suppose that we assess that the certainty equivalent for an option giving, say, a 50% chance of $Y = 5$ and a 50% chance of $Y = 10$ does not depend on the level at which the cost X is fixed. As long as our preferences for lotteries in the completion-time attribute are the same (as, say, measured by their certainty equivalents) regardless of the fixed level of cost, then completion time is utility independent of cost.

Keeney and Raiffa (1976) discuss an example in which utility independence might not hold. Suppose that X and Y are the rates of serious crime in two precincts of a metropolitan police division. In determining the joint utility function for this region's police chief, the issue of utility independence for X and Y would be faced. With Y fixed at 5, a relatively low rate of crime, he may be quite risk-averse to rates of crime in region X. He may not want to appear as though he is neglecting a particular precinct. Thus, his certainty equivalent for an option giving a 50% chance of $X = 0$ and a 50% chance of $X = 30$ may be 22 when Y is fixed at 5. If Y were fixed at the higher rate of 15, however, his certainty equivalent may be less risk-aversely assessed at 17. Thus, one must not assume that utility independence will hold in all cases. Even so, there are many reported practical multiattribute studies that assume utility independence, and in many cases it may be realistic.

◆ DETERMINING WHETHER INDEPENDENCE EXISTS

How can you determine whether your preferences are preferentially independent? The simplest approach is to imagine a series of paired comparisons that involve one of the attributes. With the other attribute fixed at its lowest level, decide which outcome in each pair is preferred. Once this is done, imagine changing the level of the fixed attribute. Would your comparisons be the same? Would the comparisons be the same regardless of the fixed level of the other attribute? If so, then preferential independence holds.

Determining whether independence holds is a rather delicate matter. The following sample dialogue is taken from Keeney and Raiffa (1976). The notation has been changed to correspond to our notation here.

ANALYST. *I would now like to investigate how you feel about various* Y *values when we hold fixed a particular value of* X. *For example, on the first page of this questionnaire [this is shown to the assessor] there is a list of 25 paired comparisons between* Y *evaluations; each element of the pair describes levels on the* Y *attributes alone. On this first page it is assumed that, throughout, the* X *evaluations are all the same, that is,* x_1 *[the fixed value for* X *is shown to the assessor]. Is this clear?*

ASSESSOR. *Crystal clear, but you are asking me for a lot of work.*

ANALYST *Well, I have a devious purpose in mind, and it will not take as much time as you think to find out what I want. Now on the second page of the questionnaire [this is shown to the assessor] the identical set of 25 paired comparisons are repeated, but now the fixed, common level on the* X *attribute is changed from* x_1 *to* x_2 *[value is shown to the assessor]. Are you with me?*

ASSESSOR. *All the way.*

ANALYST. *On page 3, we have the same 25 paired comparisons but now the common value of the* X *value is* x_3 *[shown to the assessor].*

ASSESSOR. *You said this would not take long.*

ANALYST. *Well now, here comes the punchline. Suppose that you painstakingly respond to all of the paired comparisons on page 1 where* x_1 *is fixed. Now when you go to the next page would your responses change to these same 25 paired comparisons?*

ASSESSOR. *Let's see. In the second page all paired comparisons are the same except* x_1 *is replaced with* x_2. *What difference should that make?*

ANALYST. *Well, you tell me. If we consider this first comparison [pointed to on the questionnaire] does it make any difference if the* X *values are fixed at* x_1 *or* x_2? *There could be some interaction concerning how you view the paired comparison depending on the common value of* X.

ASSESSOR. *I suppose that might be the case in some other situation, but in the first comparison I prefer the left alternative to the right no matter what the* X *value is . . . as long as they are the same.*

ANALYST.   *Okay. Would you now feel the same if you consider the second paired comparison?*

ASSESSOR.   *Yes. And the third and so on. Am I being naive? Is there some trick here?*

ANALYST.   *No, not at all. I am just checking to see if the X values have any influence on your responses to the paired comparisons. So I gather that you are telling me that your responses on page 1 carry over to page 2.*

ASSESSOR. *That's right.*

ANALYST.   *And to page 3, where the X value is held fixed at x₃ [shown to assessor]?*

ASSESSOR. *Yes.*

ANALYST.   *Well, on the basis of this information I now pronounce that for you attribute Y is preferentially independent of attribute X.*

ASSESSOR.   *That's nice to know.*

ANALYST.   *That's all I wanted to find out.*

ASSESSOR.   *Aren't you going to ask me to fill out page 1?*

ANALYST.   *No. That's too much work. There are less painful ways of getting that information.*

[*Source:* Keeney, R., and H. Raiffa *Decisions with Multiple Objectives: Preferences and Value Tradeoffs*, pp. 299–300. Copyright © 1976 by John Wiley & Sons, Inc. Reprinted by permission.]

The dialogue describes how to check for preferential independence. Checking for utility independence would be much the same, except that the paired comparisons would be comparisons between lotteries involving attribute *Y* rather than sure outcomes. As long as the comparisons remain the same regardless of the fixed value for *X*, then *Y* can be considered utility independent of *X*. Of course, to establish mutual preferential or utility independence, the roles of *X* and *Y* would have to be reversed to determine whether paired comparisons of outcomes or lotteries in *X* depended on fixed values for *Y*. If each attribute turns out to be independent of the other, then mutual utility or preferential (whichever is appropriate) independence holds.

◆ USING INDEPENDENCE

If a decision maker's preferences show mutual utility independence, then a two-attribute utility function can be written as a composition of the individual utility functions. As usual, the least preferred outcome (x_0, y_0) is assigned the utility value 0, and the most preferred pair (x_1, y_1) is assigned the utility value 1.

Under mutual utility independent preferences, the two-attribute utility function can be written as:

$$U(x, y) = k_X U_X(x) + k_Y U_Y(y) + (1 - k_X - k_Y) U_X(x) U_Y(y),$$

where

1. $U_X(x)$ is a utility function on X scaled so that $U_X(x_0) = 0$ and $U_X(x_1) = 1$.
2. $U_Y(y)$ is a utility function on Y scaled so that $U_Y(y_0) = 0$ and $U_Y(y_1) = 1$.
3. $k_X = U(x_1, y_0)$.
4. $k_Y = U(x_0, y_1)$.

The product term $U_X(x) U_Y(y)$ in this utility function is what permits the modeling of interactions among attributes. The utility functions U_X and U_Y are *conditional utility functions*, and must be assessed with the other attribute fixed at a particular level. (For example, in assessing U_Y, imagine that X is fixed at a specific level.) To understand conditions 3 and 4, all we must do is plug the individual utilities into the equation. For example,

$$U(x_1, y_0) = k_X U_X(x_1) + k_Y U_Y(y_0) + (1 - k_X - k_Y) U_X(x_1) U_Y(y_0)$$
$$= k_X(1) + k_Y(0) + (1 - k_X - k_Y)(1)(0)$$
$$= k_X.$$

This multiattribute utility function, called a *multilinear* expression, is not as bad as it looks! Look at it from the point of view of the X attribute. Think about fixing Y at a value (say, y_a); you get a conditional utility function for X, given that Y is fixed at y_a:

$$U(x, y_a) = k_Y U_Y(y_a) + [k_X + (1 - k_X - k_Y) U_Y(y_a)] U_X(x).$$

Because Y is fixed at y_a, the terms $k_Y U_Y(y_a)$ and $[k_X + (1 - k_X - k_Y) U_Y(y_a)]$ are just constants. Thus, $U(x, y_a)$ is simply a scaled version of $U_X(x)$. Now change to another y (y_b). What happens to the utility function for X? The expression now looks like:

$$U(x, y_b) = k_Y U_Y(y_b) + [k_X + (1 - k_X - k_Y) U_Y(y_b)] U_X(x).$$

This is just another linear transformation of $U_X(x)$, and so $U(x, y_b)$ and $U(x, y_a)$ must be identical in terms of the way that lotteries involving the X attribute would be ranked. We have scaled the utility function $U_X(x)$ in two different ways, but the scaling does not change the ordering of preferences. Now, notice that we can do exactly the same thing with the Y attribute; for different fixed values of X $(x_a$ and $x_b)$, the conditional utility functions are simply linear transformations of each other:

$$U(x_a, y) = k_X U_X(x_a) + [k_Y + (1 - k_X - k_Y) U_X(x_a)] U_Y(y)$$
$$U(x_b, y) = k_X U_X(x_b) + [k_Y + (1 - k_X - k_Y) U_X(x_b)] U_Y(y).$$

No matter what the level of one attribute, preferences over lotteries in the second attribute (Y) stay the same. This was the definition of utility independence in the last section. We have mutual utility independence because the conditional utility function for one attribute stays essentially the same no matter which attribute is held fixed.

♦ ADDITIVE INDEPENDENCE

Look again at the multiattribute utility function:

$$U(x, y) = k_X U_X(x) + k_Y U_Y(y) + (1 - k_X - k_Y) U_X(x) U_Y(y).$$

If $k_X + k_Y = 1$, then the utility function turns out to be simply additive:

$$U(x, y) = k_X U_X(x) + (1 - k_X) U_Y(y).$$

If this is the case, we only have to assess the two individual utility functions $U_X(x)$ and $U_Y(y)$ and the weighting constant k_X. This would be convenient: It would save having to assess k_Y. In fact, you should recognize this additive utility function; it is just the weighted-scoring technique that we had from Chapter 15, with utility functions for the individual scores. How is this kind of multiattribute utility function related to the independence conditions? To be able to model preferences accurately with this additive utility function (or the weighted-scoring technique), we need *additive independence*, an even stronger condition than utility independence.

The statement of additive independence is the following: Suppose X and Y are mutually utility independent, and that you are indifferent between Lotteries A and B:

    A (x_0, y_0) with probability 0.5.

            (x_1, y_1) with probability 0.5.

    B (x_0, y_1) with probability 0.5.

            (x_1, y_0) with probability 0.5.

If this is the case, then the utility function can be written as the weighted combination of the two utility functions, $U(x, y) = k_X U_X(x) + (1 - k_X) U_X(y)$. You can see by writing out the expected utilities of the lotteries that they are equivalent:

$$\text{EU}(A) = 0.5[k_X U_X(x_0) + (1 - k_X) U_Y(y_0)] + 0.5[k_X U_X(x_1) + (1 - k_X) U_Y(y_1)]$$
$$= 0.5[k_X U_X(x_0) + (1 - k_X) U_Y(y_0) + k_X U_X(x_1) + (1 - k_X) U_Y(y_1)].$$

$$\text{EU}(B) = 0.5[k_X U_X(x_0) + (1 - k_X) U_Y(y_1)] + 0.5[k_X U_X(x_1) + (1 - k_X) U_Y(y_0)]$$
$$= 0.5[k_X U_X(x_0) + (1 - k_X) U_Y(y_1) + k_X U_X(x_1) + (1 - k_X) U_Y(y_0)]$$
$$= \text{EU}(A).$$

The intuition behind additive independence is that, in assessing uncertain outcomes over both attributes, we only have to look at one attribute at a time, and it does not matter what the other attribute's values are in the uncertain outcomes. This sounds a lot like utility independence. The difference is that, in the case of additive independence, changes in *lotteries* in one attribute do not affect preferences for lotteries in the other attribute; for utility independence, on the other hand, changes in *sure levels* of one attribute do not affect preferences for lotteries in the other attribute. Here is another way to say it: When we are considering a choice among risky prospects involving multiple attributes, if additive independence holds, then we can compare the alternatives one attribute at a time. In comparing Lotteries A and B above, we are indifferent because (1) for attribute X, each lottery gives us a 50% chance at x_0 and a 50% chance at x_1; and (2) for Y, each lottery gives us a 50% chance at y_0 and a 50% chance at y_1. Looking at the attributes one at a time, the two lotteries are the same.

The additive utility function, or weighted-scoring technique from Chapter 15, requires additive independence of preferences across attributes in order to be an accurate model of a decision maker's preferences. Think back to some of the examples or problems. Do you think this idea of additive independence makes sense in purchasing a car? Think about reliability and quality of service, two attributes that might be important in this decision. When you purchase a new car, you do not know whether the reliability will be high or low, and you may not know the quality of the service. To some extent, however, the two attributes are substitutes for each other. Suppose you faced the hypothetical decision shown in Figure 16.4. Would you prefer Lottery A or B? Most of us probably would take A. If you have a clear preference for one or the other, then additive independence cannot hold.

Von Winterfeldt and Edwards (1986) discuss reports from behavioral decision theory that indicate additive independence usually does not hold. If this is the case, what is the justification for the use of the weighted-scoring procedure developed in Chapter 15? Many multiattribute decisions that we make involve little or no uncertainty, and evidence has shown that the weighted-scoring procedure is a reasonable model of most people's preferences under conditions of certainty. And in extremely complicated situations with many attributes, the weighted-scoring procedure may be a useful rough-cut approximation. It may turn out that considering the interactions among attributes is not critical to the decision at hand.

Finally, it is possible to use simple approximation techniques to include interactions within the additive utility framework or the weighted-scoring technique. For example, suppose that we have a decision problem with many attributes that are, for the most part, additively independent of one another. The additive representation of the utility function does not allow for any interaction among the attributes. If this is appropriate for almost all of the possible outcomes, then we may use the additive representation while including a specific "bonus" or "penalty" (depending on which is appropriate) for those outcomes with noticeable interaction effects.

Raiffa (1982) has an interesting example. Suppose a city is negotiating a new contract with its police force. Two attributes are (1) increase in vacation for

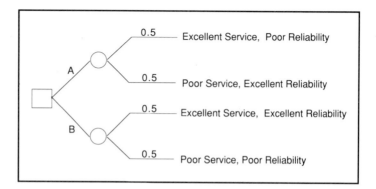

FIGURE 16.4 *An Assessment Lottery for a Car Purchase*
If you have a clear preference for A or B, then additive independence cannot hold.

officers who have less than five years of service, and (2) increase in vacation for officers who have more than five years of service. The city loses points in an additive value function for increases in vacation for either group. If either group is held to no increase, then the city loses no points for that particular group. But the city would be happy if all its officers could be held to no increase in vacation time; thus, no precedent is set for the other group. To capture this interaction, the city gets a "bonus" of some points in its weighted score if there is no increase in vacation for either group.

◆ SUBSTITUTES AND COMPLEMENTS

In the multiattribute utility function, the interaction between the attributes is captured by the term $(1 - k_X - k_Y)\,U_X(x)\,U_Y(y)$. How can we interpret this? Keeney and Raiffa (1986) give an interesting interpretation of the coefficient $(1 - k_X - k_Y)$. The sign of $(1 - k_X - k_Y)$ can be interpreted in terms of whether x and y are complements or substitutes for each other. Suppose $(1 - k_X - k_Y)$ is positive. Now examine the multiattribute utility function:

$$U(x, y) = k_X\,U_X(x) + k_Y\,U_Y(y) + (1 - k_X - k_Y)\,U_X(x)\,U_Y(y).$$

Preferred values of X and Y will give high values to the conditional utility functions, and the positive $(1 - k_X - k_Y)$ will drive up the overall utility for the pair even higher. Thus, if $(1 - k_X - k_Y)$ is positive, the two attributes complement each other. On the other hand, if $(1 - k_X - k_Y)$ is negative, high values on each scale will result in a high product term, which must be subtracted in the multiattribute preference value. In this sense, preferred values of each attribute work against each other. But if one attribute is high and the other low, the subtraction effect is not as strong. Thus, if $(1 - k_X - k_Y)$ is negative, the two attributes are substitutes.

Keeney and Raiffa (1976) offer two examples. In one, imagine a corporation with two divisions that operate in different markets altogether, and let profits in each division represent two attributes of concern to the president. To a great extent, success by the two divisions could be viewed as substitutes. That is, if profit from one division was down while the other was up, the firm would get along fine. Financial success by one division would most likely ensure the overall success of the firm.

For an example of the complementary case, Keeney and Raiffa consider the problem a general would face in a battle being fought on two fronts. If we let the consequences on the two fronts represent two distinct attributes, then these two attributes may be complementary. That is, defeat on one front may be almost as bad as defeat on both fronts, and a completely successful outcome may be guaranteed only by victory on both.

◆ ASSESSING A TWO-ATTRIBUTE UTILITY FUNCTION

Now that we have seen the basics of two-attribute utility functions, we are ready to assess one. The procedure is relatively straightforward. First, we determine whether mutual utility independence holds. Provided that it does, we then assess the individual utility functions. Finally, the scaling constants are determined in order to put the individual utility functions together.

THE BLOOD BANK

In a hospital blood bank it is important to have a policy for deciding how much of each type of blood should be kept on hand. For any particular year, there is a "shortage rate," the percentage of units of blood demanded but not filled from stock because of shortages. Whenever there is a shortage, a special order must be placed to locate the required blood elsewhere or to locate donors. An operation may be postponed, but only rarely will a blood shortage result in a death. Naturally, keeping a lot of blood stocked means that a shortage is less likely. But there is also a rate at which blood is "outdated," or kept on the shelf the maximum amount of time, after which it must be discarded. Although having a lot of blood on hand means a low shortage rate, it probably also would mean a high outdating rate. Of course, the eventual outcome is unknown because it is impossible to predict exactly how much blood will be demanded. Should the hospital try to keep as much blood on hand as possible so as to avoid shortages? Or should the hospital try to keep a fairly low inventory in order to minimize the amount of outdated blood discarded? How should the hospital blood bank balance these two objectives? [*Source:* Keeney, R., and H. Raiffa (1976) *Decisions with Multiple Objectives: Preferences and Value Tradeoffs.* New York: Wiley.]

◆

The outcome at the blood bank depends on uncertain demand over the year as well as the specific inventory policy (stock level) chosen. Thus, we can think of each possible inventory policy as a lottery over uncertain outcomes having two attributes, shortage and outdating. Shortage is measured as the annual percentage of units demanded but not in stock, while outdating is the percentage of units that are discarded due to aging. A high stock level probably will lead to less shortage but more outdating, and a low stock level will lead to more shortage and less outdating. To choose an appropriate stock level, we need to assess both the probability distribution over shortage and outdating outcomes for each possible stock level and the decision maker's utility function over these outcomes. Because each outcome has two attributes, we need a two-attribute utility function. Here we focus on the assessment of the utility function through the following steps:

1. The first step was to explain the problem to the nurse in charge of ordering blood. Maintaining an appropriate stock level was her responsibility, so it made sense to base an analysis of the problem on her personal preferences. She understood the importance of the problem and was motivated to think hard about her assessments. Without such understanding and motivation on her part, the entire project probably would have failed.

2. It was established that the annual outdating and shortage rates might range from 10% (worst case) to 0% (best case).

3. Did mutual utility independence hold? The nurse assessed a certainty equivalent for uncertain shortage rates (Attribute X), given a fixed outdating rate (Attribute Y). The certainty equivalent did not change for different outdating rates. Thus, shortage was found to be utility independent of outdating. Similar procedures showed the reverse to be true as well. Thus, shortage and outdating were mutually utility independent, implying the multilinear form for the utility function.

4. The next step was to assess the conditional utility functions $U_X(x)$ and $U_Y(y)$. In each case, the utility function was assessed conditional on the other attribute being held constant at 0. To assess $U_X(x)$, it was first established that preferences decreased as x increased. Using the lotteries that had been assessed earlier in the utility independence step, an exponential utility function was determined. Setting $U_X(0) = 1$ (best case) and $U_X(10) = 0$ (worst case), the utility function was

$$U_X(x) = 1 + 0.375(1 - e^{x/7.692}).$$

Likewise, the second utility function was determined using the previously assessed certainty equivalents, and again an exponential form was used. The utility function was

$$U_Y(y) = 1 + 2.033(1 - e^{y/25}).$$

This utility function also has $U_Y(0) = 1$ and $U_Y(10) = 0$.

5. Assessing the weights k_X and k_Y is the key to finding the two-attribute utility function. The trick is to use as much information as possible to set up equations based on indifferent outcomes and lotteries, and then to solve the equations for the weights. Because we have two unknowns, k_X and k_Y, we will be solving two equations in two unknowns. To set up two equations, we will need two utility assessments.

Recall that the multilinear form can be written as

$$U(x, y) = k_X U_X(x) + k_Y U_Y(y) + (1 - k_X - k_Y) U_X(x) U_Y(y).$$

We also know that

$$U(10, 0) = k_Y$$
$$U(0, 10) = k_X.$$

These follow from conditions 3 and 4 above, substituting $x_0 = 10$, $x_1 = 0$, $y_0 = 10$, and $y_1 = 0$.

The nurse determined that she was indifferent between the two outcomes ($x = 4.75$, $y = 0$) and ($x = 0$, $y = 10$). This first assessment indicates that, for her, avoiding shortages is more important than avoiding outdating. We can substitute each one of these points into the expression for the utility function, establishing the first equation relating k_X and k_Y:

$$U(4.75, 0) = k_X U_X(4.75) + k_Y U_Y(0) + (1 - k_X - k_Y) U_X(4.75) U_Y(0)$$
$$= k_X U_X(4.75) + k_Y(1) + (1 - k_X - k_Y) U_X(4.75)(1).$$

Because she was indifferent between $(4.75, 0)$ and $(0, 10)$, we have

$$U(4.75, 0) = U(0, 10) \qquad \text{(because she is indifferent)}$$
$$= k_X \qquad\qquad \text{(from } U(0, 10) = k_X, \text{ above)}.$$

Substituting, we obtain:

$$k_X = k_X U_X(4.75) + k_Y + (1 - k_X - k_Y) U_X(4.75)$$
$$= k_Y + (1 - k_Y) U_X(4.75)$$
$$= k_Y + (1 - k_Y) [1 + 0.375\{1 - e^{4.75/7.692}\}]$$
$$= k_Y + (1 - k_Y) 0.68$$
$$= 0.68 + 0.32\, k_Y. \tag{16.1}$$

In the second assessment, the decision maker concluded that she was indifferent between the outcome $(6, 6)$ and a 50–50 lottery between the outcomes $(0, 0)$ and $(10, 10)$. Using this assessment, we can find $U(6, 6)$:

$$U(6, 6) = 0.5\, U(0, 0) + 0.5\, U(10, 10)$$
$$= 0.5\, (1) + 0.5\, (0)$$
$$= 0.5.$$

This is just a standard assessment of a certainty equivalent for a 50–50 gamble between the best and worst outcomes. Now substitute $U(6, 6) = 0.5$ into the two-attribute utility function to find a second equation in terms of k_X and k_Y:

$$0.5 = U(6, 6)$$
$$= k_X U_X(6) + k_Y U_Y(6) + (1 - k_X - k_Y) U_X(6)\, U_Y(6).$$

Substituting the values $X = 6$ and $Y = 6$ into the formulas for the individual utility functions gives

$$U_X(6) = 0.56$$
$$U_Y(6) = 0.45.$$

Now plug these into the equation for $U(6, 6)$ to get:

$$0.5 = k_X (0.56) + k_Y (0.45) + (1 - k_X - k_Y) (0.56) (0.45),$$

which simplifies to

$$0.248 = 0.308\, k_X + 0.198\, k_Y. \tag{16.2}$$

Now we have two linear equations in k_X and k_Y — Equations (16.1) and (16.2):

$$k_X = 0.680 + 0.320\, k_Y$$
$$0.248 = 0.308\, k_X + 0.198\, k_Y.$$

Solving these two equations simultaneously for k_X and k_Y, we find that $k_X = 0.72$ and $k_Y = 0.13$. Thus, the two-attribute utility function can be written as

$$U(x, y) = 0.72\, U_X(x) + 0.13\, U_Y(y) + 0.15\, U_X(x)\, U_Y(y),$$

where $U_X(x)$ and $U_Y(y)$ are given by the exponential utility functions defined above. Now we can find the utility for any (x, y) pair (as long as the x's and y's are each between 0 and 10, the range of the assessments). Any policy for ordering blood can be evaluated in terms of its expected utility. Table 16.1 shows utilities for different possible outcomes, and Figure 16.5 shows the indifference curves associated with the utility function. From Figure 16.5, we can verify the conditions and assessments that were used:

$U(0, 0) = 1$ $\qquad\qquad$ $U(10, 10) = 0$

$U(10, 0) = 0.13 = k_Y$ $\qquad$ $U(0, 10) = U(4.75, 0) = 0.72 = k_X$

$U(6, 6) = 0.50.$

The final assessed utility function is readily interpreted. The large value for k_X relative to k_Y means that the nurse is much more concerned about the percentage of shortage than she is about the percentage of outdating. This makes sense; most of us would agree that the objective of the blood bank is primarily to save lives, and we probably would rather throw out old blood than not have enough on hand when it is needed. The fact that $k_X + k_Y < 1$ means that the two attributes are complements rather than substitutes. We can see this in Figure 16.5. For example, imagine an outcome of $(8, 8)$, for which the utility is 0.27 (Point A). Now imagine improving the shortage percentage to zero. This would increase the utility value to $U(0, 8) = 0.79$, for an approximate net increase of 0.52. On the other hand, improving the outdating percentage the same amount results in $U(8, 0) = 0.40$, for a net increase of 0.13. If we increased both at the same time, we would have $U(0, 0) = 1.00$, an increase of 0.73. The increase in utility from increasing both at once is greater than the sum of the individual increases ($0.73 > 0.52 + 0.13 = 0.65$). This is the sense in which there is an interaction. This kind of phenomenon is impossible in the weighted-scoring method or the additive utility function.

x Values (Shortage)	y Values (Outdating)					
	0	2	4	6	8	10
0	1.00	0.95	0.90	0.85	0.79	0.72
2	0.90	0.86	0.81	0.76	0.70	0.64
4	0.78	0.74	0.69	0.64	0.59	0.54
6	0.62	0.58	0.54	0.50	0.45	0.40
8	0.40	0.37	0.34	0.31	0.27	0.23
10	0.13	0.11	0.08	0.06	0.03	0.00

TABLE 16.1   *Utility Values for Shortage and Outdating in the Blood Bank*

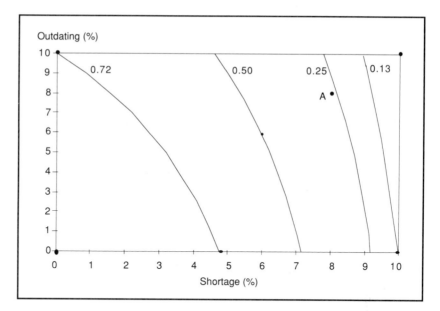

FIGURE 16.5   *Indifference Curves for Nurse's Utility Function for Shortage and Outdating*
The numbers are U(x, y) for the corresponding indifference curve.

♦ THREE OR MORE ATTRIBUTES (OPTIONAL)

When the decision problem involves three or more objectives, modeling preferences is more difficult. Building a utility function that will permit interactions across many attributes can become complex. Under certain conditions, however, the *multiplicative* utility function can be used. Let X_i denote the ith attribute, and $U_i(x_i)$ and k_i the corresponding individual utility function and scaling constant. The multiplicative utility function for n different attributes is

$$U(x_1, x_2, \cdots, x_n) = \prod_{i=1}^{n} [k\, k_i\, U_i(x_i) + 1],$$

where k is a nonzero solution to the equation

$$1 + k = \prod_{i=1}^{n} (1 + k\, k_i).$$

The k_i's have the same meaning they had in the two-attribute case. That is, if $x_{i,0}$ indicates the worst level on attribute X_i, and $x_{i,1}$ represents the best, then

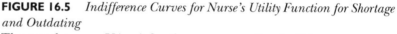

That is, k_i is the utility of an outcome having the best level on attribute X_i and worst on all others. Thus, we can assess the k_i's directly through our standard reference-lottery approach, which is shown in Figure 16.6. We have the refer-

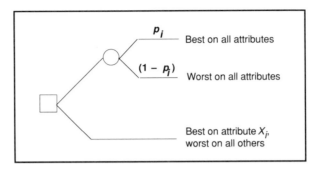

FIGURE 16.6   *Assessing Scaling Constants for the Multiplicative Utility Function*
The p_i that makes the decision maker indifferent between the lottery and the sure thing is the utility of the sure outcome and hence equals k_i.

ence lottery with the best possible and worst possible outcomes versus the sure thing having the best level on attribute X_i and the worst level on all others. The probability p_i that makes us indifferent between the lottery and the sure thing is our utility for the sure thing and hence is equal to k_i. The decision maker can assess each of the k_i's in this way and then find the scaling constant k that satisfies the condition given above. Finally, putting the individual utility functions together with the scaling constants gives the overall utility function.

The multiplicative utility function requires a fairly strong version of utility independence. Strictly speaking, each subset of the attributes must be utility independent of the remaining attributes. This essentially means that we should be able to partition the attributes into two subsets in any way we want, and then consider lotteries in one subset, holding the attributes in the other subset fixed. As long as preferences for the lotteries do not depend on the level of the remaining attributes, the multiplicative utility function should provide a good model of the decision maker's preferences. If the multiplicative model is not appropriate, then a more general version of the multilinear model may be a possibility. For more details, consult Keeney and Raiffa (1976).

◆ WHEN INDEPENDENCE FAILS

We have just dealt in depth with situations in which the assumption of mutual utility independence results in a reasonable model of preferences. This is not always true. Suppose we are interested in assessing a two-attribute utility function over attributes X and Y, but have found that neither X nor Y is utility independent of the other. Then neither the multilinear nor additive forms for the utility function are appropriate. How can we obtain a reasonable $U(x, y)$ for decision-making purposes? Several possibilities exist. One is simply to perform a direct assessment as described at the beginning of this chapter. Pick the best and worst (x, y) pairs, assign them utility values of 1 and 0, and then use reference gambles to assess the utility values for other points.

A second approach is to transform the attributes and proceed to analyze the problem with the new set. Of course, the new set of attributes still must capture the critical aspects of the problem, and they must be measurable. Take the example discussed above in which X and Y designate measures of the crime rates in two sections of a city. There may be a complicated preference structure for (x, y) pairs. For political reasons, the relative ordering of hypothetical lotteries for criminal activity in one section may be highly dependent on the level of crime in the other section. But suppose we define $s = (x + y)/2$ and $t = |x - y|$. Then s may be interpreted as an average crime index for the city and t as an indicator of the balance of criminal activity between the two sections. Any (x, y) outcome implies a unique (s, t) outcome, so it is easy to transform from one set of attributes to the other. Furthermore, even though x and y may not be utility independent, it may be reasonable to model s and t as being utility independent, thus simplifying the assessment procedure.

One of the most difficult and subtlest concepts in multiattribute utility theory is the notion of interaction among attributes. To use the weighted-scoring technique from Chapter 15, we need to have no interaction at all. To use the multilinear utility function discussed in this chapter, we can have some interaction, but it must be of a limited form. (Any interactions must conform to the notion of utility independence.) The blood bank example demonstrated the nature of the interaction between two attributes that is possible with the multilinear utility function. In this section, we are concerned with situations in which the interactions are even more complicated than those that are possible in the multilinear case. Fortunately, evidence from behavioral research suggests that it is rarely, if ever, necessary to model extremely complex preference interactions.

Chapters 15 and 16 have presented many of the principles and decision-analysis techniques that are useful in making decisions in the face of conflicting objectives. Given the complexity of the techniques, it is important to keep in mind the modeling perspective that we have held all along. The objective of using the multiattribute decision-analysis techniques is to construct a model that is a reasonable representation of a decision maker's value structure. If minimal interactions exist among the attributes and little or no uncertainty is involved in the decision, then the weighted-scoring technique from Chapter 15 is appropriate. If uncertainty comes into play, then scores should be based on assessed utility functions, and the weights should be assessed on the basis of indifference among lotteries. When there is both uncertainty and interactions among attributes, then it may be necessary to consider multiattribute utility theory, just as we have in this chapter.

◇ SUMMARY

We have continued the discussion of making decisions in the face of conflicting objectives. Much of the chapter has been a rather technical discussion and treatment of independence conditions: preferential independence, utility independence, and additive independence. The differences among these have to do with the presence or absence of uncertainty. Preferential independence says that preferences for sure outcomes in one attribute do not depend on the level of other attributes. Utility independence requires that preferences for gambles or lotteries in an attribute do not depend on the level of other attributes. Additive independence is still stronger: Preferences over lotteries in one attribute must not depend on lotteries in the other attributes. The blood bank example showed how to apply mutual utility independence to assess a two-dimensional utility function that includes an interaction term. We saw that the attributes of shortage and outdating were complementary; they work together to increase the decision maker's utility. Finally, we briefly saw what to do when there are three or more attributes, and what to do if no independence properties hold. ◆

◇ EXERCISES

16.1 Explain what is meant when we speak of interaction between attributes. Why would the weighted-scoring technique from Chapter 15 be inappropriate if two attributes interact?

16.2 What are the advantages and disadvantages of directly assessing a multiattribute utility function?

16.3 Explain preferential independence in your own words. Can you cite an example from your own experience in which preferential independence holds? Can you cite an example in which it does not hold?

16.4 Explain in your own words the difference between preferential independence and utility independence.

16.5 Explain in your own words the difference between utility independence and additive independence. Why is it important to understand the concept of additive independence?

16.6 Suppose that a company would like to purchase a fairly complicated machine to use in its manufacturing operation. Several different machines are available, and their prices are more or less equivalent. But the machines vary considerably in their available technical support (Attribute X) and reliability (Attribute Y). Some machines have a high degree of reliability and relatively low support, while others are less reliable but have excellent field support. The decision maker determined what the best and worst scenarios were for both attributes, and an assessment then was made regarding the independence of the decision maker's preferences for these attributes. It was determined that utility independence held. Individual utility functions $U_X(x)$ and $U_Y(y)$ were assessed. Finally, the decision maker was found to be indifferent in comparing Lottery A with its alternative B:

    A   Best on both reliability and support with probability 0.67.

           Worst on both reliability and support with probability 0.33.

    B   Best on reliability and worst on support.

The decision maker also was indifferent between:

    C   Best on both reliability and support with probability 0.48.

           Worst on both reliability and support with probability 0.52.

    D   Worst on reliability and best on support.

a. What are the values for k_X and k_Y? Write out the decision maker's full two-attribute utility function for reliability and support.

b. Are the two attributes substitutes or complements? Explain, both intuitively and on the basis of k_X and k_Y.

◊ QUESTIONS AND PROBLEMS

16.7 A hospital administrator is making a decision regarding the hospital's policy of treating individuals who have no insurance coverage. The policy involves examination of a prospective patient's financial resources. The issue is what level of net worth should be required in order for the patient to be provided treatment. Clearly, there are two competing objectives in this decision. One is to maximize the hospital's revenue, and the other is to provide as much care as possible to the uninsured poor. Attributes to measure achievement toward these two objectives are (1) prospective revenue (R), and (2) percentage of uninsured poor who are treated (P).

The two attributes were examined for independence, and the administrator concluded that they were mutually utility independent. Utility functions $U_R(r)$ and $U_P(p)$ for the two attributes then were assessed. Then two more assessments were made. Lottery A and its certain alternative B were judged to be equivalent by the administrator:

    A   Best on revenue, worst on treating poor with probability 0.65.

            Worst on revenue, best on treating poor with probability 0.35.

    B   Levels of revenue and treatment of poor that give $U_R(r) = 0.5$ and $U_P(p) = 0.5$.

In the second assessment, Lottery C and its certain alternative D were judged to be equivalent:

    C   Best on both revenue and treating poor with probability 0.46.

            Worst on both revenue and treating poor with probability 0.54.

    D   Worst on revenue and best on treatment of poor.

a. Find values for k_R and k_P. Should the administrator consider these two attributes to be substitutes or complements? Why or why not?

b. Comment on using an additive utility model in this situation. Would such a model seriously compromise the analysis of the decision?

16.8 Suppose you face an investment decision in which you must think about cash flows in two different years. Regard these two cash flows as two different attributes, and let X represent the cash flow in Year 1, and Y the cash flow in Year 2. The maximum cash flow you could receive in any year is $20,000, and the minimum is $5000. You have assessed your individual utility functions for x and y, and have fitted exponential utility functions to them:

$$U_X(x) = 1.05 - 2.86\, e^{-x/5000}$$
$$U_Y(y) = 1.29 - 2.12\, e^{-y/10,000}.$$

Furthermore, you have decided that utility independence holds, and so these individual utility functions for each cash flow are appropriate regardless of the amount of the other cash flow. You also have made the following assessments:

♦ You would be indifferent between a sure outcome of $7500 each year for two years and a risky investment with a 50% chance at $20,000 each year, and a 50% chance at $5000 each year.

♦ You would be indifferent between getting (1) $18,000 the first year and $5000 the second, and (2) getting $5000 the first year and $20,000 the second.

a. Use these assessments to find the scaling constants k_X and k_Y. What does the value of $(1 - k_X - k_Y)$ imply about the cash flows of the different periods?

b. Use this utility function to choose between Alternatives A and B in Problem 15.26 (Figure 15.15, page 465).

c. Draw indifference curves for $U(x, y) = 0.25, 0.50$, and 0.75.

16.9 Refer to Problem 15.28 (page 466). A decision maker who prefers Chemical B might be said to be sensitive to equity between the two groups. The eventual outcome with Chemical A is not equitable; one group is better off than the other. On the other hand, with Chemical B, both groups are treated the same. Let X and Y denote the expected increase in the number of deaths in Groups 1 and 2, respectively, and denote a decision maker's utility function as

$$U(x, y) = k_X U_X(x) + k_Y U_Y(y) + (1 - k_X - k_Y) U_X(x) U_Y(y).$$

What can you say about the value of $1 - k_X - k_Y$? Are X and Y complements or substitutes?

16.10 In Problems 13.11 (page 392) and 14.10 (page 424) you assessed individual utility functions for money (X) and computer reliability (Y). In this problem, we will use these assessed utility functions to put together a two-attribute utility function for use in a computer-purchase decision. (If you have not already worked Problems 13.11 or 14.10, do so before continuing. Even if you already have assessed these utility functions, review them and confirm that they are good models of your preferences. When you assessed them, did you consciously think about keeping all other important attributes at the same level?)

a. Are your preferences mutually utility independent? Your utility for money probably does not depend on your computer's level of reliability. But would you be less nervous about computer reliability if you had more money in the bank? Imagine that you have $5000 in the bank. Now assess a certainty equivalent (in terms of computer downtime) for a 50–50 gamble between your computer being down for 20 days next year or not breaking down at all. Now imagine that you have $30,000 in the bank, and reassess your certainty equivalent. Is it the same? Are your preferences for money and computer reliability mutually utility independent?

b. Regardless of your answer to part a, let us assume that your preferences for money and computer reliability are mutually utility independent. Now make the following assessments:

i. Assess a certainty equivalent (in terms of both attributes: computer downtime and money) for a 50–50 gamble between the worst outcome ($1000 in the bank and 50 days of computer downtime) and the best outcome ($20,000 in the bank and no downtime).

ii. Imagine the outcome that is $1000 and no downtime (worst level in money, and best level in computer reliability). Assess a dollar amount x so that the outcome x dollars and 50 days of downtime is equivalent to $1000 and no downtime.

c. Using your individual assessed utility functions from Problems 13.11 and 14.10 and assessments i and ii from part b, calculate k_X and k_Y. Write out your two-attribute utility function.

(*Note:* This problem can be done without having fit a mathematical expression to your individual utility function. It can be done with a utility function expressed as a table or as a graph.)

16.11 Someday you probably will face a choice among job offers. Aside from the nature of the job itself, two attributes that are important for many people are salary and location. Some people prefer large cities, others prefer small towns. Some people do not have strong preferences about the size of the town in which they live; this would show up as a low weight for the population-size attribute in a multiattribute utility function.

Assess a two-attribute utility function for salary (X) and population size (Y):

a. Determine whether your preferences for salary and town size are mutually utility independent.

b. If your preferences display mutual utility independence, assess the two individual utility functions and the weights k_X and k_Y. Draw indifference curves for your assessed utility function. If your preferences do not display mutual utility independence, then you need to think about alternative approaches. The simplest is to assess several utility points as described at the beginning of this chapter and "eyeball" the indifference curves.

c. What other attributes are important in a job decision? Would the two-attribute utility function you just assessed be useful as a first approximation if many of the other attributes were close in comparing two jobs?

16.12 Refer to Problem 15.19 (page 462). For some of the attributes in your computer decision, you face uncertainty. The weighted-scoring procedure essentially assumes that additive independence among attributes is reasonable.

a. Check some of your attributes with formal assessments for additive independence. Follow the example in the text in setting up the two lotteries. (One lottery is a 50–50 gamble between best and worst on both attributes. The other is a 50–50 gamble between (i) best on X, worst on Y; and (ii) worst on X, best on Y.)

b. How could you extend this kind of assessment for additive independence to more than two attributes?

16.13 Show that when $n = 2$, the multiplicative utility function is equivalent to the two-attribute multilinear utility function. (*Hint:* This is an algebra problem. You must show that one utility function is a scaled version of the other. Start by solving for the scaling constant k in the multiplicative function when $n = 2$. Then substitute your expression for k into the multiplicative utility function and simplify.)

16.14 In many cases a group of people must make a decision that involves multiple objectives. In fact, difficult decisions usually are dealt with by committees composed of individuals who represent different interests. For example, imagine a lumber mill owner and an environmentalist on a committee trying to decide on national forest management policy. It might make sense for the committee to try to assess a multiattribute "group utility function." But assessment of the weights would be a problem because different individuals probably would want to weight the attributes differently. Can you give any advice to a committee working on a problem that might help it to arrive at a decision? How should the discussions be structured? Can sensitivity analysis help in such a situation; if so, how?

16.15   In making a land-use policy decision, a planner had to consider three objectives: the development of the best economic mixture of industrial and residential uses, the preservation of sensitive environmental areas, and satisfying the largest industrial firm in the community. Attributes to measure achievement along these three objectives were developed. Let k_{econ} represent the scaling constant for the economy, k_{env} the scaling constant for the environmental concerns, and k_{firm} the scaling constant for satisfying the firm. After careful thought, the planner assessed $k_{econ} = 0.36$, $k_{env} = 0.25$, and $k_{firm} = 0.14$. Use the equations for the multiplicative utility model to verify that the scaling constant k is approximately 1.303.

CASE STUDY

A Mining-Investment Decision

A major U.S. mining firm faced a difficult capital-investment decision. The firm had the opportunity to bid on two separate parcels of land that had valuable ore deposits. The project involved planning, exploration, and eventually production of minerals. The firm had to decide how much to bid, whether to bid alone or with a partner, and how to develop the site if the bid were successful. Overall, the company would have to commit approximately $500 million to the project if it obtained the land.

Figure 16.7 shows a skeleton version of the decision-tree model for this decision. Note that one of the immediate alternatives is not to bid at all, but to stay with and develop the firm's own property. Some of the key uncertainties are whether the bid is successful, the success of a competing venture, capital-investment requirements, operating costs, and product price.

Figure 16.8 shows cumulative distribution functions for net present value (NPV) from four possible strategies. Strategy 25 — develop own property with partner — stochastically dominates all of the other strategies considered, and hence appears to be a serious candidate for the chosen alternative. The decision makers realized, however, that while they did want most to maximize the project's NPV, they also had another objective, the maximization of product output (PO). Because of this, a two-attribute utility function for NPV and PO was constructed. The individual utility functions were assessed as exponential utility functions:

$$U_{PO}(po) = 1 - e^{-po/33.33}$$
$$U_{NPV}(npv) = 1 - e^{-(npv + 100)/200}.$$

The scaling constants also were assessed, yielding $k_{NPV} = 0.79$ and $k_{PO} = 0.16$. Using this two-attribute model, expected utilities and certainty equivalents — a

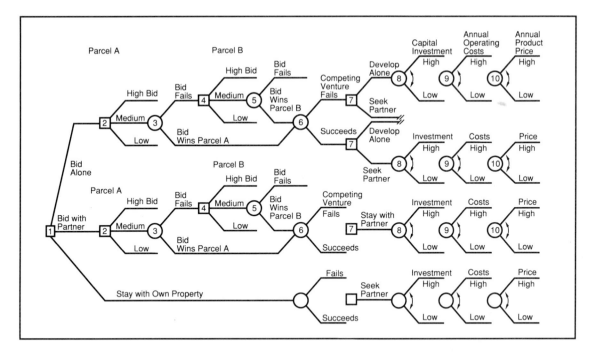

FIGURE 16.7   *Skeleton Decision Tree for Mining-Investment Decision*

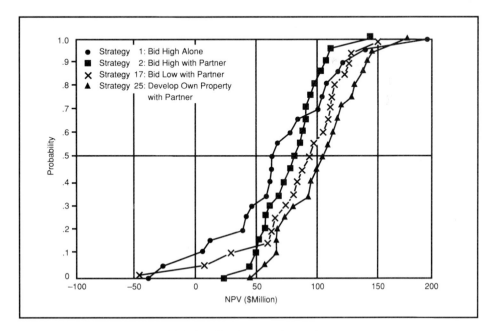

FIGURE 16.8   *Cumulative Risk Profiles for Four Strategies in Mining-Investment Decision*

	Bid High Alone	Bid High with Partner	Bid Low with Partner	Develop Own Property with Partner	Do Nothing
EU	0.574	0.577	0.564	0.567	0.308
CE (NPV, in $million, PO = 50)	51	52	45	47	—

TABLE 16.2   *Expected Utilities (EU) and Certainty Equivalents (CE) for Strategies in Mining-Investment Decision*

certain (NPV, PO) pair, with PO set to a specific level — were calculated. Table 16.2 shows the results for some of the strategies.

QUESTIONS

1. Which of the alternatives should be chosen? Why? Discuss the apparent conflict between the stochastic dominance results (Figure 16.8) and the results from the utility model.
2. The values of the scaling constants suggest that NPV and PO are viewed by the firm as complements. Can you explain intuitively why these two attributes would be complements rather than substitutes?

Source: Hax, A. C., and K. M. Wiig (1977) "The Use of Decision Analysis in a Capital Investment Problem." In D. Bell, R. L. Keeney, and H. Raiffa (eds.), *Conflicting Objectives in Decisions*, pp. 277–297. New York: Wiley. Figures 16.7 and 16.8 reprinted by permission.

◆

◇ REFERENCES

Chapter 16 represents only the tip of the iceberg when it comes to multiattribute utility modeling. If you are interested in reading more, the standard reference for multiattribute utility theory is Keeney and Raiffa (1976). Keeney (1980) covers most of the same material and is a little easier to read. Bunn (1984) provides a somewhat less technical summary of many of the techniques, and von Winterfeldt and Edwards (1986) has extensive discussion with an emphasis on behavioral issues. Further references and examples of applications can be obtained from all of these texts.

BUNN, D. (1984) *Applied Decision Analysis.* New York: McGraw-Hill.

KEENEY, R. (1980) *Siting Energy Facilities.* New York: Academic Press.

KEENEY, R., and H. RAIFFA (1976) *Decisions with Multiple Objectives.* New York: Wiley.

RAIFFA, H. (1982) *The Art and Science of Negotiation.* Cambridge, MA: Harvard University Press.

VON WINTERFELDT, D., and W. EDWARDS (1986) *Decision Analysis and Behavioral Research.* Cambridge: Cambridge University Press.

◇ EPILOGUE

THE MINING-INVESTMENT DECISION.   Hax and Wiig (1977) reported that the decision was to adopt Strategy 2 — bid high with a partner. Just looking at NPV left the decision maker feeling uneasy. But with the product volume included in the two-attribute analysis, the decision maker was satisfied that the important objectives had been considered, so it was easy to adopt the strategy with the highest EU.   ◆

Conclusion and Further Reading

We all have to face hard decisions from time to time. Sometimes we must make difficult personal decisions such as how to care for an elderly loved one or which one of several job offers to accept. Many policy decisions for corporations or governmental agencies are hard to make. In fact, as time goes by, it becomes increasingly clear that as a society we must grapple with some particularly thorny problems, such as competitiveness in the world marketplace, the risks associated with new technologies, and trade-offs between short-term economic benefits and long-term environmental stability.

The argument all along has been that decision analysis can help with such hard decisions. The cycle of structuring the decision, modeling uncertainty and preferences, analyzing and then performing sensitivity analysis can lead a decision maker systematically through the issues that make the decision complicated and toward a requisite decision model, one that captures all of the essential elements of the problem. The objective is to arrive at a model of the decision that explicates the complex parts in a way that the decision maker can choose from the alternatives with insight and understanding.

At the same time that decision analysis provides a framework for tackling difficult decisions, it also furnishes the decision maker with a complete tool kit for the construction of the necessary models of uncertainty and preferences. We have spent much time in considering probability and how to use it to model the uncertainty that a decision maker faces. Subjective assessment, theoretical models, and the use of data and simulation are all tools in the decision analyst's kit. We also discussed the tools available for modeling preferences. We considered in some depth the fundamental trade-off between risk and return. Finally, the last two chapters focused on the modeling of preferences when the decision maker must try to satisfy conflicting objectives.

Throughout the book the view of decision making has been optimistic. We all are subject to human foibles, but a person interested in making better decisions can use the principles and tools that we have discussed in order to do a better job. In day-to-day decisions, it may be simply a matter of thinking in terms of an informally decomposed problem: What is the nature of the problem? What are the objectives? Are there trade-offs to make? What uncertainties are there? Is it a risky situation? More complicated situations may warrant considerable effort and careful use of the modeling tools.

Finally, in the process of reading the text and working through the problems, you may have learned something about yourself. You may have learned how you personally feel about uncertainty in your life, how you deal with risky situations, or what kinds of trade-offs are important to you. If you have learned something about the tools of decision analysis, gained an understanding of what it means to build a model of a decision problem, and learned a little about your own decision-making personality, then your work has been worthwhile. If you feel that you are more prepared to face some of the complicated decisions that we all must face as we move into the next century, then the goal of this text has been achieved.

Where should you go from here? The references at the end of each chapter can lead you to more information on specific topics. You undoubtedly noticed that many of the references reappeared several times. Several textbooks cover decision analysis at a variety of levels and from different perspectives. Here are some favorites:

- Derek Bunn (1984) *Applied Decision Analysis.* New York: McGraw-Hill. An excellent book written at about the same level as this one, although more theoretical and somewhat more terse. Excellent problems.
- Robyn Dawes (1988) *Rational Choice in an Uncertain World.* San Diego, CA: Harcourt Brace. An easy-to-read introduction to the behavioral issues in decision analysis.
- Simon French (1986) *Decision Theory: An Introduction to the Mathematics of Rationality.* London: Wiley. If you liked the chapter on utility axioms, you would love this book. The text covers a lot of new material, including consensus, group decisions, and non-Bayesian approaches. The problems are good, tending to be technical and theoretical rather than applied.
- Robin M. Hogarth (1987) *Judgement and Choice,* 2nd ed. New York: Wiley. An excellent introduction to behavioral decision theory, this is decision analysis from a psychological perspective. This book covers a broad range of topics and is very easy to read.
- Ronald A. Howard and James Matheson (eds.) (1983) *The Principles and Applications of Decision Analysis* (2 volumes). Palo Alto, CA: Strategic Decisions Group. Since the early 1960s, Ron Howard has been practicing decision analysis and teaching the principles to students in the Engineering–Economic Systems Department at Stanford University. This two-volume set contains many papers that present the principles and techniques that make up the "Stanford School" of decision analysis.

- Ralph Keeney and Howard Raiffa (1976) *Decisions with Multiple Objectives: Preferences and Value Tradeoffs*. New York: Wiley. This is *the* standard reference for multiattribute utility theory, although it also is good for decision analysis in general. Many applications are described. Much of the material is highly technical, although the mathematics is not difficult. Gems of insight and explanation are scattered through the technical material. Unfortunately, no problems are included.
- Dennis V. Lindley (1985) *Making Decisions*, 2nd ed. New York: Wiley. A classic by a founder in the field. Professor Lindley explains difficult concepts well. The problems tend to be somewhat abstract.
- Howard Raiffa (1968) *Decision Analysis*. Reading, MA: Addison Wesley. Professor Raiffa also is a founder of decision analysis, and like Lindley, he explains the material well. The problems tend to be abstract. The text covers the basics (and then some), and still is worthwhile after more than 20 years.
- Detlof von Winterfeldt and Ward Edwards (1986) *Decision Analysis and Behavioral Research*. Cambridge: Cambridge University Press. An up-to-date and in-depth treatment of decision analysis from a behavioral perspective. Professor Edwards has been involved in decision analysis since its beginnings, and his history (Chapter 14) is an eye opener. The authors have a strong slant toward applications and behavioral research that provides evidence on the applicability of decision-analysis tools. Like Keeney and Raiffa, there are no problems.
- Robert L. Winkler (1972) *Introduction to Bayesian Inference and Decision*. New York: Holt, Rinehart, & Winston. An excellent introduction to decision theory. Professor Winkler is especially interested in Bayesian models of information, and the book is slanted more toward inference and statistics than toward applied decision analysis.

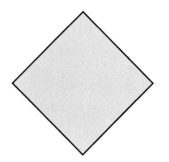

Appendixes

APPENDIX A. Binomial Distribution: Individual Probabilities

$$P_B(R = r \mid n, p) = \frac{n!}{r!(n-r)!}\ p^r\ (1-p)^{n-r}$$

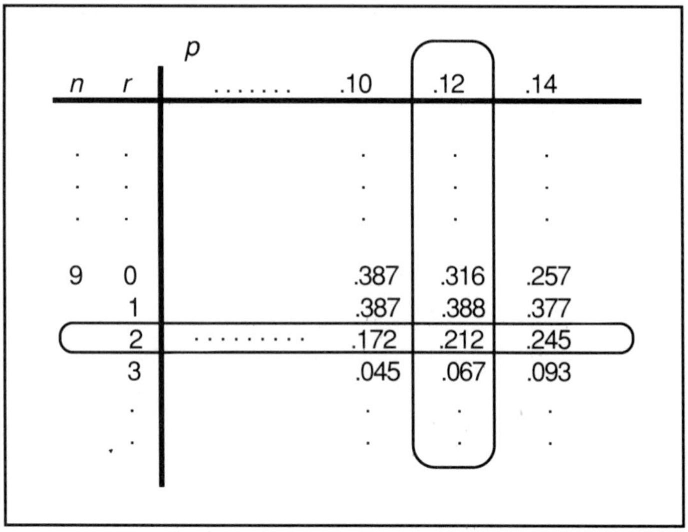

n	r	p			
		....	.10	.12	.14
	·		·	·	·
	·		·	·	·
	·		·	·	·
9	0		.387	.316	.257
	1		.387	.388	.377
	2	....	.172	.212	.245
	3		.045	.067	.093
	·		·	·	·
	·		·	·	·

Figure A.1 *Using Appendix A to find $P_B(R = 2 \mid n = 9, p = 0.12)$*

n	r	p=.01	.02	.04	.05	.06	.08	.10	.12	.14	.15	.16	.18	.20	.22	.24	.25	.30	.35	.40	.45	.50
2	0	.980	.960	.922	.903	.884	.846	.810	.774	.740	.723	.706	.672	.640	.608	.578	.563	.490	.423	.360	.303	.250
	1	.020	.039	.077	.095	.113	.147	.180	.211	.241	.255	.269	.295	.320	.343	.365	.375	.420	.455	.480	.495	.500
	2	0	0	.002	.003	.004	.006	.010	.014	.020	.023	.026	.032	.040	.048	.058	.063	.090	.123	.160	.203	.250
3	0	.970	.941	.885	.857	.831	.779	.729	.681	.636	.614	.593	.551	.512	.475	.439	.422	.343	.275	.216	.166	.125
	1	.029	.058	.111	.135	.159	.203	.243	.279	.311	.325	.339	.363	.384	.402	.416	.422	.441	.444	.432	.408	.375
	2	0	.001	.005	.007	.010	.018	.027	.038	.051	.057	.065	.080	.096	.113	.131	.141	.189	.239	.288	.334	.375
	3	0	0	0	0	0	.001	.001	.002	.003	.003	.004	.006	.008	.011	.014	.016	.027	.043	.064	.091	.125
4	0	.961	.922	.849	.815	.781	.716	.656	.600	.547	.522	.498	.452	.410	.370	.334	.316	.240	.179	.130	.092	.063
	1	.039	.075	.142	.171	.199	.249	.292	.327	.356	.368	.379	.397	.410	.418	.421	.422	.412	.384	.346	.299	.250
	2	.001	.002	.009	.014	.019	.033	.049	.067	.087	.098	.108	.131	.154	.177	.200	.211	.265	.311	.346	.368	.375
	3	0	0	0	0	.001	.002	.004	.006	.009	.011	.014	.019	.026	.033	.042	.047	.076	.111	.154	.200	.250
	4	0	0	0	0	0	0	0	0	0	.001	.001	.001	.002	.002	.003	.004	.008	.015	.026	.041	.063
5	0	.951	.904	.815	.774	.734	.659	.590	.528	.470	.444	.418	.371	.328	.289	.254	.237	.168	.116	.078	.050	.031
	1	.048	.092	.170	.204	.234	.287	.328	.360	.383	.392	.398	.407	.410	.407	.400	.396	.360	.312	.259	.206	.156
	2	.001	.004	.014	.021	.030	.050	.073	.098	.125	.138	.152	.179	.205	.230	.253	.264	.309	.336	.346	.337	.313
	3	0	0	.001	.001	.002	.004	.008	.013	.020	.024	.029	.039	.051	.065	.080	.088	.132	.181	.230	.276	.313
	4	0	0	0	0	0	0	0	.001	.002	.002	.003	.004	.006	.009	.013	.015	.028	.049	.077	.113	.156
	5	0	0	0	0	0	0	0	0	0	0	0	0	0	.001	.001	.001	.002	.005	.010	.018	.031
6	0	.941	.886	.783	.735	.690	.606	.531	.464	.405	.377	.351	.304	.262	.225	.193	.178	.118	.075	.047	.028	.016
	1	.057	.108	.196	.232	.264	.316	.354	.380	.395	.399	.401	.400	.393	.381	.365	.356	.303	.244	.187	.136	.094
	2	.001	.006	.020	.031	.042	.069	.098	.130	.161	.176	.191	.220	.246	.269	.288	.297	.324	.328	.311	.278	.234
	3	0	0	.001	.002	.004	.008	.015	.024	.035	.041	.049	.064	.082	.101	.121	.132	.185	.235	.276	.303	.313
	4	0	0	0	0	0	.001	.001	.002	.004	.005	.007	.011	.015	.021	.029	.033	.060	.095	.138	.186	.234
	5	0	0	0	0	0	0	0	0	0	0	.001	.001	.002	.002	.004	.004	.010	.020	.037	.061	.094
	6	0	0	0	0	0	0	0	0	0	0	0	0	0	0	0	0	.001	.002	.004	.008	.016
7	0	.932	.868	.751	.698	.648	.558	.478	.409	.348	.321	.295	.249	.210	.176	.146	.133	.082	.049	.028	.015	.008
	1	.066	.124	.219	.257	.290	.340	.372	.390	.396	.396	.393	.383	.367	.347	.324	.311	.247	.185	.131	.087	.055
	2	.002	.008	.027	.041	.055	.089	.124	.160	.194	.210	.225	.252	.275	.293	.307	.311	.318	.298	.261	.214	.164
	3	0	0	.002	.004	.006	.013	.023	.036	.053	.062	.071	.092	.115	.138	.161	.173	.227	.268	.290	.292	.273
	4	0	0	0	0	0	.001	.003	.005	.009	.011	.014	.020	.029	.039	.051	.058	.097	.144	.194	.239	.273
	5	0	0	0	0	0	0	0	.001	.001	.001	.002	.003	.004	.007	.010	.012	.025	.047	.077	.117	.164
	6	0	0	0	0	0	0	0	0	0	0	0	0	0	.001	.001	.001	.004	.008	.017	.032	.055
	7	0	0	0	0	0	0	0	0	0	0	0	0	0	0	0	0	0	.001	.002	.004	.008

n	r	.50	.45	.40	.35	.30	.25	.24	.22	.20	.18	.16	.15	.14	.12	.10	.08	.06	.05	.04	.02	.01
8	0	.004	.008	.017	.032	.058	.100	.111	.137	.168	.204	.248	.272	.299	.360	.430	.513	.610	.663	.721	.851	.923
	1	.031	.055	.090	.137	.198	.267	.281	.309	.336	.359	.378	.385	.390	.392	.383	.357	.311	.279	.240	.139	.075
	2	.109	.157	.209	.259	.296	.311	.311	.305	.294	.276	.252	.238	.222	.187	.149	.109	.070	.051	.035	.010	.003
	3	.219	.257	.279	.279	.254	.208	.196	.172	.147	.121	.096	.084	.072	.051	.033	.019	.009	.005	.003	.001	0
	4	.273	.263	.232	.188	.136	.087	.077	.061	.046	.033	.023	.018	.015	.009	.005	.002	.001	0	0	0	0
	5	.219	.172	.124	.081	.047	.023	.020	.014	.009	.006	.003	.003	.002	.001	0	0	0	0	0	0	0
	6	.109	.070	.041	.022	.010	.004	.003	.002	.001	.001	0	0	0	0	0	0	0	0	0	0	0
	7	.031	.016	.008	.003	.001	0	0	0	0	0	0	0	0	0	0	0	0	0	0	0	0
	8	.004	.002	.001	0	0	0	0	0	0	0	0	0	0	0	0	0	0	0	0	0	0
9	0	.002	.005	.010	.021	.040	.075	.085	.107	.134	.168	.208	.232	.257	.316	.387	.472	.573	.630	.693	.834	.914
	1	.018	.034	.060	.100	.156	.225	.240	.271	.302	.331	.357	.368	.377	.388	.387	.370	.329	.299	.260	.153	.083
	2	.070	.111	.161	.216	.267	.300	.304	.306	.302	.291	.272	.260	.245	.212	.172	.129	.084	.063	.043	.013	.003
	3	.164	.212	.251	.272	.267	.234	.224	.201	.176	.149	.121	.107	.093	.067	.045	.026	.013	.008	.004	.001	0
	4	.246	.260	.251	.219	.172	.117	.106	.085	.066	.049	.035	.028	.023	.014	.007	.003	.001	.001	0	0	0
	5	.246	.213	.167	.118	.074	.039	.033	.024	.017	.011	.007	.005	.004	.002	.001	0	0	0	0	0	0
	6	.164	.116	.074	.042	.021	.009	.007	.005	.003	.002	.001	.001	0	0	0	0	0	0	0	0	0
	7	.070	.041	.021	.010	.004	.001	.001	.001	0	0	0	0	0	0	0	0	0	0	0	0	0
	8	.018	.008	.004	.001	0	0	0	0	0	0	0	0	0	0	0	0	0	0	0	0	0
	9	.002	.001	0	0	0	0	0	0	0	0	0	0	0	0	0	0	0	0	0	0	0
10	0	.001	.003	.006	.013	.028	.056	.064	.083	.107	.137	.175	.197	.221	.279	.349	.434	.539	.599	.665	.817	.904
	1	.010	.021	.040	.072	.121	.188	.203	.235	.268	.302	.333	.347	.360	.380	.387	.378	.344	.315	.277	.167	.091
	2	.044	.076	.121	.176	.233	.282	.288	.298	.302	.298	.286	.276	.264	.233	.194	.148	.099	.075	.052	.015	.004
	3	.117	.166	.215	.252	.267	.250	.243	.224	.201	.174	.145	.130	.115	.085	.057	.034	.017	.010	.006	.001	0
	4	.205	.238	.251	.238	.200	.146	.134	.111	.088	.067	.048	.040	.033	.020	.011	.005	.002	.001	0	0	0
	5	.246	.234	.201	.154	.103	.058	.051	.037	.026	.018	.011	.008	.006	.003	.001	.001	0	0	0	0	0
	6	.205	.160	.111	.069	.037	.016	.013	.009	.006	.003	.002	.001	.001	0	0	0	0	0	0	0	0
	7	.117	.075	.042	.021	.009	.003	.002	.001	.001	0	0	0	0	0	0	0	0	0	0	0	0
	8	.044	.023	.011	.004	.001	0	0	0	0	0	0	0	0	0	0	0	0	0	0	0	0
	9	.010	.004	.002	.001	0	0	0	0	0	0	0	0	0	0	0	0	0	0	0	0	0
	10	.001	0	0	0	0	0	0	0	0	0	0	0	0	0	0	0	0	0	0	0	0
11	0	.000	.001	.004	.009	.020	.042	.049	.065	.086	.113	.147	.167	.190	.245	.314	.400	.506	.569	.638	.801	.895
	1	.005	.013	.027	.052	.093	.155	.170	.202	.236	.272	.308	.325	.341	.368	.384	.382	.355	.329	.293	.180	.099
	2	.027	.051	.089	.140	.200	.258	.268	.284	.295	.299	.293	.287	.277	.251	.213	.166	.113	.087	.061	.018	.005
	3	.081	.126	.177	.225	.257	.258	.254	.241	.221	.197	.168	.152	.135	.103	.071	.043	.022	.014	.008	.001	0
	4	.161	.206	.236	.243	.220	.172	.160	.136	.111	.086	.064	.054	.044	.028	.016	.008	.003	.001	.001	0	0
	5	.226	.236	.221	.183	.132	.080	.071	.054	.039	.027	.017	.013	.010	.005	.002	.001	0	0	0	0	0

n	r	.50	.45	.40	.35	.30	.25	.24	.22	.20	.18	.16	.15	.14	.12	.10	.08	.06	.05	.04	.02	.01
11	6	.226	.193	.147	.099	.057	.027	.022	.015	.010	.006	.003	.002	.002	.001	0	0	0	0	0	0	0
	7	.161	.113	.070	.038	.017	.006	.005	.003	.002	.001	0	0	0	0	0	0	0	0	0	0	0
	8	.081	.046	.023	.010	.004	.001	.001	0	0	0	0	0	0	0	0	0	0	0	0	0	0
	9	.027	.013	.005	.002	.001	0	0	0	0	0	0	0	0	0	0	0	0	0	0	0	0
	10	.005	.002	.001	0	0	0	0	0	0	0	0	0	0	0	0	0	0	0	0	0	0
	11	0	0	0	0	0	0	0	0	0	0	0	0	0	0	0	0	0	0	0	0	0
12	0	.000	.001	.002	.006	.014	.032	.037	.051	.069	.092	.123	.142	.164	.216	.282	.368	.476	.540	.613	.785	.886
	1	.003	.008	.017	.037	.071	.127	.141	.172	.206	.243	.282	.301	.320	.353	.377	.384	.365	.341	.306	.192	.107
	2	.016	.034	.064	.109	.168	.232	.244	.266	.283	.294	.296	.292	.286	.265	.230	.183	.128	.099	.070	.022	.006
	3	.054	.092	.142	.195	.240	.258	.257	.250	.236	.215	.188	.172	.155	.120	.085	.053	.027	.017	.010	.001	0
	4	.121	.170	.213	.237	.231	.194	.183	.159	.133	.106	.080	.068	.057	.037	.021	.010	.004	.002	.001	0	0
	5	.193	.222	.227	.204	.158	.103	.092	.072	.053	.037	.025	.019	.015	.008	.004	.001	0	0	0	0	0
	6	.226	.212	.177	.128	.079	.040	.034	.024	.016	.010	.005	.004	.003	.001	0	0	0	0	0	0	0
	7	.193	.149	.101	.059	.029	.011	.009	.006	.003	.002	.001	.001	0	0	0	0	0	0	0	0	0
	8	.121	.076	.042	.020	.008	.002	.002	.001	.001	0	0	0	0	0	0	0	0	0	0	0	0
	9	.054	.028	.012	.005	.001	0	0	0	0	0	0	0	0	0	0	0	0	0	0	0	0
	10	.016	.007	.002	.001	0	0	0	0	0	0	0	0	0	0	0	0	0	0	0	0	0
	11	.003	.001	0	0	0	0	0	0	0	0	0	0	0	0	0	0	0	0	0	0	0
	12	0	0	0	0	0	0	0	0	0	0	0	0	0	0	0	0	0	0	0	0	0
13	0	.000	.000	.001	.004	.010	.024	.028	.040	.055	.076	.104	.121	.141	.190	.254	.338	.447	.513	.588	.769	.878
	1	.002	.004	.011	.026	.054	.103	.116	.145	.179	.216	.257	.277	.298	.336	.367	.382	.371	.351	.319	.204	.115
	2	.010	.022	.045	.084	.139	.206	.220	.245	.268	.285	.293	.294	.291	.275	.245	.199	.142	.111	.080	.025	.007
	3	.035	.066	.111	.165	.218	.252	.254	.254	.246	.229	.205	.190	.174	.138	.100	.064	.033	.021	.012	.002	0
	4	.087	.135	.184	.222	.234	.210	.201	.179	.154	.126	.098	.084	.071	.047	.028	.014	.005	.003	.001	0	0
	5	.157	.199	.221	.215	.180	.126	.114	.091	.069	.050	.033	.027	.021	.012	.006	.002	.001	0	0	0	0
	6	.209	.217	.197	.155	.103	.056	.048	.034	.023	.015	.008	.006	.004	.002	.001	0	0	0	0	0	0
	7	.209	.177	.131	.083	.044	.019	.015	.010	.006	.003	.002	.001	.001	0	0	0	0	0	0	0	0
	8	.157	.109	.066	.034	.014	.005	.004	.002	.001	.001	0	0	0	0	0	0	0	0	0	0	0
	9	.087	.050	.024	.010	.003	.001	.001	0	0	0	0	0	0	0	0	0	0	0	0	0	0
	10	.035	.016	.006	.002	.001	0	0	0	0	0	0	0	0	0	0	0	0	0	0	0	0
	11	.010	.004	.001	0	0	0	0	0	0	0	0	0	0	0	0	0	0	0	0	0	0
	12	.002	0	0	0	0	0	0	0	0	0	0	0	0	0	0	0	0	0	0	0	0
	13	0	0	0	0	0	0	0	0	0	0	0	0	0	0	0	0	0	0	0	0	0
14	0	.000	.000	.001	.002	.007	.018	.021	.031	.044	.062	.087	.103	.121	.167	.229	.311	.421	.488	.565	.754	.869
	1	.001	.003	.007	.018	.041	.083	.095	.122	.154	.191	.232	.254	.276	.319	.356	.379	.376	.359	.329	.215	.123
	2	.006	.014	.032	.063	.113	.180	.195	.223	.250	.272	.287	.291	.292	.283	.257	.214	.156	.123	.089	.029	.008
	3	.022	.046	.085	.137	.194	.240	.246	.252	.250	.239	.219	.206	.190	.154	.114	.074	.040	.026	.015	.002	0

n	r	.01	.02	.04	.05	.06	.08	.10	.12	.14	.15	.16	.18	.20	.22	.24	.25	.30	.35	.40	.45	.50
14	4	0	0	.002	.004	.007	.018	.035	.058	.085	.100	.115	.144	.172	.195	.214	.220	.229	.202	.155	.104	.061
	5	0	0	0	0	.001	.003	.008	.016	.028	.035	.044	.063	.086	.110	.135	.147	.196	.218	.207	.170	.122
	6	0	0	0	0	0	0	.001	.003	.007	.009	.012	.021	.032	.047	.064	.073	.126	.176	.207	.209	.183
	7	0	0	0	0	0	0	0	.001	.001	.002	.003	.005	.009	.015	.023	.028	.062	.108	.157	.195	.209
	8	0	0	0	0	0	0	0	0	0	0	0	.001	.002	.004	.006	.008	.023	.051	.092	.140	.183
	9	0	0	0	0	0	0	0	0	0	0	0	0	0	.001	.001	.002	.007	.018	.041	.076	.122
	10	0	0	0	0	0	0	0	0	0	0	0	0	0	0	0	0	.001	.005	.014	.031	.061
	11	0	0	0	0	0	0	0	0	0	0	0	0	0	0	0	0	0	.001	.003	.009	.022
	12	0	0	0	0	0	0	0	0	0	0	0	0	0	0	0	0	0	0	.001	.002	.006
	13	0	0	0	0	0	0	0	0	0	0	0	0	0	0	0	0	0	0	0	0	.001
	14	0	0	0	0	0	0	0	0	0	0	0	0	0	0	0	0	0	0	0	0	0
15	0	.860	.739	.542	.463	.395	.286	.206	.147	.104	.087	.073	.051	.035	.024	.016	.013	.005	.002	.000	.000	.000
	1	.130	.226	.339	.366	.378	.373	.343	.301	.254	.231	.209	.168	.132	.102	.077	.067	.031	.013	.005	.002	.000
	2	.009	.032	.099	.135	.169	.227	.267	.287	.290	.286	.279	.258	.231	.201	.171	.156	.092	.048	.022	.009	.003
	3	0	.003	.018	.031	.047	.086	.129	.170	.204	.218	.230	.245	.250	.246	.234	.225	.170	.111	.063	.032	.014
	4	0	0	.002	.005	.009	.022	.043	.069	.100	.116	.131	.162	.188	.208	.221	.225	.219	.179	.127	.078	.042
	5	0	0	0	.001	.001	.004	.010	.021	.036	.045	.055	.078	.103	.129	.154	.165	.206	.212	.186	.140	.092
	6	0	0	0	0	0	.001	.002	.005	.010	.013	.017	.029	.043	.061	.081	.092	.147	.191	.207	.191	.153
	7	0	0	0	0	0	0	0	.001	.002	.003	.004	.008	.014	.022	.033	.039	.081	.132	.177	.201	.196
	8	0	0	0	0	0	0	0	0	0	.001	.001	.002	.003	.006	.010	.013	.035	.071	.118	.165	.196
	9	0	0	0	0	0	0	0	0	0	0	0	0	.001	.001	.003	.003	.012	.030	.061	.105	.153
	10	0	0	0	0	0	0	0	0	0	0	0	0	0	0	0	.001	.003	.010	.024	.051	.092
	11	0	0	0	0	0	0	0	0	0	0	0	0	0	0	0	0	.001	.002	.007	.019	.042
	12	0	0	0	0	0	0	0	0	0	0	0	0	0	0	0	0	0	0	.002	.005	.014
	13	0	0	0	0	0	0	0	0	0	0	0	0	0	0	0	0	0	0	0	.001	.003
	14	0	0	0	0	0	0	0	0	0	0	0	0	0	0	0	0	0	0	0	0	0
	15	0	0	0	0	0	0	0	0	0	0	0	0	0	0	0	0	0	0	0	0	0
16	0	.851	.724	.520	.440	.372	.263	.185	.129	.090	.074	.061	.042	.028	.019	.012	.010	.003	.001	.000	.000	.000
	1	.138	.236	.347	.371	.379	.366	.329	.282	.233	.210	.187	.147	.113	.085	.063	.053	.023	.009	.003	.001	.000
	2	.010	.036	.108	.146	.182	.239	.275	.289	.285	.277	.268	.242	.211	.179	.148	.134	.073	.035	.015	.006	.002
	3	0	.003	.021	.036	.054	.097	.142	.184	.216	.229	.238	.248	.246	.236	.218	.208	.146	.089	.047	.022	.009
	4	0	0	.003	.006	.011	.027	.051	.081	.114	.131	.147	.177	.200	.216	.224	.225	.204	.155	.101	.057	.028
	5	0	0	0	.001	.002	.006	.014	.027	.045	.056	.067	.093	.120	.146	.170	.180	.210	.201	.162	.112	.067
	6	0	0	0	0	0	.001	.003	.007	.013	.018	.023	.037	.055	.076	.098	.110	.165	.198	.198	.168	.122
	7	0	0	0	0	0	0	0	.001	.003	.005	.006	.012	.020	.030	.044	.052	.101	.152	.189	.197	.175
	8	0	0	0	0	0	0	0	0	.001	.001	.001	.003	.006	.010	.016	.020	.049	.092	.142	.181	.196

n	r	.50	.45	.40	.35	.30	.25	.24	.22	.20	.18	.16	.15	.14	.12	.10	.08	.06	.05	.04	.02	.01
16	9	.175	.132	.084	.044	.019	.006	.004	.002	.001	.001	0	0	0	0	0	0	0	0	0	0	0
	10	.122	.075	.039	.017	.006	.001	.001	0	0	0	0	0	0	0	0	0	0	0	0	0	0
	11	.067	.034	.014	.005	.001	0	0	0	0	0	0	0	0	0	0	0	0	0	0	0	0
	12	.028	.011	.004	.001	0	0	0	0	0	0	0	0	0	0	0	0	0	0	0	0	0
	13	.009	.003	.001	0	0	0	0	0	0	0	0	0	0	0	0	0	0	0	0	0	0
	14	.002	.001	0	0	0	0	0	0	0	0	0	0	0	0	0	0	0	0	0	0	0
	15	0	0	0	0	0	0	0	0	0	0	0	0	0	0	0	0	0	0	0	0	0
	16	0	0	0	0	0	0	0	0	0	0	0	0	0	0	0	0	0	0	0	0	0
17	0	.000	.000	.000	.001	.002	.008	.009	.015	.023	.034	.052	.063	.077	.114	.167	.242	.349	.418	.500	.709	.843
	1	.000	.001	.002	.006	.017	.043	.051	.070	.096	.128	.167	.189	.213	.264	.315	.358	.379	.374	.354	.246	.145
	2	.001	.004	.010	.026	.058	.114	.128	.158	.191	.225	.255	.267	.278	.288	.280	.249	.194	.158	.118	.040	.012
	3	.005	.014	.034	.070	.125	.189	.202	.223	.239	.246	.243	.236	.226	.196	.156	.108	.062	.041	.025	.004	.001
	4	.018	.041	.080	.132	.187	.221	.223	.221	.209	.189	.162	.146	.129	.094	.060	.033	.014	.008	.004	0	0
	5	.047	.087	.138	.185	.208	.191	.183	.162	.136	.108	.080	.067	.054	.033	.017	.007	.002	.001	0	0	0
	6	.094	.143	.184	.199	.178	.128	.116	.091	.068	.047	.031	.024	.018	.009	.004	.001	0	0	0	0	0
	7	.148	.184	.193	.168	.120	.067	.057	.040	.027	.016	.009	.007	.005	.002	.001	0	0	0	0	0	0
	8	.185	.188	.161	.113	.064	.028	.023	.014	.008	.004	.002	.001	.001	0	0	0	0	0	0	0	0
	9	.185	.154	.107	.061	.028	.009	.007	.004	.002	.001	0	0	0	0	0	0	0	0	0	0	0
	10	.148	.101	.057	.026	.009	.002	.002	.001	0	0	0	0	0	0	0	0	0	0	0	0	0
	11	.094	.052	.024	.009	.003	.001	0	0	0	0	0	0	0	0	0	0	0	0	0	0	0
	12	.047	.021	.008	.002	.001	0	0	0	0	0	0	0	0	0	0	0	0	0	0	0	0
	13	.018	.007	.002	.001	0	0	0	0	0	0	0	0	0	0	0	0	0	0	0	0	0
	14	.005	.002	0	0	0	0	0	0	0	0	0	0	0	0	0	0	0	0	0	0	0
	15	.001	0	0	0	0	0	0	0	0	0	0	0	0	0	0	0	0	0	0	0	0
	16	0	0	0	0	0	0	0	0	0	0	0	0	0	0	0	0	0	0	0	0	0
	17	0	0	0	0	0	0	0	0	0	0	0	0	0	0	0	0	0	0	0	0	0
18	0	.000	.000	.000	.000	.002	.006	.007	.011	.018	.028	.043	.054	.066	.100	.150	.223	.328	.397	.480	.695	.835
	1	.000	.000	.001	.004	.013	.034	.041	.058	.081	.111	.149	.170	.194	.246	.300	.349	.377	.376	.360	.255	.152
	2	.001	.002	.007	.019	.046	.096	.109	.139	.172	.207	.241	.256	.268	.285	.284	.258	.205	.168	.127	.044	.013
	3	.003	.009	.025	.055	.105	.170	.184	.209	.230	.243	.244	.241	.233	.207	.168	.120	.070	.047	.028	.005	.001
	4	.012	.029	.061	.110	.168	.213	.218	.221	.215	.200	.175	.159	.142	.106	.070	.039	.017	.009	.004	0	0
	5	.033	.067	.115	.166	.202	.199	.193	.175	.151	.123	.093	.079	.065	.040	.022	.009	.003	.001	.001	0	0
	6	.071	.118	.166	.194	.187	.144	.132	.107	.082	.058	.038	.030	.023	.012	.005	.002	0	0	0	0	0
	7	.121	.166	.189	.179	.138	.082	.071	.052	.035	.022	.013	.009	.006	.003	.001	0	0	0	0	0	0
	8	.167	.186	.173	.133	.081	.038	.031	.020	.012	.007	.003	.002	.001	.001	.000	0	0	0	0	0	0
	9	.185	.169	.128	.079	.039	.014	.011	.006	.003	.002	.001	0	0	0	0	0	0	0	0	0	0
	10	.167	.125	.077	.038	.015	.004	.003	.002	.001	0	0	0	0	0	0	0	0	0	0	0	0
	11	.121	.074	.037	.015	.005	.001	.001	0	0	0	0	0	0	0	0	0	0	0	0	0	0

n	r	.01	.02	.04	.05	.06	.08	.10	.12	.14	.15	.16	.18	.20	.22	.24	.25	.30	.35	.40	.45	.50
18	12	0	0	0	0	0	0	0	0	0	0	0	0	0	0	0	0	.001	.005	.015	.035	.071
	13	0	0	0	0	0	0	0	0	0	0	0	0	0	0	0	0	0	.001	.004	.013	.033
	14	0	0	0	0	0	0	0	0	0	0	0	0	0	0	0	0	0	0	.001	.004	.012
	15	0	0	0	0	0	0	0	0	0	0	0	0	0	0	0	0	0	0	0	.001	.003
	16	0	0	0	0	0	0	0	0	0	0	0	0	0	0	0	0	0	0	0	0	.001
	17	0	0	0	0	0	0	0	0	0	0	0	0	0	0	0	0	0	0	0	0	0
	18	0	0	0	0	0	0	0	0	0	0	0	0	0	0	0	0	0	0	0	0	0
19	0	.826	.681	.460	.377	.309	.205	.135	.088	.057	.046	.036	.023	.014	.009	.005	.004	.001	.000	.000	.000	.000
	1	.159	.264	.364	.377	.374	.339	.285	.228	.176	.153	.132	.096	.068	.048	.033	.027	.009	.003	.001	.000	.000
	2	.014	.049	.137	.179	.215	.265	.285	.280	.258	.243	.226	.190	.154	.121	.093	.080	.036	.014	.005	.001	.000
	3	.001	.006	.032	.053	.078	.131	.180	.217	.238	.243	.244	.236	.218	.194	.166	.152	.087	.042	.017	.006	.002
	4	0	0	.005	.011	.020	.045	.080	.118	.155	.171	.186	.207	.218	.219	.210	.202	.149	.091	.047	.020	.007
	5	0	0	.001	.002	.004	.012	.027	.048	.076	.091	.106	.137	.164	.185	.199	.202	.192	.147	.093	.050	.022
	6	0	0	0	0	.001	.002	.007	.015	.029	.037	.047	.070	.095	.122	.146	.157	.192	.184	.145	.095	.052
	7	0	0	0	0	0	0	.001	.004	.009	.012	.017	.029	.044	.064	.086	.097	.153	.184	.180	.144	.096
	8	0	0	0	0	0	0	0	.001	.002	.003	.005	.009	.017	.027	.041	.049	.098	.149	.180	.177	.144
	9	0	0	0	0	0	0	0	0	0	.001	.001	.003	.005	.009	.016	.020	.051	.098	.146	.177	.176
	10	0	0	0	0	0	0	0	0	0	0	0	.001	.001	.003	.005	.007	.022	.053	.098	.145	.176
	11	0	0	0	0	0	0	0	0	0	0	0	0	0	.001	.001	.002	.008	.023	.053	.097	.144
	12	0	0	0	0	0	0	0	0	0	0	0	0	0	0	0	0	.002	.008	.024	.053	.096
	13	0	0	0	0	0	0	0	0	0	0	0	0	0	0	0	0	.001	.002	.008	.023	.052
	14	0	0	0	0	0	0	0	0	0	0	0	0	0	0	0	0	0	.001	.002	.008	.022
	15	0	0	0	0	0	0	0	0	0	0	0	0	0	0	0	0	0	0	.001	.002	.007
	16	0	0	0	0	0	0	0	0	0	0	0	0	0	0	0	0	0	0	0	0	.002
	17	0	0	0	0	0	0	0	0	0	0	0	0	0	0	0	0	0	0	0	0	0
	18	0	0	0	0	0	0	0	0	0	0	0	0	0	0	0	0	0	0	0	0	0
	19	0	0	0	0	0	0	0	0	0	0	0	0	0	0	0	0	0	0	0	0	0
20	0	.818	.668	.442	.358	.290	.189	.122	.078	.049	.039	.031	.019	.012	.007	.004	.003	.001	.000	.000	.000	.000
	1	.165	.272	.368	.377	.370	.328	.270	.212	.159	.137	.117	.083	.058	.039	.026	.021	.007	.002	.000	.000	.000
	2	.016	.053	.146	.189	.225	.271	.285	.274	.247	.229	.211	.173	.137	.105	.078	.067	.028	.010	.003	.001	.000
	3	.001	.006	.036	.060	.086	.141	.190	.224	.241	.243	.241	.228	.205	.178	.148	.134	.072	.032	.012	.004	.001
	4	0	.001	.006	.013	.023	.052	.090	.130	.167	.182	.195	.213	.218	.213	.199	.190	.130	.074	.035	.014	.005
	5	0	0	.001	.002	.005	.015	.032	.057	.087	.103	.119	.149	.175	.192	.201	.202	.179	.127	.075	.036	.015
	6	0	0	0	0	.001	.003	.009	.019	.035	.045	.057	.082	.109	.136	.159	.169	.192	.171	.124	.075	.037
	7	0	0	0	0	0	.001	.002	.005	.012	.016	.022	.036	.055	.076	.100	.112	.164	.184	.166	.122	.074
	8	0	0	0	0	0	0	0	.001	.003	.005	.007	.013	.022	.035	.051	.061	.114	.161	.180	.162	.120
	9	0	0	0	0	0	0	0	0	.001	.001	.002	.004	.007	.013	.022	.027	.065	.116	.160	.177	.160
	10	0	0	0	0	0	0	0	0	0	0	0	.001	.002	.004	.008	.010	.031	.069	.117	.159	.176

r	n	.50	.45	.40	.35	.30	.25	.24	.22	.20	.18	.16	.15	.14	.12	.10	.08	.06	.05	.04	.02	.01
11		.160	.119	.071	.034	.012	.003	.002	.001	0	0	0	0	0	0	0	0	0	0	0	0	0
12		.120	.073	.035	.014	.004	.001	.001	0	0	0	0	0	0	0	0	0	0	0	0	0	0
13		.074	.037	.015	.004	.001	0	0	0	0	0	0	0	0	0	0	0	0	0	0	0	0
14		.037	.015	.005	.001	0	0	0	0	0	0	0	0	0	0	0	0	0	0	0	0	0
15		.015	.005	.001	0	0	0	0	0	0	0	0	0	0	0	0	0	0	0	0	0	0
16		.005	.001	0	0	0	0	0	0	0	0	0	0	0	0	0	0	0	0	0	0	0
17		.001	0	0	0	0	0	0	0	0	0	0	0	0	0	0	0	0	0	0	0	0
18		0	0	0	0	0	0	0	0	0	0	0	0	0	0	0	0	0	0	0	0	0
19		0	0	0	0	0	0	0	0	0	0	0	0	0	0	0	0	0	0	0	0	0
20		0	0	0	0	0	0	0	0	0	0	0	0	0	0	0	0	0	0	0	0	0
0	25	.000	.000	.000	.000	.000	.001	.001	.002	.004	.007	.013	.017	.023	.041	.072	.124	.213	.277	.360	.603	.778
1		.000	.000	.000	.000	.001	.006	.008	.014	.024	.038	.061	.076	.094	.140	.199	.270	.340	.365	.375	.308	.196
2		.000	.000	.000	.002	.007	.025	.031	.048	.071	.101	.139	.161	.183	.228	.266	.282	.260	.231	.188	.075	.024
3		.000	.000	.002	.008	.024	.064	.076	.104	.136	.170	.203	.217	.229	.239	.226	.188	.127	.093	.060	.012	.002
4		.000	.002	.007	.022	.057	.118	.132	.161	.187	.206	.213	.211	.205	.179	.138	.090	.045	.027	.014	.001	0
5		.002	.006	.020	.051	.103	.165	.175	.190	.196	.190	.170	.156	.140	.103	.065	.033	.012	.006	.002	0	0
6		.005	.017	.044	.091	.147	.183	.184	.179	.163	.139	.108	.092	.076	.047	.024	.010	.003	.001	0	0	0
7		.014	.038	.080	.133	.171	.165	.158	.137	.111	.083	.056	.044	.034	.017	.007	.002	0	0	0	0	0
8		.032	.070	.120	.161	.165	.124	.112	.087	.062	.041	.024	.017	.012	.005	.002	0	0	0	0	0	0
9		.061	.108	.151	.163	.134	.078	.067	.046	.029	.017	.009	.006	.004	.001	0	0	0	0	0	0	0
10		.097	.142	.161	.141	.092	.042	.034	.021	.012	.006	.003	.002	.001	0	0	0	0	0	0	0	0
11		.133	.158	.147	.103	.054	.019	.015	.008	.004	.002	.001	0	0	0	0	0	0	0	0	0	0
12		.155	.151	.114	.065	.027	.007	.005	.003	.001	0	0	0	0	0	0	0	0	0	0	0	0
13		.155	.124	.076	.035	.011	.002	.002	.001	0	0	0	0	0	0	0	0	0	0	0	0	0
14		.133	.087	.043	.016	.004	.001	0	0	0	0	0	0	0	0	0	0	0	0	0	0	0
15		.097	.052	.021	.006	.001	0	0	0	0	0	0	0	0	0	0	0	0	0	0	0	0
16		.061	.027	.009	.002	0	0	0	0	0	0	0	0	0	0	0	0	0	0	0	0	0
17		.032	.012	.003	.001	0	0	0	0	0	0	0	0	0	0	0	0	0	0	0	0	0
18		.014	.004	.001	0	0	0	0	0	0	0	0	0	0	0	0	0	0	0	0	0	0
19		.005	.001	0	0	0	0	0	0	0	0	0	0	0	0	0	0	0	0	0	0	0
20		.002	0	0	0	0	0	0	0	0	0	0	0	0	0	0	0	0	0	0	0	0
21		0	0	0	0	0	0	0	0	0	0	0	0	0	0	0	0	0	0	0	0	0
22		0	0	0	0	0	0	0	0	0	0	0	0	0	0	0	0	0	0	0	0	0
23		0	0	0	0	0	0	0	0	0	0	0	0	0	0	0	0	0	0	0	0	0
24		0	0	0	0	0	0	0	0	0	0	0	0	0	0	0	0	0	0	0	0	0
25		0	0	0	0	0	0	0	0	0	0	0	0	0	0	0	0	0	0	0	0	0

APPENDIX B. Binomial Distribution: Cumulative Probabilities

$$P_B(R \leq r \mid n, p) = \sum_{i=0}^{r} \frac{n!}{i!(n-i)!} \, p^i \, (1-p)^{n-i}$$

n	r	p	.10	.12	.14
9	0		.387	.316	.257
	1		.775	.705	.634
	2	....	.947	.917	.880
	3		.992	.984	.973

Figure A.2 *Using Appendix B to find $P_B(R \leq 2 \mid n = 9, p = 0.12)$*

512

n	r	.50	.45	.40	.35	.30	.25	.24	.22	.20	.18	.16	.15	.14	.12	.10	.08	.06	.05	.04	.02	.01 (p)
2	0	.250	.303	.360	.423	.490	.563	.578	.608	.640	.672	.706	.723	.740	.774	.810	.846	.884	.903	.922	.960	.980
	1	.750	.798	.840	.878	.910	.938	.942	.952	.960	.968	.974	.978	.980	.986	.990	.994	.996	.998	.998	—	—
	2	1	—	—	—	—	—	—	—	—	—	—	—	—	—	—	—	—	—	—	—	—
3	0	.125	.166	.216	.275	.343	.422	.439	.475	.512	.551	.593	.614	.636	.681	.729	.779	.831	.857	.885	.941	.970
	1	.500	.575	.648	.718	.784	.844	.855	.876	.896	.914	.931	.939	.947	.960	.972	.982	.990	.993	.995	.999	.999
	2	.875	.909	.936	.957	.973	.984	.986	.989	.992	.994	.996	.997	.997	.998	.999	.999	—	—	—	—	—
	3	1	—	—	—	—	—	—	—	—	—	—	—	—	—	—	—	—	—	—	—	—
4	0	.063	.092	.130	.179	.240	.316	.334	.370	.410	.452	.498	.522	.547	.600	.656	.716	.781	.815	.849	.922	.961
	1	.313	.391	.475	.563	.652	.738	.755	.788	.819	.849	.877	.890	.903	.927	.948	.966	.980	.986	.991	.998	.999
	2	.688	.759	.821	.874	.916	.949	.955	.964	.973	.980	.986	.988	.990	.994	.996	.998	.999	.999	.999	—	—
	3	.938	.959	.974	.985	.992	.996	.997	.998	.998	.999	.999	.999	—	—	—	—	—	—	—	—	—
	4	1	—	—	—	—	—	—	—	—	—	—	—	—	—	—	—	—	—	—	—	—
5	0	.031	.050	.078	.116	.168	.237	.254	.289	.328	.371	.418	.444	.470	.528	.590	.659	.734	.774	.815	.904	.951
	1	.188	.256	.337	.428	.528	.633	.654	.696	.737	.778	.817	.835	.853	.888	.919	.946	.968	.977	.985	.996	.999
	2	.500	.593	.683	.765	.837	.896	.907	.926	.942	.956	.968	.973	.978	.986	.991	.995	.996	.998	.999	—	—
	3	.813	.869	.913	.946	.969	.984	.987	.990	.993	.996	.997	.998	.998	.999	.999	—	—	—	—	—	—
	4	.969	.982	.990	.995	.998	.999	.999	—	—	—	—	—	—	—	—	—	—	—	—	—	—
	5	1	—	—	—	—	—	—	—	—	—	—	—	—	—	—	—	—	—	—	—	—
6	0	.016	.028	.047	.075	.118	.178	.193	.225	.262	.304	.351	.377	.405	.464	.531	.606	.690	.735	.783	.886	.941
	1	.109	.164	.233	.319	.420	.534	.558	.606	.655	.704	.753	.776	.800	.844	.886	.923	.954	.967	.978	.994	.999
	2	.344	.442	.544	.647	.744	.831	.846	.875	.901	.924	.944	.953	.961	.974	.984	.991	.994	.997	.998	—	—
	3	.656	.745	.821	.883	.930	.962	.967	.976	.983	.988	.993	.994	.995	.997	.999	.999	—	—	—	—	—
	4	.891	.931	.959	.978	.989	.995	.996	.997	.998	.999	.999	—	—	—	—	—	—	—	—	—	—
	5	.984	.992	.996	.998	.999	.999	—	—	—	—	—	—	—	—	—	—	—	—	—	—	—
	6	1	—	—	—	—	—	—	—	—	—	—	—	—	—	—	—	—	—	—	—	—
7	0	.008	.015	.028	.049	.082	.133	.146	.176	.210	.249	.295	.321	.348	.409	.478	.558	.648	.698	.751	.868	.932
	1	.063	.102	.159	.234	.329	.445	.470	.522	.577	.632	.689	.717	.744	.799	.850	.897	.938	.956	.971	.992	.998
	2	.227	.316	.420	.532	.647	.756	.777	.816	.852	.885	.913	.926	.938	.958	.974	.986	.994	.996	.998	—	—
	3	.500	.608	.710	.800	.874	.929	.938	.954	.967	.977	.985	.988	.991	.995	.997	.999	.999	—	—	—	—
	4	.773	.847	.904	.944	.971	.987	.989	.993	.995	.997	.998	.999	.999	—	—	—	—	—	—	—	—
	5	.938	.964	.981	.991	.996	.999	.999	.999	—	—	—	—	—	—	—	—	—	—	—	—	—
	6	.992	.996	.998	.999	—	—	—	—	—	—	—	—	—	—	—	—	—	—	—	—	—
	7	1	—	—	—	—	—	—	—	—	—	—	—	—	—	—	—	—	—	—	—	—

n	r	.01	.02	.04	.05	.06	.08	.10	.12	.14	.15	.16	.18	.20	.22	.24	.25	.30	.35	.40	.45	.50
8	0	.923	.851	.721	.663	.610	.513	.430	.360	.299	.272	.248	.204	.168	.137	.111	.100	.058	.032	.017	.008	.004
	1	.997	.990	.962	.943	.921	.870	.813	.752	.689	.657	.626	.563	.503	.446	.392	.367	.255	.169	.106	.063	.035
	2	—	—	.997	.994	.990	.979	.962	.939	.911	.895	.877	.839	.797	.751	.703	.679	.552	.428	.315	.220	.145
	3	—	—	—	.999	.999	.998	.995	.990	.983	.979	.973	.960	.944	.924	.900	.886	.806	.706	.594	.477	.363
	4	—	—	—	—	—	—	—	.999	.998	.997	.996	.993	.990	.984	.977	.973	.942	.894	.826	.740	.637
	5	—	—	—	—	—	—	—	—	—	—	—	.999	.999	.998	.997	.996	.989	.975	.950	.912	.855
	6	—	—	—	—	—	—	—	—	—	—	—	—	—	—	—	—	.999	.996	.991	.982	.965
	7	—	—	—	—	—	—	—	—	—	—	—	—	—	—	—	—	—	—	.999	.998	.996
	8	—	—	—	—	—	—	—	—	—	—	—	—	—	—	—	—	—	—	—	—	—
9	0	.914	.834	.693	.630	.573	.472	.387	.316	.257	.232	.208	.168	.134	.107	.085	.075	.040	.021	.010	.005	.002
	1	.997	.987	.952	.929	.902	.842	.775	.705	.634	.599	.565	.499	.436	.378	.325	.300	.196	.121	.071	.039	.020
	2	—	.999	.996	.992	.986	.970	.947	.917	.880	.859	.837	.790	.738	.684	.629	.601	.463	.337	.232	.150	.090
	3	—	—	—	.999	.999	.996	.992	.984	.973	.966	.958	.938	.914	.886	.852	.834	.730	.609	.483	.361	.254
	4	—	—	—	—	—	—	.999	.998	.996	.994	.993	.988	.980	.971	.958	.951	.901	.828	.733	.621	.500
	5	—	—	—	—	—	—	—	—	—	.999	.999	.998	.997	.995	.992	.990	.975	.946	.901	.834	.746
	6	—	—	—	—	—	—	—	—	—	—	—	—	—	.999	.999	.999	.996	.989	.975	.950	.910
	7	—	—	—	—	—	—	—	—	—	—	—	—	—	—	—	—	—	.999	.996	.991	.980
	8	—	—	—	—	—	—	—	—	—	—	—	—	—	—	—	—	—	—	—	.999	.998
	9	—	—	—	—	—	—	—	—	—	—	—	—	—	—	—	—	—	—	—	—	—
10	0	.904	.817	.665	.599	.539	.434	.349	.279	.221	.197	.175	.137	.107	.083	.064	.056	.028	.013	.006	.003	.001
	1	.996	.984	.942	.914	.882	.812	.736	.658	.582	.544	.508	.439	.376	.318	.267	.244	.149	.086	.046	.023	.011
	2	—	.999	.994	.988	.981	.960	.930	.891	.845	.820	.794	.737	.678	.617	.556	.526	.383	.262	.167	.100	.055
	3	—	—	—	.999	.998	.994	.987	.976	.960	.950	.939	.912	.879	.841	.799	.776	.650	.514	.382	.266	.172
	4	—	—	—	—	—	.999	.998	.996	.993	.990	.987	.979	.967	.952	.933	.922	.850	.751	.633	.504	.377
	5	—	—	—	—	—	—	—	—	.999	.999	.998	.996	.994	.990	.984	.980	.953	.905	.834	.738	.623
	6	—	—	—	—	—	—	—	—	—	—	—	—	.999	.998	.997	.996	.989	.974	.945	.898	.828
	7	—	—	—	—	—	—	—	—	—	—	—	—	—	—	—	—	.998	.995	.988	.973	.945
	8	—	—	—	—	—	—	—	—	—	—	—	—	—	—	—	—	—	.999	.998	.995	.989
	9	—	—	—	—	—	—	—	—	—	—	—	—	—	—	—	—	—	—	—	—	.999
	10	—	—	—	—	—	—	—	—	—	—	—	—	—	—	—	—	—	—	—	—	—
11	0	.895	.801	.638	.569	.506	.400	.314	.245	.190	.167	.147	.113	.086	.065	.049	.042	.020	.009	.004	.001	.000
	1	.995	.980	.931	.898	.862	.782	.697	.613	.531	.492	.455	.385	.322	.267	.219	.197	.113	.061	.030	.014	.006
	2	—	.999	.992	.985	.975	.948	.910	.863	.809	.779	.748	.684	.617	.551	.487	.455	.313	.200	.119	.065	.033
	3	—	—	.999	.998	.997	.991	.981	.966	.944	.931	.915	.880	.839	.792	.740	.713	.570	.426	.296	.191	.113
	4	—	—	—	—	—	.999	.997	.994	.988	.984	.979	.967	.950	.928	.901	.885	.790	.668	.533	.397	.274
	5	—	—	—	—	—	—	—	.999	.998	.997	.996	.993	.988	.981	.972	.966	.922	.851	.753	.633	.500

n	r	.50	.45	.40	.35	.30	.25	.24	.22	.20	.18	.16	.15	.14	.12	.10	.08	.06	.05	.04	.02	.01
11	6	.726	.826	.901	.950	.978	.992	.994	.996	.998	.999	—	—	—	—	—	—	—	—	—	—	—
	7	.887	.939	.971	.988	.996	.999	.999	—	—	—	—	—	—	—	—	—	—	—	—	—	—
	8	.967	.985	.994	.998	.999	—	—	—	—	—	—	—	—	—	—	—	—	—	—	—	—
	9	.994	.998	.999	—	—	—	—	—	—	—	—	—	—	—	—	—	—	—	—	—	—
	10	—	—	—	—	—	—	—	—	—	—	—	—	—	—	—	—	—	—	—	—	—
	11	—	—	—	—	—	—	—	—	—	—	—	—	—	—	—	—	—	—	—	—	—
12	0	.000	.001	.002	.006	.014	.032	.037	.051	.069	.092	.123	.142	.164	.216	.282	.368	.476	.540	.613	.785	.886
	1	.003	.008	.020	.042	.085	.158	.178	.222	.275	.336	.405	.443	.483	.569	.659	.751	.840	.882	.919	.977	.994
	2	.019	.042	.083	.151	.253	.391	.422	.489	.558	.630	.701	.736	.770	.833	.889	.935	.968	.980	.989	.998	—
	3	.073	.134	.225	.347	.493	.649	.680	.739	.795	.845	.889	.908	.925	.954	.974	.988	.996	.998	.999	—	—
	4	.194	.304	.438	.583	.724	.842	.862	.898	.927	.951	.969	.976	.982	.991	.996	.998	—	—	—	—	—
	5	.387	.527	.665	.787	.882	.946	.955	.970	.981	.988	.994	.995	.997	.999	.999	—	—	—	—	—	—
	6	.613	.739	.842	.915	.961	.986	.989	.993	.996	.998	.999	.999	—	—	—	—	—	—	—	—	—
	7	.806	.888	.943	.974	.991	.997	.998	.999	.999	—	—	—	—	—	—	—	—	—	—	—	—
	8	.927	.964	.985	.994	.998	—	—	—	—	—	—	—	—	—	—	—	—	—	—	—	—
	9	.981	.992	.997	.999	—	—	—	—	—	—	—	—	—	—	—	—	—	—	—	—	—
	10	.997	.999	—	—	—	—	—	—	—	—	—	—	—	—	—	—	—	—	—	—	—
	11	—	—	—	—	—	—	—	—	—	—	—	—	—	—	—	—	—	—	—	—	—
13	0	.000	.000	.001	.004	.010	.024	.028	.040	.055	.076	.104	.121	.141	.190	.254	.338	.447	.513	.588	.769	.878
	1	.002	.005	.013	.030	.064	.127	.144	.185	.234	.292	.360	.398	.439	.526	.621	.721	.819	.865	.907	.973	.993
	2	.011	.027	.058	.113	.202	.333	.364	.430	.502	.577	.654	.692	.730	.802	.866	.920	.961	.975	.986	.998	—
	3	.046	.093	.169	.278	.421	.584	.618	.684	.747	.806	.859	.882	.903	.939	.966	.984	.994	.997	.999	—	—
	4	.133	.228	.353	.501	.654	.794	.818	.863	.901	.932	.956	.966	.974	.986	.994	.998	.999	—	—	—	—
	5	.291	.427	.574	.716	.835	.920	.932	.954	.970	.982	.990	.992	.995	.998	.999	—	—	—	—	—	—
	6	.500	.644	.771	.871	.938	.976	.981	.988	.993	.996	.998	.999	.999	—	—	—	—	—	—	—	—
	7	.709	.821	.902	.954	.982	.994	.996	.998	.999	—	—	—	—	—	—	—	—	—	—	—	—
	8	.867	.930	.968	.987	.996	.999	—	—	—	—	—	—	—	—	—	—	—	—	—	—	—
	9	.954	.980	.992	.997	.999	—	—	—	—	—	—	—	—	—	—	—	—	—	—	—	—
	10	.989	.996	.999	—	—	—	—	—	—	—	—	—	—	—	—	—	—	—	—	—	—
	11	.998	.999	—	—	—	—	—	—	—	—	—	—	—	—	—	—	—	—	—	—	—
	12	—	—	—	—	—	—	—	—	—	—	—	—	—	—	—	—	—	—	—	—	—
	13	—	—	—	—	—	—	—	—	—	—	—	—	—	—	—	—	—	—	—	—	—
14	0	.000	.000	.001	.002	.007	.018	.021	.031	.044	.062	.087	.103	.121	.167	.229	.311	.421	.488	.565	.754	.869
	1	.001	.003	.008	.021	.047	.101	.116	.153	.198	.253	.319	.357	.397	.486	.585	.690	.796	.847	.894	.969	.992
	2	.006	.017	.040	.084	.161	.281	.311	.376	.448	.526	.607	.648	.689	.768	.842	.904	.952	.970	.983	.998	—
	3	.029	.063	.124	.220	.355	.521	.557	.628	.698	.765	.826	.853	.879	.923	.956	.979	.992	.996	.998	—	—

n = 14

r	.50	.45	.40	.35	.30	.25	.24	.22	.20	.18	.16	.15	.14	.12	.10	.08	.06	.05	.04	.02	.01
4	.090	.167	.279	.423	.584	.742	.770	.824	.870	.909	.941	.953	.964	.980	.991	.996	.999	1	—	—	—
5	.212	.337	.486	.641	.781	.888	.905	.934	.956	.973	.984	.988	.992	.996	.999	1	—	—	—	—	—
6	.395	.546	.692	.816	.907	.962	.969	.980	.988	.994	.997	.998	.999	.999	1	—	—	—	—	—	—
7	.605	.741	.850	.925	.969	.990	.992	.995	.998	.999	.999	1	—	—	—	—	—	—	—	—	—
8	.788	.881	.942	.976	.992	.998	.998	.999	1	—	—	—	—	—	—	—	—	—	—	—	—
9	.910	.957	.982	.994	.998	1	—	—	—	—	—	—	—	—	—	—	—	—	—	—	—
10	.971	.989	.996	.999	1	—	—	—	—	—	—	—	—	—	—	—	—	—	—	—	—
11	.994	.998	.999	1	—	—	—	—	—	—	—	—	—	—	—	—	—	—	—	—	—
12	.999	1	—	—	—	—	—	—	—	—	—	—	—	—	—	—	—	—	—	—	—
13	—	—	—	—	—	—	—	—	—	—	—	—	—	—	—	—	—	—	—	—	—
14	—	—	—	—	—	—	—	—	—	—	—	—	—	—	—	—	—	—	—	—	—

n = 15

r	.50	.45	.40	.35	.30	.25	.24	.22	.20	.18	.16	.15	.14	.12	.10	.08	.06	.05	.04	.02	.01
0	.000	.000	.000	.002	.005	.013	.016	.024	.035	.051	.073	.087	.104	.147	.206	.286	.395	.463	.542	.739	.860
1	.000	.002	.005	.014	.035	.080	.094	.126	.167	.219	.282	.319	.358	.448	.549	.660	.774	.829	.881	.965	.990
2	.004	.011	.027	.062	.127	.236	.264	.327	.398	.477	.561	.604	.648	.735	.816	.887	.943	.964	.980	.997	1
3	.018	.042	.091	.173	.297	.461	.498	.573	.648	.722	.791	.823	.852	.904	.944	.973	.990	.995	.998	1	1
4	.059	.120	.217	.352	.515	.686	.719	.781	.836	.883	.922	.938	.952	.974	.987	.995	.999	.999	1	—	—
5	.151	.261	.403	.564	.722	.852	.873	.910	.939	.961	.977	.983	.988	.994	.998	.999	1	—	—	—	—
6	.304	.452	.610	.755	.869	.943	.954	.970	.982	.990	.995	.996	.998	.999	1	—	—	—	—	—	—
7	.500	.654	.787	.887	.950	.983	.987	.992	.996	.998	.999	.999	1	—	—	—	—	—	—	—	—
8	.696	.818	.905	.958	.985	.996	.997	.998	.999	1	—	—	—	—	—	—	—	—	—	—	—
9	.849	.923	.966	.988	.996	.999	.999	1	—	—	—	—	—	—	—	—	—	—	—	—	—
10	.941	.975	.991	.997	.999	1	—	—	—	—	—	—	—	—	—	—	—	—	—	—	—
11	.982	.994	.998	1	—	—	—	—	—	—	—	—	—	—	—	—	—	—	—	—	—
12	.996	.999	1	—	—	—	—	—	—	—	—	—	—	—	—	—	—	—	—	—	—
13	—	—	—	—	—	—	—	—	—	—	—	—	—	—	—	—	—	—	—	—	—
14	—	—	—	—	—	—	—	—	—	—	—	—	—	—	—	—	—	—	—	—	—
15	—	—	—	—	—	—	—	—	—	—	—	—	—	—	—	—	—	—	—	—	—

n = 16

r	.50	.45	.40	.35	.30	.25	.24	.22	.20	.18	.16	.15	.14	.12	.10	.08	.06	.05	.04	.02	.01
0	.000	.000	.000	.001	.003	.010	.012	.019	.028	.042	.061	.074	.090	.129	.185	.263	.372	.440	.520	.724	.851
1	.000	.001	.003	.010	.026	.063	.075	.103	.141	.189	.249	.284	.323	.412	.515	.630	.751	.811	.867	.960	.989
2	.002	.007	.018	.045	.099	.197	.223	.283	.352	.430	.516	.561	.607	.700	.789	.869	.933	.957	.976	.996	.999
3	.011	.028	.065	.134	.246	.405	.442	.519	.598	.678	.754	.790	.824	.884	.932	.966	.987	.993	.997	1	1
4	.038	.085	.167	.289	.450	.630	.666	.735	.798	.854	.901	.921	.938	.965	.983	.993	.998	.999	1	—	—
5	.105	.198	.329	.490	.660	.810	.836	.881	.918	.947	.968	.976	.983	.992	.997	.999	1	—	—	—	—
6	.227	.366	.527	.688	.825	.920	.934	.957	.973	.985	.992	.994	.996	.998	.999	1	—	—	—	—	—
7	.402	.563	.716	.841	.926	.973	.979	.987	.993	.996	.998	.999	.999	1	—	—	—	—	—	—	—
8	.598	.744	.858	.933	.974	.993	.994	.997	.999	1	—	—	—	—	—	—	—	—	—	—	—

n	r	.01	.02	.04	.05	.06	.08	.10	.12	.14	.15	.16	.18	.20	.22	.24	.25	.30	.35	.40	.45	.50
16	9	—	—	—	—	—	—	—	—	—	—	—	—	—	—	.999	.998	.993	.977	.942	.876	.773
	10	—	—	—	—	—	—	—	—	—	—	—	—	—	—	—	—	.998	.994	.981	.951	.895
	11	—	—	—	—	—	—	—	—	—	—	—	—	—	—	—	—	—	.999	.995	.985	.962
	12	—	—	—	—	—	—	—	—	—	—	—	—	—	—	—	—	—	—	.999	.997	.989
	13	—	—	—	—	—	—	—	—	—	—	—	—	—	—	—	—	—	—	—	.999	.998
	14	—	—	—	—	—	—	—	—	—	—	—	—	—	—	—	—	—	—	—	—	—
	15	—	—	—	—	—	—	—	—	—	—	—	—	—	—	—	—	—	—	—	—	—
	16	—	—	—	—	—	—	—	—	—	—	—	—	—	—	—	—	—	—	—	—	—
17	0	.843	.709	.500	.418	.349	.242	.167	.114	.077	.063	.052	.034	.023	.015	.009	.008	.002	.001	.000	.000	.000
	1	.988	.955	.853	.792	.728	.601	.482	.378	.290	.252	.219	.162	.118	.085	.060	.050	.019	.007	.002	.001	.000
	2	.999	.996	.971	.950	.922	.850	.762	.665	.568	.520	.473	.387	.310	.243	.188	.164	.077	.033	.012	.004	.001
	3	—	—	.996	.991	.984	.958	.917	.862	.793	.756	.716	.633	.549	.467	.389	.353	.202	.103	.046	.018	.006
	4	—	—	—	.999	.997	.991	.978	.955	.922	.901	.878	.822	.758	.687	.612	.574	.389	.235	.126	.060	.025
	5	—	—	—	—	—	.999	.995	.989	.977	.968	.958	.931	.894	.849	.795	.765	.597	.420	.264	.147	.072
	6	—	—	—	—	—	—	.999	.998	.994	.992	.988	.978	.962	.940	.911	.893	.775	.619	.448	.290	.166
	7	—	—	—	—	—	—	—	—	.999	.998	.997	.994	.989	.981	.968	.960	.895	.787	.641	.474	.315
	8	—	—	—	—	—	—	—	—	—	—	—	.999	.997	.995	.991	.988	.960	.901	.801	.663	.500
	9	—	—	—	—	—	—	—	—	—	—	—	—	—	.999	.998	.997	.987	.962	.908	.817	.685
	10	—	—	—	—	—	—	—	—	—	—	—	—	—	—	—	.999	.997	.988	.965	.917	.834
	11	—	—	—	—	—	—	—	—	—	—	—	—	—	—	—	—	.999	.997	.989	.970	.928
	12	—	—	—	—	—	—	—	—	—	—	—	—	—	—	—	—	—	.999	.997	.991	.975
	13	—	—	—	—	—	—	—	—	—	—	—	—	—	—	—	—	—	—	—	.998	.994
	14	—	—	—	—	—	—	—	—	—	—	—	—	—	—	—	—	—	—	—	—	.999
	15	—	—	—	—	—	—	—	—	—	—	—	—	—	—	—	—	—	—	—	—	—
	16	—	—	—	—	—	—	—	—	—	—	—	—	—	—	—	—	—	—	—	—	—
	17	—	—	—	—	—	—	—	—	—	—	—	—	—	—	—	—	—	—	—	—	—
18	0	.835	.695	.480	.397	.328	.223	.150	.100	.066	.054	.043	.028	.018	.011	.007	.006	.002	.000	.000	.000	.000
	1	.986	.950	.839	.774	.706	.572	.450	.346	.260	.224	.192	.139	.099	.069	.048	.039	.014	.005	.001	.000	.000
	2	.999	.995	.967	.942	.910	.830	.734	.631	.529	.480	.433	.346	.271	.208	.157	.135	.060	.024	.008	.003	.001
	3	—	—	.995	.989	.980	.949	.902	.838	.762	.720	.677	.589	.501	.418	.341	.306	.165	.078	.033	.012	.004
	4	—	—	.999	.998	.997	.988	.972	.944	.904	.879	.852	.788	.716	.639	.559	.519	.333	.189	.094	.041	.015
	5	—	—	—	—	—	.998	.994	.985	.969	.958	.945	.911	.867	.813	.751	.717	.534	.355	.209	.108	.048
	6	—	—	—	—	—	—	.999	.997	.992	.988	.983	.969	.949	.920	.883	.861	.722	.549	.374	.226	.119
	7	—	—	—	—	—	—	—	.999	.998	.997	.996	.991	.984	.972	.954	.943	.859	.728	.563	.391	.240
	8	—	—	—	—	—	—	—	—	—	.999	.999	.998	.996	.992	.985	.981	.940	.861	.737	.578	.407
	9	—	—	—	—	—	—	—	—	—	—	—	—	.999	.998	.996	.995	.979	.940	.865	.747	.593
	10	—	—	—	—	—	—	—	—	—	—	—	—	—	—	.999	.999	.994	.979	.942	.872	.760
	11	—	—	—	—	—	—	—	—	—	—	—	—	—	—	—	—	.999	.994	.980	.946	.881

APPENDIX B BINOMIAL DISTRIBUTION: CUMULATIVE PROBABILITIES

n	r	.50	.45	.40	.35	.30	.25	.24	.22	.20	.18	.16	.15	.14	.12	.10	.08	.06	.05	.04	.02	.01
18	12	.952	.982	.994	.999	—	—	—	—	—	—	—	—	—	—	—	—	—	—	—	—	—
	13	.985	.995	.999	—	—	—	—	—	—	—	—	—	—	—	—	—	—	—	—	—	—
	14	.996	.999	—	—	—	—	—	—	—	—	—	—	—	—	—	—	—	—	—	—	—
	15	.999	—	—	—	—	—	—	—	—	—	—	—	—	—	—	—	—	—	—	—	—
	16	—	—	—	—	—	—	—	—	—	—	—	—	—	—	—	—	—	—	—	—	—
	17	—	—	—	—	—	—	—	—	—	—	—	—	—	—	—	—	—	—	—	—	—
	18	—	—	—	—	—	—	—	—	—	—	—	—	—	—	—	—	—	—	—	—	—
19	0	.000	.000	.000	.000	.001	.004	.005	.009	.014	.023	.036	.046	.057	.088	.135	.205	.309	.377	.460	.681	.826
	1	.000	.000	.001	.003	.010	.031	.038	.057	.083	.119	.168	.198	.233	.317	.420	.544	.683	.755	.825	.945	.985
	2	.000	.002	.005	.017	.046	.111	.131	.178	.237	.309	.394	.441	.491	.597	.705	.809	.898	.933	.962	.994	.999
	3	.002	.008	.023	.059	.133	.263	.297	.372	.455	.545	.638	.684	.729	.813	.885	.940	.976	.987	.994	—	—
	4	.010	.028	.070	.150	.282	.465	.506	.590	.673	.752	.824	.856	.884	.931	.965	.985	.996	.998	.999	—	—
	5	.032	.078	.163	.297	.474	.668	.705	.775	.837	.889	.930	.946	.960	.980	.991	.997	.999	—	—	—	—
	6	.084	.173	.308	.481	.666	.825	.851	.897	.932	.959	.977	.984	.989	.995	.998	—	—	—	—	—	—
	7	.180	.317	.488	.666	.818	.923	.937	.960	.977	.987	.994	.996	.997	.999	—	—	—	—	—	—	—
	8	.324	.494	.667	.815	.916	.971	.978	.987	.993	.997	.999	.999	.999	—	—	—	—	—	—	—	—
	9	.500	.671	.814	.913	.967	.991	.993	.997	.998	.999	.999	—	—	—	—	—	—	—	—	—	—
	10	.676	.816	.912	.965	.989	.998	.998	.999	—	—	—	—	—	—	—	—	—	—	—	—	—
	11	.820	.913	.965	.989	.997	—	—	—	—	—	—	—	—	—	—	—	—	—	—	—	—
	12	.916	.966	.988	.997	.999	—	—	—	—	—	—	—	—	—	—	—	—	—	—	—	—
	13	.968	.989	.997	.999	—	—	—	—	—	—	—	—	—	—	—	—	—	—	—	—	—
	14	.990	.997	.999	—	—	—	—	—	—	—	—	—	—	—	—	—	—	—	—	—	—
	15	.998	.999	—	—	—	—	—	—	—	—	—	—	—	—	—	—	—	—	—	—	—
	16	—	.999	—	—	—	—	—	—	—	—	—	—	—	—	—	—	—	—	—	—	—
	17	—	—	—	—	—	—	—	—	—	—	—	—	—	—	—	—	—	—	—	—	—
	18	—	—	—	—	—	—	—	—	—	—	—	—	—	—	—	—	—	—	—	—	—
	19	—	—	—	—	—	—	—	—	—	—	—	—	—	—	—	—	—	—	—	—	—
20	0	.000	.000	.000	.000	.001	.003	.004	.007	.012	.019	.031	.039	.049	.078	.122	.189	.290	.358	.442	.668	.818
	1	.000	.000	.001	.002	.008	.024	.030	.046	.069	.102	.147	.176	.208	.289	.392	.517	.660	.736	.810	.940	.983
	2	.000	.001	.004	.012	.035	.091	.109	.151	.206	.275	.358	.405	.455	.563	.677	.788	.885	.925	.956	.993	.999
	3	.001	.005	.016	.044	.107	.225	.257	.329	.411	.503	.599	.648	.696	.787	.867	.929	.971	.984	.993	.999	—
	4	.006	.019	.051	.118	.238	.415	.456	.542	.630	.715	.794	.830	.863	.917	.957	.982	.994	.997	.999	—	—
	5	.021	.055	.126	.245	.416	.617	.657	.734	.804	.864	.913	.933	.949	.974	.989	.996	.999	—	—	—	—
	6	.058	.130	.250	.417	.608	.786	.816	.870	.913	.946	.970	.978	.985	.993	.998	.999	—	—	—	—	—
	7	.132	.252	.416	.601	.772	.898	.917	.946	.968	.982	.990	.994	.996	.999	—	—	—	—	—	—	—
	8	.252	.414	.596	.762	.887	.959	.968	.981	.990	.995	.998	.999	.999	—	—	—	—	—	—	—	—
	9	.412	.591	.755	.878	.952	.986	.990	.995	.997	.999	.999	—	—	—	—	—	—	—	—	—	—
	10	.588	.751	.872	.947	.983	.996	.997	.999	.999	1	1	—	—	—	—	—	—	—	—	—	—

n	r	p .01	.02	.04	.05	.06	.08	.10	.12	.14	.15	.16	.18	.20	.22	.24	.25	.30	.35	.40	.45	.50
20	11															.999	.999	.995	.980	.943	.869	.748
	12															1	1	.999	.994	.979	.942	.868
	13															1	1	1	.998	.994	.979	.942
	14															1	1	1	1	.998	.994	.979
	15															1	1	1	1	1	.998	.994
	16															1	1	1	1	1	1	.999
	17															1	1	1	1	1	1	1
	18															1	1	1	1	1	1	1
	19															1	1	1	1	1	1	1
	20															1	1	1	1	1	1	1
25	0	.778	.603	.360	.277	.213	.124	.072	.041	.023	.017	.013	.007	.004	.002	.001	.001	.000	.000	.000	.000	.000
	1	.974	.911	.736	.642	.553	.395	.271	.180	.117	.093	.074	.045	.027	.016	.009	.007	.002	.000	.000	.000	.000
	2	.998	.987	.924	.873	.813	.677	.537	.409	.300	.254	.213	.147	.098	.064	.041	.032	.009	.002	.000	.000	.000
	3	1	.999	.983	.966	.940	.865	.764	.648	.529	.471	.416	.317	.234	.168	.117	.096	.033	.010	.002	.000	.000
	4	1	1	.997	.993	.985	.955	.902	.827	.733	.682	.629	.523	.421	.328	.248	.214	.090	.032	.009	.002	.000
	5	1	1	1	.999	.997	.988	.967	.929	.873	.838	.800	.712	.617	.518	.423	.378	.193	.083	.029	.009	.002
	6	1	1	1	1	.999	.997	.991	.976	.949	.930	.908	.851	.780	.697	.607	.561	.341	.173	.074	.026	.007
	7	1	1	1	1	1	.999	.998	.993	.983	.975	.964	.934	.891	.834	.765	.727	.512	.306	.154	.064	.022
	8	1	1	1	1	1	1	1	.998	.995	.992	.988	.975	.953	.921	.877	.851	.677	.467	.274	.134	.054
	9	1	1	1	1	1	1	1	1	.999	.998	.997	.992	.983	.967	.944	.929	.811	.630	.425	.242	.115
	10	1	1	1	1	1	1	1	1	1	1	.999	.998	.994	.988	.978	.970	.902	.771	.586	.384	.212
	11	1	1	1	1	1	1	1	1	1	1	1	.999	.998	.996	.992	.989	.956	.875	.732	.543	.345
	12	1	1	1	1	1	1	1	1	1	1	1	1	1	.999	.998	.997	.983	.940	.846	.694	.500
	13	1	1	1	1	1	1	1	1	1	1	1	1	1	1	.999	.999	.994	.975	.922	.817	.655
	14	1	1	1	1	1	1	1	1	1	1	1	1	1	1	1	1	.998	.991	.966	.904	.788
	15	1	1	1	1	1	1	1	1	1	1	1	1	1	1	1	1	1	.997	.987	.956	.885
	16	1	1	1	1	1	1	1	1	1	1	1	1	1	1	1	1	1	.999	.996	.983	.946
	17	1	1	1	1	1	1	1	1	1	1	1	1	1	1	1	1	1	1	.999	.994	.978
	18	1	1	1	1	1	1	1	1	1	1	1	1	1	1	1	1	1	1	1	.998	.993
	19	1	1	1	1	1	1	1	1	1	1	1	1	1	1	1	1	1	1	1	1	.998
	20	1	1	1	1	1	1	1	1	1	1	1	1	1	1	1	1	1	1	1	1	1
	21	1	1	1	1	1	1	1	1	1	1	1	1	1	1	1	1	1	1	1	1	1
	22	1	1	1	1	1	1	1	1	1	1	1	1	1	1	1	1	1	1	1	1	1
	23	1	1	1	1	1	1	1	1	1	1	1	1	1	1	1	1	1	1	1	1	1
	24	1	1	1	1	1	1	1	1	1	1	1	1	1	1	1	1	1	1	1	1	1
	25	1	1	1	1	1	1	1	1	1	1	1	1	1	1	1	1	1	1	1	1	1

APPENDIX C. Poisson Distribution: Individual Probabilities

$$P_P(X = k) = \frac{e^{-m} \, m^k}{k!}$$

Figure A.3 *Using Appendix C to find $P_P(X = 2 \mid m = 1.5)$*

m

x	0.00	0.00	0.00	0.00	0.01	0.01	0.01	0.01	0.01	0.01	0.02	0.03	0.04	0.05	0.06
0	.999	.998	.997	.996	.995	.994	.993	.992	.991	.990	.980	.970	.961	.951	.942
1	.001	.002	.003	.004	.005	.006	.007	.008	.009	.010	.020	.029	.038	.048	.057
2	0	0	0	0	0	0	0	0	0	0	0	0	.001	.001	.002

m

x	0.07	0.08	0.09	0.10	0.15	0.20	0.25	0.30	0.40	0.50	0.60	0.70	0.80	0.90	1.00
0	.932	.923	.914	.905	.861	.819	.779	.741	.670	.607	.549	.497	.449	.407	.368
1	.065	.074	.082	.090	.129	.164	.195	.222	.268	.303	.329	.348	.359	.366	.368
2	.002	.003	.004	.005	.010	.016	.024	.033	.054	.076	.099	.122	.144	.165	.184
3	0	0	0	0	0	.001	.002	.003	.007	.013	.020	.028	.038	.049	.061
4	0	0	0	0	0	0	0	0	.001	.002	.003	.005	.008	.011	.015
5	0	0	0	0	0	0	0	0	0	0	0	.001	.001	.002	.003
6	0	0	0	0	0	0	0	0	0	0	0	0	0	0	.001

m

x	1.1	1.2	1.3	1.4	1.5	1.6	1.7	1.8	1.9	2.0	2.1	2.2	2.3	2.4	2.5
0	.333	.301	.273	.247	.223	.202	.183	.165	.150	.135	.122	.111	.100	.091	.082
1	.366	.361	.354	.345	.335	.323	.311	.298	.284	.271	.257	.244	.231	.218	.205
2	.201	.217	.230	.242	.251	.258	.264	.268	.270	.271	.270	.268	.265	.261	.257
3	.074	.087	.100	.113	.126	.138	.150	.161	.171	.180	.189	.197	.203	.209	.214
4	.020	.026	.032	.039	.047	.055	.064	.072	.081	.090	.099	.108	.117	.125	.134
5	.004	.006	.008	.011	.014	.018	.022	.026	.031	.036	.042	.048	.054	.060	.067
6	.001	.001	.002	.003	.004	.005	.006	.008	.010	.012	.015	.017	.021	.024	.028
7	0	0	0	.001	.001	.001	.001	.002	.003	.003	.004	.005	.007	.008	.010
8	0	0	0	0	0	0	0	0	.001	.001	.001	.002	.002	.002	.003
9	0	0	0	0	0	0	0	0	0	0	0	0	0	.001	.001

x	m 2.6	2.7	2.8	2.9	3.0	3.1	3.2	3.3	3.4	3.5	3.6	3.7	3.8	3.9	4.0
0	.074	.067	.061	.055	.050	.045	.041	.037	.033	.030	.027	.025	.022	.020	.018
1	.193	.181	.170	.160	.149	.140	.130	.122	.113	.106	.098	.091	.085	.079	.073
2	.251	.245	.238	.231	.224	.216	.209	.201	.193	.185	.177	.169	.162	.154	.147
3	.218	.220	.222	.224	.224	.224	.223	.221	.219	.216	.212	.209	.205	.200	.195
4	.141	.149	.156	.162	.168	.173	.178	.182	.186	.189	.191	.193	.194	.195	.195
5	.074	.080	.087	.094	.101	.107	.114	.120	.126	.132	.138	.143	.148	.152	.156
6	.032	.036	.041	.045	.050	.056	.061	.066	.072	.077	.083	.088	.094	.099	.104
7	.012	.014	.016	.019	.022	.025	.028	.031	.035	.039	.042	.047	.051	.055	.060
8	.004	.005	.006	.007	.008	.010	.011	.013	.015	.017	.019	.022	.024	.027	.030
9	.001	.001	.002	.002	.003	.003	.004	.005	.006	.007	.008	.009	.010	.012	.013
10	0	0	0	.001	.001	.001	.001	.002	.002	.002	.003	.003	.004	.005	.005
11	0	0	0	0	0	0	0	0	.001	.001	.001	.001	.001	.002	.002
12	0	0	0	0	0	0	0	0	0	0	0	0	0	.001	.001

x	m 4.1	4.2	4.3	4.4	4.5	4.6	4.7	4.8	4.9	5.0	5.1	5.2	5.3	5.4	5.5
0	.017	.015	.014	.012	.011	.010	.009	.008	.007	.007	.006	.006	.005	.005	.004
1	.068	.063	.058	.054	.050	.046	.043	.040	.036	.034	.031	.029	.026	.024	.022
2	.139	.132	.125	.119	.112	.106	.100	.095	.089	.084	.079	.075	.070	.066	.062
3	.190	.185	.180	.174	.169	.163	.157	.152	.146	.140	.135	.129	.124	.119	.113
4	.195	.194	.193	.192	.190	.188	.185	.182	.179	.175	.172	.168	.164	.160	.156
5	.160	.163	.166	.169	.171	.173	.174	.175	.175	.175	.175	.175	.174	.173	.171
6	.109	.114	.119	.124	.128	.132	.136	.140	.143	.146	.149	.151	.154	.156	.157
7	.064	.069	.073	.078	.082	.087	.091	.096	.100	.104	.109	.113	.116	.120	.123
8	.033	.036	.039	.043	.046	.050	.054	.058	.061	.065	.069	.073	.077	.081	.085
9	.015	.017	.019	.021	.023	.026	.028	.031	.033	.036	.039	.042	.045	.049	.052
10	.006	.007	.008	.009	.010	.012	.013	.015	.016	.018	.020	.022	.024	.026	.029
11	.002	.003	.003	.004	.004	.005	.006	.006	.007	.008	.009	.010	.012	.013	.014
12	.001	.001	.001	.001	.002	.002	.002	.003	.003	.003	.004	.005	.005	.006	.007
13	0	0	0	0	.001	.001	.001	.001	.001	.001	.002	.002	.002	.002	.003
14	0	0	0	0	0	0	0	0	0	0	.001	.001	.001	.001	.001

x	5.6	5.7	5.8	5.9	6.0	6.1	6.2	6.3	6.4	6.5	6.6	6.7	6.8	6.9	7.0	x
0	.004	.003	.003	.003	.002	.002	.002	.002	.002	.002	.001	.001	.001	.001	.001	0
1	.021	.019	.018	.016	.015	.014	.013	.012	.011	.010	.009	.008	.008	.007	.006	1
2	.058	.054	.051	.048	.045	.042	.039	.036	.034	.032	.030	.028	.026	.024	.022	2
3	.108	.103	.098	.094	.089	.085	.081	.077	.073	.069	.065	.062	.058	.055	.052	3
4	.152	.147	.143	.138	.134	.129	.125	.121	.116	.112	.108	.103	.099	.095	.091	4
5	.170	.168	.166	.163	.161	.158	.155	.152	.149	.145	.142	.138	.135	.131	.128	5
6	.158	.159	.160	.160	.161	.160	.160	.159	.159	.157	.156	.155	.153	.151	.149	6
7	.127	.130	.133	.135	.138	.140	.142	.144	.145	.146	.147	.148	.149	.149	.149	7
8	.089	.092	.096	.100	.103	.107	.110	.113	.116	.119	.121	.124	.126	.128	.130	8
9	.055	.059	.062	.065	.069	.072	.076	.079	.082	.086	.089	.092	.095	.098	.101	9
10	.031	.033	.036	.039	.041	.044	.047	.050	.053	.056	.059	.062	.065	.068	.071	10
11	.016	.017	.019	.021	.023	.024	.026	.029	.031	.033	.035	.038	.040	.043	.045	11
12	.007	.008	.009	.010	.011	.012	.014	.015	.016	.018	.019	.021	.023	.025	.026	12
13	.003	.004	.004	.005	.005	.006	.007	.007	.008	.009	.010	.011	.012	.013	.014	13
14	.001	.001	.002	.002	.002	.003	.003	.003	.004	.004	.005	.005	.006	.006	.007	14
15	0	.001	.001	.001	.001	.001	.001	.001	.002	.002	.002	.002	.003	.003	.003	15
16	0	0	0	0	0	0	0	.001	.001	.001	.001	.001	.001	.001	.001	16
17	0	0	0	0	0	0	0	0	0	0	0	0	0	.001	.001	17

x	m=7.1	7.2	7.3	7.4	7.5	8.0	8.5	9.0	9.5	10.0	11.0	12.0	13.0	14.0	15.0
0	.001	.001	.001	.001	.001	.000	.000	.000	.000	.000	.000	.000	.000	.000	.000
1	.006	.005	.005	.005	.004	.003	.002	.001	.001	.000	.000	.000	.000	.000	.000
2	.021	.019	.018	.017	.016	.011	.007	.005	.003	.002	.001	.000	.000	.000	.000
3	.049	.046	.044	.041	.039	.029	.021	.015	.011	.008	.004	.002	.001	.000	.000
4	.087	.084	.080	.076	.073	.057	.044	.034	.025	.019	.010	.005	.003	.001	.001
5	.124	.120	.117	.113	.109	.092	.075	.061	.048	.038	.022	.013	.007	.004	.002
6	.147	.144	.142	.139	.137	.122	.107	.091	.076	.063	.041	.025	.015	.009	.005
7	.149	.149	.148	.147	.146	.140	.129	.117	.104	.090	.065	.044	.028	.017	.010
8	.132	.134	.135	.136	.137	.140	.138	.132	.123	.113	.089	.066	.046	.030	.019
9	.104	.107	.110	.112	.114	.124	.130	.132	.130	.125	.109	.087	.066	.047	.032
10	.074	.077	.080	.083	.086	.099	.110	.119	.124	.125	.119	.105	.086	.066	.049
11	.048	.050	.053	.056	.059	.072	.085	.097	.107	.114	.119	.114	.101	.084	.066
12	.028	.030	.032	.034	.037	.048	.060	.073	.084	.095	.109	.114	.110	.098	.083
13	.015	.017	.018	.020	.021	.030	.040	.050	.062	.073	.093	.106	.110	.106	.096
14	.008	.009	.009	.010	.011	.017	.024	.032	.042	.052	.073	.090	.102	.106	.102
15	.004	.004	.005	.005	.006	.009	.014	.019	.027	.035	.053	.072	.088	.099	.102
16	.002	.002	.002	.002	.003	.005	.007	.011	.016	.022	.037	.054	.072	.087	.096
17	.001	.001	.001	.001	.001	.002	.004	.006	.009	.013	.024	.038	.055	.071	.085
18	0	0	0	0	0	.001	.002	.003	.005	.007	.015	.026	.040	.055	.071
19	0	0	0	0	0	0	.001	.001	.002	.004	.008	.016	.027	.041	.056
20	0	0	0	0	0	0	0	.001	.001	.002	.005	.010	.018	.029	.042
21	0	0	0	0	0	0	0	.001	0	.001	.002	.006	.011	.019	.030
22	0	0	0	0	0	0	0	0	0	0	.001	.003	.006	.012	.020
23	0	0	0	0	0	0	0	0	0	0	.001	.002	.004	.007	.013
24	0	0	0	0	0	0	0	0	0	0	0	.001	.002	.004	.008
25	0	0	0	0	0	0	0	0	0	0	0	0	.001	.002	.005
26	0	0	0	0	0	0	0	0	0	0	0	0	.001	.001	.003
27	0	0	0	0	0	0	0	0	0	0	0	0	0	.001	.002
28	0	0	0	0	0	0	0	0	0	0	0	0	0	0	.001

APPENDIX D. Poisson Distribution: Cumulative Probabilities

$$P_P(X \le k) = \sum_{i=0}^{k} \frac{e^{-m} m^i}{i!}$$

k	m	1.4	1.5	1.6
0		.247	.223	.202
1		.592	.558	.525
2	....	.833	.809	.783
3		.946	.934	.921
.		.	.	.
.		.	.	.

Figure A.4 *Using Appendix D to find $P_P(X \le 2 \mid m = 1.5)$*

x	m 0.00	0.00	0.00	0.00	0.00	0.01	0.01	0.01	0.01	0.01	0.02	0.03	0.04	0.05	0.06
0	.999	.998	.997	.996	.995	.994	.993	.992	.991	.990	.980	.970	.961	.951	.942
1	1	1	1	1	1	1	1	1	1	1	1	1	.999	.999	.998
2													1	1	1

x	m 0.07	0.08	0.09	0.10	0.15	0.20	0.25	0.30	0.40	0.50	0.60	0.70	0.80	0.90	1.00
0	.932	.923	.914	.905	.861	.819	.779	.741	.670	.607	.549	.497	.449	.407	.368
1	.998	.997	.996	.995	.990	.982	.974	.963	.938	.910	.878	.844	.809	.772	.736
2	1	1	1	1	.999	.999	.998	.996	.992	.986	.977	.966	.953	.937	.920
3				1	1	1	1	1	.999	.998	.997	.994	.991	.987	.981
4								1	1	1	1	.999	.999	.998	.996
5										1	1	1	1	1	.999
6															1

x	m 1.1	1.2	1.3	1.4	1.5	1.6	1.7	1.8	1.9	2.0	2.1	2.2	2.3	2.4	2.5
0	.333	.301	.273	.247	.223	.202	.183	.165	.150	.135	.122	.111	.100	.091	.082
1	.699	.663	.627	.592	.558	.525	.493	.463	.434	.406	.380	.355	.331	.308	.287
2	.900	.879	.857	.833	.809	.783	.757	.731	.704	.677	.650	.623	.596	.570	.544
3	.974	.966	.957	.946	.934	.921	.907	.891	.875	.857	.839	.819	.799	.779	.758
4	.995	.992	.989	.986	.981	.976	.970	.964	.956	.947	.938	.928	.916	.904	.891
5	.999	.998	.998	.997	.996	.994	.992	.990	.987	.983	.980	.975	.970	.964	.958
6	1	1	1	.999	.999	.999	.998	.997	.997	.995	.994	.993	.991	.988	.986
7	1	1	1	1	1	1	1	.999	.999	.999	.999	.998	.997	.997	.996
8													.999	.999	.999
9															1

m

x	2.6	2.7	2.8	2.9	3.0	3.1	3.2	3.3	3.4	3.5	3.6	3.7	3.8	3.9	4.0
0	.074	.067	.061	.055	.050	.045	.041	.037	.033	.030	.027	.025	.022	.020	.018
1	.267	.249	.231	.215	.199	.185	.171	.159	.147	.136	.126	.116	.107	.099	.092
2	.518	.494	.469	.446	.423	.401	.380	.359	.340	.321	.303	.285	.269	.253	.238
3	.736	.714	.692	.670	.647	.625	.603	.580	.558	.537	.515	.494	.473	.453	.433
4	.877	.863	.848	.832	.815	.798	.781	.763	.744	.725	.706	.687	.668	.648	.629
5	.951	.943	.935	.926	.916	.906	.895	.883	.871	.858	.844	.830	.816	.801	.785
6	.983	.979	.976	.971	.966	.961	.955	.949	.942	.935	.927	.918	.909	.899	.889
7	.995	.993	.992	.990	.988	.986	.983	.980	.977	.973	.969	.965	.960	.955	.949
8	.999	.998	.998	.997	.996	.995	.994	.993	.992	.990	.988	.986	.984	.981	.979
9	1	.999	.999	.999	.999	.999	.998	.998	.997	.997	.996	.995	.994	.993	.992
10	1	1	1	1		1	1	.999	.999	.999	.999	.998	.998	.998	.997
11	1	1	1			1	1	1	1	1		1	.999	.999	.999
12	1	1												1	1

m

x	4.1	4.2	4.3	4.4	4.5	4.6	4.7	4.8	4.9	5.0	5.1	5.2	5.3	5.4	5.5
0	.017	.015	.014	.012	.011	.010	.009	.008	.007	.007	.006	.006	.005	.005	.004
1	.085	.078	.072	.066	.061	.056	.052	.048	.044	.040	.037	.034	.031	.029	.027
2	.224	.210	.197	.185	.174	.163	.152	.143	.133	.125	.116	.109	.102	.095	.088
3	.414	.395	.377	.359	.342	.326	.310	.294	.279	.265	.251	.238	.225	.213	.202
4	.609	.590	.570	.551	.532	.513	.495	.476	.458	.440	.423	.406	.390	.373	.358
5	.769	.753	.737	.720	.703	.686	.668	.651	.634	.616	.598	.581	.563	.546	.529
6	.879	.867	.856	.844	.831	.818	.805	.791	.777	.762	.747	.732	.717	.702	.686
7	.943	.936	.929	.921	.913	.905	.896	.887	.877	.867	.856	.845	.833	.822	.809
8	.976	.972	.968	.964	.960	.955	.950	.944	.938	.932	.925	.918	.911	.903	.894
9	.990	.989	.987	.985	.983	.980	.978	.975	.972	.968	.964	.960	.956	.951	.946
10	.997	.996	.995	.994	.993	.992	.991	.990	.988	.986	.984	.982	.980	.977	.975
11	.999	.999	.998	.998	.998	.997	.997	.996	.995	.995	.994	.993	.992	.990	.989
12	1	1	.999	.999	.999	.999	.999	.999	.998	.998	.998	.997	.997	.996	.996
13	1	1		1	1	1	1	1	.999	.999	.999	.999	.999	.999	.998
14									1	1	1	1	1	1	.999
15															1

x	m 5.6	5.7	5.8	5.9	6.0	6.1	6.2	6.3	6.4	6.5	6.6	6.7	6.8	6.9	7.0	x
0	.004	.003	.003	.003	.002	.002	.002	.002	.002	.002	.001	.001	.001	.001	.001	0
1	.024	.022	.021	.019	.017	.016	.015	.013	.012	.011	.010	.009	.009	.008	.007	1
2	.082	.077	.072	.067	.062	.058	.054	.050	.046	.043	.040	.037	.034	.032	.030	2
3	.191	.180	.170	.160	.151	.143	.134	.126	.119	.112	.105	.099	.093	.087	.082	3
4	.342	.327	.313	.299	.285	.272	.259	.247	.235	.224	.213	.202	.192	.182	.173	4
5	.512	.495	.478	.462	.446	.430	.414	.399	.384	.369	.355	.341	.327	.314	.301	5
6	.670	.654	.638	.622	.606	.590	.574	.558	.542	.527	.511	.495	.480	.465	.450	6
7	.797	.784	.771	.758	.744	.730	.716	.702	.687	.673	.658	.643	.628	.614	.599	7
8	.886	.877	.867	.857	.847	.837	.826	.815	.803	.792	.780	.767	.755	.742	.729	8
9	.941	.935	.929	.923	.916	.909	.902	.894	.886	.877	.869	.860	.850	.840	.830	9
10	.972	.969	.965	.961	.957	.953	.949	.944	.939	.933	.927	.921	.915	.908	.901	10
11	.988	.986	.984	.982	.980	.978	.975	.972	.969	.966	.963	.959	.955	.951	.947	11
12	.995	.994	.993	.992	.991	.990	.989	.987	.986	.984	.982	.980	.978	.976	.973	12
13	.998	.998	.997	.997	.996	.996	.995	.995	.994	.993	.992	.991	.990	.989	.987	13
14	.999	.999	.999	.999	.999	.998	.998	.998	.997	.997	.997	.996	.996	.995	.994	14
15	1	1	1	1	.999	.999	.999	.999	.999	.999	.999	.998	.998	.998	.998	15
16	1	1	1	1	1	1	1	1	1	1	.999	.999	.999	.999	.999	16
17	1	1	1	1	1	1	1	1	1	1	1	1	1	1	1	17

x	m 7.1	7.2	7.3	7.4	7.5	8.0	8.5	9.0	9.5	10.0	11.0	12.0	13.0	14.0	15.0
0	.001	.001	.001	.001	.001	.000	.000	.000	.000	.000	.000	.000	.000	.000	.000
1	.007	.006	.006	.005	.005	.003	.002	.001	.001	.000	.000	.000	.000	.000	.000
2	.027	.025	.024	.022	.020	.014	.009	.006	.004	.003	.001	.001	.000	.000	.000
3	.077	.072	.067	.063	.059	.042	.030	.021	.015	.010	.005	.002	.001	.000	.000
4	.164	.156	.147	.140	.132	.100	.074	.055	.040	.029	.015	.008	.004	.002	.001
5	.288	.276	.264	.253	.241	.191	.150	.116	.089	.067	.038	.020	.011	.006	.003
6	.435	.420	.406	.392	.378	.313	.256	.207	.165	.130	.079	.046	.026	.014	.008
7	.584	.569	.554	.539	.525	.453	.386	.324	.269	.220	.143	.090	.054	.032	.018
8	.716	.703	.689	.676	.662	.593	.523	.456	.392	.333	.232	.155	.100	.062	.037
9	.820	.810	.799	.788	.776	.717	.653	.587	.522	.458	.341	.242	.166	.109	.070
10	.894	.887	.879	.871	.862	.816	.763	.706	.645	.583	.460	.347	.252	.176	.118
11	.942	.937	.932	.926	.921	.888	.849	.803	.752	.697	.579	.462	.353	.260	.185
12	.970	.967	.964	.961	.957	.936	.909	.876	.836	.792	.689	.576	.463	.358	.268
13	.986	.984	.982	.980	.978	.966	.949	.926	.898	.864	.781	.682	.573	.464	.363
14	.994	.993	.992	.991	.990	.983	.973	.959	.940	.917	.854	.772	.675	.570	.466
15	.997	.997	.996	.996	.995	.992	.986	.978	.967	.951	.907	.844	.764	.669	.568
16	.999	.999	.999	.998	.998	.996	.993	.989	.982	.973	.944	.899	.835	.756	.664
17	1	1	.999	.999	.999	.998	.997	.995	.991	.986	.968	.937	.890	.827	.749
18	—	—	1	1	1	.999	.999	.998	.996	.993	.982	.963	.930	.883	.819
19	—	—	—	—	—	1	.999	.999	.998	.997	.991	.979	.957	.923	.875
20	—	—	—	—	—	—	1	1	.999	.998	.995	.988	.975	.952	.917
21	—	—	—	—	—	—	—	—	1	.999	.998	.994	.986	.971	.947
22	—	—	—	—	—	—	—	—	—	1	.999	.997	.992	.983	.967
23	—	—	—	—	—	—	—	—	—	—	1	.999	.996	.991	.981
24	—	—	—	—	—	—	—	—	—	—	—	.999	.998	.995	.989
25	—	—	—	—	—	—	—	—	—	—	—	1	.999	.997	.994
26	—	—	—	—	—	—	—	—	—	—	—	—	1	.999	.997
27	—	—	—	—	—	—	—	—	—	—	—	—	1	.999	.998
28	—	—	—	—	—	—	—	—	—	—	—	—	1	1	.999
29	—	—	—	—	—	—	—	—	—	—	—	—	1	1	1

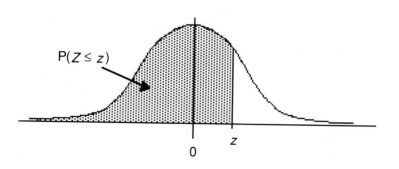

$P(Z \leq z)$

z	$P(Z \leq z)$
....	....
1.20	.8849
1.21	.8869
1.22	.8888
1.23	.8907
1.24	.8925
1.25	.8944
1.26	.8962
1.27	.8980
1.28	.8997
1.29	.9015
....	....

Figure A.5 *Using Appendix E to find $P_N(Z \leq 1.25)$*

z	$P(Z \le z)$	z	$P(Z \le z)$	z	$P(Z \le z)$	z	$P(Z \le z)$	z	$P(Z \le z)$
-3.49	.0002	-2.99	.0014	-2.49	.0064	-1.99	.0233	-1.49	.0681
-3.48	.0003	-2.98	.0014	-2.48	.0066	-1.98	.0239	-1.48	.0694
-3.47	.0003	-2.97	.0015	-2.47	.0068	-1.97	.0244	-1.47	.0708
-3.46	.0003	-2.96	.0015	-2.46	.0069	-1.96	.0250	-1.46	.0721
-3.45	.0003	-2.95	.0016	-2.45	.0071	-1.95	.0256	-1.45	.0735
-3.44	.0003	-2.94	.0016	-2.44	.0073	-1.94	.0262	-1.44	.0749
-3.43	.0003	-2.93	.0017	-2.43	.0075	-1.93	.0268	-1.43	.0764
-3.42	.0003	-2.92	.0018	-2.42	.0078	-1.92	.0274	-1.42	.0778
-3.41	.0003	-2.91	.0018	-2.41	.0080	-1.91	.0281	-1.41	.0793
-3.40	.0003	-2.90	.0019	-2.40	.0082	-1.90	.0287	-1.40	.0808
-3.39	.0003	-2.89	.0019	-2.39	.0084	-1.89	.0294	-1.39	.0823
-3.38	.0004	-2.88	.0020	-2.38	.0087	-1.88	.0301	-1.38	.0838
-3.37	.0004	-2.87	.0021	-2.37	.0089	-1.87	.0307	-1.37	.0853
-3.36	.0004	-2.86	.0021	-2.36	.0091	-1.86	.0314	-1.36	.0869
-3.35	.0004	-2.85	.0022	-2.35	.0094	-1.85	.0322	-1.35	.0885
-3.34	.0004	-2.84	.0023	-2.34	.0096	-1.84	.0329	-1.34	.0901
-3.33	.0004	-2.83	.0023	-2.33	.0099	-1.83	.0336	-1.33	.0918
-3.32	.0005	-2.82	.0024	-2.32	.0102	-1.82	.0344	-1.32	.0934
-3.31	.0005	-2.81	.0025	-2.31	.0104	-1.81	.0351	-1.31	.0951
-3.30	.0005	-2.80	.0026	-2.30	.0107	-1.80	.0359	-1.30	.0968
-3.29	.0005	-2.79	.0026	-2.29	.0110	-1.79	.0367	-1.29	.0985
-3.28	.0005	-2.78	.0027	-2.28	.0113	-1.78	.0375	-1.28	.1003
-3.27	.0005	-2.77	.0028	-2.27	.0116	-1.77	.0384	-1.27	.1020
-3.26	.0006	-2.76	.0029	-2.26	.0119	-1.76	.0392	-1.26	.1038
-3.25	.0006	-2.75	.0030	-2.25	.0122	-1.75	.0401	-1.25	.1056
-3.24	.0006	-2.74	.0031	-2.24	.0125	-1.74	.0409	-1.24	.1075
-3.23	.0006	-2.73	.0032	-2.23	.0129	-1.73	.0418	-1.23	.1093
-3.22	.0006	-2.72	.0033	-2.22	.0132	-1.72	.0427	-1.22	.1112
-3.21	.0007	-2.71	.0034	-2.21	.0136	-1.71	.0436	-1.21	.1131
-3.20	.0007	-2.70	.0035	-2.20	.0139	-1.70	.0446	-1.20	.1151
-3.19	.0007	-2.69	.0036	-2.19	.0143	-1.69	.0455	-1.19	.1170
-3.18	.0007	-2.68	.0037	-2.18	.0146	-1.68	.0465	-1.18	.1190
-3.17	.0008	-2.67	.0038	-2.17	.0150	-1.67	.0475	-1.17	.1210
-3.16	.0008	-2.66	.0039	-2.16	.0154	-1.66	.0485	-1.16	.1230
-3.15	.0008	-2.65	.0040	-2.15	.0158	-1.65	.0495	-1.15	.1251
-3.14	.0008	-2.64	.0041	-2.14	.0162	-1.64	.0505	-1.14	.1271
-3.13	.0009	-2.63	.0043	-2.13	.0166	-1.63	.0516	-1.13	.1292
-3.12	.0009	-2.62	.0044	-2.12	.0170	-1.62	.0526	-1.12	.1314
-3.11	.0009	-2.61	.0045	-2.11	.0174	-1.61	.0537	-1.11	.1335
-3.10	.0010	-2.60	.0047	-2.10	.0179	-1.60	.0548	-1.10	.1357
-3.09	.0010	-2.59	.0048	-2.09	.0183	-1.59	.0559	-1.09	.1379
-3.08	.0010	-2.58	.0049	-2.08	.0188	-1.58	.0571	-1.08	.1401
-3.07	.0011	-2.57	.0051	-2.07	.0192	-1.57	.0582	-1.07	.1423
-3.06	.0011	-2.56	.0052	-2.06	.0197	-1.56	.0594	-1.06	.1446
-3.05	.0011	-2.55	.0054	-2.05	.0202	-1.55	.0606	-1.05	.1469
-3.04	.0012	-2.54	.0055	-2.04	.0207	-1.54	.0618	-1.04	.1492
-3.03	.0012	-2.53	.0057	-2.03	.0212	-1.53	.0630	-1.03	.1515
-3.02	.0013	-2.52	.0059	-2.02	.0217	-1.52	.0643	-1.02	.1539
-3.01	.0013	-2.51	.0060	-2.01	.0222	-1.51	.0655	-1.01	.1562
-3.00	.0013	-2.50	.0062	-2.00	.0228	-1.50	.0668	-1.00	.1587

z	P(Z≤z)	z	P(Z≤z)	z	P(Z≤z)	z	P(Z≤z)	z	P(Z≤z)
-0.99	.1611	-0.49	.3121	0.01	.5040	0.51	.6950	1.01	.8438
-0.98	.1635	-0.48	.3156	0.02	.5080	0.52	.6985	1.02	.8461
-0.97	.1660	-0.47	.3192	0.03	.5120	0.53	.7019	1.03	.8485
-0.96	.1685	-0.46	.3228	0.04	.5160	0.54	.7054	1.04	.8508
-0.95	.1711	-0.45	.3264	0.05	.5199	0.55	.7088	1.05	.8531
-0.94	.1736	-0.44	.3300	0.06	.5239	0.56	.7123	1.06	.8554
-0.93	.1762	-0.43	.3336	0.07	.5279	0.57	.7157	1.07	.8577
-0.92	.1788	-0.42	.3372	0.08	.5319	0.58	.7190	1.08	.8599
-0.91	.1814	-0.41	.3409	0.09	.5359	0.59	.7224	1.09	.8621
-0.90	.1841	-0.40	.3446	0.10	.5398	0.60	.7257	1.10	.8643
-0.89	.1867	-0.39	.3483	0.11	.5438	0.61	.7291	1.11	.8665
-0.88	.1894	-0.38	.3520	0.12	.5478	0.62	.7324	1.12	.8686
-0.87	.1922	-0.37	.3557	0.13	.5517	0.63	.7357	1.13	.8708
-0.86	.1949	-0.36	.3594	0.14	.5557	0.64	.7389	1.14	.8729
-0.85	.1977	-0.35	.3632	0.15	.5596	0.65	.7422	1.15	.8749
-0.84	.2005	-0.34	.3669	0.16	.5636	0.66	.7454	1.16	.8770
-0.83	.2033	-0.33	.3707	0.17	.5675	0.67	.7486	1.17	.8790
-0.82	.2061	-0.32	.3745	0.18	.5714	0.68	.7517	1.18	.8810
-0.81	.2090	-0.31	.3783	0.19	.5753	0.69	.7549	1.19	.8830
-0.80	.2119	-0.30	.3821	0.20	.5793	0.70	.7580	1.20	.8849
-0.79	.2148	-0.29	.3859	0.21	.5832	0.71	.7611	1.21	.8869
-0.78	.2177	-0.28	.3897	0.22	.5871	0.72	.7642	1.22	.8888
-0.77	.2206	-0.27	.3936	0.23	.5910	0.73	.7673	1.23	.8907
-0.76	.2236	-0.26	.3974	0.24	.5948	0.74	.7704	1.24	.8925
-0.75	.2266	-0.25	.4013	0.25	.5987	0.75	.7734	1.25	.8944
-0.74	.2296	-0.24	.4052	0.26	.6026	0.76	.7764	1.26	.8962
-0.73	.2327	-0.23	.4090	0.27	.6064	0.77	.7794	1.27	.8980
-0.72	.2358	-0.22	.4129	0.28	.6103	0.78	.7823	1.28	.8997
-0.71	.2389	-0.21	.4168	0.29	.6141	0.79	.7852	1.29	.9015
-0.70	.2420	-0.20	.4207	0.30	.6179	0.80	.7881	1.30	.9032
-0.69	.2451	-0.19	.4247	0.31	.6217	0.81	.7910	1.31	.9049
-0.68	.2483	-0.18	.4286	0.32	.6255	0.82	.7939	1.32	.9066
-0.67	.2514	-0.17	.4325	0.33	.6293	0.83	.7967	1.33	.9082
-0.66	.2546	-0.16	.4364	0.34	.6331	0.84	.7995	1.34	.9099
-0.65	.2578	-0.15	.4404	0.35	.6368	0.85	.8023	1.35	.9115
-0.64	.2611	-0.14	.4443	0.36	.6406	0.86	.8051	1.36	.9131
-0.63	.2643	-0.13	.4483	0.37	.6443	0.87	.8078	1.37	.9147
-0.62	.2676	-0.12	.4522	0.38	.6480	0.88	.8106	1.38	.9162
-0.61	.2709	-0.11	.4562	0.39	.6517	0.89	.8133	1.39	.9177
-0.60	.2743	-0.10	.4602	0.40	.6554	0.90	.8159	1.40	.9192
-0.59	.2776	-0.09	.4641	0.41	.6591	0.91	.8186	1.41	.9207
-0.58	.2810	-0.08	.4681	0.42	.6628	0.92	.8212	1.42	.9222
-0.57	.2843	-0.07	.4721	0.43	.6664	0.93	.8238	1.43	.9236
-0.56	.2877	-0.06	.4761	0.44	.6700	0.94	.8264	1.44	.9251
-0.55	.2912	-0.05	.4801	0.45	.6736	0.95	.8289	1.45	.9265
-0.54	.2946	-0.04	.4840	0.46	.6772	0.96	.8315	1.46	.9279
-0.53	.2981	-0.03	.4880	0.47	.6808	0.97	.8340	1.47	.9292
-0.52	.3015	-0.02	.4920	0.48	.6844	0.98	.8365	1.48	.9306
-0.51	.3050	-0.01	.4960	0.49	.6879	0.99	.8389	1.49	.9319
-0.50	.3085	0.00	.5000	0.50	.6915	1.00	.8413	1.50	.9332

z	$P(Z \leq z)$	z	$P(Z \leq z)$	z	$P(Z \leq z)$	z	$P(Z \leq z)$
1.51	.9345	2.01	.9778	2.51	.9940	3.01	.9987
1.52	.9357	2.02	.9783	2.52	.9941	3.02	.9987
1.53	.9370	2.03	.9788	2.53	.9943	3.03	.9988
1.54	.9382	2.04	.9793	2.54	.9945	3.04	.9988
1.55	.9394	2.05	.9798	2.55	.9946	3.05	.9989
1.56	.9406	2.06	.9803	2.56	.9948	3.06	.9989
1.57	.9418	2.07	.9808	2.57	.9949	3.07	.9989
1.58	.9429	2.08	.9812	2.58	.9951	3.08	.9990
1.59	.9441	2.09	.9817	2.59	.9952	3.09	.9990
1.60	.9452	2.10	.9821	2.60	.9953	3.10	.9990
1.61	.9463	2.11	.9826	2.61	.9955	3.11	.9991
1.62	.9474	2.12	.9830	2.62	.9956	3.12	.9991
1.63	.9484	2.13	.9834	2.63	.9957	3.13	.9991
1.64	.9495	2.14	.9838	2.64	.9959	3.14	.9992
1.65	.9505	2.15	.9842	2.65	.9960	3.15	.9992
1.66	.9515	2.16	.9846	2.66	.9961	3.16	.9992
1.67	.9525	2.17	.9850	2.67	.9962	3.17	.9992
1.68	.9535	2.18	.9854	2.68	.9963	3.18	.9993
1.69	.9545	2.19	.9857	2.69	.9964	3.19	.9993
1.70	.9554	2.20	.9861	2.70	.9965	3.20	.9993
1.71	.9564	2.21	.9864	2.71	.9966	3.21	.9993
1.72	.9573	2.22	.9868	2.72	.9967	3.22	.9994
1.73	.9582	2.23	.9871	2.73	.9968	3.23	.9994
1.74	.9591	2.24	.9875	2.74	.9969	3.24	.9994
1.75	.9599	2.25	.9878	2.75	.9970	3.25	.9994
1.76	.9608	2.26	.9881	2.76	.9971	3.26	.9994
1.77	.9616	2.27	.9884	2.77	.9972	3.27	.9995
1.78	.9625	2.28	.9887	2.78	.9973	3.28	.9995
1.79	.9633	2.29	.9890	2.79	.9974	3.29	.9995
1.80	.9641	2.30	.9893	2.80	.9974	3.30	.9995
1.81	.9649	2.31	.9896	2.81	.9975	3.31	.9995
1.82	.9656	2.32	.9898	2.82	.9976	3.32	.9995
1.83	.9664	2.33	.9901	2.83	.9977	3.33	.9996
1.84	.9671	2.34	.9904	2.84	.9977	3.34	.9996
1.85	.9678	2.35	.9906	2.85	.9978	3.35	.9996
1.86	.9686	2.36	.9909	2.86	.9979	3.36	.9996
1.87	.9693	2.37	.9911	2.87	.9979	3.37	.9996
1.88	.9699	2.38	.9913	2.88	.9980	3.38	.9996
1.89	.9706	2.39	.9916	2.89	.9981	3.39	.9997
1.90	.9713	2.40	.9918	2.90	.9981	3.40	.9997
1.91	.9719	2.41	.9920	2.91	.9982	3.41	.9997
1.92	.9726	2.42	.9922	2.92	.9982	3.42	.9997
1.93	.9732	2.43	.9925	2.93	.9983	3.43	.9997
1.94	.9738	2.44	.9927	2.94	.9984	3.44	.9997
1.95	.9744	2.45	.9929	2.95	.9984	3.45	.9997
1.96	.9750	2.46	.9931	2.96	.9985	3.46	.9997
1.97	.9756	2.47	.9932	2.97	.9985	3.47	.9997
1.98	.9761	2.48	.9934	2.98	.9986	3.48	.9997
1.99	.9767	2.49	.9936	2.99	.9986	3.49	.9998
2.00	.9772	2.50	.9938	3.00	.9987	3.50	.9998

APPENDIX F. Beta Distribution: Cumulative Probabilities

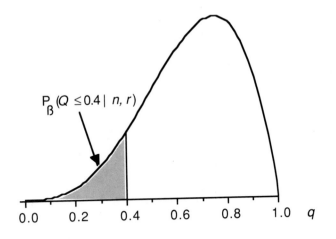

				Values for Q:		
n	r	....		0.16	0.18	0.20
				.	.	.
				.	.	.
20	2			.83	.88	.92
	4			.36	.45	.54
	6	....		.07	.11	.16
	8			.01	.01	.02
				.	.	.
				.	.	.

Figure A.6 *Using Appendix F to find* $P_\beta(Q \leq 0.18 \mid n = 20, r = 6) = 0.11$

n	r	.50	.48	.46	.44	.42	.40	.38	.36	.34	.32	.30	.28	.26	.25	.24	.22	.20	.18	.16	.14	.12	.10	.08	.06	.04	.02	0
2	1	.50	.48	.46	.44	.42	.40	.38	.36	.34	.32	.30	.28	.26	.25	.24	.22	.20	.18	.16	.14	.12	.10	.08	.06	.04	.02	0
3	1	.75	.73	.71	.69	.66	.64	.61	.59	.56	.54	.51	.48	.45	.44	.42	.39	.36	.33	.29	.26	.22	.19	.15	.12	.08	.04	0
	2	.25	.23	.21	.19	.18	.16	.14	.13	.12	.10	.09	.08	.07	.06	.06	.05	.04	.03	.03	.02	.01	.01	.01	0	0	0	0
4	1	.87	.86	.84	.82	.80	.78	.76	.74	.71	.68	.66	.63	.59	.58	.56	.52	.49	.45	.41	.36	.32	.27	.22	.17	.11	.06	0
	2	.50	.47	.44	.41	.38	.35	.32	.30	.27	.24	.22	.19	.17	.16	.15	.12	.10	.09	.07	.05	.04	.03	.02	.01	0	0	0
	3	.13	.11	.10	.09	.07	.06	.05	.05	.04	.03	.03	.02	.02	.02	.01	.01	.01	.01	0	0	0	0	0	0	0	0	0
5	1	.94	.93	.91	.90	.89	.87	.85	.83	.81	.78	.76	.73	.70	.68	.67	.63	.59	.55	.50	.45	.40	.34	.28	.22	.15	.08	0
	2	.69	.66	.63	.59	.56	.52	.49	.45	.42	.38	.35	.31	.28	.26	.24	.21	.18	.15	.12	.10	.07	.05	.03	.02	.01	0	0
	3	.31	.28	.26	.23	.20	.18	.16	.14	.12	.10	.08	.07	.06	.05	.05	.04	.03	.02	.01	.01	.01	0	0	0	0	0	0
	4	.06	.05	.04	.04	.03	.03	.02	.02	.01	.01	.01	.01	0	0	0	0	0	0	0	0	0	0	0	0	0	0	0
6	1	.97	.96	.95	.94	.93	.92	.91	.89	.87	.85	.83	.80	.78	.76	.74	.71	.67	.63	.58	.53	.47	.41	.34	.26	.18	.09	0
	2	.81	.79	.76	.73	.70	.66	.63	.59	.55	.51	.47	.43	.39	.37	.35	.30	.26	.22	.18	.15	.11	.08	.05	.03	.01	0	0
	3	.50	.46	.43	.39	.35	.32	.28	.25	.22	.19	.16	.14	.11	.10	.09	.07	.06	.04	.03	.02	.01	.01	0	0	0	0	0
	4	.19	.16	.14	.12	.10	.09	.07	.06	.05	.04	.03	.02	.02	.02	.01	.01	.01	0	0	0	0	0	0	0	0	0	0
	5	.03	.03	.02	.02	.01	.01	.01	.01	0	0	0	0	0	0	0	0	0	0	0	0	0	0	0	0	0	0	0
7	1	.98	.98	.97	.97	.96	.95	.94	.93	.92	.90	.88	.86	.83	.82	.81	.77	.74	.69	.65	.59	.53	.47	.39	.31	.22	.11	0
	2	.89	.87	.85	.82	.80	.77	.73	.70	.66	.62	.58	.54	.49	.47	.44	.39	.34	.30	.25	.20	.16	.11	.08	.05	.02	.01	0
	3	.66	.62	.58	.54	.50	.46	.41	.37	.33	.29	.26	.22	.19	.17	.15	.12	.10	.08	.06	.04	.03	.02	.01	0	0	0	0
	4	.34	.31	.27	.24	.21	.18	.15	.13	.11	.09	.07	.06	.04	.04	.03	.02	.02	.01	.01	.01	0	0	0	0	0	0	0
	5	.11	.09	.08	.06	.05	.04	.03	.03	.02	.01	.01	.01	.01	.01	0	0	0	0	0	0	0	0	0	0	0	0	0
	6	.02	.01	.01	.01	.01	0	0	0	0	0	0	0	0	0	0	0	0	0	0	0	0	0	0	0	0	0	0
8	1	.99	.99	.98	.98	.98	.97	.96	.95	.94	.93	.92	.90	.88	.86	.85	.82	.79	.75	.70	.65	.59	.52	.44	.35	.25	.13	0
	2	.94	.92	.91	.89	.87	.84	.81	.78	.75	.71	.67	.63	.58	.56	.53	.48	.42	.37	.31	.26	.20	.15	.10	.06	.03	.01	0
	3	.77	.74	.70	.66	.62	.58	.54	.49	.44	.40	.35	.31	.26	.24	.22	.18	.15	.12	.09	.06	.04	.03	.01	.01	0	0	0
	4	.50	.46	.41	.37	.33	.29	.25	.22	.18	.15	.13	.10	.08	.07	.06	.05	.03	.02	.02	.01	.01	0	0	0	0	0	0
	5	.23	.20	.17	.14	.12	.10	.08	.06	.05	.04	.03	.02	.02	.01	.01	.01	0	0	0	0	0	0	0	0	0	0	0
	6	.06	.05	.04	.03	.02	.02	.01	.01	.01	.01	0	0	0	0	0	0	0	0	0	0	0	0	0	0	0	0	0
	7	.01	.01	0	0	0	0	0	0	0	0	0	0	0	0	0	0	0	0	0	0	0	0	0	0	0	0	0

n	r	.52	.54	.56	.58	.60	.62	.64	.66	.68	.70	.72	.74	.75	.76	.78	.80	.82	.84	.86	.88	.90	.92	.94	.96	.98	1.0
2	1	.52	.54	.56	.58	.60	.62	.64	.66	.68	.70	.72	.74	.75	.76	.78	.80	.82	.84	.86	.88	.90	.92	.94	.96	.98	1
3	1	.77	.79	.81	.82	.84	.85	.87	.88	.90	.91	.92	.93	.94	.94	.95	.96	.97	.97	.98	.98	.99	.99	1	1	1	1
	2	.27	.29	.31	.34	.36	.38	.41	.44	.46	.49	.52	.55	.56	.58	.61	.64	.67	.71	.74	.77	.81	.85	.88	.92	.96	1
4	1	.89	.90	.91	.92	.94	.94	.95	.96	.97	.97	.98	.98	.98	.99	.99	.99	.99	1	1	1	1	1	1	1	1	1
	2	.53	.56	.59	.62	.65	.68	.70	.73	.76	.78	.81	.83	.84	.85	.88	.90	.91	.93	.95	.96	.97	.98	.99	1	1	1
	3	.14	.16	.18	.20	.22	.24	.26	.29	.31	.34	.37	.41	.42	.44	.47	.51	.55	.59	.64	.68	.73	.78	.83	.88	.94	1
5	1	.95	.95	.96	.97	.97	.98	.98	.99	.99	.99	.99	.99	.99	1	1	1	1	1	1	1	1	1	1	1	1	1
	2	.72	.74	.77	.80	.82	.84	.86	.88	.90	.92	.93	.94	.95	.95	.96	.97	.98	.99	.99	.99	1	1	1	1	1	1
	3	.34	.37	.41	.44	.48	.51	.55	.58	.62	.65	.69	.72	.74	.76	.79	.82	.85	.88	.90	.93	.95	.97	.98	.99	1	1
	4	.07	.09	.10	.11	.13	.15	.17	.19	.21	.24	.27	.30	.32	.33	.37	.41	.45	.50	.55	.60	.66	.72	.78	.85	.92	1
6	1	.97	.98	.98	.99	.99	.99	.99	1	1	1	1	1	1	1	1	1	1	1	1	1	1	1	1	1	1	1
	2	.84	.86	.88	.90	.91	.93	.94	.95	.96	.97	.98	.98	.98	.99	.99	.99	1	1	1	1	1	1	1	1	1	1
	3	.54	.57	.61	.65	.68	.72	.75	.78	.81	.84	.86	.89	.90	.91	.93	.94	.96	.97	.98	.99	.99	1	1	1	1	1
	4	.21	.24	.27	.30	.34	.37	.41	.45	.49	.53	.57	.61	.63	.65	.70	.74	.78	.82	.85	.89	.92	.95	.97	.99	1	1
	5	.04	.05	.06	.07	.08	.09	.11	.13	.15	.17	.19	.22	.24	.25	.29	.33	.37	.42	.47	.53	.59	.66	.73	.82	.90	1
7	1	.99	.99	.99	.99	1	1	1	1	1	1	1	1	1	1	1	1	1	1	1	1	1	1	1	1	1	1
	2	.91	.92	.94	.95	.96	.97	.97	.98	.99	.99	.99	.99	1	1	1	1	1	1	1	1	1	1	1	1	1	1
	3	.69	.73	.76	.79	.82	.85	.87	.89	.91	.93	.94	.96	.96	.97	.98	.98	.99	.99	1	1	1	1	1	1	1	1
	4	.38	.42	.46	.50	.54	.59	.63	.67	.71	.74	.78	.81	.83	.85	.88	.90	.92	.94	.96	.97	.98	.99	1	1	1	1
	5	.13	.15	.18	.20	.23	.27	.30	.34	.38	.42	.46	.51	.53	.56	.61	.66	.70	.75	.80	.84	.89	.92	.95	.98	.99	1
	6	.02	.02	.03	.04	.05	.06	.07	.08	.10	.12	.14	.16	.18	.19	.23	.26	.30	.35	.40	.46	.53	.61	.69	.78	.89	1
8	1	.99	1	1	1	1	1	1	1	1	1	1	1	1	1	1	1	1	1	1	1	1	1	1	1	1	1
	2	.95	.96	.97	.98	.98	.99	.99	.99	.99	1	1	1	1	1	1	1	1	1	1	1	1	1	1	1	1	1
	3	.80	.83	.86	.88	.90	.92	.94	.95	.96	.97	.98	.98	.99	.99	.99	1	1	1	1	1	1	1	1	1	1	1
	4	.54	.59	.63	.67	.71	.75	.78	.82	.85	.87	.90	.92	.93	.94	.95	.97	.98	.98	.99	.99	1	1	1	1	1	1
	5	.26	.30	.34	.38	.42	.46	.51	.56	.60	.65	.69	.74	.76	.78	.82	.85	.88	.91	.94	.96	.97	.99	.99	1	1	1
	6	.08	.09	.11	.13	.16	.19	.22	.25	.29	.33	.37	.42	.44	.47	.52	.58	.63	.69	.74	.80	.85	.90	.94	.97	.99	1
	7	.01	.01	.02	.02	.03	.04	.04	.05	.07	.08	.10	.12	.13	.15	.18	.21	.25	.30	.35	.41	.48	.56	.65	.75	.87	1

n	r	.50	.48	.46	.44	.42	.40	.38	.36	.34	.32	.30	.28	.26	.25	.24	.22	.20	.18	.16	.14	.12	.10	.08	.06	.04	.02	0
9	1	.99	.99	.99	.99	.98	.98	.98	.97	.96	.95	.94	.93	.91	.90	.89	.86	.83	.79	.75	.70	.64	.57	.48	.39	.28	.15	0
	2	.96	.96	.94	.93	.91	.89	.87	.85	.82	.78	.74	.70	.66	.63	.61	.55	.50	.44	.37	.31	.25	.19	.13	.08	.04	.01	0
	3	.86	.83	.80	.76	.72	.68	.64	.60	.55	.50	.45	.40	.35	.32	.30	.25	.20	.16	.12	.09	.06	.04	.02	.01	0	0	0
	4	.64	.59	.55	.50	.45	.41	.36	.32	.27	.23	.19	.16	.13	.11	.10	.08	.06	.04	.03	.02	.01	.01	0	0	0	0	0
	5	.36	.32	.28	.24	.21	.17	.14	.12	.09	.07	.06	.04	.03	.03	.02	.02	.01	.01	0	0	0	0	0	0	0	0	0
	6	.14	.12	.10	.08	.06	.05	.04	.03	.02	.02	.01	.01	.01	0	0	0	0	0	0	0	0	0	0	0	0	0	0
	7	.04	.03	.02	.02	.01	.01	.01	0	0	0	0	0	0	0	0	0	0	0	0	0	0	0	0	0	0	0	0
	8	0	0	0	0	0	0	0	0	0	0	0	0	0	0	0	0	0	0	0	0	0	0	0	0	0	0	0
10	1	1	.99	.99	.99	.99	.99	.98	.98	.97	.97	.96	.95	.93	.92	.91	.89	.86	.83	.79	.74	.68	.61	.52	.42	.30	.16	0
	2	.98	.97	.97	.96	.94	.93	.91	.89	.87	.84	.80	.77	.72	.70	.67	.62	.56	.50	.43	.37	.30	.23	.16	.10	.05	.01	0
	3	.91	.89	.86	.84	.80	.77	.73	.69	.64	.59	.54	.48	.43	.40	.37	.32	.26	.21	.16	.12	.08	.05	.03	.01	0	0	0
	4	.75	.71	.66	.62	.57	.52	.47	.42	.37	.32	.27	.23	.18	.17	.15	.11	.09	.06	.04	.03	.02	.01	0	0	0	0	0
	5	.50	.45	.40	.36	.31	.27	.23	.19	.16	.13	.10	.08	.06	.05	.04	.03	.02	.01	.01	0	0	0	0	0	0	0	0
	6	.25	.22	.18	.15	.12	.10	.08	.06	.05	.03	.03	.02	.01	.01	.01	.01	0	0	0	0	0	0	0	0	0	0	0
	7	.09	.07	.06	.04	.03	.03	.02	.01	.01	.01	0	0	0	0	0	0	0	0	0	0	0	0	0	0	0	0	0
	8	.02	.01	.01	.01	.01	0	0	0	0	0	0	0	0	0	0	0	0	0	0	0	0	0	0	0	0	0	0
	9	0	0	0	0	0	0	0	0	0	0	0	0	0	0	0	0	0	0	0	0	0	0	0	0	0	0	0
12	2	.99	.99	.99	.98	.98	.97	.96	.95	.93	.91	.89	.86	.82	.80	.78	.73	.68	.62	.55	.47	.39	.30	.22	.14	.07	.02	0
	4	.89	.86	.83	.79	.75	.70	.65	.60	.55	.49	.43	.37	.31	.29	.26	.21	.16	.12	.08	.06	.03	.02	.01	0	0	0	0
	6	.50	.45	.39	.34	.29	.25	.20	.17	.13	.10	.08	.06	.04	.03	.03	.02	.01	.01	0	0	0	0	0	0	0	0	0
	8	.11	.09	.07	.05	.04	.03	.02	.01	.01	.01	0	0	0	0	0	0	0	0	0	0	0	0	0	0	0	0	0
	10	.01	.01	.01	.01	.01	0	0	0	0	0	0	0	0	0	0	0	0	0	0	0	0	0	0	0	0	0	0
14	2	1	1	1	.99	.99	.99	.98	.97	.97	.95	.94	.92	.89	.87	.86	.82	.77	.71	.64	.56	.47	.38	.28	.18	.09	.03	0
	4	.95	.94	.92	.89	.87	.83	.79	.75	.70	.64	.58	.52	.45	.42	.38	.32	.25	.19	.14	.10	.06	.03	.02	.01	0	0	0
	6	.71	.66	.60	.54	.48	.43	.37	.31	.26	.21	.17	.13	.09	.08	.07	.05	.03	.02	.01	.01	0	0	0	0	0	0	0
	8	.29	.24	.20	.16	.13	.10	.07	.05	.04	.03	.02	.01	.01	.01	0	0	0	0	0	0	0	0	0	0	0	0	0
	10	.05	.03	.02	.02	.01	.01	.01	0	0	0	0	0	0	0	0	0	0	0	0	0	0	0	0	0	0	0	0
	12	0	0	0	0	0	0	0	0	0	0	0	0	0	0	0	0	0	0	0	0	0	0	0	0	0	0	0

Cumulative probabilities of the beta distribution (entries give the cumulative probability; values shown as "1" denote 1.00). Column heads are values of q; rows are indexed by n and r.

n	r	.52	.54	.56	.58	.60	.62	.64	.66	.68	.70	.72	.74	.75	.76	.78	.80	.82	.84	.86	.88	.90	.92	.94	.96	.98	1.0
9	1	.99	1	1	1	1	1	1	1	1	1	1	1	1	1	1	1	1	1	1	1	1	1	1	1	1	1
9	2	.97	.98	.98	.99	.99	.99	1	1	1	1	1	1	1	1	1	1	1	1	1	1	1	1	1	1	1	1
9	3	.88	.90	.92	.94	.95	.96	.97	.98	.98	.99	.99	.99	1	1	1	1	1	1	1	1	1	1	1	1	1	1
9	4	.68	.72	.76	.79	.83	.86	.88	.91	.93	.94	.96	.97	.97	.98	.98	.99	.99	1	1	1	1	1	1	1	1	1
9	5	.41	.45	.50	.55	.59	.64	.68	.73	.77	.81	.84	.87	.89	.90	.92	.94	.96	.97	.98	.99	.99	1	1	1	1	1
9	6	.17	.20	.24	.28	.32	.36	.40	.45	.50	.55	.60	.65	.68	.70	.75	.80	.84	.88	.91	.94	.96	.98	.99	1	1	1
9	7	.04	.06	.07	.09	.11	.13	.15	.18	.22	.26	.30	.34	.37	.39	.45	.50	.56	.63	.69	.75	.81	.87	.92	.96	.99	1
9	8	.01	.01	.01	.01	.02	.02	.03	.04	.05	.06	.07	.09	.10	.11	.14	.17	.20	.25	.30	.36	.43	.51	.61	.72	.85	1
10	1	1	1	1	1	1	1	1	1	1	1	1	1	1	1	1	1	1	1	1	1	1	1	1	1	1	1
10	2	.99	.99	.99	.99	1	1	1	1	1	1	1	1	1	1	1	1	1	1	1	1	1	1	1	1	1	1
10	3	.93	.94	.96	.97	.97	.98	.99	.99	.99	1	1	1	1	1	1	1	1	1	1	1	1	1	1	1	1	1
10	4	.78	.82	.85	.88	.90	.92	.94	.95	.97	.97	.98	.99	.99	.99	.99	1	1	1	1	1	1	1	1	1	1	1
10	5	.55	.60	.64	.69	.73	.77	.81	.84	.87	.90	.92	.94	.95	.96	.97	.98	.99	.99	1	1	1	1	1	1	1	1
10	6	.29	.34	.38	.43	.48	.53	.58	.63	.68	.73	.77	.82	.83	.85	.89	.91	.94	.96	.97	.98	.99	1	1	1	1	1
10	7	.11	.14	.16	.20	.23	.27	.31	.36	.41	.46	.52	.57	.60	.63	.68	.74	.79	.84	.88	.92	.95	.97	.99	1	1	1
10	8	.03	.04	.04	.06	.07	.09	.11	.13	.16	.20	.23	.28	.30	.33	.38	.44	.50	.57	.63	.70	.77	.84	.90	.95	.99	1
10	9	.01	.01	.01	.01	.01	.01	.02	.02	.03	.04	.05	.07	.08	.08	.11	.13	.17	.21	.26	.32	.39	.47	.57	.69	.83	1
12	2	1	1	1	1	1	1	1	1	1	1	1	1	1	1	1	1	1	1	1	1	1	1	1	1	1	1
12	4	.91	.93	.95	.96	.97	.98	.99	.99	.99	1	1	1	1	1	1	1	1	1	1	1	1	1	1	1	1	1
12	6	.55	.61	.66	.71	.75	.80	.83	.87	.90	.92	.94	.96	.97	.97	.98	.99	.99	1	1	1	1	1	1	1	1	1
12	8	.14	.17	.21	.25	.30	.35	.40	.45	.51	.57	.63	.69	.71	.74	.79	.84	.88	.92	.94	.97	.98	.99	.99	1	1	1
12	10	.01	.01	.02	.02	.03	.04	.05	.07	.09	.11	.14	.18	.20	.22	.27	.32	.38	.45	.53	.61	.70	.78	.86	.92	.97	1
14	2	1	1	1	1	1	1	1	1	1	1	1	1	1	1	1	1	1	1	1	1	1	1	1	1	1	1
14	4	.97	.98	.98	.99	.99	.99	1	1	1	1	1	1	1	1	1	1	1	1	1	1	1	1	1	1	1	1
14	6	.76	.80	.84	.87	.90	.93	.95	.96	.97	.98	.99	.99	.99	1	1	1	1	1	1	1	1	1	1	1	1	1
14	8	.34	.40	.46	.52	.57	.63	.69	.74	.79	.83	.87	.91	.92	.93	.95	.97	.98	.99	.99	1	1	1	1	1	1	1
14	10	.06	.08	.11	.13	.17	.21	.25	.30	.36	.42	.48	.55	.58	.62	.68	.75	.81	.86	.90	.94	.97	.98	.99	1	1	1
14	12	.01	.01	.01	.01	.01	.02	.03	.03	.05	.06	.08	.11	.13	.14	.18	.23	.29	.36	.44	.53	.62	.72	.82	.91	.97	1

n = 16

q	r=2	r=4	r=6	r=8	r=10	r=12	r=14
.50	1	.98	.85	.50	.15	.02	0
.48	1	.97	.81	.44	.12	.01	0
.46	1	.96	.76	.38	.09	.01	0
.44	1	.95	.71	.32	.07	.01	0
.42	1	.93	.66	.26	.05	0	0
.40	.99	.91	.60	.21	.03	0	0
.38	.99	.88	.53	.17	.02	0	0
.36	.99	.85	.47	.13	.02	0	0
.34	.98	.81	.40	.10	.01	0	0
.32	.98	.76	.34	.07	.01	0	0
.30	.96	.70	.28	.05	0	0	0
.28	.95	.64	.22	.03	0	0	0
.26	.93	.57	.17	.02	0	0	0
.25	.92	.54	.15	.02	0	0	0
.24	.91	.50	.13	.01	0	0	0
.22	.87	.43	.09	.01	0	0	0
.20	.83	.35	.06	0	0	0	0
.18	.78	.28	.04	0	0	0	0
.16	.72	.21	.02	0	0	0	0
.14	.64	.15	.01	0	0	0	0
.12	.55	.10	.01	0	0	0	0
.10	.45	.06	0	0	0	0	0
.08	.34	.03	0	0	0	0	0
.06	.23	.01	0	0	0	0	0
.04	.12	0	0	0	0	0	0
.02	.04	0	0	0	0	0	0
0	0	0	0	0	0	0	0

n = 18

q	r=2	r=4	r=6	r=8	r=10	r=12	r=14	r=16
.50	1	.99	.93	.69	.31	.07	.01	0
.48	1	.99	.90	.62	.26	.05	0	0
.46	1	.98	.87	.56	.21	.04	0	0
.44	1	.98	.83	.49	.16	.02	0	0
.42	1	.97	.79	.43	.12	.02	0	0
.40	1	.95	.74	.36	.09	.01	0	0
.38	1	.94	.68	.30	.07	.01	0	0
.36	.99	.91	.61	.24	.05	0	0	0
.34	.99	.88	.55	.19	.03	0	0	0
.32	.99	.84	.47	.14	.02	0	0	0
.30	.98	.80	.40	.10	.01	0	0	0
.28	.97	.74	.33	.07	.01	0	0	0
.26	.96	.68	.27	.05	0	0	0	0
.25	.95	.65	.23	.04	0	0	0	0
.24	.94	.61	.20	.03	0	0	0	0
.22	.92	.53	.15	.02	0	0	0	0
.20	.88	.45	.11	.01	0	0	0	0
.18	.84	.37	.07	.01	0	0	0	0
.16	.78	.28	.04	0	0	0	0	0
.14	.71	.21	.02	0	0	0	0	0
.12	.62	.14	.01	0	0	0	0	0
.10	.52	.08	0	0	0	0	0	0
.08	.40	.04	0	0	0	0	0	0
.06	.27	.02	0	0	0	0	0	0
.04	.15	0	0	0	0	0	0	0
.02	.04	0	0	0	0	0	0	0
0	0	0	0	0	0	0	0	0

n = 20

q	r=2	r=4	r=6	r=8	r=10	r=12	r=14	r=16	r=18
.50	1	1	.97	.82	.50	.18	.03	0	0
.48	1	1	.95	.77	.43	.14	.02	0	0
.46	1	.99	.93	.71	.36	.10	.01	0	0
.44	1	.99	.91	.65	.30	.07	.01	0	0
.42	1	.98	.88	.58	.24	.05	.01	0	0
.40	1	.98	.84	.51	.19	.04	0	0	0
.38	1	.97	.79	.44	.14	.02	0	0	0
.36	1	.95	.73	.37	.10	.01	0	0	0
.34	1	.93	.67	.30	.07	.01	0	0	0
.32	.99	.90	.60	.24	.05	.01	0	0	0
.30	.99	.87	.53	.18	.03	0	0	0	0
.28	.98	.82	.45	.13	.02	0	0	0	0
.26	.97	.77	.37	.09	.01	0	0	0	0
.25	.97	.74	.33	.08	.01	0	0	0	0
.24	.96	.70	.30	.06	.01	0	0	0	0
.22	.94	.63	.23	.04	0	0	0	0	0
.20	.92	.54	.16	.02	0	0	0	0	0
.18	.88	.45	.11	.01	0	0	0	0	0
.16	.83	.36	.07	.01	0	0	0	0	0
.14	.77	.27	.04	0	0	0	0	0	0
.12	.68	.19	.02	0	0	0	0	0	0
.10	.58	.11	.01	0	0	0	0	0	0
.08	.46	.06	0	0	0	0	0	0	0
.06	.32	.02	0	0	0	0	0	0	0
.04	.18	.01	0	0	0	0	0	0	0
.02	.05	0	0	0	0	0	0	0	0
0	0	0	0	0	0	0	0	0	0

n = 30

q	r=4	r=8	r=12	r=16	r=20	r=24	r=28
.50	1	1	.87	.36	.03	0	0
.48	1	.99	.82	.28	.02	0	0
.46	1	.99	.75	.21	.01	0	0
.44	1	.98	.68	.15	.01	0	0
.42	1	.96	.60	.11	0	0	0
.40	1	.94	.51	.07	0	0	0
.38	1	.91	.42	.05	0	0	0
.36	1	.87	.34	.03	0	0	0
.34	1	.82	.26	.02	0	0	0
.32	.99	.76	.19	.01	0	0	0
.30	.99	.68	.13	0	0	0	0
.28	.98	.59	.08	0	0	0	0
.26	.96	.49	.05	0	0	0	0
.25	.95	.44	.04	0	0	0	0
.24	.94	.39	.03	0	0	0	0
.22	.91	.30	.01	0	0	0	0
.20	.86	.21	.01	0	0	0	0
.18	.79	.14	0	0	0	0	0
.16	.70	.08	0	0	0	0	0
.14	.59	.04	0	0	0	0	0
.12	.47	.02	0	0	0	0	0
.10	.33	.01	0	0	0	0	0
.08	.20	0	0	0	0	0	0
.06	.09	0	0	0	0	0	0
.04	.03	0	0	0	0	0	0
.02	0	0	0	0	0	0	0
0	0	0	0	0	0	0	0

n	r	.52	.54	.56	.58	.60	.62	.64	.66	.68	.70	.72	.74	.75	.76	.78	.80	.82	.84	.86	.88	.90	.92	.94	.96	.98	1.0
16	2	.99	.99	.99	1	1	1	1	1	1	1	1	1	1	1	1	1	1	1	1	1	1	1	1	1	1	1
	4	.88	.91	.93	.95	.97	.98	.98	.99	.99	1	1	1	1	1	1	1	1	1	1	1	1	1	1	1	1	1
	6	.56	.62	.68	.74	.79	.83	.87	.90	.93	.95	.97	.98	.98	.99	.99	1	1	1	1	1	1	1	1	1	1	1
	8	.19	.24	.29	.34	.40	.47	.53	.60	.66	.72	.78	.83	.85	.87	.91	.94	.96	.98	.99	.99	1	1	1	1	1	1
	10	.03	.04	.05	.07	.09	.12	.15	.19	.24	.30	.36	.43	.46	.50	.57	.65	.72	.79	.85	.90	.94	.97	.99	1	1	1
	12			0	0	.01	.01	.01	.02	.02	.04	.05	.07	.08	.09	.13	.17	.22	.28	.36	.45	.55	.66	.77	.88	.96	1
	14																										1
18	2	.98	.99	.99	1	1	1	1	1	1	1	1	1	1	1	1	1	1	1	1	1	1	1	1	1	1	1
	4	.86	.90	.93	.95	.96	.98	.99	.99	.99	1	1	1	1	1	1	1	1	1	1	1	1	1	1	1	1	1
	6	.57	.64	.70	.76	.81	.86	.90	.93	.95	.97	.98	.99	.99	1	1	1	1	1	1	1	1	1	1	1	1	1
	8	.23	.29	.35	.42	.49	.56	.63	.70	.76	.82	.87	.91	.92	.93	.95	.97	.98	.99	.99	1	1	1	1	1	1	1
	10	.05	.07	.09	.12	.16	.21	.27	.33	.40	.47	.55	.63	.67	.70	.77	.84	.89	.93	.96	.98	.99	1	1	1	1	1
	12		.01	.01	.02	.03	.05	.07	.10	.13	.18	.23	.28	.31	.35	.44	.53	.62	.72	.79	.86	.92	.96	.98	.99	1	1
	14						.01	.01	.01	.01	.02	.03	.04	.05	.06	.08	.12	.16	.22	.29	.38	.48	.60	.73	.85	.96	1
	16																										1
20	2	1	1	1	1	1	1	1	1	1	1	1	1	1	1	1	1	1	1	1	1	1	1	1	1	1	1
	4	.98	.99	.99	1	1	1	1	1	1	1	1	1	1	1	1	1	1	1	1	1	1	1	1	1	1	1
	6	.86	.90	.93	.95	.96	.98	.99	.99	1	1	1	1	1	1	1	1	1	1	1	1	1	1	1	1	1	1
	8	.57	.64	.70	.76	.81	.86	.90	.93	.95	.97	.98	.99	.99	.99	1	1	1	1	1	1	1	1	1	1	1	1
	10	.23	.29	.35	.42	.49	.56	.63	.70	.76	.82	.87	.91	.92	.94	.96	.98	.99	.99	1	1	1	1	1	1	1	1
	12	.05	.07	.09	.12	.16	.21	.27	.33	.40	.47	.55	.63	.67	.70	.77	.84	.89	.93	.96	.98	.99	1	1	1	1	1
	14		.01	.01	.02	.02	.03	.05	.07	.10	.13	.18	.23	.26	.30	.37	.46	.55	.64	.73	.81	.89	.94	.98	.99	1	1
	16			.01						.01	.01	.02	.03	.03	.04	.06	.08	.12	.17	.23	.32	.42	.54	.68	.82	.95	1
	18																										1
30	4	1	1	1	1	1	1	1	1	1	1	1	1	1	1	1	1	1	1	1	1	1	1	1	1	1	1
	8	.98	.99	.99	1	1	1	1	1	1	1	1	1	1	1	1	1	1	1	1	1	1	1	1	1	1	1
	12	.91	.94	.96	.98	.99	.99	1	1	1	1	1	1	1	1	1	1	1	1	1	1	1	1	1	1	1	1
	16	.44	.53	.61	.69	.77	.83	.88	.92	.95	.97	.98	.99	.99	1	1	1	1	1	1	1	1	1	1	1	1	1
	20	.05	.07	.11	.16	.21	.28	.36	.45	.54	.64	.72	.80	.83	.86	.91	.95	.97	.99	1	1	1	1	1	1	1	1
	24						.01	.02	.04	.06	.09	.14	.20	.23	.27	.36	.46	.57	.68	.79	.87	.94	.97	.99	1	1	1
	28																.01	.02	.04	.07	.12	.20	.31	.47	.68	.89	1

n	r	.50	.48	.46	.44	.42	.40	.38	.36	.34	.32	.30	.28	.26	.25	.24	.22	.20	.18	.16	.14	.12	.10	.08	.06	.04	.02	0
40	4	1	1	1	1	1	1	1	1	1	1	1	1	1	.99	.99	.98	.97	.94	.89	.81	.70	.56	.38	.20	.07	.01	0
	8	1	1	1	1	1	1	.99	.99	.98	.96	.93	.89	.83	.79	.75	.65	.53	.40	.28	.17	.09	.04	.01	0	0	0	0
	12	1	.99	.98	.97	.95	.91	.86	.80	.72	.62	.52	.41	.30	.25	.21	.13	.07	.04	.02	.01	0	0	0	0	0	0	0
	16	.90	.85	.78	.70	.61	.51	.41	.31	.22	.15	.09	.05	.03	.02	.01	.01	0	0	0	0	0	0	0	0	0	0	0
	20	.50	.40	.31	.22	.16	.10	.06	.04	.02	.01	0	0	0	0	0	0	0	0	0	0	0	0	0	0	0	0	0
	24	.10	.06	.04	.02	.01	.01	0	0	0	0	0	0	0	0	0	0	0	0	0	0	0	0	0	0	0	0	0
	28	0	0	0	0	0	0	0	0	0	0	0	0	0	0	0	0	0	0	0	0	0	0	0	0	0	0	0
	32	0	0	0	0	0	0	0	0	0	0	0	0	0	0	0	0	0	0	0	0	0	0	0	0	0	0	0
	36	0	0	0	0	0	0	0	0	0	0	0	0	0	0	0	0	0	0	0	0	0	0	0	0	0	0	0
60	4	1	1	1	1	1	1	1	1	1	1	1	1	1	1	1	1	1	1	.99	.97	.93	.85	.70	.48	.21	.03	0
	8	1	1	1	1	1	1	1	1	1	1	1	1	.99	.99	.98	.96	.93	.86	.75	.60	.41	.23	.10	.02	0	0	0
	12	1	1	1	1	1	1	1	1	.99	.98	.97	.93	.87	.84	.79	.67	.53	.37	.23	.11	.05	.01	0	0	0	0	0
	16	1	1	1	1	.99	.99	.97	.94	.90	.83	.73	.61	.47	.40	.33	.21	.12	.05	.02	.01	0	0	0	0	0	0	0
	20	1	.99	.98	.96	.92	.86	.78	.68	.56	.42	.30	.19	.11	.08	.06	.02	.01	0	0	0	0	0	0	0	0	0	0
	24	.94	.90	.83	.74	.63	.51	.38	.27	.17	.10	.05	.02	.01	.01	0	0	0	0	0	0	0	0	0	0	0	0	0
	28	.70	.58	.46	.34	.24	.15	.09	.05	.02	.01	0	0	0	0	0	0	0	0	0	0	0	0	0	0	0	0	0
	32	.30	.20	.13	.07	.04	.02	.01	0	0	0	0	0	0	0	0	0	0	0	0	0	0	0	0	0	0	0	0
	36	.06	.03	.01	.01	0	0	0	0	0	0	0	0	0	0	0	0	0	0	0	0	0	0	0	0	0	0	0
	40	0	0	0	0	0	0	0	0	0	0	0	0	0	0	0	0	0	0	0	0	0	0	0	0	0	0	0
	44	0	0	0	0	0	0	0	0	0	0	0	0	0	0	0	0	0	0	0	0	0	0	0	0	0	0	0
	48	0	0	0	0	0	0	0	0	0	0	0	0	0	0	0	0	0	0	0	0	0	0	0	0	0	0	0
	52	0	0	0	0	0	0	0	0	0	0	0	0	0	0	0	0	0	0	0	0	0	0	0	0	0	0	0
	56	0	0	0	0	0	0	0	0	0	0	0	0	0	0	0	0	0	0	0	0	0	0	0	0	0	0	0

Values in the body are cumulative probabilities indexed by q (column headings) for each n, r combination.

n	r	.52	.54	.56	.58	.60	.62	.64	.66	.68	.70	.72	.74	.75	.76	.78	.80	.82	.84	.86	.88	.90	.92	.94	.96	.98	1.0
40	4	1	1	1	1	1	1	1	1	1	1	1	1	1	1	1	1	1	1	1	1	1	1	1	1	1	1
	8	1	1	1	1	1	1	1	1	1	1	1	1	1	1	1	1	1	1	1	1	1	1	1	1	1	1
	12	.94	.96	.98	.99	.99	1	1	1	1	1	1	1	1	1	1	1	1	1	1	1	1	1	1	1	1	1
	16	.60	.69	.78	.84	.90	.94	.96	.98	.99	1	1	1	1	1	1	1	1	1	1	1	1	1	1	1	1	1
	20	.15	.22	.30	.39	.49	.59	.69	.78	.85	.91	.95	.97	.98	.99	.99	1	1	1	1	1	1	1	1	1	1	1
	24	.01	.02	.03	.05	.09	.14	.20	.28	.38	.48	.59	.70	.75	.79	.87	.93	.96	.98	.99	1	1	1	1	1	1	1
	28	0	0	0	0	0	.01	.01	.02	.04	.07	.11	.17	.21	.25	.35	.47	.60	.72	.83	.91	.96	.99	1	1	1	1
	32	0	0	0	0	0	0	0	0	0	0	0	0	.01	.01	.02	.03	.06	.11	.19	.30	.44	.62	.80	.93	.99	1
	36																										1
60	4	1	1	1	1	1	1	1	1	1	1	1	1	1	1	1	1	1	1	1	1	1	1	1	1	1	1
	8	1	1	1	1	1	1	1	1	1	1	1	1	1	1	1	1	1	1	1	1	1	1	1	1	1	1
	12	1	1	1	1	1	1	1	1	1	1	1	1	1	1	1	1	1	1	1	1	1	1	1	1	1	1
	16	1	1	1	1	1	1	1	1	1	1	1	1	1	1	1	1	1	1	1	1	1	1	1	1	1	1
	20	1	1	1	1	1	1	1	1	1	1	1	1	1	1	1	1	1	1	1	1	1	1	1	1	1	1
	24	.97	.99	.99	1	1	1	1	1	1	1	1	1	1	1	1	1	1	1	1	1	1	1	1	1	1	1
	28	.80	.87	.93	.96	.98	.99	1	1	1	1	1	1	1	1	1	1	1	1	1	1	1	1	1	1	1	1
	32	.42	.54	.66	.76	.85	.91	.95	.98	.99	1	1	1	1	1	1	1	1	1	1	1	1	1	1	1	1	1
	36	.10	.17	.26	.37	.49	.62	.73	.83	.90	.95	.98	.99	.99	1	1	1	1	1	1	1	1	1	1	1	1	1
	40	.01	.02	.04	.08	.14	.22	.32	.44	.58	.70	.81	.89	.92	.94	.98	.99	1	1	1	1	1	1	1	1	1	1
	44	0	0	0	.01	.01	.03	.06	.10	.17	.27	.39	.53	.60	.67	.79	.88	.95	.98	.99	1	1	1	1	1	1	1
	48	0	0	0	0	0	0	0	.01	.02	.03	.07	.13	.16	.21	.33	.47	.63	.77	.89	.95	.99	1	1	1	1	1
	52	0	0	0	0	0	0	0	0	0	0	0	.01	.01	.02	.04	.07	.14	.25	.40	.59	.77	.90	.98	1	1	1
	56	0	0	0	0	0	0	0	0	0	0	0	0	0	0	0	0	0	.01	.03	.07	.15	.30	.52	.79	.97	1

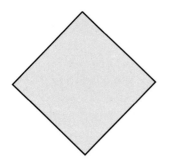

Answers to Selected Numerical Exercises

The following are answers to selected numerical *exercises* only. Solutions and answers to *all* exercises, questions, and problems can be found in the instructor's manual.

Chapter 2   **2.7.** $158.78. **2.8a.** $23.71, –$28.44. **2.8b.** 14.5%. **2.9.** $2003.90, 19.2%. **2.10a.** –$25.60. **2.10b.** $25.60. **2.10c.** –$0.08.

Chapter 4   **4.4.** 3.0, 3.2. **4.6.** 8.1, 3.2. **4.8.** 5.08, 4.5.

Chapter 7   **7.3.** 0.12, 0.29, 0.41, 0.65, 0.35, 0.29, 0.18, 0.17. **7.4.** 0.94. **7.6.** j, c, c, c, j, c, c, c, c, c, j. **7.7.** σ_B = $3.72 million. σ_C = 0. **7.8.** 0.58, 0.34, 0.75, 0.42, 0.58, 0.66, 0.34, 0.25, 0.75. **7.9.** 0.90, 0.61, 0.61, 0.39, 0.61, 0.10, 0.90, 0.10, 0.90. **7.10.** 0.70, 0.98, 0.21, 0.79, 0.970, 0.030, 0.603, 0.397. **7.11.** 0.56. **7.12a.** 2.65, 0.728, 0.853. **7.12b.** 26.40, 2255.04, 47.49. **7.12c.** 0.632, 0.233, 0.482. **7.15a.** $7000, 12250. **7.15b.** $42,895, 41871. **7.16.** $1594, 430,575. **7.17.** 0.24, 0.795, 0.001. **7.19.** 0.779, 0.041, 0.656, 0.134.

Chapter 9   **9.1.** 0.915. **9.2.** 0.0918, 0.0918. **9.3.** 0.027, 0.706, 0.001. **9.4.** 0.33. **9.5a.** 0.037, 0.971, 0.191, 0.157; 0.205, 0.514, 0.317, 0.108.

9.5b. 0.180, 0.594, 0.099, 0.068; 0.336, 0.130, 0.190, 0.310. **9.5c.** 0.993, 0.471, 0.0; 0.368, 0.002, 0.368. **9.5d.** 0.6915, 0.2604, 0.0062, 0.0; 0.9525, 0.1056, 0.5363, 0.6915. **9.5e.** 0.39, 0.01, 0.36; 0.31, 0.30, 0. **9.6.** −1.645, 0; 0.675, 1.28 **9.7.** $\mu = 200$, $\sigma = 111.11$. **9.8.** 0.2854. **9.9.** 5.4. **9.10.** 1.743.

Chapter 10   **10.3.** 275, 400.

Chapter 12   **12.2.** 1.2. **12.4.** 3.04, 1.20, 3.22.

Chapter 13   **13.5.** $236. **13.6a.** 0.56, 0.48, 0, −1.81. **13.6b.** 0.052. **13.6c.** $64.52, $270.98. **13.6d.** $106.18. **13.6e.** $2363.

Chapter 15   **15.8.** 1, 0.4, 0. **15.10.** 0.41, 0.59. **15.12.** 0.25, 0.34, 0.41.

Chapter 16   **16.6.** 0.48, 0.67.

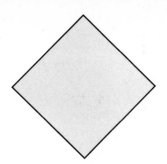

Index